THE SAILOR AND THE SERMON

HADAR SHMARYAHU YA'AKOV

STRATTON PRESS

Publishing Life

THE SAILOR AND THE SERMON

Stratton Press Publishing
831 N Tatnall Street Suite M #188,
Wilmington, DE 19801
www.stratton-press.com
1-888-323-7009

ISBN (Paperback): 978-1-64895-055-1
ISBN (Hardback): 978-1-64895-057-5
ISBN (Ebook): 978-1-64895-056-8

Printed in the United States of America

To Mom and Dad, Ron (Bay), Lawrence, and Fred,
my siblings, and my military comrades

The events in this book are based on a true story.
The names have been changed to protect the innocent.
Some real-life names have been used with the express
permission of the individual, either in writing or verbally.

Preface

Gratitude is expressed to people who have been directly influential in the life of TJ in a positive way. His two older brothers touched his life as a boy in ways they would never know or imagine on this side of heaven. Frederick E. was a direct mentor to TJ as a boy and practically cracked open the mind of TJ and introduced him to be open-minded and sparked his desire to learn and grow. In the eyes of TJ, Fred was a strong role model and positive thinker. His energy and tenacity to fight the odds to succeed and make it through life's challenges strongly influenced TJ as a boy. Ron, a.k.a. Bay, unknowingly set TJ on a path of skill, military interest, and manhood. When he shouldn't have introduced TJ to the world of licentiousness, he did it anyways, and TJ's first experience of the world, though a novice experience in comparison with what was to come later in life, shattered his little-boy innocence. Brothers in the navy during his first enlistment influenced TJ both negatively and positively. He loved and respected both his parents endlessly, but when he began to grow and mature and to experience the unforgettable trials of life, his respect and love for his parents became jumbled with deep hellish painful emotions of hurt and sorrow. Yet he could not stop loving them, and many times after their passing, he sometimes desired to hug them just because…the sleeper in him had awoken.

INTRODUCTION

In the year 1972, on a cold December evening at a small local church, TJ did what older *Christians* called "giving your heart to the Lord." He did not fully understand what that meant but was taught as a child that giving your heart to the Lord is what God expected of all men and women. From those early *Christian* days till now, he has seen and experienced the best of life to the extreme malicious crimes of life—with a *Christian* background experience, called the anointing of the Holy Ghost and the unquestionable presence of the spirit of God, to the deep sexual sins of fornication and adultery and all-night partying. In fact, if he could have known the future and could have looked into the proverbial crystal ball, he would have turned in absolute horror and run like a man fleeing from hell to avoid what lay ahead. On the other hand, TJ is thankful to God that he could not know the future about his life. Truth be known, many would probably run in the opposite direction of their destined path of growth and maturity. But through it all, God graciously keeps all his children and enables them to become what he created us to become. We were all created by Elohym, called God by most of the world, to impact a life—to impact many lives or impact the world. This book is the humble contribution to impacting someone's life, be it a member of the armed forces, a member of a religious organization, or your typical everyday citizen. This book is about spiritual and mental growth. It's also about the deep unforgiving abyss of sin, the United States Armed Forces, and the depth of confusion in the mind of TJ about religion.

TJ is the main character in this book, and his testimony is strictly about the battles and struggles he had to overcome along the path of maturity. All men and women make choices, and we all make mistakes. But most men and women believe they have made the right choice until faced with the outcome of our choices. As a youth, the decision to accept the call to the ministry of the Gospel was the farthest thought in the mind of TJ. In fact, there were many secular professions he desired, and becoming a minister of the Gospel was not one of them. His own perception was that there was no way at all that he would be worthy of becoming a messenger of God and proclaiming the truth of his Word. But then who knows the will of God in their lives until one begins to mature on the predetermined path of their life. One thing for sure is a devoted child of God matures to a place in him where the power of his Holy Spirit becomes increasingly real and alive. The reality of the presence of God and the anointing of his Spirit is not about a charismatic emotional hype, a kind of "falling out in the spirit" sort of thing. The ability and power of God's Spirit to awaken the spirit of men and women is what is talked about in this book. That deep change ultimately brings one into the presence of Messiah while facing and overcoming the evils of the devil himself. It is an experience that brings the true essence of the Gospel message of Christ into the heart of God's creation. The spirit of Christ that he predetermined before the foundation of the world to change his creation into his image. Only the Father of lights, who created all things through the love of his Son, accomplishes the great feat of regenerating a man and women into the image of his only begotten Son. *The Sailor and the Sermon* is strictly about the inner struggles and demons confronted along the way. TJ would learn in the ensuing years who God had determined for him to become. Many times, he failed God and walked unnecessary paths, but because of the grace of God, he managed through and returned to the right path over and over again. Such is the work and purpose of grace. Nonetheless, as life's experiences are learned, individual lives are about how God brought you through. But each personal testimony always involves other people to some degree or another. It must be understood while family members, friends, enemies, and all manner of people are mentioned in this book, it is only because TJ's fight to overcome his own shortcomings and weaknesses always involved other people. No one can absolutely experience anything in life without someone else being involved to some degree. We are all interconnected to one another; if not by direct genealogy, we are connected as far back as Adam and Eve in the Garden of Eden. The Bible says we all have been made of one blood (Acts 17:26). So in a divine way, all of God's creation of man and women come from Adam and Eve some six thousand-plus years ago. We all are interconnected by virtue of the eternal creative act of God, and we all have a story to tell about our interconnection.

The following pages of this book will take you through a choppy, sometimes uncontrollable emotional roller coaster ride that seemingly has no end. The ride at times becomes so heart-wrenching that the author wept while writing the story. The author repented over and over again as his mind was slingshot back into his own dreadful past of mistrust, ungodliness, and wickedness. Now TJ can assuredly confess that he completely understands why the Bible says, *"Forgetting what is behind and reaching out for what lies ahead. I press on toward the goal for the prize of the high calling of Elohym in Messiah הושצי"* (Phil. 3:13–14).

1

THE PROJECTS ON CAMERON STREET

The Sailor and the Sermon is about the life of a young man who grew up thinking he knew everything about life, only to discover later that he knew nothing at all. Many of the titles and names reflect actual places and events. For identification purposes in this book, the young man will be referred to as TJ up to the point when "Sailor" emerges. His life begins with the days of innocence in a place called the projects, a community of row homes divided up into sections listing from *A* to *Z*, with separate house address numbers. The projects on Cameron Street in Harrisburg, Pennsylvania (officially named MW Smith Homes), was a restricted-income family community. Smith Homes began housing tenants in 1959, making it essentially brand-new at the time TJ lived there. During those days in the projects, the ethnic ratio was an estimated 98 percent black, 1 percent white, and 1 percent other. These overwhelming high and low percentages are drawn because TJ rarely saw a white person or any person of other nationality in the projects during the 1960s. In fact, he could not comprehend or see the world any further than what he was seeing in the projects. That was the world of TJ, and he knew nothing beyond Cameron Street and the projects. Still, he grew up thinking he knew everything. TJ's world was a conglomeration of make-believe, desire, secrecy, lies, religious hype, and fear of the future. His story and world of confusion grants others a glimpse into the crevices of his soul. Traditional Christianity was the driving force and fulcrum on which all other experiences hinged.

His memory stretches back to the age of six in the projects. TJ and his family lived there from the time he was two or three. One of his brothers had shown him a picture of himself scrambling up the steps outside of their home at 38MW Smith Homes, and they told him that he was about two or three at that time. His youngest brother was born in 1965, and he remembered that his younger brother was two years old when they moved on the Hill to North 18th Street, which at that point would have been 1967. Memory prior to six is sketchy and clouded, to say the least. Different events from when he was six and older, he would remember quite vividly, as the saying goes, "like it was yesterday."

Cowboys, Indians, and Model Cars

A couple of sketchy memories remain almost like a dream in his mind. Fred was playing outside with their neighbors in the front yard, or maybe it was the backyard—he was not quite sure which was the front or back of the house. Fred and the other boys couldn't have been more than two steps away from the entrance. It was a nice sunny afternoon filled with the carefree sound of project children laughing and playing outside. The sound of other children got TJ's attention, and very quickly, he bolted outside to see what was going on. He did not remember what he was doing before he ran outside. Once he got outside, he could see Fred sitting on the ground with the other boys playing cowboys and Indians with those old plastic miniature toy cowboys. That was his very first time seeing the toy cowboys, and he was elated! Sprinting at full speed to get to his brother (who was only about four feet from the door), he ran directly into Fred's back and rebounded on the ground wearing the biggest smile, the type of smile a kid at a carnival with cotton candy smeared on his face would have worn. The plastic cowboys were the single most cool toys he had ever seen—ever.

The projects as they appear now

But Fred obviously did not enjoy TJ's demolition of his precise formation of cowboys and Indians. Not to mention the detailed dirt fort that Fred had formed on the ground had now been obliterated. Man, oh man, he blew it! There were cowboys scattered as far as his little eyes could see, and Fred's fortress had been demoted back to plain old project dirt. One of the last things he remembered was getting up off his butt about two feet away from Fred. At this point, Fred snatched TJ up and thrust his little body in the opposite direction. TJ had made the number one spot on Fred's hit list of pain-in-the-butt, annoying little child. In response, TJ jumped up, ran toward Fred, kicked the remainder of the cowboys down, and dashed in the house. The rest is a blur.

A similar set of circumstances existed involving Fred and the other boys. Fred was outside in precisely the same spot. The weather conditions that day were almost identical to the previous encounter with Fred's cowboys and Indians. Once again it was a nice sunny afternoon, but this time the attraction was not the cowboys. This time, it was shiny plastic model cars. Fred had two or three shiny plastic model cars on the ground, and the other boys were in complete admiration. On this encounter, TJ was walking, but he could not walk exact or stable. His only intention was to get close to those shiny plastic model cars. He simply had to examine them more closely, and of course, he had to enlist his services to play with the big boys. Unfortunately, it happened again. He got too close and in fact stepped on one of the cars, crushing it to smithereens. Deep in his heart, TJ was really, really sorry for destroying the cars that he so eagerly wanted to play with. His singular fault was being a clumsy little boy who only wanted to hang out with the big kids. Surprisingly, Fred's only response was one of deep pain and sorrow. Fred erupted into painful tears. TJ could do nothing more than run in the house, and once he was inside, that moment was forever etched into his memory. His mom was in the kitchen. He couldn't remember what she was doing, but he could remember that she was there. Her response astounded him. She didn't spank him, nor did she yell at him. Her only response to Fred was, "Let your little brother play with you." Fred, in great grief, struggled to tell his side of the story. He attempted to explain how his new shiny plastic model car world had just been destroyed by a meteor shower in the form of a clumsy little boy. But his mom did not hear how much Fred was hurting inside from the destruction of his newfound pride and joy. TJ never did understand why his mom did not listen to Fred's side of the story and why she just casually told him to let his little brother play with them. That day became an eternal deposit in TJ's memory.

Up the Stairs and around the Corner

From about six years old, TJ would run up and down the stairs always in a hurry to do something. Sometimes he would go outside or maybe he would go to his room and just stare dreamily out the window. Many times, he would run up the stairs to the second floor and envision what the third floor looked like. A couple of his older brothers slept on the third floor. In his mind, that was the grown-up level. TJ always revered his older brothers and had grand imaginations about going to the third floor. Of course, he was too young at that time to go up there. TJ felt shunned many times by his older brothers. He felt his brothers did not like him, and he didn't know how to fit in with them or how to get them to accept him. On every occasion, TJ's persistence and love for his brothers inspired him to keep trying time after time to hang out with them. As far as TJ was concerned, they were his big brothers, and he looked to them for advice. Desperately, he sought their acceptance. He idolized them so much that he imagined himself to be just like them when he grew up. To TJ, his big brothers knew everything, and there were no other big brothers on earth that could compare to them. He would mimic them. He walked every placed they walked. He did everything they did, and in turn, they were always irritated with him. They were annoyed at him for trying to hang around and fit in. At this point in TJ's life, their display of irritation toward him did not matter. What mattered the most to TJ was their acceptance and their approval.

That is a glimpse into the world of TJ prior to the experience as both the Sailor and the Sermon. His desires, feelings, and thoughts were very green. His thoughts conceived nothing more than to be accepted by his big brothers.

Running up and down the stairs, always being in a hurry to do something, was motivated by a diverse set of thoughts and emotions—mostly curiosity. He just could not explain it and still would have a hard time explaining it now.

At the top of the stairs and around the corner to the right was his parents' room. That room was the most private and hallowed place in the house. He always wanted to go in, even if for no other reason than to stand in the center and just look around. But there was a sense of top secrecy to that hallowed room. Just the thought of going in there catapulted an emotion through his mind of extreme discipline. This caused the bones in his body to shiver. But something drove him. It was that rush one feels from living on the edge. The rush compelled him to run up and down the stairs for that one opportunity to glance into their room. There was an open storage section with shelves at the top of the stairs where his mom kept all the clean bath towels. (The memory is so vivid, even the scent of clean towels is clear). One day TJ ran up the stairs, and when he stopped at the top of the stairs and slowly looked to the right, he noticed their door was open a little. His heart began to beat at a pace so fast it seemed like his chest was expanding from the rush of blood pumping through his small body. Within a few seconds, he froze in his spot! He was afraid! He was excited! He was in shock to find the door open, and the temptation to peek inside their room was sinfully hard to resist.

At that time in his life, he had no respect for or understanding of the Bible, nor did he appreciate the value of life. TJ was, in many ways, in deep search for something. He was not quite sure what he was searching for but knew something was lacking in his life. He did not realize that the fundamental part of what was lacking was the relationship he longed for from his parents. He searched upstairs and downstairs trying to find the place where they fit into his life. TJ sought out a spot in his brothers' lives as a substitute. As a young boy, he longed for a deep relationship with his parents. He could not materialize what he was looking for, but he searched all aspects of his environment while living in the projects. Somehow, he thought what he was looking for was inside their room.

The compelling drive to walk toward their room and peek inside was overwhelming him. The temptation to peek, to fulfill his curiosity, and to be nosy was irresistible. Certainly, he had no other choice but to fulfill his desire. He mentally prepared himself to see whatever he might see by looking inside their room. The most dreadful factor of the cracked doorway incident is that he heard them snoring, yet he was still compelled to walk toward their room and risk a peek inside. Funny, isn't it? While other children where outside playing, TJ is running up and down the stairs in the house trying to find something. It was something he couldn't even identify, yet he searched diligently for it. About two feet from their room, he was getting ready to open the door a little bit more when an unexpectedly thunderous voice sounded from the direction of their room.

"Boy, get downstairs and stop running up the steps!"

At that moment, it seemed as if his heart skipped a few beats. All the blood that was pumping just a few seconds earlier plummeted down to his feet. His feet became as heavy as two concrete pillars. But then within seconds, he was running in the opposite direction toward the steps, at the same time yelling out, "Okay, okay." He could remember how he sprinted back to the stairs and how he ran down them so quickly. The voice had come as a surprise attack. The voice exploded in his mind, and it frightened him. As a matter of fact, it discouraged his search for anything in his parents' direction for decades.

Sticks and Stones Will Break You

How many times did TJ's dad tell him and all his siblings not to play with sticks? TJ especially did not understand why it was so dangerous. So in typical carefree childhood manner, they all played with sticks when they thought they could get away with it.

Dad was employed at the Pennsylvania State Hospital, which was located all the way up Cameron Street just before entering the freeway. It was TJ's understanding that Dad walked to work because he did not have a car. Whether Dad did or did not walk to work, TJ does not remember. He could only rely on what his older brothers told him. There were certain times of the day Dad was not at home, and during those times, there was a small amount of freedom to play. This freedom carried with it a sense of restriction. At the time, TJ did not even know anything about the concept of an all-seeing eye," but he felt there was something watching over them. They dared not to disobey Dad. One thing they all knew was they had to be very careful with that limited freedom to play with sticks. TJ remembers seeing Dad both before and after he came home from work. Dad was always dressed from head to toe in all white, with white shoes on. He thought Dad's clothes had something to do with him being a preacher. The white clothes he wore to work painted a picture in TJ's mind that Dad was faultless. Perfect! Always right! Untouchable and sinless. Almost as if a halo or aura of goodness encapsulated the person of his dad. Thirty years into the future would destroy this perception of his father and lay a path for TJ toward the brink of a nervous breakdown. Thirty years into the future would drop a hydrogen bomb of information that would be earth-shattering. Thirty years into the future would unquestionably define sin and the works thereof bringing TJ face to face with Satan himself. Thirty years into the future began the drastic, purging, painful, change of his every belief. It would change the very perception and ideas about life by which TJ previously learned to live. Thirty years can alter a lot of things that seemed unalterable before.

And now, back to the sticks. While Dad was at work, TJ and his siblings played with dead branches they found on the ground. Laughing and joking and mimicking Dad, trying to imitate Dad's voice, "Didn't I tell you not to play with sticks?" They thought that was funny, and they would drop the sticks and run around outside laughing to the extreme. To TJ and his brothers and sisters, it was good clean fun. No harm is done. No one was ever hurt or injured. But to Dad, it was disobedient, hardheaded, unruly behavior. One specific event remains in TJ's memory—he remembers once they got caught with the sticks by Dad, and he remembers hearing the screams of his brothers as Dad vehemently tore into their backside with a belt. Diligently and persistently searching his young mind, TJ could not figure out how, when, and from what place Dad saw them with the sticks, but he unquestionably remembers his brothers, Bay and Fred—they were older than him—getting spanked almost without mercy. As for TJ, he was exempt from the spanking because in Dad's mind, the young lad was influenced and was not responsible for his actions of disobedience. His brothers were the instigators, the leaders of misbehaving. You might say Dad was being just toward the younger lad, but still, TJ did not understand the reason for his brothers' scolding. After that incident of getting caught by Dad, the memory of playing with sticks in the projects fades into his next memory of the projects.

Other Memories of the Projects

The projects are full of memories; however, as it goes, only the more significant ones remain in TJ's memory. The significant memories are the ones that define his life and the lack of love he had for others. TJ was searching to find and understand love for anyone. Here are a few significant memories of the projects that TJ clearly remembers:

Their first TV got delivered by the delivery people. There is no memory of the name of their company, what type of vehicle the TV was delivered in, or whether black or white men delivered it. The more pronounced memory is how the TV was delivered on a nice sunny day early in the morning (most likely on a Saturday because children were out on the street playing). A truck pulled up in the parking space on Calder Street, and two men got out and unloaded a funny-shaped box with a small screen in it. Children were all in the way trying to see what it was. TJ was right among them, trying to see and understand what it might be able to do. Mom was signing some papers, and the men were frustrated because the children were in the way of them doing their job. You know what the projects are like—everybody's business is your business, and your business is everybody's business. Nonetheless, the TV was delivered, and he does not remember what took place the remainder of that day or what they ever watched on TV in the projects. Television was new, and playing outside was routine and old to the project children. Those days were the epitome of good social interaction and fun. Besides, there was not much to watch on TV during those days. As far as television goes, it took a few years for the "couch potato" concept to catch on. In his day, children were socially connected with one another playing outside. Anyhow, TJ was more concerned with Dad's cars than with any old TV set.

Dad's cars had to be the coolest and most exciting events in TJ's young mind. The first car in the memory of TJ was a blue-and-white 1957 Chevrolet Bel Air. The second car was a 1960 Buick Electra 225, dark blue, sharp, streamlined, and absolutely beautiful. TJ does not remember if Dad kept the 1960 Bel Air or if he just test drove it home from the car dealer. TJ doesn't remember ever riding in the 1960 Bel Air. TJ does remember how Dad stood beside it and how the neighbors gawked at it and whispered among themselves. They were probably wondering how his dad could afford a nice car like that with all those kids. That was TJ's assumption; however, that's not a difficult assumption to come up with living in the projects. That day, just that one day, he did remember the 1960 Chevrolet Bel Air. Fred was goofy in those days. He always came up with clever things to do and made up songs. One day Fred stood beside the 1960 Bel Air and sang a whole made-up song about the car. Fred said, "Diamond in the back, wing back tails, Batman." Diamond described the opera window on the Bel Air. Wing back tails described the back sides of the car as it was designed like wings in an upward motion. But then "Batman," TJ had no idea why Fred was referring to Batman. But then Fred was older than TJ, and Fred seemed much bigger and taller. Fred had access to DC and Marvel comic books. Fred's friends had hundreds of comic books, and every now and then TJ would see one laying on the porch or in Fred's back pocket. TJ never thought anything of it, and he was not interested at the time. Later on, TJ presumed that's where Batman fit into the song because the Buick Electra 225 in some ways resembled the Batmobile. Come to think of it, TJ does not remember riding much in the Chevy Bel Air except for one event that remains to this day. But the memory of playing with his Matchbox toy cars on Dad's cars remains intact. TJ would take his Matchbox cars and play like they were driving up hills through the creases of Dad's cars. But he must have ridden in the Chevy because going to church every Sunday was mandatory, and the Chevy would have been the means in which TJ and his siblings got to church.

As far as TJ was concerned, there was no one like Dad. He was tall, slender, well dressed (all the time), and a man to be respected. He was reliable, dependable, and faithful. During those days, TJ had only one view and perception about his dad. When Dad spoke, his words were saturated with wisdom. When he spoke, one had to give attention to what he said. To TJ, he was the perfect dad, and he and his siblings never went hungry and never went without clothes on their back. Every time he went shopping for food, he would come home with bags and bags of groceries. Dad would go to the store and buy the grocery, bring it home, and take it to the kitchen. TJ's older brothers had to help bring the groceries in the house, and it was always an exciting time. Dad was always experimenting with some new food to try out to see if his children liked it. If the new food went over good, he would buy more the next time.

In regard to TJ's own children, I'm sure they probably saw him in a similar light because in many ways, TJ's life followed in the footsteps of his father. Only by the grace and mercy of God can TJ tell his story. There are many failures, sinful crevices, mountains to climb, and personal demons he had to slay and displace. His choices and decisions in life were drawn from the choices and decisions of his father and his older brothers. Their choices and their decisions immensely aided TJ in avoiding certain pitfalls while at the same time experiencing similar consequences. In the eyes of a young boy, the greatest thing TJ's dad ever did in the projects was to rescue him from death and a potential brain-damaging accident.

The Race, the Fall, the Rescue

In those days, the projects did not have much grass to play on. It was mainly concrete sidewalks from one house to another. The only place where grass may have grown was on the hill behind his house, 38 MW Smith Homes, that led to what was called "the old homes" (officially, William Howard Day Homes). The old homes were an earlier version of the projects that were positioned slightly higher on a bank than the newer Smith Homes. But the hill was played on so much by the project children that grass wouldn't grow. The hill that led to the old homes was nothing but dirt and tracks from children running up and down on it back in those days. There was a baseball field across Calder Street that had grass, but at TJ's age, that was too far for him to walk. To get to the baseball field, he had to cross Calder Street, and he was not daring enough then to take the chance. Many times he wanted to cross the street but hadn't developed the spirit of adventure at that point in his life. TJ must have been six years old, and his only object then was to impress his father. He was the sole reason TJ lived during those days, and in everything TJ did, he wanted to make Dad proud of him—everything. In the most genuine way, TJ looked up to him. TJ admired him. TJ respected him in the godliest way he knew at the time. Dad was the coolest and the chief role model that TJ yearned to connect with. TJ knew nothing else about life's woes and disappointments and to this day wishes he would have never learned anything otherwise.

The most exciting race of TJ's toddler life was with Fred, the second person in his sight to follow after and win his affection. Next to Dad came Fred because Fred was cool and also his older brother. The boyish activity in TJ's life was directly influenced by Fred. TJ had an unchangeable perspective of Fred and held immoveable pride deep in his heart of his older brother. He especially held Fred as the guarding and role model of his youthful days. He thought nobody better mess with him because Fred is his brother. The view young TJ held of Fred lasted pretty much into adulthood even as a married man. But that view would all be ground to powder as the years progressed on. Religion and age difference became a wedge of distrust and utter godless separation between the two.

The day TJ and Fred raced was a very, very nice summer day while the sun brightened their morning and Dad was about to go to work. The memory remains as clear as something that just occurred yesterday. TJ can still see Dad in his mind's eye. Dad was dressed in his white uniform about to go to work at the Pennsylvania State Hospital. Dad was standing on the porch with one leg on the banister of the porch leaning over, looking at Fred and TJ enjoy the carefree bliss of life as youngsters. Fred was chasing TJ around on the concrete sidewalks. Dad was smiling, and Fred, in a taunting way, wouldn't catch TJ; Fred made it seem like TJ was running too fast for him. Fred was being really goofy and clowning around, and young TJ did not realize the psychological fun Fred engaged him in. TJ thought he was running fast and his big brother Fred couldn't catch him. The memory in young TJ's mind was destined to last forever, possibly into eternity, if that is permissible. The last thing TJ remembers was the stirring words of Fred, "Let's race." Little did both of them know that day would turn into a nightmare of almost deadly and crippling proportions. Fred, in his playful, fun, agitating way, decided to give TJ a head start.

Finally, Fred said, "On three! One, two, three!"

TJ and his older brother Fred started running. TJ was racing Fred, his big brother, his idol, his friend, and TJ was in the lead. He was so overcome with joy that he could not keep focus on the path of their race, and he kept looking back at Fred as Fred seemed to be running very slowly. The entire time TJ was running, he was laughing and laughing and laughing deep from within his untainted soul.

Then totally unexpectedly, and in some ways evil and devilish, the laughs were abruptly ended. The remainder of that day was filled with tears deep from within the child's unpolluted and undamaged soul. The tears would not stop, and he could not make them stop. TJ literally cried the rest of the day all the way into the night until he fell asleep. He went from running to staggering like a drunkard out of control.

The actual impact, both physically and mentally, remains intact in his memory to this day. TJ remembers it like frames in a picture—one, two, three steps and he was at the bottom of the stairway that led into the house. Providentially, Dad was still standing on the porch, and to this day it appears Dad's arms were six feet long. TJ remembers looking up at Dad, and for the first time since the accident, he heard himself crying. Dad took one step, it seems, and reached down toward the young child and picked him up into his arms like a shovel scoops up snow. Between the tears and blood in his eyes, TJ got a glimpse of Dad's face, and that face remains in the clear memory of TJ to this day. Dad's face was chiseled with extreme seriousness. Dad wore a face of compassion. A face of responsibility. A face of love. He held TJ so closely and tightly to his bosom until TJ heard Dad's heart beating with every stride. He was not sure if he heard only his heart beating or both his and Dad's beating in one accord.

Within seconds—no, milliseconds, no, all one motion, TJ was lifted into Dad's arms and Dad was running with him toward the Chevy Bel Air. As TJ recalls the event, he could not explain the progression of things, but when Dad got in the car after he put him in the back seat—no seatbelts during those days—Mom was holding TJ in her arms. All he can guess is that Fred ran in the house and told Mom what happened, and within seconds, she dropped everything she was doing and was on the heels of Dad as he was running to the car. This is one of those times that, TJ concluded as he got older, that angels intervene in some cases to preserve lives for the glory of the Most High's service. Fred running inside to tell Mom is the only explanation TJ could think of later in life. He also believed that Dad broke every traffic law transporting him to the emergency room at the Harrisburg Hospital. But the Most High showered his grace upon the entire event because a police officer stopped Dad and quickly assessed the situation and escorted Dad the remainder of the way.

TJ's crying was erratic because he would hear himself cry and then he would hear his mother saying, "Son, son." He kept blacking out from the fall. After arriving at the hospital, his next memory was lying on a bed while the doctors stitched his forehead from the fall. There is no memory of pain. Was it because of the medicine given by the hospital, or was it because his young body was going numb? Everything moved at a face rate of speed. His life at that time sped, like everything was being fast-forward. Dad said to him while lying on the operating table, "Wake up, son. Wake up, son."

TJ continued to fade out into nothingness that held zero memories. His memories of the blackness was a space in time that was void of any form of life. It was the same blackness when he fell. TJ does not remember the fall, but he does remember blackness, then light, then staggering like a drunkard, then Dad lifting him into his arms. The sequence of events occurred in this manner.

The concrete in the projects during those days was not what it looks like today. Concrete was chipped, broken, and uneven, and on that day during his exciting run with Fred, his foot happened to trip on an uneven section of the sidewalk. At the precise moment that he was turning around from looking back at Fred, he was at the uneven concrete, and he does remember tripping and going airborne, about three, maybe four feet in the air. In his mind, he was deathly afraid of what was about to happen and had no control over what came next. TJ's forehead slammed into the concrete sidewalk and was the only part of his body that broke the fall. No arms, knees, or legs, just his forehead broke the fall. That's when the blackness came, then the light, then the staggering, and the rest you already know about.

Dad was the ultimate savior in his life during those days. TJ thought Dad was an angel temporarily placed on this earth to raise him and his siblings. He never thought Dad able to do anything wrong, not for one second. Dad rescued his life from the arms of death. What negative can anyone think of a person who rescues their life from death? Not only did his dad rescue him, he showed great compassion for him after the accident. TJ felt compassion and love were genuine from the heart of his father. If there ever was a time his dad was compassionate, godly, and truly of a loving spirit, it was the time he shared TJ's pain and rescued his life from the potentially deadly accident in the projects. For decades, TJ could not see his father other than as a loving compassionate dad. It was not until he became a full-grown man that his view of his father changed. But TJ respected him even more. As time moved on and his understanding became fruitful, all that was confusing and unknown to him in the projects and on North 18th Street became clear. The scar from the fall serves as a reminder of the grace of the Most High. Even as a young child, TJ believed in God's grace. He also respected the stewardship of his father, REGARDLESS of both his and his father's personal shortcomings. The reason for the early attempt from the powers of darkness to kill young TJ becomes apparent in the future—TJ unknowingly idolized his father, and his father, a Christian evangelist, was a constant threat to the powers of darkness and the enemy of his soul.

The Name of Churches

Going to church is very, very sketchy during the days of the projects. There were three churches TJ attended—Mt. Calvary COGIC on 3rd Street, Lingo Memorial on Cameron Street, and Emmanuel on 16th and Liberty Street. It was not until TJ was grown in his early thirties that he began to understand why that was so. Of course, he thought his dad was well-liked and a sought-after preacher for all those churches. He was clueless about other things involved in churches that would be the underlying reason for a preacher to go from one church to another. Dad had accepted the calling in the ministry as an evangelist but was not supported by any church to evangelize the lost. The cliques that were so typical in many of those churches was one of many challenges his dad had to face. TJ was blind beyond blind and would have never thought of the church as anything other than a good thing. His novice understanding was that all Christian churches were the epitome of Christ himself, only to learn some thirty years later the true nature and motivation of all those churches. Church and church services, Christianity, and the Bible would become the elite defining aspect of *The Sailor and the Sermon*. TJ's life exploded into a myriad of constructive criticism in the years to come about church and Christianity. As he matured, his spiritual eyes were centered on Christianity as the true religion until the falseness of the beliefs and practices of Christianity would be revealed to him. His experience with the Church of God and Christ as described by the hierarchy solidified in his mind the authenticity of Christianity. TJ's conclusion of going to church while growing up in the projects all the way through the days of North 18th Street was typical. Church was routine, a formality, and religious misleading and preacher power struggles. TJ termed those days as the deepest form of religiosity and churchianity he would ever experience. Since those days, he developed a genuine passion to enlighten the unenlightened but failed in the worst way. That failure allowed the Most High Yahuah to chart his path in the direction of the ancients.

Georgia and the UFO

Living in the projects was filled with numerous unexplained events in his life. Just about every event that occurred had a reason and an explanation. But then none of it made sense to TJ. He was so naive until the concept of naive had nothing to do with him. He lived in a blissful world of make-believe and an unexplained eventful childhood world. There was no direction, no purpose or reason for anything he did during those days. Understanding then for the things that were done and experienced in his life was totally unfruitful during the days of the projects. For instance, the first time he heard of a place called Atlanta, Georgia, is because Dad would travel there. Much of the time he would travel alone every year or so. Leo Jr., Dad's eldest son, told him that Dad would sometimes go to Georgia three and four times in one year. Well, that explained the times when TJ didn't see Dad around, and during those times, TJ was filled with anxiety. He thought Dad was working a lot. Nonetheless, Dad would go to Atlanta, Georgia, to visit his mother, and TJ learned from Leo Jr.—they called him Junior for short—that Dad told Mom as long as his mother was alive, he would go visit her. At the first hearing of that, it sounds very noble and strong attachment to family, but the future would reveal a startling, upsetting, deceptive, almost unbelievable reason for the Atlanta trips. In time, TJ learned, according to the Word of the Most High Elohym Yahuah, when a man leaves his father and mother, he is by precept to cling unto his wife.

When Dad went to Atlanta, Georgia, to visit his mother, there was a feeling of sadness in all of them because he was leaving his children and going away. When Dad was on his way home (he used to call and tell them he was coming home), as far as TJ could tell, there was excitement, anticipation, and they were unable to sleep on the eve of his return. Going to Atlanta, Georgia, with Dad became an unexplained frustration with TJ, and he used to always wonder why they couldn't go with Dad. Once when he was about six or seven years old, TJ asked Dad if he could go. Dad said to him, "You're not old enough." Like a person who had smoked too much marijuana or drunk too much alcohol or sniffed too much glue, TJ's little mind had been blown to the moon and back. Dad did not explain why he was not old enough, and TJ certainly did not understand what that meant. The result was TJ never went to Atlanta with Dad during those days. He couldn't figure it out. What was old enough? Dad would always tell TJ, "Maybe next year."

But next year never came, even until Dad's mother passed away. TJ was about ten or eleven years old then. If memory serves, Dad did take Fred and Bay a couple of times while living in the projects. TJ never had the privilege. All he could do was imagine in his mind what Atlanta must look like and what it must be like to go there. He wanted so desperately to go to Atlanta with the best dad he thought he had in those days.

One summer while Dad was in Atlanta and Bay and Fred was with him, TJ was totally lost. He was homesick for them and afraid. He does not remember much interaction with his sisters that well in the projects. Glimpses of his sisters remain as a memory simply because he and his sisters didn't play much together. He just knew he had sisters, and every now and then they would appear in his life. Don't get me wrong, TJ loved his sisters and all his siblings, but the relationship he had was mostly with his two idolized brothers, Fred and Bay, it was not the same as with his sisters. Sisters were sisters. That's all they were to TJ then because at that time, he did not see them as having much in common other than their parents. His brothers, in the mind of TJ, on the other hand, were to be sought after. He wanted to be like them and be accepted by them.

The summer that Dad, Bay, and Fred was in Atlanta, there was little activity in TJ's life and he didn't do much of anything. He had some friends by that time, and they would play hide-and-seek in the boiler room, the section of the projects that supplied the heat and hot water. TJ lived about five houses from the boiler room. He and MB would play imaginary games, much of which he does not remember. He would stay in the house most of the time because he didn't have his brothers to irritate or play with. Even though the summers were gorgeous summer days, TJ had no desire to stay outside playing while his brothers were away.

One day he remembers hearing or seeing something on the not-too-popular TV about comets and meteorites, and at first he thought he dreamed this, but he came to learn later that it was an actual event. One particular night, he was out back and was gazing up in the sky, looking for something, anything. He expected and anticipated to see something because he had heard about comets and meteorites. There were other children out that night along with him, and they were all looking. His new friend MB was there also, and they looked and looked and expected and hoped to see a comet. Then in a flash, out of nowhere traveling from south to north, an object appeared in the sky right above the bank of dirt leading to the "old homes." As the Most High sits on his throne, TJ was positive he saw an object that was shaped like a missile about the size of a small plane with no wings and flashes of red, yellow, green, and white lights on it. The object seemed to be gliding in the air but was on a descent. As it flew by his position, either his mind was playing a serious trick on him because of what he was hoping to see or he saw what he saw.

There was, midway of this flying craft, what seemed to be a glass bubble and a man sitting in it or a dummy. This dummy/man appeared to be flying the unidentified object. TJ couldn't believe it! He thought earth had contacted extraterrestrials. Who would believe what he just saw? How would he explain what he just saw? What would he tell anyone about what he just saw? What words would he say? He didn't know much of the English vocabulary. How would he explain a UFO? He didn't even understand the concept of UFOs. He didn't even know what a UFO was or what the initials stood for. He didn't even know that people were searching and studying alleged UFO encounters. He knew absolutely nothing about anything involving possible UFO sightings and the fact that humans are fascinated about alleged UFO experiences. TJ knew nothing other than what he saw! But then it doesn't matter what he knew or didn't know about UFOs, what mattered is the response of the other children; they saw it too!

"Wow! What was that?"

"Where is it going?"

"Who was in it?"

Children running in all directions and some toward the direction of the flying object. Some in the other direction of the object and some gazing in the sky, trying to figure out what just happened. That perhaps was the most unusual highpoint of the projects' experiences that to this day remains unanswered. Were they, as low-income families, taunted with by some secret government experiment? Were they being used as some kind of test to control the mind and thinking of private citizens? Who knows the truth of those days?

From that experience, his sadness and homesickness for Dad and his brothers seemed to fade into the back of his mind. But he could not wait to tell them about the event, though he did not know how to explain what he saw. Vocabulary and communication was not a strong point in his life then. He had just witnessed something that impacted his memory all the way into adulthood. TJ was not able to intelligently explain what he saw to his brothers or his dad. He does not even remember if he talked much about that experience anymore.

But to solidify his experience, he came across a certain article written in the *Paranormal PA & Beyond* magazine titled "1967: PA's Capital Becomes the UFO Capital," in association with UFORCOP, UFO Research Center of Pennsylvania. In this article, the author speaks about Harrisburg, Pennsylvania, and the surrounding areas experienced a flood of UFO sightings during the late 1960s. That article places the time frame in which TJ tells his story of something he was not sure of, nor did he understand.

The blotches of life-defining memories in the projects would become the foundation of the emerging of Sailor, who becomes the man of the Sermon, who embraces all the lies and all the vices of the heart and hidden man, who becomes humble. The teen years are exploratory and includes searching for his lost, confused soul. That launches him into the armed forces, where the battle between the Sailor and the Sermon rages. The conflict between the two is sort of like when the apostle Paul penned these words:

> For that which I do, I allow not: for what I would, that do I not: but what I hate, that do I... Now then it is no more I that do it, but sin that dwelleth in me. (Rom. 7:15, 17)

2

NORTH 18TH STREET TRANSITION

When TJ and his family moved from the projects to North 18th Street, he felt like they were moving up in the world. The move itself generated questions in his mind of all the "don't play with sticks" and restrictions imposed by Dad. How is it that Dad allowed him to ride in the back of the U-Haul truck from the projects to the hill what was safe about that? Anyways, he did not question Dad's judgment because everything was exciting in those days and it was not unusual to see grown men in the back of a U-Haul truck. Sometimes TJ sat up front, enjoying the sensation of feeling grown and special, and other times he sat in the cargo section of the truck, enjoying liberty and freedom. Seat belts did not become specifications in American vehicles until January of 1968, and it did not matter where you sat in a moving vehicle up until the seatbelt law. TJ was moving to "the hill," and in many ways, they were literally moving up, in the mind of TJ. It was only then that TJ became aware of the fact that he had an older brother, Jr., who he did not know was related to him while living in the projects. Rarely did TJ remember seeing his oldest brother in the projects, but he showed up during the move to help and, TJ suspects, to keep in touch with his people. TJ remembers seeing him walk in the house on North 18th Street but did not hear much of what he talked about and was unaware of his reason for not being around in the projects, at least from what he could tell. But he does remember that when he met him for the first time, his oldest brother struck him as one of the coolest brothers, apart from Fred and Bay. Sad to say that TJ would learn rather quickly in time that he and his oldest brother had almost nothing in common. TJ felt he and his oldest brother would never connect with each other in life. At that time, it became somewhat of a mission of his to get to know his oldest brother and become his friend. Jr. was a tall slim-jim, well-dressed professional of some sort, he thought. His appearance was one of intelligence and worldly experience. Jr. appeared to be well off and an adviser of sorts to both their mom and dad until thirty years later, the nasty truth of all things would erupt.

Dysfunctional is a word that most people do not like, nor do they willingly accept dysfunctional as it may apply to their family. If TJ were a cursing man, he probably would use another word as it applied to his perception and his own ignorance of the truth concerning the family that he dearly loved. TJ honestly thought there was none like his family on the planet. He thought Jr. was the coolest ever in his youthful eyes all the way into his adult life. Nonetheless, Jr. still holds that "coolness" to the grown-up TJ. It's just that the reality of what is can many times overwhelm what one perceives. When TJ first became aware of who Jr. was and the way he carried himself, his desire to be like all his brothers grew inside his soul. Jr. carries within his soul the potential of a Beauford Delaney, Sargent Claude Johnson, John Coltrane, Sonny Rollins, and even Lionel Hampton. He is musically inclined and endowed with practical wisdom beyond measure. There were many times TJ felt a sense of fatherhood while confiding in him and even expressed to him how his wisdom encouraged him in many ways. Two different worlds with two different parents. While Jr. and TJ were born of the same parents, both were raised by different people, so to speak. Jr. sees life from a perspective that is foreign to the young TJ. Jr.'s views were shaped and formed in many ways by wayward parents while TJ's views were shaped and formed by Charismatic Christian parents.

Moving to North 18th Street was one of the most thrilling and memorial events in TJ's youthful life. North 18th Street was located atop a major city street named Herr Street and sometimes called Herr

Street Hill. Literally, you had to drive up a hill about a quarter of a mile. Another direction of getting on the hill was to cross what many times was called State Street Bridge. Its actual name is Soldiers and Sailors Memorial Bridge. State Street Bridge was elevated some fifty or so feet from the level of the projects, which was located right off Cameron Street. But when TJ and his family moved from the projects, Dad took the route of Herr Street Hill, which took them up to 17th Street, turn right on 17th down to Briggs Street, turn left up Briggs Street, then turn left down onto North 18th Street. The move took place around 1967 because TJ's younger brother was born in May of 1965, and when the family moved to North 18th Street, the baby was two years old. Jon would run around in the house enjoying the larger space of their new home, running up and down the long hallway on the second floor, being chased by Dad and laughing with the greatest happiness those days could offer. Jon's laughter often reminded TJ of his laughter while running with Fred in the projects. TJ enjoyed the laughter coming from his younger brother for a myriad of reasons. Those days were good times in the truest sense. Living on North 18th Street was more or less a step above the low-income community. Everything about North 18th Street was almost a picture-perfect environment. The trees were tall and fully grown, casting a calming shadow on the house. The street was clean and free of potholes and chips in the concrete, inviting a respectable community. North 18th Street at that time reminded TJ of a place out of a Norman Rockwell picture, pleasing to the eye, friendly neighbors, a place you wanted to live in for a while. The growing experiences on North 18th Street in many ways were pretty mundane. However, there were things that occurred while living there that impacted TJ's life all the way into adulthood, and they are the ones that will be cited in this book. Upon leaving North 18th Street, TJ was catapulted into a phase of having to mature and break the childhood connection. He was not aware of his preparedness, nor was he cognitive of how to tap into what his older brothers inputted into his mind. Maturing into adulthood was emotionally painful and mentally unsettling. TJ fought against a lifetime of realities and sought to hold on to his past. He held as long as he could to the projects and North 18th

Street. He perceived his family to be the best family in the whole wide world. Every single feeling and every perception he had of his family would be shattered and pulverized into tiny pieces in the years to come. Every shattered piece of his perception would be impossible to retrieve or rebuild nor where they advisable to attempt to rebuild. It was if all he knew and learned was either fake, a dream, or outright lie. He had difficulty sorting out what was true and what was a lie. At one point in his life, he had concluded that everything and everybody was a lie and everybody was lying. The prospect of suicide became a thought he would entertain often. Many times he was overwhelmed by his shattered perspective of life and deceptive and seemingly misleading view of growing up.

Good Memories First

From the projects, all the way through growing up on North 18th Street, his mom was the dearest person to his heart. TJ did love his father but was closer to his mom probably because she was always making every attempt to individually and personally keep her children happy. Dad worked two eight-hour jobs and also preached the Gospel of Jesus Christ at different churches, which kept him out of the house on a regular basis. Mom was always home until she began working jobs cleaning people's homes. She finally landed a permanent job with the Commonwealth of Pennsylvania as a janitor working in the evenings. TJ dearly loved her with all his heart and thought the world of her and clung to her every word, not doubting anything she spoke.

Thirty years later would introduce TJ to the first of several proverbial explosive realities that his mom was struggling with. There were many personal issues and situations brought upon her by his father, her husband, things that he wishes he had NEVER been privy to; essentially, he would have preferred to keep his own perception of his family. While growing up, he was clueless of his mom's personal struggles, and it was good he didn't know the things his older siblings already knew. After having been made aware of the struggles and sins in life, it answered the bitterness harbored in the heart of his older siblings. But as far as TJ was concerned, his mom was the greatest mother of all, and he thought she was full of the wisdom of God. The stuff they both went through somehow would encourage TJ to view the larger picture of life's woes and shortcomings of men and women. The development of TJ could be divided up into four quarters: he took some of his mother's genes and some of his father's genes but walked in the steps of his two brothers Fred and Bay, whom he idolized.

June 19, 1958, must have been a special time for his mom because every June 19th, she always gave TJ a birthday gift. When he became an adult and got married, she still gave him a birthday gift, even if it was a birthday card with money in it. The ultimate naiveté in TJ's life was from about eight years old up to about thirty, whatever his mom would do for him or buy for him was perfectly all right because to TJ, it was her expression of love toward him, and he would do anything for her. As a boy, TJ murmured and complained often, but deep inside his heart was the satisfaction that he made his mother happy because he pretty much obeyed her every word and did whatever she asked him to do.

One birthday, she brought a brown teddy bear for him, and he does not remember if she brought the teddy bear because he said he wanted one or if she thought it was a nice stuffed animal for him. He doesn't know the reason, but he clearly remembers the teddy bear largely because of how continuously his older brothers degraded him. Every older brother of TJ came down hard on him, and I mean hard, with jokes and sneers and laughing and calling him a "momma's boy." From Melvin down to Fred, Lawrence, and Bay. They all gave him a genuine hard time. Every single time they spotted him with that teddy bear, he would catch hell from them. TJ would hug the teddy bear and lay the teddy bear in the bed with him when he went to sleep. He walked around the house with the teddy bear and showed his gratitude and happiness to his mom for buying him that teddy bear. Jr. made a comment not directly to TJ, but the words found their way to his ears when he said to their mom, "You shouldn't give that boy a teddy bear. Buy him a football or a basketball, even hockey sticks, but not a teddy bear."

Mom laughed it off and told Jr. to be quiet before he hurts TJ's feelings. TJ did not play sports growing up, nor was he a socially active child. He did not go to house parties at all and did not go to the movies until about fifteen years old. Crowds frightened him, and he felt everybody was either making fun of him or did not like him because he was slim. His muscles had not developed, and he was shy, timid, and nonaggressive. While in high school, he decided on his own to join gymnastics and use the skills learned in gymnastics along with Isshin-ryū karate. His sensei became a role model of sorts in self-defense, and later on, having become interested in Bruce Lee, he changed over to practicing a style of kung fu called Sim Lum Pai under Sensei Brown (RIP). TJ took up martial arts to feel a sense of self-control and discipline in his own life and to develop the confidence to withstand bullies in school.

On another birthday, TJ remembers like it was yesterday, his mom came into the house with his older sister. He was either eight or nine years old, and it was toward the end of the day, but he had the undying faith and confidence in his mom coming through with a birthday gift for him. She arrived in the dining room with shopping bags in her hand, and his older sister also had shopping bags in her hands. Two of his older sisters were always bossy and pushy toward their younger siblings, and this particular older sister seemed to especially have an ax to grind with TJ. She told the young lad to "stand back and let us get all the way in the house—be patient, Timothy." He knew when any of his older siblings addressed him as Timothy, they were serious, and he better not play around with them. As a young boy, TJ was exceptionally playful and boasted a very smart mouth. He could irritate the most irritable person with his antics. TJ was basically happy being around his family, and his way of expression was joking around with them. He did not understand why Mom would allow his older sisters to get away with bossing them around. Nonetheless, he pretty much rolled with the punches then and took things as they would come. He stood back from his older sister with all respect. Yet he was filled with excitement anticipating what Mom was going to pull out of the bag and give to him for a birthday gift. In haste, his mom reached inside and pulled out a small box nicely wrapped and handed it to TJ. He does not remember if his younger siblings were standing around or not, but then they had to be because with eight brothers and sisters in the house, there weren't too many places they could have been. With a gleam in his eyes and excitement in his heart, TJ slowly and politely took the box out of his mom's hand. His mom said, "What do you say?"

"Thank you, Mom!" He couldn't wait to open the box to see what was inside. When he opened the box, he was thrilled that his mom had bought him his first wristwatch with a Mickey Mouse on the face of the watch. Looking back, TJ is not sure if his mom wanted her children to remain children or if she was just looking for nice things to give to her children. Either way, he quickly put the watch on his wrist and advertised a smile the remainder of the day, a smile so noticeable angels in heaven were able to see. He went to sleep with that watch on, went to church with that watch on, and always had his watch on when he left the house. That Timex watch was his pride and joy up to the point his older brothers got wind of it and the bustin' started again. His brothers could not resist the sneers and jokes about their "momma's boy" little brother. But this time, their jokes about him made him cry. He conveniently began to forget to put his watch on because of the embarrassment he felt from his older brothers. He did not know whether to show his gratitude toward his mom or seek his brothers' approval. The Mickey Mouse wristwatch was one of those birthday gifts from his mom that faded into eternity past. He does not know what became of that Mickey Mouse Timex watch to this day.

The Breathtaking and Remarkable Eliminator

Mom worked house cleaning jobs during those days, and TJ can only guess that she scrounged up the money to provide things for her children, things she thought a mother was supposed to buy. Dad always worked, but Dad's money paid the rent, provided for clothes, food, and transportation, from what TJ could tell then. TJ thought that Mom wanted to work to provide for her children's wants and desires and probably to have a piece of money for herself. Not to mention helping Dad pay bills, he could only guess. There was a store downtown market square called Miller's Furniture Store located exactly where the downtown Hilton is today. Miller's Furniture Store was kind of the upper-class furniture store during those days, and it was a nice furniture store. Not far from Miller's Furniture Store was an automobile place called Joe The Motorist. Once he began to drive a car, he would frequent Joe The Motorist for this and for that. He enjoyed riding the city bus with his mom to go pay bills, and he learned the responsibility of paying bills by going with his mother on the city bus. Between the ages of nine and twelve, TJ went with his mother on every opportunity he could to pay bills. She even graduated him to the point that she started giving him bills to pay and TJ would ride the bus alone, fifteen cents bus fare to pay Mom's bills. As a youngster, he felt like he was doing something worthwhile and gaining experience in becoming responsible. His emphasis shifted, kind of drifted from the desire to please Dad to the satisfaction of pleasing his mom. He wanted nothing more in the world than his parents to be proud of him and see him as a good child. His attachment to his mother began to develop and substitute for what he longed for in his father. Dad was, for the most part, always working, except on Sunday mornings, but his respect and reverence for him *never* diminished. It's just that Mom was ALWAYS there, and he was becoming old enough to help her with whatever she needed. He was fulfilled knowing that Mom had confidence in him and his ability to follow instructions and get things done.

His tenth birthday yielded an unexpected incredible, unbelievable gift from Mom. One day Mom told him to get ready because they were going downtown to pay bills. That's just how she said it, "pay bills." Excited and moving with rapid speed, TJ was ready before she finished telling him to get ready. Riding the bus and going downtown was one of the most exciting things he did as a young boy. His mother and father did not have any money to involve them in an extracurricular activity, and they didn't, for the most part, have any interest. They all seemingly still had the project mentality of survival and one day at a time. Extra things like Boys' Club, Girls' Club, and a member of a swim club or bike club NEVER entered his mind. Those activities were as far from TJ's mind as the expanse of heaven is from earth. But that didn't matter to him. He was happy just riding the Capital Area Transit (CAT) bus and going downtown with mom. Riding the bus was exciting enough during the days of the civil rights movement in Harrisburg, Pennsylvania. TJ and his mother typically would ride the number 12 State Street Bus because it was a straight route across State Street Bridge into downtown. Occasionally he and his mother would ride the number 8 Herr Street Bus into downtown, a downtown that resembled a leftover from the 1950s and one that appeared as though it would remain that way forever.

On that day TJ and his mom stopped at the G.C. Murphy's store on Market Street and Pomeroy's, the largest and most sophisticated downtown store at that time. What he liked about G.C. Murphy's was the meal his mom occasionally bought for him. Inside Murphy's store toward the rear of the building, off to the left was a restaurant with a counter and bar stools. At nine years old all the way through to twelve years old, he thought they made the best hamburgers in the world, at least the world he knew. Every now and then TJ and his mom would stop at Murphy's before catching the bus to go home, and his mom would buy him a big fat juicy Murphy's hamburger and fries. Those days were among the best days of his life as a boy, and he truly DID NOT want to grow up. He was not in a hurry for those days to end. Mom had a job cleaning apartments at a place called The Town House located on 6th and Forester Street. TJ remembers she cleaned the apartment of a well-to-do Jewish lady whom he never ever met. Mom's boss reminded him of Charlie's Angels when their boss always talked to them over the phone. Every time they were in her apartment, either she would call his mom or his mom would call her, and they conducted business over the phone. He never laid eyes on her, and he thought there was something secretive about her and the special way she wanted her apartment cleaned. Every time they went to her apartment, she was never there. She would give his mom special instructions over the phone, and TJ would hear his mom saying, "Yes, ma'am, I'll do that. Thank you, ma'am."

The town house restaurant on the first floor also made big fat hamburgers but nothing like the burgers at G.C. Murphy's. Part of TJ's excitement of going to pay bills with his mom was knowing his mom would buy him a fat juicy hamburger at one of those restaurants. Kind of silly, but at nine years old in 1967, moving from the low-income project lifestyle to "the hill" and now able to go downtown was an absolutely harmless, innocent "stay-out-of-trouble" good thing for a boy to do. There was minimal risk of getting in trouble with the law or becoming involved in drug trafficking, virtually an unheard-of thing for boys and girls in those days. Back then boys and girls were boys and girls, and family was family at least in the mind and world of TJ.

After paying a bill at Pomeroy's, Mom and TJ walked up to Miller's Furniture store, and he remembers entering Miller's Furniture Store and the memories remain "just like it was yesterday." Market Square today has a fancy Hilton Hotel, and Miller's furniture store was located EXACTLY in the same spot in 1967–1974? At some point when they left the furniture store, there was a bill that had to be paid at Joe The Motorist store. That was the automobile store, and TJ could not figure out why Mom was paying a bill at an auto store. Perhaps Dad had something laid away, or perhaps Mom was picking an item up for Dad's car. Nonetheless, when they entered the store, a bicycle was the first thing facing you in the center of the floor on display for all that set foot in the building. TJ didn't know, nor did he think, why there was a bicycle in an automobile store. He just knew when he walked in the store, the bicycle arrested his attention and captivated his mind. He became oblivious to everything else in the store and everyone else around him.

Mom said, "I'm going to pay this bill. Don't touch anything. Be a good boy."

Funny, he heard her but he didn't hear her, and subsequently, he failed to obey her, not out of disrespect or disobedience for that matter, but he had become captivated by a dream bicycle. The possibility of owning that bike, though very slim, overwhelmed his thoughts. At least, at best, *let me get a closer look. Let me touch it please,* he thought.

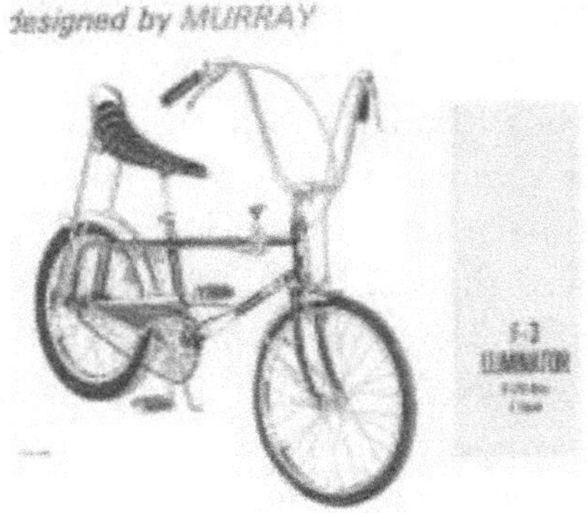

TJ carefully and clandestinely approached the bicycle awed by its beauty. Its color, its size, its style—everything about the F3 Eliminator bicycle appeared to be futuristic. It had a shine to it that would captivate any child, and in TJ's mind, the possibility of owning that bicycle was like a dream that never ended and a dream that would never come to past. Mom and Dad didn't have extra money to purchase something like that for him. Besides, there were seven other siblings in the house, so what made him think he would be the chosen one to deserve such a gift? So he dreamed, and his heart skipped several beats due to the overwhelming excitement and exposure to a dream that he wished and wished might become a reality. For about ten minutes, the dream of owning that bicycle obsessed his mind, and he couldn't control his wishful thinking. In a truly innocent disobedient manner, he slowly, carefully, unworthily, reached his hand forward, and touched the handlebar. The bike had a feel of quality and perfection he never thought possible. Never in the projects or anywhere else had he seen a bicycle like the F3 Eliminator.

Before he had the chance to finish his examination of the F3 Eliminator, and maybe because he was not paying attention to anyone or anything, Mom and a white male salesclerk were standing over him, both smiling. Mom said, "It's time to go, baby, let's go."

Mom reached forth to take his hand and escort him out of the store, but he didn't want to leave just yet. Seems like she paid that bill fast.

Give me more time. I'm not finished inspecting the bike, he thought. His thoughts were uncontrollable, and he wanted so desperately to speak those thoughts to Mom. He looked that bike over from top to bottom. Smelled the tires. Looked at the reflection of his face in the fenders. He took a close look at the chain guard that boldly displayed the word F3 Eliminator (in italics). He took a detailed sharp mental picture of the color of the bike—soft red, silver chrome fenders, racing tires with white unique red stripes on the tires. Three-speed gear shifter on the center bar with the numbers 1, 2, 3. The shifter was white, and the chain guard was red, with white letters of F3 Eliminator. The color scheme of the bicycle was unmatched by ANY bicycle he had ever seen, but it was time to go home. TJ specifically remembers riding the bus home sitting next to Mom, and she would occasionally look over at him on the ride home. He was trying very hard to hold back the tears that had welled up in his eyes and the excitement of a dream he deeply wished would somehow or another come true. Mom never said a word. She would just look at his face and smile, and he would smile back at her. Though he was sad, her smile reassured him and comforted his heart in ways he could not explain. It was if Mom had a secret but was unwilling to disclose even a hint to him. A surge of disappointment flooded his heart because he wanted desperately to tell her about the bicycle to solicit a response from her, but he was satisfied with her smile.

June 19, 1968

The day began like any other day, a gorgeous morning (those days were pretty much all gorgeous to TJ). In a word, his childhood was nice, very nice. TJ enjoyed being a child. He cannot think of one day that he lacked anything. At least he had no knowledge of the fact that they may have been lacking because everything seemed to be running well. He ate every day and had clothes on his back every day. He just did not have the niceties that others may have had. He did not have the privilege of going on vacations or to the beach. His parents did not have two cars until TJ was grown and out of the house and married. He did not miss what he did not have. As far as he was concerned, he was completely happy with what he had. He desired things and wanted things, but he did not press the issue with his parents because he felt deep within his soul that they were doing the best they knew how and the best they could. He was not fully cognizant of the effect of their lack of formal education, so he did not attribute his parents' lack to him and his siblings' lack. He felt his family was a straight-up godly, God-fearing, special kind of family, ordained by God to be a living testimony and witness of Jesus Christ. In TJ's heart, he was content with his family being a Christian family and serving the Lord. He was totally oblivious to the reality behind the scenes of the deep emotional scarring taking place and hellish personal issues that would boldly show its ugly face in the years to come. But that is later in the story of his life.

While riding the bus on their way home, all he could see in his mind was that bicycle, and he embraced wishful thinking until June 19, 1968, arrived.

When he woke up, he expected and wanted a surprise; it didn't matter what, it was his birthday, and he always looked forward to his birthday. He felt his birthday was special. His mom ALWAYS surprised him with something on his birthday, and that day would be the crescendo of surprises. That June 19, he was turning ten years old. The memory remains almost like yesterday. And it went like this:

"Timothy! It's time to get up, son. Happy birthday," his mom said.

He slept on the second floor in the room to the left as soon as you went up the stairs. Mom's room was to the right facing the front of the house. TJ popped up out of the bed with strength and energy to last for the next ten years.

"Wash your face and come downstairs to eat breakfast, baby!"

This was the one time she didn't have to repeat herself. He knew something was up, but he didn't have a clue to the extent of joy and happiness this birthday would bring. He never even thought for one second what he was about to see.

"Yes, ma'am, I'm up!" After brushing his teeth and washing his face fast, he hurried down the stairs. He was hoping to get a feel of what kind of day this was about to become. It was not until he was all the way downstairs that he noticed something unusual out of the corner of his eye. Something got his attention and skyrocketed his emotions to the throne of heaven beside Almighty God and left him speechless for what seems like an eternity.

Image from website ratrodbikes.com

He had fallen into excitement paralysis; he couldn't believe it! He thought maybe he was still sleeping and dreaming. He stopped at the bottom of the stairway and stared for maybe five to ten minutes before he realized he was not dreaming.

In the living room, propped up on its own stand, was a brand-spanking-new Murray F3 Eliminator! You could smell the newness from the tires. A flood of questions barraged his thoughts. How? When? How did she get this past him? When did she bring it home? Who helped her bring it in the house? Many questions that were irrelevant, but TJ had always been the type of child that had to know the who, what, when, and how of things.

His thoughts were equal to the thoughts he had the day he first laid eyes on the F3 Eliminator. He'd thought the ownership of that bike was an impossibility. But this time the thoughts were positive in nature and filled with unanswered questions that DID NOT MATTER. The F3 Eliminator was in his living room, and it was his personal property! Almost unbelievable, considering his mom and dad's financial state and the fact his mom worked part-time jobs, cleaning apartments and houses. Also considering the fact there were seven other siblings in the house. How did he deserve this wonderful once-in-a-lifetime gift?

The F3 Eliminator belonged to him, and it set the pace for the remainder of his boyhood. When he finally stopped admiring the bike in the living room, it was time to present his new bike to the boys on North 18th Street. It was time to take her outside and show off. Normally, he was a quiet boy, very unassuming, respectful, and friendly. But this day, he felt a sense of pride and childhood power. He felt he was special and had a "you can't tell me anything" kind of thinking. He didn't mean any harm. That's just how he felt once it settled in that he had something NO ONE on North 18th Street had or could compare to. TJ was the proud owner of the F3 Eliminator, and it was an eye-catcher and worthy of being touched by only the most respectful and decent children of the neighborhood.

Every birthday thereafter, from ten to about twenty, he expected a surprise from his mom, and every birthday thereafter, she always came through. He thought she was the greatest mom in the world. He thought the world of her and loved her with all his heart. He would do anything for her and stand in harm's way for her. She had placed his heart in her hands, and his umbilical cord, in many ways, was still attached. He thrived off her every word, and whenever she became upset about something, to him the foundation of his world was unstable. He looked to her for almost everything and expected good direction and guidance from her. He believed she knew God and Jesus Christ personally, as though she and God ate breakfast together or went to the local diner to chat over a cup of tea. He thought God was like an old friend of hers and she could get whatever she wanted or needed to satisfy the desires of her children. Of all the Christians in the world, to TJ, there was none closer to God than his mother. She was the single most influential person in his life that set him on the path of seeking to know the truth of the Bible. Essentially, he could thank her for developing him into the man of God in the decades to come. She was a mother of mothers, and it was extremely comforting just to be in her presence. Every day when he came home from anywhere and from doing anything, he always made it a point to see his mom and talk to her about anything. She was patient enough to listen to his silly escapades and adventurous travels around the neighborhood. She was his mom, and there was none like her in his eyes.

Ah yes! The F3 Eliminator was the first of dreams in his life that came to pass, a dream that he truly did not expect to come true. He could not see a way at all that his parents would be able to purchase that bike for him. Call it a blessing, call it goodness, he was clueless, but he believed as a boy that God was satisfying a boyhood desire of his because of how he viewed his mother and father. God enabled his mom to be able to lay away and pay in full his first bicycle. He had no clue that while they were going downtown to pay bills that his mom was paying on the F3 Eliminator. She really did a good job keeping that secret from him all those bill trips. He never learned who picked out the bike for him. Was it his mom or one of his older brothers? He kind of thought his mom picked it out, and if so, she had very good taste and made sure she got him the best.

The remainder of that day, June 19, 1968, was one of the longest days of his boyhood life. Mom allowed him to stay outside riding his bicycle way into the night. He was finally told to come inside the house around 11:30–12:00 p.m. You could do that back in those days without fear of police brutality and real danger, especially where they had moved to on "the hill."

Taking the Bike Out

He didn't need any help to get his bicycle outside. He propped the door open with one hand and held the door and with the other hand while carefully and slowly guiding his bicycle onto the porch. Once he got on the porch, he closed the door and began to take his bike down the three steps that led to the sidewalk in front of his house. He got down to the sidewalk holding the handlebars of his bike all the while inside feeling like he was ten feet tall with a glow on his face equal to the sun. A smile from ear to ear, yes, ear to ear. When he got on the sidewalk, all he did was straddle his new bike across the center bar and looked around to see who was outside. He gazed up the street and down the street and looked across the street until he spotted some of his new friends—MB, Calvin, and PJ. They spotted him also and came running over to his house.

"Wow, that's a slick bike," said Calvin.

"When did you get that?" asked MB and PJ. "You think you bad now, don't you?"

PJ was always the tough one of the group, but for some reason or another, he and TJ never bumped heads. "Hey, I just got it today. Today is my birthday."

"Oh, birthday boy! Well, you got a nice birthday present. Let's see what you can do with it," said MB.

Both Brothers MB and Calvin seemed to be a step ahead of everyone else on North 18th Street. MB and Calvin were the first to get a motorized minibike, a motorized go-cart, and always had a piece of money in their pocket—things TJ never had at that age. The F3 Eliminator was the best of good things about TJ's childhood on North 18th Street. MB and Calvin's father owned a barbershop and cut hair from clients all over the city. TJ supposed that was one of their means of income that enabled them to get a lot of stuff. Mr. Barbershop seemed to have good connections, and everybody knew him. MB and Calvin already had bicycles, but theirs was no match for TJ's. They had plain black bikes. TJ's bike, on the other hand, was cool. It had fenders, shiny fenders, red strips on the tires to match the color of the bike, and the F3 Eliminator was a three-speed.

TJ said to them, "Go get your bikes! We can ride."

Without hesitation, they darted across the street and within seconds came riding down the street in the stand-up position on their bike, looking tall and everything, chests poked out, head high, like they were looking for TJ and like they were going to show him up.

"Good," he said. "Let's get it on!"

At the corner of North 18th Street and Briggs, they started what would become an all-day event of bike racing the length of one block on North 18th Street. However, the block seemed way longer than what it is. You know what I mean. When you're a young person, *everything* seems big. It takes longer to get to your destination so on and so forth. But when you become older and revisit old familiar territory, you realize that things weren't as big as they seemed. Starting at the corner of North 18th Street and Briggs Street, one half of a block up the street from his house, they started racing the course. The maneuvers they did to outdo one another ranged from popping wheelies on the sidewalk and racing down the sidewalk to darting between parked cars. TJ and his new friends raced and raced and raced literally all day. He may have stopped to go into the house around 4:00 or 5:00 p.m. to get something to eat, but that memory is not clear. The F3 Eliminator lived up to its name—it was one smooth bicycle. The gear shift for changing speeds shifted precisely in sync with the chain, driving the wheels forward. The bike was ahead of its time and setting the pace for speed. TJ and his friends raced that day well into the night and also rode beyond the block of North 18th Street to racing around the block to see who would return to the starting point first. The concept of the "good ol' days" was true to its definition of the good memories on North 18th Street. They were truly days of good, clean, innocent fun. There was nothing of a sexual nature or drugs or thievery until they started getting older—fifteen, sixteen, and onward. While the projects were the days of innocence, North 18th Street was a mixture of good, bad, and very ugly as more exposure to the vice of life appeared. The experiences on North 18th Street was preparing him for the next phase of his life in the United States Navy. The Sailor and the Sermon began to take on heart-wrenching experiences that were unimaginable to TJ while living on North 18th Street. Every other experience prior to entering the military were preliminary to the real life-shaping, mind-growing spiritual battles that would construct his faith in God. Encounters the likes of which he could have never imagined in all his life. Spiritual and physical battles on the level of certain death and his faith in the Lord would be tried to the point of nonexistence. Physical death became a reality and an expectation in his heart on numerous occasions but was unsuccessful for reasons not clearly understood or known. There were times in TJ's naval career that, by all scientific data and odds of survival, he should be dead. There are many who can say that about themselves, but his experiences were more than just a near miss from an automobile accident. The Sailor metamorphizes into the Sermon, and the Sermon the Sailor thought he had was definitely under continuous construction.

But for now, the F3 Eliminator was the king and star of his life in childhood adventures. TJ, MB, Calvin, PJ, and all the North 18th Street gang that could hang tough learned the city of Harrisburg and would ride everywhere on their bikes. TJ and his bike was his sole source of getting around and socializing with one another nurturing good healthy friendships. The temptations that presented themselves to TJ and his new friends as they got older began to reveal what was dwelling in their hearts. But until that time came, they rode their bikes on North 18th Street, parts of North 19th Street, parts of North 17th Street, and the 17th Street churchyard. The Pennsylvania State Police Troop H Headquarters is located on Elmerton Avenue in Harrisburg, Pennsylvania. At the time the gang rode their bikes, Elmerton Avenue was congested with huge, tall forest-looking trees. In fact, they thought that area of town was the woods, and they felt they had ridden quite a distance from North 18th Street to get to Elmerton Avenue. Today Elmerton Avenue is entirely made up of private business: the Commonwealth of Pennsylvania State office buildings, a Susquehanna township park, and the United States Post Office Main Distribution Center. Back then nothing but woods filled the entire area, and TJ and his friends would ride their bikes through the woods, trying to get to the other end of the extremely narrow forest area. The crazy thing about riding on Elmerton Avenue was the fight with the little tiny red beetles. They had no clue what type of bug it was, but they came out of the trees and would literally fly after them, some connecting and biting the gang on the neck, leg, and arms. TJ and his friends would swat at them, laughing the entire time and riding at top speeds, attempting to ride faster than the beetles were flying. In hindsight, they were some very aggressive beetles, and he never learned what they actually were, but they were some mean bugs.

Very Ugly Memories

The Good, the Bad and the Ugly was the name of an old Western movie TJ watched as a boy. But he decided to modify the name based on the following experience and call this the "good, bad, and very ugly." The very ugly contributed greatly to his perception of educators and developed a mistrust of teachers. The bad was the last horrific event on North 18th Street before he left for the United States Navy. From the bad, an unexpected changed occurred involving one of his greatest mentors that influenced his decision to enter the navy. Working in reverse, we will look at the very ugly, and the bad will be coherent with the rest of the story. While in the fourth grade, amid fresh affirmative action and civil right laws marches led by emerging well-known black leaders who came forth during the 1960s. Among them were Dr. Martin Luther King, Jr., Rev. Jesse Jackson, and Ralph Abernathy. TJ did not completely understand the full impact of the civil rights movement, nor did he realize the effects it would have on his unlearned mind. But the time had come for him to slowly and gradually move into a world of conflict and a nation divided. All the while he was becoming aware of these things, he struggled to hold on to the memories of the projects and most recently the good and fun life of North 18th Street. Even though he was becoming aware of these things, he purposely ignored them and did not face them until he was forced to face the aggressive and prevailing spirit of racism and division. He was in the infancy stage of waking up in an era that plagued the United States of America and would shine the light on the hypocrisy of a hypocritical nation. So much racism and hypocrisy right under his nose and right in his face, and he was clueless of the impact it would have on his life.

Woodward Elementary school was two blocks from the house on North 18th Street, right at the corner of North 18th and Herr Streets. At the time, Woodward was predominately black children with some black teachers. TJ enjoyed attending school at Woodward because it was within walking distance of his house, and going to school at Woodward was fun. The beginning of the fourth grade brought about life-altering changes for the young lad. The experience didn't appear much to worry about for TJ, but to mom, it was a taste, a regurgitating of hellish unjust social practices in America. Mom remembers the times of Jim Crow laws in the south. Mom, originally from Atlanta, Georgia, and raised in the south, was very familiar with acts of racism that continued to be alive and well between black and white. Prejudiced acts largely were instigated by white society and white America. Mom received a letter in the mail from the school district that her child would be the first among a new government program to integrate schools. She cried and earnestly prayed to God on her knees to protect and keep her son from the evils of racism. When his mom read the letter and told TJ that they were going to bus him to another school, the concept did not make sense to his novice mind. To TJ, bussing sounded like children were being outcast and singled out, like something was wrong with him.

"Why are they sending me to another school? Why can't I stay at Woodward? I don't want to leave my friends."

He thought for sure his mom could get the ear of God because God always heard her. Surely he would answer and stop this foolishness of bussing. From what he could tell at the time, this was one time his mom's prayers did not get answered. Sadness apprehended his heart and left an unexplained nervousness in his stomach and a weakness his knees. He thought going to a predominately white school in the late 1960s would surely mean trouble—name-calling, fights, arrest, suspensions, and threats at home. His negative thinking was the national climate at the time, but all that stuff was new to TJ. The spirit of racism in the land had invaded his thoughts, and his mind was slowly beginning to break into very ugly things going on in the United States of America. He was scared, and it seemed that bussing was the way of the future for all schools, and there was nothing his mom or he could do to stop it. Once the government had made up their mind to attempt to solve the issue of racism and prejudice that they themselves created and once it was signed into law, the evolution of change had been put in motion. Historically, America has NEVER really given a damn about black people, and integration was one of the results that were birthed out of the civil rights movement. At that time, integration was an uncharted thing, but the country had already lived through desegregation for years that integration was dubbed as the most reasonable solution. The natural response of many white Americans was resistance on every level. Resistance in employment, education, the military, and sadly Christian churches in the name of Jesus Christ. It has been said by many scholars that Sunday morning is the most segregated day of the week.

TJ's first ride on a yellow school bus took place in the month of September 1968. Typically, today, a fourth grader riding the big yellow school bus is an exciting thing, and usually, mom and or dad walks the child to the bus, maybe with a camera in their hand to capture memories. Years later parents will look at their child's first school bus ride and enjoy the memories. But at the bedrock level of school bussing, this was not the case. TJ's mother walked him down the street in front of Woodward school along with other mothers. No camera. No excitement. No oohs or ahhhs. Silence. A sort of deadening, unpredictable, unhappy, lifeless silence of what might go wrong. Black children attending white schools in 1968. Civil rights movement had achieved a small victory, but this thing was very brand new, with a mountain of mixed feelings nationwide. The dust had not completely settled from centuries of the storm racism caused in America. School bussing became the law of the land in the wake of the Supreme Court's decision in *Brown v. Board of Education.* Marshall Elementary School, exactly four miles away in comparison to two blocks would be the secondary education institute for TJ for the next three years. The first bus ride to Marshall School remains a clear memory as yesterday. He remembers arriving at the school on Hale Street, and Marshall looked longer wider and somewhat modernized than Woodward. It was a gorgeous day outside but a gray dreary overcast inside his soul. When the children got off the school bus, there were two white teachers on either side of the bus door.

"Stand in a straight line, children. Don't push, don't rush," one teacher said.

"When I call your name, answer me loudly and clearly," the other teacher said. She went down the list until arriving at his name.

TJ spoke loudly! He spoke clearly as his mother taught him to speak, "Here!"

The children were literally marched into the school hallway, and immediately he noticed that Marshall was significantly larger than Woodward. Once they arrived inside the school, they were marched to the rear of the building to their classroom. All the children stood in single file quiet as mice, with a good mixture of black children and white children. The system had integrated black children and white children as planned and almost looked like half and half black and white. At least with Marshall Elementary school, someone did their planning very well, TJ thought.

From that day, the experience of Marshall Elementary School quickly went from bad, to not a good thing, to not so bad, to "I like it out here." However, there were many unanswered questions and not knowing what to expect or what would happen at this predominately white school. The most horrific thing that happened at Marshall Elementary school is mainly why this section is in the book. In reality, Marshall Elementary school turned out to be an overall good experience for TJ. The teachers were nice, and the female teachers were pretty. At Marshall, TJ was allowed to flourish in reading, spelling, and the beginning of fair to good verbal skills? The new children he came to know at a predominately white school were nice and easy to get along with. All his fears were totally unwarranted. But his fears were developed by the racism and division in the country and largely the fears of his mother. Mom was not purposely encouraging fear but the love TJ had for his mother was so deep that he felt what she felt and hurt with her pain. His mother's fear was actually his fear, and her fear was born DEEP within the Southern states involving Jim Crow laws and lynching black people and Ku Klux Klan activity. Who can blame her for what she feared, and who cannot understand why she feared those atrocious, heinous, dreadful, terrible acts of racism condoned by the American government? White leadership in America and justified racism is what TJ's mother knew and experienced firsthand. One can only imagine the tenacity and strength and hard times it took for her and many other blacks to not only deal with such atrocities but strive to let the evils of man remain in the past—not an easy task.

The education TJ received at Marshall Elementary School challenged in a good way to excel. At Marshall, he discovered the interest in reading and writing. TJ desired to become one day a poet and an author; hence, he first got the idea of writing a book while at Marshall Elementary School. He didn't know what to write about then, but he knew he wanted to write about something simply because all his teachers said he was a good reader and could pronounce words well. His teachers inspired him to always want to improve on whatever ability he would discover within himself. He liked all his teachers at Marshall and cannot recall one bad experience as the sixties moved into the seventies and the spirit of racism now had man's laws to constrain it. Laws do not eliminate injustices or prejudice acts. Man's law constrains the perpetrator of the acts by certain legal consequences based on the infraction. The laws of man are like a vicious dog on a long chain waiting for an opportunity to strike and chew your legs off. The chain would represent the law, and the dog would represent man, and every now and again, dogs can break the chain and run amuck. Marshall turned out to be a nice school to attend, and he began looking forward to riding the bus to go to school. One might say that God did hear mom's prayer, like always. Overall, Marshall Elementary School was a very good start of an educational experience that would last a lifetime for TJ. But that was the dream world had to be brought back to reality when he ran into the one lady he would never forget. The one lady who held on to her personal ugly racist beliefs and demeanor regardless of man's law. This lady was the manifestation of the dog breaking the chain, and her actions and reputation were widely known. She repeatedly broke the chain and received little consequences to her actions, as far as TJ knew.

The Ugly Racist Educator

One time at the end of the school year going into summer, TJ came face-to-face with the ugliest racist act personally targeted against his young flesh. All the teachers at Marshall loved TJ, and he had no problem with his school mates. He couldn't understand why the principal of Marshall could not see that he was a well-liked child who respected authority and was not disruptive in class at all. Reflecting back on one of the darkest days in his life, he discovered the principal was not a good people person with most, but especially with black children. Ms. GW was the principal of Marshall Elementary School and Woodward Elementary School and always appeared to have a scowl look on her face. TJ's view of Ms. GW was one of apprehension and on guard of all white people. Imagine Ms. GW as a hyena with a certain smirk on her face. The eyes of a crocodile lurking slightly above the surface of the water looking over the rims of her glasses. A scowl look as though she had a mouth full of lemons or sour grapes. He does not ever remember seeing Ms. GW smile. She looked like she would hurt a child if you got in her way or disobeyed her at any time. TJ made it his point to stay out of her way whenever he spotted her in the school building. Her appearance was always professional and her manner of walking was a proud look, erect, noticeable, about six feet tall. It appeared the teachers respected her or were fearful of her, and she seemed to always demand her staff's attention.

One day the children were lined up marching to the front door to leave the building. Most of the class was already at the door in the line. TJ was not paying attention that day, and he was holding up the line. Somebody yelled, "TJ, let's go" He turned around and began walking at a fast past to catch up with the line at the door. He was in such a hurry to leave school because this was the summer break coming up and he couldn't wait. He was walking forward and looking behind talking to the children behind him. He had plans to ride his bike every day and enjoy the summer. As he was walking at a child's pace, he suddenly and abruptly came to a screeching halt. He turned around to see who he had bumped into. He knew he bumped into a person because when he came to an abrupt stop, it was a soft stop, not hard, not as though he had walked into the wall, but soft like walking into human flesh. He turned around to see who he had bumped into, then everything sped up extremely fast. He never saw it coming. It was like one slow-fast motion. Before he could think, breath, or get his composure, the hands of Ms. GW were tightly wrapped around his neck, and she was shaking his head like you shake a bottle of ketchup to losing the contents. You would have thought she was all alone on a distant island trying to shake herself free from the bondage of being trapped among oversized weeds. She was still living on her own island wrapped up in the weeds of ugly racism. Unbelievable; in the midst of a multitude of witnesses the elementary school principal was vigorously choking a student in plain sight. She physically accosted, disrespected, abused, abuse of power and authority, harassed and racially demoralized a little black boy at Marshal Elementary School in 1968.

TJ felt he was getting a small taste of what it must have been like to have been a slave in this country. If Ms. GW was able to accost young TJ in public in broad daylight, it seems like no one was able to stop her, what of the slaves who endured untold brutality and death in these United States of America? To this day, he can see crystal clear her face in his mind's eye and the rapid back-and-forth of his little head shaking uncontrollably as she was choking him for unintentionally bumping into her. The school principal, Ms. GW, actually choked tears from his eyes. Whether that is possible or not, it remains the experience of young TJ. She choked him so hard that tears erupted from his eyes streaming down his face into his mouth and on his shirt like a geyser ejects water from the ground. TJ's anticipation of summer was ripped to pieces. Hell had erupted in another human being's heart and arrested his soul, creating an untold amount of anguish. The anguish he felt as a fourth grader was absurd and intensely traumatic. He could not breathe. His vision was quickly going blurry. He had no defense against a six-foot tall full-grown woman trying to choke the life out of him. He needed help in a desperate way. He gripped the books he was carrying, as if to hold on to some form of life support. It was his way of realizing he was still conscious. He could not breathe. His vision was blurry. Immediately he hated white people from that point onward and would never, ever from that day forward turn his back on another white person as long as he was alive. TJ did not know how to define what prejudice was and did not fully understand the issues of civil rights. But on that day, unbeknownst to him, he received a revelation inserted into his soul from a grown-up women. The message was clear; this is what it feels like to hate and to hate another race of people. Ms. GW gave him the definition of hate and demonstrated to him the anger and practice of prejudice that was very much still alive in America. His lesson was personally taught to him by a state certified educator. It would take decades to overcome that spirit in his life and even longer to understand the reason behind such unreasonable atrocities. He would become a full-grown man with children of his own before he would overcome what Ms. GW taught him. She took great strides to demonstrate to him how to hate. Essentially every day at Marshall was a beautiful day and wonderful educational experience. He anticipated going to school and did not like missing school up until the time the school principal taught him a lesson he did not deserve or sign up for. She epitomized the role of an educator and purposely taught him a lesson on hate with the intent to maim, disable, or kill. Her actions were undeniably evil to the core.

Obviously, she realized after a few shakes what she was doing because she pulled back her hands in a jerking motion and released him from her hellish grip. She offered no remorse or apology or anything else. She turned her head without uttering a word, and she looked toward the school bus. He does not remember if she even said a word at all. As the victim, it seemed to TJ she choked him for almost fifteen to thirty minutes.

The walk from the school door to the bus at the curb was about 35–40 feet, but it seemed like a mile. He tried to walk straight with the confidence his mom instilled in him, but he couldn't. He tried to be strong and shake it off, but he couldn't. He looked up toward heaven out of the corner of one eye and thought in his mind, *Why?*

He knew the other children were laughing, and he just knew everyone was watching him as he walked away. In other words, he was the butt of the joke. You know how it is in elementary school; kids joke, they make fun, and they laugh. He felt like he was walking to the bus in slow motion. All he wanted to do was sit down and turn his head in shame and look out the window and forget everybody around him. His thoughts were, *I got to get to that bus, I need to get to that bus so I can sit down and look out the window and forget about what just happened. I have to get to that bus!*

But his legs would not move fast enough. In the midst of the shock and evil unleashed upon him, he did not realize until he sat down that his pants were wet, not from tears but from the extreme debauchery brought on by the finest educator Harrisburg School System had to offer. His bladder could not hold the liquid content it was created to hold. That day he came face-to-face with fear for the second time in his young life. The paralysis of fear seized his mind as anxiety rushed through his heart at an uncontrollable pace. He had emptied whatever urine that was inside his body. He was blindsided by evil, hit upside the head by an entire country of so-called intelligent, educated leaders. He did not understand why and why him. TJ had been totally, inhumanly, unjustifiably, shamed, and demoralized by the principal of Marshall Elementary school.

Breathing was increasingly difficult. With each breath, his lungs were trying to catch up with his heartbeat. Frightening stress and unexplainable confusion overtook his thoughts. Ms. GW held him captive what seemed like hours. Her actions toward TJ were *deeply* personal and in sync with the hypocrisy of America. He did not understand why he felt shame. He did nothing wrong other than being in the wrong place at the wrong time crossing paths with the wrong person. He had no composure and his entire body was vigorously shaking like a falling leaf from a tree.

TJ thought maybe he had displeased God someway but couldn't figure in which way. He felt anger, like he wanted to do something to retaliate but didn't know how or what to do. He hoped something bad would happen to Ms. GW but felt wrong for thinking that way. He wanted someone to feel sorry for him but was afraid to tell anyone what happened.

Strangely enough, the other children were absolutely silent. Perhaps they also feared the same thing could happen to them. Not a soul on the bus snickered, joked, laughed, or even looked in his direction, from what TJ can remember. The ride home on the yellow school bus was filled with deafening silence, almost like every child on that bus felt the pain and humiliation. Ms. GW's evil spirit captivated, in the worst way, every single black child that day. Racism was still alive and well during those days. Every black child could relate to the pain and hatred they felt from a hypocritical America. Ms. GW demonstrated the epitome of hypocrisy in a hypocritical nation.

By the time the bus had driven to Market and Hale streets about two city blocks away, the memory of the remainder of that day faded into darkness. That day is one of those days he wishes he could erase so that it never existed. But as you know that is impossible, and every experience of our lives must be dealt with and overcome one day at a time.

Whenever TJ would ride by Marshall Elementary School, he could not help but see in his mind's eye the most shameful act by an adult woman toward a young fourth-grade child. He does not know if Ms. GW had children of her own, but ANY good mother would first think of their own child before accosting another women's child. Each drive-by resurrects in his mind the yellow school bus. He can see and hear the children in line standing at the door. He can see the teachers standing around, and he can see a dark menacing mist surrounding Ms. GW, standing with a scowling look on her face. There is no hatred, anger, or unanswered questions anymore. The memory, however, is rock solid, and TJ remembers it without a doubt. His heart has been changed, and his understanding is clear—the acts of racism are the bedrock of this country. The perpetrators of such acts must answer to God on the day of reckoning. The late 1960s into the 1970s were turbulent times for all people while racism flourished on both sides of the fence. The oppressor who feared the potential of those being oppressed and the oppressed who simply desired to be treated equally. The rights for dignity and respect continued to be a fight against racism and prejudiced acts spawned from the pit of hell itself. Even the leaders of this country in the twenty-first century continue to promote deep-seated racist acts. The current president of the United States of America, simply addressed by some blacks as "45," verbally encouraged, promoted, and sanctioned racist activity during his campaign for the presidency.

The Unjustified Spanking

Mom rarely spanked her children she would leave that form of discipline up to Dad. Of course, Dad seemed to be a master at it. Whether he enjoyed it or not, he taunted his children with spankings. He would say things like "I owe you a spanking."

TJ thought that was cruel, but he did not question Dad's method of discipline or his judgment. TJ was afraid to question Dad's judgment, and his younger siblings thought Dad was a picture-perfect, straight-out-of-the-pages-of-the-Bible man of God. TJ thought the same thing about Dad. On the other hand, he did not think Dad knew how to balance that authority and leadership. TJ was clueless that his father was a man with like tendencies and shortcomings. But TJ, being a child, simply tried to do what he was told. As he got older, he noticed that some of his siblings withstood Dad. Others outright disobeyed him, and others still disrespected him.

But back to Mom, she hardly ever spanked TJ, and this one day he got the spanking of his life from the mother he loved so very much. Years later, to vindicate her, TJ concluded the other things going on in her life contributed to the merciless spanking he received from her that day. Spanking her children was something she rarely did. But that day, if she was angry or frustrated about something else, she uncontrollably took out her frustration on TJ. He will never forget the unmerciful spanking he received from Mom. She spanked him so hard to the point she became very sick afterward. He didn't go to school the following day because he missed the bus, and he missed the bus on purpose. He was slow getting up out of the bed and dragging along so the bus would leave without him. He could hear the bus coming down North 18th Street, and he could hear children running to the bus stop. He looked out of his mom's window and saw the bus at the bus stop and knew whether or not he had time to make it to the stop. He did not tell his mom about Ms. GW choking him, and he does not remember telling her right away. One thing for sure, he did not want to go to school that day even though he enjoyed Marshall Elementary school, and he enjoyed being around his new white friends. The summer vacation had not yet kicked in, and there were still a few days left in school. But he was afraid of Ms. GW and did not want to see her even walking down the hall. He was not articulate enough to explain to his mother what had happened and was kind of hoping everything would blow over.

He took his time walking down the steps through the living room toward the front door. By the time he opened the front door, he heard the bus pulling away from the bus stop. He looked down the street toward Woodward Elementary School where the bus stop was located and noticed not a single soul standing outside. All the children were on the bus, and the bus was on its way to Marshall Elementary School. He hated to miss that bus. He also feared and hated to go back to school.

Slowly walking up the steps toward his mom's room, he ran into Fred. Fred looked at him and said, "You missed the bus, didn't you?"

"Yes."

"You're going to get in trouble because I know you did that on purpose." Fred was in middle school at Edison Junior High, and he walked to school and could leave the house much later than TJ. But

Fred had not left for school at the time TJ missed the bus, and once Fred discovered that TJ missed the bus on purpose, things would drastically change.

On one hand, Fred was cool, on the other hand, Fred was sort of a snitch and seemed to enjoy his siblings getting in trouble. Fred delayed his leaving for school just to make sure TJ got what he thought TJ deserved; a spanking. TJ could not get a word in edgewise, and he wished that somehow he could smooth Fred over and get Fred on his side, but Fred was not listening. Fred decided, in his own mind, to be the gavel of justice. Never once did TJ expect what was about to occur, even with Fred's unsolicited involvement over his deliberate action not to go to school that day. Both his mom and Fred had no idea how TJ had been traumatized by an educator sworn to teach and lead children to excel.

Mom was in her bedroom, and Fred ran to her bedroom and knocked on her door, and before TJ could explain anything or appeal to his mother, Fred blurted out, "TJ missed the bus, and I know he did it on purpose. He just didn't want to go to school."

Why didn't Fred leave for school himself and leave it up to him to tell their mom what happened? Deep inside, inarticulate or not, TJ believed had he been able to explain to Mom what happened at school, he may have gotten sympathy and leniency. At any rate, when his mom heard that TJ was still home by the loose lips of Frederick E., she opened her door and said, "What! You missed the bus, Timothy?" Whenever she addressed TJ as Timothy, he knew he was in deep trouble. "You did that on purpose!"

Tongue-tied and already distraught, he attempted to explain to his mom the real reason why he missed the bus. He also added to his unheard explanation, "I don't feel well." Failing to have the skill of negotiation in those days, coupled with a limited vocabulary, did not help TJ to plead his case.

Besides, Fred was right behind him, almost breathing down his neck, saying, "Yes, he did. He knew that bus was out there, and he knew he could make it. He missed that bus on purpose. I think he should get a spanking!" Those words coming from the lips of Fred, with such convincing persuasion, threw TJ into a level of unimaginable anxiety. The odds were wrongly stacked against the young lad because Fred was on a mission to edge their mom on to spank him, and his mother would not stop for two seconds to listen to him. The situation was a conspiracy against the lad, and pardon for his actions was unthinkable for his mom.

Fred continued to grind the ice pick by yelling, "Spank him!"

What a cool, uncool brother he was that day. Almost in sync with Fred's unjust suggestions, his mom shocked young TJ when she said, "I'm going to spank you. You missed that bus on purpose." Many times Mom would be playful with her children, and they all had come to accept her as a mother that loved her children and had every intention of keeping her family together. But this time, TJ could not believe what got into her, or if it was even possible that Fred's words were so forceful and so suggestive that Mom became someone else and something else when she decided to spank TJ.

Up to the point the first strike of the leather belt tore across TJ's backside, he thought and hoped this would be one of those playful moments, and he had a little smirk on his face, but then she said, "I'm not playing. You are going to get a good spanking for missing that bus." Still, he was not a believer of her words, because she always would take it to the limit and never actually spank. But he quickly realized that this was the one time his mother was not playing when she told Fred to "grab him and pull his pants down!"

"WHAT! Mommy I didn't mean to miss the bus on purpose! I'm sorry, I'm sorry! Please, Mommy, don't spank me! I didn't mean to miss the bus!" He might as well have been talking to himself, because neither she nor Fred considered his cry to "please, listen to my explanation!" He wanted so very much to explain to her why he missed the bus but lacked the assertiveness to withstand the onslaught of the negative words of Fred. The devil imputed into the mind of Fred to convince Mom that TJ needed a spanking. Any hope of intelligent listening was lost in the mind of TJ, and he was left with these words, "I'm sorry, Mommy. Please don't spank me, please!"

Fred was stronger than TJ because he was a little older and a little rougher. He caught hold of TJ, and with one motion, pulled his pants down. Mom said to him, "Pull them down, all the way down!"

By that time, she had a leather belt in her hand, and all doubt was dispelled in the mind of TJ that this was not going to be one of those playful times. Fred was rambunctious and excited that he had convinced Mom to spank TJ. Fred pulled not only TJ's pants down but his underpants as well. The young lad stood there squirming and crying uncontrollably and butt naked as his mother began to strike his bare backside with nasty blows. Each strike seemed to be harder than the last. He wondered if it were possible that the evil spirit of GW had somehow transferred to his mother. She swung the wicked belt on his undeserving body with blows that were generated from hell. The trauma experienced from the evil vise grips of Ms. GW at Marshall Elementary school induced by the school principal had now turned into rejection and deep unexplainable hurt and pain. Almost like an unseen evil force wanted to demoralize TJ and swipe his mind of the thought of loving anyone. This unsolicited devil was convincing him, *Nobody in the entire world cares about what you go through, so suck it up, boy, and cry like a baby.*

Fred held on to TJ with an evil force, much tighter than GW's grip. Painfully tight! Mom was striking the young lad from center field with blows he could not believe she could wield. There were times the belt caught his legs and times the belt caught his back and times the belt caught his buttocks. The strikes were not precisely on his butt but seemed to fall wherever she could connect. The spanking of his young smooth flesh seemed to be endless when in reality, she must have hit him with the belt no more than three or four times. It just seemed long because he could not believe she was spanking him! He just could not believe it!

Then she said to Fred, "Let him go. That's enough. Go to your room and don't come out for the rest of the day."

He struggled to pull his pants up, which were now drenched with urine and tears. He was weeping from deep within his soul, his human spirit crushed by the two people he loved. He felt there was no one in the entire world he could talk to because his mother was the closest person to him in those days, and Fred, he thought, was his friend and cool big brother. The love in his heart for them was without measure. When he turned to walk out her room to this day, he will never forget her reaction to spanking him. At this point, Fred kind of fades in memory, and now the memory is solidly focused on Mom. As he was walking out of her room, he shamefully looked back at her. He purposely looked directly into her eyes while his eyes were flooded with tears, as to say, "Why didn't you listen to what I had to tell you?"

For the first time in his life, his spirit had been reduced to untold hopelessness. His mind suffered the emptiness of thought and expression. He noticed that she was shaking and tears running down her face, and she said to him, "Go to your room and don't come out!" EVERY experience in the life of TJ up to that point had immediately become confusing. Feelings of boiling anger against Fred. He did not like Fred at the moment, and of course, he really wanted to die. If his mother, the dearest woman he knew and the dearest woman in his life at the time, rejected his plea and would not consider his words, who else could he turn to? He wished very much that something, anything, would happen that would take his life. He wanted to get hit by a car and die. He had seen other children get hit, and he wanted that to happen to him. He wanted to jump out the third-floor window but was afraid of heights. He wanted to run away from home and purposely lose his way. He was painfully starving for sympathy and did not know why NO ONE heard his plea and why no one would consider his voice.

His room, for the remainder of the day, crowded in on him. The more he cried, the smaller the room seemed to become. He sniffed and cried while curled up on the bed like a newborn infant. He was on the verge of physical convulsions. Uncontrollably, and with hellish frightening emotion, he cried himself to sleep. He woke up late at night, because he had slept all day, to the fresh memory of the spanking that his mother gave him earlier. The remainder of the day was a painful reminiscing of the spanking. Totally lost for any sense of explanation, he began to cry again until he cried himself to sleep into the next morning.

Cookie was the one sister that TJ found solace confiding in. He believes Cookie revealed to Mom what happened. When Mom got wind of the story, she began to question TJ, and she asked him, "Why didn't you tell me?" and to his defense, he blurted out, "I was trying to tell you when you spanked me that day, but you wouldn't listen."

She immediately burst into tears and hugged her son with the hugs he was most familiar with and begged his forgiveness for not listening. TJ then detailed everything Mrs. GW did and how he was endlessly shamed. GW embarrassed him without mercy. She physically hurt him and made him feel like a lost unwanted child. Both he and his mother cried, and with that her tears became TJ's acceptance of her plea to forgive her for not listening. In TJ's mind, his mother was quickly elevated back to the level of the greatest mother of all. What happened after Mom found out that grown white women accosted her child would turn the prissy Marshall Elementary School into a place that might as well have been a back alley street brawl. One very angry black woman too familiar with Jim Crow laws tore into the school and brought years of anger, plus her personal issues against the uppity life of white America. Mom reminded TJ of the scene in *The Color Purple* when actress Oprah Winfrey is storming through the cornfields toward her mother-in-law and says, "You had Harpo beat me!" Mom was about the same size then as the actress Oprah Winfrey was in that movie. Mom stormed into Marshall Elementary yelling, "Who's the white cracker that put their hands on my child?" I will beat your ass into hell itself!" She used a few other choice words on the day she met Ms. GW. TJ had never seen his mother fight or angry to the level of using profanity. He was stunned but satisfied. He was ecstatic that she took such a stand to defend her child in a time of great racial division nationwide. Immediately other teachers and a few men restrained her and made attempts to reason with her. Talking was out of the question with Mom. The beatdown of Ms. GW was all she had in her eyes. TJ often thought about what she may have been capable of or what she intended to do to Ms. GW. On that day he would not want to be Ms. GW. In telling his story, TJ must be respectful to his mother because he only heard her use profanity once or twice in his life. He heard other teachers pleading with Mom to "calm down, Mrs. DD."

TJ was frantic and excited at the same time to see his oppressor being debased and verbally demoralized. Mom never got her hands on Ms. GW, but the principal sure did take a verbal beating that day, the likes she probably never saw from black women, and TJ is confident Mom left a reverential fear in the heart of that lady. He stood alongside the wall outside the office wondering what his mother was going to do. Some teachers barricaded Ms. GW and shielded her from the angry Southern black woman. Mom had revengeful death in her eyes against one pompous white lady. GW did not appear to give a damn about anything but her own agenda. TJ noticed through the barricade that GW was standing with her hands folded, as to imply "you can't touch me." But he also noticed a slight twitch in GW's eyes, who was perhaps glad the other teachers were there to shield her. Mrs. DD was a battering ram that day, ready to mow the white racist educator down. TJ was hoping that Mom would get at least one blow in and crack Ms. GW upside her salon-styled head. At the same time, he was fearful for his mother had she struck that white woman with several white witnesses. Over time as TJ gained knowledge of the Most High, he would become convinced that all the Most High wanted in that situation was to put fear into the heart of Ms. GW. She had to know that you can't go around putting your hands on anyone's child.

There was one other time when TJ remembers seeing his mother that angry, and that was when his second grade teacher at Downey Elementary School smacked him in the face. He does not remember why she smacked him, but he remembers she left a handprint on his youthful face and his mother noticed the handprint. Now that is too deep, the handprint. From that day on, TJ never had any problems with Ms. GW again, and he was no longer afraid of her after seeing his soft-hearted, soft-spoken Christian mother turn into a lion, tiger, bear. Oh my! He believed if other teachers had not gotten a hold of Mom, he would have witnessed a smackdown—a screaming, hair-pulling, old-school back alley brawl. And he also was convinced who the victor would have been, none other than his sweet little Christian mother. The young lad then realized that the stern, mean, evil Ms. GW could be gotten to. Sort of like in the epic movie, *The Book of Eli*, when Carnegie, the searcher of the mysterious book being transported by Eli, shoots Eli and says, "You see, he's just a man." His spirit arose within him as he realized that Ms. GW was "just a woman" not worthy of being afraid of. All you needed was one angry black mother, and there were a lot of them back in those days.

Mockery, Laughs, and Jokes

Courtesy of Harrisburg Pa Archives

Courtesy of Harrisburg Pa Archives

Fast-forward a little to the seventh grade at Edison Junior High School, a time where hormones and fleshly pride were beginning to develop. But Edison was interesting and fun, to say the least. Edison was a time of growing into young adulthood and a time of competition in many areas. The Temptations, Sly and the Family Stone, The Jackson 5, The Isley Brothers, Marvin Gaye, Gladys Knight & the Pips, even a little bit of Parliament and on and on. Girlfriend-boyfriend childish games. Everyone has experienced those games to some degree or another. It's a child's world, but unbeknownst to the seventh grader, they are just a little bigger than elementary children. While TJ was in the seventh grade, his older brothers were in high school, attending John Harris High School. Both Ron and Frederick E. had become elevated in TJ's mind as the mentor of mentors. He idolized them in every way and in everything. He thought they were the coolest and Ron the fiercest. TJ believed they both were streetwise and swam upstream without getting eaten by the sharks. He wanted to be just like them all the way. Fred grew an afro, and

TJ grew an afro. Bay was smooth with the girls, and TJ tried to be smooth with the girls. Young TJ had a problem matching his style of clothes. His brothers kind of left him on his own when it came to style. He actually believed they didn't notice him until he was about fifteen years old. The way TJ dressed was up to him. The 1970s maxi coat era was during the time of the Super Fly era and the movie starring Ron O' Neil. Brothers were walking around with long leather coats, big wide-brimmed hats, and platform shoes. There were even a couple brothers in town who thought they were Super Fly. One brother drove a white Rolls Royce, and another brother drove a white Eldorado, with big front lights typifying what might resemble large eyes on the front of a car. These brothers' cars looked just like the car Super Fly drove in the movie.

In those days, there was a lot of wannabe Super Fly's around town, and Fred, for the most part, fell into that category. When it came time for TJ to get his maxi coat, you can only guess who purchased it for him. There was a store called Robert Halls at 19th and Paxton streets where many urban families purchased clothes for their children. TJ's family was no different living on North 18th Street. Mom knew he wanted a maxi coat, so they went to Robert Halls to buy one. TJ did not know quality clothes back then, and Mom's budget wouldn't allow name-brand clothes. The substitute then was a long reddish-brown "imitation" leather. The seventh-grade kids busted something fiercely on TJ about wearing what they called pleather.

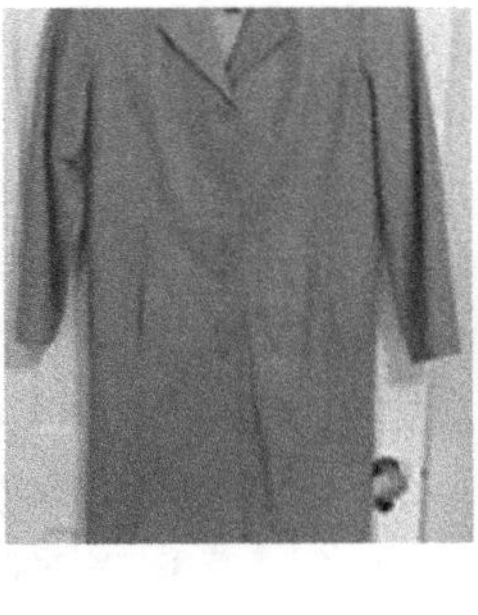

The coat was stiff, like it had been sprayed with starch. The coat did not move gracefully and feel soft; instead the coat was stiff and shiny. There was no loosely flowing movement of the coat while walking. It was if TJ were wearing a fancy reddish stiff straight jacket. But nonetheless, he believes he was styling until his older brothers had a word or two to say about his pleather. TJ thought he was cool; schoolmates thought he was a stand-up comedian and a novice when it came to style. Busting on one another was the minor side of events of those days. TJ was so naive that he took in stride all the busting slung at him because of his pleather and the multicolor dashiki Mom had made for him in the seventh grade. He also had the nerve to wear high water pants, pants he really liked. He thought nothing of how they looked. Even a schoolteacher had the nerve to bust on his dashiki. A black female teacher in Edison Junior High called another teacher over to where they were standing and pointed at TJ's dashiki and said to the other teacher, "Look, his mother made this. Isn't it nice?"

TJ took the comment as a compliment, but looking back, he does remember the teacher with a smirk on her face while asking the other teacher, and he does remember both of them sort of snickering while he walked away. But there was something more threatening that occurred during those days that would make busting seem like child's play. The conflict and ongoing issues between the Uptown and the Hill boys of Harrisburg, Pennsylvania, involving girls. TJ did not know if there were actually gangs or not, but he knew the Uptown and Hill did not get along. And from what he understood, the issues had to do with girls and who was dating who. Was a Hill guy dating an Uptown girl, or was an Uptown girl dating a Hill guy? There may have been more involved than that, but that's all TJ knew at the time. The summer of 1970, August, to be exact, was one that would saturate his mind long into adulthood and one that would elevate his view of Ron and Frederick E. from being just cool to being street-smart, terrible "sons of thunder." What took place in the summer of 1970 would be the clashing of sumo wrestler. The knockout of a heavyweight boxer. The ultimate fighter of explosive proportion. A combination of earthquakes and tornadoes mixed with the likes the devil himself never imagined. It would be the quintessential of what TJ thought of his brothers and how terrible he viewed them, and that night remained in his mind throughout his career in the United States Navy.

3

BOYS AND GANGS

Noise in Front of the House

Deacon and Mother P. were the next-door neighbors who lived in the duplex house next to TJ and his family. The Ps were an elderly couple who TJ supposed at that time were probably in their mid to late fifties. They projected a holier-than-thou type image. All the Commonwealth of Pennsylvania church of God in Christ respected them as a God-fearing holy couple. They were loved by many and hated by others, but they were very influential in the Commonwealth of Pennsylvania church District. Mother P., as she was called a mother of the Church of God in Christ, would pray and sing aloud at night to the point that you could hear her speaking through the wall. You could also hear her talking about certain people of the church and how God would "take care of them" for whatever reason, either for disrespecting her or talking about her. She appeared like she was without sin, and they both appeared to be the holiest people in the eyes of TJ. Many times TJ questioned her personal witness of Jesus Christ and the persona she must have given to the world. Nonetheless, because of who she was and what she stood for and how TJ had been raised, he respected them both with godly respect. He never personally got a hard time from them. In fact, many times he believed Mother and Elder P. had a genuine parental liking toward him. He will never know on this side of heaven why they took a personal liking toward him, but he was glad they did. Maybe they were parental toward all TJ's brothers and sister, he did not know, but in his eyes, they were a fantastic couple to know, especially in August of 1970. Only the Son of the Most High has the authority to judge their witness while living on this earth. But one night TJ thought their actions to be the actions inspired, motivated, and led by an untold power beyond theirs. Elder P., on the other hand, demonstrated a quiet and meek spirit and very laid-back personality. Deacon P. was a stoic type and distinguished well-dressed respectable gentleman. He was about 5 feet 9 and was built like a locomotive. Stocky, broad shoulder, deep voice and distinguished, to say the least. He had a way about himself that made you want to respect him. He didn't seem like he always agreed with Mother P., but then he didn't always speak up, nor seem to be the assertive aggressive man that you might think him to be. That same problem with headship and authority is prevalent in the world today due largely because of the silent voice of Adam. In the book of Genesis, God gave Adam his Word and distinctly told Adam, "DO NOT EAT of the tree of knowledge of good and evil." Adam failed to take authority over his wife and failed to obey the Word of God. TJ would learn that such has been the case with many men throughout his life's experience.

Both Elder and Mother P. stepped into a realm that evening the likes TJ never would have imagined from them, nor has he ever seen it again in any Christian, young or old, since that night. Perhaps both Elder and Mother P. did not even expect themselves to walk in the role of divine intercession. Mom and Dad were at Emanuel Church of God in Christ at 16th and Liberty streets that evening. It was a Sunday evening, and both Ron and Frederick E. were at the Penway movie theater at North 18th and State Street. TJ and his siblings were in the house in the living room watching TV. Cookie, Gloria, Dewitt, and Jon may have been sleeping. Both of them were still little boys. TJ was twelve years old in 1970, and he understood a little bit about what was going on. Some black-and-white TV show was on TV. It was quiet in the house, perhaps one of the quietest nights ever in TJ's house, and they all were basically chillin', living in their comfort zone, waiting for Mom and

Dad to come home from church. That silence they were enjoying, without warning, was broken into what seemed like an all-out war!

The first sound TJ heard was like objects being thrown against cars, then loud yelling and screams, screeching, horrific screams. Girls' voices yelling. What sounded like slaps, maybe punches and objects, maybe human bodies, repeatedly being thrown up against cars. All sorts of noise that was not easily distinguishable were happening right in front of his house on North 18th Street. Noise on a level that forced everyone who was home to come outside their house to investigate what was going on. TJ jumped up from the floor in front of the TV and ran to the door. Cookie was behind him, and his younger brothers and sisters were roused up out of sleep. Cookie and TJ tried to restrain them in the living room. When TJ opened the front door, he was faced with what seemed like a multitude of people walking, running, standing, screaming, yelling, and throwing things. He immediately saw baseball bats, a few sticks here and there. Then like a flash of lightning, there was a collision of two, three, maybe even four guys throwing fists back and forth, striking each other with unbelievable blows. Two guys and one guy up against a car punching what seemed like precision blows. It wasn't sissy kind of fighting. These boys were hitting one another face-to-face with precision. TJ looked swiftly to the left and to the right. He looked up the street, down the street, trying to identify who's who but was not able to. There was too much going on way too fast. There were too many people in front of the house and too much noise and chaos. Pandemonium had filled North 18th Street. What's going on? He stood on the front wall of the house trying to see. He was excited about what was happening but quickly became deeply saddened when he realized both Bay and Fred were at the center of the conflict. Bay was one of the guys up against the car. He did not immediately spot Fred, but his eyes became fixed on the guys up against the car. Like a punctured fountain erupting, tears filled his eyes. The tears were uncontainable, without restraint, but he kept watching, wanting to know the outcome. Wanting to see what was going on. Wanting to help but couldn't. He looked over at two other guys up against a car and one guy in front of them throwing blows left and right with rapidity and precision of a trained professional boxer. The two guys up against the car were being busted upside the head and thrown around like amateur fighters. The one guy that was kicking their butts was broad shouldered, about 5 feet 4 and solid as a rock. TJ came to learn later he was Bay and Fred's best friend. They called him "Speaks."

His punches could have been clocked with radar to ascertain the speed at which he was throwing them. It did not appear as though the guys up against the car were able to get a punch in at all. Speaks had his head tucked down, sort of like he was running in a race. He had his shoulders back, and his elbows looked like two precision pistons operating a turbocharged well-oiled engine. TJ was mesmerized by Speaks' fighting ability and focused on his battle for about five minutes or so. It seemed that's how long Speaks were kicking butt of two, NOT ONE but TWO guys. TJ concluded that Speaks was one of THE meanest street brothers he had the privilege to know. He watched until somehow, the guys got away from under his blows and ran down the streets. Speaks then turned to another guy and slammed him up against a car and like an encore performance, measured every punch and every blow. TJ thought then that Speaks was invincible and nothing or no one could stop him! The crowd moved along down the street as one body. Punching, swinging weapons, pushing one another. It was about 10:00 p.m., but it seemed like midnight because the spirit of mayhem hovered over North 18th Street that evening demonstrating pure lawlessness. He now believes that Satan had launched an attack that was targeted at his father and his household. While both parents were attending church service on a Sunday evening, the devil was at war with their children with the goal of taking a life or two that night. That August night reminisced of a dark cloud that would not go away and seemed to linger on and on. It was one of the longest nights ever at that point in TJ's life. Everyone who entered into the radius of the fighting was quickly engulfed in its rage. You either felt anger, hurt, pain, despair, frustration, and death—any one of those feelings could have quickly consumed your heart and swept you into the fray. Or God would have to miraculously intervene in your spirit and put inside you resilience and power beyond human ability.

A miraculous ability and resilience did demonstrate itself in two of the most unlikely people. As if on cue, both Mother and Elder P. swung their front door open as if to say "enter the P's!" They rushed outside from their home with courage beyond their own strength to be courageous. They were employed by a divine calling and assisted by angels that evening. It was their time. It was their day to be transformed into a character of angelic proportion. Had TJ not seen it for himself, he would not have believed it. When the Ps entered into the mix, TJ was standing against the wall, and his eyes were filled with tears that seemed to nestle in his eyelids. A man by the name of Deacon P. rushed out of his house looking like a bull, his chest out and his head held high. He had confidence in himself that was far beyond human flesh. It was confidence as though he may or may not have known. He had been drafted into the army of God and the Spirit of the God-endowed his physical ability times seven. TJ believes the Ps may have come outside because the noise was directly in front of both their houses, and they knew their brand-new Cadillac may become damaged. They were very particular about their possessions, especially their Cadillac. But once they stepped outside, TJ was fully persuaded that God had dispatched one of his warrior angels to endow them with heavenly ability. God immediately elevated their spirit on a heavenly plane and turned their heart toward the lives of youthful men and women. They may have come outside with one thing on their mind but quickly stepped into chaos stirred by the devil himself. They were immediately enabled to genuinely engage hell in this conflict, and God made them become something they could have never become on their own. Deacon P. boldly walked into the midst of the fray and began to displace fighters like a shovel scoops up snow and puts it aside. Deacon P. did not strike anyone because there was no need. With God on his side and his warrior angel, the Deacon was compassionate, bold and battle-worthy without injuring one soul. But TJ did see the Deacon pick boys up one, two at a time and move them away from Bay. When Deacon P. realized Bay and Fred were involved, all TJ heard from that point from Deacon P. was, "Bay! Bay! Bay! Bay! Come on, son, get yourself together! Let's get out of here, son."

He was a quiet man, but that night he thundered like the voice of many waters. Then like a flash of lightning, Mother P. was on the heels of her husband, "Deacon, Deacon,!" Where did she get the strength and courage to engage the fighters? As Deacon P. was displacing fighters, Mother P. was holding them back—holding them back! How was she able to do that? And while she was holding them back, NOT A FIST WAS SWINGING toward her. TJ observed Mother P. chase a couple boys down the street as she was praying aloud in a manner that was unlike any prayer he had ever heard her pray through the wall. With her right hand held toward heaven, she yelled out, "The Lord is my light whom shall I fear the Lord is the strength of my life of whom shall I be afraid!"

The Spirit of God, in a real, undeniable way, took over her body and spoke using her tongue. It could have easily been compared to the spirit of Elisha and the day of Pentecost when the outpouring of the Holy Ghost fell on the disciples. Both she and Deacon P. were anointed of a different kind just for that night. Maybe the boys heard thunder or a language of heavenly proportion and we just heard the voice of Mother P. Like when Jesus asked the Father to glorify his name and a voice came from heaven, which said, "I have both glorified it, and will glorify it again." But it sounded like thunder to the people (John 12:27–29). She and Deacon P. were not themselves—at all! They had been possessed, endowed with a divine presence and righteous indignation the likes of which TJ has never seen again in two human beings. He longed to witness such a presence of the spirit of Messiah, if not in himself at least in someone else. The *Ps'* response and involvement in rescuing those boys that night remain undeniable and forever recorded in the eternal record of heaven.

There were thoughts in the mind of TJ, all kind of thoughts: *If only Mom and Dad could see what Deacon and Mother P. are doing. If they were only here to stop this madness. Where are the police?*

Oh, the police did not show up until after everything was over (typical, especially in a predominately black neighborhood of mediocre income). Both Deacon and Mother P. had cleared the street of the worst fighting TJ ever witnessed on North 18th Street. As the fight progressed on, Deacon P. made his way down the street after Bay, continuing to call his name out.

Then a cry rang out, "He's shot, Bay is shot!"

TJ's heart sank into a deep chasm of a lifeless freezing pit. His body became numb, and he ran into the house, thinking, *No! No! He can't die! Why is this happening? Why Bay?*

The words kept ringing on the street from one corner to the next. "Bay is shot! Somebody shot Bay."

Deacon P. was there who again courageously intervened and somehow or another got a hold of Bay and rescued him from the cruel sickle of hell's death grip. Deacon and Mother P. walked into the enemy's camp and into the enemy's presence and snatched out from the grips of Satan two boys that death was in the process of taking. Grace, sovereignty, the will of God, providence—all those attributes were present and implemented that night. Subsequently, Messiah used two of his servants in his own way that most of Harrisburg, Pennsylvania, and the world probably have never known. TJ learned later that Bay was shot in the shoulder with a pellet gun, which made the shooting less severe than what it appeared to be. Even the weapon used that night by the assailant was orchestrated by God to be less threatening to the life of one of TJ's idles. Yet the miracles continued when the fighting had subsided and the police finally arrived. From what TJ could tell, both Deacon and Mother P. had not one scratch on their body. They were completely unharmed in the middle of the worst fighting TJ had ever seen as a boy. They walked right smack into the heart of pandemonium and quelled the storm. Both were used as regulators against evil and transformed into angelic police. They not only displaced humans, but they put Satan on the run and every evil spirit involved that night. The Ps, by their obedience to God and fearless actions, sent Satan, the devil, running back to his headquarters in shame. Deacon and Mother P. had the spirit of David, the anointing of Elijah and Elisha, and the faith of the apostle Paul. That night they moved mountains and walked on the sea of death dispelling the cloud of fear and they put the devil on the run. They were well equipped beyond a simple religious experience. They were truly godsent, and God commissioned to do what they did. For all time and memorial may their work of courage and obedience on that Sunday night in August 1970 be eternally remembered. After the fights broke up, several guys stood directly across the street way into the wee hours of the morning. They were casing the house out waiting for Bay or Fred to step in or out the house.

Still Fighting

Seems both Bay and Fred were always involved in some conflict with the uptown boys. In those days, a constant rivalry existed between what was known as "the hill" and "uptown." Ideally, uptown boys didn't go out with hill girls, and hill boys didn't go out with uptown girls. Whenever that unspoken agreement was violated, fighting was always the outcome. That whole immature act is quite silly now as you look back on it, but it was reality then. Bay and Frederick E. went to John Harris High School, and TJ was being bussed to William Penn High School in the eighth grade. One day, from playing basketball at 19th and Forester street playground, Bay came storming in the house yelling, "I'm going to get him, I'm going to get him."

Fred was right behind him. Everyone wanted to know what or who was he talking about. By the time he got to the dining room, everyone understood his anger. His nose was busted wide open, blood streaming down everywhere.

Fred yelled out, "A guy hit him in the face and had a rock in his hand!" Fred continued on, "They were fighting, and the guy picked up a rock and hit Bay in the face."

Mom was scurrying around attempting to restrain Bay from his anger and the retaliatory urge to go back outside with a bat or some sort of weapon.

Bay kept yelling out, "I'm going to get him!"

It was a day of unrest and confusion inside the house. All sorts of anger filled the heart of young TJ. He did not know what to make of all this fighting and seemingly stupid stuff to him. What is the fighting for? Over girls? Didn't make sense to TJ, not at all! His only concern was for the well-being of his brothers. They kept getting into trouble and seemed to wear fighting as a badge of pride. But TJ concluded that fighting was the only way to establish yourself in the community and to hold your own with the women. Or maybe fighting was a way for them to express displeasure and anger built up inside them? Or maybe fighting was the result of Dad not being there mentoring and teaching and guiding as the Bible says fathers are supposed to do. The answer was not clear to TJ then, but at any rate, God had mercy on all of them during those turbulent times.

Mom eventually calmed Bay down, and TJ does not remember how or who took them both to the hospital, but they did go to the hospital to get treatment for Bay's injury. The questions in the mind of TJ was about to be answered with the personal training and mentoring he was about to receive from Bay. Fred was the loyal follower of Bay, and wherever and whenever something kicked off, if it involved Bay, Fred was there. It became clear to TJ later on, around sixteen years old, that Bay was the leader and sort of godfather of his crew he hung out with, and Fred was his disciple. Nonetheless, both men, the brothers of TJ, were his idols for decades to follow. He wanted to be like them in just about every way. He looked up to them and trusted their every word and sought their guidance in just about everything. He looked for in them what he longed for in his father. Not to take away from his father at all; it was his father that gave the impression that there was nothing wrong with following brothers as long as they did not lead down the wrong path. Dad worked sixteen hours a day on two different jobs. He was not always there to monitor and father his boys. Sad to say, he didn't know what path TJ's brothers were leading him down. Under normal circumstances, siblings will stick together and will not reveal to Mom and Dad the things they are learning and doing. Such was the case with Bay and Frederick E. mentoring the young TJ. He NEVER disclosed to his mother and father the things he was learning. He just followed and learned from the lover, fighter, and mentor of his life. He didn't know any better and thought his acts of sin were normal growing up. In many ways, the practices and choices he made because of the great influence of his brothers were normal as sin goes. It appears to be a normal process in most family to learn how to commit sin. But then again, what family on earth is exempt from committing sinful acts? Whatever Frederick E. said, TJ felt it was all right repeating. By this time, TJ had overcome the dreadful spanking that Fred influenced Mom to give him when he missed the school bus. As far as mentoring goes, Fred was back at the top of the list next was Bay. To TJ, Bay was just a tad bit more complicated than Fred, and Bay required some "bonding," so to speak. Anyways, whatever Bay did, TJ felt it was all right for him to do. Whatever and whenever they talked and walked, TJ found great honor to be allowed to talk and walk the same path. They could do no wrong in his eyes and were essentially the two men his life would model. Be it good or bad, he strove to walk in their steps. In the future, the break away from their ownership, so to speak, would be emotionally earth-shattering.

The Boys from Uptown

The time had come for TJ to experience his personal encounter with Uptown boys. One incident scared him a little bit, and he was expecting something bad to happen. On his way home from his best friend's house, James Jones at 1402 State Street, he encountered some guys. There were these guys about six or seven of them, and they were walking about twenty feet in front of TJ. In fact, they were far enough in front of him that he could have walked slower and drifted back from them out of danger, placing them even farther in front of him. But with the so-called street spirit, he wanted to test his worthiness and did something very stupid and almost got swooped—that's when several guys jump you at once and beat you up. These guys were walking and talking, laughing among themselves, and seemed to be minding their own business. TJ was behind them a few steps, and he kept walking until he overtook them. They took up the entire sidewalk because there was about seven of them. They were strolling, seemed like they were not in a hurry to get to wherever they were going. And TJ, to this day, does not know why he was in such a hurry. Nonetheless, when he walked past them, he had to step in the dirt and really does not remember if he brushed up against the closest guy to him or not. But when he walked past them, he DOES remember saying very softly, kind of under his breath, "Excuse me."

No sooner had he walked past them when one of them said out loud, "Cut your stroll!"

TJ kept walking, thinking nothing of it and trying to ignore them, but they said it again, "I said, cut your stroll!"

At this point, he knew these guys were up to no good and he was about to get into something he knew he would not be able to handle. He started walking faster, and another yelled out, "LET'S GET HIM!"

TJ started walking a little faster, and they started walking faster. TJ started running, and they started running, and at this point, his heart was racing. TJ's encounter with the Uptown boys took place after the North 18th Street fight, and he does not remember how far apart the two events were, but he knew it was afterward. In his mind, he was thinking "Uptown and Hill rivals." He quickly ran across North 17th Street and turned up a little alley called Miller Street, which was the worst decision he could have made. They quickly caught up with him and cornered him between a building.

Looking back at his lessons learned, he envisioned a sort of daredevil move he wished he would have attempted. If he could have maintained his cool, he would have run in a totally unsuspecting zig zag way. For instance, he would have run directly into the middle of State Street in the face of oncoming traffic to throw them off. TJ was in familiar territory, and they were not. He would have run up the middle of the street while traffic was coming down to see how many could have kept up with him. He would have jumped on the backside of a moving vehicle. In those days, he was a bit of a foolish daredevil. If the driver would not have stopped, he would have ridden the car up to North 18th Street, hopped off, and run down North 18th Street as fast as he could. Once on North 18th Street, it would have been straight clear running and in those days TJ was a strong sprinter. They would not have caught up with him, and he would have run directly into his friends on North 18th Street. But it did not happen that way. In fact, days afterward he thought about what he could have done differently by getting away from those guys.

But he ran up Miller Street alley, and they caught up with him and cornered him between a house and the cross alley. It was just his luck to get swooped by seven guys when he was alone. He supposed the ringleader was the one who got in his face and said to him, "Yo, you bumped into my homeboy."

"I didn't realize I did."

"Well, I'm telling you, you bumped into my homeboy. Now tell him you're sorry."

Nose to nose, TJ and the ringleader had a stare down for about five seconds. Everything inside TJ DID NOT want to say I'm sorry. For what? There were seven of them and one of him. *Why do I have to tell a guy I have never seen before in my life and will probably never see again that I'm sorry?* he thought.

The bigmouthed ringleader said again, "Are you going to tell him you're sorry?"

Only God knows the youthful pride of TJ did not want to comply. He wanted to say, "HELL NO!" But he was compelled to swallow his pride. The reality was, he was outnumbered, and at fifteen years old, he found a little bit wisdom within his soul. He looked at one of the guys. He didn't even know who he was saying sorry to, but he humbled himself and said, "I'm sorry."

The bigmouthed leader then had the nerve to say, "Don't let it happen again."

And TJ said, "Okay."

The whole thing was like something out of a comedy scene. What were the chances that he would ever see those guys again in similar circumstances?

That was funny, really funny. TJ did not laugh then, but to this day will cry laughing, thinking about the whole encounter. Call it what you want, but the grace of God intervened in the silliest acts of TJ that day. The encounter was extremely silly because it is 90 percent certain a young boy will not get off that easily in today's street world. On the other hand, the mercy of God kept TJ through all the potentially dangerous and harmful situations while growing up in the projects and North 18th Street.

But do you think TJ was going to let that go? He was filled with crazy youthful pride in those days and very proud of his brothers Bay and Frederick E. and the things they, directly and indirectly, taught him on the streets. Those Uptown boys had to pay, and they had to pay today! As soon as that dialogue was over between TJ and the bigmouthed ringleader, they turned and began walking away. Immediately, TJ broke out into a sprint. He ran as fast as he could between the houses and up to North 18th Street and sprinted down North 18th street with enough speed to win the Olympic gold medal. When the Uptown boys turned to walk away, he looked over his shoulder and noticed they started running the other way, like they knew they may have stirred something up. He couldn't figure out why they were running. There were seven of them and only one TJ. Why did they run the other way after they had threatened him and tried to put fear in his heart? Why did they run?

TJ ran down North 18th Street, not missing a step and tripling his stride. He had to find his 18th Street boys, and he had to find them NOW! Considering this stage play, so to speak, sometimes it seems that God must allow us to have fun while at the same time teaching us the necessity of needing his protection. As soon as TJ hit the vicinity of his neighborhood, all his North 18th Street friends were outside, EVERY one of them! He yelled to them while still running down North 18th Street, "MB, PJ, Calvin," and there were a few others who joined in the call. "Hey!

there were some guys that were about to jump me a few seconds ago! Help me! Let's get them!"

Chains, sticks, monkey wrenches and other things that could have been used as weapons immediately were in the hands of the North 18th Street gang. TJ figured considering where they cornered him that they must have run down North 17th Street trying to take a shortcut back to uptown. He thought strategy and said to his crew, "Let's run down Forester Street and head them off at North 17th Street."

The entire crew of North 18th Street got to running, and some were even on bikes. They ran down Forester Street, and wouldn't you know it, TJ spotted them walking down North 17th Street like they were on a Sunday afternoon stroll.

He yelled out at the top of his voice, "THERE THEY ARE, LET'S GET THEM!"

Just like a scene out of *Three Stooges* or some other black-and-white comedy, those guys dispersed in all directions and ran toward Herr Street. TJ and his crew were on their heels. Some of TJ's friends picked up stones and threw at them. The North 18th Street gang chased them to the top of Herr Street Hill, and those guys were running like they were breaking out of prison. That incident by far ranks as number one of the funniest things that ever happened on North 18th Street. But it could easily have been a duplicate of the epic fight involving Bay and Frederick E. But those guys obviously were not the true real street thugs because all seven of them ran like a spanked dog. But then again, maybe they were not on the hill for trouble. Maybe they were just on a nice summer stroll in the wrong place at the wrong time. The pride of TJ was humbled, but his lesson still was not learned yet.

Big Brother Fred and Lawrence

The unknown antagonist somehow enlisted his antagonistic ways toward TJ. For this account, we will call him Rip Off because TJ does not remember his name, and he was but a passing experience in TJ's life. What Rip Off did was significant enough to warrant inclusion in this book because it severely disrupted TJ's life. Rip Off lived somewhere on South 14th Street right off State Street. TJ's church homeboy James Jones lived at 1402 State Street, and they kicked it just about every day. They would both visit each other almost on an equal basis. TJ, however, spent a significant amount of time at his house than he did TJ's, but that did not make a difference they were genuine friends. And Rip Off, the guy you are about to read about, lived literally around the corner from James. Back in those days, there wasn't a big concern about kids stealing things, although it did happen. TJ was aware thievery would happen, but it wasn't an overly big concern. But after being introduced to Rip Off, TJ thought it necessary to buy a bicycle lock. Rip Off did not like TJ, and TJ believes it had something to do with him practicing kung fu with James and him walking around with Bruce Lee nunchucks. It was not uncommon for wannabe Bruce Lees to have either homemade nunchucks or the real thing. TJ had a pair of homemade nunchucks that were pretty lightweight, and the speed at which he could whirl them was impressive. Rip Off saw TJ and James in white karate gees and TJ with nunchucks. Rip Off also studied karate. TJ did not know who his sensei was and didn't care. Apparently, Rip Off had a competitive spirit and a spirit of jealousy because TJ didn't know Rip off. TJ hadn't done anything to Rip Off that he knows of. But every time Rip Off saw TJ walking up the street or down the street or when Rip Off was with a couple of his boys, Rip Off ALWAYS gritted on TJ something fiercely. After seeing his brothers Bay and Fred in action and bonding with them, TJ was not afraid of anything or anyone. He said to his friend James, "If Rip Off wants to bump heads with me, I am willing and ready at any minute. Tell the pussy to bring it on. We are about the same weight class. Let's see who is the better man."

TJ concluded that Rip Off didn't want to bump heads with him because he was too sissy to come right out and step up to the plate. Rip Off attempted another approach to get TJ's attention. Rip Off made his move one day and to TJ, it was a punk move. Nonetheless, TJ gladly answered the call and silenced the facial expressions and mouth of Rip Off thereafter. TJ was about sixteen years old because he remembers getting his driver's license shortly thereafter. In fact, he had them after the summer vacation into the eleventh grade. Most of the time he would ride his bike over to James's house and kickstand it right outside his friend's house. He did that for the entire time he would visit his church homeboy. But this one day would invite something he did not expect, though he was not surprised it happened.

After visiting James, he walked outside to get on his bike the F3 Eliminator, and it wasn't there. He could not believe that his prized possession was stolen. The F3 Eliminator bike that his mother bought for him, the bike that he never dreamed he would own, was now in the hands of a thief! He yelled in the house to James, "Yo, James! Somebody stole my bike. Where is it at, James? Do you hear me?"

James came running to the door and said, "Damn! Who took your bike, bro?"

TJ could not believe that his most coveted bicycle was stolen. James's aunt casually said, "A guy from across the street came over and took your bike. I thought he was just taking it for a ride." She gave TJ and James the information they needed by loosely describing the guy. TJ immediately knew who it was. James's aunt gave them the lead as to where his bike was possibly located. This suggested to TJ that she possibly knew what was going on and wanted to see how TJ would respond. The pieces fell into place almost immediately. Her description and location of the bike were surprisingly accurate. Invite God again into a seemingly insignificant earthly event because TJ believed that God engaged a spiritual satellite location of the bike. In other words, TJ believed with all his heart that divine intervention took them directly to where the bike had been taken. Amid tall untrimmed trees and row duplex houses, they went DIRECTLY to where the bike was at. How else do you explain it?

James' aunt, who had kind of an unexplained crush on TJ, was much older than both James and TJ, that's why TJ calls it unexplained. Nonetheless, TJ questioned her intensely and vehemently "Who took my bike? Did anybody see anything?" She was free to give up the information and said that she saw a guy take the bike across the street down such and such alley between two houses. The silly irony about this information is, why didn't she question the guy or come in James' house and alert TJ that some guy was taking his bike, why? She knew the bike belonged to TJ. She saw him on it every time he came over the house. She always had something flirtatious to say to TJ. Why did she see the thief and do or say nothing? Who knows? At that time, that did not matter to TJ. His only concern was retrieving his rightfully owned property. He was glad she had valuable accurate information. Upon receiving that info, TJ again sprinted to his house to commandeer good solid backup. He did not want to find himself alone again when facing the enemy; he was not afraid, just plain ol' practical wisdom. He ran home and told Fred what had happened, and Fred almost jumped to attention and said, "WHERE IS IT AT, AND WHO TOOK IT? LET'S GO GET YOUR BIKE!"

It was as if someone had stolen the bike from Frederick E. himself and all hell could not stop him from retrieving it. TJ was furious when he ran in the house, and Mom heard TJ telling Fred about his bike being stolen and noticed both TJ and Fred storming out of the house. He heard her in the background, "You boys be careful! Don't get into trouble!" TJ was confident that she must have prayed the entire time they were away from the house. He can only imagine the things she must have held in her heart during those days and the concerns and prayers she must have prayed. But all honor is given to God for hearing the prayers of TJ's mother. She deserves all the honor for her faithfulness in praying for her children.

When Frederick E. and TJ arrived back at the location of the crime, James was still outside, and his aunt repeated, "I seen a guy with your bike walk over in that direction." James pointed out the direction precisely, and Fred started marching like a trained street soldier, ready to do battle. TJ marched directly beside his brother Fred with resolve and fearlessness that surprised even him. He knew they were about to either kick some butt and take the bike back or kick some butt anyway. Fred was almost leaping forward as he walked, with his shoulders back and high and his head plunged forward like a lion on the attack. He was absolutely fearless that day, and TJ was walking in the shadow of Fred, mimicking Fred's precise body movement as they crossed State Street headed toward South 14th Street. Frederick E. said, "Where is it at, which house?" and James lagging behind pointed out the house and said, "I believe the guy lives there."

Frederick E. boldly and arrogantly marched down the alley between two houses toward the backyard, and TJ remained in the shadow of his brother Frederick E. Both man and teenager were walking with chest poked out and fist clenched in a manner to welcome anything and anyone. TJ heard a Doberman pinscher growling and barking in the backyard, only to learn later that the Doberman was in the neighbor's yard. But that didn't seem to matter to Frederick E. He kept strutting like a special forces soldier ready to take on whatever resistance we would encounter. Whether he had to deal with the Doberman or a human being, he was ready, and TJ simply tailed his older brother and mentor. He walked in the shadow of Fred's confidence and the aura of Fred's valiant spirit. Fred was a lion, and TJ was a lion's whelp. When they arrived at the rear of the house through the narrow alley, right inside the fence was TJ's bike on the kickstand like it belonged to the owner of that house. Like yesterday, as the saying goes, TJ can see Frederick E. filled with confidence. Clothed with boldness and walked with impressive victory. As far as TJ was concerned, Fred was taking him to school on the streets of Harrisburg, Pennsylvania.

When TJ spotted his F3 Eliminator, he yelled out, "THERE IT IS! THERE IS MY BIKE!"

Rip Off then arrived at the back door of his porch, and TJ heard his mother in the background.

"Hey, what are you doing? That's my son's bicycle! What are you doing? You can't take that bike! That belongs to my son!"

Rip Off just stood on his back porch looking at them, not saying a word but had a look of fear on his face. Frederick E. then reached over the fence and with one hand, lifted the bike over the fence in one sweeping motion, placing the bike in front of TJ and said, "Here is your bike. Take it home!"

If Frederick E. and Bay meant the world to TJ up to that point, Frederick E. had just conquered the universe and now had become the ultimate leader and role model in TJ's youthful life. His worth in the life of TJ was now equal to the universe as opposed to just the world. Frederick E. was a super cool, street-suave, fearless "son of thunder!"

And to top that episode off, Frederick E. did not immediately turn and walk away. The mother was yelling out, "You can't take my son's bike."

The nerve, the stupidity, and the arrogance of somebody taking someone else's property and getting upset when the true owner claims the property!

Little did she know, she had unleased the anger and hell in the soul of Frederick E. He unleashed a tactic that compelled TJ to admire him the rest of his life. Although the sleeper has awakened, TJ will always remember Fred as a fearless street-suave big brother. Even though their lives strayed galaxies apart in the future, TJ strives to retain the good things about Frederick E.

Rip Off's mother was yelling and sounding like a fool because she couldn't have believed she purchased the F3 Eliminator Bike for her son. Nonetheless, from the moment she starting yelling, Fred put a spirit of fear in both her and Rip Off standing on the porch. As TJ was walking back down the alley with his bike, Fred was still standing there and TJ stopped walking. He was not about to leave his brother who stood in the hellish gap for him. TJ waited for Fred and witnessed the fearlessness of a lion. TJ heard Fred speak with the confidence and authority that almost made him afraid.

"You know you did not buy this bike, you dumb bitch! Come on outside, you and your man, and stop yelling from the house. You are a dumb bitch! I will kick you and your man's ass! C'mon outside! I'm standing here waiting. GET THE FUCK OUTSIDE OR SHUT YOUR DUMB ASS MOUTH, YOU STUPID CUNT!"

She was going on and on how she was going to call the cops, and Frederick E. encouraged her. All along he continued to belittle her with ungodly names and especially the B-word. When he challenged her and her man to come outside, silence prevailed. Rip Off, standing on the porch, was admittedly in a state of shock as TJ and Fred walked away with TJ's bike. Fred, all the while calling her names while he and TJ were walking out of the alley with TJ's prized possession; the F3 Eliminator. How is what TJ and Frederick E. did right? How do you figure that? Either what they did was justified in the eyes of God, or God allows his mercy to cover us in the things we feel are justified and right. God beheld the entire situation before time began. At any rate, nothing happened while TJ and Fred walked away, and there were no actual repercussions except for what appeared to be coincidental involving big brother Lawrence.

Lawrence, the Other Guy, and Rip Off?

You would think this situation was unrelated to the previous one, but the set of circumstances and faces involved would lead one to think it had a sense of retaliation. At 1402 State Street at another time on a similar type of day in the summer, TJ was at James' house. They were kickin' it like they typically did, watching some TV going out back in his yard and practicing some kung fu moves with the nunchucks. They spent a little time out back sparring with each other. Out of nowhere, James's same aunt came running in the house all frantic and seemingly ready to have a nervous breakdown. She was shaking and yelling, "TJ, TJ, some guy is about to fight your brother. Get outside!" She ran back through the house and out the front door yelling, "Please stop them, TJ, stop them." She was really deeply concerned and did not know what to do, but she felt she had to let TJ know. TJ and James stopped sparring and within seconds ran outside and next door to where James's aunt lived. The ruckus appeared to have begun there. TJ immediately spotted his older brother Lawrence. Lawrence's girlfriend was attempting to hold him. There was gathering a small crowd because of the yelling going on, and someone was holding back the other guy who wanted to fight Lawrence. TJ calmly and slowly walked up to the scene and asked what was going on while Rip Off was taking off his jacket, ready to rumble. Betty, Lawrence's girlfriend, chimed in, "They going to fight. TJ, stop them!"

Lawrence then said, "I'm not afraid of him! I'll kick his dumb ass!" The street mentality that had been put in TJ over the years from both Frederick E. and Bay rose up inside him and rose up without fear. TJ stepped between both of them and sort of shielded his older brother Lawrence and put great distance between the other guy and his brother and said, "*Nobody* here is going to fight my brother!"

The other guy had taken his jacket off like he was ready.

TJ yelled "Didn't you hear me, nigga? Nobody is going to fight my brother. If you want to fight somebody, you will fight me, and I don't think you want that because I will kick your black ass!"

TJ had pushed his brother far behind him and had advanced to the other guy with his hands up, ready to fight. He quickly went into a kung fu front-leaning stance and said, "Now c'mon, let's get it on. It's going to be you and me, not my brother! You want somebody to fight? It will be me, I'm ready. Are you? Let's get it on and stop standing there like a pussy!"

The retaliatory situation did not come as a surprise when TJ noticed Rip Off, the guy who stole TJ's bike, was standing behind the guy that wanted to fight Lawrence.

Huh! What the hell is going on here? TJ thought. But since he was already poised and ready to bang some heads, he pointed to Rip Off and said, "And what are you looking at, punk? You can get some of this also. Both you pussies, c'mon!"

What happened the most in those days is that both TJ and his brothers knew how to put fear in people's heart because neither one of those guys answered the challenge. TJ effectively had stolen the show, and both Lawrence and the other guy backed down. Everybody gathered up their friends and family and quietly drifted away from the scene. TJ happened to have his homemade nunchucks on him and pulled them out. While the crowd was standing there, he went into a five-minute exhibition, swinging, catching, and twirling as fast as he could. The objective was met, and fear seized the heart of the enemy. The other guy started putting his jacket back on while gritting on TJ, but he backed down, nonetheless. TJ looked at Lawrence and asked him if he were all right. Lawrence was looking at TJ, and Lawrence asked TJ the question, "You were going to fight for me?" and TJ said, "I was going to kick his ass, quick, fast, and in a hurry."

Lawrence was amazed at TJ standing up for him for the longest time. But in those days TJ's brothers were like the terror of the streets with a reputation of a street fighter—at least, that's how he saw them. His brothers, being older than him, never really hung out with him, but he was always learning from their actions and their ways on the street. He wanted to be like them and wanted their acceptance as a younger brother. One of his mission in those days was to prove to them that he could hang in their world. When it boils down to the real truth, one would have to say the mercy and grace of God prevailed throughout TJ's life and his brothers' lives in those days.

The First Sin

There were sins committed in the projects, but as a young boy, TJ did not understand the concept of sin. He just thought it was natural to explore certain vices. But this one he understood what he was doing but followed the lead of his mentor. He idolized Bay, who had a 1965 Buick Skylark convertible.

When TJ first laid eyes on Bay's car, his sense of idolatry of Bay escalated to another level. Bay had a sky blue car, and it was a nice convertible with white seats and an 8 track tape deck player. His car smelled good on the inside, and he couldn't wait to ride in it. Soon after Bay got his new car, he decided to take TJ for a ride. It was a gorgeous summer morning. Bay pulled up in front of the house, and TJ was outside minding his own business, playing and having fun. Bay drove up and got out of his car and went into the house for something. Two of Bay's friends were sitting in the back seat of the car. Bay hung out regularly with his friend, Speaks and Patrick, who was sitting in the back of the car. When Bay came out of the house, he looked at TJ and said, "Want to go for a ride?"

TJ thought, *Well, that's a silly question, coming from his idol and mentor!* His eyes lit up like a neon sign, and a smile came across his face like a five-year-old birthday boy.

"Yeah!" That's all he said. What else was there to say? TJ was about to take a ride in his brother's hot-looking convertible car for the first time. The other guys in the back really didn't matter. TJ paid little attention to them. He was respectful and spoke to them as he jumped in the front seat. They might as well have been props or manikins sitting in the back. In the mind of TJ, this was about his older brother and him going for a ride in his new car. Only God in heaven knows the only action and excitement TJ was looking forward to was a good, honest, innocent ride in his brother's car up the street, down the street, and return home. But the nature of sin knows nothing of a sort, and he was about to be introduced to sinful practices and the works of the flesh. TJ was about to be given a ride that would open the door and pathway to disobedience, disrespect, lying, lust, and ungodliness of life.

Once in the car, he sat up front without the requirement of seat belts, and Bay popped an 8 track in the tape deck. The first time he heard Isaac Hayes and the song that was playing was called "The Look of Love." The music was hip and the sound captivating. They didn't travel far from the house. TJ figured Bay had to get back to where he was going somewhat in a hurry, but he had enough time to lead his younger brother down the path of sin and the indulges of the flesh. While driving the car, Bay was drinking what looked like a soda, and he looked over to TJ and said, "Want some of this?"

Of course, anything Bay would say to TJ, ask TJ about, or suggest to TJ, he saw as a privilege to have any conversation with Bay. To TJ, Bay was definitely the man. So he reached over and took Bay's glass and began to drink what looked like Coca-Cola. The taste was kind of different. It was sweet and bitter and tangy at the same time, but it was good. TJ drank some more and then began to guzzle the rest down like drinking a bottle of water. Bay reached over and stopped him and said, "Careful, champ. Not too much at one time."

TJ asked Bay, "What is this stuff?" and Bay said, "Rum and Coke."

"Okay," TJ said, but it still did not register to the young lad what was sinfully unfolding. It was his very first experience of becoming intoxicated. What TJ was drinking was good, and he couldn't wait to have more. Bay drove his younger brother around for about fifteen to twenty minutes drinking rum and Coke. Isaac Hayes was getting louder and louder in the 8 track player, and the sound became more captivating and stimulating to TJ's mind. Within minutes, light-headedness crept upon him, not in a painful manner but in a relaxed and sensual manner. He began to drift down into the seat, sort of leaning back with his head leaning to one side and looking out the convertible window. Isaac Hayes got louder and louder, and the instrumental section of that song "The Look of Love" was the crescendo as the lead guitarist with the "Wawa" peddle serenaded his mind into an intoxicated blissful high. At fifteen years old, he was drunk and didn't really understand the implications of being drunk or the future problems it would solicit in his soul and the overpowering temptation it would invite.

4

SIN

The problem with sin is, the nature of sin has no respect for anyone, and its only purpose is to sink you into the dark ravishes of its evil binding chains. Here is the problem that unfolded that day, Bay, after getting TJ drunk, took him home right in front of North 18th Street and dropped him off. You would think Bay would have kept TJ with him for a while just to monitor him being it was his first alcoholic experience. Later in the day, after TJ made a complete fool of himself, he thought about why his brother dropped him off instead of staying with him. Sin has its own way of demoralizing its victims and in time will completely destroy the participants thereof. Bay said to TJ when he dropped him off, "Be careful. Just be cool. Don't talk too much." Looking back, he supposes Bay was instructing him with "words to the wise," as street learning goes. But TJ could not keep his mouth shut. He was slowly stepping outside of his box and comfort zone and especially after witnessing his brothers in action. The first thing he did was sprint into the house and go directly to the kitchen where Mom was straightening Cookie's hair with a hot iron. He walked in the kitchen all loud and stuff, saying, "I feel good, I feel good."

By the grace of God or Mom's unsuspecting awareness of his intoxication, or she simply wasn't paying attention to TJ, all she said was, "Good, now get out of here so I can finish your sister's hair."

He did not leave immediately because he was feeling so good and in his ignorant state, wanted them to know how good he felt. He pranced around in the kitchen a few more times spatting off at the mouth and noticed Cookie looked up at him out of the corner of her eye with this big-sister look that spoke a million words. The look was, "Get out of here, TJ, get out!"

At least he was able to pick up on what she was gesturing and turned and bolted out of the kitchen and out of the house.

But the spirits inside that drink was not finished with TJ. There are no limits to sinful practices and intoxication; they will drive you into the grave if you do not conquer the weakness of the flesh. The weakness of the flesh is inherent in all men and women. When TJ left the house, he saw a neighbor girl he was friends with, strictly platonic friendship, nothing more. Up to that age in his life, pretty much all of the North 18th Street crew were friends nothing serious or sexual then. But sin, mixed with a little intoxication, has a way of bringing out of you all the potential of evil that resides in the heart of men.

The neighbor girl's name, looks, and voice all remain vivid in TJ's mind. He went up to her and asked her how she was doing, and she politely responded, probably thinking he just wanted to talk and maybe just hang out. But TJ had other things in mind, though he had never approached her in this manner before. They were just friends. He carefully and quickly inched himself closer and closer to her. She started laughing, thinking he was acting silly. He grabbed her butt, and all she did was laugh and to him, that was the okay to proceed. He began to massage her and had his hands all over her. He kissed her, and she responded back without resistance. He thought to himself, *This was easier than expected.*

But then, instinctively, she stopped all the action and looked in his face and said, "You're drunk."

He thought to himself, *How did she know I am drunk? How could she tell?*

He could not figure out how she knew, perhaps the direct strong advance TJ made on her. She knew that was not TJ's style or personality. They were the same age. Maybe inexperience and lack of control in TJ clued her of the fact of his intoxication. Not only did he feel embarrassed, he started crying and sincerely apologizing to her. The old maxim that girls are more mature than boys or mature faster than boys was very much true on that day. Though she was accepting his advances, she didn't want it in a drunken stupor. Her presence of mind and strength of heart saved the young man from foolishness and protected her from the ignorance in his life and the potential of becoming pregnant. Immaturity and youthful foolishness, coupled with sinful ways, did not care about TJ. He stumbled in speech and reasoning while communicating with her. She responded in the most mature manner toward him, softly caressing his back. Her kindness brought TJ back to reality and help to sober up his mind. She then said to him in the most authoritative manner, "Wait here and I'll be right back."

She went into the house and prepared some coffee, and TJ sat exactly where she told him and did not move a muscle. He just sat there crying, upset with Bay and upset with himself for acting like a fool toward his friend and pissed off at the whole situation. When she returned, she had in her hand a steaming hot cup of coffee. She handed it to him and even assisted him to drink the first few sips. Once he held the cup on his own, she let go and told him to drink all the coffee.

"Don't leave a drop. Drink it all."

Soberness began to return to him from the intoxicated state. He began to gain control of his reasoning and realized the disrespectful and potentially harmful ways in which he was acting. He begged her to forgive him, and without hesitation, she accepted his request for forgiveness. For the next hour or so, he sat there while she talked to him about the whole experience. From what TJ could tell, she was not bitter toward him at all. To this day, he has no idea if she ever told anyone about what he did because he never heard it repeated by his friends or family. TJ felt that he disrespected his father's home. He disrespected his mother and her authority. He disrespected his friend, and he disrespected himself. He was upset with Bay and did not speak to him for a while, but that didn't last too long. Both TJ and his friend were essentially children, so to speak, but she had to be the most mature and understanding female friend at that time in his life.

The Departure of Bay

Soon afterward, Bay would enlist in the United States Air Force, and the wheels of great change in TJ's life would be put in motion. One day TJ would follow in the footsteps of Bay. At some point, before Bay left for the air force, TJ found unconditional forgiveness for how he felt Bay let him down. Not talking to Bay was a difficult and painful emotional experience because TJ always looked up to his older brothers and particularly idolized both Bay and Fred. After a few weeks of not talking to Bay, TJ could take the absence no longer. The conversation of karate came up with Bay, and TJ found himself back in the loop with his idolized, mentor brother. On a nice summer day, on the steps of North 18th Street, Bay introduced an unexpected thought into the mind of TJ when he said, "It's time to get between those legs."

He was talking about two of TJ's friends—the one who helped him come out of a drunken stupor and another neighbor girl who was also very pretty. The second girl had a very nice figure, was very attractive, and flaunted herself with boys. They were all the same age, and all they did, for the most part, was play, talk, and ride bicycles.

Looking over at his two friends, he did not really think of them in that way, but because he was fifteen going on sixteen, Bay thought he should begin exploring the possibilities and seizing the opportunities of sinful lust. In fact, his eyes lit up, and he was delighted with the idea. A sense of excitement and possibility erupted deep inside his heart. A sort of forbidden desire was ignited by the words of his mentor. Because Bay suggested it, TJ wanted to live up to Bay's suggestion. TJ held no blame toward Bay for introducing him to the vices of life. The void of consistent fatherly attention was captured by a brother who, in all respects, was his mentor and advisor. In the years to come, Bay's mentoring would become a serious, serious confrontational issue decades later.

Bay began to lay down the smooth talk of how to get the attention of the girls. How to talk nice to them and tell them how nice they look, so on and so forth. He said, "TJ, you have to get them alone, just you and them, and take your time to impress them with words. Tell them good stuff about them and how long you have been looking at them and thinking about them at night…"

Of course, these were all lies filled with the desire to fulfill the lust inside a young boy's heart. A lust he had not discovered on his own, but once the lust got his attention, he fed it with desire and desire and desire. From that point on, TJ sought an opportunity to be alone with the two girlfriends that all the boys of North 18th Street played with. Prior to the introduction of lustful thoughts, it was good clean fun, nothing sexual at all until the problem with sin came alive inside his heart.

After Bay had left for the air force sometime later, TJ learned that Mom and Dad were pleased that he joined the air force because apparently, Bay was racking up trouble points that were leading to possible jail time. TJ did not know the details of what led Bay into the air force, but what he understood is that it was a good thing for him to leave and come off the streets of Harrisburg, Pennsylvania. The unfortunate thing for TJ is that a legacy of sinful acts and lustful thoughts would follow him for decades, a legacy that had attached itself to his family generations ago, a sinful legacy he was ignorant of, nor did he have any idea of how to overcome its thoughts. When Bay left, he became a distant advisor for TJ. It was then TJ's sights turned to Fred for immediate mental gratification. TJ, like all his siblings, was raised to believe in God, but at this point in his life, his brothers were kind of a god to him. He trusted, believed, loved, and idolized both Bay and Fred. He respected them and would accept just about every word they spoke to him and would follow their every advice. They could do no wrong, and he would have defended their character to death on any accusations of them doing wrong. As for the two female friends, he found time to be alone with them and explored in the basement of their house. But nothing serious involving penetration, because actually, TJ was a young novice at physical intimacy. In every case, the circumstances always led them being in a hurry. But the touching, kissing, and pulling down of pants had been awakened in TJ by his older brother whom he unknowingly idolized.

1974, 1975, 1976

The mid-seventies brought about a change that would catapult TJ into the next level of growing and maturing and becoming the man he would one day become. With Bay gone, Frederick E. became the man of words the man of wisdom the man of style and philosophical thinking. Every word Fred spoke was about positive thinking. He would repeatedly say to TJ daily, "Do not let anyone control your mind. Take charge of yourself. Always be yourself in whatever you pursue. Be your own thinker and your own man." For some time, TJ wondered as he became aware of the control and influence Bay had over Fred. Perhaps that was Fred's cry to be released from the control of Bay. In time, certain events would reveal that in some sense, he himself failed to live by his own philosophy. Fred admired Bay, and Bay was a mentor to him. Fred also knew that Bay, in many ways controlled him. What an irony, what a sad and enchanting irony. For TJ, though, it was nice learning those philosophical thoughts and perspectives. He felt like he was learning something from Fred, who had taken up the vacancy left by Bay. TJ's brothers, to him, were like the gurus of life, and he thought the world of them. Funny, when you're a youngster in mind and body, it is easy to make an impression on the mind of those younger than you. But when you become a man those impressions, though useful, are now elementary, like grade school lessons. Nonetheless, what TJ learned from both of them seriously sustained his sanity when he entered the United States Navy and left home for the first time on his own. Leaving home was a great cultural shock and painful growth for the young lad. Homesickness became TJ's friend in the first twelve months of his life when he left home. Like peeling the skin off a banana, he felt he was being peeled apart from his body at times. Like sawing his brain into pieces, his thoughts were jumbled in his head, and he was having a difficult time recapturing old thoughts and memories. Like a tornado ripping through the playpen of an infant, TJ felt helpless and thrown about in the sea of life. Nonetheless, both the life and example of Bay and Fred greatly helped sustain him through his first tour of duty in the United States Navy.

Fred, in his usual way, spoke positively about everything, criticized anything, and questioned everything. But to TJ, Fred held the potential of accomplishing any and everything he wanted. Fred, at that time, was attending a school in Reading, Pennsylvania, and TJ does not remember what his course of study was. But to the impressionable mind of TJ, it did not matter what Fred was learning, TJ yearned for a conversation about life with Fred every day. Fred sported one of the largest Afros back then. Every hair perfectly in place. Line up perfectly straight. Always profiling in the mirror to maintain his polished look and appearance. He was the essence of the definition of wearing an Afro and the personification of a clean brother. TJ and Fred talked about everything during those days except girls. TJ does not remember holding any conversation with Fred about girls—that was Bay's department. Bay prided himself in attracting the attention of girls. But Fred, it was the mind, philosophy, Jonathan Livingston Seagull, poetry, positive thinking.

"Be strong, never stoop to your enemy's level. Never seek revenge. Be honest. Never lie. Do not steal not only material possessions but do not steal time. Be where you are supposed to be. Do what you are supposed to do. Be dependable and respectable. Respect yourself and others will respect you."

That was Fred talking to TJ, and he certainly filled TJ's mind with that type of thinking. TJ diligently pursued and tirelessly sought to attain every principle and concept of believing. When it came to the mind, Fred was the man who fundamentally shaped the thoughts of TJ in every respect. TJ had a genuine love and admiration for Fred all his life.

When TJ studied kung fu, Fred's philosophical way of thinking contributed greatly to TJ's understanding of control and discipline. Fred, in many ways, was proud of TJ for developing into a controlled and disciplined young man. He said to TJ on many occasions how proud he was of him. Fred boosted TJ's esteem of himself into higher levels. TJ always sought to impress both Bay and Fred. He thought it normal to admire them the way he did. He sincerely believed they were the best brothers in the whole wide world. Mental spars with Fred and karate spars with Bay was the most competitive and privileged mind-to-mind and hand-to-hand interaction he enjoyed with them brothers. You see, they were streetwise and had engaged in many a scrapple on the streets and could hold their own without a problem. TJ, on the other hand, was being trained in hand to hand martial arts of Isshin-ryū karate and kung fu. This became a significant challenge to Bay, who had taken up Thai kickboxing in Thailand. There was a time when Bay came home on furlough from the air force and learned of TJ learning kung fu. Of course, Bay decided he wanted to spar with TJ to test TJ's skill and ability to defend himself. TJ and Bay were in the house clowning around while Fred was looking on, and Bay threw a couple of punches directly at TJ within arm's length. Surprisingly to Bay, TJ effortlessly blocked his punches and started laughing. TJ had this way about himself that he was always in a laughing or playful mood. These are the guys he watched fight on the streets. These are the guys he heard speak fear into their opponent's heart. These are the guys he admired and looked up to. Now it was his turn to prove to them what he learned. TJ noticed the fury in Bay's eyes because he was able to block, weave, and dodge all of Bay's blows. Bay then began aggressively kicking, punching, and running toward TJ in an attempt to confuse or overwhelm the young lad. Kung fu is basically offensive with some defensive moves. What TJ had learned in the absence of Bay was how to utilize the opponent's frustration and maintain his composure and be strictly offensive. The famous martial artist Bruce Lee termed it "the art of fighting without fighting." Bay could not strike TJ at all. TJ continued to block, duck, sway. He was swift as lightning, simulating defensive blows while utilizing offensive techniques. TJ finally ran out of the house because there was not enough room inside with all the kicking and punching going on. When they got outside in front of the house on North 18th Street, they continued to spar. TJ was throwing roundhouse kicks, spinning back kicks, front snap, and sidekicks at his leisure rather effortlessly. Bay became a little upset because he could not hit TJ while TJ was laughing the entire time. Bay suddenly ceased his attack and admitted to TJ, "You're good. Keep training."

That was all TJ needed to hear. Fred was standing off to the side smiling from ear to ear. He was impressed with what TJ had learned. Fred said, "You have good speed, and your punches are pretty accurate. The way you wield your kicks will hurt someone when you connect."

That's it! He finally got their attention, and he was delighted with their approval. He was no longer the nuisance little boy trying to hang out with the big boys. TJ felt he had finally gained the acceptance of the two most important men in his life at that time. The confidence in himself skyrocketed to an all-time high. He would not come down from that high until some twenty-four years later. His downfall would be heart-wrenching, to the point of strongly wanting to commit suicide. Everything he did in his life from the point of hearing Bay say he was good, he did with the motivation of impressing both Bay and Fred. In TJ's heart, it was always, "Hey, brothers, look at me! Look at who I have become! Look how you taught me to think and become!" But it seemed in the years to come, they failed to see the heavy impression they made in his soul. They were oblivious to the positive results of their influence in his life. Bay's furlough was coming to an end, and he was about to transfer from sunny California to South Dakota. His leaving would be another sad time in TJ's life. But at this point with Fred still around, TJ was obsessed and made every attempt to become who he thought they wanted him to become.

At seventeen years old, TJ got his first vehicle. As far as he knows, he was the first child of Mom and Dad that got a vehicle by the hand of his parents. Mom suggested and Dad offered to relinquish his 1967 Ford Galaxie 500 to TJ with a $1 transfer through the

Pennsylvania Department of Transportation. The car was nice and clean and smelled good inside, with an 8 track tape deck player with good music playing. Amid the groovy sounds of the Temptations, the Jackson 5, some jazz tunes like Bob James, Royer Ayers, Grover Washington Jr., TJ would pop his Isaac Hayes track and play the song, "The Look of Love," reminiscing of the earlier days with Bay and the introduction to alcohol.

The time had come for TJ to drive Bay to the Middletown Airport in Middletown, Pennsylvania. Mom and TJ took Bay to the airport to catch his flight, and since this memory is squarely focused on Bay, TJ does not remember if Fred went along for the ride. But it is hard to believe that Fred did not go to the airport with them. Both Fred and Bay were inseparable. Nonetheless, before they left for the airport, there was a song playing that TJ had come too really like, especially the lyrics and not just the tune. He did not know all the lyrics to the song, but he really liked that song. The song made him happy and made him sad and made him feel good all at the same time. Once arriving at the airport, Bay boarded the plane, and Mom and TJ hung around for a bit until the plane taxied down the runway. TJ pulled the car over to the side of the road, and both he and Mom got out of the car and stood by the fence and watched until the plan was out of sight. Mom was crying and she said, "There goes my baby, dear Lord. Keep him safe."

TJ's eyes had watered up as he watched the red taillights of the plane fly out of sight.

For years, TJ did not understand why and how certain events unfold. He thought perhaps God uses events of this world to teach a lesson good or bad. When Mom and TJ got back in the car to drive home, TJ turned the radio on just to try and take his mind off the fact that Bay just left home again, and he did not know when he would see him again. The thought of not seeing Bay anytime soon was essential because TJ had decided to try the military himself. He knew he would be leaving home before Bay returned, and when he and Mom got back in the car to go home, ironically, the song he had come to love was playing on the radio. He purposely drove slowly all the way home so he could reminisce about Bay and lose his thoughts in the song that was playing on the radio.

It was not until some weeks later that he heard the song again. Fred was nearby, and he asked Fred who was singing the song. Fred said without hesitation, "Elton John," and Fred said the name of the song was "Daniel." Fred also said, "That song reminds me of Bay when he left for the air force and I could see the red taillights on the plane."

TJ was speechless when Fred said that. What were the odds that Fred liked the very song TJ liked that reminded both TJ and Fred of Bay? Fred was still teaching and leading him because he told TJ who the artist was singing the song and what the song was about.

"Daniel is traveling tonight on a plane, I can see the red taillights headed for Spain."

Everything about that song was in the heart of both TJ and Fred at different times about the same brother. Bay was older than both of them, and they both could feel their own pain and scars that took decades, at least for TJ, to heal. And when the pain and scars healed, all three of them were miles apart geographically, spiritually, and mentally. The connection they had as young men waded, waned, and strained apart over the years, and while TJ yearned for restoration with them, they chose a path TJ refused to walk. "Bay was traveling tonight on a plane, I could see the red tail lights...Lord I miss Bay, oh I miss him so much," was TJ's on version of "Daniel," by Elton John, 1973.

Time to Leave Home

June 26, 1976, Mount Calvary Church of God in Christ had dinner in TJ's honor of leaving for the US Navy. Funny how experiences and friendships in life can change drastically over time. At the time Mount Calvary Church of God in Christ was his Christian family, and he held them dear to his heart. Twenty years into the future, he would not have much to do with Mount Calvary or its religious practices. Not because he thought he was better than them, but spiritual growth separated TJ from the belief and practices of the people he knew as a youth. He sang on the church choir of Mount Calvary from 1972 through 1976. He felt Mount Calvary church choir was the best church choir in Central Pennsylvania. He had great times together with the choir members. Singing, "shouting," listening to what he thought and understood to be great preaching of the Gospel of Jesus Christ. One of the exciting highlights of the church was going out to dinner with his church friends. Most of the relationships with the girls were on a friendly, nonsexual level. But as he got older and temptations were stirred up, platonism began to fade at every opportunity to be alone with a church girl. The weekend before he left, there was a festive dinner held on his behalf in the basement of 5th and Kelker Streets of Mount Calvary Church of God in Christ. The food was great, and the entire church members attended the dinner. TJ received over fifty cards that he held on to till this day. The comments were all encouraging to the point that many of his church friends said, "You better come back home safely and in one piece." Some even blurted out "Don't try to be a hero, come back home."

His sister-in-law presented him with a beautiful white Bible that traveled with him for twenty-four years while in the United States Navy. TJ placed that particular Bible among his books in his personal library of learning as a hallmark of his growth in God. The Bible has smears of ink and faded letters and words from its constant use throughout the years. His sister-in-law had no knowledge that his spiritual growth all began with the Bible she gave to him.

June 27, 1976, Sunday church service for TJ seemed to be heavenly inspired in many respects. Mount Calvary Church of God in Christ is a traditional charismatic Pentecostal believing church in every aspect. Its doctrine, teaching, practices, and programs are the epitome of religious tradition. But even with that mundane form of worship, there have been times that in his ignorance, God intervened among men and a brief moment of his goodness fell among the people. Sort of like when Moses demanded of God to allow him to see him God's response was "I will make all my goodness pass before thee" (Exod. 33:19). On that Sunday morning, "the goodness" of the Lord fell among the people, and there have been trickles of his goodness throughout the naval career of TJ. What TJ was going to experience in the years to come were times when the goodness and mercy of God would be present simultaneously. In charismatic Pentecostalism, what they call "shouting," a form of emotional expression of dancing on the floor, was a regular at Mount Calvary Church of God in Christ. In a fully charismatic church, the leadership interprets "shouting" as "the spirit" moving in and upon a person to compel them to "dance." The "shouting" expression is purely emotional by many and this is known by testimonies of different church people. TJ had firsthand knowledge of a contradictory lifestyle of these different church people. Many unanswered questions were prevalent in the mind of TJ concerning the Christian church. But for now, that's all he knew, and that's all he embraced. Nonetheless, on that Sunday after the preaching was done, the music frenzy began, and the people began singing, dancing, clapping, and having church much in the traditional Black Christian manner. But when the music subsided and it appeared as though the church was about to end service, the presence or goodness of God fell upon the entire choir. There was a strong sense of the presence of the Lord, not in your traditional emotional expression but an overpowering serenity of mind, a cleansing of heart, a weeping among the people. Some were sitting, others standing in one spot not jumping or running around the church. There was no dancing on the floor but a deep sense of surrender. And then the spirit of God "moved" upon TJ like no other experience at Mount Calvary Church of God in Christ. As compassionate hands lifted him up from his choir seat and gracefully raised his arms, he felt compelled to express his liberty in the Lord by dancing in the center of the floor for about ten to fifteen minutes. The rest of the church was praising God in a heightened crescendo. The pastor stood gazing at the people in submission to the spirit, and his words intermittently were "praise him, praise him." As TJ danced before the Lord, the spirit danced inside his soul. He was very much cognizant of his actions, but felt loose of his control and liberty in Christ, but yet he was not out of control. At times he felt like he was weightless and could become airborne, but he knew he was inside the church building. His mind and soul and body felt enraptured in the "goodness" of what he was feeling. His dancing was more than a traditional emotional expression. He concluded that at that time God was reassuring him and giving peace inside his heart in ways that he understood. God was also reassuring him the decision he made to enlist in the United States Navy was a good decision. Deep inside, he felt that he had God's blessings and God was directing him to leave home to join the armed forces. There was much, much, much to learn not only about himself but about the evil and wickedness of man. God was also reassuring TJ that he would lift him up at times during his naval career, and he would guide his steps and raise his hands in submission to him...as long as he obeyed him and believed his Word. The time had come for TJ to leave home and NEVER return.

But before leaving he had to stop by the church one more time during noonday prayer and a 5'4" petite lady leading noonday prayer noticed him walking in the building and motioned to him to come up front. TJ had every intention of coming upfront because he believed in prayer and he believed that she was a prayer warrior. Nevertheless, he obeyed her word and quickly made it to the front of the church in the center of the floor. There were only a couple people there that day at noonday prayer, but she felt a need to pray only for TJ knowing he was about to enter the armed forces. She prayed one of the most anointed heartfelt prayers he had ever heard. As far as he can recall, no prayer has matched that prayer since. TJ experienced some *good* and anointed times among other believers and witnessed the outpouring and "goodness" of the Lord since then, but *none* have compared to the urgency and heartfelt prayer that prayer warrior mother prayed that day. The prayer was so intense that he remembers a good portion of what she prayed on his behalf:

"Lord remember this son of yours and protect him from dangers seen and unseen. Keep his mind stayed on you as he travels the world. Give him experience and knowledge of your word beyond his years and help him to remain faithful and true to you."

Then she elevated the tone and urgency in her prayer. She began to discharge a mighty flow of words that came with power and anointing as if God himself was praying for TJ as she said:

> Favor! Give him favor with his officers and men! Favor, Lord, favor, Lord, give him favor! Let the enemy be stopped at every path and give him favor, Lord! Oh my God! Dear God, give this young man favor, not just to have a testimony but to bear your name and Holy Word. Give him favor, Lord!

Did favor grace TJ during his military career, or was favor just a temporary thing? One thing for sure is that when he walked away from that noonday prayer on that day, he walked away with a confidence that was not his own and a direction he was sure of. His thoughts then were, if there are additional rewards given at the judgment seat of Christ for his ministers, missionaries, and praying women, he would hope the prayer warrior mother is in the eternal Hall of Fame of God. The experience he would gain while in the United States Navy will reveal if favor was given and when favor was ignored by TJ himself. In the decades to come, TJ would become sharply discerning that the favor of God never left him. But many decisions he made throughout his naval career took him out from under God's favor. Solid truth and strong prayers were imputed into his spirit as a youth. There was a purpose to develop him into the man of God, God would have him to become as the years passed by.

1976: Time to Grow Up

Life on North 18th Street had come to an end, and in a few short months, it would all seem like a dream as if it never existed. It was at this time that certain Bible truths began to resonate in the spirit of TJ, such as "For what is your life? It is even a vapor, that appears for a little time, and then vanishes away" (James 4:14). Bay had now become a distant adviser, and Fred was the immediate role model in the life of TJ. Fred's words continued to stand as monuments holding up a skyscraper. All the bicycle rides up and down North 18th Street, hanging out with his friends Calvin, MB, PJ, Harold, James Jones—also, his church friends, DC, Freddie, and the choir of Mount Calvary Church of God in Christ—was about to come to an abrupt end. Life in the projects in the Smith Homes and life on North 18th Street were elementary phases in the growth of TJ, but they were phases he truly enjoyed. It all was preliminary to the Sailor and the Sermon but would catapult him into manhood. TJ never felt prepared for the next phase of his life, but in all aspects, he was fully prepared. The last few weeks on North 18th Street, he spent intensely talking to Fred about everything. Suggesting certain scenarios to Fred to get Fred's take and his response on how to handle potential conflicts. He spent time with his choir friends at church having enjoyed the special going away dinner they had for him. He also enjoyed the special prayer the church held for him about to enter the armed forces. The days at Mount Calvary Church of God in Christ were special in regard to upholding what he had learned and had been taught of the Bible. There appeared to be a genuinely loving concern about his well-being from everyone! But the launching into the armed forces and the final preparations came from none other than Frederick E.

Every day up until June 28, 1976, for about a couple of weeks Fred had something to say to TJ about "life." Fred's words were comforting and strengthening TJ's mind, giving him perspective, preparing him for the dragons and serpents he would face. One particular thought Fred dropped into TJ's mind was, "Don't be afraid of it. It can't hurt you." At first, that seemed presumptuous and an ungodly perspective. But a few short years later, when he would repeat those words, they were like steel plates inserted into TJ's spine and concrete walls wrapped around his brain. Fred and TJ talked about the possible experiences that he would go through, and Fred said in many ways he wished he were the traveler. TJ did not quite understand why Fred would wish he was leaving for the military. But then he remembered that Fred had a knee cap replacement, and the military would not accept him without being physically fit. Fred was persistently preparing TJ in ways that had profound impact years later. Fred and Bay's bearing on the life of TJ was so profound he believed it was the primary cause of contention that would separate them in the years to come. Another word Fred dropped into the mind of TJ left him hanging for the moment. But Fred was a specialist and provoking one to think and to think as deep as a well of water. Fred, in a cool and calm way, said, "When you leave, you can never come back." The thought of NEVER coming back was deep and philosophical. The depth of what Fred said did not immediately register in the young lad. He yearned to experience the world, something, anything other than Harrisburg Pennsylvania. The thought of never coming back gradually became clear. Having experienced and discovered what he was searching for, TJ began to understand it was not the physicality of his return. Rather Fred was referring to the mental, the spiritual, and actual life of a child and little boy was over. He could NEVER return to the project boy or the North 18th Street bicycle riding boy full of smiles and fun. But he would become a man of worldly experience, and the need or desire to return would become null and void. Many of the words Fred spoke to TJ frightened him, but he was compelled within his soul to go and learn for himself what Fred was talking about. His heart had been gripped with pursuing his life at any cost and untold danger. He had to do it! He had to leave! He had to grow up in a manner that would become the anchor of his soul. The United States Navy was the ticket into the school of life. The United States Navy was the financier of the world classroom experience. The United States Navy was the door that would open and remain open for 2.5 decades, more than enough time to learn and grow up. It was time for TJ to grow up and transition into the Sailor. Natural fear and anxiety of the unknown introduced themselves into the mind and heart of TJ. But in many ways, he couldn't wait to get started. He hated to leave home but couldn't wait to leave and there was a happy, sad, anticipatory feeling deep inside the young lad's soul.

The morning TJ left home, his family had gotten up early to see him off, a memorable occasion. Dad was sitting on the rocker porch furniture, and Mom was standing beside him on the porch.

Cookie was there, Jonathan, Raymond, Gloria, and Jackie, and of course, Frederick E. TJ craved for a word from Fred; anything! Any word!

TJ then looked up the street on North 18th Street and spotted the White Ford Torino, with headlights on, slowly making its way toward his house. Anxiety hit TJ like an unexpected barrage of arrows straight to his heart. At the precise moment he spotted the navy vehicle approaching, he thought, *Fred, say something, anything to calm my spirit.*

He was panting, craving, silently desiring a word or two from Fred. Fred then grabbed TJ by the shoulders, looked him straight in the eyes, and said to him, "Don't be afraid of it. It can't hurt you."

How is it that Fred could find words that were so calming and reassuring to TJ then and in the future, prior to Fred's demise, they would not even be speaking to each other? How?

5

TOUR OF DUTY: BOOT CAMP

Leaving Home for the First Time

A white Ford Torino made its approach down North 18th Street, the driver looking for TJ's house. It was not difficult for him to locate the house because TJ and all his people were standing on the porch. TJ remembers they were talking about everything from the projects to growing up on North 18th Street. What they talked about was extemporaneous memories as they entered the mind of his siblings.

One would blurt out, "Remember when we moved up here?"

Another would say something like, "Hey, TJ, you going to miss your bike?"

Someone even said, "I'll keep your bike safe."

And then there were a few lyrics mentioned from church songs. Obviously, the psychology was an attempt to keep TJ's mind off leaving, even though he was committed to leaving at this point. TJ was on his quest into an unknown world, a world he often dreamt about as a boy, a world that was about to quickly become reality. His heart was pounding almost uncontrollably. He was feeling nervous excitement. He was zealous and strong, but his heart was beating and throbbing in such a manner virtually making an imprint through his rib cage. While he stood there on the porch gazing at his family and also in deep, deep anticipation to leave, time seemed to move in slow motion. He looked up North 18th Street and spotted the white Ford Torino. The words painted on the side were, "United States Navy (Be all you can be)." As it slowly approached the house, he looked at his family on the porch, and while their lips were moving, he does not remember much of what they were saying. He remembers the earlier outburst of comments and questions, but nothing more from that point. He gazed at the Ford Torino as it got closer to the house driving about two miles per hour with front headlights on. He looked back at his family again, and they were like manikins frozen in his mind. A mental picture of them fading into the past almost like they were not there. With every word they spoke, they were becoming like silhouette images. But then Fred spoke up and said, "You can't come back home."

TJ heard Fred's words but was not upset at his words because he had become accustomed to Fred dropping words of knowledge into his psyche. A faint smile came across his face when he spoke, and faint the smile was—a lifeless smile. Within seconds, it seemed, the Torino had stopped in front of the house and a second class petty officer got out of the car and slowly opened the back door of the car, inviting TJ to enter in.

TJ does not remember the petty officer ever speaking to his family. It was as if this was military business, and on this mission, courtesy was not part of the armed forces. He solicited one last look and word from either Dad or Fred before he would take that life-changing walk down the steps toward the Ford Torino. Any word from Dad would suffice. Without TJ speaking a word, Dad reached out and grabbed the hand of TJ and said, "You can make it, son." That was all Dad said to him, and that was all TJ needed, but like the days of the projects running up and down the steps, he wanted more words than "You can make it, son." Nevertheless, it would have to do for now.

TJ began walking down the steps toward the car and heard his brothers and sisters and Mom and Dad saying, "Bye, bye, TJ."

He looked back once. That one look was too many times to look back, and he was afraid to respond and say bye. With each step, great apprehension flooded his soul. But he was drawn, hypnotized by the great desire to launch out into the unknown world. He was filled with uncontrollable, apprehensive, nervousness, and he could not wait to leave. Walking almost at a snail's pace, he was mummified and magnetized to walk toward the Ford Torino. TJ knew to leave home to join the military was something he had to do. It was a time of discovery in his life. By the time he got to the car, the back door of the car standing wide open, the words of his family were distant voices fading in his mind with each step. He did not hear them any longer. The memories with them as a child, as a boy and teenager, somehow had already faded into the past. A nervous fear seized his mind, and he was afraid to look back. He felt that if he looked back they would not be standing there. But he took the chance as soon as he sat down in the Torino. The driver closed the door and pulled off traveling what seemed like two miles per hour. TJ wanted him to speed up and get this thing over with. But it appeared as though the driver was conscious of what TJ was experiencing, and he permitted him to savor the feeling. Funny, real funny that was. As he drove away, TJ took the chance and sluggishly turned around to take one more look, but the driver had reached North 18th and Forester Streets. From where TJ was sitting in the car, he did not have a clear view of his family. It was at that moment the first wave of sadness struck deep within his heart. Tears immediately filled his eyes, and his stomach felt a deep emptiness inside. The driver turned the corner toward North 17th Street, and the view of them was gone, but the memory and image of them would last the remainder of TJ's life, into the Sailor and the Sermon.

Mom and Some Choir Members

Mom had to go to work that evening. She worked at the finance building at the capitol complex in the evenings as a cleaning woman. She was a janitor for the Commonwealth of Pennsylvania. She had a nice job with nice benefits. TJ continued to maintain the closeness with his mother, and he loved her with a genuine son's love. He thought she was a great mother despite her shortcomings and issues, which he would come to learn later in life. She was Mom, and he loved her with all his heart. He was glad to have a mother whom he knew. She was always there for him when he needed her while growing up. He wanted her to accept every decision he made. She did not immediately agree with his decision to enlist in the navy, but she accepted it and encouraged him to go and be the best he could ever be. She had nothing but positive things to say to him. As time crawled along, the recruiter driving the Torino had to stop and pick up two more recruits. Afterward, they drove directly to what was called the Armed Forces Examining and Entrance Station (AFEES). The station was located at New Cumberland Army Depot in New Cumberland, Pennsylvania. All the new recruits were there in processing from about 10:00 a.m. until 5:00 p.m. when they all took the patriotic oath: "Do you solemnly swear (or affirm) that I will support and defend the constitution of the United States…"

Officially sworn in to the military, they were driven back to Harrisburg, Pennsylvania, with their orders in hand and dropped off at the train station. TJ and a couple of other recruits were left there to board the train when it was time to leave. TJ seized those few minutes to make last-minute phone calls. He got on the phone, and the first person he called was Mom. When he spoke with her on the phone, she told him that she would stop down shortly to see him. After the call, he waited patiently to see her arrive at the train station. Boarding time for the train was fast approaching, and she hadn't arrived. TJ was beginning to stress, thinking she wouldn't make it in time. Homesickness began to tempt him with cowardly thoughts like, *If she does not make it in time, will I still board the train before I see my mother once more?* He began to pray, asking God to allow his mother to *please make it down here before I leave.* He did not want to leave without seeing her.

She did arrive at the station shortly before he had to board the train to give him one last hug and kiss. She looked more beautiful than ever. She was lovely, and her motherly love was a boost to him to board the train that afternoon. She kissed TJ on the cheek and said, "I have to go to work now, son. I just wanted to see my baby off." She didn't stay long, but she was satisfied just to see him once more. She turned around and walked out of the train station, and TJ did not see her again for another nine weeks and twelve days. He learned later from her that when she turned and walked away, she cried all the way to her job. Obviously, TJ cried when she left, and he watched her until she was out of his sight. But the excitement of leaving overtook his sad feelings. Then the sad feelings of leaving overtook his excitement. Mixed feelings swished around in his mind and heart like a washing machine cleaning clothes.

A few Mount Calvary church choir members had arrived at the train station to see him off—his homeboy, James Jones, DC, L. Dorsey, Freddie C, Aretha, and a few of his sisters. Although he was trying very hard to enjoy them seeing him off, deep inside he wanted to depart the station and get this thing started, as if he were going to an appointment and would return in a few hours. He still did not fully comprehend the deep changes in his life and his relationship with them that would unfold over the years to come. He did not want his departure to be a permanent memory, but he could not control the memory from becoming a lifelong one. Back and forth within his soul were the overwhelming excitement and the uncontrollable sadness. He smiled and played along with his church friends while they were there to see him depart Harrisburg, Pennsylvania, into a world of absolute unknown. When TJ sang on the choir at Mount Calvary, he led a song titled "You Know Lord." When he sang that song at church, he put his all into it. Very amateur voice, but he put his all into it. The lyrics to the song were, "You know Lord, whether I'm right, you know, Lord, whether I'm wrong. I want you to search me, search me Lord" and the chorus "search me, search me, Lord." That was TJ's song, and he sang it well back then on the choir at Mount Calvary Church of God in Christ. Little did he know, he was entering an experience that would not only search his heart but rip to shreds everything he thought and *everything* he believed. Christianity, church, and the Bible would become an unveiling of a maze of things on an unbelievable scale. A novice extraordinaire he was. Yes, the Lord DID search him, and only God, as he knew him them, knew how wrong and sinful the young TJ was. TJ was oblivious of his true spiritual state.

Before he boarded the train, he hugged everyone standing on the landing that day—James, DC, Lynette, Aretha, Freddie C, and his sisters. Other than his siblings, those hugs would be the last of an era he knew with his friends at Mount Calvary Church of God in Christ. He had a brief reunion with them after boot camp, but upon leaving Harrisburg for his permeant duty station, he would never reconnect with them again in life. They would never return to a level of trusted friends. Little did he know then that was the beginning of the end of the relationship he had with them. His growth and maturity were about to skyrocket him beyond their lifestyle and religious beliefs and Christian faith. He boarded the train as the conductor yelled out, "Last call, all aboard!"

He quickly made it to a window so he could see them as the train was pulling away from the station. He did not want to make the same mistake when the Torino drove away from North 18th Street when he could no longer see his family standing and waving on the porch. He made sure he could see them. They were the last memory of home he would have for a long time. When the train pulled off, they all ran alongside the train as far as they could run, singing to the top of their voice, "You know Lord, whether I'm right, you know Lord, whether I'm wrong. I want you to search me, search me, Lord, search me, search me, Lord, search my heart, search my mind"

Those words faded along with them into the eternal past forever. TJ had left home on his own, headed someplace and somewhere he was absolutely ignorant of. He speculated deep within his soul, quivering with fear and disbelief. He was not sure within his heart whether he had made the right decision. He was a lonely traveler on the train that day, entering into a whole new world of mystery and full of lies. Deceit, anger, and hatred would become the menu of the day. Death and devastation were looming in the near future, the likes he had only seen in movies. But his audition was rapidly approaching as he would become indoctrinated into the sinful world of adulthood. TJ would become the star of the show. The target of the bull's-eye for the crucifixion of his life. The butt of the joke and the world traveler with all its benefits and curses.

Tears on the Train

He quickly discovered that he did not realize the human tear ducts could release the number of tears he cried on that day. The last time he cried so intently and cried for hours was when he injured his head in the projects running from Fred. His boyhood life was good. His teenage life was fun, and his high school days were interesting. But during those growing years, he never cried or felt so alone and lost about everything like he did on the train on his way to boot camp at Naval Training Center, Great Lakes, Illinois. What worsened matters is the train ride took longer than anticipated. The train left Harrisburg, Pennsylvania, on June 28, 1976, but did not arrive in Chicago until the morning of June 29, 1976, due to an alleged mechanical problem on the train. They had traveled up north, miles away from Harrisburg. The temptations that entered his mind were relentless and unbearable. Thoughts were entering his mind of how to get off the train and find his way back home. All he cared about at the moment was nursing his sadness. He began to experience the first wave of homesickness, and it struck with a vengeance and unyielding attitude. The mechanical issue with the train did not help matters. It just gave him more time to think. Thoughts that were bathed in extreme negativism. They were not good at all. He entertained uncourageous thoughts—thoughts of running, thoughts of what will everybody think about him if he were to get off the train and find his way back home. Absent without leave (AWOL) before ever arriving at boot camp. What should have been a ten- to twelve-hour trip turned out to be a twenty-hour trip.

This is horrible, he thought. *What is wrong with this train?* He desperately tried to hold back the tears while talking to the other recruits on board. One guy, whose name he does not remember, noticed tears in his eyes and was trying to big brother TJ and was attempting to speak positive words like, "It's not that bad, homey. We all are facing the same thing. You'll be all right. Come out with the rest of the guys and let's play some cards." That guy must have been out of his mind as far as TJ was concerned.

Didn't he realize who he was talking to? TJ thought. Didn't he know the kind of person he was? First of all, TJ did not drink, did not play cards, and there was nothing that guy could possibly say to him that could remotely match the words of Frederick E. TJ had yet to learn that the words of Fred and the words of *all* his friends and family was but a teaspoon of countless views and perspectives of the entire world. In a respectful way, he ignored the guy and closed the curtains to his cube on the train. He leaped into his bed, curled up like a child, and put the pillow over his face and wept until he could weep no more. He was experiencing the newness of homesickness. The cup of homesickness was painful to his soul, but he had to drink the bitterness of what he did not understand. For the remainder of the trip to Chicago, Illinois, he occasionally looked out the window into the darkened night and resumed soaking his pillow with tears.

He could not believe what he had just done. *Why in the hell didn't somebody stop me? Why did they let me do this? They didn't really love me as they said?* Undisciplined thoughts ran through his mind, looking to blame someone for his own decision. An extreme novice who failed to understand the pain he was feeling. It was but a small taste of the spirit of loneliness and homesickness that he was compelled to overcome. His sad experience was no more than the little boy inside that had started down the road of maturing. Never taught in a classroom or spoken about between family members. He had embarked on his own to learn on his own. But in the early stages of learning, he was not taking it too well. The projects, North 18th Street, high school, Mount Calvary Church of God in Christ, and everything he knew about home was quickly fading. Each sound of the steel wheels pressing against the steel train tack was hammering his past away. He had entered the inescapable phase of life at an accelerated pace and did not understand what it was he was feeling. His first experience of homesickness was entirely agonizing for him. He was clueless of what homesickness looked like and what it felt like and the rigid adjustment of maturing. He wondered about the men in his life and why Fred, Bay, or even Dad failed to tell him about the unkind adjustment. For a brief moment, he felt like Fred's words was a bunch of mumbo jumbo. *All that talk, but why didn't he tell me about this?* He would learn later on that homesickness was something he had to experience on his own.

Years later, he realized they may not have been able to adequately explain how to identify homesickness. He believed they understood what he would personally go through. But he reasoned in his mind they also knew he would have to become familiar with and endure homesickness on his own. He would soon realize that their words actually prepared him for the greatest personal battle he would have to overcome. All other battles thereafter would be understood and overcome having conquered his own personal fears.

The train ride seemed to take extra-long while traveling to Chicago, Illinois. Stressing himself, he forced thoughts of reliving his life from the projects to the point he boarded the train in Harrisburg, Pennsylvania. The memories he embraced and mentally fed escalated his sadness beyond any resolution he could imagine. He thought about the time as a toddler when he ransacked Fred's cowboys and Indians fort in the projects. He thought about the time he crushed Fred's beautiful model cars in the projects. He thought about the time he injured himself in the projects in front of 38 MW Smith Homes while running from Fred. He thought about the time he was in the U-Haul truck with Dad when they moved to North 18th Street. He thought about riding the CAT bus downtown to go pay Mom's bills. He thought about Miller's Furniture Store and the day he walked in the lobby of Joe the Motor's and Friends and laid eyes for the first time on the F3 Eliminator bicycle. He thought about the day he walked down the steps on June 19, 1968, and spotted the F3 Eliminator in the living room. He thought about taking the bike outside and showing off with his friends and how they rode all day into the night. He thought about his first car, the Galaxy 500 and his second car, the Ford Torino. He thought about Mount Calvary Church of God in Christ and the friends he had on the choir and the times they went out to eat. He thought about the times they spent together and the departure from the train station on June 28, 1976. Evoking these thoughts was detailed in the memory banks of his mind, and he thought intensely about each moment. The day, the time of day, the temperature on that day, even managed to capture the emotions of each thought in detail, reliving in his mind every moment and weeping every second of every moment he thought of. He made matters worse by isolating himself from the other recruits onboard the train and purposely thinking about his childhood and his life growing up. Nothing wrong with remembering but everything wrong with dwelling on the past and detailing each memory to the point of tears and isolating oneself from others. This was his first experience with having a depressed spirit coupled with homesickness. TJ was an immature young man without any focus whatsoever. He aimlessly sought direction on a quest to find the man that God had envisioned in his own mind on the day TJ was created. Each thought of his past propelled his heart into a painful thrust to pump blood throughout his veins. He cried and cried and cried until he could cry no more and until he cried himself into a weary broken sleep. He felt like he forgot how to go to sleep, and staying awake and mentally reminiscing kept him close to the recent past. His body became tired from crying literally all night until the break of day. When morning arrived, he wanted to sleep all day, but he heard the screeching sound of the train coming to a stop. He did not want to get off the train but knew deep inside his heart this is what he longed for, and with the presence of mind, he signed up for Uncle Sam's world of the armed forces. TJ, in a mummified state, gazed out the window and was able to see tall buildings of Chicago, Illinois. He heard the bustling of the other recruits waking up and preparing themselves to disembark the train. Somebody yelled out "We're here! Get up! Get out of the bunks. Baby time is over."

You can't imagine what thoughts flooded his mind when he heard those words. Thoughts and feelings that almost sent him over the edge. Instantly he became angry, wondering who spoke those words and if they heard him crying. He wanted to grab the big-mouthed, loud-talking chump and punch them in the mouth. But for what? Whoever spoke those words spoke the shameful truth. Baby time was over and time to enter the first step of manhood. That kind of thinking was a reminiscent of Fred speaking to him, and that was the first of many times thereafter Fred's words began to sink deep into his soul. He could see the face of Fred and could hear his words and embrace his thoughts. With that surge of mental acuity, he stood up and got himself together and quickly, kind of with an anxious zeal and excitement to get off the train. He had to get away from the cube he was sleeping in and away from the thoughts inside that cube and ready to grow and face the challenges of life. Inside that cube on the train was his own personal shell he was breaking out of, and the initial crack in the shell was heart-wrenching. The shell would not totally break wide open and the new man step forward until some months later. He was tired, hungry, and a little angry at himself because he fell apart under such a common emotion. Homesickness would attack several times throughout his career, but the next would be more intense than the train ride. He was bordering on a nervous breakdown and actually desired one in order to have an excuse for being mentally unstable for military service. But for now, he was ready to get started with whatever faced him for the next six years.

Baby time is over. Time to grow up, he thought.

Navy Terminology

The new world of TJ's life was the introduction to navy terminology irritated him for the first few weeks. He had entered a whole new world with new terminology and a regimented intense disciplined new lifestyle. When they arrived at Chicago, there was transportation for them to board the local train that would take the recruits to Great Lakes, Illinois, about a good hour's train ride. TJ was tired and exhausted from crying all night, but something inside him was anxious to get on the train for Great Lakes. He had survived the initial leg of his journey taking him far away from for the first time in his youthful life. After the train ride, he knew he had to accept the reality of his new life. Now he wanted to get even further away from the train that brought him to this new life. He paced and paced in the train station on pins and needles to get on board. Didn't take long before the conductor yelled, "Great Lakes departing in fifteen minutes." TJ made his way to the train and quickly got on board. The excitement and great anticipation flooded his heart as the recent memories of home began to diminish. He was on his way to a world of no return, as Fred put it, and the train pulled away from the station. Recruit Training Center (RTC) Great Lakes, Illinois, was the next stop. His anticipation was further frustrated because they were not on the express train, and the train stopped at every interchange, taking every bit of one hour to arrive at RTC. The crew from Harrisburg had rendezvoused with more recruits throughout the nation, and they all headed toward RTC Great Lakes, Illinois. TJ remembered everyone on board that train up to about two years after boot camp, and faces began to fade and names became unknown. The events of those days entering into the United States Navy world at RTC are clear in TJ's memory, and other events are like shadowy figures. Nonetheless, the Recruit Company, as they were identified then, was his new family. TJ develop a relationship with other recruits by wanting to meet whoever held the same or similar beliefs as his. Even beyond that, he began to connect with different ones in his group to help fight off loneliness. The episode on the train was his personal private hatching from a sheltered life and youthful mind. He had embarked on an experience that would literally bring him face-to-face to the entire world. Much was told to TJ while growing up, and the practice and belief of Sunday church services are what he was familiar with. The homesickness and depression spirit came as a great surprise beyond his ability to control. But all that, church, homesickness, and depression—would become battle scars in his future. He would learn things and become exposed to different perspectives and views that would unquestionably change his life. In a real sense, he would become born again and the reality of the Most High would be *the* most significant pivotal change in his life.

Ten hundred (1000) hours, they arrived at Recruit Training Center Great Lakes, Illinois, on Tuesday, June 29, 1976, and the first sign he spotted was "Naval Station Great Lakes, Ill." When the new recruits arrived at Recruit Training Center, Great Lakes, Illinois, the first face they were introduced to was their company commander.

The first words out of his mouth were, "Greetings, gentlemen, and welcome to the United States Navy. I am your new company commander, and you will learn things my way, the navy way. Forget about home and your girlfriend and your wife. If the navy wanted you to have a wife, they would have issued you one. If the navy wanted you to have a girlfriend, they would have put her in your seabag and issued you one."

Kind of cold and insensitive, TJ thought, but then he reasoned within himself and thought, *Well, this is boot camp. I guess I have to get used to that kind of talking.*

Then came the first of navy terminology that deeply irritated him. He was furious at every mention of certain navy terminology. The CC (company commander) said, "I want you all to get nut to butt."

They were scrambling around like two-year-old's with two left feet. They didn't know what he meant, and he didn't like that. He yelled to the top of his voice, "You ninnies better get it together! I said 'nut to butt,' and that's what I mean!"

Then in an instructional way, the CC began to demonstrate. He took two new recruits and stood one here and stood the other one directly behind him about one-fourth of an inch from his backside.

TJ thought in his mind, *The first nigger or white boy that touches my butt, I am going to go off. I don't care that this is boot camp. No one had better even breathe down my back or I will fight them like a bear.*

He was not adjusting well to the new changes. But thanks to God, all went well that day. They eventually figured out nut to butt and got it together and tried to march in unison, but marching was horrible for the new recruits. Nuts and butts were all over the place. They were spaced out as far as six to seven feet. Then they were on top of each other, stepping on the heel of the guy in front of them and bumping into the guy in front and the guy in back, stumbling and tripping over heels. It was a sight to see for the rest of that day. The new Recruit Company 76-169 just couldn't seem to get together nut to butt and march at the same time. What an amusing event that provoked the CC, and he yelled and yelled and yelled all day at the new recruits in Recruit Company 76-169.

As the days crept along, TJ couldn't believe how much he was beginning to enjoy the newness, the challenge, and the excitement. He knew deep inside his heart the recruit company he was attached to would develop into a fine marching company in boot camp. But the night times were the ghost from hell in the form of memory and reminiscing in his mind. Every night it seems when he lay down, he ran through his mind some portion of home. The thoughts of detailing different times in his life growing up haunted him again and again every night when he lay down. Homesickness attacked TJ at night, but he would fight it and fight it until he fell off to sleep. When he awoke in the mornings, there was great anticipation in his soul of what the day was going to be like. Excitement became his morning friend, which enabled him to endure each day. But at night the fight was on again all the way through nine weeks of boot camp. He could not shake the homesickness throughout boot camp. It was during the day he enjoyed the experience of basic training, but he hated being in Great Lakes, Illinois, at nighttime. When the recruits had free time, guys would sit around either writing letters or talking about home or talking about their girlfriend. It took TJ about two weeks before he really began mingling with the other guys. In his mind, he was there to learn a skill and gain knowledge and travel the world. He did not have to like the people he was around, so he thought. Not only was basic training for the work of the United States Navy, but it was the tool he came to believe was used by God. The circumstances of navy boot camp became the catalyst of waking his mind and soul. All his life growing up, he was a sleepwalker living in a sheltered world. He sincerely believed his life and his family was a silver-spoon family. Later on, he was unsure if he would have been able to deal with and handle the things he learned about his family had he not gone away, far away. He did not know if he would have become successful in life had he taken a local job or had he gone off to college for two or four years. When all was said and done, he believes his experience in the United States Navy for twenty-four years, without a doubt, widened his perspective of the world, like taking a can opener and opening a can of food. God had food to serve him the likes he or *anyone* else could not have possibly imagined. Later on, in life, he believed that God carefully and methodically opened the top of his head and filled his mind with higher learning. He began to accept that God peeled the baby fat from his body like you peel a banana. He likened his separation from his brothers and mother like a physician cuts the cord from a newborn. He was slowly embracing his new life and accepting his new birth, naturally so and then spiritually so. What he thought he had in terms of salvation while living at home was but a microscopic crust of bread that caused his soul to salivate for the true bread from heaven.

Raisin

The term *raisin* was humiliating to him for the first few weeks of boot camp. To think of a raisin, one might picture a dried-up, shriveled fruit. Very small and insignificant. To TJ, *raisin* sounded humiliating and degrading, but everyone went through the same humiliation. The fact that all new recruits were called raisins helped him deal with the term. The concept of raisins is because new recruits were clean-shaven and the fact of being dry, not knowing cadence or how to march. Raisins were shriveled up because they were always stopping too late of the cadence call or bumping into one another while flanking. To the rear march was nothing but a fiasco early on. Or just tripping and bumping into one another for no apparent reason. In addition to being called raisins, they wore a white badge a little larger than a silver dollar on a white string hooked on to a front shirt pocket button. The message was clear to all other recruits they came in contact with—they were brand-new recruits or raisins.

What a humiliating thing, TJ thought, and to top it off, senior recruits (those ready to graduate) got pleasure out of calling them, "Raisins, step aside!"

TJ thought, *Our day is coming, and I'm sure I will do the same thing when I run into a raisin.* He was struggling to learn navy terminology, and he looked forward to the day that he could call new recruits "Raisin, step aside."

For instance, two short weeks into boot camp after their hair had begun to grow back, different ones in TJ's company began pointing out and yelling out to new recruits, calling them raisin. New recruits did not have a name, their name was Raisin, and that's what they were called, and that's what TJ pridefully called them: raisin!

There was a navy term that TJ embraced and felt affection for. It was a new way of saying, "You are my friend, and we have many things in common." The first he heard the term *shipmate* was when the CC was speaking to another CC and called him "shipmate." TJ was not sure if the word was derogatory in nature or harbored feminine characteristic. Having heard negative stories about sailors in close quarters, he just was not sure. What he did not completely understand at the time that if there were any ungodly promiscuity on board a naval vessel, it would not have been because of close quarters but because of what was in the heart of the individuals. The vices of the heart is a truth he did not come to learn until years later. Nonetheless, he got the boldness to ask the company commander what *shipmate* means, and the CC must have been in a good teaching mood because he actually took the time to explain to him. He led TJ to the Blue Jackets Manual (a kind of Bible for new recruits). The CC said, "*Shipmate* means 'you are my friend, my confidant, the one I can trust.' We are on the same path together. Reliability, dependability, so on and so forth."

TJ gladly embraced the term *shipmate* and from that point, began calling his new friends in Recruit Company 76-169 his shipmate.

Company 76-169: The Original Company

The newness and cultural shock and the experience of boot camp in the summer of 1976 were thrilling and enjoyable. Basic training alone catapulted the life of TJ years beyond his friends back home and the choir at Mount Calvary Church of God and Christ. He had overcome the train ride up to Chicago, which became like a dark tube or channel full of memories and sadness and homesickness that he had to travel through. And the traveling for the remainder of his life had only just begun. The spirit of pride was birthed in him because of the mentality of military thinking and developing an independent thinker mind-set. After getting over the long train ride from Harrisburg, Pennsylvania, to Chicago, Illinois, and arriving at Naval Station Great Lakes, Illinois, he settled in his mind the navy was his new life. About the third or fourth week of boot camp, he began to adjust to his new life and began to enjoy the physical aspect of exercise and competition. Boot camp was becoming fun, and if he had to do it all over again, as the saying goes, he would return to basic training at Great Lakes, Illinois. In fact, years later, that's exactly what he did but in a different capacity. Extensive and comprehensive tour of duty would bring the young boy from the projects through countless experiences and graduate him to the man envisioned in the mind of God. That's what this is all about—the path he chose was the path chosen by God. The crew he rode the train with were processed as recruit company 76-169, and they had come to know one another fairly well. New friendships were made, and they talked about their backgrounds, where they grew up, girlfriends, cars, and the prospect of making the navy a career.

Smoke and Coke time was free time in a large room for guys who smoked to smoke their cigarettes. Guys who didn't smoke enjoyed the luxury to drink a Coke. The drawback with smoke and Coke is that everyone had to be in the same room together amid the great cloud of cigarette smoke. Secondhand smoke in those days was not talked about much, and smoking inside buildings was permissible. It was nothing for anyone to light up a cancer stick inside a building in those days. When smoke and Coke was authorized, all recruits had to participate. Drawing on his Christian background, TJ felt smoke and Coke infringed upon his "religious" beliefs, but back then Uncle Sam was not hearing that. Nevertheless, he had developed friendships with many of the guys and had come to rely on his friends as a team. Two weeks into boot camp with his original Company 76-169, he developed the team concept and learned to work as a unit. Company 76-169 encouraged one another to be the best recruit company at Great Lakes, Illinois. TJ began to consider himself adjusted when a heartbreaking and almost disastrous setback occurred for him. Immediately he would interpret the setback as a life setback but could not help view the setback as the result of a bad decision. Bad thoughts would resurge, and the United States Navy now appeared to be a bad decision.

Being ASMO'd would crush his spirit. At the time, he thought it was a tragedy, and his perspective of boot camp and the navy became frazzled when TJ was "ASMO'd". A recruit receives Assignment Memorandum Orders (ASMO) when they fail a test or a violation of the Uniform Code of Military Justice (UCMJ). TJ was ASMO'd for failing to pass the swim test. He had never learned to swim well and only dove off a diving board once or twice in his life at the YMCA on 6th Street in Harrisburg, Pennsylvania. Even then he didn't swim to well but well enough to get out of the water. At basic training, you had to swim the width of the pool to be classified class C swimmer and swim the length of the pool to be classified class A swimmer. TJ did neither one. He was classified class D for "didn't do it." It was not that he could not swim at all, but the fear of not having the ability like the other recruits somehow electrified him with the inability to swim. For that reason, he could not continue on with his original company 76-169. Now he would be separated from the guys he rode the train with from Harrisburg, Pennsylvania, and the new friends he had made. TJ felt they were a tight unit and always helped each other study and formed study groups to learn navy terminology and the Blue Jackets Manual. He had become pretty close with many of them, and his closeness significantly contributed to the enjoyment and excitement he was having in boot camp. He was told he would be set back two and a half weeks, and he even tried to reason with the CC, explaining his nervousness about the pool. But the CC was not hearing that. There seemed to be no negotiation in the navy in boot camp. "Set back" sounded like tons of bricks falling upon every cell in his brain, as if his heart was removed from his rib cage and placed in vise grips. Like bits and pieces of TJ's heart were being chipped away with every word the military processor spoke. A tight knot formed in his belly, and tears filled his eye ducts, but he held them back because of shame, pride, and youthful ego. A lump developed in his throat, making it hard to swallow. He did not know where the lump came from, but man, was it hard for him to swallow. He felt like he was going into a mild shock. He could not believe what was happening; just when he thought things were getting better, he is slingshot back two and half weeks in training.

He became nervous, numb, teary eyed, and uncertain as to his success and progress in the United States Navy. His thoughts were, *If I am getting set back two and a half weeks in boot camp, what will the remainder of my naval career be like?* Jumbled-up thoughts like a locomotive out of control flooded his mind. Reminiscing like the time on the train in the cube where he slept, but not as stressful as then. Being set back in boot camp was embarrassing and traumatic at the same time because he was solid and in shape. He proudly brandished a six-pack abdomen. As a young man, failing the swim test smashed his pride for a moment. He imagined he would be starting over with a group of raisins. He imagined he would be starting over from the beginning getting his hair cut again. He envisioned himself standing at the entrance of Recruit Training Center Great Lakes, Illinois. He thought it would be like his first day with a new recruit company in civilian clothes tripping over one another. Thoughts of the clumsiness of his first company when they arrived in Basic Training. His thoughts ran wild, filled with all sorts of negativity and had no logical order at all. For the second time since leaving home, he felt the ugly spirit of deep loneliness and depression and embracing total loneliness. At least in Company 76-169, he knew most of those guys because they rode from Harrisburg, Pennsylvania, together. At least they had something in common, if it was only being from Harrisburg or York and the surrounding area of Pennsylvania. In his new company, if he would make it to the new company, he thought, the company he would be ASMO'd into, he did not know anyone. He would literally be starting over to develop new friendships. Stress on a level of anger and frustration filled the soul of the young lad, and disturbing thoughts plagued his mind. Almost instantaneously, he went from adjustment and acceptance of boot camp to agonizing with every thought of being in boot camp. He was worried and nervous with every second of time as to what he might have to learn over and who he would have to get to know. "What about this and what about that and what about so and so," he wondered and worried. He didn't know what to think, so his thoughts were nothing but unanswered questions that beset his mind. Homesickness overtook him like an unsuspecting thief and stole his confidence and severed the connection with his new friends. It was not easy for him to leave his original company 76-169 and his new friends. Ironically, "my way and the navy's way" resonated in the mind of TJ when he thought about what his company commander said on the first day of boot camp. The navy's concept of being ASMO'd is a mark of maturity when a recruit can make new friends in another company and work with them to attain the ultimate goal of graduation to the fleet. That was the navy's definition, and TJ strove to embrace the navy's concept of ASMO. But he would have to wrestle with the mental struggle and vehemently fight to overcome a quitting spirit. He struggled back and forth whether to flow with the change or throw up his hands and harbor the idea of quitting and fabricating some kind of story to get discharged.

The ASMO Unit

One of *the* most depressing times of TJ's entire naval career was the day he was ASMO'd. He was placed in a holding unit until assigned to a new recruit company. He would first have to pass the swimming test to be reassigned. While a recruit was in ASMO, basically they were in limbo between remaining on active duty or getting discharged for cause. After dinner in the galley on a day of the week, so depressing, he does not remember what day. TJ had to report to the ASMO unit, which was clear on the other side of the training center. ASMO'd recruits were kind of outcast to a remedial section on post; in the mind of TJ. Trying to draw from Bible stories, TJ felt like he was in the leprosy colony of biblical times. ASMO recruits had little to no contact with active recruits other than seeing them in the chow hall. Recruits in the ASMO unit did not participate in scholastic competition or athletic competition. They did not enjoy the privilege of making phone calls or going to the exchange. In TJ's mind, ASMO recruits failed the navy and were worthless out processing for discharge. There was no company commander or a senior enlisted man that called cadence to ASMO recruits. They were marched back and forth to the chow hall and sort of looked in on by the active-duty sailor assigned to the ASMO unit. Having been in boot camp for a few weeks, TJ had not yet mastered the ranking structure and was prone to saying "yes, sir" to anyone that had stripes on their shoulder. Funny thing, the sailor assigned to look in on the ASMO unit was a white man, a meager E3 (airman). When TJ discovered the rank of the airman, he did not respect him as he should have because the airman was only one rank higher than TJ. Immaturity and ignorance kicked into the mind of TJ, and he thought the airman did not have his best interest in mind.

TJ can recall the ASMO unit barracks as if it were yesterday, and the barracks to him was extremely depressing. The walls were what the navy calls "shipboard" gray. A dull depressing gray color that helped to contribute to the really bad attitude TJ had now developed. The barracks was quiet, depressingly quiet, void of activity as simple as talking, laughing, and sharing hometown experiences. There was anywhere from ten to twenty people in the ASMO unit at any given time. TJ knew everyone in the ASMO unit was a failure in some activity or competition during training, and for the most part in some strange way, they did not talk about their failure to one another. Consequently, they did not talk much to one another at all. Pins and needles as to the fate of their continuing in the navy or given a second chance to correct their deficiency. All they did in the ASMO unit was go to chow and study the Blue Jackets Manual and practice marching drills. They did not have a leader they were expected to perform their task when told to. The E3 assigned to the unit would pop in every now and then to look in on the ASMO'd recruits, and with every rousing moment, TJ sank deeper and deeper into self-pity and nurtured his anger of the United States Navy. The ASMO unit was long eight to twelve hour days of nothing but thoughts, nasty, ugly, bad, unproductive thoughts. TJ was done with the navy and really, really wanted to get out of the navy after the second day in the ASMO unit.

Amid the long days in the ASMO unit, he had to report for remedial training at the pool to pass that phase of training to become reassigned. He was weeping almost every night but able to maintain most of his composure during the day. He didn't want to seem weak and spineless, so he held back the tears. But at night when nasty, ugly, bad and unproductive thoughts flooded his mind, he wept.

Thoughts of attempting murder, suicide, stealing something, anything, cursing out the E3, attacking the E3 the next time he showed up, wetting the bed on purpose—these thoughts were entirely not the person he thought himself to be; nevertheless, he entertained hopeless thoughts in hopes to find one that would release him from his failure and bring peace to his soul. He did not want to think of himself as a quitter or an evil person. Nor did he want to believe he was surrendering to drastic measures to plead his case and warrant a discharge. He did not want to go home but wanted to get out of the navy. He did not like the circumstance he was in and sought to attempt any measure to get himself out of what he thought was a bad ill-advised decision. At this point, enlisting in the United States Navy plunged his life into a type of hell on earth. Pretty drastic thoughts and unbecoming a Christian. But what he was unaware of and hadn't learned then was the great depravity of his own heart. As he would learn in years to come, the heart of TJ desperately needed the right direction. His soul yearned for true healing, and his mind starved for intelligent thinking.

The Great Escape (Attempt) and the Angel

While marching to the chow hall on a daily basis, TJ looked at the fence around the training facility (an indication of how far away he was from the active successful recruits). The fence was not visible when he was in his original company 76-169. The active drilling companies are deep in the heart of the training center far away from the outskirts of the facility. It would appear to him that the navy placed temptation in his lap and every other ASMO recruit by housing them near the perimeter and the gate to the facility. TJ imagined in his mind what it would be like to scale the fence and run for his life. He imagined scaling the fence and what he would do once over the fence. He dreamed at night how to get out of the barracks without being noticed and run for the fence. He even heard stories of recruits attempting to escape, like they were in prison. Recruits did make attempts to go absent without leave (AWOL). Stories were circulating of recruits who went AWOL but were captured and immediately placed in the brig on bread and water for three days. He heard stories of recruits who were captured after attempts of going AWOL and were sent to hard time in federal prison five to ten years. As far as TJ knew, these were just stories, all in an effort to put fear in their minds that any attempts of going AWOL would be foiled. However, the stories worked if that's all they were designed to do. TJ did not make any attempts to scale the fence and run for his life. All those thoughts were just tormenting thoughts trumped in his own mind due to his own failure. Besides, the problem with the fence connected at the top is what looked like fresh, shiny, sturdy barbed wire, almost identical to a prison hold. The barbed wire was sparkling silver almost like it had been newly installed. The barbed wired was unmistakably noticeable. TJ had jotted down at one point on paper a quasi-plan of escape. He became delusional, like he was a criminal. Totally forgetting that he signed the dotted line fully aware of his own decision to enlist. ASMO, by far, was one of the weakest and depressing time in his life. The ASMO unit elicited bad thoughts from deep within his heart. Thoughts he never imagined would spring forth from within his soul. Thoughts that one day would define who he really was and why the struggle to "know thyself" was one of THE greatest challenges he faced at the time. TJ wrestled and wrestled every night with evil satanic thoughts of himself and of the prospect of quitting. But he struggled most of how to confess his failure to the world, his friends, and his family, but most of all to God. The God he was taught loved him so much and desired him to be "saved." Why did he let him get into this situation? Blaming God for his decision entered the mind of TJ. Feeling like the tunnel had closed in on him and there was *no* light *anywhere*. Answers to TJ's mundane questions would become apparent to him as time moved on. The answers to all the mundane questions would also reveal to him the real man inside that he was oblivious to and the fearful, uncertain man that had to be crucified. Boredom and mental weariness plagued him daily. Back and forth to chow, studying the Blue Jackets Manual with no real purpose, it seemed, began to take its toll. TJ concluded it was time to make his decision and make his move to get discharged from the

United States Navy. It did not matter to him what type of discharge he would receive, all he thought was, *I want out of this shit!*

One day on a typical depressing quite Sunday afternoon, there was very little activity going on the grinder. Guys were writing letters, reading letters, studying the Blue Jackets Manual when the E3 assigned to the ASMO unit to "look in" on them popped in. The mind of confusion that had now become the ruling factor in the life of TJ thought, *Now is the time to make my move.*

TJ decided to go for broke but was clueless that he was about to become broken like the Scriptures say about a "broken heart and a contrite spirit" (Ps. 34:18). Brokenness and contrition both became very real to the young lad the day he decided to act a total fool. The mental battle he was about to engage in would be one of many brokenness experiences throughout his navy career. Frustrated and angry, he decided that he hated the navy and hated company commanders and hated his shipmates and wanted to go home and get out of the navy.

Essentially, that's what he told the airman E3 assigned to look in on the ASMO unit recruits. The airman gave TJ time to speak with him, and TJ expected a different response than what the airman gave him, and if he did not get the response he wanted from the airman, he was prepared to initiate plan B. TJ had every intention to attack the airman and strike him in the face to hasten his discharge and satisfy his hatred of the navy. His encounter with the airman would be the first of countless "school of life" training seminars he would attend. TJ's perspective of the airman would change from the white E3 assigned to look in on them to the angel who pointed him back in the right direction. TJ looked at the E3 as an angel because his responses to TJ's immaturity took him completely by surprise. It would be the first of countless engagements on the scale of mercy and angelic guidance. The E3's response was instructive, informative, intelligent, and assuring in many ways. That day brought comfort in the confused young lad. At the time, TJ did not understand, nor was he aware of the biblical injunction of being careful how you entertain strangers because some have entertained angels unaware (Heb.13:2). In the mind of TJ, it seemed a little esoteric to call an E3 airman recruit an angel in boot camp, but TJ chose to accept the airman's response to him in an angelic manner. As a young Christian believing that type of rhetoric was not uncommon for TJ. The airman's response was one of good understanding and exactly what TJ needed at that unstable time in his life. In other words, he was just what God sent his way on that day at that time. TJ had become delusional and was fostering a coward spirit. But for the grace of God, a man with good reason and sensibility was sent to help a young man find his way. The airman's response and words were reminiscent of talking to Fred or listening to Bay. Obviously, TJ was still at the baby stage of maturing, and God was still carrying him and nursing his soul until he sent the angel.

"Sir, can I talk to you about the navy?"

"Sure, but you don't have to call me sir."

TJ walked into a small room that had a gray desk. The chair the airman sat in and the one chair in front of where TJ sat to face him across the desk all the color of grey. The room was empty of any other furniture, and the walls were bare. There were no pictures on the wall of ANY sort. There were no file cabinets and not even a window. It appeared to be a small 10 × 12 room with a desk and two chairs. Obviously, that environment was designed to offer zero distractions. What occurred that day was pure, an unquestionable focus for one distraught delusional young man.

"What do you need, recruit?" the airman asked.

"Well, I want to get out of the navy, I decided I don't like the navy, and I feel angry toward everyone around me."

"And how long have you been feeling like this?" said the airman.

"For about a couple of weeks."

"Do you mean a couple of weeks before you came to the ASMO unit or since you came to the ASMO unit?"

"I don't know, probably since I came here to this unit. I hate the navy, and I want to get out." TJ even had the audacity to tell the airman, who had done nothing to him at all, that he hated him also, trying to elicit a negative response from the airman, but to no avail. The airman was very levelheaded and cool, and not once did the airman ever raise his voice or look down on TJ.

"I would like to speak to a psychiatrist. I miss my family and friends back home, and I don't think I can do this anymore."

The airman shifted into another gear, one of purpose, seriousness, and skillfully armed to massage the thoughts and emotions of the young ignorant TJ. The first question he then asked TJ was, "What is your first name?"

TJ found it hard to believe that he would ask his first name, but he reluctantly told him, and he addressed him as TJ the remainder of the conversation. The airman then sat up straight in his chair and began to speak to TJ very skillfully. Skilled in the art of persuasion, the airman spoke reason and common sense to TJ. But at the time, for TJ at eighteen years old, the airman appeared to be way beyond the maturity years of TJ. "I want you to think about what you're feeling. Before you were ASMO'd, how did you feel about the navy?"

"Well, it was fun and exciting, but now..."

"But now, you are experiencing homesickness on a profound level, and you are also experiencing feelings you are afraid to face—feelings that are deep inside your soul and feelings you are having a difficult time sorting out. It isn't that you hate the navy as it is the feelings you hate. The navy and the people around you are the tools being used to bring out of you what you need to face and overcome."

TJ was stunned, mesmerized, speechless, and in awe at what the airman said to him. *Who is this guy, and what gives him the right to speak to me like he knew me? How is it that he is so calm and patient with my immaturity and ignorance? Why didn't I just walk in his makeshift office and cap him right in the face and then follow up with a couple of jabs and beat him until he bleeds? Why didn't I end this thing immediately?* TJ thought.

The airman had impressive control and spoke with authority and a calmness TJ least expected. To TJ, the airman was a skilled warrior with words and good judgment of human behavior even though TJ misjudged him based on his appearance. TJ expected yelling and derogatory comments like, "Get yourself together and stop whining like a little girl! Your momma is back home. She ain't here, recruit! Now get out there and get yourself together!"

But on the contrary, the airman was anything but loud and degrading and disrespectful. Rather, he was compassionate, surprisingly intelligent, understanding, skilled, and most of all, he exhibited what TJ interpreted as godly wisdom. The mannerism and articulation ability of the airman left a lasting impression on the mind of TJ. As the conversation neared the end, the eyes of TJ became teary, like a well of water had gushed up through to his eyelids. The airman counseled TJ in an angelic manner and was very understanding and compassionate toward the immaturity and ignorance of the young lad. To this day, the airman is clear in the mind of TJ. The counselor airman leaned back a little in his chair and said, "Now take a few minutes and get yourself together, and I want you to go back out there and overcome this deep personal challenge inside your soul and conquer yourself and overcome your challenges. You are meant to win and not lose. You are in good hands, and you are a strong shipmate." The fact that he addressed TJ as his shipmate placed him on equal terms with TJ. Sitting down and talking with the airman that day turned out to be astounding and totally the opposite of what he expected. That one talk humbled TJ, encouraged him, and instructed and refocused him on his goals and learning how to engage his own spirit in personal conflict. The pathway to maturity for TJ was an eye-opener and deep soul searcher experience. Oddly enough, as though the talk with him that day was surprising and instructional in every respect, TJ does not recall seeing the airman much after that day. What happened to him? He did not pop in anymore to look in on them. TJ never saw him walk through anymore. TJ was in the ASMO unit almost two weeks, and his talk with the airman was near the end of the first week.

Having passed the swim test and returned back to the ASMO unit one day another E3 showed up and called out TJ's name, "Seaman Apprentice TJ, front and center."

TJ was then given a "walking chit" and directions to his new company. He was told to pack his seabag and get stepping to Company 76-179 located in Black Cat Battalion. That was all the way on the other side of the training facility. One good thing, they marched the entire ASMO unit to the chow hall first and afterward

TJ had to report to his new company right across from the chow hall. It was like the sun had risen in his heart and the clouds had dried up along with his depression of tears. The excitement he once embraced being in the navy had returned with a renewed confidence and things were beginning to look new. TJ had been reassigned back into an active drilling company and back in competition with other recruits. Felt good! Really good. In many ways, he thanked his counselor, whom he thought of as an angel, whom he never ever seen again at Naval Training Center Great Lakes, Illinois. TJ did not see him walking down the street at the training facility. He did not see him in the post exchange. He did not see him at graduation. He did not see him again at all. Maybe he transferred to another duty station, or maybe, just maybe, he was an angel sent there for TJ and other recruits. The idea of him being an angel and the thought of him being there to assist TJ and other recruits, for TJ, was, at least, an exciting thought. The prayer of the church Mother came to mind after speaking about five minutes in that small office with the airman. Is this what she meant, and were there more encounters like this to come? TJ wondered how effective that prayer was, and he would learn the answer to be yes, much more on a magnificent scale.

Company 76-179: Color Company

After making it through the ASMO unit, he becomes refocused and time to report to his new company, who was already two weeks behind his original company. TJ felt like he had been wronged and that he was supposed to be with the guys he rode the train to boot camp with. Sort of like a "buddy" system, and "the system" was tearing them apart. He had no redress, no one to complain to, no one to air his grievance. He had to do what the navy wanted. He remembers the words of his original CC when they arrived, "You will learn things my way, the navy way." ASMO was the navy's way of doing things for remedial training for recruits.

After dinner in the galley, TJ had to report to Company 76-179, 13th Black Cat Battalion, ten companies behind his original company, which meant if he remained in Company 76-179, he would be graduating two weeks later than his original company. Man, what a serious heartbreaker that was for TJ. He felt like a loser and on the road to failure in the navy. Dead thoughts began to resurrect in his mind, the kind of thoughts he had when he first left home. Thoughts like, *Why?* and *Somebody should have stopped me from enlisting*. Like a private pity party. A small pond of his own tears of sympathy. When he stepped inside Black Cat Battalion and laid eyes on his new shipmates, he had to look mean. He had to look like he was ready for the challenge. He did not crack a smile, not even a hello. First of all, he didn't like them because he didn't know them and didn't want to get to know them. He struggled to get inside the battalion carrying his seabag and packed to the rim on his shoulder. The new company commander (EM1 Lundquist) introduced TJ and told him where to put his seabag.

"Unpack and get your linen and make your bunk," the CC said.

Some of the guys spoke, others just looked at him, and some nodded their heads in a gesture of speaking. TJ was brief. A look here a look there, but no smiles from him. No "sir," no smiles at all. At the time, little did he know that his transfer to company 76-179 was *the* best move for him while in boot camp at Great Lakes, Illinois. It would be the most exciting experience that apparently would not have been experienced in Company 76-169, the crew from home. This transfer would be *the* very first step toward the mark of maturity for the young lad.

King of the Hill

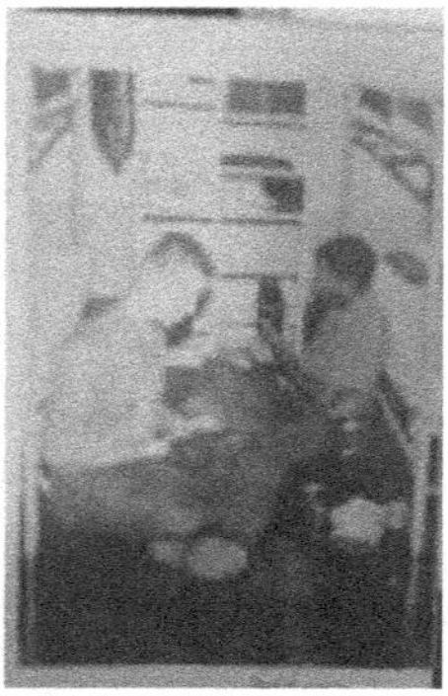

Remember playing the game "King of the hill" when you were a child? TJ played that game often in the projects and on North 18th Street. The game was fun and made you feel kind of big and bad and in charge. About a week being on board with his new company, TJ had to prove himself to some people. There is ALWAYS one person who wants to see what you are made of and offer you a personal challenge. Are you a wimp? Are you a bully? Can you hold your own, or can you be taken down? TJ expected that kind of reception from some and knew one day he would have to deal with somebody's challenge.

He stayed on guard of his thoughts, his emotions, and his personal feelings. He knew the day would come when he would have to square off with one of his shipmates. It did not take long, say, after about a week or so. He could have easily picked out the guy he would have to prove himself to. Actually, he imagined picking him out in a police lineup. The guy TJ would have to confront was the cockiest, loudmouthed, strong Southern accent draw. It was his first experience with such a deep Southern accent. He had not met many people at this point in his life not being anywhere other than Philadelphia, Pennsylvania, and Atlanta, Georgia. The challenge, including the change of recruit companies, was his first step into the "competitive adult world." He was not sure if he was ready, but he had to become quickly ready very fast! Turned out TJ and the cocky guy became pretty good friends after the square off, and a certain amount of respect was gained all the way through graduation day. TJ missed that guy and most of his fellow recruits years after graduation. His new recruit company would go through a lot together and mature into working as a team and watching each other's back. For purposes of identification and also protect the guy's privacy, we will call the guy Calvin. During free time, everyone was sort of lying around writing letters and shining boots, folding clothes, chitchatting as Calvin was making noise. He was acting silly and immature, wanting to be seen and heard—laughing aloud, crackin' jokes, and pushing smaller guys around. Nothing really threatening, he was all about getting attention and being the center of attraction. The last thing TJ remembers before Calvin challenged him was Calvin and another recruit wrestling. The other guy was a little bigger than Calvin; in fact, Calvin was not that much bigger than TJ. The guy Calvin was wrestling around with wrestled Calvin to the floor, and Calvin began laughing really loud, and when he stood up, the episode was over. Then, as TJ expected, Calvin came over to where he was sitting while he was writing a letter minding his own business. TJ remembers that his mentors Fred and Bay, and even his recruiter, advised him to mind your own business. Calvin tapped TJ on the shoulder and said, "What about you, TJ? You never talk, and you flunked out and ended up with us. What about you?"

TJ said to Calvin, "I'm part of the unit now. Doesn't matter where I came from."

Apparently, Calvin did not like his response and said, "Let's see what you know."

Other guys started egging the whole thing on, getting louder and louder. TJ tried within all his power to ignore the challenge and commence to finish writing his letter when Calvin attempted to tap him again on the shoulder. TJ had been watching Calvin out of the corner of his eye, and he would not take his eye off him even when he was clowning around with the other recruits. Calvin's hand came near TJ's shoulder for the second time. TJ immediately stood up. He probably should not have stood up in the manner he did because he was boldly accepting Calvin's challenge. But then the challenge was on, and at the time TJ was feeling very good and enjoying having to prove myself. Calvin began swinging like he was shadow boxing and laughing loud and just acting silly. TJ played and played with him, blocking every one of his wild swings until he became bored and tired with the game Calvin had initiated, which did not take very long.

When TJ stood up, the other recruits' eyes were on him. They were all expecting to see some kind of defensive skill, hoping TJ would embarrass Calvin and shut him up once and for all. TJ immediately decided to give everybody what they wanted, including loud-mouthed Calvin. All TJ did was go into a front leaning stance, and the other recruits went crazy. Yelling and screaming and saying to

Calvin, "You in trouble now. Looks like you pushed the button of the wrong person!"

"Oh, so you know that stuff?" Calvin said. He took another swing at TJ, continuing to act silly, but TJ was not joking. He swung at TJ in a manner that it was impossible for him to connect, sort of like when a father plays with his son, swinging at him but never close enough to actually hit him. But for TJ, he urgently welcomed Calvin's challenge. Although Calvin was not close enough to hit TJ, the instant he swung, TJ knew he was way off. But TJ accommodated him and swiftly stepped into the radius of Calvin's cocky swing and purposely blocked his punch. Calvin was taken by surprise because the wild swings he was throwing all of a sudden was blocked by a rock solid forearm, and Calvin stepped back and said, "Wow! You're good!" But Calvin would not stop at that, he starting clowning around and began to through crazy, wild, almost girly-like swings. TJ repeatedly and purposely stepped into his wild punches and blocked every single one of them.

By that time, the entire unit was excited, wooing the whole situation on, yelling, "Get him, TJ! Get him, TJ." Calvin did a stupid thing, thinking he was going to intimidate young TJ by charging at him and attempting to wrestle him to the ground. TJ had just learned a knew kung fu hold and had perfected it before leaving home. Even to this day, he remembers the hold and have demonstrated the hold to a few people and how to apply it. James Jones, his closest friend back home, admired TJ for swiftness and accuracy and the ability to catch on quickly. James and TJ use to practice often in James's backyard and TJ's yard with what they learned in kung fu. Neither one of them ever took martial arts anywhere in their lives, but both loved to do exhibitions. Anyways, when Calvin charged TJ without any form whatsoever, TJ could see it coming because he was not advancing on TJ with his sissy swinging. In a desperate move, Calvin ran toward TJ like an out-of-control ox. TJ flanked to the right, because he was left-handed, to throw him off balance and immediately grabbed Calvin around the torso. He quickly slipped his arm around Calvin's midsection and locked his hand into his other arm, giving him sort of an "L" shape around Calvin. He then positioned himself directly behind Calvin. He continued to hold the locked left hand on the right arm.

The sleeper hold is designed to have the right hand free to take the right hand and push down on the opponent's head. Then in one swift motion, lift the opponent off the floor. If applied correctly, *any* opponent can be lifted off the floor. Interestingly enough, was an angel with TJ in such a childish, careless act? The clowning around was not to be taken seriously, but Calvin did not realize that when TJ was much younger, he was bullied a lot. After becoming a karate and kung fu student, TJ did not take bulling lightly. The flank he did to the right and grabbing Calvin around his torso worked PERFECTLY! So perfect that it astounded TJ himself, but he dared not to show his surprise. TJ then lifted Calvin off the floor and held him for about, maybe thirty seconds. By this time everyone was screaming and yelling "TJ, TJ, TJ!"

Calvin was squirming like a baby trying to wiggle his way from the hold. Little did Calvin know the more the victim squirms and wiggles, attempting to get released from the hold, the harder it is to breathe. The victim would be shortening his own breath by his own actions. The entire event lasted perhaps a millisecond but was giving TJ a satisfying victorious pleasure. Then the assistant recruit petty officer in charge (RPOC) noticed what was going on and said to TJ in the most authoritative voice he could muster, "Put him down, TJ, right now! That's an order!"

TJ was furious, thinking to himself, *What's wrong with the RPOC? Didn't he see how this whole thing unfolded? Didn't he see that I was minding my own business? Nothing was ever said to Calvin and all the attention he needed. Why am I getting a direct order? But of course, I'm the new kid on the block and in order to save face for their own, I get ordered.*

TJ dropped Calvin directly to the floor without apology, and Calvin stood up coughing and gagging and had the nerve to say, "Man, can't you take a joke? I gotta watch out for you. I was just playing and you tried to kill me."

"Yeah, I will not be pushed around by you or anyone else," TJ said.

The RPOC and the assistant RPOC called themselves, rebuking TJ by taking him to another table and telling him not to take things personal. TJ had to set them straight and let them know, "Hey, I will not be bullied or pushed around by anyone, and if Calvin wants to talk to me, then he must talk intelligently and I will respond in kind."

Assistant RPOC, "Yeah, but you could have hurt the man. He was only kidding."

"Then you tell the man, RPOC: *do not kid with me like that*!"

The entire situation ended at that, and everyone resumed what they were doing and the excitement was over. However, the remainder of boot camp, TJ never had any confrontation, not even a disagreement with Calvin and TJ had instantaneously gained the respect of the entire Recruit Company 179. But it was never, ever the intent of TJ to show off or get others to like him. He just wanted respect and would gladly give respect to others. Ironically, though, TJ and Calvin became good friends, and Calvin repeatedly asked TJ to show him that move he laid on him. Reluctantly, at some point in time, TJ showed Calvin one of the deadliest kung fu holds he had ever learned. TJ felt it was like entrusting the proverbial "button" that would launch a nuclear weapon into the hands of the wrong person. Calvin was the kind of guy you didn't want to turn your back on because he may sneak up on you and play some practical joke. Calvin was a jokester, and TJ was not. He was perhaps a little bit too serious for his age; nonetheless, that's who TJ was. Letting up on that seriousness would not become a reality in the life of TJ for decades to come. But on that day, TJ established to the entire Company 76-179 that he was not a jokester and could hold his own without question. Calvin, on the other hand, continued to clown around with others, and it became sort of a sidebar, "We're going to sic TJ on you if you don't stop clowning around."

Calvin would laugh at those comments, and everyone who heard the comment would laugh together. For that one day in boot camp, TJ became "king of the hill" and was gladly accepted as a permanent member of Company 76-179. His new company and new shipmates would become color company at Recruit Training Center, Naval Training Center Great Lakes, Illinois.

Color Company

TJ never would have imagined that his transfer and two-and-half-week setback would land him in one of the best graduating company of boot camp. He had lost all enthusiasm for joining the navy and began the long journey of questioning God as to why he made the decisions he made, all the while God was orchestrating his life for his own purpose.

Company 76-169, the original company TJ arrived with, did not attain color company status, nor did they graduate with honors as far as he knew. But Company 76-179 was a group of efficient, articulate, and educated recruits. The expertise in which they executed marches was not too far from being a drill team. Recruit company 76-179 had developed into ideal recruits, which manifest in their performance and competition. They would become color company of the graduating companies on September 3, 1976. Color company is the flag that is won by the company that attains the highest overall average of the group of companies that it will graduate. Upon realizing that Company 76-179 was developing into becoming color company, the enthusiasm of TJ began to return and the spirit of pride came alive in his soul. He began to feel a sense of belonging and accomplishment like he made the right decision to enter the navy. The two-and-a-half-week setback and ASMO was one of many valleys that turned out to become a mountain of success while he walked on the peak of the mountain top. Boot camp turned out to be one of a small portion of personal success of where his experience and level of maturity would take him. While in the ASMO unit, many times he would think, *Why did I leave home for this?* But little did he know the two-and-a-half-week setback was actually catapulting him forward. The challenge and excitement contributing to becoming color company inspired him to march with pride. He developed character and self-worth, as he understood it to be. The navy taught "pride, honor, and integrity." Pride in the heart of TJ was an attribute that would be cut down to its lowest denominator some years into his future. He could not help but feel those emotions within himself, and in those days, it was all about TJ, "myself and I." He had become a part of an organization that taught many elements of life.

Marching along with his shipmates became regimented, soldierly, disciplined, and extremely competitive. Recruit company 76-179, with every step, every stride, and every training session, was quickly developing into one of the sharpest recruit companies. They were "just what the navy ordered" marching group of men. Recruit company 76-179 stopped on a dime, pivoted on ball and heel effortlessly, flanked like a well-oiled vessel and always to the rear marched in perfect unison. Recruit company 76-179's hard training and discipline was beginning to become evident and beginning to reap special dividends in boot camp.

About the fifth week into boot camp, the unit was starting to get special privileges to the exchange, the recreation room and even allowed to make up to ten-minute phone calls back home. TJ did not make too many phone calls because he was just beginning to adjust to his new surroundings. He feared the onslaught of reminiscent feelings and the resurrection of homesickness and having to readjust. He did not want to relapse back into feeling homesick after somewhat adjusting to boot camp. He decided to leave the phone alone and engage his mind into meeting the challenge of becoming a United States Navy sailor. The athletic competition was extremely fun and challenging in every respect. An eighteen-year-old pristine physical condition lean body structure. He had a perfect body fat percentage for his height and weight. Textbook blood pressure and no physical ailments at all. Had practiced kung fu from the tenth grade through high school graduation. Track and field, climbing the ropes, and every physical activity was like a walk in the park for TJ. He contributed 100 percent in the area of athletics to Company 76-179 becoming color company. He was a member of track and field and proudly demonstrated his ability to run the sprint and 440 in record-breaking time. TJ would run in competition, relay, sprint and 440 and would not even break a sweat. Ah yes, those were the days of a healthy young specimen who looked forward to every physical competition he engaged in as a recruit. Climbing the ropes with and without the knots on the ropes and running relays and sprints at a competitive speed. Even tug-of-war was fun to TJ, a conspicuous display of testosterone.

Line Captain

Week 6 of boot camp every recruit was assigned special duty called service week. They served in some function supervising or leading other recruits much junior in the training process. TJ does not remember if he had the privilege to pick the duty he wanted or if he was assigned the duty. Nevertheless, he served as line captain in the galley and at this point in boot camp had become very proud of what he was doing and what he was accomplishing. He at least felt like he was accomplishing something. He walked tall, with his head up his back straight in sort of a marching manner. He saluted every officer and drill instructor with razor-sharp salutes. He placed his feet solid on the ground when he walked. His shoulders were back and defined, proudly walking tall everywhere he went on the training facility. You would have thought he had just conquered the entire world—at least in the early stages of conquering his own world. TJ was in a battle of the world of homesickness, self-pity, doubt, fear, and uncertainty. And what he felt was a conquering then was just a smidgen of what personal battles and military engagements lay ahead. But this supposed conquering was actually masked with adjusting and not a true conquering of his world. Little did he realize that in just a few short months, another episode of homesickness would strike. But even still, he was a proud young sailor on his way to showing everybody back home what he had grown into. He felt he was going places and would have a lot to talk about upon returning home. He felt he made quantum leaps into the world of maturity. His experience was being gained in shopping cart style. The kids back home still standing on the corning were stuck in a world of the past and afraid of the future. But TJ, oh yeah, he had jumped into a proud, exciting, wonderful, career. He was ignorant of the unsuspecting, divisive, cruel, and fast-paced sinful world. It would be a world that would captivate the young lad's mind. The mind of TJ would become engulfed in a shrewd, unmerciful, sometimes good, sometimes bad way of maturing boys into men. Every day as line captain, he looked forward to performing his duties. He was in charge. He assigned recruits their duties on the food line. He delegated duties to junior recruits to keep the galley floor and tables glistening clean. "Keep the tablecloths on each table uniformed and smelling clean. Make sure the food on the line was steaming hot and every server behind the line must wear razor-sharp creases in their shirts and pants." It was TJ's line, and he was proud to be the line captain. He kept everything in place and everything placed where it was supposed to be. When the recruits marched into the chow hall, he was ready to give them the service they deserved. In military and stoic manner, he ordered those under him "get this line replenished with hot food! More juice is needed in the dispenser. Fill up that milk dispenser. Don't let the drink run out we have recruits to feed here!" TJ was in leadership heaven, as he thought. Everything was running smoothly every day and he was beginning again to like boot camp and the United States Navy. He thought, *If the rest of the navy is like this, I'm going to have fun.*

Judging by the obedience of his team in following his orders, he naively presumed everybody liked him, or at least accepted him. He really gave no thought how he may have been rubbing someone the wrong way or even being the cause of someone getting angry with him. TJ did not know anything about leading people; he was just doing what he was told to do. He sincerely thought he was doing a fantastic job supervising those who served under him. Of course, he was not made line captain immediately. He was trained by the outgoing line captain, a recruit who was in his seventh week one week from graduating from boot camp.

TJ thought, *One day I'll be in that position one week from graduation.*

Nonetheless, he walked in his trainer's shoes and did not ask many questions. He was told, in boot camp, just look, listen, and learn. In fact, that's what his recruiter told him before he left home, Keep your mouth shut and do what you're told. TJ followed the orders of his navy recruiter and did what he was told. The outgoing line captain that TJ learned from was a proud military man, and for the most part, TJ copied him, enjoying the whole idea of leading people. The outgoing line captain was strict and demonstrated a great deal of pride serving "his country." Likewise, TJ confirmed easily into his mold by feeling deep inside that he was serving his country by becoming like his instructor line captain. At this juncture in his naval career, all that good feeling of pride, commitment, honor, and integrity felt good and was good for his soul. But after more than twenty years of serving in the navy, nursing his personal feelings, he expected his life to become razor sharp. But his pride would turn into deep gratefulness. His commitment would turn into duty and responsibility. His honor would turn into respect and his integrity remain. Decades into the future he would absolutely change his entire perspective about his life. He would experience a series of heart-wrenching falls from grace until he would personify the Sermon.

Sugar Tastes Better Than Salt

Around his seventh week of boot camp, things were going good. The young TJ was developing into the new man at the grass roots level. Every morning before he began his duties as line captain, he would always sit down at one of the clean tables with a clean white tablecloth and eat a bowl of Kellogg's Corn Flakes. That was the start of his day in a humble harmless sort of childhood way. TJ loved cornflakes and would always enjoy them as a child whenever his Dad would buy some. In the navy, TJ could have cornflakes every day without a problem or concern of their availability. He would sit at his own personal table observing the fruit of his leadership. The line was clean, and hot steaming food was ready for recruits to come in and dine. The galley floor was sparkling clean and waxed every day. The tables were uniformed and lined up perfectly, and the galley smelled fresh in almost restaurant presentation. This was his work and his doing.

His first shot at leading and guiding people. Each table had a restaurant-style glass sugar jar on the table filled to the brim with clean white cane sugar. TJ filled his bowl up with Kellogg's Corn Flakes, grabbed a jar of sugar, and began to pour like crazy. He loved his cornflakes sweet and crunchy. While serving as line captain, eating cornflakes was his daily routine before he began ordering recruits around. He was totally unsuspecting of anyone not liking him or possibly playing a practical joke on him.

One particular day toward the end of service week on a morning when he was very hungry, he was looking forward to sitting down and enjoying his cornflakes. But someone else had something else in mind that disrupted TJ's routine. Was it a personal attack, or was somebody screwing with not just him but every recruit that entered the galley that day? He don't know the why or wherefores. He just knew his routine was disrupted by a not-funny practical joke.

That day, TJ's morning was thrown the proverbial monkey wrench along with nuts, bolts, and screwdrivers. He sat down to eat and like any other day, began to pour sugar almost like pouring a glass of water to sweeten his crunchy Kellogg's Corn Flakes. His mouth was salivating for the first spoon full of crunchy flakes. He positioned and settled a spoon full of crunchy flakes into his mouth; instantaneously, he felt an extreme upset stomach coming on, and the whole contour of his face changed. His cheekbones twisted in a manner to make him look deformed. His entire face changed from its look of satisfaction to utter dissatisfaction.

"What the hell! Who is the dumb son of a bitch!? This is not funny! Damn you recruits!"

The foul language coming from the lips of TJ was not normal, but the actions of some practical jokers can awaken the dark regions of the heart of men. These words were shouted out loud, and it was the first time TJ lost his cool and used language unbecoming of who he thought he was. He felt the words rushing through the neurons of his brain. Like a dam that had burst over an unsuspecting city full of occupants, he snapped to attention from his chair, drops of milk and flakes hanging out of his mouth. He looked at the faces of the recruits, trying to see who was smirking or laughing or pointing at him. Several faces came to mind of possible suspects. He thought about Calvin, but Calvin was nowhere in the galley. Actually, he did not know where Calvin performed his service week. But he thought maybe Calvin came over to the galley just to get back at him. He accused every recruit on the floor that day trying to solicit an admission from someone. He suspected all and trusted no one in his crew from that day until the completion of service week. That day he did not feel as authoritative as before. He didn't even want to be on the job. He was angry and saddened and even disappointed that someone would fill the sugar glass with salt. What a childish and immature act that was, and he wanted to know who would stoop so low and for what purpose. He wanted to stand in their face and order them to do something. He did not know what order to give, but any kind of punishment would be worthy in TJ's eyes. He was upset for the remainder of the day. He felt controlled by others because he lost his cool in an uncivilized way and was angry at himself because he lost his cool. He was mad with everyone on the line that day and did not perform his duties with fairness. He suspected everyone and showed little mercy toward anyone. He asked around, but to no avail. He did receive a satisfactory response. He ordered the recruits on the floor to check every table and "make damn sure each sugar glass is filled with pure grain sugar and not salt!" That's the way he put it, "make damn sure" and "pure grain sugar."

Since the angry and profound juices were already flowing, coupled with profanity, he figured, might as well demonstrate his anger in the language he thought everyone understood. *Damn* was pretty much the extent of profanity he used in those days. Hard cursing would manifest itself sometime in the near future, and his language would become profane, to say the least.

The remainder of his service week dragged along, losing some of the excitement and luster it once had. He realized that everyone was not going to merely and blindly follow his orders. He also realized that not everyone held the same perspective as he held of pride, integrity, and commitment. From that day on until the end of service week, when he sat down to enjoy his Kellogg's, he would always perform a taste test to verify the contents in the sugar jar. He wanted to make sure it was "pure grain." He felt sad that he had to do that, but he quickly learned that people are as varied in their view of life as much as the variety of animals in the entire world. His view of the navy did not atrophy into negativism. He was still enjoying the navy, feeling like he had made a good decision and had overcome his initial introduction to homesickness. There were more homesickness experiences to come, but he was able to identify the feeling and would appropriately handle what lay ahead. Yet there was one more homesickness attack that would top the train ride to Chicago, Illinois. A few days after he calmed down from the salt prank, a thought came to him that he had not considered and thought maybe he was seriously rationalizing with his own thoughts. But maybe, just maybe, some young recruit actually thought he was filling the sugar jar and did not realize it was salt. Kind of dumb, though, because every bag was properly labeled. But then he thought maybe, just maybe, the bag from the vendor was labeled incorrectly and maybe the recruit that filled the jars could not read that well. In his Christian manner, he was trying to exonerate any wrongdoing from his crew because he really wanted to believe that someone simply made a mistake. This would reveal a sign of TJ's naïveté.

The Epic Experience of All

On a gorgeous summer Friday morning on September 3, 1976, the temperature was about 80 degrees. Recruit Company 76-179 was preparing to graduate from Basic Training in the United States Navy. The rush of excitement all the recruits felt was a high that lasted for weeks prior to and long afterward. Every recruit shared the same excitement that sent a rush of adrenaline that did not allow them to sleep sound the night before. TJ was full of pride not only of himself but for his entire company achieving the status of senior recruits. They were allowed to stay up late and shine shoes, prepare their uniforms, or just sit around talking about what they were going to do once leaving boot camp. Different ones talked about how they were going to grab their girl when they see her and hug and kiss her. Others talked about how they will be glad to see their parents. Others still did not seem too excited about leaving their new friends from boot camp. Almost like they really did not have anyone back home to share their excitement with and they would rather remain together. As for TJ, he just laid around in his bunk reminiscing about his entire trek from home: The train ride. The arrival with his original company. The time when he was ASMO'd, to becoming "king of the hill," service week, and now graduation.

TJ, for once in boot camp, basked in quiet excitement and almost could not believe that he made it through the United States Navy Basic Training. The physical part of boot camp—the running, pushups, and field competition—was an absolute breeze. The emotional part being introduced to and dealing with homesickness was his greatest internal battles. He examined his life and decision he made to enter the navy and sought whether the Lord had anything to do with the direction he chose. He pondered many things throughout his naval career, and this was only the beginning of years of almost unbelievable experiences that lay ahead. He said a word or two to his shipmates and in some way felt a little sadness knowing they were about to part ways. He had developed a bond with most of them and developed new friendships along the way. James, DC, Lynette, Aretha, Freddie, though they were his friends back home, he was trying to figure out in his mind how that friendship with them would pan out. At this point in his life, the commonality he once had with them had changed drastically. He was in the United States Navy and intended to stay as long as he could. Back home they did not appear to be in a hurry to transit from and travel through the doorway of life that presented the great change to him. TJ had begun traveling down a road that would present great internal challenges and extreme external challenges and exposure to the world on an unfathomable scale. Boot camp was the means in which God introduced TJ to himself. The growth TJ would experience would be akin to ripping the bark from a tree. His life would become bare and naked as it was already naked in the eyes of God. It appeared at times mercy was void of his tears and he was thrown into outer darkeners of worldliness. Boot camp was a crash course mainly involving his own fears, his weaknesses, his doubts, his likes and dislikes of other people. For TJ, boot camp was not physically challenging at all; the physical aspect, as already mentioned, was a walk in the park. Graduation was a time to prepare to reenter society as trained military men. He had just spent eight grueling weeks learning to work as a team with people of all nationalities. Now he was about to return home for a short leave period. Other recruits would go directly to their "A" school training, and some would report directly to their first command. The Friday morning of graduation was the first time in boot camp that they were able to put on cologne. Every sailor had the same cologne on. There was an overwhelming smell of either Old Spice or Blue Velvet. The smell of the same cologne on fifty different guys was overpowering, but for some strange reason, it smelled good, almost like a small step back into civilization and becoming free to do what you wanted to do and go where you wanted to go. The cologne was the first step, and it seems every recruit sported cheap-smelling aftershave on the Friday morning of September 3, 1976.

THE KEEL

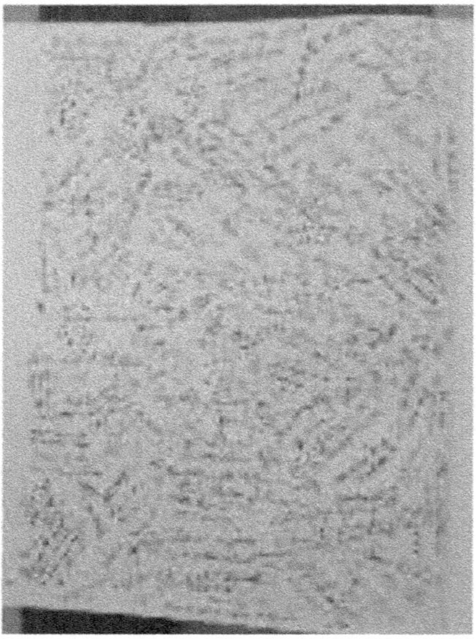

6

TOUR OF DUTY NAVAL AIR STATION

San Diego, California

New experience after new experience was rapidly taking the place of excitement as a boy. The projects and teenager on North 18th Street were becoming dreams of the eternal past. Traveling to San Diego, California, was TJ's third airplane flight. Flying in airplanes had now become the most exciting thing in his life. The days riding the bus with Mom to go downtown had become elementary warm and fuzzy memories. Back in those days, the threat of planes blowing up and crashes due to international terrorist takeover was practically unheard of. Homeland Security and TSA agents did not exist at the time and would not become an agency until decades into the future. It was fun and adventurous and exciting to fly on airplanes during those days. Both the projects and North 18th Street had become historical relics in the mind of TJ. North 18th Street was still fresh in his mind, but much of what occurred there had become like a dream. The projects was simply ancient history, as far as he was concerned, and he didn't think much about those days anymore. Every time TJ had an airplane trip, it was always a nice flight, and he always looked forward to flying. He saw himself as some important government dignitary working for Uncle

Sam. Having been raised in the projects, with his father as the only income bearer, not once did TJ ever think he would be flying on airplanes. Nor did he imagine flying throughout the nation and also internationally at the government's expense. In perspective, it seemed everything moved along at a fast rate of speed. He transitioned rapidly from the growing pains and fights that occurred on North 18th Street, to traveling as a member of the United States Navy. The awakening of a prideful spirit that occurred while in boot camp was beginning to impress TJ about himself. His new experiences up to this point was a great shock to himself adjusting to navy life, and he would try to imagine what lay ahead of his uncertain future.

Traveling in the air onboard US Airways to the West Coast had now exposed TJ to America and literally opened up a new world to him. He was euphoric to be traveling solo. The time difference alone between the East Coast and the West Coast was an eye-opener for him. While flying, he was repeatedly looking at his wristwatch, calculating in his mind what time it would be back in Harrisburg, Pennsylvania. TJ had now launched out into the world of many experiences and opportunities. North 18th Street was a sheltered world. and no other world existed in his mind at the time. Of the projects era, TJ knew nothing about life and slowly began to realize how much he did not know, and he supposed that would hold true for any child. On North 18th Street, his experience and thoughts were all limited to the small events that occurred between State Street, North Street, Briggs Street, Forster Street, and Herr Street—a tiny centralized area in comparison of what lay ahead. North 18th Street was a little larger area than the projects but a mere speck in comparison to the entire world. The West Coast experience and travel started TJ on the road to knowledge and excelled his growth. His spirit and his body were becoming riveted into complete maturity. His future experiences would overflow his mind that cannot be gained from a textbook. West Coast, San Diego, California, was one of the most exciting times of his life. TJ was young, single, adventurous, and getting paid for easy work. He enjoyed the thought of being missed at home and enjoyed visiting home when he could. The things he was learning in the early stages of traveling was giving him stories to tell because he loved to tell of his experiences. TJ had new world experiences to take back home to share with family. He was excited about learning new things and going to different places and being able to say that he has traveled to such and such place and experienced so and so. He was glad his brothers prepared him somewhat for walking the path of the world and was beginning to learn the world on his own. He terribly missed his family at times and was glad to put to use the positive things they told him. His brain was becoming filled with knowledge, knowledge, and more knowledge. TJ soaked his brain with learning and read any and every time he had the opportunity. He also was hard-pressed to advance in rank whenever he was eligible. He had left behind all the growing pains of the projects and the sheltered naive world of North 18th Street. Much of North 18th Street stayed with him for a while. He knew he had to ultimately let it go but was not always willing to do so. There were too many good memories, and the memories were alive and fresh with every thought. His memories had become stored in his mind for a lifetime. TJ had entered another chapter in his life, and the pages turned kind of sloppy and almost without purpose in the beginning. As the pages of his life unfolded, they became more exciting and full with each turn. Halfway during his naval career, each chapter became a crash course of adult maturing and seemingly at times with no mercy or compassion from anyone. It was as if those who had already walked the path he was on, would look at him and ask the question "What's the problem, kid? Grow up." And of course, growing up is much easier said than done for most people. The things one is compelled to learn, and the difference between what is true and what is a lie, can be devastating. The Christian foundation that was instilled in the life of TJ enabled him to keep positive sight and believe in God. But even with that foundation, a traveler can be tripped up because the enemy of our soul is way more cunning and crafty against the affairs of men. So as TJ moved forward in life, he held on to the cord of Christianity to the best of his ability.

Air Antisubmarine Squadron 41 (VS-41)

Creativity was sparked in TJ because of the influence of Fred during the days of North 18th Street. TJ dabbled a little writing poetry all because he was mimicking Fred. His idol Fred wrote poetry and participated in church plays and local community activities. The first few years of TJ's new life in the navy was in many ways mentally tied to the umbilical cord of both Bay and Fred. He sought them out by phone calls and letters looking for advice, and at times any word from either of them would suffice. It was a brother relationship blooming for the first time, and there was a lot of back-and-forth with both Bay and Fred. After TJ's youthful years trying to get their attention, and even the brief encounters with them, it appears they finally recognized him. He could discern they began to love the idea that he took much of their advice, and he became their student. But the student-teacher relationship one day would be strained to an unbelievable break in a sibling relationship. What would unfold in the future held the potential of sending TJ over the deep end. But the thin cord of Christianity helped him through the separation that would happen between him and his brothers. Both Bay and Fred readily accepted taking TJ under their wings, and both Bay and Fred were a large part of TJ making it through his first tour of duty with the United States Navy. It is nice for a young man to have a good role model, but it quickly can become a bad thing when the teacher begins to take the liberty of their influence in a manner to control the student the rest of their life. One of the greatest disappointments of all time between blood brothers is when both Bay and Fred's influence would one day abruptly end. It would be the quintessential necessary tragic severing of an idolatrous friendship. TJ literally idolized Bay and Fred and desired greatly to be like them in every way. But he was destined to learn and face the great insecurity and weaknesses they themselves wrestled within their own lives. TJ would learn the scriptural injunction that says, "Put not your trust in princes, nor in the son of man, in whom there is no help" (Ps. 146:3). He was constantly blinded by his brother's words and impressed by their "worldly" ways. He was years away from developing a foundation in the truth for himself. He had built what foundation he had on shady, sinking marsh ground. What he could not see then was the early days of the Sermon being outlined. The stage had been set almost strategically by his two brothers. Fred was the street-suave brother, and Bay, the lover, always had pretty ladies hanging on his arms. Both men were brutal fighters when it came to bumping heads on the street against their enemies. But Bay and Fred were an intriguing part of TJ's life for decades into adulthood. But there would come a time when he would wake up. But even then, waking up was not easy. It's almost like he wanted to stay asleep. Remember in the epic movie *Dune*, starring Kyle MacLachlan as Paul Atreides, when Paul (Maudee) travels into the desert with the Fremen and drinks the spice and the worms ascend out of the desert sand? Maudie looks up to heaven and cries aloud, "Father, the sleeper has awoken!"

TJ was a sleeper from the days of his youth all the way up to the time he discovered the need to break away from the dependency of his two older brothers. His first tour of duty in San Diego, California, began that breaking-away process. It was a very slow breaking but would crescendo in time. The steps of a good man are ordered by the Lord, but those steps are not always clear to see or follow. Many times, the steps of a good man are long months and years in their stride. They can be arduous to walk and can be lonely to tread. TJ began to discover those steps while stationed at Naval Air Station San Diego, California.

TJ arrived at San Diego's airport in September 1976 at about 5:00 p.m., and it was one of the most gorgeous days ever. Of course, his renewed perspective and excitement enhanced those days. Almost like he had discovered new land and ready for the new experiences awaiting him. TJ had become electrified with excitement, rambunctious with discovery, and virtually free to do and go anywhere his heart desired. He was on his own and could not be still if he were offered a million dollars. There were military orders, civil laws, local state, and United States laws that TJ would violate all in the name of exploring. VS-41, which stood for "Air Anti-Submarine Squadron 41," was TJ's first active duty tour in the United States Navy and his first experience with an active duty after graduating from boot camp. Naval Air Station at San Diego, California, North Island (NAS), perhaps was one of the best and most professional commands and tour of duty for a young eighteen-year-old new recruit. The one lure of such command right out of boot camp is the misconception of the entire navy being like that. The barracks were nice, and the chow hall resembled a commercial restaurant a far cry from the chow hall in boot camp. The food was cooked very well and tasted really good. The appearance of the chow hall was more than he expected, and

TJ could have stayed in there all day. The proud spirit introduced to him in boot camp was being fed to his mind day after day while stationed at NAS North Island, California. Periodically he would mentally assess his accomplishments after finishing boot camp. The ASMO unit reminisced like a bad dream but a necessary awakening to his soul. He was very proud to be stationed on the west coast for a brief moment. He looked forward to going to lunch and dinner because the place was immaculate and beyond what he anticipated the military to be. He remembers hearing stories from Lawrence and Melvin about their tour of duty in Vietnam, and their description of the food was horrible. Both Lawrence and Melvin did not experience the type of opportunities presented to TJ in the navy. Lawrence and Melvin were drafted at a time the nation of America was divided and countless controversy within the nation concerning Vietnam. They both ate from rations and ate food cooked by nonprofessional soldier cooks much like themselves. Civil rights was at the forefront on the shores of America while American soldiers were dying by the hundreds on the shores of Vietnam. On the other hand, the military had made some improvements and advancements toward equal opportunity and programs to foster race relations and so on and so forth. During TJ's tour of duty, the opportunities were limitless, especially as a black American. The attention the civil rights movement got from the government of the United States, did make things a lot more competitive and somewhat easier as far as equal rights were concerned. But all the efforts of the government could never eliminate prejudice. TJ did not know if the cooks at the chow hall at NAS North Island, San Diego, California, were professional cooks or military cooks. Either way, the food was great.

TJ was assigned to VS-41 Shamrocks training on the Lockheed S3A Viking as a plane captain to work onboard a United States aircraft carrier. Carriers are one of the most powerful warships on the face of the planet earth. Nothing but excitement filled his heart and mind at this point. TJ was pumped up at an accelerated rate. He was a young air dale about to enter a world that was worlds apart from the projects and North 18th Street. San Diego, California, was nothing but fun in the sun, and his memory of that time remains like a good movie you would go see over and over again. The impact San Diego and the navy life made on TJ has been recorded on digital disc in the memory banks of his mind. Compared to the East Coast, specifically Harrisburg, Pennsylvania, San Diego was like a tropical land with tall trees and summer-like perfect weather. Dramatic leaps made from the days of a youngster to the days of bicycle riding to the appetizer of a taste of the world. In TJ's mind, he had arrived at a place he only dreamed about staring out the window from his mother's room. He trained during the day in the hangars and on deck learning the skills of an aircraft mechanic. TJ had learned very minimal about engine mechanics in high school. How did he end up in the navy training as an aircraft mechanic? His Armed Service Vocational Aptitude Battery test (ASVAB) did not qualify him for any technical schools or cryptic type jobs, so he accepted Aircraft Mechanic (AD), just so he could enter the navy. Heck, he did not know any better and did not have anyone coaching him along in his decision-making process when he decided to enter the navy. The entrance into the United States Navy was pretty much TJ's own decision, and everyone allowed him to travel that road on his own. Bay and Fred were closely involved in the life of TJ. Bay was already in the air force, and neither one of them discouraged TJ from joining the navy.

Courtesy use of image

Fred had no advice for what training to pursue in the military, so TJ was left up to his own decisions. His mother and father were neutral about him going in the navy, and they also had no advice what job he should pursue while in the navy. Mom did express her disagreement at first because TJ initially wanted to quit high school to join. But in her usual way, she talked him into finishing school, and she eventually accepted his decision to enter the navy. The navy recruiter was able to convince TJ to enter the navy as an air dale. The chances were good of not being stationed on board as ship's company. The idea offered a little bit more liberty than in the mind of TJ. It also decreased the chances of being on board, what navy terminology called "small boy, or tin can." Colloquially speaking, "tin cans" are the much smaller vessels of war. TJ was sold and thought it would be exciting working on the deck of an aircraft carrier. His navy recruiter was successful in selling TJ on the idea of becoming an aircraft mechanic and convinced him of the excitement and travel onboard an aircraft carrier. San Diego, California, was the place TJ learned how to repair and work on million-dollar, high-tech, Anti-Submarine Lockheed S3A seek and destroy aircraft. The S3A's mission was to drop sonar buoy tubes into the ocean—certain radio frequencies of the buoy would identify the location of enemy submarines. The sonar buoy would send depth, longitude, and latitude information back to the aircraft. Once the submarine's location was identified, certain destructive weapons could be used to render the submarine incapable to inflict any return attack. High-tech expensive and exciting stuff for a young eighteen-year-old straight from a sleepy life of childhood. Life was nothing but adventure after adventure while stationed at NAS San Diego, California, in the late summer and fall of 1976. At this particular point in the naval career of the young TJ, he loved being in the United States Navy and felt he had made the best decision at the time for his life.

Off Limits and Handcuffed

After eight grueling weeks of boot camp and two weeks Advanced Training Division in Great Lakes, Illinois, in the summer of 1976, TJ was ready to begin experiencing what lay ahead of him. So far, San Diego, California, was painting a pretty picture and setting his hopes very high because "if this is the navy, I don't ever want to get out, NEVER!" he thought. He learned the bus routes and how to go downtown and would ride the bus downtown just about every weekend and sometimes during the week. He met another brother in San Diego who became a good friend and was enrolled in the same training. The orders of his new friend would take them both to the same duty station after completing training at VS-41. After the tour of duty in San Diego, California, and the upcoming tour in Jacksonville, Florida, TJ lost contact with him and was unable to get his okay to mention his name. Therefore, he is identified as brother C. He was a good brother that welcomed the friendship with TJ. Over the weeks and months, they shared stories and discovered they both had a similar Christian upbringing. That was the recipe TJ needed then, a friend he could confide in and someone that would help to keep him out of trouble. Brother C. sort of took the place of James Jones back home and in some ways reminded TJ of James. His mannerism and speech was almost an exact replica of James'. How is it in life you meet people who remind you of someone you either loved or greatly admired? That was the type of relationship TJ had with Brother C. He was a good friend, and TJ had no problem trusting him. They would hang out together riding the city bus to downtown San Diego. There was a park called Balboa Park, and when they learned of its location, they frequented Balboa Park on the weekends. They would spend whole weekends at Balboa Park. The park was quintessential of family gatherings and picnics, almost like a picturesque painting on canvas done by Norman Rockwell. Balboa Park was nothing but good clean family gatherings, from what TJ could tell. TJ loved Balboa Park, and if there is one leisurely thing he did often while stationed at Naval Air Station San Diego, California, it was going to Balboa Park.

But the overwhelming adventurous spirit and exploring tendencies resident in the heart of TJ would lead him down a path of disobedience. He would be introduced to the other end of the law. TJ had never been in any trouble with the law and made it an attempt to avoid such attention. Except the time he contemplated a criminal act by wanting to attack the airman in boot camp. But apart from that immature thought, he did not have any police record at all, not even a speeding ticket or parking ticket. For the most part, he was a clean young man with a clean record with the law. It would have been advisable for him to enjoy the clean because one day he would manifest all the filthiness life had to offer. Can he blame someone for not telling him what to do in certain situations or could he draw from what was already inputted into his spirit? Growing up he received countless instructions from Bay, Fred, and his father? Even with him making bad decision after bad decision, the mercy of God sheltered him and protected him year after year after year. What is it that God would have of this young man because with the stuff he would become engaged in, his days should have been numbered, so to speak. But something about being on his own and at liberty to make his own decisions, coupled with a little bit of cockiness, he was destined to receive an electric shock of life to get his attention.

The beauty and serenity of San Diego would introduce TJ to a bad side that brought the electric shock of life directly to him. There were dangers all around him that he was unmindful of. In those days, TJ lived in a rollick state of mind in the midst of what appeared to be a tropical land. He remembers details of one of the most frightening events in his life that took place many years ago involving a group of sailors visiting Tijuana, Mexico. During the orientation for new recruits, and not just recruits but new incoming personnel assigned to the training unit of VS-41, they were told to be careful while traveling to Tijuana and to use the buddy system.

The buddy system is basically two people traveling together who remain with one another at all times. Certain areas of Tijuana were off limits, and military personnel were told not to go to those areas. TJ, eighteen years old, with an adventurous spirit, hooked up with other sailors. They not only influenced his disobedience but incited him to do something he knew he was not authorized to do. They all caught a bus on its way to Tijuana and got on board. His new friend Brother C. was with him on this excursion, and everything started out fine. He felt pretty good about getting on the bus because at least he was with someone he liked as a friend. Just in case something would happen in Tijuana, his friend would be able to tell the story and get the report back to his family. He never considered that something could happen to both of them. But anyways, TJ did have mustard seed faith that everything was going to be just fine. Traveling to Tijuana was thrilling for TJ and was the beginning of his world experiences that would last his lifetime. Tijuana was also a wakeup call that quickly refocuses TJ's attention and spirit to follow orders for a long while. The first and last time TJ ever traveled to Tijuana was on a Saturday morning as he and his Sailor's made their trek into Mexico just inside the border. All that was necessary for those days was to flash their military ID card and they were across the border. TJ thought that was a little simplified to cross the US, Mexican border, but nonetheless, that's all that was necessary back then. In 1976 terroristic acts against the United States as a nation were in the embryo and planning stages and a military ID stood for something then. A noticeable difference was brewing in those days in comparison to twenty-first century times beginning with the late 1990s. TJ and Brother C. did not venture deep into Tijuana; in fact, they were just inside the border, maybe a couple of miles. Once they were in Mexico, the group of about ten guys dispersed and went in all directions. Brother C. and TJ made their way down through the dusty hot roads on a September afternoon exploring for the first time in his life the land of another country.

TJ and Brother C. got separated from each other, and TJ thinks it happened because he wanted to go in one direction and Brother C. another direction. They hadn't been friends too long because they just met at VS-41, so their friendship was not as solidified as with James Jones back home. TJ considered Brother C. to be a good friend, but they had not yet reached the level of trust and commonality. Going in different directions for TJ was not unusual because he had to prove to himself that he could handle being in another land on his own. He walked around head high and chest out like he knew what he was doing and where his feet were taking him. On that day in September, it was very hot, and there was minimal shade around. He remembers hearing someone say it gets hot in Tijuana in the summer. That day was going to prove to TJ just how hot it could become, and he would quickly learn that "hot" was more than just temperature. After he walked around about a few hours, doing nothing, he became concerned about where the other sailors were and especially Brother C. He thought he spotted one of the sailors that were on the bus, but he did not know him, so his arrogant pride got the best of him and he didn't speak to the guy. Full of pride, he did not try to find out where the other sailors were. He was lost in a foreign land, just over the border from the United States and starting a "cool" panic, if that's possible. The heat from the sun was becoming unbearable, and there appeared to be no shade in sight. Not to mention he was alone and beginning to hear Mexicans speak in their native tongue whenever he walked by a shop on the street. He heard a few snickers, like they may have been laughing at him or maybe planning some attack once the sun went down. Perhaps he was just paranoid, but it sure did seem like they were laughing at him as he walked by shop after shop. He attempted to play it cool by not looking at them and like he was window-shopping until a guy ran by him like he was in a hurry to get somewhere. The guy blazingly brushed up against TJ like some scene right out of a movie chase, and the guy did not even attempt to apologize he just kept running.

A small disturbance erupted on the street in the vicinity that TJ was, and the disturbance just happened to be directly in the path he was walking. There were a few guys who looked like Americans who seemed to be at the center of the disturbance. There were a few guys who took off running. TJ had no idea what was going on. He just knew that it was extremely hot, no shade. He was very hungry and lost. The "cool" panic he felt earlier had now instantaneously became fear and stress and deep anxiety. All the coolness he thought he had how now vanished. Fear, extreme temperature, and hunger took its toll on the young lad. Delirium began to set in his mind, and he was quickly losing his sense of direction. Fear seized his mind and became the ruling factor. TJ didn't know what was happening. He did not know where to get anything to eat, and all he could think of was surviving. Some trouble was happening in Tijuana, Mexico, that he had nothing to do with, but the trouble found TJ in the eye of the mayhem and quickly engulfed his mind, soul, and body. He could not distinguish between what he was feeling. Was it fear, hunger, delirium, confusion, loss, or a combination of them all? He was no longer cool, calm, and collected. He was becoming increasingly agitated by the second about every little sound around him. The action of those walking by him greatly disturbed him. He had never really sweated things in his life up to this point, but this situation was causing him deep concern in a hurry. He picked up the pace in his steps, trying to get across the street. He had to get away from the ruckus up ahead of him in the path he was walking. He had to get away from where a disruptive crowd was quickly gathering. He had no idea where he was going or in which direction he was walking. He shouted out an extemporaneous prayer to God, hoping he would run into shore patrol, knowing that if he spotted shore patrol, he would be in deep trouble. But that type of trouble he welcomed. He then realized that he had wandered off into an area military personnel were not authorized to be in. About this time, the sun was starting to set, and he became very afraid for the first time in his life. It was a different fear unlike he had ever felt. It was not like the time the Uptown boys cornered him in the alley, that was a cocky fear. Not really afraid, but just wanted to prove something to himself and the Uptown boys. But that evening in Tijuana, in a section of town where Mexicans were laughing as he walked by them, he felt a genuine fear of enormous proportion. Some type of disturbance involving American sailors was becoming worse by the minute, and he had no clue what was going on. He was lost, hot, sweaty, hungry, and delirious. The dominant thought in the mind of TJ was, *If something happens to me, no one will know how it happened or what happened.*

THIS IS NOT TJ'S PICTURE. BUT IT LOOKS **EXACTELY** LIKE THE LOCATION HE WAS IN. **IT WAS GETTING DARK!**

He was becoming petrified and afraid for his life. He thought all the weirdest thoughts possible. *Will I be robbed? Will I be murdered? Will I be buried somewhere or dismembered?* His mind was visualizing all the horror movies he had ever seen. He was alone in Tijuana, which was the results of being disobedient to the orders of the commanding officer.

But as providence would have it, his panicking returned to a cool sweat, and his fear turned into rescue. It would seem to him he received an answer to a prayer that should have never been prayed. He spotted two shore patrol making their way over to the center of the ruckus and chaos that was happening on the street. He froze in his tracks, reasoning to himself how he could make himself known to the shore patrol. The decision resting on the synapsis of his brain was imperative and the difference between life and death for the shore patrol to spot him. Afraid to yell out to them, but necessary to be apprehended by them. He knew he was in deep trouble for being in territory that was off-limits to military personnel, but he dare not run the other way because he had absolutely no sense of direction where to go. The horrific thoughts rushing through the mind of TJ might have come true had he not turned himself in. His final thought and decision became obvious as the shore patrol were making their way over to the disorder. TJ did an immediate about-face and without haste, made his way over to where the shore patrol was standing and made it his point to be noticed by them. The training and years of gymnastics in high school and running track in boot camp reaped the best benefits he could have ever needed at that moment in Tijuana, Mexico. TJ sprinted across the street like never before only to stop directly in front of the shore patrol before they left the scene. He knew it would be impossible for shore patrol to mistake him for a tourist or a Mexican. His sprint across the street was momentarily hindered by almost uncontrollable vehicular traffic. The motorist was yelling out the window of their vehicles at him in their native language. He almost got run over several times, but nothing would or could stop TJ. His only objective was to get to where the shore patrol was so they would see him and apprehend him. In other words, TJ purposely ran into the arms of military law to get arrested for being disobedient and breaking the law.

A brief panic lay hold on his thoughts as he was concerned the shore patrol would get control of the situation and leave the scene. It was getting dark, and he did not know where Brother C. was or when the next bus would be returning to Naval Air Station San Diego. Only one mission was prevalent in his life at that time, in that place, in Tijuana, Mexico, on a hot September night in 1976. There was absolutely no alternative. He was in deep trouble, lost, and paranoid. He was afraid for his life, he was disobedient, and most importantly, he needed to get caught. The mission was simple: get caught by the shore patrol and face whatever consequence the commanding officer issued him. Or second-guess his decision to get caught and face what inevitable fate of being lost in Tijuana, Mexico, would serve him. The latter option was out of the question. He could not allow those two shore patrol to leave the scene without getting in their face. Hustle! Run! Dodge car after car! Almost right out of a movie scene, sprinting, running across the street…just to get arrested. TJ literally ran into the arms of the law on that steamy hot summer night in Mexico. Providence and mercy prevailed in the entire Tijuana experience. He did not get run over by the unfamiliar traffic pattern and driving habits of the Mexicans. The shore patrol seemed to linger at the scene, like they were going to remain there as long as it took to get the situation under control. It was an irony that TJ became one of their prisoners. Would one say he was in the wrong place at the right time or the right place at the wrong time? He made it to the shore patrol, and the most unusual thing totally unexpected occurred once he was spotted by them. You know the old street vernacular how you say something is a "trip," old street slang? What happened after the shore patrol spotted TJ was the trip of all trips. There is no other explanation other than God shook the young lad up for being disobedient and taught him a valuable lesson of the deadly potential the results of disobedient may ensue. When TJ got within an arm's length of the shore patrol, all the ruckus ended just as fast as it began. The shore patrol spotted TJ before he could say a word and asked him, "What are you doing in this section of town, recruit?"

They could tell he was wet behind the ears and straight out of boot camp. TJ told them that he lost his way, and they asked for his military ID card. He quickly and without hesitation handed them his military ID card with a smile and was glad to confess his disobedience and wrongdoing. They took his ID and told him to turn around and slapped handcuffs on his wrist and told him to sit down at the curb and wait. Within five minutes, a white paddy wagon showed up, and the shore patrol placed TJ in the rear of the paddy wagon and drove off. It was TJ's first experience ever being handcuffed and transported in the rear of a steamy hot, uncomfortable white paddy wagon as the sole prisoner of the United States Navy Shore Patrol in Tijuana Mexico.

By that time, darkness had blanketed the area, and the temperature was in the high nineties, with almost unbearable humidity. Being inside the paddy wagon was like being inside a sauna with clothes on, and sweat began to run down TJ's face and back, as if someone doused him with a bucket of water. His shadow was as paranoid as his mind and soul, and he basked in a pool of fear of a different kind. He was full of anxiety, not knowing what his fate would be once returning to the naval air station and only being on active duty four months. His mind was blank, and he was unable to piece together what just happened that day while being transported back to the base. From head to toe, the young man was drenched with perspiration, fearing he would receive the worst once the commanding officer learned of his disobedience. If you consider wondering to be valid thoughts, that's all he had on his mind. He wondered and wondered and wondered what just took place in Tijuana, Mexico, in a section of town he was not supposed to be in. But was his fear and anxiety necessary having not pleaded his case to the commanding officer yet? He hoped the CO would be lenient to the adventurous spirit of the young lad. He began to strategize in his mind how to summarize his life's story up to the present moment and hoped he could find the words to articulate his case.

When the military police arrived back to Naval Air Station North Island with their prisoner on board, they opened the rear door of the steamy hot van and escorted TJ inside to the master at arms' office. Frazzled by the experience and sitting at attention, he was panting heavily, ready to speak, to beg for leniency. He was expecting a boot camp type of interrogation.

The master at arms began questioning him. "Son, what is your full name? How long have you been here, sailor, and where do you work? SN TJ, I understand that you were in a location that is unauthorized for military personnel. You should be thankful the shore patrol spotted you because, under normal conditions, Shore Patrol do not police that area."

TJ was drilled with question after question to the point that he left a residue of sweat in the chair he was sitting on. He knew the next word out of the master at arms' mouth would be, "Take him to the brig until tomorrow morning, then he can explain his situation to the CO."

TJ thought he was about to get thrown in the brig, locked up for the stupidest thing he could have ever done. After asking a series of direct questions, the master at arms kindly handed TJ his military ID card and told him, "Report for duty on time tomorrow and be careful and stay out of trouble, young man."

Almost in a daze, TJ asked, "You mean I can leave?"

"Yes! Be careful and stay out of trouble, sailor."

Unbelievable! He was speechless. *What was all that sweat for*, he wondered. TJ had just undoubtedly experienced a compassionate "spanking" from God for him to pay attention to orders and cease from trying to do your own thing. He then reasoned in his mind that angels were continuing to preserve his way, much like the time when he was in the ASMO unit and wanted to go berserk. God showed great mercy for the naïveté of the young disobedient TJ who had now transitioned from a sheltered world of codependency on others to expect the protection of God. There was no other reason for him doing what he did in disobedience other than being a naive eighteen-year-old man. For that, he believed that God had mercy on his ignorance, and plus it was not the time for his life to end. As for the other sailors, he cannot begin to speculate their fate or whether or not they were the sailors he rode with on the bus to Tijuana. The entire disturbance on that unknown street in an unfamiliar country erupted within a split second and ended as immediately as it began.

As for Brother C, TJ met with him the next day and learned that Brother C. returned to the base way before dark. TJ unloaded to Brother C. what happened and how there were no charges filed against him. Brother C. laughed and said, "God was watching over you, TJ I heard there were a couple of guys that got hurt real badly in some big fight on the street." Brother C. further said, "There were a lot of shore patrol at the scene."

A lot! he thought. TJ only spotted two shore patrol, or maybe there was another disturbance somewhere else. He asked Brother C., "When and where did it happen?"

He named the location, and it turns out the location was exactly where TJ was lost. Brother C. said, "It was about dark time. I know they said the sun had just gone down."

TJ was speechless, and Brother C. looked at him and said, "TJ, are you all right?"

TJ had no reply to his question and only said to him, "Let's go to work, man."

For the remainder of his time at Naval Air Station San Diego, North Island, he thought about that event. He examined it from every possible angle. Where the two shore patrol that cuffed him actually angels in disguise? Where the two shore patrol that cuffed him actually real men that providence allowed to be in the exact location that he was? Was the entire situation orchestrated by God to wake him up of his disobedience? At any rate, something happened in Tijuana, Mexico, in September 1976 that he liked to believe was the providential work of God on behalf of a young man whose heart was ignorantly and innocently learning the world. On his transfer from Naval Air Station North Island, California, on the plane flight to his next tour of duty, he analyzed and analyzed in his mind deeply about that day in Tijuana, Mexico. The entire event was sobering beyond what TJ could comprehend, and he chose to retain the experience for the remainder of his natural life and chose to thank God for his undying mercy.

7

TOUR OF DUTY NAVAL AIR STATION CECIL FIELD, FLORIDA

Air Antisubmarine Squadron 31 (VS-31)

As if it were yesterday, TJ could see images in his mind. He envisioned the clouds from his seat on board the airplane. Brother C. and TJ went to the airport together to catch their flight back home. They separated once arriving at San Diego International Airport. They were flying to different states. Brother

C. was headed back to his home for a few days on annual leave. TJ was headed to Harrisburg, Pennsylvania, for a few days of R and R. TJ was happy that he met Brother C. and became friends with him. TJ's flight itinerary was nonstop to Washington BWI and then from Washington to Olmstead airport in Middletown, Pennsylvania. The flight back to the East Coast was one more his flying experience that turned out to be another exciting flight. The sun shone perfectly on the return flight to the East Coast. The temperature was just right, and the flight was perfectly smooth. Couldn't ask for a more perfect beginning in the United States Navy.

Occasionally, after a training school in the navy, Uncle Sam would allow travel time and some leave time if you have enough leave on the books. Often sailors wind up "in the hole" because they take leave and end up with negative days on the books. It took TJ sometime to understand that concept of "leave on the books." But it turned out TJ could take a one-week leave from San Diego before reporting to his permanent duty station. After leave, he would be reporting to VS-31 at Naval Air Station Cecil Field, Jacksonville, Florida. He enjoyed the old surprise thing when he would return home and got great pleasure out of surprising his family. His family seldom knew when he would be coming home, and he would arrive at the front door totally unexpected, stepping out of a taxicab full of pride and accomplishment. In those days, he was confident that he made the best decision of his life to join the United States Navy. But the strangest thing occurred each time he went home on leave; home was not the same as when he left in June of 1976. Something was different, and he was not able to identify the difference. It was home on North 18th Street, but something was different about being home. Years later, the revelation of the difference would become clear for TJ, but until that time arrived, he searched deep within his soul for the difference every time he went home.

The flight from San Diego to Washington, DC, was long, but everything in those days took long. Nothing happened fast, except for the time he was home. When he would go home on furlough, he was full of anxiety to report back to duty. The time he spent at home became more arid and stagnant. He was enjoying his new experiences and recording every new page of his military career. TJ ALWAYS strutted through the airport walking tall like a proud sailor. Oftentimes he wore his uniform when traveling so he would stand out and get compliments and so on and so forth. He was young and boasted a strong spirit of self-pride. His pride was about who he had become. To TJ, it was not about comparison between other people, but about where he came from and the personal battles he recently overcame. Looking back on the road he had just traveled, he was feeling good about himself and wanting to say to his brothers, "Look at me now, laugh now, make fun of me now." But none of that ever occurred. In the mind of TJ, he earned the respect and love that he always wanted from his older brothers. He hoped that his younger siblings would view him as someone to look up to. Little did he know the respect that he yearned from his younger siblings would be a tall order that would one day reap years of angry emotions. TJ loved *all* his brothers and sisters like there was no one else in the entire world that could compare to them. He took them faults and all because they were his brothers and sisters and he would fight and die for them. He felt great happiness knowing how deep his feelings were for them and in his mind, his relationship with them was as a closely knit family. He thought the world of his siblings, all twelve of them and would proudly tell people, "Yeah, my parents had thirteen children." That was his signature identification, and he wore that fact as a family badge of pride.

Every time TJ would go home on leave, it was brief and time to return back to duty. But oftentimes he was faced with the dilemma that something was different about home, and he could not figure it out in those days. Spiritual insight would not become clear to him until some ten to fifteen years later. But while he was home, he went to his church, gave his "testimony," visited old friends, and proudly walked around the neighborhood of North 18th Street. The change in scenery was very noticeable, almost like looking at a faded picture. Were his new feelings a glimpse into what Fred told him about returning home? What he felt was troubling. Because while he was home, he could not wait to leave again! He never expressed this to anyone during those days, but he knew inside his spirit, he felt something he could not explain. Fred's words were engrained in his mind: "When you leave, you cannot come back home." Were those words prophetic or simply Fred's own life's experience that he chose to share with TJ? Fred had spoken those words to TJ only four months ago, and TJ was beginning to feel and experience the effects of those words but did not yet understand the depth of their meaning. This was the first of many times Fred's words would resurrect in the mind of TJ. "When you leave, you cannot come back home," would become more alive on a deeper and personal level each time TJ would visit home. The feeling would intensify with each visitation. TJ became like a lone traveler reaching back in the past of his life attempting to bring his family along with him. He single-mindedly held on to the life of North 18th Street as long as he could. Making every attempt to keep his siblings up to date of his new experiences. But it seemed, they could not, or would not keep up with his new life. What he failed to understand and realize that while he was experiencing his new life, they were walking in their own experiences. He failed to see at the time, that he had to travel his road alone. His siblings were quickly becoming deep friends of his soul that he knew once upon a time. The United States Navy was merely a vehicle in which God used to sign him up into "his army." The army of God made absolutely no sense to TJ in those days. TJ would come to love the navy and hate the navy. He would come to enjoy visiting home to becoming bored while at home. He would come to looking forward to going abroad to becoming out of touch with the experiences of home, his church, and his family. He had entered the portal that led to the master's training camp of life and was meticulously guided, carried, stripped of certain attachments, and exposed to the entire world. He was becoming not so much Uncle Sam's man but the man of God. The world was God's training ground, and TJ's fellow human beings are the instructors and students at the same time. TJ would transition from student to teacher and at times become both simultaneously. After spending a few days at home and marching around old stomping grounds and going to church, he was ready to leave home once more and could not wait. His spirit tugged at him to get back to where he was supposed to be and beckoned to him to stop trying to live in the past. His fruitless efforts of trying to bring his past with him into his present would resonate for years to come. At certain times while home, it appeared to him that no one cared or was not that excited about who he had become. They were all glad to see him, but there was no roll out the red-carpet thing because he was home. A few hugs here and there. A little bit of chatting here and there, and people went about their own business. That kind of reception was surprising to TJ at the time, but he kind of, sort of, brushed it off and anticipated leaving home to report to his next duty station.

Cecil Field and the Navy Bunk

When TJ arrived at his permanent command located at Cecil Field, Florida, the duty driver was at the airport to pick him up. In fact, the duty driver was the guy he would be bunking with as roommates. For one reason or another, TJ clearly remembers the duty driver and his roommate. Neither of them had anything in common. It's just that the memory of him is clear.

PO3 Bender was none other than the first person TJ met at his permanent duty station assignment. Bender and TJ were no more than coworkers in the same unit. Nevertheless, the duty driver, PO3 Bender, picked him up from the airport in a white Chevy van. He then drove TJ to Naval Air Station Cecil Field, Florida, about a good hour's ride from the Jacksonville, Florida, airport. The remainder of that day remains fuzzy in his memory, but TJ can never forget the balance of that week. It was the week of unfathomable sadness and a week of nauseating homesickness. A rush of homesickness flooded his mind almost ten times greater than the train ride from Harrisburg. After arriving at boot camp and adjusting to his surroundings, then traveling to California and loving the East Coast, West Coast travel, then adjusting to the surroundings on the West Coast, he thought he was all but done with crying. When he arrived at Cecil Field, Florida. and checked in to his permanent command and got settled in with his new roommate, EVERYTHING sunk in. TJ had left home and not just on a casual visit, he had four years of uncertain events facing him, and for the most part, he was afraid to face those years alone.

On the first night sleeping in the navy bunk bed at his permanent command, homesickness struck with a vengeance. This would be the most stirring and emotional homesickness of all and would be the finality of the homesickness trauma. The room was just big enough for two people and had one small window. The smell of another human being's body odor wasn't disgusting, he just was not used to living with anyone else outside his immediate family. It needed much adjusting to get used to, and he was not taking the adjusting well. The first night, he cried and cried and cried with his pillow tightly wrapped around his face. He was too embarrassed to let his roommate notice or even get a hint of him crying. His crying was softly but painfully emanating from deep within his belly. His tears were mammoth size and unending, like a rushing river out of control overflowing its banks against the shoreline. His face was wrinkled with unhappiness, and his abdominal muscles were tight from the stress of weeping. His stomach was as tight as though he had just completed two hundred sit-ups in less than one minute. Every muscle within his physical body was tight as a rope stretched to its limit and ready to snap at any moment. Thank God his roommate did not stay in the room. PO3 Bender dropped TJ off and was pretty much gone for the remainder of the evening into the wee hours of the morning. By the time Bender returned, TJ had cried himself to sleep. He felt like he totally drained his tear ducts, if that is possible. There was no more tear left inside the young lad. The balance of that week was a repeat of the first night of crying in the navy bunk bed. He was now permanently assigned to VS-31, Air Antisubmarine Squadron at Naval Air Station, Cecil Field, Florida.

TJ does not remember much about his roommate other than he talked with a Southern slur and he spoke fast and often with a stutter. The impression TJ had of Bender was of someone who may not have liked black people but had learned how to mask his true feelings. TJ never got a hard time from Bender mostly because PO3 Bender was not around often. TJ pretty much had the room to himself in the evenings and especially on weekends. Every night for the remainder of the week was a deep reminiscing of growing up on North 18th Street. He tossed and turned almost every night wishing that he would wake up from a bad dream. But he was consciously aware of being on active duty, and he prayed to God that all this was only a dream. He hoped for some reason or another he would find himself home on the third floor, in his room hearing Fred telling him to wake up for school. The mental state and homesickness TJ was experiencing were emotionally painful than he possibly imagined. In fact, he had no idea that homesickness and stressing himself with loneliness would be anything like he was feeling day after day. For seven days straight, each night he cried a deep, long, hard cry, and for seven days straight he acutely dreamed about home as if he were there. It was the most he had ever dreamed consistently in his entire life. His dreams were penetrating. They were concentrated. His dreams were alive and real, to the point every morning that he woke up, he swore his waking up was a dream. Consciously, he knew he was on active duty in the United States Navy. The real-time active duty military was nothing like he imagined and nothing like basic training. He had a roommate who was never around, and in the mornings, his roommate was attempting to wake him up. You see, TJ had not adjusted to getting up on his own and wanted to sleep long and stay in the bunk. PO3 Bender would either make noise like opening and closing his closet, not in a disruptive way, but just enough to disturb the sleep of TJ and wake him up. And there were times that Bender would said, "Hey, TJ, time to get up." But Bender would not continue to try to rouse TJ. He would say it one time, then Petty Officer 3rd Class Bender would get dressed and leave the room. TJ was on his own and would be held accountable for his own actions, and all Bender had to say to the commanding officer was, "I told him to get up." An epiphany struck in the mind of TJ after a couple of days of Bender telling him to get up. TJ noticed the consistency of Bender's action: call TJ once out of sleep, get dressed, leave the room. It was then the proverbial light came on in TJ's mind. TJ knew he had to protect his butt, and all the training he had received up to this point, he was duty-bound to put in action. When PO3 Bender left the room, TJ was on his own, and he was compelled to adjust rapidly to his new life. He could not continue to expect the type of leniency he had received in boot camp and at the master at arms shack in San

Diego, California. At some point, he thought, his laziness and not following orders would take a good chunk out of his black ass. There was no more mommy calling for her "baby" to "get up, it's time to eat." TJ was now an enlisted sailor in the United States Navy, and everything was about discipline. Hardcore military, senior enlisted and commissioned officers telling him what to do and when to do it, and they were not listening to any excuses.

A dream he once had remains vividly to this day, causing him not to sleep the remainder of the night. The dream was detailed to every color, smell, touch, and sound. When he woke up and realized that he was in the navy bunk with the sounds of fighter aircraft flying overhead, he burst into the most emotional crying session ever since the train ride from Harrisburg, Pennsylvania. He dreamed he was with his mom on the bus on their way downtown to pay bills. He now began to understand that his soul was brutally entrenched in the past of his life. But his spirit was attempting to grow into the future of his life, and the war going on inside his soul was causing cerebral casualty after casualty. There were times he thought he would lose his mind and times he wanted to fake a nervous breakdown. Nervous breakdown is the intense uncontrollable emotions of past and present events in one's life that appear impossible to overcome. The war raging inside his mind to get himself together was not only his state of mind at Naval Air Station Cecil Field but on several occasions in the early days of his naval career. His face was not a happy face in those early days of maturing, and his eyes were filled with bags from sleepless nights over a seven-day period. But the dream he had was all too real and lifelike. Every part about the dream was precise down to the minute. Mom and TJ arrived downtown and went to Miller's Furniture store to pay a bill, and *everything* in the dream went *exactly* as it did in the real life of his recent past. He entered the furniture store with his mother, and after paying the bill, they both went over to Joe the Motorist to pay a bill. As the real account took place, so did the dream. TJ noticed a bicycle in the middle of the floor the likes of a bicycle he had never seen before and the dream goes through every scene and every touch and every feeling and look like the day it occurred back in 1968. In the dream, he enjoyed thrilling peace and contentment because he was with his mother and he was home. The dream went as far as TJ and Mom getting on the bus to go home and TJ sitting beside her. He looked up at her with baby tears in his eyes, and she looked over at him, never saying a word and rendered unto TJ her motherly smile. At that, he woke up in the middle of the night and immediately wept and wept and wept. He woke up into the real world he so desperately wanted it to be a dream and desperately wanted the dream to end. He dreamed again that he was taking the bicycle out for the first time on North 18th Street and showing off his bike to his new friends. The dream followed the *exact* scene and every touch and every feeling and look like the day it occurred back in 1968. The dreams were becoming tremendously stressful to him and psychologically weary. He could not withstand a continuation of the dreams any longer and wished to end his life or go absent without leave (AWOL) (Art. 86). The feelings of homesickness he experienced when traveling on the train from Harrisburg, Pennsylvania to Chicago, Illinois, had returned in force. Double, triple, quad the feelings he had on the train. He wanted. He desired. He thought a nervous breakdown was looming over his head. He could not endure the dreams and embrace the homesickness feelings much longer. The dreams at night and thoughts during the day were running amuck in his mind. The negative and unproductive thoughts he was harboring a few months ago had returned with a new vitality and with an attitude. He strongly considered quitting and giving up on everything he thought he wanted in life. The anger and blame he felt while in boot camp had returned with a renewed attack and vengeance. He was angry with himself and angry with all his family and so-called friends who did not talk him out of joining the navy. He wanted to get dressed and walk off the base to 103rd Street about a deeply wooded ten-mile area.

He was afraid of what might befall him had he taken that walk. Fear seized his mind, and he quickly dismissed that idea. He wanted to walk off the base for just a couple of miles and hitch a ride into Jacksonville and find his way anywhere! He was mentally deranged, afraid, angry, and striving to break away from his unstable soul. Everything about home seemed to be a dream or possibly a story he read in a book somewhere. TJ could not find the book to stop reading it, and he was loss finding his way in the world he voluntarily entered.

After seven straight days of arduous weeping and sorrowfulness and self-pity, the thought came to TJ to pray. A novel thought, wouldn't you agree? And for the very first time since leaving home, instead of continuing to harbor his selfish immature feelings of sorrow and homesickness, he seriously began to pray to God, "Please, please let me adjust and let these dreams cease." He had no fancy words, no deep spiritual warfare confession, nothing but genuine, pure, honest faith that God would hear him. He sought the Master's mercy to take him to the place he was destined to arrive. He knew nothing about positive confession and hardly knew the Bible for that matter. He was brand-new fresh meat "church" boy for Satan. TJ knew *nothing* about anything! He was taught growing up that the God of heaven and earth loves to respond to genuine prayers in one's hopeless state.

God knows when we have come to our wit's end and when we have stepped into the place where we are totally helpless without him. TJ remembered a sermon he once heard entitled, "Man's Extremity Is God's Opportunity." Kind of a catchy thought, but a place TJ had entered without knowing he was there. TJ had reached his wit's end and was frustrated that he lacked control over his emotions, his thoughts and the plaguing of his dreams. He learned quickly what the apostle Paul meant when he penned the words, "When I am weak, then am I strong" (2 Cor. 12:10). For the first time in his life at eighteen years old, TJ had become undeniably mentally and physically weak. He was lost. He felt hopeless. He lacked focus. Aimlessly was he searching and trying to figure out and make sense of who, what, where and how he arrived at Cecil Field, Florida, in the United States Navy. But when he finally obeyed the spirit of God to pray, a wondrous, speechless, undeniable change began to take place. The likes he could have never imagined combatting what he was feeling and the sense of loneliness and self-pity he was harboring. His soul would become transformed, and his spirit would become awakened to the reality and eternal existence of God.

The First Awakening

He closed his eyes and continued his simple, unimpressive prayer that took him into the sleep world on the seventh night of weeping. He fell off to sleep asking God to "please, please have mercy on me. Although this is a minuscule thing to you, you know it is new to me, and I am here with no advice or direction. Please have mercy on my soul and please, please, God, help me. I don't know what to do, and these feelings have overwhelmed my mind. What should I do God, what should I do?"

The last thing the young lad remembered is asking God that question, what should I do? The next thing he remembered was God answering him in such a way that may be difficult for you, the reader, to accept or believe. But his answer from God was in his own way that left TJ without any question and awakened his spirit to a new level of relationship with the mercy of God. The Master of heaven and earth was about to introduce TJ to a new birth of sorts, at the baby level, but a birth that would place TJ on the path he was destined to follow. The manner in which God answered TJ left no question at all in his mind that God was answering his prayer. It was late September in Florida, and the days were still hot and the nights warm. But TJ was convinced the geographical location or the temperature had nothing to do with the way his prayer was answered. After all, God is the creator of everything, and with that, TJ concluded, he can answer prayers in a manner of his choosing and in a way that would be unquestionable. He remembers hearing the older preachers say that your alarm clock does not wake you up, but the Master in heaven wakes us up every morning. While that is true, the Master does wake us up, it's not that he personally wakes us up each day, but that his grace and mercy allows us to see another day. His grace is eternal, and when his grace was initiated toward mankind, his grace continues to operate day in and day out. The scriptural injunction in Lamentations 3:23 says, "They are new every morning: great is thy faithfulness." We do physically hear alarm clocks, but it is the unmerited favor of God that allows us to be aroused to see another day. But on that eighth morning, TJ's alarm clock did not ring. God chose another way to wake the young lad on the eighth morning. TJ was aroused from sleep in the most peaceful, gorgeous, divinely, and supernatural manner that he had ever known. That wakeup call from heaven literally buried every negative thought from the day he first left home up to the point he was awakened in the eighth morning.

From that day forward, the outline of the sermon was beginning to form. He did not know that, but God knew what he was doing and the plans he had for TJ. Those days were filled with complete trust and dependency of the reality and legitimacy of an eternal Heavenly Father. It was also the beginning of severing the codependency he had of his brothers, whom he idolized.

The wakeup occurred on a Sunday morning, on a weekend that PO3 Bender was not around. The day of worship that TJ was familiar with and had been taught all his life. Apparently, he had turned over in his bed during the night and was lying on his back. He was awakened feeling a soothing warmth on his entire body as the warmth began at his feet and ran up his entire body to cover his face. A fresh new morning was unfolding, and a fresh new awakening was in process. Like a baby waking up from sleep not having to toil or labor, babies just wake up opening their eyes, gazing at their surroundings. That's how TJ woke up on the eighth morning, only to be astounded to find the sun shining DIRECTLY through the one window in that room and shinning DIRECTLY on his entire body, from his feet to his face. A blanket of natural light was shown through the window at the precise longitude and latitude to strike the person of one TJ Sailor. The experience was undeniably breathtaking and irrefutably an answer straight from heaven that spoke without speaking and said, "Yes, I hear you. Time to arise from sleep. Get up."

TJ snapped to attention by sitting up in the bed beholding the sun, while the sun was beholding him, in all its glory and splendor as if to say, "You asked for direction and help, didn't you." He sat up in the bed for a minute or two contemplating what was happening and thinking about his prayer before he fell off to sleep. For the first time in his life, TJ was introduced to the results of what genuine prayer could accomplish. He did not question at all if God was speaking to him using his splendorous created heavenly body, having dug his heels into the quicksand of his self-pity, his weeping, doubtful mind, and returning to the seed of faith planted in him long ago. TJ got a response that was probably waiting for him since the early days he left Harrisburg, Pennsylvania, on the train to Chicago, Illinois. He questioned himself as to what took so long for him to turn his attention away from his own self-pity and selfishness and come to know the God in heaven that he longed to know. From that day forward throughout the military career of TJ, God began to teach him in his own way and in his own time. He was learning from the Master's school of life, and his school has no rivals. From that point, TJ arose from the top bunk and got on his knees and wept. But the weeping this time was from a renewed spirit and renewed perspective as to why he entered the navy in the first place. This was the third wave of homesickness experienced and was by far, the toughest pity-party that Satan unleashed on the young lad. If the prince of darkness was going to be successful in deceiving his mind in the guise of a nervous breakdown, his initial try was TJ's first days assigned to VS-31 at NAS Cecil Field, Florida. TJ's next strategy from then on was to begin reading his Bible and marking EVERY verse in the Bible he read. He initiated the underline, highlight, memory method, quoting of the Scriptures. He enthusiastically fell in love with the Word of God, day by day. Following that brutal attack, his mind, soul, and spirit had become all too familiar with the entire emotional entourage. In the future, he would quickly identify the characteristics therewith and would surrender his emotions to the Spirit of God. Homesickness experiences in the future would be NOTHING like the initial attack on his mind and soul at NAS Cecil Field, Florida. Renewed in spirit and focused in mind, he was feeling ten feet tall. The remainder of that day was a day of deep reflection about everything from boot camp through two weeks additional training at Great Lakes through San Diego, California, and Tijuana, Mexico. In a real way, God answered the desperate cry of TJ and placed him on the right track. That day was a day of great reflection and devotion to the God of the Bible he had learned about all his life. Sometime shortly thereafter, he ran into Brother C. at Cecil Field. It was a good thing, a nice reunion. They began to hang out, not every day because TJ still had a little rough edge that needed to be shaved off. He was still a little standoffish and leery of getting too close with anyone. Although he thought Brother C. to be a good friend, he had only known him since meeting him in San Diego, California. TJ's own personal life was still at the starting line of maturing. But for now, Brother C. was good to have around and a good brother to hang out with.

A Brother from Home

While assigned to VS-31 stationed at Cecil Field, Florida, time crept along slowly in those days and every day seemed to drag along; nothing went terribly fast. It seemed the initial three-year enlistment in the United States Navy for TJ would be a long time away from home. He would not be discharged until April of 1979, and that was a long way away in the mind of TJ. But at eighteen years old, nothing moves terribly fast, and you feel as though you have all the world ahead of you, like you will live forever. There was much about Cecil Field TJ enjoyed once he adjusted to being away and overcame the persistent wave of homesickness. Brother C. and TJ became good friends, and they would talk about church go to church and read the Bible a lot. TJ began to trust Brother C. as a faithful and sincere brother about living a godly life. In fact, while at Cecil Field, TJ met several brothers who appeared to be serious about God and the things of God relative to the Bible. He was always leery about getting too close to anyone not of the Negro descent, and many times he walked around with a scowling look on his face and was extremely sharp with his answers to questions people would ask him. He only felt comfortable talking with his black brothers and those of the Christian faith.

There was one brother he met that always relaxed TJ's spirit when around him. He *never* expected to meet or know anyone from Harrisburg, Pennsylvania, or close to Harrisburg. The thought *never* crossed his mind. One day in the chow hall with Brother C., he introduced TJ to a good brother not too far from Harrisburg, Pennsylvania. When Brother C. introduced TJ to him, the questions and familiarity began.

"TJ is my name."

"Where are you from?"

"York, Pennsylvania."

"Wow! I'm from Harrisburg."

At that point, there was a smile on TJ's face big enough for the entire air station to see. Darnell Bowman was from York, Pennsylvania, and he smiled likewise and began to laugh. Darnell had a kind, happy, reassuring, carefree godly laugh. TJ had met someone practically neighbors with him who had already been at Cecil Field before his arrival. They made their acquaintance by mentioning familiar names like, Elder Wise, Elder Wilson, Bishop Jones, and even TJ's Father. At this point, TJ was elated and beginning to feel not only relieved but like the sunshine that shone in his room that day was now beginning to shine the way and mark the path of his life. He was not as alone as he thought, and he was not the only person from Pennsylvania believing in the Father, the Son, and the Holy Ghost.

But there were brothers he knew nothing about but quickly came to know and regard as his brand-new family. While at Cecil Field, Florida, Darnell, Brother C., and Jamie, another brother who was biblically astute was the needed spiritual support and "two by two" (Luke 10:1) he so desperately needed at that time in his life. Brother C. was a good friend who kept TJ focused on godliness. Brother Darnell was a serious brother about the things of God who kept TJ challenged to excel to greater heights. The other brothers were simply there for fellowship. TJ has never been aware of much of what those brothers may have been going through in their personal relationship, but he was glad they were in his life, and he was glad to know them. When he may have wanted to give up and launch out into the deep of "sin," they restrained him. When he may have wanted to quit the United States Navy and go AWOL, they encouraged him. And when he may have wanted to give in to homesickness, they assured him he was not alone. Funny thing is that they were probably not aware of the timeliness and the positive effect just knowing them had on his life in those days. They all spent fantastic times together attending different churches in Jacksonville, Florida.

Every church they attended was because Darnell took them. Darnell had a sweet-looking 1975 Plymouth Road Runner that sounded like it could go from zero to sixty in a minute. TJ thought Darnell's Road Runner was a car that was ahead of its time. Darnell seemed to always have it together, and TJ felt that he could never fill his shoes. Darnell seemed to be advance in everything and seemed to have good things going for himself. All the brothers would go to Faust Temple and other COGIC churches, and each experience then was very much suited for what TJ needed at that time in his life. Every now and then, they would go over church members' homes on Sundays to eat dinner. Sometimes they would go back to church in the evening, and other times they would return to the base. TJ really, really enjoyed those days and the church folks he met. He met a young lady at Faust Temple who appeared to be virtuous, untouched, and serious about going to church and the Christian life. Given his background and the direction his life was headed, God kept him from contaminating her, and the relationship he was trying to start with her never got off the ground. He didn't even get on the launching pad when it came to that sister. Not to mention an older minister by the name of Elder Timothy was watching over her soul and her best interest. One day while at Elder Timothy's house, he called TJ on the carpet and asked him a good amount of questions about how serious he was starting a relationship with her. TJ ALWAYS respected ministers in his life and knew he better answer the minister straight. The minister didn't play around with useless questions or try to use a lot of analogies. He came right out and asked, "Are you serious, Brother TJ? Do you plan to put a ring on her finger?"

Of course, TJ could not answer his question with confidence that he was serious, so he said to TJ, "If you are not serious, I would suggest you leave her alone. No need to date and write letters and expect her to wait for you. Let's not play with this!"

TJ became frustrated with the questions the minister put to him, but after thinking about it, TJ did appreciate his approach and cutting to the chase. Instability with relationships was not what he needed and would not have been fair to her. TJ respected him and respected the God in him because he appeared to be, what Christians would say, "for real in God." Of what TJ knew and understood then, there was nothing he could see of Elder Timothy that did not line up with the Word of God.

The Ford Pinto and KS

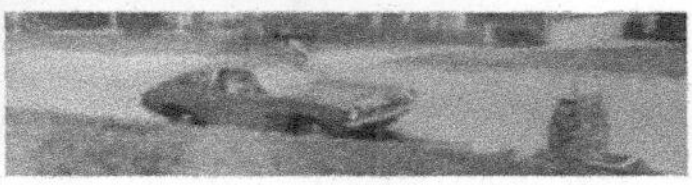

But Darnell Bowman, his new friend from York, Pennsylvania, was needed in TJ's life at the precise time he was needed. Brother C. and the other Christian brothers he met was the best side of meeting new people and new friends he was acquiring. But there was always that lingering temptation and test to explore sin further looming over his head from the brothers he met in the squadron. In his new squadron at his permanent duty station of approximately one hundred unit members, only six were black men, TJ included among the six. In 1976–1979, civil rights, affirmative action, and all social upward mobility programs were fairly new. They were pretty much just getting off the ground and beginning to gain some momentum. It was not entirely too strange for the demographics to be that drastic. And of the six black men assigned to VS-31, only one black man was a commissioned officer. That black officer was not there much longer after TJ checked on board. For the entire time he was assigned to VS-31, there was only one other black commissioned officer. TJ was among a small minority in the midst of old social beliefs and political systems and personal perspectives and prejudices that reared its ugly head from time to time. What amazed TJ with the five black brothers as he was getting to know them is that to his knowledge, they *all* respected him as a "man of God." TJ walked among them in such a manner as to present the Lord in the face of bigotry and unfairness. He spoke what little of the Word of God and limited understanding he knew at the time. Despite his own personal struggles and the adjustments he was experiencing, he strove to be a light in a very dark world, both internally and externally. Much of what he spoke to the squadron brothers was a combination of Fred's words, the Bible, and what he learned from his mother. He did not see himself as a wise sage, but apparently, they perceived him as a levelheaded young man with some words of wisdom to drop on them from time to time. Simultaneously, TJ continued to struggle with indecisiveness, immature emotions. He continued to be unsettled. He was mentally challenged in such a way of contemplating quitting and giving up. On one hand, he strove to walk the walk among his peers and black brothers, but secretly and privately on many occasions, he literally cried out to God every minute of the day because his own soul was lost. He *never* gave serious thought as to how his life could possibly have a positive effect on someone else. In fact, he thought it impossible for him, scrawny, uneducated, indecisive, unstable, and lost soul to have any positive effect on anyone's life. Obviously, God knew and thought otherwise about him and understood the depths of his soul and all that lay in his heart. TJ would come to understand in the years to come that God had placed him there and charted his life for a reason greater than his own selfishness and self-pity. The Bible says in Psalm 37:23, "The steps of a good man are ordered of the Lord," and in those days TJ's steps were logistically and strategically ordered of God. Much depth of soul-searching and the fall he would experience from an extreme height of pride. But revival and resurrection would occur in the years to come. But then 1976 through 1979, *everything* going on in the life of TJ was about what God was doing to teach him his ways and uncover and dispose the darkness lurking deep within his soul.

There was not one brother TJ met in those days that he did not like, *not one*! There were a couple of brothers who he thought would be difficult men to convince of the words he spoke concerning the existence of God. It was difficult for him to get to know certain brothers, but even they would soon give in to the wave of the spirit of God in those days. Straddling the fence because he just did not know how to remain focus and walk the path of the mission. At times, the squadron brothers would influence TJ to become careless, and TJ nursed the "accept me" type of relationship with them. Similar to the "please accept me" type of relationship he longed for with his own natural brothers when he was much younger. He stood some distance from their lifestyle as he wanted to convince them of the validity of the Bible. He did not always know how to explain truth and the Bible to them. Years later with the explosion of the internet and membership sites, TJ contacted a white coworker from VS-31 via the internet on a navy shipmate site.

The guy texted TJ and said, "I always thought you were straitlaced. The guy's response was hilarious to TJ because he *never* thought of himself as being straitlaced, because TJ knew full well that he committed things worthy of being called a chief sinner. He also engaged in things that were not godly at all. The earlier part of TJ's military career was filled with what the older saints called "straddling the fence." Therein lies the reality of who TJ thought himself to be and at what depth he knew of himself back then. Straitlaced, as the guy termed it, was a gross misnomer on his part, but TJ understood where he was coming from. Most of the brothers in the squadron were single men just like TJ, so in his youthful mind, hanging out with them from time to time was not necessarily wrong. TJ hung out with the squadron fellows Friday and even Saturday nights, but the things the squadron brothers were into was not the lifestyle of TJ, nor did he want to keep giving into their lifestyle. But at eighteen and wanting to befriend and wanting to explore his new "free" life, TJ found himself giving into smoking marijuana. He started drinking alcohol like water, and he attended house parties with the squadron fellows. Drinking *never* was TJ's interest, and he *never* could adjust to it or go to the bar or state store just because it was the weekend. But those brothers also knew that their lifestyle and the lifestyle of TJ *did not* agree even when TJ took a swag here and there. They themselves knew it just did not fit who TJ was. It was TJ searching for who he was and on what grounds he was destined to stand. But strangely enough, they seemed to be quite comfortable with TJ around and included him in with their smoking, drinking, and laughing. TJ found personal pleasure in smoking marijuana because that was introduced to him, along with drinking, by his older brother Bay. He took smoking marijuana as being cool and hip. He enjoyed the marijuana experience and would embrace it for years to come, though deep in his spirit he *knew* it was wrong because he was defiling the temple of the vices of the world. But did not have the spiritual fortitude and soundness of mind to withstand the temptation and onslaught.

One onslaught and great temptation happened when TJ and a brother by the nickname KS drove down 103rd Street to another brother's place to hang out for the weekend. TJ thought that was pretty cool hanging out with the brothers from the squadron and was looking forward to that evening. KS said to TJ earlier during the day that he wanted to go over to a brother's apartment that lived off base. Living on base was like confinement for guys who did not have transportation because Cecil Field was located miles and miles away from the nearest town. Cecil Field was also a good half hour drive to Jacksonville, Florida. The base was literally out in the boonies, as it was called. The only transportation in those days for TJ was the lemon Ford Pinto he had purchased. TJ was not stationed at Cecil Field long before he realized that he needed transportation, and out of desperation and advice from older sailors, he joined the Navy Federal Credit Union and immediately got a loan approved. TJ searched diligently in the auto magazine searching for a cheap car that he could purchase right away. A 1972 Ford Pinto for $700 from a car dealer not too far off the expressway but still miles from Jacksonville, Florida. The car dealer had junk cars behind a fence on his lot and broken-up cars with flat tires sitting on his lot. It was almost like a bartering type of dealership where car mechanics probably purchased vehicles to work on and sell for cash. TJ was eighteen years old, trying so hard to navigate through life on his own. Bad decision after bad decision would plague TJ for years into the future, and purchasing the 1972 Ford Pinto would be the first of many. The car salesman, if you want to call him that, was an overweight, cover-all-wearing, deep Southern draw, with a big cigar in his mouth and a huge belly. If it weren't for the business transaction, TJ perceived the car salesman as a man who might see him in distress, take a couple of puffs on his cigar, and turn his head the other way. Perhaps the perspective of TJ was totally wrong, but considering his limited uneducated, sheltered background and negative experience in race relations, a good portion of his perception of people had been rooted in ignorance.

KS was a little bit smaller than TJ and scrawny as well but had a large head and most of the guys made fun of him and would call him big head. As much as TJ can remember, it was all done in fun, and they all pretty much laughed at how he was picked on and KS himself would laugh. If there ever was a time that KS took it seriously, TJ never knew about it. Funny thing is, KS was the one who found the car dealer and convinced TJ that "we gotta get a car, we gotta get off this base."

TJ wanted to be friends with the squadron brothers. Simultaneously, he wanted to be a preacher of sorts around his Christian brothers. His life in those days was like mixing sand and oil floating on water. TJ was the epitome of the parable of the sower and the seed told by Messiah in Matthew's Gospel of what TJ understood then. TJ would not experience the eighth verse that talks about "good ground" and bringing for "good fruit" until decades later after God had rid TJ of himself. Funny thing, though, about the car "they" had to get was paid for 100 percent from TJ's money and the car "they" had to get was registered solely in TJ's name. It was quintessential of the epitome of compromise, a classic demonstration of "straddling the fence," as it is called in charismatic Christianity.

TJ had now associated with some new friends, black brothers, some older than he, some his age, that he found himself wanting to befriend them all. So he compromised and compromised and compromised just to have friends or people he could get to know, and he felt good about his new friends. Actually, the 1972 Ford Pinto was TJ's personal transportation off the confined base of Naval Air Station Cecil Field, Florida. One of the older sailors, Brooks, was a man TJ admired and enjoyed being around him as a blood brother. Brooks convinced TJ that he needed to become a member of the Navy Federal Credit Union and TJ got a loan for $1,000 to purchase that car. He was eighteen years old and just starting off to establish credit. He had no mortgage or dependents, and he was full-time active duty, making about $650 every two weeks. Funny then, the loan was approved in one hour. TJ began to feel that freedom he was longing for knowing that he could literally go anywhere he wanted and practically whenever he wanted. He now had transportation, and the 1972 Form Pinto was *nothing* but transportation. Nothing at all fancy about the car, and TJ would soon learn the car was the true definition of a "lemon." The BEST thing about the Pinto is that it would start and get TJ from point A to point B.

It was not the concern of KS that TJ had multiple problems on top of multiple problems with the Pinto, KS only concern was getting off the base to have fun. They had discussed going out on Friday, and TJ was sort of hoping KS would change his mind or forget. But what were the odds of KS changing his mind? One Friday, KS went to TJ's barracks and knocked on his door.

"Hey, T, you ready?"

Among his Christian brothers, they addressed each other as "brother" so and so or by their full name. The facade of being one way around one group and another way around another group is misleading, but that was all TJ knew to survive in the military and face his own weaknesses. Those were the days of serious growth that was lonely and exciting at the same time. Years would pass, and countless experiences would be gained before TJ would get the revelation of who he is and how to develop into who God made him. At the time KS knocked on TJ's door, he was lying on his bunk praying and hoping that KS would forget that he promised they would go to the brother's apartment. TJ was locked up in his barracks room hoping that KS would not show up. But KS was very, very assertive and persistent in his approach to everything as far as TJ knew. KS knocked and knocked, increasing the hardness of his knock and began yelling, "T, come on, man. We gotta go. Let's get out of this place."

TJ heard other guys yelling at KS, "Hey, stop that yelling. Some guys do work third shift and you up there yelling like you some kind of madman!"

"Ah, shut up!" KS said. "We'll be out of here soon."

TJ prolonged the time because he did not want to go, but he had given his word that he would take KS to the brother's apartment and hang out a bit. He finally answered the door with a fake smile and a "cool and hip" response like, "Yeah! I'm ready. Time to roll. Let's go, bro, let's get off this base."

Walking down the hallway of the barracks hoping something, anything would stop them from going out. Hoping the car would not start because it was not unusual for the Ford Pinto not to start, and that would not have surprised TJ. KS, on the other hand, was extremely excited and was passing cassette tapes back and forth to TJ of what he wanted to listen to in the car. To the chagrin of TJ, nothing hindered them from going out that evening to the brother's apartment, it would be a night of great onslaught against his unstable, weak, immature embryo Christian walk and Christian testimony. He wanted to explore and launch out into sin, but not too far because in his heart he tried to hold on to some conviction of what he believed to be right and wrong. But his trying was not good enough as compared to true faith and trust in God along with the convictions in his soul. That night would further reveal to TJ that he lacked the necessary biblical life of a true believer. Of all the church services he had attended in his life to that point, he had not yet truly surrendered his soul to the Lord but was on the path of discovering the depth of uncleanliness in his own heart.

The Pinto started up with no problem, and KS reminded TJ of a kid in a candy store talking and laughing about anything he said and could not wait to get off the base. KS popped in a cassette, and they began their long drive on their way off the base and turning right to 103rd Street listening to Kool & the Gang. A mixture of feelings overtook the mind of TJ, and he was feeling excited, happy, sad, and could not wait for the night to end. A jumble of feelings and thoughts, and he was not sure which ones were right or wrong. He reasoned in his mind of being young and thought, *I'm a young man who never lived a worldly life. What's wrong with having a little fun?* Considering his upbringing, conviction began to set in his mind, and he also felt what he was doing was wrong, but his flesh and curiosity urged him on. His flesh prevailed that night, and he was on his way living his life as a back and forth Christian experience. He did not know what to expect at the brother's apartment but was looking forward to having fun and trying to enjoy himself and have a good time with a couple of brothers from the squadron. When they arrived at Mack's apartment, Mack gladly opened the door. TJ and KS walked up a set of steps into an almost bare apartment with a couple of chairs and a few things here and there. TJ was not used to a place being as empty as that apartment because back home, Mom had a full house of furniture. When TJ walked into Mack's apartment, it looked and felt strange to him. But the brothers had exactly what they wanted. They had freedom from the base and a good time liquefied inside a bottle and twirled inside Tops wrapping paper. Everyone was laughing, and the music was playing loud and four brothers were already in the apartment not counting TJ and

KS. Everyone seemed to have the same idea of party, fun, and relaxation away from the squadron. Drinking alcohol never interested TJ, when he did drink, it was only because of the crowd he was with and also to fit in. But the "Jay," or marijuana, TJ had a liking to, and immediately he and KS began puffing a few Jays as the music blazed louder and louder. TJ was becoming a little uneasy about the entire scene but maintained his cool and appeared to be enjoying the so-called fun. Then a knock on the door and Mack yelled out, "That must be them!"

KS responded in kind, "Oh, yeah, now the fun begins!"

TJ was wondering what these brothers were talking about. When Mack opened the door, TJ heard the sound of female voices laughing and entering the apartment. He thought to himself, *I hope this does not turn out to be something involving sex.* At that time in his life, he didn't have a real interest in engaging in a sexual relationship with a woman. He held on to being abstinent for a long time. Not to mention an uncertain relationship he had with a woman back home that had begun to stir up much controversy in his life. All TJ wanted to do then was leave the apartment and return back to his cozy room in the barracks. No matter how high he had become, he maintained sense enough to realize that he was about to engage deeply into something he was not interested in. He actually thought that he and the brothers were just hanging out (kind of like he hung out with James Jones) and just "chillin'." But little did he know and as naive as he was, the hang out in their mind was a different world of interpretation from the mind of young TJ.

The women walked up the steps very skimpily dressed, with breasts bulging and hot pants painted on their bodies, looking sensual and sexually enticing. TJ was very nervous, unwilling, and wanted to leave because the so-called fun had now become a concern of his. He was high from smoking marijuana and had to drive back to the base on a dark, poorly lit street—straight drive, no turns or curves, about ten miles long. The women came in and immediately became the life of the party and center of attraction. What TJ thought earlier to be brothers hanging out turned out to be a world he had little experience with at this point. There were two women and six guys, and the music was loud. They were laughing and touching, and he was looking and wanting to get involved but was too nervous and sanctimonious in his own mind. KS, on the other hand, was all into the onslaught against the mind of TJ and thoughts unbeknownst to him. TJ took the entire experience very personally and blamed KS for the longest time of trying to "corrupt him." When the women showed up, everything escalated and seemed to shift gears, as it were. The feeling TJ had of not wanting to leave the barracks suddenly was a fainting thought, and he was smack dab in the middle of a house party—a party involving liquor, marijuana, women, and sex. What to do? KS was enjoying himself relentlessly, and TJ thought the brothers would probably make fun of him and have nothing to do with him if he left. He did not want to leave KS there because he knew no one would bring him back to the base, and he felt stuck in a situation he did not like while he continued to wrestle with deeply mixed feelings.

Should I forget everything I learned about church, fidelity, honesty, integrity, and sin and go ahead and take advantage of this situation involving these women and bond with these brothers into their world, or what? What should I do? he thought.

One of the girls came over to the couch where he was sitting and sat down with legs crossed, exposing just about every part of her body. There was nothing left to the imagination. She did not strip, but what was exposed to TJ left his mind with very little to imagine. Then a knock on the door, and KS went wild. "Oh yeah, we bout to blow this thing up!"

Three more women showed up—two black women and one white woman. At that point, TJ stood up, unstable, sort of rocking back and forth while the girl that sat beside him attempted to pull him back down to the couch. He slumbered on the couch, not out of control, just high and giggling like an ignorant child. The girl then began touching, rubbing, and whispering in the ear of TJ. Actually, he did not focus on what she was saying. His mind was preoccupied with leaving.

The music was blaring at this point, and all he heard was what appeared to be pointless laughter and senseless chatter. KS and the other brothers were enjoying themselves like children at an amusement park with two handfuls of cotton candy. Deep within the soul of TJ, regardless of the thoughts running through his mind, he blurted out to KS, "Hey, it's time to go. I need to leave."

Maybe one or two seconds passed by, and it got silent. TJ wondered why the hell everyone got silent for.

Then with one accord, *everyone* in the room burst into roaring laughter of the most humiliating kind. They must have laughed for about five minutes. Different ones blurted out, "Hey, it's time to go. I need to leave."

And they repeated and repeated what TJ said for about five minutes, over and over again. The women just chuckled and resumed their temptation of the other brothers. The lady that sat down beside TJ aggressively pulled him back down on the couch, hands all over him, and whispered in his ear, "Don't leave yet, handsome. We can have fun, and you will not regret it."

All TJ was doing initially was enjoying his jay and feeling good. He made no moves on any of the girls and was trying to figure out why this pretty black woman was all but throwing herself on him. Every now and then, some of the brothers would blurt out, "It's time to go, it's time to go," and then with unified laughter, they would repeat the words again. He wanted so desperately to take advantage of the girl that sat beside him, but was now embarrassed and shame saying what he said. While struggling to get up again, she continued to restrain him, and he kindly said, "Look, I don't want to stay, and I'm leaving."

Surprisingly, she said to him, "At least take my number. Perhaps you and I can meet up outside of these conditions. I can tell you are very uncomfortable being here."

He thought her reaction was strange, and she kind of reminded him of the situation with his neighbor girlfriend when he got drunk on North 18th Street at fifteen years old. He remembered how his neighbor girlfriend calmed him down with intelligent conversation and a hot steamy cup of coffee. He waited for a few seconds, and she reached in her pocketbook, pulled out a piece of paper, jotted her phone number down, and handed it to TJ and said, "PLEASE don't stand me up. Give me a call, handsome."

At that point, TJ slowly stood up again, politely walked to the door and walked down the steps, measuring each step so as not to trip. The lady that was coming on to him smelled especially good, a fragrance he was not familiar with but a fragrance that was captivating, and he thought she was very pretty. TJ wrestled with the fact that she was giving him attention like that. Usually, the pretty girls with education did not pay TJ any attention in the projects and North 18th Street.

What was different about now? he thought. He enjoyed the attention and was liking it and afraid of it at the same time.

Weeks later, he mentally beat himself down by not following up with her invitation and in the annals of time, he could not tell you what happened to her phone number. Over time, her number vanished away. While he was walking down the steps, crowds of men and women were passing him, walking up the steps into the house party. KS yelled out, "T, don't leave me! I'll be there in a few."

TJ did not care if KS would follow him or not. There was too much going on too fast and too many thoughts rushing through TJ's mind, and he was not sure which one he should obey. Impulsively, TJ left the party because he was doing all within his power to run from what he perceived as wrong, but he could not run too far from himself until it would catch up with him. He did not care about KS or the brothers or the women. When he got outside and got to his car and got inside and sat down to turn the key, he looked up and KS was at the passenger door about to open the car door. Obviously, KS must have come right behind him. But TJ did not care, and he was not looking back for him. He wanted to get out of that place. When KS got in the car, he was still laughing and said, "Let's go somewhere else. Let's go to the mall."

TJ did not feel like going *anywhere* but back to the base inside the barracks in his room and curl up in his bunk. TJ remembers driving down the highway, high as a kite for hours until they arrived back at the base. They never went to the mall they just drove around listening to music and 103rd Street *never* looked darker, as if TJ was attempting to escape from the dark life of the desires of his heart and the pleasure of a sinful world. TJ expected something to jump out from between the tall pine trees and pursue them, particularly to get him for giving in to the marijuana from the brothers and falling prey to the temptation of the women. He analyzed and questioned himself and doubted his Christianity and feared the man being revealed from within his heart. He sought answers, and he knew the answer could only come from God. He also would seek answers from family members as he began visiting Bay and his older sister in Atlanta, Georgia. His decision to begin visiting family that was not too far from him renewed his thoughts. Almost like aftermath from his great desire to visit Atlanta with his father as a boy. As far as the pretty lady on the couch, well, he thought about her for months thereafter. In time, he would regain some focus, and even she, and the fragrance of her "fleshly love" began to fade.

The Barbershop ladies

TJ has always been a young man that prided himself in sharp grooming standards. He frequented the barbershop like clockwork every two weeks. Of course, no matter where he traveled he made it a point to find a good barbershop with black barbers. It did not matter if other barbers in the shop where of a different nationality, just as long as a black barber would cut his hair. With all respect, he would purposely wait for a black barber if there were other barbers in the shop that was not black. That is not unusual or disrespectful, every barber understands if a customer wants to wait on a specific barber. Nothing personal, just business. One Sunday after attending church service at Faust Temple in Jacksonville, FL. he decided to explore around town looking for a barbershop. No sooner than he turned the corner from the church he seen a barbershop sign in the window of what looked like someone's house. The shop was not located in a separate spot detached from other buildings. There was no barber pole anywhere to be found. It looked like somebody's house with a small sign in the window – barbershop.

He slowed down and did a double-take. He rode around the corner and returned to the location and stopped to get a closer look. The last thing he wanted was to walk up to someone's house and knock on the door feeling like a fool if it were not a legitimate business. The house almost resembled his house on North 18th Street in Harrisburg, PA. Being that it was a nice summer day in the early noontime, he decided to park his car and walk close enough to either get the hours or see if he could see customers inside. He noticed a man sitting in a barber chair and he also was able to see their working hours. He had his information and was satisfied that he had located a barbershop in a black neighborhood. He kind of fast pace back to his car and rode away. That was on a Sunday after church and he had to return to the base. He planned to return the following weekend to get himself a nice haircut and he could not wait. Paying close attention to the street name because that's all he needed to find the barbershop again. Although, in his mind, the shop was inconspicuous among other resident's houses. He was confident though that he could find the shop again because he needed that haircut.

The surprise of all surprises smacked him right in the face when he returned the following weekend in the evening to get his haircut. When he walked into the shop there were 4 barber chairs, if he remembers correctly and not one male barber in the house. There were two women in the shop. One standing in front of a full-body mirror, playing with her hair and talking about the clothes she had on. She appeared to be asking aimless questions that warrant attention. "How do I look?" Is this nice or should I wear the other?" She was not talking to TJ, rather just talking out loud and the barber, the other female was answering her giving her very little attention. Both women sort of looked at TJ with the biggest smile as if he were a long lost friend or relative for that matter. TJ smiled and was making his way to a chair to sit down. While he was walking to a customer chair, the woman looking in the mirror kind of pranced over by TJ and said "you can sit here handsome, boy! You are cute!" From that moment the girl in the mirror continued to talk about nothing, all the while looking at TJ. She didn't stare but TJ could see she kept looking over at him. The other female barber would occasionally look at TJ while cutting the gentlemen's hair and ask questions that may have been obvious. "Where you from?" How old are you? Are you in the service? TJ had a mixture of feelings that ranged from excitement, nervous and uncertain. Reason for the uncertainty is that he never had his hair cut by a woman. . . never! This would be the very first time. But he was not overly concerned about that because the barber appeared to know what she was doing. Secondly, he was already in the shop sitting down and he was not about to leave. He needed a haircut and he was the next customer up for service. The other two concerns he had both women seemed to be older than him, if they were around his age, he may have been interested. The mirror lady was very flirtatious and kept profiling in front of the mirror and walking in front of TJ. He wore a smile of satisfaction amidst his concerns while his male ego was brewing knowing these older women seemed to be interested in more than just giving a haircut. The two women in the barbershop experience occurred before TJ made his first trip overseas. If he had been exposed to what he would be exposed to with his travels overseas, he knows meeting the two women in the barbershop would have turned out differently. His main concern with the women in the barbershop is that both, not one, but both women had breast the size of Dolly Parton. The barber woman cutting the gentleman's hair, her breast may have even been larger than Dolly Parton. The mirror woman wore a very tight blouse and tight jeans revealing every curve and form. The barber woman was not wearing a braw because as she moved her breast moved fluidly. It was a difficult time for TJ because while he was interested in their obvious advances he struggled and reasoned about the clear temptation. What about being a Christian and what about his girlfriend back home? He should have left and was two seconds from leaving and started to say, "look, I will come back later." Knowing he did not intend to return. But he gawked and reasoned and waited too late to make his move to leave.

The barber was done with the customer in the chair and she immediately withdrew her cape from around the customer as he was getting out of the chair. He said to her "I will see you next week Mary." That wasn't her name but TJ does not remember and her name is irrelevant. As the last customer was walking out the door, he noticed something strange but played it off like, "no she didn't!" TJ was standing up to get in the barber chair and the barber lady quickly unbuttons a few buttons in her blouse as she was walking towards the door, then she locked the door and turned around and said, with the biggest smile . . . next! TJ was in the barber chair at this point and he understood that when the shop is about to close, barbers will lock the door to prevent other people from walking in. That was not strange or unusual. But the unbuttoned blouse was a very loud suggestion. TJ thought, "what the hell?" Effectively, the action of both women had hypnotized TJ and he could not take his eyes off them. His excitement was raised to the roof, but his struggle was between right and wrong, considering his girlfriend and his Christianity. But he stayed and endured the advances and wanted desperately to accept, but was afraid because of obvious reasons. The mirror lady then turned the music up loud on the radio and started dancing back in forth in front of TJ sitting in the barber chair. She was moving and shaking and suggesting sensual and sexual moves. Her dancing had no shame in front of a young man they had never seen before in life. Perhaps there was more involved in those women than just cutting hair. The barber was laughing and telling her to stop clowning around, "our customer will think you crazy." The barber lady stood directly in front of TJ smiling with a clear amount of cleavage showing and asked him, "Now sweetie, what can I do for you, you handsome thing!" The entire experience was THE strangest encounter for the young lad at this point in his life, but he was excited, hopeful and afraid. He was not sure of their real intent but concluded it was about sex. He was no way prepared for their advances and did not expect any of that. He just wanted a haircut, that's all he wanted. He must admit though, they both smelled very good and one could tell whatever they were wearing in the way of perfume, was undoubtedly expensive.

TJ was bizarrely uncomfortable because the barber was unashamedly rubbing her breast against TJ's face and at times pressing in under the guise of cutting his hair. When she moved to the front of TJ to do his front line up, she took every bit of 10 minutes. Trimming slowly and talking at the same time. The problem with that front line up is that her breast was purposely dangling directly in front of TJ. There were times her breast unquestionably smacked TJ in the face and other times they were loosely dangling. He was not sure how to respond to the obvious sexual temptation mainly because these were two women he did not know. He wasn't sure if they would attack him if he tried and he wasn't sure if men were hiding in the other rooms. It was one of the most awkward situations of his youthful life. He wanted to grab, kiss and manhandle the barber but was afraid of the possible negative response and or attack. What to do? So he calmly relaxed while sitting in the chair as the barber with huge breasts was sexually abusing him and the other woman was giving him an unsolicited dance. Music loud, women smelling good and tits and big asses all in his face. He was excited, hopeful, nervous and afraid, all in one. The entire situation was one of the weirdest experiences for a 19-year-old inexperienced young lad.

It is not to exaggerate to estimate that the barber took every bit of 1 hour to cut his hair. Between talking to the other lady, asking TJ questions and cutting slowly, TJ estimates a full hour had passed by the time she was finished cutting his hair. When she finished, she slowly removed the cape from around his neck, asked him a few more questions, like "what are you going to do tonight?" as she purposely stood in front of him, now revealing more cleavage than before. As TJ was walking toward the door attempting to leave, the other lady was still dancing, almost enjoying herself. The barber still standing by her chair, not in a hurry to unlock the door, smiling, fixing her hair and said – "you don't have to leave yet, its early sweetheart." TJ immediately said, "Oh yes mam, I have to get back to the base." She strutted over to the door, unlocked the door and said, "please come back soon darling." She unlocked the door and let him free from their hot on fire booty and boobs. No sooner than TJ had gotten in his car with the key in the ignition, he noticed the barber running towards his car. He couldn't be rude and pull off, so he sat there until she got to the passenger's window. She then reached between her breast, pulled out a wad of money, exposing all but her nipples and said, "please don't leave, we can have fun and I promise you will not regret staying awhile!" With all the strength and fight he could muster up he said, "no mam, I have to go." "You will come back won't you, I can't wait to see you again and give you a nice haircut." "Ok then, I'll be back!" That was the first and last time he ever encountered the barbershop ladies. He held onto that encounter he had with them for months trying to make sense out of the whole thing. Where they that "HOT" or desperate, or maybe they needed a young stud to satisfy their physical physique?

Atlanta, Georgia, and the Cathedral of Faith

TJ was eighteen years old at the time of the vicious onslaught involving the brothers with the drinking, marijuana, and women. Air Anti-submarine Squadron 31 at Naval Air Station Cecil Field, Florida, was TJ's second tour of duty. Smoking marijuana was put on hold for a long while. Getting back on track was now his renewed focus. He did not smoke marijuana from that time for a long while. Smoking marijuana would resurface later on and would actually be the crowning point that put the fear of God inside him. He would become convinced by certain events to cease smoking marijuana and truly seek the Lord. The house party experience compelled him to ask forgiveness and restitution with the Lord. He began searching for a Bible-believing church to attend and started spending more time with his Christian brothers. But strangely enough, the brothers at the squadron did not reject him as much as he thought they would. There were no jokes or comments made the following workday. They greeted each other as nothing had happened. It was business as usual at work. KS wanted to continue to go out somewhere but would find another brother to take him off the base. TJ purposely began spending more time with his new Christians friends and began attending church with them on a regular basis. They would frequent Faust Temple Church of God in Christ, and many of their songs and worshipping was exactly like back home. He felt at home going back to church with brother Darnell and Brother C. They would even go over different church member's house for dinner on Sunday's evenings. TJ was much more familiar with the church life, and he embraced the church scene and crying at the altar and jumping and shouting on the floor. He had, for a moment, returned home in his cozy little world of church service and mingling with the "saints."

But something continued to lack in his church experience, and something was still missing. Something of depth and eternal substance of the one he worshipped as God. There appeared to TJ to be a superficial experience with the church scene or at least the church back home and the church in Jacksonville Florida. He visited other churches and even decided to travel to Atlanta, Georgia, where his oldest sister and his boyhood mentor lived. Both Bay and his oldest sister were only a few hours or so from where TJ was stationed. He learned the most direct route from NAS Cecil Field to Atlanta, Georgia. Interstate 10 west to Interstate 75 north took him right smack dab into the heart of Atlanta, Georgia. If for no other reason to purchase that Ford Pinto, it was for TJ to travel to Atlanta, Georgia, on a regular basis to refocus his sights on God and to fill his spirit with an experience that remains second to none to this day as it relates to church service. Once he mapped out the travel route to Atlanta, he contacted Bay and oldest sister and told them he would be coming up to Atlanta. Jacksonville, Florida, is just a few miles south of the Peach State. They were both very glad to know that TJ would be visiting. They were both very glad to welcome their young brother from boot camp and his first duty station not too far from them. His first trip ever to Atlanta on his own was a monumental feat. At first, he could not believe that the city he longed to visit as a boy, with Dad, he was about to visit on his own at eighteen years old. He could not sleep the night before. Of *all* the times Dad went to Atlanta while TJ lived in the projects and on North 18th Street, he only visited Atlanta with Dad one time for a funeral. He attended the funeral of his grandmother, whom he did not know at all and met her briefly as she lay in the coffin. This would be the very first time he would be traveling to the state he longed to see as a boy. But this time he was calling the shots. He was doing the driving, he was on his own, and he knew where he was going.

In those days, no cell phone or tablets or laptops existed, only paper maps. TJ had learned how to read maps very well from the confidence instilled in him by military training. He purchased a large Rand

McNally Road map and began to read and map out his route. It took him exactly five hours and twenty minutes to reach his destination of Atlanta, Georgia, the very first time on his own. He knows that he exceeded the speed limit of the controversial 50–55 mph even in the late 1970s. The problems with the "lemon" Ford Pinto presented itself every twenty miles or so. The car had a terrible problem retaining engine oil, and TJ often had to pull alongside the highway to pour oil into the engine. But that did not hinder him from going to Atlanta to "meet God." The faith of TJ at that time was such that he believed God providentially allowed that vehicle to make the trips. Perhaps during the evening, a guardian angel touched the engine with his baby finger to allow the car to make the frequent trips back and forth to Atlanta. The thought of a supernatural occurrence upon a material man-made item was at least a comforting thought for TJ. How else do you explain an unreliable old vehicle with an oil leak to make the round trip? TJ carried a box of Castrol engine oil in the trunk of his second-, third-, or fourth-hand ford Pinto. TJ took that drive as frequently as he could. In the Bible, God parted the Red Sea, caused an ax head to float, poured out fire from heaven with the prophet Elijah and raised people from the dead. Was it difficult for him to allow a "lemon" of a car to make a ten-hour round trip highway drive? The Ford Pinto was not a reliable vehicle at all, but every time that vehicle successfully made the trip. TJ drove to Atlanta in that car and had *no problem whatsoever*! In those days, the relationship he had with his oldest sister whom he adored and his older brother whom he idolized. They both kept him encouraged. Atlanta was not home in the sense of North 18th Street, but there were two people in Atlanta, who were family members and part of the background of home. TJ lived the entire five-day workweek in those days just to get a long weekend in order to travel to Atlanta, Georgia, as often as he possibly could.

As God does in his own way because the Bible says his ways are past finding out and his thoughts are not our thoughts. As high as heaven is from the earth so are his thoughts and his ways from our ways (Isa. 55:8–9; Rom. 11:33). Through all the emotional drama and homesickness and sinful things he experienced in the early days at Cecil Field, Florida, God placed TJ in a strategic location. TJ was compelled to enter a slightly open crack in the doorway of the beginning of a new relationship with God. That relationship would start at a church in Atlanta, Georgia, under the ministry of a man who at the time to TJ appeared to be genuinely called of God and lead of the spirit of the Lord. Dr. Jonathan Greer of Cathedral of Faith would be the man of God TJ would become introduced to in those days. In those days, what little TJ knew of Dr. Greer would greatly impact his life and his faith. After attending Cathedral of Faith on a Sunday morning through Sunday school and morning worship, TJ would return to Cecil Field, Florida, with a renewed vitality and expectation of quantum leaps in God beyond what he knew.

There was something about that Church of God in Christ in those days that left TJ spellbound and electrified and hopeful and expecting. The Showers of Blessings choir was a wonderful choir. Each singer on the choir, every single choir member, had a look on their face while singing and radiance as if heaven itself shown down its approval of their singing. Up to that point in his life, never had he experienced a choir so melodious and voices so trained and complete with zealous fire for the Lord. They sang as if they were truly free from the cares of this world. TJ began to realize that *everyone* in life has things to overcome and issues they may be dealing with. But to observe the expressions on the face of each choir member and to listen to them sing, it appeared they did not have a care in the world. Maybe it was the singing that helped to put them in that state of mind. Maybe the church itself was so pleasing to God that everyone that stepped foot in that place really experienced "showers of blessings." Maybe they just were really saved, born again, and living godly lives and not perpetrating a Christian experience. Nonetheless, Cathedral of Faith in Atlanta, Georgia, formerly Jones Avenue in the days of TJ's parents, became the place of a deep well of deliverance for him in those days. Even though he had to travel many hours, the long travel up and down Interstate 10 was well worth the time spent. The highway driving compelled him to think about his life as a youth and to think long and hard of the decisions he would make in the future.

The first Sunday TJ visited was the most unforgettable church service he had ever experienced in his life. Maybe because his spirit was drenched and deeply parched with sorrowful emotions and the life of sin. Maybe because his mind was in such a roller coaster ride and indecisive thoughts that his spirit yearned for what he knew of Christianity. Or maybe because God saw fit to logistically have him stationed in Jacksonville, Florida, that if he were thirsty and hungry enough he would search out God. And search him out did the young man do without reluctance and without fear. He knew he needed a turning of the soil in his heart because his ground was sinfully broken up. He was in need of a fresh visitation in spirit, mind, and soul from that which he believed to be true and right. That first Sunday would dash him with just a teaspoon of what would come later. Sunday school was refreshing, soothing, and enlightening. He remembers his older sister, telling him to go over to the men's class, and that's where he would see the pastor of the church. Cathedral of Faith was a large church with four aisles, if he remembers correctly. A large red brick church that appeared to be in very good condition. The red bricks on the outside of the church looked to be pointed precisely and freshly cleaned, and the windows of the church appeared to be airtight and glistening with cleanliness. The windows appeared not to even have a fingerprint on them. The inside of the church was immaculately maintained, natural wood pews with a large hundred-foot-wide stage with the choir directly behind the quorum of ministers. There was wide white molding gracing the trim of the ceiling and what appeared to be newly perfectly red carpet throughout the church. Each classroom was in pristine condition, and the inside of the church actually had a soft soothing fragrance. The first church for him to have a nice fragrance inside that he had ever experienced. The church smelled fresh and clean. Cathedral of Faith in Atlanta, Georgia, in those days was an exceptional Church of God in Christ. He stepped into a place that his mind and spirit were all too familiar with. Perhaps in the scheme of things, God meets his children where they are in their understanding.

Dr. Greer and the Blessing

The entrance of Dr. Greer into the already in progress Sunday service was captivating without any fleshly or human fanfare that TJ could tell. The choir was singing, and people were in the pews, some standing and clapping along with the choir, others sitting and singing or rocking back and forth. Still, others who appeared to be completely satisfied to be in that church. When Dr. Greer made his entrance, everyone stood to acknowledge him as he walked down the aisle TJ was able to get a glimpse of him. He made his entrance down the center aisle, and TJ was one aisle over from where Dr. Greer walked with a crowd of people blocking his view. But as providence would have it, as he passed by TJ's section of the pew, TJ was able to gaze for a brief moment at him and what appeared to be a regal man ready to engage in spiritual matters caught his eye. He wore what looked like a tailor-made robe green and white in color with a short cape down to his waist and a longer robe that covered his entire body. He held his Bible in his right arm as if to be carrying his tried and true weapon. He did *not* "strut" down the aisle but rather confidently, in a respectable manner. He was erect, tall, and stately looking as he walked. When Dr. Greer took his position on the pulpit, everyone was bid to take their seats as the choir continued to sing with the full intensity of spirit and soul. The choir sang until TJ imagined the walls to roar and loosen their foundation. The choir sang until the entire congregation, whether people were believers or not, was in the spirit of praise and worship with one mind. For TJ, the experience at Cathedral of Faith that summer Sunday was a church experience phenomenon. After the choir finished singing, there were a few preliminaries before Dr. Greer got up to speak. There where announcements, more singing, offering, and other typical church business. The heart of TJ was palpitating because he was in DEEP expectation of the words the man of God was prepared to serve to the children of God. TJ sat through the preliminaries, but his spirit was yelling from within, "I'm ready, I'm ready! Speak to me! Please speak to me!"

But there was one more song the choir had prepared to sing before the man of God would become immersed in the Word and speak into the spirit of the expecting audience.

"We Are Receiving Showers of Blessings" was the name of the song and the name of the choir. Amazingly enough, not only did that song minister to TJ, the song reached into the bottomless darkness of TJ's heart and resurrected his spirit as he became almost lifeless while taking it in. TJ had walked a path of disobedience while stationed at NAS San Diego, California. With presence of mind, he engaged in sinful practices while at Cecil Field, Florida. The deep chasms of his soul knew he needed a revival that only a real and true God could give. Actually, he was clueless of how deeply the revival would take place inside his soul and spirit, and he did not even know what to expect of a revival in spirit. But Showers of Blessings set the tone of what he was about to hear and what he was about to experience. In fact, the upcoming experience was so mind-blowing and so direct that TJ was speechless the entire ride back to Cecil Field, Florida. For five hours and twenty minutes on the ride back to Cecil Field, for the first time in his life, TJ was "in the spirit of the Lord. His mental acuity seem to be razor-sharp while driving back to Cecil Field for five hours and twenty minutes straight. The song, the preaching, and the total experience the first day he visited Cathedral of Faith imprinted an indelible mark deep down inside his soul. "We are receiving showers of blessings, that are sent to us from Heaven above. The Lord has promised that he would bless us, not just our souls, but our bodies as well" He could never know the blessings that awaited him from that day forward and the lyrics of that song rang and rang in TJ's mind and heart for weeks on end. For once, TJ had found what he desired and wanted from God; "assure me you are with me." Everyone who would obey the voice of the Lord through the man of God would receive unmitigated showers of blessings throughout the week and month. Little did TJ know the blessings he received from that visit continued for the entire time he was stationed at Cecil Field. When the choir began to sing the song "We are Receiving Showers of Blessings," TJ's eyes immediately, and I mean immediately, filled with tears. His eyes were so filled he was unable to clearly see the choir or anyone around him. The tears did not run down his face; they kind of sat there, almost waiting for a cue. So he gave them the cue. When he slightly touched his face, the tears ran like a stream. His heart was beating like a jackhammer inside as if to break up and evict an unauthorized visitor who had taken up residence. The Showers of Blessings choir sung and sung and sung to the top of their voices without missing a note or straying off-key. They sang with perfect sound, perfect pitch, perfect highs, and soothing lows. They sang the song "We are Receiving Showers of Blessings," as if angels from heaven were directing their queue and leading them. They sang that song with perfect praise that TJ was convinced the devil himself was gruelingly angry that TJ was in that church on that day. TJ also believed that Showers of Blessings drove any presence of the devil from that place. Not that the presence of the devil could ever have taken up residence at Cathedral of Faith. But just in case he hitched a ride inside someone's heart, in TJ's mind, the devil *could not have stayed*! The blessings from heaven that day made the devil run like a jackal without a home and without a place to hide.

As if the entire experience was not earth shaking enough, there was breaking up of fallow ground after fallow ground in the life of TJ. When Dr. Jonathan Greer stood up to speak the message for that Sunday, the first words out of his mouth were spectacular! The spirit of TJ became captivated as he physically sat at attention in the pew.

Dr. Greer said, "The Lord brought you hear today to revive your spirit and to set you on the right track!"

This may have been a common saying of Dr. Greer, and someone may call it a coincidence that he would say that. But at that time, on that day, when TJ was there, he said that. TJ refused to accept *any* of those rationales. Dr. Greer, through the leading of the spirit of God, spoke directly to TJ on that Sunday morning just prior to TJ going overseas for the first time. TJ was sitting in the pew with his Bible open, ready for the reading of the Scripture from him, but he never looked down at his Bible from that point on. His eyes were fixed on Dr. Greer, and his face was broken up and drenched with uncontrollable tears. Why did Dr. Greer say "you"? Why didn't he say, "Welcome to Cathedral of Faith," or something along those lines? But Dr. Greer said, "The Lord brought you!" TJ took that very personally and rightfully so because he knew the Lord led him to attend that church that day to get revived. He knew that he was sinking and sinking fast into a life of sin and wicked practices, and he seemed to be enjoying pleasing his flesh. The remainder of Dr. Greer's message was all about how the Lord was going to revive "YOU" and to look for total blessings the remainder of the week throughout the month. After the church service, he purposely lagged way behind his sister so he could shake Dr. Greer's hand. It was a daunting task because Dr. Greer was protected, sort of guarded as he was standing to the rear of the sanctuary. TJ's sister would occasionally look at him with a smile of approval, sensing that TJ was getting revived in spirit. She was satisfied that TJ had come to Atlanta and attended her church. Through the hustle and bustle of the congregants that day, finally, TJ was at the exit of the church. Dr. Greer was standing their sort of waiting to greet TJ, and TJ shook the hand of the man of God that spoke deep into his heart. His impression of Dr. Jonathan Greer exploded into devout respect, and he was honored that Dr. Greer acknowledged him. TJ was full of anxiety because he felt like Dr. Greer would be able to discern the backslidden state TJ had come in with, and TJ anticipated a rebuke from the minister. On the contrary, the minister was very kind and almost reverentially and fatherly compassionate. What Dr. Greer said to TJ as they shook hands, for the first and last time ever in TJ's life, "Take the Lord with you, son, everywhere you go, because he will never leave you no matter where you go!"

TJ was convinced beyond convinced that God directed him to Cathedral of Faith and particularly used the lips and tongue of his servant Dr. Jonathan Greer in that one visit alone to resurrect his life. Cathedral of Faith was a brief experience in the life of TJ, but what an unbelievable godly impression the entire experience deeply impressed itself in TJ's spirit.

"Take the Lord with you son everywhere you go, because he will never leave you no matter where you go"—that personal word from the man of God would be added with the prayer of the prayer warrior mother, "Favor! Give him favor with his officers and men! Favor, Lord, Favor, Lord, Give him favor!"

The words of faith spoken by Dr. Greer carried TJ year after year after year as he pondered the experience. He spoke to his sister of how awesome the entire visit to Cathedral of Faith was on the way back to her house. On his drive back to NAS Cecil Field, Florida, he began receiving the first wave of blessings. His Ford Pinto, by today's standards, would be considered a safety hazard on the road, but back then you did not have strict vehicle inspection requirements, nor did you have emissions testing, especially in the state of Florida.

The Pinto was a four-speed transmission in the floor, and the gear shifter would actually come out of the housing into TJ's hand *while* the car engine was running and the car was in motion. At sixty miles per hour, TJ floundered with the gear shifter, trying to put it back into the housing to continue driving the car. All the while the car would be slowing down because he could not change gears. On the long five-hour drive back to Cecil Field, this particular time took him every bit of six hours because he took his good ol' time savoring the experience at cathedral. The total opposite of the experience on the train ride to boot camp where he wanted to leave his sleeping quarters to get far away from the freshness of home in his mind. On this trip, he wanted to stay close to the freshness of the experience at Cathedral of Faith. Concerning the Pinto, for six hours not once did the gear shifter come out of the housing, until he arrived at Cecil Field, Florida! Normally the gear shifter would come out of the housing regularly while operating that car, but that time, it remained intact for the six-hour trip. Was that a blessing? TJ considered it blessing number 1. Not that he was counting blessings. It was just the first of several throughout the month. Within the month, he got promoted to 3rd class petty officer, equivalent to a corporal in the army and marines. That was blessing number 2. The promotion gave him an increase in pay to help pay off his new car loan. Then he received a check for $500 that was owed to him from Uncle Sam. He was not expecting the check and therefore had no expectations of getting money, which he considered blessing number 3. And the blessings continued to flow all the way up to his experience onboard the USS *Independence* (CV-62) at the port of call in Naples, Italy. The roller coaster ride with sin would resurrect and capture his five senses. He would drift away from the Lord in the most horrible and worst way possible. Sort of like a child sliding down a sliding board—backward. The drifting was not just his personal experience but an experience that would involve other people and threatened to bring serious military infractions.

Grace is the word in the Bible to describe God's unmerited favor toward his creation. TJ would discover that God showed a double, if not a quadruple, measure of grace toward him throughout his entire naval career. Time after time, TJ believes the grace and mercy of God should have run out on him. But there was the real actual living God of the Bible that he was yet to meet in a personal relationship. TJ sang about God in church services, danced on the church floor because of God, and read the Bible about God. But he was yet to meet God. The experiences the young lad would face overseas for the first time at nineteen years old would be things that never entered his mind as a boy. In fact, he had no clue that such experiences could be had in life. TJ was like a young chicken just hatched, attempting to fly everywhere on his own. Never would he ever have known or thought possible the things he would do or learn while in Italy, France, Spain, and many European countries and cities. But these experiences were all used by God, the God whom TJ would come to understand as the Most High Elohym Yahuah instead of the plain and simple "God" identification.

The Most High Elohym Yahuah would form and fashion the person of Yahusha HaMashayak inside the spirit of TJ in the years to come. Christianity identifies Messiah by the name Jesus Christ. But the understanding TJ would gain over the years of the name would become the most explosive truth ever in all his life. The ignorance of life and living from the days of the projects through North 18th Street were his entrenched learning experience. Many times TJ fought like hell to remain ignorant. As the apostle Paul said that Mashayak would be formed in us (Galatiyim 4:19, Galatians). TJ longed for that forming but was clueless as to how it would arrive and with what life's experience it would manifest.

8

TOUR OF DUTY THE USS *INDEPENDENCE* (CV-62)

Norfolk, Virginia

Having visited Atlanta, Georgia, on several occasions before boarding the ship for the first time, TJ had become revived in spirit and renewed focus. He was now ready for whatever lay ahead. The next few chapters in his life will open and end with youthful excitement having been away from home for months at a time. Surviving Basic Training and becoming very familiar with homesickness and overcoming the onslaught. Committing sinful acts and got revived at Cathedral of Faith but continued to be tempted by the flesh. In those days, TJ prayed the same prayer over and over, "God, please help me not to do wrong. Please help me." It is perhaps the most mundane prayer in anyone's life. Nonetheless, TJ prayed in pure ignorant humility. TJ's mundane prayer was answered by God on many occasions. The prayer may not seem too passionate for some and may seem like a lifeless and faithless prayer, but it was all he knew. He strove to maintain his level and understanding of the church experience of Christianity. On every occasion of God answering him, he did not always identify that it was God answering his prayer. But in the long run, he began to acknowledge God and began to accept every time he thought God was answering his prayer.

Every new experience during his first enlistment was captivating down to loading and handling navy cruise boxes. Cruise boxes were large metal storage containers about the size of a footlocker and some even larger. These containers were used to pack items from each department that would be taken on board the ship. TJ was very excited when it came time to pack the cruise boxes. He was excited and anticipated boarding the ship the entire time they were packing. The anticipation of going aboard the ship were days full of both excitement and anxiety. He could not wait to see the real aircraft carrier and board his first aircraft carrier and naval vessel. In his mind, he was ready to travel and ready to handle the challenges he would face in the future. Prior to getting on board the ship, he worked half days because much of the office equipment was either stored in a cruise box ready to be shipped or already shipped to the boat. TJ used the free time he had to get the most out of the road hazard Ford Pinto and would drive around throughout Jacksonville, Florida. He would go to the mall and drive around to other places. He even attended several Churches of God in Christ through the week. He was trying to take in as much spiritual food that he could while he was still on land in the United States of America. In those youthful days, his worldly experience was greater than his understanding of the Bible. On his first deployment onboard the USS *Independence* (CV-62), short for *Indy*, he left his car in Atlanta at his sister's house while he was deployed. One day the time arrived for the remaining personnel of VS-31 to fly up to Norfolk, Virginia, to embark onboard the USS *Independence* (CV-62). The remaining squadron members boarded a navy aircraft from Cecil Field, Florida, just like boarding a commercial civilian airline with the exception that everyone onboard the plane was military from the pilot to the flight attendants. Kind of a different experience altogether to say the least, but very exciting. The early days of TJ's military career were simultaneously filled with homesickness and excitement. After being away from Harrisburg for almost a year, he had learned how to adjust to the homesickness. Excitement, pleasure, and total enjoyment became his life during those days and a life he learned to love very much. This was his first time in Norfolk, Virginia, and at this point, he had six different cities and states under his traveling belt and one foreign land before he had reached the age of twenty years old. The projects and North 18th Street were becoming relics in his mind and at the same time difficult memories to overcome. TJ had traveled to Chicago, Illinois (Great Lakes), San Diego, California, Tijuana, Mexico, Jacksonville, Florida, and Atlanta, Georgia. Atlanta, Georgia, was his boyhood dream state. Now he would be traveling to Norfolk for the first time. He did not get to know the cities and states he passed through very well starting with Chicago on his way to Great Lakes. He was able to explore some of San Diego due to a little bit of recruit freedom. He experienced an unforgettable experience in Tijuana, Mexico. Passed through Jacksonville, Florida, on his way to Cecil Field and was able to explore Jacksonville having purchased the unsafe Ford Pinto. He would travel to Atlanta, Georgia, and explore the peach city on long weekends. He would not learn Norfolk, Virginia, until returning from his first Mediterranean cruise. TJ was beginning to feel like he had matured by leaps and bounds and was quickly becoming very proud of himself and travels into the world. His life's experience was broadening exponentially and had leaped outside of the textbook beginning to enter the lands he dreamed of and imagined as a boy. During his first tour of duty between the ages of eighteen and twenty, he went to every city, state, and country he wanted to visit and did everything he wanted to do. He often dreamt about those places while living on North 18th Street. As far back as the seventh grade at Edison Junior High School, he read about the West Coast and places in Europe like Italy and Spain. He would sit in his mother's room when she was sick, waiting for her to get better and would read books about Europe and traveling abroad. He wanted so desperately to visit those places, and for years he sought to understand the providence of having those dreams and desires fulfilled. He would not come to understand until decades later how these things unfolded. This was his path to travel, and he was about to be launched into a world he could have *never* known otherwise. Fred, Bay, Dad, Mom and his other siblings would not even begin to imagine the experiences that lay ahead for him. TJ's life was about to experience the enormous depth of purging and growth he would come to know. Seeing the

USS *Independence* (CV-62) for the first time and boarding her to cross the mighty Atlantic Ocean, was the official beginning of TJ becoming the Sailor. His life would be unlocked on untold levels of experience. The words of Fred, "When you leave, you can never come back" would resonate with each waking moment and become relevant for the first time in the life of TJ, the Sailor.

The USS Independence (CV-62)

March 1977, the squadron arrived at Norfolk Naval Air Station from Naval Air Station Cecil Field, Florida. The squadron crew debarked the aircraft just like a civilian commercial airline but all military personnel. The squadron personnel entered the passenger section of the building to claim their luggage and get mustered in for roll call after everyone had picked up their luggage. Once all personnel had been accounted for, they boarded a bus waiting for them outside the front entrance of the terminal. The bus was the size of a large Greyhound bus with space for luggage underneath.

From the moment the aircraft touched down on the runway, TJ was about to explode with excitement, attempting to get a feel of Norfolk Naval Air Station. It was huge and was spread out a lot larger than Cecil Field, Florida. There seemed to be a lot going on at Norfolk Naval Air Station along with their transport from Florida to Norfolk. TJ could not wait for the bus to be on its way to get to the pier where the *Indy* was docked. He heard all sorts of stories about being on board the ship from KS and the other brothers in the squadron. Most of them did not like the ship and pretty much had negative things to say. TJ gives KS credit for being objective about the ship. Of all the childish ways KS displayed and ridiculous things he did, he told TJ that he could not explain the ship to him, that he would have to experience it himself. Looking back on the comments of KS, TJ gained a good deal of respect for KS from that point on. Even though he continued to do and say things he did not agree with or approve of, KS dropped a tad bit of wisdom on him when he made that statement. TJ would have to experience the ship himself and draw his own conclusions.

A brother they called Mac was senior to TJ in rank and worked in the administrative office along with TJ. Mac liked TJ as a good friend, but Mac had absolutely no spiritual advice and did not seem to be interested in religion or the Bible. Mac was strictly a lady's man with a high tolerance of the disco era, and Mac boarded on imitating the likes of a "superfly" of the 1970s. Mac was a little over six feet tall and pretty much lived the life of a lover. He drove a sweet, always clean, blue Cadillac and had a coolness about him and swag that TJ was drawn to. Mac walked with a strut and drove his car with a certain lean to one side. TJ did not particularly agree with Mac's lifestyle, but Mac was a good brother. All the white senior officers and white enlisted petty officers did not like Mac, and TJ slowly began to understand why. From what TJ could tell, Mac did not let them get to him, and they just did not like Mac's self-confidence and the fact that he was a black man with a certain swag and drove a fresh light blue Cadillac. Anyways, Mac said to TJ, "The ship was nice, and you just have to get used to it, young sailor."

There were times Mac would call TJ, Tim and other times he would call him Timmy. But TJ particularly liked the identification of Sailor. From that point, while boarding the USS *Independence* (CV-62), TJ began to see himself as a Sailor of the sea. When he met Mac and rode in his Cadi for the first time, Mac was playing an eight-track tape of the rock group the Bee Gees. Surprisingly enough, the stereo inside Mac's car sounded nice. He did not ride much in his car, nor did any other brother in the squadron. Mac was very particular about his Cadi, and it was rare to see *anyone* sitting in the passenger seat.

There was a small detachment that stayed on board whatever ship the squadron was assigned to and would maintain squadron quarters and other duties as assigned. Subsequently, there were other squadron members TJ had not met but would meet during the cruise, and their influence on his life would become monumental in a good way. Frank was the other brother TJ would meet, and he would influence TJ in a sibling type of way. At this point in TJ's life, only God knew the future of his life and repeatedly poured his grace on him during those days. That cruise would reveal that TJ, the Sailor, was like a ship without a sail. He would become tossed and driven on the ocean of life, seemingly at will.

TJ had been schooled by Mac, and even KS, on how to board the naval vessel. As a Sailor there are certain protocols boarding and leaving the ship. You can't just walk on the ship without respecting her and requesting permission. Sailors, like many, liked to personify man-made things as "her," as though the ship is a living, breathing person of the feminine characteristics. The late rear admiral Francis D. Foley, US Navy (retired), wrote "Ships are referred to as "she" because men love them, but this encompasses far more than just that…She is greatly admired when freshly painted and all decked out to emphasize her cardinal points. If an aircraft carrier, she will look in a mirror when about to be arrested, and will wave you off if she feels you are sinking too low or a little too high, day or night. She will not hangar around with duds, but will light you off and launch you into the wild blue yonder when you muster a full head of steam."

When TJ first set eyes on the USS *Independence* (CV-62), docked at pier 12 at Naval Station Norfolk, Virginia, he fell in love with her! When the bus arrived at pier 12 and squadron members were getting off the bus, he sort of lagged behind in the rear of the bus full of nervous, anticipatory, unknown excitement. Mac yelled out. "C'mon, young sailor, get a move on it! We have to check in and put our stuff away so we can leave this boat!"

Incidentally, *boat* was the slang name for a naval seagoing vessel. Although it was a massive man-o'-war ship the length of three football fields, oftentimes sailors would call it "the boat." The excitement welling up in the young sailor was as if he were about to enter an amusement park for the first time in his life. All kinds of butterflies were loosely flying around in his belly. He felt an electrical charge of energy shoot from the depths of his stomach, up through his spine when he laid eyes on the ship for the first time. He did not want to board the ship along with everyone else. He wanted to stand on the pier and gawk at the massive steel man-made war vessel. Taking his good old time until everyone was off the bus and struggling with his seabag, step by step, disembarking the bus. His feet hit the ground, and he slowly made his way around the bus to get a clear full view for the first time ever the USS *Independence* (CV-62). Time began to slip away as he stood there gazing. But how long did he stand there with mouth slightly open, seabag dropped on the ground? As he slowly scanned the ship from bow to stern, from keel to mast, from port to starboard, completely spellbound. Precisely at this point, he was not sure if growing up in the projects and North 18th Street was a dream, or if standing on the pier glaring at the *Indy* was a dream. Analytical thinking was birthed inside his mind from that day forward. TJ, the Sailor, had to decide that one of the two realities of his life was the past and the other was the present. The site of the USS *Independence* (CV-62) consumed his past, and his future appeared unending. He did not want to return to Harrisburg, Pennsylvania, and was afraid of the thought to revisit North 18th Street. The times and experiences of growing up had now qualified for several chapters in a book in the mind of TJ. The United States Navy would fill a good portion of that book. The sight of the USS *Independence* (CV-62) had opened a gateway that was unimaginable, unbelievable, and totally unsuspecting. TJ entered the doorway full of anticipation as the sailor was born.

First Mediterranean Cruise

The young Sailor struggled up the gangplank, the last one boarding the vessel, and observed the other sailors before him so he could follow proper boarding protocol. Mac said, "Do everything I do." The young Sailor was like a child in a brand-new world, the world of the United States Navy. He would become a member of representing the United States government on behalf of the president of the United States. The military world and the world of politics are closely intertwined, and Sailor was about to receive a slow, step-by-step lesson on how to live and survive in the military's world. There were times learning and survival was fast-paced, and other times seemed to drag along. Understanding how the military and politics intertwine would be a revelation sometime later in his career. In fact, during his second and third tour of duty, the revelation would come as a shock. Sailor watched Mac and did everything Mac did, and when Sailor got to the brow of the ship, he immediately dropped his seabag on deck, turned, and saluted the ensign. He then turned and saluted the officer of the deck (OOD). With a drill team, snap salute, for the first time Sailor said, "Request permission to come aboard, sir!"

The OOD replied by saying, "Permission granted!"

Lifting up his seabag in a quick motion and basically on the heels of Mac, he was enthusiastically strutting down the passageway toward his new quarters for the next 7 months. From that point on, the young TJ had transitioned from one life into another life as the United States Navy Sailor. Basic Training, West Coast, East Coast, Naval Air Station, and ultimately boarding the ship made him a Sailor. For the next three years, he was a proud member of the United States Navy and proud to be an American. Pride would become his thriving heartbeat with every step he took. The emotional changes and homesickness of the past year had now taken its place as a memory in his mind. The homesickness was sealed in his thoughts as an experience of growing up. Unfathomable sadness and ardently charged self-pity were no longer the ruling emotions in his life. Excitement about traveling and gaining knowledge of the world had now taken a seat in the frontal lobe of Sailor's brain. He could not wait for the ship to get underway. He anticipated what it would sound like, what it would feel like sailing on the massive war vessel of the USS *Independence* (CV-62). He looked forward to the everyday sounds and activity on a war vessel. What would the evenings be like confined to a war vessel at sea? How would he feel leaving the United States of America, the only place he had known and the best country in the world? Although Sailor had much to learn and would adjust his views in the years to come, for the moment, his pride as an American sailor was immutable in his mind. He wondered for a moment how much would he think about home and his experience growing up? Every thought was powerful and charged with moving feelings. Sailor had now convinced himself that the projects and North 18th Street were not a dream. Those days were simply leftovers of reality that had lost its power to enthrall him in the past. The reality of being onboard the naval vessel was so overwhelming to the young Sailor, that EVERYTHING about growing up seemed to be something that was experienced by someone else and not TJ, the Sailor. The Mediterranean Cruises of 1977, 1978, and 1979 would be the crowning, the most joyful, memorable, and thrilling tours of duties in the United States Navy. TJ would transition in full form to become Sailor, who had traveled the world. Both Med. cruises were beyond any college courses he could have ever taken. His life's experiences during those tours of duty catapulted his growth in such a way he would have *never* known had he gone straight to college, or if he had gotten employed on some mediocre job. At least, that was the conclusion in the mind of Sailor after a few years of traveling the world. A further conclusion of Sailor was that joining the United States Navy was his decision but one, he believed, which was sanctioned by God. The world became his platform and course of learning. States, countries, the ocean, and naval vessels of war was his classroom, and his teacher was the spirit of God. The angels of God were dispatched to be his hall monitors to keep him on task. Angels also served as protectors over Sailor's sometimes foolish choices and childlike exploratory heart. He would go astray often and walk the wrong path willingly. His going astray was disobedience to the Word of God, yet compliance to being a youth. And in that state of disobedience and compliance, he began to see God in an unexplained and unpreached light that none of his mentors spoke of.

During the Med. cruise of 1977, Mac sort of took on the role as Sailor's mentor. Sailor worked side by side with Mac in the admin office, and he looked to Mac for worldly advice. Sailor hadn't totally relinquished his upbringing and religious beliefs at this point, but since he had entered the world of the military and the world of travel, he sought advice from a man of the world. When the two sailors arrived at their sleeping quarters, other squadron members were passing out linen and pillows. Everything was fresh and clean. The navy was starting to impress the young Sailor, and he couldn't get enough of it. He gladly received his sheets, pillow, and gray US Navy blanket and quickly finding a bunk to claim as his own. He chose the middle bunk of a three-tier bunk system. He was able to move to the top bunk later on in the cruise when a sailor transferred from the squadron. At once, the training received at boot camp was starting to make sense and everything was coming together. In boot camp, all the recruits slept in an open barracks with a two-bunk tier system. Little did he know at the time, it was a pattern of what quarters would be like onboard a naval vessel. A satisfying smile came upon his face as he thought about the excessive emotional changes he had endured and overcome. Sailor made his bunk with perfect forty-five-degree angles at the corners. He flipped a quarter in the air over his bed so that it would fall on the made-up bunk to see if the quarter would bounce. The quarter did bounce. Sailor was personally and deeply proud of himself. Over the past year, he traveled places he only dreamed about and had conquered soul-searching areas of his heart, areas that he was clueless existed. For the first time since leaving home, Sailor felt that he had adjusted into the United States Navy. The spirit of pride began to flood his soul. Sailor could not control, nor was he aware of how proud he had become and would embrace the spirit of pride for the next thirty-years plus.

Everything was in place, and Sailor had emptied his seabag and put all his stuff away into the locker bed and stand up lockers for his uniforms. He then asked Mac how to get to the chow hall, and Mac said, “Follow me and I will take you there.” Learning the ship involving frame numbers, forward, aft, topside, hangar bay, flight deck, port, starboard, captain’s mast, crow’s nest was easy as reading a book. It seemed to all come naturally to Sailor. Maybe because of his youthfulness, maybe because of his excitement or maybe because of a good memory. Nonetheless, Mac and Sailor went down below, starboard side, and stood in line at the aft galley. The ship had a distinct smell. It was not a smell of stench, rather a smell of seafarer, but the smell had to grow on him. He was taking it all in as it was defining his memory of the past and developing his memory of the future. The ship, the bunk, the crew, the galley, and the galley line had somehow or another launched him into becoming independent onboard the USS *Independence* (CV-62). He was ready for the world, with his chest poked out, his shoulders arched, and a stride in his walk was saturated with fleshly pride. He had come a very long way down the road of maturity and had even a longer road to travel toward humility. Not knowing that one day he would experience an incredible fall laced with ego, pride, and selfishness. But until then, the experiences that lay ahead on board the *Indy* would become lifelong memories.

Underway "Shift Colors"

The transit from the United States of America at Hampton Roads, Virginia, to the Mediterranean Sea through the Straights of Gibraltar, was the most exciting and memorable experience then. On the morning of March 31, 1977, the USS *Independence* (CV-62) got underway for the first time with the new Sailor onboard. Unhooking that massive ship from the pier was sort of like disengaging his soul from the recent past of North 18th Street. He was been released from a world of childhood into a world of incredibly awesome adventure. True to the United States Navy's slogan: "It's not just a job, it's an adventure." A world of untold and unimaginable experiences lay ahead. A world of unknown danger and a world of sin and debauchery unbeknownst to Sailor at the time. Like in the projects looking a distance over to state street bridge, Sailor knew nothing of the world beyond the projects, and he knew nothing of the world he was entering. But somehow or another, the unknown world was calling to him to explore the vices of life and enjoy the mind-broadening experiences to be had. The boatswain's mate called away, "Now set the sea and anchor detail." This meant the crew assigned to unmooring the ship went to work to release the tie-down moors from the chocks on the pier and allow the ship to slowly move away from the pier to set sail. When the last moor was released, the boatswain's mate sounded the most thrilling announcement over the 1 Main Circuit, or short for 1MC, "Underway, shift colors!" This meant the ship was moving—it was sailing! As unnoticeable as it may have been, once the ship was unmoored and undocked, she was underway. Sailor ran up on deck to view the scenery as they were moving away from the pier and to get one last glance at Norfolk Naval Station. He had begun his quest to enter the journey of a lifetime. The life of extreme naïve childhood quickly became extinct. In many respect, the childhood boy was still alive inside the heart of Sailor because the whole event of being onboard the USS *Independence* (CV-62) was almost like being outside playing with a new toy. Amid all his excitement, he wanted his brothers Fred and Bay to be with him and see what he was seeing. He imagined running in the house at North 18th Street and yelling, "Hey, look at me! I'm on the ship and I'm about to travel the world!" He held on to the childhood fantasy locked inside his soul as long as he could. But in a few short months, essentially, the child of TJ would be crucified, never, ever, to rise again.

He stayed on deck for as long as he could, knowing he had to go down below to his workspace and get to work. Incidentally, his immediate supervisor, sort of like his personal instructor, was a five-foot-four chubby white man. Sailor perceived that he may have been a nerd in high school, and only God knows how much Sailor tried to like that guy. But he was a constant irritant and slightly intimidated Sailor. The guy was not that brilliant, but the struggle Sailor had was learning how to deal in the white man's world with the very limited knowledge and experience he had. Funny thing about his supervisor is that he was only one rank higher than Sailor, but the guy took the rank structure and limited authority he had *very, very* seriously. In hindsight, Sailor thought the guy was being rated by his supervisor on how he trained him in navy administration duties. Nonetheless, before Sailor made his way back down to his working space, he realized that he could feel the massive keel of the ship sailing and making her way toward Hampton Roads Tunnel. He stood on deck taking mental picture after mental picture of the shoreline of Virginia as frame after frame passed through his mind. It was amazingly exciting beyond his most imaginable dream. As if the dreams he had while sitting in mom's bedroom, gazing out her window, wishing to be able to travel the world, had providentially come true. Nothing could outdo the excitement he was experiencing then. Boatloads of excitement and unforgettable brushes with death awaited him as time moved on. The deep emotional past was still in his hip pocket, and he could pull them out every now and then like a man pulls his wallet out of his pocket. He would scan through sections of his past and slowly, slowly began to archive them. Sailor was growing up in almost a mind-blowing manner. Events, situations, places he visited and things he did were being recorded deep inside his soul in living color. Memories were being formulated and experiences were being embraced as two lovers perpetually embrace one another in the early stages of a relationship. Sailor was in love with being in the United States Navy and called the USS *Independence* (CV-62), "my ship" and personified the boat as "her."

The Storm of 1977

Of all the experiences and love affair Sailor developed with the boat, the sea, and the squadron, none was more poignant than crossing the great Atlantic Ocean on April 7, 8, and 9, 1977.

The storm on the Atlantic Ocean would be the experience of a lifetime. One of those events that as a youngster only comes once because the circumstances will never exist again. The pictures are actual US Navy official pictures taken by the photographers on board the *Indy* during the storm. From keel to the mast, the USS *Independence* (CV-62) measures in height to a twenty-five-foot story building. The following official report from a navy website attempts to capture the intensity of the storm.

The USS *Independence* (CV-62) was one of the United States Navy's largest aircraft carriers. She measured twenty stories high, and this report says the seas were twenty feet high. This is a clear indication of the enormity of the storm. It was exciting! It was adventurous! It was scary! All in a matter of nine days from leaving the pier at Norfolk Naval Station, his first harrowing experience in the US Navy involved the mighty ocean unleashing her uncontainable might. It would seem the task group would have waded out the storm, but going through the storm and overcoming its formidable threat is the mark of a true Sailor. On the morning of April 7, 1977, over the 1MC the OOD announced the probability of sailing into a storm. Later that day the OOD called away, "General Quarters, general quarters, all hands man your battle station, now set condition Zebra throughout the ship." *GQ* and *Condition Zebra* meant the ship was armed and ready for battle. But what battle?

For about a millisecond, Sailor sat in his workspace wondering, *Is this for real?*

Immediately the OOD came back on the 1MC and said, "This is not a drill!"

This is not a drill seemed to happen frequently on board the *Indy*. Anyways, at that, all hands were on the mark, donning the oxygen breathing apparatus (OBA). Fire stations were immediately getting in place. Hatches were battened down in almost lickety-split speed. Personal clothing was being fixed for floatability in preparation for any incident that would breach the hull of the ship and take on water. The *Indy* and the task force continued to sail forward toward the destination of the Mediterranean Sea. As the day went on, the storm became boisterous. The caption of the images reads as follows:

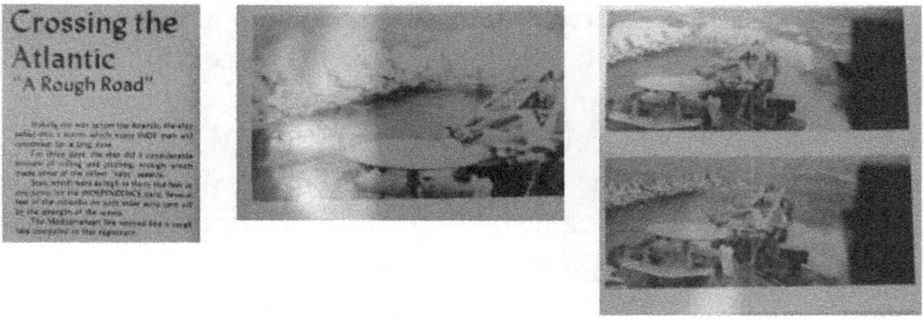

> April 7, 1977 – 1,000 miles west Rota Spain – All nine ships in US Navy Task Group 21.2 including USS Independence suffer varying amounts of damage when they encounter a storm with 20-foot seas. Some Independence planes land at Lajes Air Base, in the Azores. http://navysite.de/cvn/cv62.htm
>
> Making our way across the Atlantic, the ship sailed into a storm, which many INDY men will remember for a long time. For three days, the ship did a considerable amount of rolling and pitching, enough which made some of the oldest "salts" seasick. Seas, which were as high as thirty-

> five feet at one point, hit the INDEPENDENCE hard. Several feet of the catwalks on both sides were torn off by the strength of the waves. The Mediterranean Sea seemed like a small lake compared to this nightmare.

This official report from *on board* the *Indy* by the photographers bears a truer account than the report on the navy website. The USS *Independence* (CV-62), in Sailor's assessment, was getting thrown around in the ocean like a small canoe. The twenty-five-foot-high steel structure was no match for the mighty ocean. But the choice and decision to sail forward to the destination was an official United States Navy choice. Without compromise, the mission had to be completed. Sailor thought about the small boys, as they are called, DDGs, FFGs, the smaller escorts of the battle group. At the beginning of the storm, Sailor could see these ships, and at times he could see only the bow of the ship. Within a second, it appeared the entire ship was submerged, then the bow would reappear. He thought, *If old experienced salts were getting sick on board the* Indy, *what of the sailors on board the smaller vessels?*

For Sailor, the storm was sort of a prediction of sorts. This was his very first time ever leaving the United States of America. The storm at sea, for Sailor, acted, sort of like, how the future of his life would unfold. The most disturbing, upsetting, and distressing of all storms lay ahead for Sailor. Whether to conquer them or surrender to them would be the decision for Sailor, laying the foundation for the Sermon.

Batten Down the Hatches, The Storm Is Raging

Day 2 would escalate the storm to an event of terror for the USS *Independence* (CV-62), as if a battle was unleashed against her from the pit of hell. Sometime during day 2, the *Indy* came to a slow crawl, and both thirty-ton anchors were dropped in the ocean. The mighty USS *Independence* (CV-62) had become virtually a sitting duck. She was being plummeted, forward, midship and aft by the mighty Atlantic Ocean. Sailor decided to take a risky tour of the ship to experience the swells and hear the sounds of the wind and sea against the *Indy*. KS had said that if you walk forward, as forward as you could go, you could feel the forward part of the ship being lifted out of the water. Sailor couldn't resist, and he made his way past the officer's staterooms feeling more and more the intensity of the waves pounding the ship. As he got forward, almost near the fo'c'sle; or, forecastle—this is where the bow of the ship and where the anchor chains are housed—there was a swift rise like in a balloon and then a quick dip as if on a roller coaster. He was literally knocked off his feet!

"Damn! This is crazy! This is awesome! This is incredible!" Sailor walked around up forward in absolute blind ignorance, not understanding the horror of what was happening and the great potential of a breach in the hull of the ship. He was unauthorized to be in that section of the ship but went there anyway, isolated, with no one else around. Had to be one of those times that God excused his novice ignorance. The USS *Independence* (CV-62) sustained extreme damage both in the bow of the ship and the forward catwalks. Sailor was foolishly enjoying the highs and lows of the ship being lifted out of the water and almost treating his foolish experience as an amusement park amid certain danger.

Day 3 would be the crescendo of battering and pounding and damage, unbeknownst to just about every sailor on board that naval vessel. *Indy* was rolling, pitching, dipping deep in the ocean, and sounding like a hellish howl outside the ship. If Satan makes ungodly sounds and can engage the elements of the sky, the sea, and the land, those three days exposed the crew to the hellish acts of Satan at sea. They could hear the loud base sounding cries of the wind passing by and through the ship like a runaway locomotive.

When the waves reached up to thirty-five feet, they slammed directly into the bridge of the ship, mercilessly splattering saltwater directly on the triple-pane windows. Visibility was nearly zero percent, as *Indy* was still anchored at sea about 1,000 miles from Rota, Spain. On day 3, Sailor's excitement melted down, and an almost uncontrollable fear rose from deep within his soul. At nineteen, and this being his first experience at sea, Sailor began to wonder if three days was a bit too long to be in the eye of a storm at sea. Thoughts of ignorant excitement now transformed into fear of what to expect. Sailor thought the *Indy* would capsize, not even knowing if that were possible with such a large vessel. He feared the hull may be compromised and the ship would begin taking on water. In his youthful ignorant state of mind, he began to worry. Like the account at Cecil Field in the barracks when the novel thought came to mind to pray, the thought surfaced once more. For the second time, this time at sea, not far from Spain, it was in his best interest and his shipmates, for Sailor to call upon the Lord. He had a very novice prayer in those days, but looking back it seemed his God replied to those novice prayers as he heard the cries from a sincere, pure heart. He beckoned to God for peace of mind and relief from the grips of the ocean. He envisioned Satan holding on to the ship and harassing everyone on board with the storm. Sailor did not know about his shipmates, but his prayer simply was, "God, don't let this ship capsize, or sink or unable to sail forward." In the midst of the storm, working duties and responsibilities were still ongoing. The only crew who did not work during those days where the sick and shut-in. The entire 3rd day, *Indy* was taking on blow after blow after blow from the wind, waves, and rain. It was unthinkable the power that storm wielded against the United States Navy Task Force of 1977. The Ocean displayed her fury against the twenty-five story high war vessel. Later in the afternoon of the third day, toward the evening, the storm began to slowly dissipate, and the howling of the wind began to lessen. The rolling and pitching lightened up, and the lifting of the *Indy* out of the water had ceased! Could it be the storm was dying? Was it possible the storm would subside enough for the ship to resume underway? At first opportunity of a weakening storm, the captain saw fit to steam full ahead and waste no time retrieving the anchors from the sea.

Sometime in the early morning of April 10th, 1977, the OOD called away over the 1MC: "Now set the sea and anchor detail!" That meant retrieve those three-ton anchors back into the bow of the ship so they can sail at full speed ahead away from that vicious, almost evil storm. Once the anchors were retrieved out of the depths of the ocean, the next command from the OOD was, "Underway! Shift colors!"

That sounded sweeter than a jar of honey, and you could hear the cheers throughout *Indy*. The young Sailor now felt ten feet tall, imagining he had graduated into a real sailor of the sea. Three days of a brand-new experience untold under the proverbial belt of life. He could hear his shipmates yelling, "Yeah, yeah, yeah!" throughout the ship, and a few halleluyahs were thrown in every now and then. Sailor decided to express his own joy by shouting off with a couple of "halleluyahs" and "praise the Lord!" His ignorant excitement those three days went from an extreme curious high to a bottomless pit of fear. He embraced reverential prayer and deep respect for the Ocean and her fury. Sailor did not know about his shipmates on board the *Indy* during the storm, but he personally learned with a crash course on how to quickly turn his attention to his God in every life-threatening situation. He had not yet fully learned, nor did he comprehend how regularly he would call upon the Lord, or even trust in him when he was afraid. His test in life had only begun, and a ship without a sail became the epitome of his life during his early days in the United States Navy.

Naples, Italy, would be the next stop for the *Indy* because repair facilities and shipments from the United States would come into Naples. The crew did not know the degree of damage the *Indy* sustained, but the crew spent more than three weeks anchored off the coast of Naples while the ship was being prepared. It was reported that the USS *Independence* (CV-62) sustained a twelve-foot hole in the bow of the ship, and Sailor, like a young fool, was running around in the bow wanting to see what the hoopla was about. He easily could have become a casualty amid his foolish excitement. *Indy* also was damaged in the forward catwalks, both port and starboard, when twelve feet of the forward catwalks were ripped off the ship and thrown into the ocean somewhere. The mighty USS *Independence* (CV-62) was down hard, real hard. The battle-torn condition of the ship saddened Sailor. But the excitement level began to rise knowing that he and the crew survived the harrowing storm with their lives.

Not only did they survive, but it was also his first solid and sound experience of a sea story that he could tell for decades to those who never heard it before. Liberty in Naples, Italy, in April of 1977, was jaw-dropping for Sailor. His mind would be blown time after time. His adrenaline would flow and reach levels of intimate excitement. Naples would begin the fulfilled youthful dreams of a lifetime. TJ had quickly become just an experience of the past. The transformation of TJ into a real Sailor occurred on the ocean and culminated overseas in the truest sense. He was immensely enjoying *every* moment of his new life—every test, every storm, and even the storms to come. He thought that God was especially smiling down on him. Sailor had made it this far maintaining a sound mind and had accepted with open arms becoming a sailor. He was loving every minute of his new life. He strutted around the foreign land of Naples as though he owned it, like he had been there before, proud to be an American and part of the United States Navy. What he previously attributed to being homesickness turned out to be no more than labor pains of the birth of the Sailor inside. Sailor was born, and the eulogy of childhood life was being read. The Sermon was still decades in the making while the Sailor was developing his sea legs—egotistical, worldly, and a master at backsliding per traditional Christianity. TJ had grown up into a sailor of the sea and a world traveler. He was grown, and no one could not tell him that he was not grown. Already before reaching twenty years old, he had a wealth of experience. The next stop in Sailor's life would last for decades to come. It would be the world in pure form, and no stone was to be unturned. The vices of the world would reveal itself to Sailor's young mind. The vices of the world would become a friend to Sailor, and he would also learn how weak his foundation of Christianity was.

The crew did not realize the extent of damage the *Indy* sustained during those three days until they had endured the merciless, unforgiving storm on the Atlantic Ocean. Once underway it felt like the entire world was lifted off their backs and like the foot of Satan was removed from their neck. *Indy* was underway once more and sailing toward the destination. To Sailor, it felt good to be sailing forward. The USS *Independence* (CV-62) and her crew had literally weathered the storm sustaining significant damage. After the storm damage control could assess the damage inflicted upon the ship. To the crew's amazement, *Indy* had sustained a twelve-foot gash in the bow of the ship, and about twelve feet of the forward catwalk was remarkably ripped off the massive steel floating vessel designed to withstand a certain number of direct hits. Unfortunately, the direct hit from the ocean ripped through the steel without apology and without respect of the *Indy*'s size Her mission had been seriously interrupted. The ocean did not care about the reputation of the mighty fighting war vessel. The ocean in its fury spares no mercy. One must endure the trial at sea. HMS *Titanic*'s passengers and crew remain one of the most tragic civilian ocean liners to understand and to know the terror of the ocean. Whether a storm, iceberg, or battle, the ocean can be very unforgiving. The crew sailed directly to Naples, back then, basically the homeport in Europe for naval vessels on deployment She docked there for three full weeks. That's a long time to be sitting in port while the ship had to be repaired. The most a naval vessel would stay at a port a call was anywhere from one to two weeks, but three full weeks in port was a long time and time well spent.

9

TOUR OF DUTY
THE USS *INDEPENDENCE* (CV-62)
NAPLES, ITALY

The USNS Truckee (AO-147) after the Storm

And if the storm of 1977 while crossing the Atlantic Ocean was not enough to cause alarm, the USNS *Truckee* (AO-147), an oiler vessel whose primary mission was to fuel naval vessels, while underway was the cause of another incident at sea. Underway replenishment, or UNREP for short, involves all hands except embarked units like Sailor's of VS-31. UNREP is for replenishing the ship with supplies and fueling. Normally UNREP would begin early in the day and would last literally all day at times, from 6:00 a.m. all the way up to 9:00, sometimes 10:00 p.m. That makes for a long day and plenty of supplies for a crew of six thousand for a period of about thirty days or less and then you're back at UNREP again.

UNREP is one event Sailor had very little participation in but was caught on the working part every now and then and found himself in a line unloading milk, food, or supplies. April 20, 1977, not even two weeks apart from crossing the Atlantic Ocean. Ten days while in the Tyrrhenian Sea and positioning the *Indy* alongside the USNS *Truckee* for a scheduled UNREP, an accident at sea occurred. This caused Sailor great concern about the fate of his first Mediterranean cruise. They had just endured a titanic storm and survived. This was Sailor's first cruise, and he was not sure if these sort of things were common or if the cruise on board the USS *Independence* in the summer of 1977 was ill-fated. Sailor was in his bunk when he heard the boatswain's mate call over the 1MC, "Reveille, reveille, heave out and trice up, smoking lamp is lit throughout all authorized spaces, now reveille!"

About the same time, he heard a very loud bang, and the entire aircraft carrier shifted to starboard a little and then immediately went to general quarters (GQ). "General quarters, general quarters, all hands man your battle stations, set condition zebra throughout the ship, now general quarters!"

Almost as an afterthought the boatswain's mate came back on the 1MC and said, "This is not a drill!" The USNS *Truckee* had collided with the USS *Independence* (CV-62) while positioning herself alongside the *Indy* in preparation for UNREP. Sailor thought to himself how can two massive military naval vessels of which you have trained professional sailors onboard collide! He did not understand how that could happen. Ships, the sea, nautical terms, and sailing, all this was very brand-new to Sailor. He also learned of past accidents and mishaps on board naval vessels. Part of the training in boot camp involved watching the documentary of the USS *Forrestal* (CVA-59) fire that occurred in July 1967. The late Senator John McCain was at the center of that naval mishap. Sailor still could not understand how these trained professional military people could collide two massive warships. He had way too much confidence in the ability and expertise of military personnel, and he believed the United States military to be the best on the planet. How could these two vessels with years of experience at sea collide with one another? How could this have occurred? Didn't upset him too much because he was eager and zealous to learn. He had an overwhelming passion to discover everything he could in his new life. He did not want anyone to become injured or loss of life, and he did not even think on those terms. He knew he was experiencing things that far exceeded his friends back home of North 18th Street. Sailor was gaining sea story after sea story in quick succession. But he discovered later that the *Truckee* had a history of colliding with other vessels. The sea and the ocean are always the same in terms of swells and waves on the ocean, and as a sailor, you learn how to navigate the seas with minimal incidents. His first Mediterranean cruise would make a true sailor out of him and would unlock the love of the sea in his heart that he never knew he had.

The First Time Overseas

The excitement and adventure of the ocean had now passed. Ships company and embarked squadrons survived a harrowing experience that gave them all a reverence for God and an appreciation of life. There was a hushed silence on board the *Indy* while enduring the violent storm. For Sailor, though, the overseas life would be an altogether different experience. Overseas experiences would be one hundred percent personal and soul-searching. Both the storm and the USNS *Truckee* were corporate experiences involving the entire crews. Sailor was about to embark on a different roller coaster ride that at times appeared to be moving at a rate of speed that even he could not keep up with. If his new experiences were an actual roller coaster, the cars on the track may not have been able to make the sharp turns and deep drops. Naples, Italy, and places in Spain was the introduction to worldliness and sinful but exploratory events. Only the grace and mercy of God sustained Sailor and brought him through. His first sight of the Rock of Gibraltar while transiting the Strait of Gibraltar gave Sailor a feeling of being a world traveler. He heard about the Rock of Gibraltar only by the mentioning of its name in passing conversations. Fred would sometimes say something was, "like the Rock of Gibraltar." He did not fully understand the correlation between what Fred said and what the Rock of Gibraltar was. But he did understand it to mean something solid, huge, and unmovable. In April of 1977, for the first time Sailor laid his eyes on the famous Rock of Gibraltar, unlocking a worldview in his mind. His excitement was escalated to an uncontrollably high. Personal dreams of his were being fulfilled as if he was destined to have them fulfilled. Sailor was capturing images in his mind like the shutter speed on an SLR camera that would last a lifetime. He took pictures as did many sailors, and it appeared it may have been also the first time for other sailors on board the *Indy* that day. Don't know, maybe they were just taking pictures to add to their portfolio of travels. But Sailor was fascinated and full of overpowering anticipation to go ashore, to see, to touch the land of overseas. A small manageable degree of sadness found its way into his thoughts when he thought about his family and friends back home, wanting them to see what he was seeing. But he knew it was impossible for family and friends to see what he was seeing because his travel was at the expense of the United States government. The military foot the bill as he singularly signed a binding contract with Uncle Sam. His family and friends were not going to enlist in America's military just to partake of his experiences. However, the whole experience of Sailor's life and travels overseas was a road that only he could travel and was compelled to travel alone. Regretfully, over the years, the road Sailor traveled would distance him from family, not because he thought he was better than them but because he did not know how to use his learning and experiences to teach others and embrace their love.

Sailor would suffer many breakages and estranged relationships with the one family he loved so very much. In judging his own heart, Sailor came to realize the deep egocentric and unloving things about his own self of which he fought day and night to overcome once aware of them. Moving forward in life, all those feelings will become apparent to Sailor as the sermon emerges. The sight of the Rock of Gibraltar expanded his mind and thinking in one view. He grasped the fact that he had just crossed the Atlantic Ocean, weathered the storm, involved in a collision at sea, and now literally overseas and entering the Mediterranean Sea. Seeing the Rock catapulted Sailor's thoughts into an accelerate maturity level. Immediately he transcended years from the days of the projects and North 18th Street. Mount Calvary Church of God in Christ became a distant memory of religious stuff. Fred's words rang deep in his heart, and Sailor, for the first time, began to understand why he said, "You cannot come back home." It wasn't the physical return home that Fred referred to, but the spirit and life of home would now take on a different perspective altogether. It was immaturity versus maturity. It was worldly experience versus childhood experience. It was living inside the proverbial box versus exposure to outside of the box. Home would *never* be the same because TJ, the Sailor, would *never* be the same. Home was his only world as a child and the revealing of the bigger world was neatly packaging home into its own little box. Home would quickly become tucked away in his mind. He would hold on to certain memories strictly for sentimental purposes. His experiences from this point on would define life for him. All life's experiences would come as crash courses compelling him to learn. He envisioned himself as a teacher in the distant future, one who perhaps could enlighten others traveling similar paths as he and hope they would avoid certain unforgiving pitfalls.

As Fred's words rang deep in his heart, a new thing was about to take place in his life. He felt that he was grown or growing into becoming grown. He felt that he was on his own and life was an open field of experience after experience. He pridefully felt he was at liberty to do whatever he wanted to do and whatever he felt like doing. His religious training was like flashes of sunburst in his mind. His upbringing would remain a seed planted that would one day reveal a monumental change. The deep change in his religious beliefs would compel the great awakening in his spirit. At the same time as he was growing and maturing, he held on to the church experience and did not want it to go away. But with every sinful act that he performed he felt starved for spiritual enlightenment. He felt like a traitor to the Christian faith for the things he engaged in while overseas. Sailor's first experience overseas would be but child's play to his second and subsequent tours of duty overseas. The first experience forced him to learn because up to that point in his life he was full of curiosity about this and about that. He was desirous of worldly things, but in many cases, he just wanted to know and see what it was like. Sailor desired immense growth in all areas of his life. He diligently sought opportunity for both spiritual and personal growth and was open to whatever he would learn. His undisciplined spirit would lead him down a road that he possibly could have avoided. Growing up on North 18th Street and passionately attached to Mount Calvary Church of God in Christ, the world of his learning was deep inside a small box. He placed no blame on any past circumstances. He places the blame squarely on his inability to see and hear the countless temptations of the world. But as the record in the Scripture says, "The steps of a good man are ordered by the Lord" (Ps. 37:23). At that time, Sailor did not know which steps to follow. Still, his steps were ordered by God even though the understanding of what resided in his heart frightened him. At times, he could not believe the acts of sin he performed, and other times he welcomed sin. You see, God does not always guide our lives in such a way that would be acceptable to other people; rather, he guides our lives to teach us the things we would not readily accept as our own shortcomings. Once we live through the sinful ways and realize the wickedness in our own heart, sin then becomes appalling and we become remorseful, sort of like the movie *Evan Almighty* starring Morgan Freeman, who portrays the part of God. The scene when Mr. Freeman is talking to Lauren

Graham, the wife of the character Evan Baxter. In the restaurant, she is distraught about her husband building the ark in New York says to her that God provides opportunities. As a young church boy, Sailor had never heard or even considered the concept of opportunity, but in hindsight, it is obvious the school of life is filled with nothing but opportunity. It was not until years later that he could put Scripture to such a concept when in the book of Ecclesiastes, the writer says in chapter 9 at verse 11 that "time and chance happeneth to them all." In other words, *everyone* is afforded the chance and time in their lives to do what is right or wrong. A person's knowledge, understanding, and spiritual rebirth determine the road that will be traveled. Morgan Freeman, portraying God, said in the movie, "If he prayed for courage, does God give him courage, or does he give him opportunities to be courageous?"

He prayed to God about many things, especially after he committed the acts of sin. He lacked all the qualities of a godly man and prayed for traits of the spirit and did not realize then how God was answering his prayer. He prayed for integrity, unwavering mind, wits, courage, and the ability to understand the things he was experiencing. He prayed for victory over his weaknesses and for strong faith. He prayed for understanding of the Holy Scripture and the ability to know the difference between evil and good and for salvation of his wretched soul. Many prayers filled his request and desire of God during his military days. During the first time spent overseas, God continuously provided opportunity after opportunity to answer Sailor's prayers. He completely failed each opportunity and could not see how he was learning from the failed opportunities until decades later. When you read the first experiences overseas, you will understand why they happened and what God was performing inside his soul and the opportunities he presented before Sailor daily.

The Reign and Terror of Sin

Sailor realized he was not just across the border when he first stepped on the ground in real foreign land. He was about to enter a different school of life, unlike the time he went to Tijuana Mexico, in September of 1976. He was miles and miles away from the United States of America for the first time in his life. He was overseas in Naples, Italy, and he was elated, inquisitive, and extremely exploratory. Everything about overseas fascinated him, and every direction he walked he knew he looked like a tourist.

April into May of 1977 were spent anchored off the coast of Naples, Italy, due to the great storm the *Indy* endured while crossing the Atlantic Ocean. Operational parts had to be ordered for the ship and repaired while in port. While the task force was anchored, there was a liberal policy on liberty. Other than rotating watches, you could go on liberty after watch and stay onshore practically all day up to the last liberty launch back to the ship.

Sailor was quite a sight to see in those days. He wore blue jeans with an off-brand pair of walking shoes, a 35mm camera around his neck. Many times he carried a boom box cassette player strapped on his shoulders. He was a sight to see, but that was his world then. Figuratively, he could conveniently reach into his back pocket and carry a piece of home with him while he listened to his music.

For the first two weeks, he did nothing but go on guided tours. He signed up for the tours just before the ship arrived in Naples and kept himself busy by going on tours and learning everything he could learn about the European continent. He especially was interested in places and relics in relation to the Bible, although during this cruise, living the life of a Christian purposely took a certain back seat. The cruise of 1977 in the Mediterranean Sea was all about Sailor and satisfying his desires and wants. During that Mediterranean cruise, he was the epitome of the definition of a Sailor and a girl in every port. Well, the girl part he did not have, but he did live a fleshly life and followed his desires and the suggestions of older sailors. He turned nineteen while on the Med cruise of 1977, and leading up to his nineteenth birthday and on his birthday, he engaged in activity that endlessly tempted him. He wanted to ignore and discard the temptations, but he also wanted to experience what it was like to do the things foolish young men do. The situations and circumstances are factual, but the unfolding of the situations may not be precise in Sailor's memory.

Standard operating procedures prior to pulling in port were to get briefed about unauthorized locations and sections of town not to go into. Just like intel prior to going to Tijuana, Mexico, SOP was the same in every country. The information given to the crew from ship intel was always good information, and he intended to abide by the rules to the best of his ability. In fact, he had no intentions of violating the orders of the United States Navy. He was so excited and fascinated about being in the navy that he did not have time to get in trouble. However, foolish youthfulness and not having totally surrendered his life to God were the two factors that overwhelmed his good intentions. Sailor's first experience overseas was a good one for the most part, and his first trip to Naples, Italy, was a travel excursion. He visited Rome, Italy, and the ancient coliseum. He went to Pompeii and learned of the horrible destruction of Mount Vesuvius some twenty-seven kilometers or so away from the vacation resort of Pompeii. He took picture after picture of those popular places and was enjoying every minute of his time. In fact, home had qualified to be called a dream at this point, as though his experiences he spoke about concerning home were the experiences of someone else. He had become pretty much acclimated into his new life and did not want it to end. On one guided tour, the group stopped at a city called Amalfi, Italy, on the coast and ate at a restaurant overlooking the Mediterranean Sea. Amalfi was one of the most exciting highlights of Sailor's youthful life and travels. He imagined himself sort of like in a James Bond movie working for the United States government overseas in Italy, sitting at a restaurant on the coast of Amalfi. He asked the tour guide for the name of the place because it was so picturesque, tropical, and exciting beyond his youthful dreams. Sailor's first tour overseas in Naples, Italy, at eighteen years old turned nineteen, was one of the best times of his young life. He experienced other times equally as exciting, but in those days between eighteen through twenty-one, he lived a life of excitement, fulfilling curiosity, travel, and at times downright ungodliness. All of this would develop the Sailor into the Sermon. As the Sermon would unfold, he had to keep in mind not to be too hard on growing young people because he discovered that he was no angel, as the saying goes.

The above image of Almafi is from www.italiamia.com/images_amalfi.html. That image was chosen because it shows a picturesque view of what Sailor saw at nineteen years old as he traveled toward Amalfi.

Naples, Italy, and Unauthorized Visits

Naples, Italy, is the home port away from home, and much time is spent there for United States naval vessels. Naples was the first port of call when the ship went back to sea and stopped over at a couple of other Italian cities, returning to Naples a second time. The second visit to Naples became the visit of fulfilling curiosity and following the lead of a couple brothers he had met in the squadron while at Cecil Field, Florida. The things they did while in Naples were unauthorized and illegal, and their names must remain undisclosed. Sailor spent two weeks in Naples on the second visit, a long time to be in port. Sailor did some exploring a little on his own throughout the streets of Naples and sometimes with a few squadron members. Back then in those days, there was no serious threat or concern about terrorist, and for Sailor to be walking alone in a foreign land was pretty much accepted and safe for the most part. Everything seemed to be open and spread out, whereas, in Mexico, shops, houses, unpaved streets made that land a little more intimidating. Also, in Italy, there was a great number of sailors ashore, and there was a United Service Organization, or USO for short, close by. USO was a nice place for US sailors and other US service members to hang out and get a bite to eat, play arcade games, make phone calls, or just chill and get a touch of America with all the amenities of American socializing. Intel always briefed everyone on not divulging information about the ship's movement or even the name of their ship. Although the people of Naples could see the ships anchored in the harbor, for safety and security reasons sailors could not tell them specifically what ship they were from. The crew was always on guard as trained military personnel, even if the threat of terrorist activity was nothing like it is today overseas. Still, some Islamic terrorist group or someone associated with such groups are always looking for opportunities to slaughter military and civilian people. Terrorist threats have immensely increased in the twenty-first century in the most horrible way. Nonetheless, the second visit to Naples was a slow time, and the days seemed to drag along. There wasn't much going on, and Sailor was getting bored and ready to go back to sea. When you're in port too long, you get used to the ship being underway, and after a week or so, you are ready to get underway and back to duty. At sea, time goes faster because there is a sense of moving forward toward the end of the cruise. But in port, time seems to creep along. After all the excitement is over from being in port, typically sailors are ready to leave and get underway. Sailor had become bored after about a week and wanted to do something different and exciting. Curiosity, boredom, and not convinced in the Christian faith led him down a path of risky living and ungodly things. He was compelled to go down the path of licentiousness. He and a couple other guys were up to no good. Mac told Sailor about a place he wanted to take him to. Sailor liked Mac and sort of walked in the pernicious steps of Mac. He was eager to try something new in his experiences. Sailor was thrilled by Mac's suggestion, and it sounded extremely satisfying. He thought his desires and feelings were only natural, and God wouldn't mind and would understand his reasoning. One of the other brothers who Sailor looked up to also was heavy into these visits and agreed with the other brothers and said, "Hey, Sailor, you know you want this!"

Many of his shipmates continued to call him TJ, although in his mind, TJ was the young novice boy who knew nothing at all about life. But because many of his shipmates adopted the nickname TJ and for friendship purposes, TJ would do. One of the guys said, "I think you will have fun and be able to release some tension."

Sailor didn't really think he had any tension, but he supposed they knew what they were talking about. Because after all they were much older than him, and at nineteen, he was still impressionable. Even though he knew what they were about to do was not right, but he was not too much concerned about right and wrong as much as fulfilling lustful youthful desires.

The desire was not strong in Sailor until they arrived at their destination. Boredom and weakness persuaded him to do something he *knew* he should not have even been thinking about doing. But he wanted to hang out with the brothers of his squadron and do what they were doing. None of them was looking for trouble, but trouble found them, and the strong arm of the law pursued them. Shortly after his second visit to Naples, Italy, a couple of the brothers in the squadron had been telling Sailor about this place. In fact, when they left Naples the first time and went back to sea, Mac was laughing and telling his story in detail about this place and how much fun it was. His story sounded exciting, and Sailor wanted to try it out. The brother talked the place up so much until Sailor couldn't wait until they returned to Naples, Italy, just to see what all the talk was about. During the second trip to Naples, the brothers had convinced him to go with them. Some night within that week, they all decided to visit the place they claimed to be so much fun. Sailor got dressed and put on his white sneakers and a nice pair of pants and windbreaker. The return back to the ship in the evening on the motor whaleboat would be a little breezy. It was advisable to wear a light jacket because at times saltwater and whatnot splashed in your face; one had to be prepared. Keep in mind the place they visited was totally off-limits and they were unauthorized to be in that area.

The night was a gorgeous dark summer night in the streets of Naples, Italy, in the summer of 1977. Usually the liberty line onboard an aircraft carrier can be very long, and there are times you just go back to your bunk and wait until the line shortens a bit before you try to get off the boat. Think of waiting to get on the roller coaster in an amusement park. Sometimes the line wraps around twice and even three times before you even get up to the boarding section for the roller coaster.

That night, the liberty line was wide open, and there was no one in line! Sailor rarely left the ship at night because he was not a night person, so it was strange for him to even notice how short the liberty line was. He also did not want to get into trouble thousands of miles away from home. Sailor believed going to the house of pleasure was an opportunity he did not want to pass up. He followed the brothers in his squadron with full excitement.

The Women in the Alley

The following image is an example of where Sailor and the brothers walked.

From an Italian website www.italiamia.com/images_naples.html.

An image of a very narrow alley with high rise houses one upon another about five to six stories high.

Like all the alleys, the alley they used ascended the side of the hill the further you walk. Sailor called it an alley because he paid no attention to whether it had a name. In fact, he did not even look for a street name; he was more concerned about the surroundings. The surface of the alley was made of uneven cobblestones, very large cobblestones, and was still under construction. There were clothing lines strung across from one house to another, with clothes out drying on the line. There were trash cans lined up along the outside of the houses, nothing particularly wrong with that other than there were large piles here and there. The alley was even more intimidating because a good portion of it was literally uphill. As they ascended, there was an intersecting alley traveling from north to south. The further up they walked, the narrower the alley became, until they were at a point where a person could literally lean out the window from one house and comfortably talk to another person across the alley in another house. Had Sailor not been a young lad, he would have been exhausted just walking up the hill to the unauthorized location.

As they were walking toward the alley, they had to clandestinely turn up the direction of the alley from the main street not far from the pier. The brothers said to Sailor, "Just keep walking and don't look around. Don't look suspicious and no one will pay attention to you."

Sailor was concerned because he spotted a couple of shore patrol, and he knew if the SP would see them turning up the alley, they may get caught, and he may end up with nonjudicial punishment (NJP) and possibly reduced in rank. Never mind the other guys, it was every man for himself if some trouble went down. But they made the turn into the alley and started their ascent, taking wide strides and stepping hard on the ground. They were brisk walking uphill in anticipation of a night of sinful pleasure. They wanted to get to the location as soon as possible without detection and have their fun and return to the boat conspicuously after having accomplished their mission. Sailor's heart was pumping like a racehorse, and his adrenaline was a continuous flow. He had readied himself and planned his escape route if they were to be pursued by the authorities. He paid close attention to the route they took and even the intersecting streets so he would not get caught should the law entered the vicinity. Now this place was at the peak of the alley that turned into a dead-end, hard up against what looked like the side of a mountain. In many ways, you could say that it looked spooky. It was about 9:30, maybe 10:00 p.m., and Sailor was over four thousand miles away from home at a dead-end alley, in a foreign country, about to do some things he knew to be wrong. Nonetheless, he could not wait to jump into the sinful way of sexual pleasure.

The closer they got to the place, the more the excitement stirred inside Sailor. They were about to enter an establishment called "Momma Rosa." As they got closer, Sailor heard loud music and people singing in Italian. It sounded like disco, but the words were in Italian, and he can see in his mind's eye almost in slow motion all of them making their approach one cobblestone at a time. Beautiful young white-fleshed smooth-skinned ladies were standing outside Momma Rosa. Each girl demonstrated an extra sensual pose as they spotted Sailor and his shipmates headed in their direction. Sadly, not one of the girls spoke English, at least not well enough for you to understand what they meant, and Sailor and his shipmates did not speak Italian, but there were one reason and one common thing both parties wanted. They knew how to say "$50" very well, and they knew how to say "want sex" very well. Other than that line of communication, both the prostitutes and the sailors were clueless in holding an intelligible conversation because of their language barrier. After being on board the ship for almost three weeks straight and not thinking about fidelity or what was right or wrong, the sight of those women was exciting and extremely tempting. Everything was sinfully wrong and sinfully exciting. Sailor looked forward to giving in to the flesh. The women had on skirts way above their knees. Sailor's immediate thought was, *Wow! They might as well not have skirts on!* Others had on hot pants so high and tight one had to imagine how they put the pants on. Some even still had on blouses that showed so much cleavage imagination was not necessary. Others were braless, nipples protruding through their blouses. There were a few women a little on the heavy side, which did not interest Sailor in those days, but most of the girls were petite and very young, ranging from at least sixteen through twenty-something. One of the brothers looked over at Sailor and said, "Didn't I tell you so? Look at all that pussy!"

Sailor broke out into a faint smile. He struggled with right and wrong, but was overcome with desire and what was wrong became right in his mind. They strolled over to the place where the prostitutes were, bright lights on in the inside and the music blaring. No sooner had they gotten close to the house than the women were all over them, rubbing and smiling and laughing and speaking a bunch of senseless chatter, attempting to speak English words but making no sense.

Sailor looked inside one of the houses and noticed a couple of white dudes with women sitting on their laps, and he thought, *Oh, we are not the only sailors who know about this place.*

The white dudes seemed to be enjoying themselves with smiles as large as the ocean. One of the brothers said to Sailor, "Just point to the woman you want and she will take you to her room." The place had a smell that was not unbearable but at the same time certainly did not smell like a fresh can of Glade air freshener. Every woman in that place had on a different fragrance of perfume that maybe was purchased at a dollar store. The smell was noticeably strong and cheap and caused the eyes of Sailor to become watery. It was the smell of vice. He was entering the place of sin of all the men who were there before him. Their smell, their sinful act, and all the partners these women had sex with from throughout the world had reached out and confiscated Sailor's mind and soul. The brothers he was with didn't seem to be bothered by the smell or anything else. One brother had two girls all over him, touching and kissing, you name it. Then in a flash, he did not see the brother any longer, both he and the girls walked a little distance and entered another house. The other brothers Sailor was with also walked away with a girl and entered another house, and Sailor was left alone in that place. His mind was overwhelmed with thoughts that must have come from out of this world. He wanted to follow their lead but was full of apprehension. He wanted to leave Momma Rosa's and return to the ship, but not down that dark alley by himself. He wanted to wait for the brothers to get done and then leave together. But then he concluded, *Damn! I was looking forward to this when we were at sea, and I could not wait to get here. I've come too far not to follow through now.*

No sooner had he finished reasoning in his mind he felt a soft hand take hold of his. He looked around only to stare into the eyes of a beautiful seventeen, maybe an eighteen-year-old, prostitute. *A beautiful young lady*, was his misguided thought. But the truth of the matter was, she was a prostitute and he was a paying customer. He wanted to say to her, "Why are you here doing this? You are too pretty." But his rationale and reasoning had no basis because the same thought applied to him: "Sailor, why are you here when you know this is wrong and you have a girlfriend back home and you are a preacher's son?"

At that reasoning, he said to himself, *To hell with the thoughts and to hell with the rationale. I might as well.*

The young prostitute had never let go of his hand and began pulling Sailor in her direction as they both walked directly across the street into another house. They traversed up the stairs that were narrower than the word *narrow*. The environment of that place was overbearingly tempting, scary, ungodly, sexually suggestive, mentally controlling, and wicked. When they got up to the room, she closed the door, and all Sailor could think about was someone coming through the other door and robbing him. He would be forced to defend himself, causing serious bodily injury, or, he may die in this godless place. His heart was pumping through his chest cavity, but the spirit of the devil and hell had taken control of him. He was clueless that an actual lustful demon had brazenly found its way into his heart. He did not know where the other brothers were because they all had tagged the women they wanted and left before Sailor fulfilled his appointment with sin. The girl he was with was gesturing to Sailor to get undressed, but he said to her, "No way, you get undressed first, and if I feel comfortable, then I will get undress."

Sailor was speaking to her while shaking his head and gesturing to her to get undressed. She laughed and then began to strip until she was totally undressed. At that time all the feelings of what hell must be like when the spirit of lust takes control of your body overtook Sailor. He had no regard for the fact that she was a human being. For about thirty minutes, he sexually abused her and treated her like a dog bowing to the lustful beckoning of the sailor. She appeared to be enjoying it while laughing and suggesting different sexual acts and causing him to become more ungodly and devilish to the core.

Afterward, he felt bad because there was no compassion, no real intimacy, and no concern about her as being a real human being. He did not care that she was someone's daughter and maybe someone's mother. He could have cared less about her well-being and felt that he had been properly served. In his deranged mind, he thought if she wanted to advertise and sell herself like that, then he as a customer can treat his product however he desired. He mentally beat himself up afterward, and then satanic thoughts entered his mind. He rationalized as to why it was all right and typical for a young sailor to carry on like that away from home. His fleshly reasoning is what took him through the rest of the night. His spirit had at that point sank in a bottomless pit of hell that seemed to have no exit. There was no light at the end of the tunnel because there was no tunnel. Sailor had entered what seemed to be hell itself and did not care to look for the exit. He remained in that hellish state for months and reasoned in his mind that it was only natural to have those desires. He took ownership of the lustful spirit as his own and nursed the spirit inside his heart. Lust was his baby, and he was enjoying it while exploring more and more ungodliness during his military days overseas.

Sailor had become, in a few short weeks, another person, one that he was ashamed of and one that he was proud of. One that he hated and one that he enjoyed. One that thought he knew everything but one that knew nothing. The summer of 1977 overseas up and down the European coast was a summer that was a mixture of genuine fun while going on guided tours. It was also one of hellish, even devilish practices when the sun went down. He thought on Christian principles of living, and he periodically read his Bible, but that night and that experience opened a world of foulness that would haunt Sailor for decades. Getting free of that lustful spirit would be a personal battle for decades, and it would seem no decent women would understand his struggle.

Sailor and the Abomination

The prostitutes were a world of sexual pleasure that was exciting each time. But the next experience in Naples, Italy, would be a frightening experience for Sailor. The life of a prostitute can be degrading. Many times, they are treated with absolutely no respect. Nonetheless, in many places, prostitutes are considered part of normal street life.

But when a man purports to be a woman and a woman claims to be a man, especially when it comes to sex, that is called an abomination in the Bible. Sailor was about to engage in, for the first time in his life, the sinful abomination of the lust of the flesh. His introduction to abomination may sound a little ambiguous, but you will immediately understand as the story unfolds.

The abomination follows sometime after the whorehouse up the dark alley on the mountain. The whorehouse visit became a lot more frequent thereafter. The brothers from the squadron played a little trick on Sailor, knowing this was his first time overseas and that he was green behind the ears. The brothers knew of Sailor's Christian background, and though there was a smidgen of respect for his religious beliefs, he had entered their world instead of convincing them of the Christian world. The problem with Sailor's faith is that he was not too convinced of his faith, thereby making it child's play for them to drag him into their world. One night while out and closer to the pier, they were bar hopping just to see what was going on in the town of Naples, Italy. The one brother who told Sailor about the whorehouse also told him about a bar that he thought would be fun and that Sailor might enjoy. He said, "Timmy T."—another nickname used only by this brother—"there are a lot of pretty girls there, and I know you will like them." He and a couple other guys headed down to a bar not far from the pier and looked inside to see what was up. They had the Bee Gees on, and back in that day, the Bee Gees were at the top of the charts. They did not have to go far into the bar because women were all outside looking for an American sailor to party with. Sailor spotted this gorgeous tall thick-legged woman with high heels on and an orange dress and long fingernails and pristine haircut. People were all around her, Italian dudes and American sailors, and Sailor was wondering who she was and why so popular. In fact, he thought she was some important person or maybe an Italian actress. She was pretty to look at, and she was giggling while guys were talking to her almost in a mocking way. He could not figure out why they were treating her like that. After all, she looked like a nice woman. The crowd around her started walking away one by one into the bar and down the street. Some were laughing, and others were just shaking their heads. One of the brothers said to Sailor, "There she is, TJ. Go say something to her."

Sailor, all big and bad, was thinking if they did not want her, he would hook up with her maybe for a few drinks and then take it from there. The brothers said, "Go ahead, TJ. What you waiting for?"

Sailor then walked over to her, and it was nothing to start talking to her and strangely enough, she could speak English well. The language barrier practically did not exist. He casually and carefully put his hands on her, trying to be smooth and suave and even grabbed her ass in a tender way, not too doggish or crazy, just trying to be smooth. She was laughing and enjoying all the attention she was getting. She put her arms around Sailor and began exploring while he was beginning to feel a little embarrassed out in public while all this was going on. Sailor said to her, "Hey, easy, not here. We don't want to advertise for the entire public."

What happened next almost made the young Sailor piss his pants from complete embarrassment and the foulness he had ignorantly dived into. She said to Sailor, "Okay, baby, what do you want to do? I have a place right down the street. Let's go now!"

But the problem was not what she said or the place she suggested. The problem was her voice was too deep to be a woman's. With that, she grabbed the hand of Sailor and immediately placed his hand on her crotch. Her actions frightened Sailor because if visiting a whorehouse was sinfully wrong, then engaging with a transvestite would be the likes of Sodom and Gomorrah. Sailor intensely felt that he had offended God Almighty and immediately pulled himself away from this man and began an intense struggle mentally and physically to get away from Satan's transvestite. Unfortunately, it was not easy because he held on to Sailor extremely tight and pulled him toward her, all along saying, "C'mon, let's go to my place. I'll make you feel good, and it will be worth your while!"

All the brothers were laughing so hard as to break stitches, if they had any. They laughed and laughed and laughed, and then they started walking away toward the pier while Sailor was struggling to get away from the sensual demonic transvestite. The struggle must have lasted for about five minutes. That was way too long outside of a bar at night in a foreign country while other people are laughing and walking by. The transvestite intended to take Sailor back to his apartment, and only God knows what then. The transvestite held on to Sailor in the most ungodly manner. When Sailor thought he was breaking free, the transvestite bear-hugged him, picked him up, and turned him in another direction. At this point, Sailor could no longer see the brothers. They had gotten to the end of the street and turned the corner. They were out of his sight, and Sailor became extremely paranoid. Sailor began to sweat, something he did not do much in his youth. As Sailor gazed around while the transvestite was wrestling with him, everyone who walked by was laughing and pointing their finger to bring more attention to his sinfully sad, ignorant, ungodly state. Sailor then wanted to fight and became belligerent—out loud! "Mother fucking ugly bitch, get your mother fucking hands off me!"

But that didn't seem to matter to the transvestite. He held on to Sailor even tighter and grabbed his crotch and whispered into his ear, "C'mon, baby, you know you want it, and I will make you enter into heaven tonight."

Was it his adrenaline, or did he become so afraid that God's mercy endowed him with extra strength? But when the transvestite said he would take him into heaven, even though Sailor was a great sinner, he still respected the truth and for this transvestite to talk about heaven, pissed him the hell off. Isn't that something, hell inside his soul hated the transvestite mentioning heaven. He managed to free himself from the transvestite, don't know how, but he felt God was merciful to him that evening and endowed him with overwhelming strength. Especially when the transvestite mentioned heaven, as though sinful pleasure is akin to heaven. Sailor thought within himself that they both were on their way to hell. "Don't tell me you will take me to heaven."

He started punching the transvestite in the chest, abdomen, and kidneys. He was swinging as hard as he could, as if he were hitting a punching bag. Oddly enough, the transvestite was laughing and taking Sailor's blows. Sailor then gave the transvestite the hardest head butt he could muster. It stunned the transvestite long enough for him to release his bear hug on Sailor, dropping him to his feet.

When Sailor broke free, the transvestite lunged toward Sailor to grab him again. Adrenaline flowing like hot lava throughout his veins, he managed to push the transvestite away. Then his youthful track and field days kicked in, and he ran like a crazy man, as if he was running among a group of bats exiting out of hell to catch up with the brothers. There was no way on God's earth that transvestite could have run after Sailor in those high heels. When he caught up with his shipmates, everything was funny to them, but he was boiling hot with anger, pissed off, ashamed, and felt like he offended God. Sailor could reason and rationalize with women because after all, a man likes a woman and a woman likes a man. But he had no justification for the encounter with the transvestite. It took him a while to calm down, but he was full of anxiety. Unlike the time in the brother's apartment outside Cecil Field, Florida, when no one talked about his leaving, this event was different. Sailor had become the butt of the joke, and it was a joke for a couple weeks throughout the squadron. Some guys just laughed it off and forgot about it after a few days, but some of the other brothers held on to it for a couple weeks. Soon enough it died down and became a passing thing in the mind of the brothers. But for Sailor, it was a lifelong experience that shook him up pretty good. He felt he was able from that point onward to discern between a woman and a transvestite.

Back to the Women in the Alley

In those days of Sailor's life overseas, he never encountered another experience with a transvestite again. Never again with touching and grabbing like the time in Naples, Italy. He learned fast and looked for certain attributes and signs to differentiate between a real woman and a man in women's clothing. The reason Sailor did not recognize the voice of the man before he grabbed him is because it was loud that night and everyone was talking and the music was blaring. If you have ever been to a bar at night in the summertime, it's not always easy to distinguish between voices and sounds. At least for Sailor, that was the case, especially after you have been drinking rum and Coke, beer, and smoking marijuana and some hashish. Recognition did not become clear to Sailor until he was directly in the man's face and he and the transvestite were directly talking. Most of the high Sailor was on from smoking "mary jane" and a few drinks seem to have flushed right through his bladder and onto the street during the struggle to get away. There was another incident with a transvestite years later but nothing like that one. Sailor would learn that sin many times is like a bottomless pit of pleasure and will severely enslave one's mind with foolish and careless acts.

On the second visit to Naples, Italy, just before the ship was about to get underway, Sailor and a few brothers decided to make another visit to the whorehouse. They had become quite comfortable walking up there and engaging in untold acts of sin. There was about six of them walking casually down the street waiting for the sun to go down. They would make their way up the hellish hill on the broad way to destruction. They found a shortcut that knocked off quite a bit of travel time. They arrived at Momma Rosa's a little earlier than the first time, intending to spend more time with the prostitutes. But all their intentions and sinful joy of committing fornication would be brought to an abrupt end. Rightfully so because there was much Sailor needed to learn and take to heart. He had entered a picnic thrown by hell and hosted by Satan. Nineteen years of age, he failed to consider the deep spiritual consequences.

On his second visit when they arrived at Momma Rosa, same as before, women were standing outside, approaching them, touching and feeling and pulling them inside the establishment. But this time Sailor decided to go window-shopping, and he looked around comparing size, voice, looks, dress. He had become too comfortable and searched for the most tempting-looking woman. On his second visit, it was not as crowded as the first time so it was almost like they had the pick of the litter. They all played around with the women while the women offered some drinks, and some of the brothers accepted their offers. Sailor was not interested in drinking, and he was only there for the sexual pleasure. He thought he had to relieve some unknown tension. He made his choice and started across the alley with his selected prostitute. It was the same route as before, directly across the street, up the intimidating narrow stairway This time Sailor happened to have his 35mm Canon camera with him. He beckoned to the girl to get undressed, and then he began taking pictures of her in different poses. He had become way too comfortable in his sinful and perverted lifestyle that a great scare was needed for him. All along he knew what he was doing was civilly and spiritually wrong. Sailor had been introduced to a different world on the other side of the planet. Everything about the church world and home was fading to the point of nonexistence. He still cared about his religious background, but at the time he was enjoying his new life. His new prostitute was very accommodating and allowed him to take picture after picture of her. The young Italian whore was not as attractive as the first girl. He did look for the first girl he was with but did not see her and simply selected a different prostitute to satisfy his fleshly desires. For that reason, he did not spend half as much time with her as he did the first girl. Each time the room was dimly lit, with one window covered by what looked like a bedsheet and one entrance and exit into the room. There was another door, Sailor thinking it was a closet door. Every time Sailor visited Momma Rosa's, he was suspicious that someone was going to come storming out through that door and rob him. But he continued to take the risk at the expense of self-gratification and selfish reasons. The room basically looked like an efficiency apartment. It was small, dimly lit, and smelly and did not look like the linen was changed for weeks. Mac told Sailor what he thought was a good thing about visiting the whorehouse. Mac was excited about the one "professional" quality they had at the whorehouse. It was standard procedure for the women to use condoms.

Okay, so condoms make it right, thought Sailor. Nonetheless, in the backslidden state Sailor was in, the use of condoms was refreshing to know. Years later as the sermon unfolds, the life of Sailor became crystal clear to the man of the Sermon. All men, including the Sailor, who commit fornication and adultery, fundamentally carry out those acts because of selfish reasons. Deep, ungodly, sinfully, selfish reasons. At nineteen years old, selfishness was not even a concept or consideration of Sailor.

When Sailor was done taking pictures of his new prostitute, she laughed and then gestured to Sailor to get on with the business. Similar to his first experience, he did not even consider this young girl to be a human being that deserved respect as a woman. Sailor treated her even worse than the first girl by sexually abusing her body. There was absolutely zero compassion or love or personal intimacy. To Sailor, it was paid service, and in his mind, she was compelled to satisfy him. Months later in retrospect, he would judge himself and repent repeatedly of the things he discovered that lay deep in the crevices of his sinful heart. After spending about five minutes with the prostitute and feeling properly served, he immediately got dressed. But God had a plan that Sailor was unaware of to shake him up a little. In retrospect, Sailor believed the events that unfolded afterward was especially for him. The prostitute did not follow Sailor down the steps like the first girl, and that made him feel really horrible. Sailor had just sexually abused and treated that prostitute like a dog and probably made her feel worthless. As long as he got served, that's all he cared about in those days. As he was walking down those narrow steps alone, he heard someone say in the loudest voice ever almost like it was yelled from heaven, "Shore patrol, shore patrol!"

Sailor had made it down the steps and ran outside to witness brothers and white dudes scattering in all directions. The brothers he went to the whorehouse with made their own route of escape. Sailor immediately slung his camera around his neck and yelled out, "Oh shit!" He was not sure if the yell of shore patrol was fake or a real-time pursuit, and then he spotted a small Italian paddy wagon on the hill.

Similar to the paddy wagon in Tijuana, Mexico. Flashback after flashback of being in the paddy wagon went through his brain like a streak of lightning. One caveat, there would be no leniency if he had gotten apprehended.

Good thing he had sneakers on, which was par for the course walking up to Momma Rosa's. The paddy wagon started riding down the hill in slow motion while the SPs were looking left to right and shining a flashlight. The youthfulness and athleticism he had gained running track in boot camp and agility learned in gymnastics would aid him in his escape. He took off as if on the starting line, taking long strides down a steep hill. That neighborhood of sin and vice had little to no street lighting at all. As for the trash cans outside the houses, he purposely ran into several of them, attempting to create a noisy diversion. He heard other trash cans being knocked down from the distance. The shore patrol began driving faster and faster, almost catching up with Sailor, and he did not know the fate of the other brothers. They all scattered in various directions. Similar to the incident with the transvestite, at nineteen years old, he began perspiring from running in the hot summer night. Running never caused him to perspire that easily, but it was totally different from a normal run. He was panicking because he was running alone. He did not know where his shipmates were, and he was becoming very paranoid. All he could think about while running was getting apprehended and receiving

Nonjudicial punishment and restriction to the ship. Sailor cut across one of the side alleys and implemented his own emergency escape route. He was determined not to get caught that night! Then he heard a siren and the sound of paddy wagon bearing down on him. He noticed red lights flashing a little bit down the base of the alley in the direction he was running. The shore patrol began to broadcast over their external speaker, "This is the shore patrol of the United states Navy! Stop! I say again, stop where you are!

Sailor thought to himself, *Yeah, they got to be crazy and lunatics if they think I am going to stop running from them so they can arrest me. To hell with those fuckers, I'm not stopping.* He had to improvise and find another way to get out of the alley without getting caught. He quickly adjusted his escape route, and to this day, he does not know how he succeeded. Running in a totally different direction, not sure where it would lead him. Fortunately, he ended up behind the Galleria Umberto I, Napoli, Italy, a shopping center and other consumer interest place, a place where families hung out.

There were people walking through the Galleria, which eased his stressful situation. Sailor slowed down, wiped some sweat off his face, loosened up his camera, and mingled in with the crowd. He ended up on the main drag about a couple of blocks from the section they entered the alley. He noticed a couple of paddy wagons at the alley's entrance and a few guys being apprehended by Italian police and shore patrol. But they did not catch Sailor. He was determined in his heart not to get caught that night in the summer of 1977, in Napoli Italy, after indulging the sins of the world in a whorehouse in an unauthorized section of Italy. He spotted the brothers a few blocks from him and yelled out their names. Swiftly, he made his way over to them and mingled in with the other people of the night. A couple of Italian police officers and shore patrols appeared to be looking in their direction. One of the brothers said, "Don't pay any attention to them. If you give them attention, they may suspect you."

With that, they walked toward the pier, and a guy pulled out a couple of "jays" and they smoked them. They made their way back to the liberty boat to return to the USS *Independence* (CV-62), anchored in the harbor of Naples, Italy. There were a few more episodes with the whorehouse of Momma Rosa's but nothing equal to the first two. At one point, Sailor went to the whorehouse with a couple of brothers, and they went inside and did their thing and Sailor left them there. Boredom began to set in with the whorehouse, and what little intelligence he had he begin to reason. He was experiencing worldliness in bucket loads while struggling to reason why sinful acts were compelling or necessary. Every visit to the whorehouse was mingling his soul with the lives of countless men who engaged in sexual acts with the same women. Sailor was ready to move on, but the addiction to fleshly pleasure plagued him. His soul connected with the prostitutes of the world would repeatedly fail him every time. When opportunities arose involving nightclubs and women, Sailor would succumb to the same old tired sin.

Of those pictures he took of prostitute girl number 2, he received three developed pictures. The boat would bring authorized vendors onboard for special services like dry cleaning, ordering gifts, buying souvenirs, and getting your pictures developed. Normally it took about two to three days to get your pictures back. That's how he got his pictures developed while in port. Sailor *knows* he took about twelve to fifteen pictures of the second prostitute. When the vendors arrived on board, he ran down to the mess decks to pick up his half-naked prostitute pictures. He was so excited that he opened the envelope right there at the vender on the mess decks. When he opened the envelope, he discovered only three pictures in the envelope. The first picture was the prostitute fully dressed. The other picture was her in her bra and underpants, and the last picture was her topless. Very disappointed because he wanted the pictures to remember her and look for her again. But oh well! He certainly could not complain as a disgruntled customer like, "Hey, where the hell is my other my pictures, you stupid son of a bitch?" To complain about the other pictures would have placed him directly in the sight of the radar for captain's mast. He couldn't inquire about the pictures because he would have been interrogated by the authorities and ultimately disciplined for being in an unauthorized location. He couldn't let anyone know that he went to the whorehouse because he surely would have been disciplined, and he could not get upset because he knew he should not have been there. Momma Rosa's and the brothers of VS-31 will forever remain in the eternal past only known to Sailor, God, the devil, the brothers, and now you, the reader. As for the three pictures, Sailor kept them for the remainder of the cruise, and they got lost somewhere in the shuffle of returning home. Funny, after the deployment ended and the task force returned to the United States and Sailor looked at the pictures, they had very little meaning to him. The sight of the prostitute on the picture provoked no feeling of sensuality! There were *no feelings whatsoever* of missing her or Momma Rosas'. Sailor *did not* care one bit about her after returning to the United States. Such is the nature and character of sin. During Sailor's second Mediterranean cruise, his desires and curiosity were somewhat tamed than the first overseas duty. He was one year older at twenty years old and was familiar with the locations and surroundings and the environment of Europe. Extreme soul-searching and repentance untold but still had not discovered the depth of impact and bevy of spirits that continued to be very much a part of his life. The personal challenges and events he had yet to experience would mount unbelievably higher than the first tour of duty overseas. There would be things and people and situations almost unparalleled to anything he had experienced thus far. For a while, when the urge would strike, he would hang out with the brothers from the squadron. That same old nasty spirit would rise, and they went searching for girls. However, there was never another experience as detailed and engaging as the prostitutes in Napoli, Italy. Other encounters with women in Spain, France, and Portugal were more on a fleshly, touching, drinking, partying, dancing level. For one reason or another, those encounters never escalated any more than touching and flirting.

The N-Word

The rock group Grand Funk Railroad became one of Sailor's favorite groups instantaneously while transiting back to the United States of America. Sailor was not aware of the group Grand Funk Railroad prior to his deployment onboard the *Indy*, but he heard a certain song from them years before entering the navy. He paid little attention to it until October 1977. But before we examine the song, there was an incident that made Sailor's heart skip a few beats. Not because he was afraid but because he could not believe what was happening especially in the United States Navy of the 1970s. As far as he was concerned, equal rights, affirmative action, and all that stuff had become the law. Racist acts, bigotry and open prejudice should not be occurring on board an American naval vessel. Sailor still had much to learn of his newfound worldly experience. Prior to boarding the *Indy* for the first time, he heard reports of racial situations on board to the point that blacks and whites slept in separate sections of the ship. Once on board, he did notice a separation, but he paid little attention to it, thinking that everyone would get along. There were reports of fights between blacks and whites and a small contingency of gangs onboard. This was a little disturbing to Sailor, but it did not terribly upset him because he had studied karate and kung fu in his senior year of high school. He did not hold a black belt and not even a brown belt but a couple notches on his white belt. He enjoyed martial arts and would exercise and work out during the cruise. The eyewitness fights and boxing with his older brothers kind of prepared him for any physical altercation. In a word, Sailor could easily hold his own, and if he had to resort to the martial arts, he had no problem with that.

In 1977 through 1979, racial issues were very much prevalent even all the way through the nineties. In the twenty-first century, they have man's laws to sort of restrain racist acts, but even those laws are vehemently disregarded by the ones sworn to uphold the law. Due justice and fair treatment will always be the cancer of the United States of America. But the laws act as a temporary and social band-aid. The N-word was when Sailor unintentionally violated a secure area involving a field day. A field day is when you clean, clean, and clean some more. Field days were held every day and for obvious reasons. A ship at sea with 4,500 souls could be a breeding ground for all kinds of germs.

One day Sailor was on his way forward of the ship to go to his workspace, and he had to pass through the galley section. He did notice the area was roped off, but the section he needed to walk through he could easily squeeze through. Well, he knew that you do not walk over a waxed floor or through an area where people are holding field day. They want to get done and want their section to pass inspection, and it is disrespectful to dirty up someone's cleaning efforts. Sailor's intent was not to be disrespectful or dirty up a shipmate's work after he so painstakingly cleaned it. He was walking through the galley, and there was a space just small enough for him to get through. He heard a guy say, "This section is secure," but Sailor arrogantly kept walking. The guy said again, "Hey! This section is secured," which basically means "it's closed down and you can't walk this way." Sailor heard the guy loud and clear, and he particularly paid attention where he was walking as not to disturb the roped-off section. But the guy paid no attention to Sailor being careful because he told Sailor the section was secured, and Sailor kept walking, essentially ignoring the guy's command. Sailor was wrong, without question and could have gone around or another way. Pride and arrogance in Sailor, along with sinful ways, had turned him into a disrespectful arrogant son of a bitch. Humility was as far from him as life and death are separated from each other. From the corner of Sailor's eye, he looked over to where the guy was working. The guy was about the same size, weight class, with a T-shirt on, intently working. The guy yelled out to Sailor in no uncertain terms, "Hey, *nigger*! I said this section is secured. Can't you hear?"

What? Sailor thought! *No, he did not call me a nigger!*

Instantly there was an eruption of anger inside the soul of Sailor that caused adrenaline from hell to flood his thoughts. Sailor was mad and furious that this white boy called him a nigger.

He was not done with his derogatory remarks. The guy said again, "Didn't you hear me, *nigger*? Come back here and I will beat your ass, you dumb-ass *nigger*! Can't you read?"

That was it! Sailor could not take anymore. He stopped dead in his tracks and began to turn around toward the guy as the guy slammed the steel watertight door and said, "That's right, come back here!"

Weeks later, Sailor did not understand why God intervened because he *did not* revere God during the cruise of 1977. Why would God unlock a still small voice inside Sailor's soul? Sailor was turning around to go back with every intent to kick the shit out of this white boy. He intended to either maim him or bash his head up against that steel door. Sailor was ready and hungry to kick his ass and then go turn himself in. But he was unable to complete his turn to go back in the guy's direction. An unseen hand stopped him, and for real, for real, a still small peaceful voice inside his soul simply posed a question, *"Is it worth it?"*

To this day, Sailor does not believe that was his thoughts. He believes it was the buried conciseness of his spirit briefly awakened by God of right and wrong, and the spirit simply posed a question to Sailor, *"Is it worth it?"*

The question was asked twice in the spirit of Sailor and answered within seconds of the challenge to fight that boy. "*No*, it is not!" He then turned back in the direction he was walking and continued his way while the guy's voice began to fade. Usually people who are upset and angry like that would get louder and louder, inciting and provoking their opponent. But the guy's voice became softer and softer to the point Sailor did not hear him anymore. His words faded, and the guy also faded in Sailor's view of him. To the man of the sermon today, such words are lifeless, having lost the intended negative racial effect.

But Sailor wondered for weeks why he did not take him up on his challenge because God knows it was not about fear. In those days, Sailor was full of pride and arrogance. He would not start a fight, but he also would not run from a fight. He told some of the brothers in the squadron what just took place, and they wanted to find the guy and start some trouble, and that's all it would have been—trouble in the worst way. The crew and embarked squadrons were on their way back home to the United States after a grueling seven-month deployment to the Mediterranean Sea. They survived without injury or loss of life of immediate squadron members, and the makings of a possible riot on board a naval vessel did not make sense to Sailor. Today he realizes why he answered that it was not worth it. But then he could not understand why God would awaken the consciousness of a spirit overgrown with weeds of sinful acts. Why would he speak into the spirit of a wayward son with a simple question, "Is it worth it?" Sailor's reaction for a few days afterward was one of deep introspection and soul-searching. He continued to ask God, "Why did you make me feel like that?" In other words, "Why did you put that question to me when I wanted to fight?"

He did not get an answer, nor did he feel like God heard him. He thought perhaps he was reasoning in his own soul as to why he did not go back and fight that guy. But he was not comfortable with the thought of reasoning because the question came to him suddenly and then left as suddenly as it came to mind. It would not be until years later, like every experience and thought in his mind in those days, that he would begin to understand the unfathomable love of God. He made it a point on the transit back to the United States of America to reflect on all his actions and ways during the Med. cruise of 1977. In his mind, reason became his worst enemy. He could not figure out why and how he strayed so drastically, in a matter of minutes. He asked questions of himself and searched his soul intently. He asked forgiveness that was pretty much lip service. He convinced himself that he did nothing wrong. In fact, it was only natural for him, a young nineteen-year-old, to do the things he did even though he was taught the ways of sin is wrong. His convincing reason to himself was, it is natural to do the things he did. After all, the first time he visited the whorehouse way up the dark alley in Naples, Italy, he enjoyed all the hype and excitement. Even though those girls were not beauty queens, the encounter with them was exciting and opened a world of future experiences. The proverbial Pandora's lustful box would now open wide to Sailor all the way into the Sermon. How deep would that box unveil and release a world of struggles in Sailor's life?

Grand Funk Railroad

Channel fever is an experience only known to sailors, and it basically is the inability to go to sleep due to thrilling excitement and great anticipation. Sort of like when you were a child and you knew you were going on vacation the next day, or you were anticipating going to the amusement park the next day. Or maybe even your birthday the next day and you were looking forward to that day arriving. Channel fever is when a naval vessel transits the Strait of Gibraltar or any strait on their way back to the United States of America. The sweetest sound coming over the 1MC was "Underway, USA, shift colors." The Atlantic crossing nonstop could take about only a few days, but training exercises and general quarter drills took the CTF Task Force about a week or so to return home. It is a time of liberal stand down but still maintaining military professionalism and readiness. When channel fever struck, guys were staying up all night playing cards, listening to music, even writing letters. It was difficult to go to sleep because of the excitement of returning home to the United States of America without a great loss of souls. To Sailor, the return home was quintessential of having grown up. There were three sailors who died on the Med. cruise of 1977 because of an aircraft fatality, and that was a few souls in comparison to 4,500 crew members. The crew was thankful and excited for the most part because it was a successful cruise by military standards. Sailor remembers those days very well because he did not go to bed until sometime in the wee hours of the morning. Sleepless nights went on from day to day while the *Indy* Battle Group was sailing the Atlantic Ocean toward Hampton Roads, Virginia. They would dock at Norfolk Naval Station, Norfolk, Virginia, pier 12.

There is a brief turnover procedure that takes place after leaving Rota, Spain, and just before entering the Strait of Gibraltar with the relieving ship's battle group. Sailor had survived his first deployment overseas without injury, punitive action, or loss of limb, and he was elated to go back home and tell his stories. When turnover was complete and once sailing through the Strait of Gibraltar, a certain song was played over the 1MC to boost already high spirits even higher. As soon as the *Indy* transited the strait and hit the Atlantic Ocean, still overseas, they played that song, and once they were within the shores of the United States of America, they played that song again. From Zulu time to Alpha time, a rock group and song that he had never paid attention to now made an indelible mark on his mind ever since. The song so moved Sailor that he immediately went to a record store back home and purchased the cassette. CDs had not yet been released in the market, and iPods did not exist. A couple of the older sailors told Sailor that it was not uncommon to play that song after a seven-month deployment, and many of the old salts were expecting the song to be played. When the song began, you could hear cheers and whistling and applauds *everywhere* throughout the USS *Independence* (CV-62). The song had not even been playing one minute and shipmates were ecstatic. A group Sailor had never heard of up to that point in his life would become the name of a group he would never, ever forget. He asked one of the brothers that he admired and looked up to what the name of the group singing that song was and what the name of the song was.

Without hesitation, the brother said, "Grand Funk Railroad, 'I'm Your Captain: Closer to Home.'"

The song was beyond a doubt the most wonderful sounding song of all time to Sailor. The entire event would stamp a world of experience in Sailor in one instant, catapulting Sailor years beyond his age while transiting the Atlantic Ocean on their way home from a grueling seven-month Mediterranean cruise. Throughout the night into the day, they played different songs by several American artists, and it's funny, Sailor does not remember any other song played but "I'm Your Captain" by Grand Funk Railroad. The song was fitting, appropriate, on time, and spoke volumes to how and what he was feeling. He could not wait to get home, and he felt ten feet tall having crossed the vast Atlantic Ocean and returning home having made it through. He had experienced what was right. He had engaged in what was wrong and ungodly. He was very impressionable by the older salts. His flesh ruled his feelings and reasoning and all sorts of experiences. If he ever experienced the true definition of the grace and mercy of God, it was most definitely during the summer of 1977 with his first experiences overseas. God sustained his mind and allowed him to continue living one more day. Each day of life was more than enough to rejoice about and appreciate more and more with each breath taken. The cruise of 1977 was a roller coaster and mountaintop and valley experience. But the cruise of 1978 and the years to come would be the encore of encores and the real development and growth in Sailor's life. He traveled a long distance from the projects off Cameron Street of Harrisburg, Pennsylvania, and the days of North 18th Street were quickly fading more and more. Each visit to home on North 18th Street on annual leave was a visit that separated him from home one slice at a time. He could feel the separation at each visit back to North 18th Street. At times, it was lonely, and it was sad and even regretful to visit North 18th Street. He would feel goose bumps of homesickness every time he left home. But by this time, homesickness would end as soon as he was on the plane headed back to his duty station. Sailor had matured into a world-traveling young man with the wind most definitely at his back. He wanted so much to retain the North 18th Street life, and he regretted so much that it all went by so fast. But at the same time, he was glad it is impossible to go back, like Fred said, "Once you leave, you can never come back."

10

TOUR OF DUTY USS *DWIGHT D. EISENHOWER* (CVN-69)

Pier 12 at Norfolk, Virginia, Naval Base

As the Command Task Forced approached Hampton Roads, all the squadron pilots flew their planes off the ship, and Sailor remembers the day they sailed into Norfolk at Hampton Roads like it was yesterday. Work in the office was very minimal because the squadron had packed up their gear in squadron cruise boxes. The squadron members had to pack, load, and take the cruise boxes to the brow of the ship to be unloaded and shipped back to Naval Air Station Cecil Field, Florida. As the *Indy* was making her approach into Hampton Roads, it was a foggy morning, around 8:00 a.m. Sailor ran up on deck over to the catwalk to sneak a peek at Norfolk, Virginia, back in the United States of America. They had a saying back then that "we are going back to the world." The entire crew was familiar with the world they had left behind. The world where they all grew up at some location in the United States of America. The world overseas in Italy, Spain, France, Portugal, and other European cities was not their world but a world they had come to know and become familiar with. But the United States of America was where the crew was from; no matter where they get dropped off in the states—Norfolk, Jacksonville, or San Diego, California—they could easily find their way home. That's what made America nice to see, and even the pollution was a weird, good, breathtaking smell.

The official word was the *Indy* would not be tied up to the pier until about twelve noon or maybe even later. Sailor was panting and feeling all sorts of ways because here he was right inside the perimeter and touching the waters of home and was still confined to the ship for another three to four hours. The ship slowly steamed toward the pier being assisted by tugboats. After getting a good view of the waters and breathing the smell of home and looking at the other ships on the pier, Sailor was convinced that he had returned to the world of the United States of America. He would soon be homeward bound to North 18th Street. Enough was enough, and he was becoming impatient with looking, and he ran back down starboard side into the ship to his bunk area and made sure all his stuff was packed. He was ready and anxious to get off this tub. Seven months ago, the tub was fascinating to see, and his heart had been filled with emotion after emotion. Now that the task force had returned home, and he had committed sins he never considered for one moment. He walked in unfaithfulness while overseas, and he began to feel the environment and the places the navy took him was now a bad thing. His view had quickly changed from excitement to get off this tub. But that perspective was only placed in his mind by the words and perspective of many of the older sailors. When he returned to his bunk to make sure that he was ready to go, he felt a little sad because at the same time of the negative feelings there were feelings of missing the boat. The USS *Indy* had taken him to places he otherwise would have never seen or experienced at the youthful age of nineteen. He knew he would be going overseas again, and there was a feeling of "can't wait to go back." And for the first time, he discovered something inside his soul that was very strange. He felt homesickness of being overseas. He missed Naples, Italy, where he spent much of the time. He missed places in France and Spain and other European locations. He had homesickness for the places he traveled overseas, and it was the craziest feeling ever, but he loved the feeling. He was missing those places he visited and could not wait to return. To Sailor, it was strange that he felt homesick for the places he traveled having for the second time stepping foot on foreign land. But for now, he wanted very much to see family and talk about the places he visited and the things he did. He did not talk about the whorehouse or the other indecent and ungodly acts, just the guided tours and the whole experience of the aircraft carrier. The whorehouses and sinful acts are first being revealed in his story. You, the reader, are among the very first people to know about the satanic suggestions, the darkness of licentiousness and the temptations of Sailor's heart. When he first visited overseas the world slung him around like a helpless infant thrown into a sea of sharks. Sailor's life was not an innocent, preacher's kid, church boy who never did anything wrong. What Sailor mostly discovered is how typical he was against the weakness of his flesh. A church experience alone was fruitless in the face of his sinful nature. He was defenseless to overcome the powers of darkness with an ordinary charismatic religious experience. But the age-old question in the mind of Sailor periodically was, "If you could do it all over again, would you?" A resounding *yes*! Only on one condition, that he would have the knowledge that he was doing it all over again because without that knowledge, the experiences would be the same with the same consequences. And even though he did know the thought of doing it all over again is the essence of vanity, the thought crossed his mind every now and again. He knew in many ways he was a great failure in life and a horrible witness of the Christianity he knew or Christ-likeness he thought he had.

Air Anti-Submarine Squadron Thirty-One (VS-31) was home, and those experiences were things of the past. The ship was about to dock, and the word was passed, "Now set the sea and anchor detail, smoking lamp is secure in all authorized spaces." Sea and anchor mean this tub is about to dock alongside pier 12 at Naval Station Norfolk, Virginia. Sailor was overjoyed to hear those words and very anxious. He was unable to keep still and more than ready to offload and get started on his way home. There was a mixture of feelings he was experiencing, some good, some bad, but a combination of feelings Sailor was able to sort out. He tried to get annual leave as soon as the ship pulled into port. He was unable to get approved leave because other squadron members with more leave on the books and more seniority were granted immediate leave. Also, the fact they were married forced him to wait his turn. The word was passed: "secure the sea and anchor detail, shift colors."

A few minutes later the most exciting word given over the 1MC, "Liberty, liberty, liberty, now liberty call for all hands. Sections 1, 3, and 4 report to the Master at Arms, liberty call."

That meant the Mediterranean cruise was officially over. The ship was docked at the pier, and everyone not on duty was free to grab their bags and go wherever they wanted to in the United States of America. Only one thing, Sailor had nowhere to go but back to Cecil Field, Florida. He had to board the bus that would take the squadron over to the air terminal at Naval Air Station Norfolk. A repeat itinerary of when they arrived seven months prior. It was that time to board and fly back to his home base in Cecil Field, Florida. Having to return to his home base did not matter at the moment. Being back in America was the focus and a copious feeling of excitement. Sailor had returned to the United States of America having obtained his sea legs and gained worldwide experience. The child of the projects, North 18th Street, and Mount Calvary Church of God in Christ, had now taken a permanent place in the memory of the young Sailor. Childhood days of the projects were now gone *forever* and would have little to no impact on the future of Sailor's life. Memories of North 18th Street was but a warm and fuzzy feeling thinking of people he once knew. It was a good feeling, and that was the extent of the feeling—good. The first thing he did was find a telephone at the pier to make a call back home. The phone booth pier was overcrowded, no such thing as cell phones then, but the patience to wait for an available phone booth was no problem. He would wait all day if he had to just to hear the voice of his mother and siblings and to tell them, "A world traveler has returned home. Remember me!" The phone booths at the pier were overcrowded, literally standing room only. Guys virtually standing on top of each other waiting to make their phone call. Sailor does not remember how long he had to wait, but it did not matter because after that long cruise he would have waited night and day just to hear his mother's voice.

Back and Forth to Home

The squadron spent two months onshore back at Cecil Field, Florida, until January 1978 when they began a shakedown cruise. That's because the Carrier Air Wing Group 7 (CAG), changed aircraft carriers. They cross decked to the navy's newest nuclear-powered aircraft carrier, the USS *Dwight D. Eisenhower* (CVN69). But before embarking on board the Eisenhower, Sailor was making every attempt to spend as much time with his family back home on North 18th Street. He was now nineteen years old and would be twenty-one years old by the time his initial tour of duty with the United States Navy would end. October 21st 1977 the USS *Independence* (CV-62) returned to the United States from Sailor's first seven-month deployment to Europe. He had to wait until Thanksgiving and Christmas time and used two weeks leave at a time. He enjoyed himself enormously making the best of a short-lived visit to North 18th Street. Sailor had now become not only a traveler but a world traveler, navigating through the airports of America and making traveling arrangements became a cinch. Sailor was back in forth in the airports without a care in the world, always flying on a plane somewhere but mostly back and forth to North 18th Street. Sailor was a young single black man making good money and had no bills. Life was exceptionally good and carefree in those days. But there was one issue with an old girlfriend that had become sort of a "thorn in the flesh." It was an issue Sailor had to deal with despite his disbelief of the reality and authenticity of a dependent daughter.

Nonetheless, when Sailor went home during Thanksgiving of 1977, it was a surprise return like he always loved doing. Going home brought immediate attention to Sailor and made him the center of attraction. He talked and talked about the cruise, the port of calls, the chow onboard the fascinating aircraft carrier and the mere fact of traveling places he only dreamed about as a boy. He felt twenty feet tall in comparison to his friends he knew from North 18th Street. He felt he had a message and a testimony to tell at church. But he also felt a deep weight of heaviness inside his soul. Sailor felt like he had something to say and something to tell, but the ghost of his recent past immensely plagued him—a spirit that had followed him across the waters and a spirit he lacked the know-how to renounce. A foul spirit was with him, and it would follow him from that day forward for many years. He was harassed often in his thoughts. His memories of the events would be vivid and emotionally stirring in a bad way. He really tried not to pay attention to it, but every night he lay down, he was reminded that he had made a pact with sin. it spoke to him almost to say, "You can't get rid of me that easily just because you are home. I am yours and you are mine. You invited me in, and I am here to stay. Welcome aboard, shipmate!"

He felt haunted by something he personally invited but was quite irritated by its presence and did not know how to get rid of them—they were legion. He knew the church experience and felt somewhat at ease as long as he was in church or around church people. He could not figure out why all the "spiritual" people in church could not or did not recognize the ugly spirit that was with him. He had feelings of a different kind because he supposed and thought everyone in church was complete with salvation and discernment. That someone would be able to guide him through these unwelcomed but invited spirits he was introduced to and returned home with. He learned quickly that the people he thought would be able to guide him through and help him get rid of these ungodly and nasty spirits were themselves in need of help. He easily mingled right back into the flow of church and kind of sported himself as one who experienced the world and a proficient traveler. One Sunday he was able to get a word in at church of how thankful he was for God keeping him and bringing him back home. In typical style as it goes in a charismatic church, 90 percent of the congregants erupted in an excited and emotional uproar of "Hallelujah, thank you, Jesus! Yes, Lord, praise God" and so on." And Sailor himself fueled the charisma by continuing to say on and say on! He knew deep inside his soul that his words were worthless because he did not take care of first business to genuinely repent of his thoughts and actions and ways while overseas. But at the same time, he did not want people to think he had failed in any way, nor did he want people to think he did not have salvation in his soul.

In typical fashion and normal response, Sailor jumped up from his pew and danced a little and even shed a few tears along with the church as they thanked the Lord for his return. His heart and intentions, though not entirely honest, nonetheless, were genuine. Church service was at least stimulating and mentally refreshing while he visited home. It would be years before his heart would truly understand his actions as his soul would become broken in a real way and contrition would flood his entire being. Sailor's struggle with salvation, faith, and the Bible was a long struggle that was hindered by a failure of religion and the institutionalized church. Many young churchmen and women embrace the same concept as TJ, the Sailor did. There is much unending truth about the Most High that goes way beyond the institutionalized church and religions of this world. By the mercy and grace of the Most High, Sailor was picked, yeah, gracefully removed from the competitive life of religion and eye pleasers and lip service. He did not say it was an easy thing to be removed from the sham of the Christian religion, but the Most High saw fit to remove him. For Sailor to reenter the institutionalized church world and religion of Christianity would be like trying to rebuild a smoldering house of ash from the same ash. Yet decades later, the attempt to rebuild a ruined house was made in the life of Sailor. The Most High would take Sailor to a place of solitaire singleness. Don't misunderstand, there is a multitude of brothers and sisters in that world whom he dearly loved as members in the family of the Most High, but there is a relationship with the Most High that unequivocally extends way beyond the church institution and religious world. It would be at least two decades later before Sailor would even approach the doorway of the entry to that relationship. Much exposure to Sailor's true heart had yet to be unveiled and realized. But for now, he took the liberty of traveling back and forth to home whenever possible on long weekends. He would take a few days here and there while back at Cecil Field, Florida, from November 1977 through January 1978, when his second Mediterranean cruise would get underway.

Shake-Down Cruise

After being disembarked from the boat in Norfolk, Virginia, and back in Jacksonville, Florida, Sailor was making every attempt to find that life of a Christian. He was enjoying the life and times of Jacksonville and reunited with his Christian friends back at Cecil Field. There was Brother C and Brother Darnell Bowman. His understanding of what a Christian is and what Christianity is all about would go through revolutionary changes over the next twenty-five years, but back then all he desired was to be a good Christian. The words *Christian* and *Christianity* were very ambiguous to Sailor. He did understand the principle and expectation, but he found little demonstration not only in his own life but in those he believed in. He hooked up again with Darnell Bowman and Brother C, and they would visit a few churches in Jacksonville, all Churches of God in Christ. Every Sunday Sailor was off work and he knew Darnell was going to church, he made it a point to be ready and tag along with him. Darnell had become the most encouraging brother of Christianity to Sailor in those days. He did not talk much about a lot of things, but they mostly went to church together, and Darnell had an awesome car. In the mind of Sailor, Darnell always seemed to be more advanced than he, and Darnell always struck Sailor as excelling in the Church of God in Christ, possibly becoming a bishop or some national leader or instructor. Not once did Sailor ever think evil of Darnell Bowman. He needed Darnell's fellowship like the fish need the ocean to stay alive. Sailor did not know how much Darnell may have been aware of it then, but Darnell was enormous encouragement to Sailor. Just knowing Darnell and that he was on the same naval air station as Sailor was inspiring by itself. He felt a strong kinship with the other Christian brothers around. But he failed to see the need for that kinship until returning to Cecil Field after his first deployment and hooking up with his Christian brothers again. Sailor does not remember ever sharing with them about the licentious and promiscuity living he engaged in while overseas. He was too embarrassed to even mention the word whorehouse, but he tried not to beat himself up much because he reasoned in his mind that it wasn't all that bad. Sailor had discovered the evil temptations of his heart that he was clueless of, but those same evils would one day resurface. Sailor did not understand the long-range consequences he would have to face. So he wrote off the licentious and promiscuous things he did overseas as a growing experience and reasoned in his fleshly mind that he would have to learn how to be stronger the next time.

The USS Dwight D. Eisenhower (CVN-69)

The time had come to embark on another aircraft carrier in August 1978 and start his travels up again. This time to he would travel to Saint Thomas of the Virgin Islands. The USS *Dwight D. Eisenhower* (CV-69) was the navy's newest nuclear-powered aircraft carrier with awesome destructive capability. The *Eisenhower* was new and even had the nerve to have a new smell. The bunks were new. The sheets, mattresses, pillows, and pillowcases were all new. The mess deck was new, and the tin cafeteria trays were new. The ship was considerably larger than the *Indy* and was the United States of America's way of flexing its military muscles. If he thought the USS *Indy* was fascinating and an awesome ship to behold, the USS *Ike* (short for *Eisenhower*), was in a class of its own. Both the inside and outside was freshly painted shipboard gray and ready for sea trials. Sailor does not remember the *Indy* having an ice cream parlor on board—maybe it did, he just does not remember that detail. But for sure the *Ike* had an ice cream parlor onboard that was always crowded just before, during, and after chow. In those days, he was always getting ice cream mainly because it was one of the amenities Uncle Sam provided for the crew on board a US warship. The ship's store was a little bigger, with a larger selection of items to purchase. You could even order through the Navy Exchange catalog without paying sales tax while deployed and receive your item through the ship's store. The barbershop on board was a little bigger and had about five barbers in the shop. The ship's servicemen brothers in the barber ran the shop, had the shop looking identical to a brother's barbershop on land. Pictures, music, posters with haircut styles, and even customer waiting chairs. The barbershop on board the *Ike* was real nice. Once you stepped inside the barbershop, you could easily forget you were on a ship. The motion of the ship sailing at sea reminded you that you were not in a barbershop on land, and at any time, general quarters could be called away. When GQ was called, you would have to get out of the barber's chair to leave the shop whether the barber finished cutting your hair or not. The USS *Dwight D. Eisenhower* (CVN69) was a really nice tour of duty with some crazy experiences and some backsliding. But all in all, the experience on board the *Ike* took Sailor a step higher and time of exploratory philosophical talking and thinking.

The shakedown cruise included return trips to the Virgin Islands of Saint Thomas and Saint Croix in August 1978 and September through October 1978. There was not much excitement while visiting the islands other than the place was very picturesque, and the weather was like a nice summer vacation on the beach. The Virgin Islands reminded Sailor of a place to visit on occasion and not so much a place he would like to live. There have been places overseas in the Mediterranean and the United Kingdom that, in hindsight, Sailor wished he would have taken orders and done a full tour of duty. But the Virgin Islands was to Sailor tourist money-making place, and he could not see himself living there. Sailor did not take many pictures of the islands. He enjoyed the islands but was ready and looking forward to returning to the Mediterranean. Sailor's excitement was like the anticipation he had of summer. When he was a boy living on North 18th Street, every summer he wished and hoped and anticipated that maybe Dad would take him and his siblings to Hershey Amusement Park, in Hershey, Pennsylvania. That same type of excitement was now the desire to return to the Mediterranean and travel up and down the Mediterranean coast. He had discovered that he loved the experience of world travel, especially after going back home and seeing guys he knew and went to school with still hanging around the streets of Harrisburg, Pennsylvania. Even many of his church friends were still stuck in Harrisburg, involved in the same old, same old. Sailor had just traveled across the vast Atlantic Ocean into the Mediterranean Sea and returned safely and felt there were real-life stories he could tell. He could not wait to go back overseas to develop more stories. Sailor was not married and had no children and was young and single and the desires and things he engaged in was affecting only his life and no one else, so he thought. The days of crying on the train and in his bunk at Cecil Field were truly the proverbial electrical shock of maturing. Sailor shed fewer tears as time moved on after his first Med cruise, although there were more tears left inside his soul. They would be nothing like the first experience of homesickness. Occasionally, he would think about when he left for boot camp and when he arrived at Cecil Field and run through his mind the thoughts he had and the feelings he experienced. He concluded that he was very young, an emotional wreck, and a youth with much to learn but eager to learn much.

Preparations to Return Overseas

The trips back and forth to home from November 1977 through December 1978 were many to the point Sailor was accumulating sky miles. He would return home as much as possible and each time he returned home the experience was like a distant person out of touch with family and friends. His mind was stuck in the recent past of Europe and the things he experienced while overseas. He strangely adopted to the life overseas, and it became a large portion of his life that he would experience repeatedly at that age. It was difficult for Sailor to relate his feelings and experiences to family members, though he so desperately wanted to. He wanted his parents and all his siblings to admire him and hear what he had to talk about. He knew his younger siblings would not relate to his experiences, so he walked among them as the big brother who traveled the world. But as for his older siblings, he wanted to tell them everything, but it seemed no one wanted to listen. He would get a word or two in whenever he could about his growing experiences and leave it at that. Those were the days he began to dabble in poetry to express what he was going through and what experiences he was having in life. How maturity had dumped itself on him, seemingly out of nowhere. Home was very much different for Sailor; it was now a place he visited. He always felt the need to check in with Fred and pick Fred's brain. He desperately wanted to demonstrate to Fred how TJ became the Sailor and how Sailor became a contender on the stage of life. Sailor and Fred would sit around in those days and figuratively and philosophically "jump off cliffs," as Fred liked to term it. Admiration of Fred and Bay was endless in those days. At times, it would be hard for Sailor to believe that his friendship with Bay and Fred could ever end. The young TJ looked to Fred and Bay all his youthful life for direction, guidance, and advice. TJ, now the Sailor, began to understand that he greatly desired from his father what Fred and Bay willingly gave to him. But he reasoned in his mind that Dad had several deficiencies and shortcomings that he did not fault him for and that Dad was all right with Sailor's older brothers mentoring him. Dad was not a high school graduate and had minimal education and was not always there in the life of TJ in ways Sailor thought he should be. Dad was a provider and breadwinner, but Sailor learned later in life a man who has children is bound by the law of the land to provide for them. But the true character and demeanor of a father spring forth deep from within the heart and soul of a man. The father's spirit is then transformed into the heart and soul of his children. Dad lacked that quality of a father, but nonetheless he was still Dad to Sailor. But Sailor did not know how to draw that quality from his father or to request it from him. So he sought it in his brothers, who so willingly wanted to be the mentor of his life. But his brothers could only take him so far. Sailor was now a man of the world. His brothers were slowly becoming like equals to him. Having been overseas and returned home, he felt he could at least get the attention of his brothers. He would purposely engage them in conversations, drawing from every word they spoke and searching for application in his own life. At least at that time, he felt he could engage them intelligently and tell them a thing or two. Sailor had learned some things and had been places his brothers probably would never see or ever have the opportunity to experience in their lifetime. In Sailor's mind, he had a unique conversation that stood alone and could not be matched by North 18th Street experiences. The projects, North 18th Street, and the European continent were all entirely in separate categories, and neither could compete with the other. Sailor had conquered his youthful fears, overcome boyish homesickness, and adjusted to a world of exponential growth and sinful ways. His newfound sinful ways would be greatly masked for years into his future. After a brief stay at home and especially enjoying his deep conversations with Fred, the time had come to return to duty. It was time for preparations to return overseas and transit the Atlantic Ocean headed for the Mediterranean Sea. The thought and excitement of sailing back overseas were overwhelmingly satisfying. Home and everything about home, packaged in a neat little box, had now become solidified in Sailor's mind as nothing more than a good memory. A memory of profound love, but a memory nonetheless. Back to duty at VS-31, his first active-duty command had cross decked to the navy's state-of-the-art nuclear aircraft carrier, the United States Ship *Dwight D. Eisenhower* (CVN-69). Sailor's view was now "fair winds and following seas." He was ready, willing, and able to handle anything the world, the Navy and being on board ship would dish out to him. In his mind, Sailor had developed into a seasoned salt and welcomed whatever onslaught the ocean and high seas would inundate him with. First thing was personal inflection and his attempt to convince himself the sinful places he visited and sinful things he did the first time overseas would not happen again. He vowed to himself to read his Bible more and to meditate more on Scripture and to become involved in more constructive activity like sightseeing and learning all he could about the European continent. When he was a young lad in middle school and high school, he would dream of going to countries of Europe. And the time had come for him to begin learning and begin living the life of a Christian he desperately failed to do over a year ago.

It seemed just like yesterday, the familiar scene of families on the pier saying their goodbyes.—children crying, husband and wife embracing, and the noisy unhindered activity of the dock crew untying the naval vessel from the chocks on the pier. On his second Mediterranean Cruise, the battle group would be leaving in the winter months and returning in the summer months. What a big difference that would be, but they would be overseas for a portion of the summer. Sailor would rather have spent the entire summer overseas like the first time from March through October. Nonetheless, the time had arrived, and the battle group was about to sail again back overseas for another long arduous seven-month deployment. But Sailor would not finish this cruise with his squadron shipmates. Instead, he would choose one of the worst decisions of his naval career. Regretfully, for years, the decision to return to the United States would haunt Sailor almost endlessly. His initial tour of enlistment with the navy would end midstream of the cruise, and instead of riding the ship back, Sailor made the first of many bad decisions in his life by leaving the ship and flying back to the United States solo. On January 16, 1979, after loved ones said their goodbyes, gave their hugs, and shed a few tears, the word was passed over the 1MC, "Now set the sea and anchor detail, smoking lamp is out in all authorized spaces." Following that command, the ship was assisted by the Norfolk Naval Base tugboats, and the word was passed, "Underway, shift colors. Secure the sea and anchor detail."

Sailor had visited home the past twelve months, gone back to Mount Calvary Church of God in Christ, given his traditional testimony of how God kept him through dangers seen and unseen, and observed his friends still standing on the corners, as if their world was at a standstill. Now he was back on his way to familiar territory—overseas. He felt twenty feet tall, having fought a relentless fight of homesickness, engaged in sinful practices, dealt with fear, worry, tears, and even the spirit of cowardice. In the mind of Sailor, he was ready to do it all over again, but this time with a new perspective and a new spirit among familiar territory. He did miss home, but being at home was becoming a distant dream of sorts. With every occasion he left home, it was becoming increasingly challenging to re-acclimate himself back into the home he left over a year and a half ago. Home would *never* be the same. Fred's word had become alive, and Sailor was beginning to understand what Fred meant when he said, "When you leave, you cannot come back." He did not think of himself as better than anyone back home, but he discovered over the years that he failed to manage the distance created in him by being in the navy. There was a certain arrogance and heir of "knowing" some things that formed inside the heart of Sailor, a selfish arrogance. A know-it-all spirit that flourished in the heart of Sailor for more than twenty-five years. One day in the distant future, the inevitable rock bottom would introduce itself to Sailor. Instead of rock bottom, Sailor likes to think of it as a slab, because it was the slab of death intended for Sailor by a barrage of demonic onslaught. When rock bottom or the slab of deaths enters one's life, it is impossible to resist falling to the slab while the purging of hell takes place. True humility replaces both hell and the slab. Sailor would not know the salvation of Messiah until he truly died to the sinful curse of self. The biblical doctrine of salvation is an act of faith, but the biblical doctrine of living that salvation is the fruit of the esteemed. On the one hand, Sailor had faith in the Doctrine of Salvation, but on the other hand, he utterly lacked the doctrine of true godliness. His second trip overseas continued to be a learning curve, and while he fought and struggled within his own spirit, he still had much ground to cover growing and maturing into the man envisioned by the Creator Elohym Yahuah.

Second Mediterranean Cruise

Crossing the Atlantic on the second trip overseas was not nearly as eventful as the first crossing. The ship conducted general quarters after general quarters, fire drill after fire drill. The USS *Dwight D. Eisenhower* (CVN-69) was the navy's newest super aircraft carrier. Uncle Sam and the ship's captain had to make sure the vessel was seaworthy and battle-worthy. Crossing the Atlantic on the second trip was a series of training exercise after training exercise. The battle group did hit some rough seas in the middle of January while crossing the vast Atlantic Ocean and sailed into thick ice caps broken off in the ocean. There were times it was a harrowing experience. But not to worry, for the massive tons of beautifully sculptured steel made by man are designed to withstand direct hits. The ship could stay afloat due to its advanced watertight integrity hatches. Sailor was excited and enjoying every minute of being on board the *Eisenhower* and on his way back overseas to his stomping grounds. The thought did cross his mind about the whorehouse, but he quickly dismissed the idea because he had every intention of walking the straight and narrow his second time overseas. He began his long journey reading the Bible every day and would mark off chapters he had read and verses he memorized. Sailor made Bible verse memorization a daily task to learn the Bible and become proficient in the pages of the Holy Word. Once the task force hit the Strait of Gibraltar, as far as Sailor was concerned, he was back overseas and had transited the Atlantic Ocean safely. The next stop would inevitably be Napoli, Italy, the place where he first gave in to the lust of the flesh and the lust of the eye and the pride of life. What struck Sailor as odd is that the closer they were to Naples, the more comfortable he became. He felt like he had returned to a place in time that was a nemesis to him, but it was also a friend to him. It was in this place that he stepped into an unknown world of sin and licentiousness beyond what he knew even existed. On North 18th Street, life was all about friends which were family, and the worst he had done back home was eyeball a *Playboy* magazine or two, nothing too out of the ordinary for a growing young man, and especially once he became aware of the spirit and influence a father has on his home. It would not be until the late 1990s before a father's profound influence would become a reality to Sailor. He mentally struggled and fought within his soul wrestling at times with sleepless nights struggling to deny the inevitable.

In other words, what Sailor began to realize is that as the father lives his life, his children partake of the father's spirit, like it or not, agree or disagree. Age and wisdom would make Sailor more exposed to the world and more aware of the darkness that resided in his own heart. In many ways, like his father for the sins of the father became more real to Sailor at each step of maturity. But he passionately denied and fought against the nasty temptation and spirit of lust. Of course, he did not understand, nor did he want to accept the reality of generational sins. The sinful thoughts that repeatedly invaded his mind in those days kept him deep in the fray. Fighting and not understanding why he had to fight something he did not like. But the fight kept him uncontrollably drawn toward that which is not right. As if the mere thought of sinful practices attracted him more to them. Having this knowledge does not excuse his sinful actions and thoughts during his naval career. But he would one day find solace knowing that his greatest enemy was himself that he was tasked to conquer. It would not be until his complete discharge from the navy and spiritual growth that he would comprehend the personal spiritual battles he was engaged in. Like the saying goes "If I only knew then what I know now!" But then where would the growth have occurred if he knew it all then? Kind of interesting thought when one thinks about it. If Sailor's knowledge and experience of personal spiritual battles and spiritual battles at large would have been clear to him at nineteen, what would he have to learn up to his current point in life? Perhaps he would have been like Enoch and walked away with God; that's a nice, pacifying thought. Without dishonoring his father, it was clear to see where the spirit of Sailor stemmed from. Sailor does not blame his father for his own actions, the blame is squarely upon Sailor. But the influence and sinful thoughts did not originate from the spirit of Sailor. And such is the life of every single human being born of earthly parents.

After passing through the Strait of Gibraltar, the next stop would be the one and only Napoli, Italy, where the USS *Dwight D. Eisenhower* (CVN-69) would spend two weeks in port. That is a long time to be in port overseas for a naval vessel. There is way too much trouble a sailor could get into, and even though they were trained military men who had some degree of self-respect and dignity, trouble would look for sailors coming off the sea. Sailor swore to himself and prayed to God not to engage in sinful acts and embrace the partying spirit while in Italy on this tour of duty. The first time overseas was a world-rocking experience, and he desired this one to be a world learning experience. He made sure that he would sign up for every guided tour he possibly could within a two-week period. He went on tour after tour within the time frame the ship was in Italy. When duty felled that Sailor had to stand watch, those hours were the most grueling time of all. On watch duty, Sailor would pace back and forth on board the ship while it was docked in the harbor of Naples, Italy. He often imagined what he would do when his watch was over and go on liberty. He pretty much hung out with the same crew during the *Indy* cruise other than the guided tours. The tours he would take alone with other crew members, people he did not know other than they were on the same ship. The tours to Rome Italy, Athens, Greece, Corinth, and other places of the Bible were very captivating to Sailor. He immeasurably enjoyed seeing those places even to this day, and they introduced him to a world of experience that significantly contributed to his thinking as an adult. It's funny now, but those days seemed extra long, and it appeared to Sailor that he would be overseas for years. Memory is strong for Sailor, and he can still smell in his mind the JP5 Jet fuel smell on board the aircraft carrier. He can hear the sounds of the ships 1MC, voices of the crew, feel the anticipation while standing in the liberty line, and sense the excitement while ashore visiting places abroad. Feel the winter turn into spring and the excitement of changing from cold to a warmer temperature. Feel the rush of excitement of each day as he started it all over again as to what his adventure would be for that day. What he discovered on the second Mediterranean cruise is that there was a sense of homesickness inside his soul for Naples, Italy, and the European continent. Much of his life growing into adulthood was experienced in foreign countries, and the quickness of his adaptation to those places made it easy for the land overseas to become a part of his soul. He could have never imagined while standing on the porch with his siblings on North 18th Street, about to leave for the navy, the profound impact traveling abroad would forever change who he was then. Never did he think while onboard the train on his way to Great Lakes, Illinois, he would be changed almost in an instant. He was clueless while lying in the bunk at Cecil Field, Florida, crying because of homesickness, that he would one day become homesick for the continent of Europe and especially Naples, Italy. Sailor realized that there are some aspects of life and growing that were not easy for him to explain.

The Nagging Temptation

Sailor was full of questions without answers and answered questions he was not sure of but acted as though he knew the answer. His thoughts plagued him as to why he had to be tempted to do things he did not want to do. Did it have something to do with weakness in mind and heart or was it that he really wanted to do those things? He did not know the answer to the question but followed what his desire and heart led him to do. He did not want to engage in sinful acts, but at the same time, the company of friends he kept was an influence to Sailor to keep alive the things that resided in his own heart. As the struggle and fight to overcome self continued, Sailor once again hung out with the same brothers from the first Med. cruise. As those brothers began to talk of their exploits and excursions in places Sailor was familiar with from the first cruise, he found himself listening to their stories.

"For that which I do, I allow not: for what I would, that do I not; but what I hate, that do I"—these are the words of the apostle Paul in his Epistle to the Romans, chapter 7 and verse 15. It would literally be years before Sailor would understand and move toward verse 24 and 25 of that chapter: "O wretched man that I am! Who shall deliver me from the body of this death?" And though he was familiar with the Holy Scripture that says, "Blessed is he that walketh not in the counsel of the ungodly" (Ps. 1), he was more led by, "But what I hate, that do I." It was much stronger in Sailor than "Blessed is he that walketh not in the counsel of the ungodly." The demons he fought against in his mind and the filth of sin in his heart was a constant challenge and pull against his soul. But he yearned to become what he understood then as a true Christian, patterned after biblical truth. But in those days, he was very much ruled by his fleshly mind. Much of the time Sailor felt like a bastard because he supposed it extremely difficult to become the person outlined in the Bible. But he valiantly struggled and fought and struggled and fought every day! He hoped the guided tours to help keep his mind occupied. He greatly desired to do what was right in the eyes of God. Romans 7:15 would be the internal struggle of Sailor for decades to come. The desire to be Christ-like and the characteristics of godliness once again became foreign to Sailor on his second cruise. Figuratively speaking, he held on to biblical truths in his hip pocket and not in his heart. He never discarded the truth of Scripture; it was just the living of that truth he was unable to attain. One day in the distant future, Sailor would know that it is not as difficult as it appeared to walk the walk. Proper training and guidance with certain tools would greatly aid him to engage in spiritual battles. It would be at least thirty years into the life of Sailor that the Sermon would make its debut. He had hoped even then that his experiences and his victories would be encouraging to some young sailor in the midst of identical temptations. That young sailor would learn of the life and times of TJ, the Sailor of days gone by, and know the victory of overcoming the wiles of the devil.

Too much listening brought about the same walk of disbelief and ungodliness. This time Sailor wavered back and forth between the nightlife with the brothers but acted like the man of wisdom during the times they were at sea. If the brothers judged Sailor as a hypocrite during those cruises, he did not know because they did not treat him any differently. Sailor continued to hang out with his squadron brothers and would continue to pull from his hip pocket some Scripture every now. While at sea, he and the brothers would discuss the unjust and prejudice issues onboard Uncle Sam's boat, the USS *Dwight D. Eisenhower* (CVN69). Sailor felt like part of a family of brothers. It was a general, almost unspoken consensus back then that they had to stick together. The reality of the matter is that Sailor and the brothers had each other's back. Sailor got along very well the brothers, and Sailor was obsessed with wanting to fit into the brothers' lifestyle. He needed to belong with men who could talk his talk and who understood him as a black man because they certainly did not reject him as a Christian. On a day that is now fuzzy in the memory of Sailor, after taking a guided tour of the ruins of Europe and pretty much exhausted, the temptation struck and struck hard. The great fault appeared when earlier he listened to the brothers' stories about the whorehouse. The whorehouse was no longer a new thing, why did he think their stories were so fascinating? He thought about the whorehouse while traveling home from the first cruise, and the place entered his mind even while back at Cecil Field, Florida. Now here he was again back in the place that shattered his religion like a battering ram destroys an entrance to a doorway. It was a nice spring evening, and the brothers had been talking most of the day about what they were going to do on liberty at night. Sailor did not want to go on liberty at night because he knew the temptation he would face. But he was also curious to see what he would do facing those same temptations. Like a flash of light in a fast-forward scene of a movie, Sailor found himself again with the brothers. They were walking down the main drag of Napoli right off the pier, up through the city toward the United Services Organization (USO). While these guys were on their licentious quest to satisfy their lust, excitement filled Sailor's heart like a child returning to the amusement park on a nice spring day. Simultaneously, he was nervous and hopeful that all they would do was have a good time. What that meant to Sailor was club hopping and dancing and drinking and smoking. He could tolerate those vices over sexual sins with a woman, which takes sinful acts to an entirely different level. The connection of soul and spirit with a strange woman is no comparison like drinking and smoking. While both are destructive to the life of any individual, one vice is personal and the other vice, in many ways, is a connection with multiple persons. Spiritual connection with multiple people is one of the craziest realities of all, and that connection operates on a level of its own. The first place they stopped at was the bar not far from the pier. It was the place where he had that weird and wacky experience with the transvestite over a year ago during the first cruise. They popped in and out of the bar just to see what was going on inside. Then they made their way further into the nightlife of Naples, Italy. They stopped at maybe a club or two, and there wasn't much going on at the clubs but some white boys from the ship doing their thing. Then out of nowhere, Mac said, "Let's cross the street and find those tight-fitting skirts up the hill." Sailor knew what he meant and what was on his mind. Sailor looked at Mac with a faint smile, and Mac laughed and said, "C'mon, T, you know you want it, and you know you've been thinking about it." Sailor became irritated because what he said, but he did not deny what his friend said because he was correct on both assessments.

Familiar ground and familiar territory was now their destination. But something about this time was not as exciting as the first time, and something about this time was almost like "Okay, let's get this over with because I actually don't want to be here." But he tagged along with the brothers he was hanging out with. Straight up the narrow cobblestone alleyway to decide which "ware" he would purchase for a cheap fifteen, twenty-minute thrill. Sailor felt like he was mummified following along while a sense of curiosity and familiarity flooded his mind. He knew and understood the circumstances, and he sort of knew what to expect anticipating going through with the "connection." He fought the thoughts about the whorehouse during the transit to the Med, and he wanted it to be over with. He and the brothers arrived at the place of licentiousness and fornication, and this time it was not as crowded as the first time. No sooner had they stepped foot into the place of whoredom than the women were all over them, just like before. Speaking broken English with a limited vocabulary like "suckie, fuckie." At this point of being familiar with that rhyming phrase and proposition, Sailor was becoming irritated with the whole encounter. The first visit overseas a year ago, that question was not only exciting by enticing. This time, the rhyming phrase was boring and degrading not only to Sailor but to the women who made the proposition. His mind was his deep battleground, and his struggling was to overcome his mind. He concluded the women thought very little or thought nothing of themselves to ask a total stranger if they wanted to have sex. Their proposition was always in vulgar street language, making the whole encounter foul in the mind of Sailor. But then, Sailor concluded that he also thought very little of himself and the lack of honesty and integrity that controlled his senses and fleshly desires. A prostitute woman will freely give up her body for a few bucks for what might be pleasurable but what might also be harmful depending on the man she would meet. Sailor had become so sexually and mentally deranged that he did not give a damn about her, nor did he care about her life. He only sought to feed his lust. In that type of situation, lust, evil, wickedness, and the total depravity of man prevails when one willingly and consciously enjoys a licentious lifestyle. Of course, Sailor was as ignorant as a classroom of infants in those days, and his reasoning was not reasoning at all but rather the epitome of fleshly pleasure and a wicked heart.

There was a difference between the first time and this new experience. Sailor had no emotions and total disregard for a human being especially a fragile woman. He entered the room with the lady of his choice, motioned to her to get undressed as she smiled like she was enjoying herself, and Sailor began to manhandle her. He threw her on the bed and proceeded like a wild dog not in heat but in anger of submission and lifeless pounding. He did not care that she was human, and he did not care that she was someone's daughter, and he did not care that she was a woman.

Sailor remembers being with the prostitute for about a half an hour in a dimly lit room. He was insensitive to her being a female. He was rough in handling her body. He was angry at his decision to pay for sex but thrilled at the encounter to be a proud sinner.

He jumped up when done and removed the prophylactic, threw it on the floor, and said goodbye! While he was going through those ungodly emotions and reactions, she was attempting to rub his back as though she was expressing intimacy. He moved even faster to get away from her as he was getting dressed. He then brazenly said to her, "You are a slut and I am a dog. Let me get out of here." He was not clear at the time as to why the experience was not as exciting as the first time. And why he even allowed himself to venture back into someplace that he repented for over and over again. Nonetheless, he quickly walked out of the very dimly lit room that smelled like a thousand musty guys had passed that way before him. While walking out of the room, he sensed he was not alone and the spirit that initially drew him there would plague Sailor for decades. As he walked down the stairs, the entranceway up to the room that he had just left appeared to be getting narrower and narrower. It was if the walls were closing in on him and the dimly lit passageway had all of a sudden become dark. This was becoming a crazy, unexplainable experience.

What happened to the lights? he thought. *Is someone playing a game on me, or am I about to get jumped and robbed this time?* He strongly felt an evil, wicked presence he sensed was about to manifest itself. Was this a three-dimensional prelude for Sailor who was about to enter into the blackness of the darkest regions of hell? Was this some kind of message God was sending his way to stop toying around with whoredom? *What in the hell is going on?* Quite an appropriate thought of Sailor to question what may be going on in hell. He truly felt he was about to die under circumstances he did not understand. He began to perspire to the point of his shirt becoming stained with his sweat. Now twenty years old, he did not sweat that easily or that quickly over any situation. But this was different, it was if Satan was walking down those steps with him and had deluded his mind. All he could do was sincerely cry out to God from his spirit, "God, please, please, *please*, permit me safe passage!" By that time, Sailor had made it through the narrow passageway out to the larger alley, and sadly, he went over to the whorehouse looking for the brothers he went up there with.

He made his way over to the entrance house to wait for the other brothers, and they seemed to be taking a bit longer than Sailor. He was done and ready to go back either to downtown Napoli or back to the boat. He became irritated and very impatient, remembering the chase of the shore patrol last time. Sailor paced and paced back and forth, thinking the brothers may have left him. The women in the entrance house propositioned him again with the same tired old phrase of "suckie, fuckie?" He was angry at himself for having followed the brothers but all along wanting to befriend them and upset with himself for screwing that girl. The prostitute probably had to either feed herself or children or entire family by selling her body to the nearest client. Every day, she is connecting her soul and spirit with multiple sailors and marines who she probably would never see again in a thousand lifetimes. And if by chance Sailor would ever run across her or the other women from the first time, it would take a divine act of God to recognize them. He did not care who they were or what their lives were about. Sailor thought they were mere dirty sluts who were united with untold numbers of men, and if they were dirty sluts, then what did that make Sailor? He swore to himself and God that this cruise would be an educational one and a tour guide visit of the ancient places of Europe. He did not want to engage sin of any kind including sex. A deep concern of Sailor was that if they were engaged in a military conflict that he would die and on his way, straight to hell nonstop. The brothers he went to the whorehouse with must have been enjoying themselves and savoring the moment. Either they left him or they were still screwing those Italian women, or maybe they went back for seconds. At any rate, Sailor became incredibly impatient and irritated and ready to leave the premises.

He did not want to be there and could not forgive himself for tagging along with the brothers. He started alone walking down the dark narrow alley in Naples, Italy, hearing all sorts of sounds and dogs barking and people. He did not care about the sounds or the dogs or people, he just wanted to get as far away from Momma Rosa's as he possibly could. The sounds became louder and louder, and the people seemed as though they were directly in the rear of his footsteps. He was looking around to see if someone was following him, and he began to walk a little faster. Looking this way, looking that way, dogs barking and cats darting out in front of him from between houses. Sailor had no problem running, though it was not the shore patrol this time but rather the guilt and magnification of probably normal sounds on any given day that pursued him. He ran like a bat out of hell, as they say, and the faster he ran, the louder the sounds became. The people that seemed to be in his footsteps now seemed to be in his ear whispering things like, "Run, you sissy, run. They are going to get you, run!"

What the hell! he thought! *What is this? Where are these thoughts and feelings of fear coming from?* He picked up the pace and began to run faster than he had ever run before, making every attempt to get away from the sounds and voices directly in his ear. And the craziest thing ever happened to Sailor—he tripped and almost fell on the ground!

I NEVER trip when I run, NEVER! What is this tripping shit? I don't trip when I run. My feet are sure, and my running is definite. But he realized the guilt and demon he was trying to run from was more than in his ear but had taken up residence in his soul. Instead of focusing on getting out of that alley, he was now focused on the demon taunting and plaguing him in a devilish way.

Mercy

Back in those days, Sailor had no confidence in his prayers to God, and he did not believe that God would even consider his godless prayers. But at that moment, he was afraid with an uneasy feeling in his soul, and he believes to this day that God saw fit to be merciful toward him while he was running. He yelled out to the top of his voice, "*God, I'm sorry...please!*" That's all he said, and like raindrops that fall from heaven, it was if drops of mercy fell into his soul and he no longer was afraid. It seemed as though his eyes became infrared, and he could see blocks ahead. His footing became sure like the hind spoken of in 2 Samuel 22:34. Funny, the voices faded, and the noisy sounds of dogs and cats ceased. The only explanation that Sailor has is that God was merciful toward him. Esoteric, one may call the experience; nonetheless, that is his explanation and reasoning. He ran the remainder of that alley all downhill as if he was being assisted sort of floating but running nonetheless. Each foot picked up and laid down on the ground was precise, and each stride was calculated, and the run down the hill out of the place of sinful pleasure was left far behind. Two things he felt when he reached the bottom of the alley and could begin to see the bright lights of Naples and families milling about: he was without question being pursued by Satan, and with mercy, God, on that night, saw fit to ease Sailor's mind. He was running from the gates of hell and the captivating pleasures of sin. Hell had assigned a demonic spirit of lust to invade his soul, and the Almighty saw fit to rescue him and sent an angel Sailor's way called Mercy. The dark alleys of Napoli, Italy, were captivating, sensual, uncontrollable, and unforgiving. He did not see an angel but the change from fear to focus, almost instantaneously. A sudden rush of adrenaline, sharpness of sight, and the confidence of getting out of that place overwhelmed what he was feeling earlier. He chose to attribute his ability to refocus to an angelic presence from Heaven. Sailor went from hell to heaven while running in that alley. Needless to say, that was the last experience he *ever* had in such a place like that while overseas. There would be more temptations in the future as the spirits attached to him would transit the Atlantic Ocean with him, just like last time. But *none* would compare to the pursuit of evil spirits and sinfulness in his recent experiences overseas. One year ago, he willingly stepped in a place that uprooted the very fiber of his soul and dislocated the neurons of his brain and confused the connection of synapses in his brain.

Navy Orders

The remainder of Sailor's second Mediterranean cruise was at this point much reflection and self-examination. He was extremely hard on himself and purposely so because it was his way then of handling the nagging temptation. He knew that hanging out with the brothers was agreeing to give in to the world of sinful lust. He appreciated the fact that when the brothers went on liberty from that time forward, they did not pressure him to come along. He knew they would be going out into the nightlife, and Sailor knew he should not be doing the things they were doing. They themselves knew Sailor should not be doing the things they were doing. It was like an unspoken separation, yet they did not tell Sailor he was supposed to be separated. They allowed Sailor to experience what they knew he wanted to. But all along they knew he was not supposed to be following in their footsteps. Those guys did not say or offer any advice, one way or another; they just let you do you, right or wrong. In some sense, when Sailor did not go with them, they appeared to be all right with it. In another sense, Sailor thought himself to be a young wise leader or example of sorts. The brothers still respected Sailor's perspective and philosophy of words. In those days, all Sailor had was words, and most of those words sprung from the conversations he had with Fred on North 18th Street. Sailor's words were not mixed with Scripture; they were just words. But they were words that appeared to encourage and instill hope of some kind to other men, both black and white. He began to take his own personal tours to ancient sites. He would go on full-day excursions, sometimes alone, and other times with a couple of other white squadron members. He knew he would not be getting into anything ungodly with them because they were more into buying souvenirs and taking pictures. Something he probably should have done a long time ago. But he could not resist to know and do what was forbidden to do. A deep wanting to know and experience things he only heard about controlled his entire body, soul, and mind. The lust of the flesh, the lust of the eye, and the pride of life nearly destroyed his faith and transformed his mind into deep worldliness. The very first experience wiped his hope of returning to the faith launching him out into the deep abyss of sin. There is a mystery of iniquity that all people face whether they give in or not the mystery of iniquity is there to terminate the soul of men and women. Sailor ran across the Scripture that says the "thief cometh not but to steal, kill and destroy." Having little depth of understanding as to the true meaning of that scripture, they were comforting alone, just knowing what the Scriptures say. Sailor's faith was stolen without mercy. He listened and considered the things the brothers told him. Scripture does say be careful of what you hear: "Take heed therefore how ye hear: for whosoever hath, to him shall be given; and whosoever hath not, from him shall be taken even that which he seemeth to have." Of course, Sailor knew nothing of that great truth in those days, so in typical youthful pride, he followed his inclinations. It wasn't their problem; it was Sailor's problem. The brothers were simply advocates used of the enemy. Once the enemy of the soul of men had secured the faith of Sailor, he sought to kill and destroy him as a human being and a so-called Christian. Sailor was on the road of the natural line of progression of death. It would be decades before the second portion of that powerful truth would become alive to Sailor "but I have come that they might have life and have it more abundantly" (John 10:10).

Sailor's first tour of duty in the United States Navy was quickly coming to an end. In retrospect, it seemed like it all went by so fast. Like fast-forwarding a tape and rewinding the tape to play it over again, it all went by fast, and to Sailor, it ended way too soon. At the end of each sentence, the event is over again just as fast as it was written. The thought of getting out of the navy did cross his mind. But when they told him he had an opportunity to go back home to Harrisburg, Pennsylvania, and still be in the navy, that sounded like music to his ears and he could not resist. He made an appointment to talk to the navy's command career counselor (CC) (the person that helps negotiate orders with the rating assignment officer, usually out of Washington, DC). The United States Navy hooked Sailor with the proverbial carrot, because at the time Sailor could not resist going back home for 3.5 years. The motive in Sailor's heart for returning to Harrisburg, Pennsylvania, was to show off who he had become and display his love and commitment to Uncle Sam. The entire experience stationed back home was about pride and revealed a heart of shame of the real person of Sailor. The navy's motto about pride, commitment, and professionalism overwhelmed Sailor. He did not know how to sort out the spirit of pride but accepted a proud spirit as his own. Little did he know that pride would become his downfall in his later years. Pride became his personal baby, and he nursed a proud spirit as though he was the creator of pride. Sailor asked the career counselor what his options were, being a petty officer third class. The CC suggested Washington, DC, or somewhere in Norfolk, VA, and then the CC mentioned NRD Harrisburg, Pennsylvania. The navy recruiting district covered all the area for central Pennsylvania. The CC then immediately said to Sailor, "But you will probably not get that."

And another senior petty officer agreed with him, "Oh no, they will not give you orders back to your home of record. You are too junior to get that kind of duty."

But Sailor has always been the type of individual that when he is told he can't have something or he can't do such and such, it becomes a challenge to him. In Sailor's mind, until God shows him that he can't do it or have it, he wants it! After the CC told him he would never get orders back home virtually in his own backyard, he said to him, "I want NRD Harrisburg. If you get me orders to NRD Harrisburg, Pennsylvania, I will reenlist."

In retrospect, in the mind of Sailor, their method could have been a psychological game to get Sailor to stay in the navy. If the psychological game was their method, then the navy achieved its goal to have Sailor reenlist. His recent experiences during his first Mediterranean cruise and on his second Mediterranean cruise divided him in his faith. For that reason, he was not sure if God would be gracious enough to grant him the request for duty in Harrisburg, Pennsylvania. Sailor did not want to get out of the navy because he was not done traveling and learning and growing. Had he gotten out of the navy at that time he felt he would be stuck in a mediocre job in the civilian sector. After all he was no more than a data entry office clerk at that point in his naval career. The CC informed the captain of Sailor's request for reenlistment, and the look on the captain's face was one of great seriousness. He said, "You ask a hard request, but we will see what we can do." The captain took the request and walked away from the administrative office workspace. The admin space was a small, 10 feet wide × 15 feet long, with six crew members working inside. This took place in the earlier part of March 1979, and from that day business as usual resumed onboard the boat. Sailor was torn as to what he should do—pray to God to let the navy approve his request or just get out of the navy because his supervisor and the captain made it seem next to impossible to have his request fulfilled. What Sailor was requesting was considered choice orders by the Navy's standards.

The protocol to request orders was to submit three requests on what the navy called a "dream" sheet for orders. Sailor listed on his request in the following order: NRD Harrisburg, Pennsylvania, Washington, DC, and Norfolk, Virginia. And quite naturally the United States Navy was going to honor a first-time re-enlistee's request and grant the first choice. Getting the orders for NRD Harrisburg, Pennsylvania, unfolded in a thrilling manner. Sailor was the senior yeoman, third class in the office having gained some experience on board ship. He was responsible for picking up the mail when mail call was called away. The sound of mail call was one of the most exciting announcements on board a naval vessel while at sea. After being deployed for a month or so, every sailor looked forward to mail call. There was a great sense of excitement and joy when the boatswain's mate called away on the 1MC, "Now mail call, mail call." There were times when the boatswain's mate would call away mail call without sounding his boatswain's pipe, and other times he would give a short sound on the pipe and then announce, "Mail call, mail call!" That call was the queue for the mail petty officer to dash down to the ships post office with ID in hand and stand in line to retrieve the mail for the unit. When the call was given, you had to be swift on your feet because other mail POs were also running throughout the ship headed toward the post office. Sometimes there would be one or two number 3 small postal bags. If there were more than three, which was seldom, you knew there was a lot of mail and possibly a letter for every squadron member. On the day Sailor received his new set of orders, there was one full bag and almost a half bag of mail for VS-31. Sailor made it down to the post office minutes after the call was made and found himself to be third in line. Sailor was full of great anticipation and sort of sad joy looking for his reply from the bureau in Washington, DC. Anxiety and excitement filled his soul to see if they gave him the orders he requested. He picked up the mail and ran back to the office in great haste with virtually two mail-bags on his back. He made a whirlwind type entry into the office. He could not wait to see what mail was in those bags. The other junior yeoman in the office helped to pull the mail out because the most important mail piece every sailor looked for was a letter from home. For that mail call, Sailor was probably the only one in the unit that was not too concerned about a letter from home. He looked for an official letter from the United States Navy, Bureau of Personnel (BUPERS). They broke open the bags and got down to the end and most of the mail was out, and he was feeling kind of disheartened because no official letter had arrived. The other yeoman yelled out to Sailor, "Hey, Sailor, this might be for you!" and he started laughing and further said, "They going to ship you to Egypt somewhere or maybe send you to California. You ain't going home, boy!" YNSN Cook was a grand jokester and typically made a joke about almost everything, but he and Sailor got along pretty good.

Sailor said to him, "Give me that envelope, chump!" and snatched it out of his hand. The return address on the envelope was Bureau of Naval Personnel, Washington, DC. Sailor's heart skipped a beat, and his palms became sweaty, something unusual for him. He thought, *This must be it because I am the only one scheduled to re-enlist, this is it!*

Untold excitement filled the heart of Sailor, and nervous anticipation flooded his mind. The CC was sitting in the office, and Sailor's supervisor was there and his friend YNSN Cook, the one who was playing around with Sailor's mail. As Sailor was opening the letter from the bureau, he reached deep within his heart and said to God, "Please, just this one time please!"

At that time, YNSN Cook interrupted his anticipation and said, "Here, here is another letter for you."

He did not expect the other letter and was not concerned about the other letter. You see, Sailor did not have many words of prayer or confession of faith in those days. He was genuinely trusting in the mercy and grace of God even in the midst of his backsliding and sinful state of mind. He knew God knew his heart, and that's what mattered most to Sailor. Sailor slowly opened the envelope from the bureau and immediately looked at the report to section which read, NRD Harrisburg, Pennsylvania, for a period of thirty-six months. Sailor exploded with uncontrollable excitement and almost hit the overhead while jumping up and down. He threw the letter on the desk and yelled, "Thank you, thank you, thank you, God!"

The CC and his immediate supervisor grabbed the orders and said, "No way, they gave it to him. Somebody upstairs must like you." You know that's how the world terms it when they don't want to acknowledge the intervention of God—they simply address him as "somebody."

The CC said, "You still have to reenlist as soon as possible or they will take the orders from you."

With boisterous, loud excitement he said, "I'll reenlist TODAY!"

At that moment in time, Sailor was in love with the United States Navy and thought it was the greatest place to serve and live out one's life. Everything he had experienced good and bad from the days of Great Lakes, Illinois, and the homesickness he wrestled with all of a sudden was worth it. Now he would get the chance to return home for three years plus while still wearing the uniform. He would be on active duty in his hometown and boasting of his experience, and he could not wait. YNSN Cook said to Sailor, "Ah, you think you bad, you think you bad now. Well, they still going to send you to Egypt when those orders are up!"

They both laughed and had a good time joking back and forth. It was like the sun had shone inside that office space on board the USS *Dwight D. Eisenhower* (CNV-69). After opening his letter from the bureau that had his first set of re-enlistment orders, he would not come down from that high for the next thirty-six months. He remembers that day vividly and remembers clearly the first sight of reading "YN3 Timothy J. Sailor, Report to NRD Harrisburg, Pennsylvania."

Unbeknownst to Sailor at the time, the words of YNSN Cook may have held some cryptic message. He was not transferred to Egypt after the tour of duty at NRD Harrisburg, Pennsylvania. But his next set of orders after NRD Harrisburg, Pennsylvania, would exceed *every* experience he had in the United States Navy and leave him with the most bitter taste he never would have imagined.

Guy, Israel, and TMI

He could not wait to reenlist, and he wanted the grandest reenlistment ceremony ever. In other words, he wanted his reenlistment officer to be someone of high rank. He liked both his commanding officer and executive officer, but they would understand if he got someone else to reenlist him. So he requested the Admiral of COMSIXTHFLT, Commander Sixth Fleet, to reenlist him. Rear Admiral Shultz (RADM) and the RADM gladly agreed.

His CC and supervisor and commanding officer said, "You are getting everything you want. Somebody up above is really in favor of you. First-time reenlistee and you got the orders you wanted. Request the admiral to reenlist you and he gladly accepted the request. What else do you want?"

It was a brief time in Sailor's life that onlookers witnessed the grace and mercy of God upon an undeserving soul: TJ, the Sailor. Almost became kind of a quasiministry to his shipmates because everything seemed to be falling in place, and in some small way, Sailor's life was a witness of God's grace. Sailor accepted the orders and now had to decide when he wanted to reenlist. The next port of call they were scheduled to visit was Haifa, Israel, and he thought a once-in-a-lifetime visit to the Holy Land of Israel. His reenlistment would be put on hold until this Holy Land visit. He was more than excited knowing that he would probably never get the opportunity again to visit Israel, especially at the age of twenty-one. He would never get a free trip to what Christians consider the holiest place on earth in the country of Israel. Guy H. was a man of great persuasive Bible influence to Sailor in those days. He was a brother in the Lord from a movement called "The Way International." Many idiosyncrasies with the Way International that Sailor could not put his finger on at the time. Nonetheless, Guy was pretty cool, and he knew his Bible very well. Guy's knowledge of the Bible intrigued and captivated Sailor's attention to him. Sailor trusted Guy's word and his advice on many occasions, especially if it had to do with the Bible. Sailor and Guy talked about what it would be like and the places we would visit while in Israel. Sailor had pretty much mapped out the tours he would take, and he planned to visit EVERY Bible location: Nazareth, Damascus, Jordon, the tomb of Christ, and wherever else he would be able to visit while there. He had not reenlisted at the point of arrival to Israel because he wanted to make sure he would be able to visit Israel. But he had accepted the orders and was overjoyed on both counts. Then the absolute unexpected thing happened that blew Sailor's mind. Blowing his mind was not an easy thing to do because Sailor had become one arrogant young man. A far cry from the little boy that left North 18th Street three years ago. His supervisor said to him on a day he does not remember, "Hey, YN3 Sailor, did you hear about your hometown? Well, actually not your hometown but close enough to melt everyone there?"

Sailor did not have a clue what he was talking about. Then he slapped a *Time* magazine on Sailor's desk, and the front cover had an image of the three stacks at Three Mile Island (TMI) nuclear reactor station. He could not believe it! You mean to tell me that Harrisburg, Pennsylvania, and the surrounding cities are about to go up in a mushroom cloud! What is this all about? What is going on? Many questions inside his head while overseas off the coast of Haifa, Israel. Totally unexpected new events of a possible meltdown were earth-shattering to him. The active news report was one of the stacks at TMI was in danger of a meltdown? He was not sure what that meant, but he knew enough that it was not good at all, *not at all*! He immediately sought out Guy and began to drill him with question after question for any possible reason this was happening. (1) "I am about to visit the most Holy Land on the face of the earth" and (2) "my family back home is about to be annihilated if the nuclear stacks at TMI meltdown." What to do? He dare not miss the opportunity to go to Israel. Who knows when he will have this opportunity again? Maybe years, maybe decades, maybe never. He immediately became filled with uncontrollable anxiety and torn as to the right decision to make. He also was not sure if the fact that he was torn was a selfish spirit. Given the significance and biblical history of Israel, who would not want to visit the holy land? Also, the fact that Uncle Sam paid for his transportation and room and board and meals. The opportune circumstances would NEVER exist again in his lifetime. Sailor concluded that he would visit Israel and ride the boat back home with their scheduled return in July 1979. He would have to trust God that his family would be safe and that TMI would not meltdown. But he struggled with that decision, and he talked to different ones in the squadron. But especially Guy, who would give him godly advice. He trusted the word of Guy. But others pretty much said the same thing: "You will undoubtedly get this chance again. The navy is ALWAYS in this part of the world." That was the general consensus of advice Sailor got, and he began to feel a little okay if he decided to reenlist and go home to his new duty station. He wanted to be near and with family if the unthinkable occurred. But what got to Sailor the most was the words of Guy who said, "You don't know, TJ, maybe God has work for you in Harrisburg and needs you there. Maybe you will be an agent of change in the lives of many people. Maybe you will build your own church, and who knows, maybe you will become a great leader in the Lord's army."

That all sounded well and good, but in the mind of Sailor, he certainly did not think about God enlisting him in any capacity of ministry. All the voices he heard and different ones he talked to convinced him to reenlist. The consensus was for him to leave the boat so he could get home to Harrisburg, Pennsylvania. In the event TMI would meltdown, he would be among the ones he loved even if they were trying to flee the city for refuge. He decided that he wanted to be with his family. He decided to retake the oath of enlistment by swearing back in with Rear Admiral Shultz, who administered the oath of enlistment to him. The ceremony took place on the bridge of the USS *Dwight D. Eisenhower* (CVN-69). Sailor felt a little regret for not staying on board to visit the one place he longed to see ever since the days of his youth. But he felt his choice to return home was an unselfish decision in the face of a potentially devastating disaster. It was a tough decision to forgo walking the streets of biblical Israel and Jerusalem. His choice was to return home to conceivably die had the worst occurred. In those days, Guy was his spiritual mentor. Guy was not well-liked by other squadron members. Guy was a third class petty officer while Sailor had just made rank to E4, equal in rank to his new friend. Guy was older than Sailor and carried himself reasonably respectful. His Bible knowledge impressed Sailor immensely, and he truly believed the Lord allowed their paths to cross for several reasons. Guy was the one man outside of his immediate family that impressed upon him to study the Bible and learn the Holy Scriptures. Guy had several shortcomings that Sailor did not approve of, but Guy could explain them away. At twenty-one years old, Sailor was a novice of novices in world events. He did not interact with other people too well. He looked for certain qualities in a person that he could connect with to befriend. Guy had that one quality that no one else had in those days: knowledge and a good understanding of the Bible.

May 1979, Sailor stood on the flight deck of the USS *Dwight D. Eisenhower* (CVN69) with his luggage bags, luggage bags that were especially hand made by one of the parachute riggers in the squadron. A vinyl type material the pilots used to carry their personal belongs on board their S3A anti-submarine aircraft. Sailor was on the flight deck talking with one of his friends that he admired and took advice from. Mr. Frank was kind of sad that Sailor was leaving and going back to the United States. Mr. Frank was also in the navy, and he had no problem with Sailor addressing him as Mr. Frank. Sailor felt very special knowing that he had gotten the orders nobody thought he would get. His excitement continued for months thereafter. He also felt special that the navy was flying him off the carrier onboard delivery, or COD, the same aircraft that delivers the mail on board ship. Mr. Frank was kind of jealous Sailor was leaving and he had to remain on board. Mr. Frank thought it necessary to get one last glimpse at Sailor and one last word with Sailor as they briefly talked about their experiences together overseas. Mr. Frank kept saying that it will be nice to go back home to the good ol' USA.

But while standing on deck, Sailor could see the coastline of Haifa, Israel, and at first sight, he regretted his decision to return home. Deep down inside his soul, he knew he would never again get this close to Israel. But he kept the words in his heart everyone passed down to him. He believed and doubted simultaneously that he would get the opportunity with the navy to return to this part of the world. He also wrestled and wrestled and reasoned in his mind that he should stay on board while he had the once in a lifetime opportunity. He completely understood the reality that the navy is always in this part of the world, but right now, *I am here, and who knows when I will get back over here again?* he thought. At the time, he was not sure if he would stay in the navy long enough to make another Med. cruise to see Israel again. But the decision was made, and he had reenlisted and accepted his orders and was already scheduled to depart the ship onboard a navy aircraft. All nonessential personnel had to leave the flight deck, and all personnel scheduled to board the plane were to prepare for departure. Sailor looked around at the *Ike*, shook Mr. Frank's hand, and watched him leave the deck and enter the ship. Sailor was making his way to his seat on the COD. Once Sailor had taken his seat, the pilot of the navy aircraft was communicating with the bridge to be cleared to launch from the flight deck. Gallons of adrenalin-filled Sailor's entire body as he was about to be catapulted off the navy's newest most awesome technological aircraft carrier. Then within seconds, the negative gravity force contoured his head to the back of the seat as that aircraft was slung into the air from 0 to 100 knots in a matter of seconds, seemed like to him. Rapidly ascending in the air, he looked back and beheld the USS *Dwight D. Eisenhower* (CVN-69) sailing in the Mediterranean Sea. Sailor looked around and beheld the coastline of Haifa, Israel, and the picturesque aerial view of the *Ike* as it all was fading second after second. It seemed the entire time he was on board the ship, including his first tour of duty, went by in a flash of a flash, and he was on his way back to the United States of America. Concerning Israel, over thirty years would pass in Sailor's life, and he would never be that close to Israel again. The opportunity for Uncle Sam to foot the bill for him to return to Israel was now a thing of the eternal past. The words spoken by his shipmates in his squadron, and surprisingly Guy, turned out to be a wrong word. Of all the influences and suggestions he ever accepted of men, that was the one time they *all* were wrong. Sailor has never seen Israel since those days and never had the opportunity everyone suggested he would have. To this day, he longs to visit the Christian holy land. Of all the countries he dreamed of visiting as a young boy, Israel crossed his mind, but he did not expect to go there. When he learned during the Med. cruise of 1979 that Israel was a scheduled port of call, he could not believe it. Oftentimes the ship schedule would change, but this time, the schedule remained the same. Providentially, he supposed, the schedule did not change and the USS *Dwight D. Eisenhower* (CVN-69) did visit Haifa, Israel, during a time Sailor did not expect them to visit. His reasoning was uncontrollable for years thereafter. "Did I not stay on board to visit the holiest of all earthly locations because I really did not expect to? Or did I not stay on board to visit because I was a sinner and did not deserve to? Or did I not stay on board to visit because I was afraid of not seeing my family and being with them in the event of a TMI nuclear meltdown?" He has not been able to find the answers to those questions to this day. He believes his decision to leave the USS *Dwight D. Eisenhower* (CVN-69) in May of 1979 was one of many wrong decisions he would make. He has forgotten and remembered and forgotten and remembered for years that he even made the decision to leave. The proverbial "If I could do it all over again, I would certainly go with the decision and desire and would have stayed on board and visited Haifa Israel." Today, Guy, Israel, and TMI are nothing more than dreams that never came true. All other travels of Sailor were paid for by the United States government. Sailor cut himself short of fulfilling the ultimate travel of most Christian. And what was it all for, just because of a feeling and fearing the unthinkable may occur in Harrisburg, Pennsylvania? But he reasoned and concluded in his own mind and thought it noble to want to be in Pennsylvania when the meltdown would happen.

The Other Letter

Amid all the excitement Sailor was enjoying, there was this other thing that attacked his mind and soul. All his excitement was not only disrupted by TMI but disrupted by a personal dear john letter, so to speak. He wanted to fight somebody and couldn't wait to get home to beat the hell out of someone. YNSN Cook handed him the other letter that was addressed to him, and he did not pay much attention to the letter. He was overjoyed about the orders from Washington,

DC, transferring him to his next duty station that nothing else mattered. After all the joy and excitement of reading his next set of orders, he remembered that YNSN Cook handed him the other letter. The letter was from his ex-fiancée, whom he did not care to hear from and who, in many ways, spoiled his excitement. A few years back after his first Mediterranean cruise, Sailor believed she infected him with a communicable disease. The other letter held within its pages her own handwritten acknowledgment of what Sailor had already suspected. When he read what she wrote, his heart actually began palpitating. He does not remember how long he retained the letter in his files, but he did keep letters written to him for years for sentimental reasons. He held on to the letter his ex-fiancé wrote to him for at least until he returned home and held it for quite some time. He mused over whether he should keep it for evidence or disregard it. He never pursued establishing maternity back in those days and blindly accepted what should have been medically confirmed. After basking in the fact that he was about to reenlist, pack his bags, board a COD (carrier onboard delivery), a dual-prop aircraft that provides shore to shore cargo runs. Catapulting from an aircraft carrier would be the excitement of excitements during the early days of his naval career. Sailor would be flying off the deck of one of the navy's newest and sophisticated aircraft carriers. The other letter was a portion of reality that stole his joy and reminded him of his disrupted life. In the letter, she wrote about how Sailor was wrong for accusing her of infecting him and that she thought he was a Christian man who was in love with her and on and on and on. Then he ran across a line or two in large letters to this effect:

"Well, I had my male friend also while you were away, so you're not the only one with a girlfriend, and if this is the way you want us to break up, then you go your way and I go my way."

In the midst of all his excitement of reenlisting, getting orders to NRD Harrisburg, anticipating flying off the ship, he became *furious*. She *confirmed* his suspicions! Why would she tell him that she had a boyfriend, just to upset him or was she speaking the truth? Knowing what type of woman she was and even her background and family, it was not unreasonable that she was telling Sailor the truth. He had no doubts that what she wrote was true to the letter. She did have a man in her life, and Sailor was not certain who it was but would have not been the least surprised who it may have been. He heard talk about this one and about that one, but he knew for a fact her son's father was still in her life to a great extent. At the time, it really did not matter because as far as Sailor was concerned, she was out of his life and his life was taking a new turn. Sailor read and read over that letter for the remainder of the day in between the excitement of going home and getting his new orders. There was this other letter that he wanted to burn, but he felt compelled to hold on to the letter for a while to make sure he was reading it correctly. Unfortunately, every time he read the letter, the same words where there. He felt a sense of relief in a weird way because the question in his mind had been answered about the sexually transmitted disease. But he still had another undying reality, a child that he had been identified as the father. Nothing was more disrupting to Sailor in his life at the time. It seemed he could convince no one that he had been entrapped and ignorantly captivated. A woman who not only had a good degree of worldly experience but also sought a young man that would be able to support not only her but her already five-year-old son. At this point, both mentally and emotionally, Sailor felt as unstable as a wingless airplane plummeting to the earth. He felt like the proverbial ship without a sail in the midst of a storm, like a lone man shut up inside a dark room standing in the corner facing the wall. As if one side of his heart and body erupted with joy because his experience in the United States Navy was good to him up to that point. But the other side of his heart and body was confused and pained because he could not figure how he got in the situation with his ex. In those days, Sailor did think of himself more highly than he should have, but he was not sure if that was all his fault. He had mentors that lead him to think positive and to pursue the best things in life and strive to be the best in everything. His problem then was how to filter out thinking more of himself as opposed to thinking more of God. He had to learn how to allow God to chart his course and see God much greater than himself. While the duty at NRD Harrisburg, Pennsylvania, was filled with excitement and joy, those days were also complete with confusion, pain, hurt, and lies in a town he should have never returned to. The other letter would one day be destroyed, and Sailor does not remember how and when the letter was destroyed. But in hindsight, he should have kept the letter, if for no other reason than evidence had he needed it. The situation of the paternal father would now follow Sailor the remainder of his life. At times the paternal father identification would become somewhat of a thorn in the flesh, a nuisance. The mother and daughter would kind of secretly pass the word around that Sailor is the father. The daughter would confidently say to other people, "He's my father." Without 99.9 percent medical evidence being established, life would continue on with the idea and reality of an unproven affirmation resulting from an inexperienced youth involved in a relationship with an experienced, worldly woman. It has become Sailor's conclusion that he had to suffer and take responsibility for his actions, the consequences of his sinful and licentious living while globetrotting up and down the European continent between the ages of nineteen and twenty-one.

11

TOUR OF DUTY NAVY RECRUITING DISTRICT HARRISBURG, PENNSYLVANIA

Rota, Spain

Seemed like in a matter of minutes, Sailor was from the *Ike* to Naval Station Rota, Spain, and forced to spend the night there. Having to spend the night at the naval station was mild torture. Sailor wanted to get back to America and not spend idle time waiting for transportation. When the COD arrived at Rota, the passengers were told they had just missed the last flight to the United States and therefore were forced to spend the night in the airport. The entire flying time from the boat toward Rota, Sailor thought and thought about how he wished he'd made the decision to remain onboard the *Ike*. On the COD flying to Rota for a connecting flight to the United States, Sailor was in a deep slumber of sadness. A surge of homesickness for the boat, Italy, and the squadron brothers rushed through the memory of his mind. He knew in his heart he should not have left the boat that soon, but he was swayed by an obligation to return home in the event TMI would meltdown. What was right, he was uncertain about, but he knew he was deeply torn inside his soul and spirit having left the boat. The flight to Rota was not that long but long enough to reminisce and entertain sad thoughts. The prevailing thought was the fact that he sailed over to the Mediterranean with his shipmates and should have sailed back to the United States of America with them. Leaving the boat left Sailor with an abandonment feeling inside. He felt like he was only thinking about himself and his desire to return home even though the navy offered him to stay on board. He was guaranteed to sail the ship back to the United States while retaining the orders to NRD Harrisburg, Pennsylvania. The crying days were a thing of the distant past, but Sailor did feel badly leaving his shipmates and the crew in the Med.

When he arrived at Rota, it was a nice, warm, sunny day. Even though he was on orders, he was unable to catch the first flight returning to the United States. For that one night and one night only, he digressed and found himself with another shipmate, engaging in the nightlife due to boredom. Curiosity struck in the heart and mind of Sailor, and once more the partying spirit prevailed. Sailor's friend, KS, was also on the return flight to the States, but he was getting out of the navy. They had to find an overnight locker to store their gear and pretty much hang out in the airport all night until the first plane leaving for the United States would taxi on the runway.

After putting their luggage in lockers, Sailor agreed with KS to leave the air terminal and go bar hopping in Rota, Spain. His only intent was to hang out with another brother that he knew instead of boredom in the airport all night. He had no interest or desire for anything other than being with someone he knew. Sailor and KS rode around in a tiny taxicab looking for nightclubs, and Sailor does not remember if the cabbie suggested a club or if they went from nightclub to nightclub on their own. At any rate, the two shipless sailors ended up going to a club that did not appear too interesting to Sailor. In other words, the clubs Sailor and the brothers visited in places like Torremolinos, Spain, places in Naples, Italy, and Toulon, France, were always hoppin'. Sailor remembers there were people crowded inside those places and on the dance floor so much that it was ridiculous. The clubs Sailor and KS hit in Rota, Spain, while waiting for their flight back to the States were boring and lifeless, to say the least. Perhaps they were there at a time when the nightlife people had gone home. There was very little interaction in the clubs of Spain, a little here a little there but nothing significant enough to write about other than admit to his personal backsliding for a minute or two. Time seemed to drag along slowly while in Rota, Spain, waiting for his flight back to the United States. Things moved at an irritating snail's pace. After all the excitement of the past few months, it felt like he was stuck in the middle of nowhere. After all his years on earth, he finally found the place in the middle of nowhere. The ship was over a thousand miles east of where Sailor was in Spain, and the United States of America was some three thousand miles West of where Sailor was in Spain. This to him was the proverbial middle of nowhere, with the Atlantic Ocean on one side and unfamiliar land on the other side. At two in the morning, he and KS found themselves in a nightclub not knowing a single soul there. KS was becoming just as impatient and bored as Sailor. Each minute on the clock seemed to click clock loud enough for Sailor to hear the sound, and he watched the clock every two minutes as if to urge time on. He thought he would lose his mind if he missed the next flight leaving in the morning to the United States. Being in a club in Rota, Spain, not knowing how soon they would be able to get a taxi to return to the air terminal was not a good thing in Sailor's mind. About 3:30 a.m. Sailor became very agitated because KS seemed to be enjoying himself at that boring club. Sailor was not about to miss the next flight, and typical of his ways, he quietly got up from the bar and left the club. Lost and a little angry, he felt he was walking in the direction he thought the terminal was. Paying attention to the landmarks when the cabbie took them to the club, he was confident he was walking in the right direction. At about 4:00 a.m., he heard a vehicle racing up behind him and the horn blaring and getting closer to him. He thought to himself, *A bunch of crazy Spaniards. Please just drive by me and don't say a word because I am minding my own business just trying to get home.*

As the car got closer and the sound of the horn got louder, the car slowed down, and he thought, *Oh my God, what's going on here and what's about to happen?*

But he did not think too long before his feet started marking its territory and he was off running faster than any sprinter. Sailor was cutting across people's lawn, jumping over trash cans, knocking over trash cans, attempting to create a diversion and wake up residents—anything to draw attention to himself from potential attackers. He was running and running and running, faster and faster. Adrenaline was flowing through him like a steam valve opened up all the way. You would have thought he was on the track field running the sprint, jumping over and running through trash cans, trying to make as much noise as possible to wake up the residents. He was hopeful the noise would startle someone from sleep and discover that he was in danger and would call the police because of the disturbance. The car picked up speed, and the occupant began yelling out of the window, "*Hey, Petty Officer sailor, Tim! TJ, Tee, Slow down*!"

Sailor was running, like the saying goes, like a bat out of hell, until he heard each nickname of his yelled out. He slowed to a walk and stopped as he looked back toward the car and discovered it was KS in the car. This is the second time he willingly abandoned KS. Both times had to do with a party or clubbing. KS was in another tiny taxicab trying to locate and pick up Sailor. His heart slowed, his pace significantly slowed, and his face bore a nice welcoming smile. The entire event and mild shake-up while in Rota, Spain, was kind of funny even to this day. Sailor was one of the most impatient young men during those days and still had much to learn regarding immaturity.

Both Sailor and KS and the cabbie all laughed till they cried, and KS said, "Why did you leave? Did you think we were going to miss our flight?"

"Well, hell yeah, and that is one flight I cannot miss!"

They laughed and laughed some more. They laughed all the way back to the air terminal. KS was a little intoxicated, and Sailor was a lot pissed off. But they laughed none the same, and the laugh was filled with several emotions. They were excited about going back to the United States of America and excited about the flight. They were also tickled about Sailor running from the car like he was a sprinter on a track field. The entire scene and event in Rota, Spain, for one night was worth laughing about even then when it actually occurred.

They made it back to the terminal in one piece and flopped onto a couple of airport chairs that were very uncomfortable. It seems within minutes, people began crowding in the terminal, and time sped up too about 9:00 a.m. The Med. cruise for these two sailors was over, and while Sailor was excited about returning to the states, he was also missing the ship and the recent visit to the Mediterranean. It was one of the most uncomfortable nights ever because the nightclubs were not worth clubbing. He thought he was about to be attacked by young hoodlums, and he was tired, hungry, sleepy, and missing the boat. As daylight was breaking and the terminal was filling up with passengers, they ran over to the lockers and got their luggage out and quickly made their way over to check-in. Even though the flight was not scheduled to depart until 11:00 a.m., because of the number of dependents and military, they could begin checking in. It seemed time sped up something fierce. Things moved along at an alarming pace, and before he knew it, he was on the plane sitting in his seat, and other passengers were hustling and bustling to board the plane. KS was seated in another section of the plane and lost contact from that moment on. Sailor did not see him again until they departed the plane and a quick good-bye and that was it, like that; all that excitement, adventure, and travel was over, for now. The flight was mixed with civilians and military in uniform. Sailor was excited to be going home, but he was still torn between wanting to stay and the anticipation of returning home having traveled "his" world. Sailor had gone to every place he dreamed of as a boy and had not expected to even be within miles of Israel. The only regret he has to this day is not remaining on board the boat to visit a place that would have been the highlight of his young life. For the entire flight, he ran through his mind *all* the places he visited and *all* the things he done. He went into a mild slumber knowing that he could see the coast of Israel but not enjoy the visitation of the land of the Bible. The hustle and bustle of people getting on board seemed to end as fast as it was happening, and the pilot passed the word: "Please fasten your seat belts as we begin to taxi down the runway."

This was it. Sailor was on his way home in a military aircraft instead of sailing back with the USS *Dwight D. Eisenhower* (CVN-

69) as he did with the USS *Independence* (CV-62) back in 1977. Even though he committed sin after sin, he did maintain his belief in God and carried his Bible everywhere he went. He thought it was good to say a brief prayer like "God, let us have a safe flight and let us arrive in America without any loss of life." Terrorism was not even a word known to most Americans or military for that matter. But the fact was, it was a military plan, and hostilities against America has always been since the days of the American Revolution in 1765. Sailor thought prayer is always a good thing.

As the plane taxied the runway and began to make its ascent into the heavens, he felt himself drifting off to sleep. He could not help but fall asleep. His body was telling him, "You are exhausted, fool. Go to sleep." He briefly woke up just to eat some food they were serving on the flight, and he only did that because he did not want to miss the "free" food. Sailor could never sleep well on an airplane for whatever reason. The flight back to America was uncomfortable. For 10–11 hours, he was back and forth into the sleep world, while his mind reminisced about his experiences in the United States Navy. He did everything he possibly could to go to sleep on that plane. He turned to the right, turned to the left, slouched down, and put his head between his legs trying to sleep. Timewise, the flight was long, and Sailor could not sleep straight through. But ironically, the flight was unexplainably short, and he heard the pilot say, "We are about to make our descent into Philadelphia, Pennsylvania. Please make sure your seats are in the upright position and your seat belt fastened."

For all practical intents and purposes, Sailor was back home in the United States of America, and though he was supposed to be excited and feel good, he did not feel all that he was supposed to feel. A huge part of him was left in another country on board a naval vessel in the Mediterranean Sea, off the coast of Haifa, Israel. The plane began to make its descent, and you could feel the negative G force against your body and then the hard landing as the landing gear touched down to the Earth. The other passengers were overjoyed, applauding the captain for a safe landing. Sailor was looking out the window pondering everything he had experienced over the past three years of his life—everything! Regretfully, his second experience overseas was brief, and little did he know that he would not see Rota, Spain, again for another five years and would never see Israel again throughout his naval career. He was home, and at this point, it did not matter to him any longer. However, he remained unhappy and displeased with his decision for leaving the ship and not visiting Israel. In many ways, he feels like he did not complete a task he was supposed to complete. He deliberately cut short an experience that was destined to be his, and he could never recapture. Even if he were travel to Israel on his own someday, *it will never be anything* like it would have been at twenty-one years old.

Home after Arduous Duty

Arrival at an air terminal always was an immediate hustle and bustle of getting everything together. Passengers always anticipated the moment the pilot turned off the "fasten your seatbelt" sign. There seemed to be this unspoken competition of trying to beat others from getting in front of you turns out to be exhausting even at a young age. He learned what jet lag was and what it meant. It's amazing that just sitting in a seat flying in the heavens and walking through a terminal can get you exhausted. Anyways, Sailor was scurrying off the plane to get his luggage because it was only checked in to Philadelphia, Pennsylvania, and he had a connecting flight to Harrisburg, Pennsylvania on US. Air. He was not too concerned about KS and did not hang around to see him or say goodbye to him. But he happened to see him at the baggage claim, and they said a few words and retrieved their luggage and left toward the US Air terminal departing flights. At the US Air terminal, that would be the end of ever seeing KS again. Sailor had no sadness, reminiscing or even looking back as KS faded into the crowd. KS seemed to be elated about being back in the United States while Sailor was sorting through all kinds of conflicting feelings. Sailor was home now, and the life and events overseas did not matter to him at the time, nor did the people he met and hung out with. Hurrying through the terminal to his connecting flight, a phenomenal event, as time seemed to be racing at a fast pace. In Sailor's mind, missing his connecting flight to

Harrisburg, Pennsylvania, was not an option. He got to his connecting flight at US Air, and people were already checking in. He did not have time to sit down and wind down, nor did he have time to think about anything else but catching that flight. It was like one motion getting off the international flight from Rota, Spain, and connecting to the domestic flight in Philly with a nonstop to Olmstead Airport. Ironically, he made it at the last minute because the plane was full and the temperature was hot. The rush of hustle and bustle through one of the busiest airports straight from Rota, Spain, was thrilling.

No sooner than he sat down on the plane and attempted to relax, the plane captains on the outside were moving the plane into the taxi position on the runway. He thought, *Time is moving fast, and it seems like my shipboard time was but a moment, including my first three years. The years went by unbelievably fast!*

He did not ponder how fast the time went by the thought was just a fleeting moment in his mind. It would not be until his naval career ended that he would understand how swift time moves and the biblical truth about time: "Your life is but a vapor that comes for a short time and then vanishes away." A sobering truth that puts life in perspective. The flight from Philadelphia, Pennsylvania, to Harrisburg, Pennsylvania, is under one hour, and it seems when the plane had reached its cruising altitude and Sailor had eaten peanuts and drank a soda, the pilot made the announcement to fasten your seatbelts because they were making the descent into Middletown, Pennsylvania, Olmstead Airport.

At that moment, he gazed out his window, only to see what had emerged into the most dreadful sight that had captured the entire world's attention. Sailor happened to be sitting on the plane with a perfect view of Three Mile Island and the Stacks that had the potential of a meltdown. This was the whole reason he returned home, cutting his visit and world experience short because he thought these nuclear stacks would not be here and there would be a mass exit from Harrisburg, Pennsylvania. He envisioned the highways packed with families departing and police vehicles lined up throughout the streets and maybe even the National Guard assisting in the evacuation. But nothing of a sort was going on. In fact, it appears it was business as usual. The pilot was making his descent, and people onboard were talking amongst themselves and a few were looking out the window at the stacks. The pilot said something about Harrisburg becoming a famous place because of the recent news with TMI.

Sailor was thinking, *What's going on here? This place was about to become nuclear dust, and I, a sailor of the armed forces, left a naval vessel in the Mediterranean Sea to be with my family and die if it came to that and folks are treating this like it was a scene out of a movie!*

Sailor immediately became angry and very upset, feeling like his decision to leave the boat to return home early was one of the worst decisions of his career. He thought, *The situation wasn't that bad after all*—TMI, that is.

Within seconds after his personal assessment of the situation, he was filled with all sorts of mixed emotions. He was glad to see for himself the stacks were still there and Harrisburg was still on the earth. He was angry because he did not stay on board the ship to visit Haifa, Israel, and he was upset because the other passengers on board the plane did not seem to be too concerned at the enormous destruction and danger to human life a meltdown would have created. And no one on board that flight could have possibly known what Sailor was feeling. All aboard was clueless of the decision he had just made to return home. His shipmates influenced his decision and the picture on the front cover of *Time Magazine* added to his decision to leave. But he had to remind himself that TMI happened in March of 1979 and he was returning in June of 1979. The terror of a meltdown had melted away from people's hearts and mind. He did not realize then how typical it is of people to quickly forget terror and the potential of destruction and continue with their lives and either make light of the terror or forget it ever happened. He was not sure if his view on that was right or wrong, it just seemed to Sailor that people should be a lot more thankful to God for every waking moment of their lives. Life is extremely fragile, and time moves at an alarming pace, as Sailor was able to conclude.

North 18th Street for a Brief Moment

The feelings Sailor wrestled with back and forth about Israel, the boat, and TMI was now, as the saying goes, water under the bridge. The decision he made to return to America was done, and now he was back home in the United States of America on his way to Harrisburg, Pennsylvania. He thought to himself, *I might as well forget it all because you CANNOT redeem time back, and though it all seems like just yesterday, years and years have passed and we are all still alive and well by the grace of God.*

However, vanity filled his heart for quite some time while on shore duty because he thought, if he could do it all over again, he certainly would. But he would vow to make different decisions and different choices. But haven't we all been there especially once you reach the good old age of forty and fifty? How many things and decision have you made that deep inside your heart you just fancifully wish you could do it differently? Nonetheless, as the pilot made his descent to the airfield, there was a sense of relief having just flown thousands of miles from overseas. Only for him to realize the negative anticipation he was feeling was, in many ways, media and people hype. He began to feel that he was the only one that took the whole thing too seriously. Once on the ground, he felt like a returning world traveler and especially a proud sailor strutting through the terminal. Immediately, though, he felt like Harrisburg, Pennsylvania, was too small for him, but it was home and he had stories to tell. But the stories he thought he had to tell had not yet reached the crescendo of what lay ahead for him in the future tour of duties. If he thought the excursions over in the Mediterranean and the promiscuous youthful lust in Italy and Spain was something to talk about, he had not yet fully grown up and still had a lot of maturing to do. But for now, he was back home and looking forward to seeing family face-to-face and checking into his new duty station directly downtown of his hometown. He would be working in an office building that was thought by many of his senior officers was unlikely for him to be assigned. Back in those days the old Olmstead airport in Middletown, Pennsylvania, was not nearly as modern as it is today and was easy to navigate through. Sailor made his way over to the luggage claim, and it took about maybe one hour to retrieve his luggage. With youthful strength, he yanked his green freshly made parachute luggage from the conveyor belt and made his way to exit the terminal. That small little airport in those days seemed to be bustling with activity of people traveling, and there was always a taxi right outside the airport. Today the airport is much larger and modernized, but it appears to be less activity than back in those days. At this point, no one knew he was back in the United States, and no one knew he was about to make his grand entrance back on North 18th Street and not just for a two-week visit but for a thirty-sixth-month tour of duty. Much cockiness filled the heart of Sailor at twenty-one years old. He required no assistance with his luggage. He did not need a skycap or anyone helping him with his luggage. As far as he was concerned, he was full of youthful strength, vitality, and pride to show off his ability to get things done. He required no assistance from anyone. He had four pieces of luggage (you could do that then), plus his seven-speaker Enviro stereo.

When the skycap asked if he needed help, he proudly said, "Oh, no, thank you. I am perfectly fine!" Then he slung the vinyl type material garment bag over his shoulder, picked up the luggage bag, and double carried the smaller luggage bag. He slung his huge boom box Enviro stereo that he purchased from the exchange at Naples, Italy. The stereo was one of a kind from the Allied Joint Forces Command, Naples, Italy (AFSOUTH). He put that big stereo on his other shoulder and got to stepping toward the exit looking for the first vacant taxicab. He spotted a vacant taxi and yelled to the driver,

"Need a cab, hey! Taxi, taxi," double timing over to the cab loaded down with luggage and a huge cassette player. He put a couple things down on the ground so he could start loading one by one inside the cab. The cabdriver then picked up one of his luggage bags and started putting it in the trunk, and Sailor quickly said, "Hey, I'm fine, I'll get that," and before he could finish his sentence, the cabdriver had loaded one of his bags, which Sailor did not like. The cockiness of Sailor made him blurt out, "Hey, I don't need help, I got it!"

The cabdriver threw his hands up in the air and backed away into his cab. In those days, Sailor was cocky to the core and was not about asking people for help because he *knew* he could handle what needed to be done.

He was on his last leg of travel to North 18th Street from an arduous tour of duty from the Mediterranean Sea from onboard the USS *Dwight D. Eisenhower* (CVN-69). But the oddest thing is that *no one* was at the airport to greet him because no one knew he was on his way home. Instead of informing his family the day and time he would be arriving, back in those days he was deeply into the surprising thing. Always wanting to surprise family and friends because he thought his old North 18th Street friends cared, and he expected family to be as excited as he was surprising them. But time would reveal another perspective of family and so-called friends. He was not sure if that new perspective was because their lives traveled different paths or if the perspective was their all alone.

When the cabdriver pulled up to North 18th Street on a nice summer day, Cookie, Raymond, and Jonathan were on the porch and the rest of the clan inside the house. Immediately, he reminisced the scene three years ago when his family (those living in Harrisburg) was on the porch when he departed for the first time in the Ford Torino with the navy recruiter. Now he was returning in a taxicab as a twenty-one-year-old man with literally a world of experience under his belt, and he wanted all of North 18th Street to know that he had returned in one piece. He had something to say but wondered who would really listen. He gazed down the street as the cabdriver was slowing up, and Sailor was giving him directions "just a couple more houses, where you see those people on the porch." And as the driver slowed to a complete stop, Sailor took his good ol' time getting himself together and about to pay the cabdriver while intermittently looking out the window of the cab to see if his brothers and sisters recognized him in the car. Ray and Jon were very young, so they paid little attention to the cab stopped in front of their house. But Cookie was older than both Sailor and them, and she was a lot more aware of a taxicab stopping. Sailor was reaching for money to pay the cabdriver while continuing to look out the window, almost in slow motion, eyeballing Cookie standing on the porch. Cookie appeared to be squinting while looking at the cab. She must have noticed the Dixie cup cover on Sailor's head, and she began to look even more intensely. Sailor noticed her eyes beginning to widen, and a faint smile appeared on her face as to gesture, "That's Sailor, Sailor is home, that's Sailor!"

When Sailor stepped out of the cab taking his time, all the while trying to savor the moment, Cookie put her hand over her mouth, that little thing she does when she is excited or surprised. Her eyes wide as saucers at this point and yelled out, "Sailor!" For that moment in time, Sailor felt on top of the world because it was announced for all the inhabitants of North 18th Street that a sailor had arrived back home. Jon and Ray, frozen in time in Sailor's mind, became the epitome of a lifelong memory. They immediately ceased from playing, and instantly Sailor became the center of *everything* going on that day. Sailor was halfway onto the sidewalk when Cookie ran to greet him, and Jon and Ray ran toward him and gave him a quick hug and tried to pick up his luggage. Sailor, proud, excited, tearful, said to his young bloods, "I got it, bro!" But they still attempted to pick up his luggage nonetheless. That arrival was all he needed to be welcomed by his family and to feel proud and ten feet tall, like he had overcome the world and now ready to tell everybody about his victories. Little did he know at the time is that he had only begun to face the world in a baby stage and all its ravishes to destroy the faith and wipe clean the integrity of a young man. Home was just a brief parenthesis in the remainder of the story waiting to be written. His new duty station at Navy Recruiting District Harrisburg would be the pressing memory more than being stationed at his hometown in Harrisburg, Pennsylvania. The problem with being stationed at home is that when the time came to leave home for the next duty station, the time was fast approaching; Sailor was not ready to leave. He then came up with a multitude of excuses to stay in Harrisburg for the remainder of his reenlistment. The navy had been assigning orders to its members way before Sailor even thought of joining, and they were masters at giving you what you want. But when the time came to give back to them, they would accept no excuses or reasons short of a bona fide hardship. Sailor had letters written on his behalf, ministers and the like when it was time for him to leave Harrisburg and enter into the second phase of his growth and maturity. But it would be three years before that time arrived and those three years stationed at home would resurrect the spirit of homesickness to battle and overcome. But at this point in time he adjusted to homesickness to the point he could maintain.

NRD Harrisburg

When Sailor checked into the recruiting district at Harrisburg, Pennsylvania, downtown at 320 North 2nd Street, he felt like a businessman, in uniform, working downtown. It was going into the summer and the chiefs and officers wore the white summer uniform while E6 and below were authorized to wear salt and pepper (white shirt and black pants). Sailor stopped down to the recruiting district prior to his official check-in to introduce himself and pretty much let his new command know that he had arrived. At this point in his life, he was excited about who he had become and the places he had visited, knowing all the while that he had not gone to all the places he should have. In the back of his mind, the image of Israel and the fact he was just in the Middle East a few hours ago was slowly fading away. He went down to the district in civilian clothes, proud to be a part of the United States Navy. He felt the navy had done him well. TJ, the Sailor, was back home and still on active duty in the United States Navy. His senior officers back on the *Ike* and his shipmates thought that was a rare combination and to enjoy it while he could because the day is coming when the navy wants payback. Sailor performance rating had been 4.0 up to this point, and he mistakenly thought the navy was looking out for him and doing him justice. The level of immaturity of Sailor was obvious, and the painful awakening he would have to face in the future was quickly arriving. But anyways, NRD Harrisburg was one of the best tours of duties he had other than NAS Willow Grove, Pennsylvania, which would not come until years later. The commanding officer of NRD at the time was from the air dale community. In other words, he was a navy pilot, and Sailor related to him extremely well being that he just reported from VS-31 a command full of navy pilots. He felt right at home (to say the least), knowing his commanding officer would appreciate his background and experience. But the chief he had to work for was another story altogether. Chief was from the surface navy, of which Sailor had *no* experience and had *no* desire to become a part of. Surface navy sailors are assigned to ships and are called ship's company. They live their entire tour of duty on board a naval vessel, including frigates (FFGs), destroyers (DDGs), and other "small boys," with a crew ranging from five hundred to a thousand men. Sailor had *no* desire to know that part of the navy having served his initial tour with the air dale community. He became spoiled because when the aircraft carrier returned to the United States, the squadrons would debark and return to their air station on land. That type of duty only spoiled Sailor instead of prepping him for the real navy involving ships at sea and sailors on board ships. Sailor could not imagine having to live on board ship as ship's company, even in the United States. YNC J. was the chief he worked for, and the chief had a surface navy's mentality and always had derogatory comments about air dale sailors. At first, Sailor took great offense toward him because the chief was his supervisor, and he had to work for him, and secondly, he was black. Sailor thought the chief would understand the pride he had serving in the navy and the excitement he had having met him and knowing he would be his boss. Thirdly, Sailor took offense to his brand of Christianity and thought he was more of a Sailor than a Christian. Though Sailor had his falling short and backsliding experiences overseas, he felt his faith was real and his desire to grow in faith was serious. To Sailor, the chief appeared not to be too serious about his Christianity, and the chief's approach of Christianity by far was the greatest thing about him that Sailor did not like. There was much Sailor was destined to learn from the chief in many ways and much he did not like about him in other ways. But the chief became an integral part of Sailor's life in those days, whether he liked it or not and whether Sailor liked him or not. As time went on, YNC J. would become one of Sailor's greatest friends and later, one of Sailor's greatest antagonists.

YNC at NRD

NRD, YNC, CPO, PO—lots of acronyms in the military that Sailor adjusted to very well. Yeoman Chief (YNC) at the Navy Recruiting District (NRD) and Petty Officer Third Class (PO) Sailor. This period of time would be one of the greatest learning lessons in Sailor's life. It would be the mental and spiritual test and growth amid hatred and religion. YNC is the rank Sailor would *never* attain but would be highly recommended for promotion to YNC with an impeccable military record. When that time came in Sailor's life to be promoted to YNC, he concluded that he did not meet the extracurricular and whatever else the navy chief board was looking for during his career. NRD Harrisburg, Pennsylvania, is where Sailor learned the bulk of his administrative acumen and developed the desire to better himself and to formally increase his education. YNC J. made it possible for Sailor to become trained in many areas. He sent Sailor to what was called a MICOM company in King of Prussia, Pennsylvania. It was a computer with no configuring capabilities; in fact, one of the hottest debates in those days was that MICOM was not a computer but rather a word processor. At any rate, YNC J. enrolled Sailor in the course to learn the ins and outs of word processing, which would be the interest and exposure to computers for Sailor. In the spring of 1980, Sailor became interested in the word processor industry. About a decade later being stationed with Reserve Intelligence Programs Office Area 16 (RIPO-16) at Naval Air Station Willow Grove would expose Sailor to the technical aspects of computers. YNC J. oversaw all Sailor's administrative work and would offer improvements here and there. He schooled Sailor on the proper way of interpreting and using navy publications and manuals. He would give Sailor manuals to lookup certain articles and give him a reply as to its meaning. He sent Sailor to training courses and classes that would aid him in advancement to second class petty officer. But the chief still had that side of him when he interacted with other shipmates at the district that made Sailor question the chief's brand of Christianity. Chief made many innuendoes and jokes that just did not settle well with Sailor. However, he did have some positive critique for Sailor when he attended the trial sermon Sailor gave at Mount Calvary Church of God in Christ in February 1980. Sailor invited the chief and several other NRD personnel to what many charismatic Christians call a trial sermon. Sailor did not think the chief would show up, but not only did he show up, several others Sailor had invited showed up. There was another chief who was a field recruiter for the navy (9585, Enlisted Classification) and a senior chief at the district who worked in Enlisted Programs Office (EPO). Senior Chief in EPO was several scales higher in his learning of the Bible and skilled in interpreting human behavior. They all attended Sailor's "trial sermon," which surprised him. Sailor simply invited them because they identified themselves with Christianity and Sailor, out of respect for his senior enlisted men, thought they might be interested in hearing the message Sailor would put out to the people. The following Monday when Sailor went back to work after the "trial sermon," they all greeted him with a sense of respect and appreciation. They all encouraged him for accepting the call into the ministry. YNC J., from that point on, was not as obvious with his innuendoes and jokes around Sailor, but every now and then the chief would revert to his seafaring ways. At that point Sailor had learned to take him and his ways as a learning experience and was compelled to endure. The senior chief, on the other hand, who appeared to be well versed in the Scriptures was an obvious encouragement to Sailor in helping him deal with YNC J. But YNC J. shocked Sailor when he told him that he enjoyed his message and Sailor's content was good but he needs to slow down when speaking and take his time. Chief offered that "people will be more acceptant and appreciate you taking your time to explain and break down the scriptures and the message you intend for them to receive." Sailor did not know what to expect from the chief, especially since he did not think the chief or others would attend. With the chief's positive feedback, Sailor drank in *every* word the chief spoke because he trusted chief's judgment and leadership ability. The working relationship Sailor had with the chief was truly a love-hate relationship in Sailor's mind. The comments chief gave to Sailor about his trial sermon allowed him to overlook the short-comings and ways about the chief he did not like. Sailor knew he was not perfect in any way. But his views of a leader and manager were held to a high standard and too strict even for Sailor himself to walk in. What TJ, the Sailor, lost in Bay and Fred he looked for in other men he became friends with while serving in the United States Navy. There was F. Sanders, Brooks, Mac, KS, Jerry, Guy H., the man who knew his Bible, and YNC J. All had great impact on Sailor's youthful life in those days. Many times, Sailor thought he would like nothing more than to meet those guys at least once more before they all pass on. He wanted to express his thanks to them for being there because he certainly needed them at that time. All his life from the projects through a complete career with the United States Navy and the greatest disagreement ever with his brothers would be the necessary ingredients needed to evolve Sailor into the Sermon. The Sermon was still decades away and waiting to teach Sailor about himself. What he recently experienced in his first tour of duty was but preschool lessons. The future was waiting patiently to strip the young man bare and bring him to the extremities of life.

The Deadly Ride

In the midst of overwhelming emotions and feelings and adjusting to his new command was his new girlfriend—another young lady from the same church as his ex-girlfriend. It was a time when controversy, lies, and deceits were at an all-time high in Sailor's life. Looks, stares and Christian conspiracy talk plagued the young man day in and day out. The ex-girlfriend was very manipulative; Sailor and Sailor's mother and his siblings were obviously uncertain what to believe. The entire time he was stationed at NRD Harrisburg, PA, Sailor was flooded with extreme uncomfortable circumstances around people he loved and people who did not love him. On one hand, NRD Harrisburg was a great tour of duty, but on the other, it was full of stress, anger, division among Christians and siblings, and hatred for *everything* happening in Sailor's life.

Now that Sailor was back home and able to spend time with his new girlfriend, he made it a point to get to know the woman he felt that he was falling in love with. While overseas during the second cruise on board the USS *Dwight D. Eisenhower* (CVN-69), he wrote his girlfriend letter after letter. He wrote her just about *every* other day and sometimes two and three times within one day. He intended to prove to her that he would not forget her and that he was falling in love with her. While attempting to get to know her, she was quite the skeptic and demonstrated her skepticism by not responding to his letters. Sailor wrote her often while deployed, and she responded to Sailor a total of two times. At times, it was kind of disheartening not to hear from her as often as he would have liked to, but the two times she did write, Sailor lit up for the remainder of that week. He felt like he had a girl back home waiting for him. He felt like he was special to her and their relationship was meant to be. He felt like she was getting an interest in him but was afraid to admit it, and he felt that his persistence would someday make her submit. During the days of 1979, Sailor talked to his girlfriend on the phone literally all night at times. Those were the days of searching for love, and maybe you have or maybe you have not been there. It was the time when you place the receiver of the phone next to your ear and fall off to sleep. Waking up minutes and sometimes a half hour later, only to ask the question "are you still there?" Really funny, but sort of cute a relationship between a man and women being developed and feeling like you do not want to be out of each other's sight or voice range, not even for a minute. Subsequently, Sailor spent a lot of time with his new girlfriend especially then developing a relationship that escalated rapidly. She and Sailor would go out to breakfast and shopping on Saturdays. They would walk down at the riverfront and always thought up something to do after work. He felt like she would be the perfect person for him to help overcome his weaknesses. He looked for genuine "helpmate," as the Scriptures mentions, and looked forward to the rest of his life with her. Sailor thought he was genuinely falling in love but was under attack from many sources, both internally and externally. Each attacker was equally as strong pulling on his soul. But he and his new girlfriend were able to wade through the muddy waters and the lies and the finger-pointing and the ugly faces and the people that did not approve of their relationship. Many of the people that fought against Sailor's relationship are either passed away or were in an unhappy relationship themselves. The entire time while stationed at NRD Harrisburg was a labyrinth of issues involving his new girlfriend, his old girlfriend, and a new baby. The worst of the worst for Sailor is the attachment of the ugly lustful spirits he had invited into his soul. It truly was a bittersweet time in his life, a time to grow, learn, and get to know the God of the Bible while still crawling on his knees.

Sailor was adjusting and fighting several battles in the same arena, on the same front. The opposition from those against his new girlfriend and their relationship was mainly launched from the Christians of the church he attended. That made the battles even more intense. While studying his Bible, going to church on a regular basis, still in the navy, and wanting to marry his girlfriend. hell waged a war against him that was controversial from start to finish. New understanding in Sailor's mind concerning the interpretation of the Bible and discussing those interpretations with his parents was a struggle. The new duty station at NRD Harrisburg, Pennsylvania, and the people he worked with there, namely YNC J., who at first was antagonistic toward Sailor, at least in Sailor's own mind he was. The possibility of having to transfer and leave it all behind in a few short years plagued Sailor day in and day out. Sailor had strong misgivings about the chief and his style of leadership, there were many times chief demonstrated great compassion and understanding. The chief learned about Sailor's engagement to marry his girlfriend, but Sailor tried to keep her away from the navy crew and the lifestyle of the navy as much as possible. In many ways, he protected her from the world of the navy when he should have indoctrinated her and packed her away with him to every duty station thereafter. That's a failure of Sailor that he chooses not to remember because the circumstances involving their relationship were too mammoth a view and perspective. In the years to come, it would be shocking to Sailor why she did not respond to the letters he wrote to her. Anyways, he mentioned to the chief that he wanted to go to Norfolk, Virginia, to see the ship pull back into port. He explained to the chief how he left the boat to come back home and to report to his new duty station. He had to mention duty station; otherwise, the chief may not have approved Sailor's request. He also told the chief that he wanted to take his girlfriend with him so she could experience the navy's way of life and see the humongous aircraft carrier return to the pier. Sailor was shocked and surprised at the chief's response because he simply said, "Okay" and "Have fun!"

He took annual leave for about one week just so that he and his girlfriend could take their time driving down to Norfolk. At that time, he was still having problems navigating through the Beltway both Baltimore and Washington, but they made it there safely. Because they were not legally married at the time, but rather engaged, they strove to walk the godly life and not stay in a hotel. The temptation did cross his mind just to stay one night in order to get a good night's sleep. But he also knew he would not be able to resist the temptation of being alone in a hotel with his fiancée. With that reasoning, they decided to drive down to Norfolk early in the morning in order to catch the ship pulling in, greet some of his shipmates, and come back home.

Nothing worked out the way he had planned and hoped. At twenty-one years, old, young, vibrant, intellectual young man, he just knew he had everything together. In his mind, what happened on that trip *should never* have happened. And his reason for it happening was more Christianized in thinking than it was sensible in reasoning. Not that you could reason away God, but some things we do and the consequences we receive, we invite and bring upon ourselves. That trip flirted with a fatality, and it did not take Sailor long to understand the unsafe factors involved.

The first thing gone wrong is that when they arrived at Naval Station Norfolk and drove up to pier 12, where the USS *Dwight D. Eisenhower* (CVN-69). The ship was *already* docked and stand down had already occurred *a day earlier*!

"My God! We missed the ship pulling into port," he said aloud.

His fiancé got her first look at naval vessels docked at the largest naval station on the East Coast. But that's all she got—a look at the ships docked at the pier. She did not experience the pomp and pageantry and music and families on the pier waiting for their sailors to return home. She did not experience the sailors "manning the rails" and hear the sound of the boatswain's mate whistle when he announces over the 1MC "shift colors, secure from the sea and anchor detail. Liberty, liberty, liberty for all hands." She did not experience the emotion and excitement and cheers and laughter and observe the long-awaited embrace between sailor and girlfriend, sailor and daughter, sailor and son, and sailor and wife. She missed it all, and his heart sank deep down into his ankles because he wanted so much for her to see his world. She brushed it off and simply said, "That's all right, honey. Just as long as we are together, that's fine. I know you wanted me to see the ship pull in, but it's nice to be here with you."

Though her words were reassuring, they were not satisfying to Sailor because he felt that he did something wrong. He did not follow up to see if there were any changes to the ship's schedule because ships movement changes often. There was nothing left to do but turn around and drive five hours back to Harrisburg, Pennsylvania. After a brief time of disappointment at having missed the ship's return to the pier at Naval Station Norfolk, they began their drive back. They traveled on to Interstate 64 West to 95 North to 495 to 695 to 83 North, which would be their last stretch toward Pennsylvania 83 North would take them past York, Pennsylvania, and then back into Harrisburg, Pennsylvania. But that drive back to Harrisburg, Pennsylvania, would be abruptly interrupted, seemingly against Sailor's will and stamina. Like all the driver training classes he had attended in high school and with the United States Navy, he learned firsthand that usually the last stretch of driving anywhere between fifty and twenty miles from home are the most crucial. It is at this point that one becomes either complacent, fatigued with complacency, or hurries to finish the trip. At twenty-one years old, Sailor made a gross misjudgment thinking that for sure he had conquered all the road tests and challenges to conquer. They had made it all the way through Washington Beltway, Baltimore Beltway and past York, Pennsylvania, and just off the beltway on the stretch of Interstate 83 North toward Harrisburg.

But he had a dream, and the dream was extremely vague and lifeless and pointless and irritating and choppy, almost like being on a roller coaster in the dark. In the dream, he realized that it was pitch black, and he felt himself moving forward at an extremely fast pace, so fast it felt like someone or something had slung him from a slingshot and he was hurtling through the air. He became *extremely* irritated and felt like he was about to jump out of his body and wanted to stand up and yell to the top of his voice, "Stop! Stop this moving!"

His spirit was not at peace, and he felt this hard tugging on his soul almost like a hand was pushing him and pulling at him at the same time. He was rocking back and forth, tumbling around in a very dark place and being thrown over bumps at a rapid speed. In the dream, the last thing he remembers is that he looked at his fiancée as she was lying across his lap while he was driving. She faintly looked up at him and said, "Are you all right?"

She had gone to sleep, and he remembers looking at the speedometer on the car registering at sixty miles per hour. And then the inevitable thing happened, but he heard a distinct loud voice say directly in his ear, "*Wake up! Wake up, Sailor!*"

It was then he realized the dream was actually his soul going through a tunnel of sorts into a chasm of death. He realized then that he had driven off the road into the middle of the highway at sixty miles per hour on wet grass! They had stopped to get a cup of coffee at a Dunkin Donut somewhere off one of the Beltways, and he really was not a coffee drinker. But he blamed it on the coffee thinking they put something in the coffee to make him drowsy. He was convinced that's what made him fall off to sleep without warning. He does not even remember his eyes becoming heavy. He does not remember his head even bobbin', giving him any indication that fatigue was getting the best of him. The last thing he remembers was looking at his fiancée and then looking at the speedometer on the dashboard.

Where did the sleep come from all of a sudden? He blamed himself for not getting enough sleep and trying to drive back home six hours back to back. He was angry at himself beyond measure that he almost killed not only himself but his bride-to-be. He vowed to himself from that day onward that he would *never* drive that kind of distance without getting at least a couple hours of rest. He vowed to God, his fiancée, and himself that kind of misjudgment would *never* happen again. From that day forward, whenever he would begin to feel himself becoming drowsy on the highway, he would pull over either in a convenient store or stop at a motel and sleep until his body feels rested. The drive back from Norfolk, having had no sleep at all, by far, was one of the most deadliest times of Sailor's life involving not only himself but his lovely fiancée. Weeks thereafter, he analyzed and questioned and considered what it was he was dreaming and where it was his soul was traveling through before the angel of mercy cried out to him to "wake up!" An intricate and detailed mammoth battle raged that day between the powers of darkness, which sought to slay two young souls from the face of the earth. But thank God his mercy prevailed.

In the dream, he was alone in a very dark place—the kind of darkness you get when you turn the lights out in a room, times 10. He was fighting with the steering wheel and focused on the direction he was going. He also felt in the dream that he was descending. The descending part really caused him great concern. He became horrified as to where he might be descending too. The uneven terrain in the grass was somehow or another the reality in his dream. He was in two worlds simultaneously. How can that be? What was happening, and where was he going? Decades would pass in Sailor's life before he would have a clue of the entire event. When he woke up, he was able to bring the vehicle to a sideways stop. Immediately he placed the car in park, opened the door, stood in the middle of the wet grassy medium, and cried and yelled to heaven, "Please forgive me, God!" That cry was for *every* sinful act in his life since departing for the navy, also for the deceptive and "religious" life he was perpetrating. But the Sermon was still in the making.

The Way International

The systematic textbook study of the Bible was introduced into the life of Sailor during shore duty in Harrisburg, Pennsylvania. Guy H had first told Sailor about The Way International while on board the USS *Independence* (CV-62) during the 1977 Mediterranean cruise. Sailor was able to locate the Branch and Twig fellowships in and around Harrisburg that brought him into contact with men who were Way members. The Way International, founded by the late Victor Paul Wierwille, was a King James Version Bible verse-by-verse teaching ministry. At the young impressionable age of Sailor, *everything* he learned in The Way *all* made good Bible sense. It all seemed to flow with biblical truth. It seemed easy to understand, and there were textbooks he had to purchase for the course written by Dr. Wierwille. The basic class was about $75 at the time Sailor took the class. In the class, he learned Bible interpretative skills and began to understand many complex and controversial lessons from the Bible, like Paul's thorn in the flesh or how many thieves were actually crucified alongside Jesus. The name of the course was PFAL (Power for Abundant Living), which included twelve three-hour sessions. The ultimate lesson, which every student couldn't wait for, was session 12, when you were taught how to speak in tongues. For every PFAL graduate (so to speak), the ultimate was to go out WOW (Word over the World). However, he could not put his finger on it then, but there was something about The Way International that did not settle well with him. He learned some good Bible study methods and learned some biblical truths that to this day are undisputed. But then there still was something that didn't settle in his heart. The crowning unrest in his soul was the actual teaching of how to speak in tongues.

The lesson on how to speak in tongues struck a negative chord against fundamental truths of faith and trusting the work of the Holy Spirit. How is it possible that anyone can teach you how to speak in tongues? Nevertheless, that's what they taught, and that's what all the students did. Sailor and about ten other students sat there in the teacher's living room, jabbering and gibberish of words from each one of them as the teacher softly said, while pacing back in forth in his living room, "Let it flow. Don't think, just speak. That's it, that's it! Speak, speak, speak!" What a ridiculous, misguided non-biblical cult practice. In any case, Sailor was unsure, but he had been impressed over the years with the strict adherence to interpreting the Bible in a systematic manner. He accepted the teaching of The Way International and had become hooked. He would remain a member in good standing of The Way International during his entire tour of shore duty at Harrisburg, Pennsylvania, and eagerly desired to go out WOW (Word over the World). But WOW would never come into fruition. Subsequently, his next tour of duty would cast every cultic practice he had learned and accepted from The Way International into the proverbial depths of the sea. The Way and its questionable practices would become clearly seen as the cult that it was.

Sailor's experience with The Way International was during a time of the height of their work. It wasn't until when he left Harrisburg traveling back overseas that he kind of got out of touch with the Branch and Twig leaders, thereby becoming like a wanderer in the wilderness again. You can find all the information you want about The Way International online. Having gone through many changes and restructuring, they have managed to continue as a ministry. Sailor was on the tape of the month subscription listening and analyzing their teaching. He diligently made every attempt trying to decide if they were genuine or genuinely cultic. He anxiously looked forward to receiving a new teaching tape each month. He could not wait to hear the sound, settled, knowledgeable, expository teaching of the great Dr. Victor Paul Wierwille. His teaching of the Bible so impressed Sailor that much of the early days of Sailor preaching was taken directly from what Dr. Wierwille taught. Sailor, however, left out certain expressions and words that had become common among Way followers. He began to understand why his friend Guy could drink alcohol and maybe used the D-word every now and then and be able to explain away the use of his profanity. Dr. Wierwille and many of the so-called reverends were known for using foul language during their preaching. Not to mention lighting up a few cancer sticks, right after a sermon on great Bible expository. That, among other things Sailor would come to find out later, greatly disturbed him about The Way International. He can now see that getting transferred miles across the ocean into hostile territory in the Middle East was God's way of "taking his mind" off the cult. Sailor, in his desire to study the Bible and "know the truth," had been captivated by The Way International. A full decade would pass before Sailor would renounce the beliefs and practice of The Way International. But what he especially learned as an avid student of that cult practice was the discerning ability to see deeper than impression. The man of the Sermon will always remember the signs of a cult and the practices of the occult.

Sailor Duty Put on Hold

The duty at NRD Harrisburg, Pennsylvania, was pretty much uneventful but not boring but also not easy to relinquish come time to transfer. Sailor enlisted in a program in 1975 while in high school called DEP, Delayed Entry Program, with a United States Navy Reserve (USNR). When he reenlisted for the duty at NRD Harrisburg, the navy ordered him to re-enlist for six years. That way the navy got their thirty-six months out of him on shore duty with an additional two years, basically unassigned. The United States Navy was then at liberty to send Sailor *wherever* they wanted to send him after his cushy thirty-six-month assignment on shore duty, at home, basically in his own back yard. What a deal (sarcastically)! YNC J. transferred before Sailor did, and the chief was quite savvy in working the billeting and assignment system in the navy. At the time the chief transferred Sailor had become close to him and relied upon his guidance and expertise immensely. He made sure he stayed in contact with the chief as he transferred to Washington, DC, to the Joint Chiefs of Staff. Sailor felt and knew that he had a friend in high places that could help if he got into a crunch and got shipped somewhere he did not like. When the chief transferred, his replacement was uncanny another YNC J. but just the opposite of his first chief YNC J. The second YNC J. was a white male who was outright antagonistic toward the Bible and suggested that the disciples were queer. His assessment was because Peter was naked on the boat at a time Jesus visited them. Sailor had a twisted look on his face, trying to understand how the new Chief J. surmised the disciples of Christ were queer because Peter was naked. Nonetheless, the new YNC J. was extremely helpful with every task and advancement path Sailor needed. The new YNC J. was very versatile and knowledgeable of his job, and he spoke with a deep raspy voice. He said he ran into a concrete bridge abutment at sixty miles per hour from falling asleep on the Pennsylvania turnpike. Sailor thought for a few minutes. What was the significance of YNC J. telling him about his accident after he himself fell asleep on the highway? Is that where he was headed when he fell asleep on the highway? But Sailor kind of blew it off and did not spend much time analyzing the parallels. When the new YNC J. told Sailor that story of how they had to cut him out of the vehicle, and he did not remember anything but waking up in the hospital. Sailor was saying "ouch" the whole time he told him his story. Although he was a good chief, his demeanor and association was *nothing* like his first chief YNC J., who transferred to Washington. The second YNC J. also furthered Sailor's training by sending him to courses at the recruiting area headquarters in New York. The new YNC J. also enrolled Sailor in seminars and other training courses locally to Mechanicsburg Naval Depot, Mechanicsburg, Pennsylvania.

The time was quickly winding down for the cushy four-year shore duty in Harrisburg, Pennsylvania, and it was about time for

Sailor to transfer. The transfer was not accepted well by Sailor, and he thought about the prayer Mother Grimmel prayed for him now seven years ago. She had vehemently asked God to give TJ favor among the officers and men that he would work for and with. Sailor made every attempt to draw from that prayer, like it was an account in the bank, hoping it was still valid. Because after all, he did get the orders to NRD Harrisburg against the odds and expectations of all his senior officers. He formally requested a two-year extension, which would have put him at NRD Harrisburg for the remainder of the six-year reenlistment. Since he was already there, he figured the navy would simply go ahead and approve his request and that would be that. His commanding officer endorsed Sailor's request highly favorable. Sailor solicited and received a letter written from the district superintendent the late Belgium B. of the Church of God in Christ. He got a letter from the late Bishop Ozro Thurston Jones from Holy Temple Church of God in Christ in Philadelphia, Pennsylvania, and he got a letter from his own Pastor Doc G. of Mount Calvary Church of God in Christ. These letters were sent as attachments to his official request and the commanding officer's highly favorable endorsement for Sailor to be granted a two-year extension. In hindsight, he supposed the commanding officer and YNC J. knew he would not be granted an extension, but because he believes they favored him, they went along with his request against the odds, on the off chance it may get approved. Sailor's grave problem with the request for extension was how he went about requesting the extension. He failed to see that the favor granted by God seemed to be for the initial enlistment and anything other than his first tour of duty would require continued petitions to God. Instead of doing his first works over like intense prayer that Mother G. taught him back in 1976 when she prayed for him, he attempted to use the system designed by man by getting letters and endorsements and hoping the request would get approved. When all along, it should have been prayer and nothing but prayer, like when Mother G. prayed.

It was nothing but genuine, true, holy spirit, honest, godly prayer that got Sailor the orders to NRD Harrisburg in the first place. What made him think anything other than prayer would get him the second request? At the time, he did not know, he just did not know or understand the power of prayer. Intense, soul-wrenching, spirit-led prayer that not only changes an individual but alters the plans of men. With all the paperwork in place and the packet put together, he personally sealed the official United States government envelope and mailed it to Bureau of Naval Personnel (BUPERS then), Washington, DC, 20370. He then comfortably sat back and waited for a reply. There was not much praying going on about the situation because he *knew* he had a good endorsement from the commanding officer and favorable letters from his clergy leaders. He did, however, say a word or two to God like, "Lord bless this request and let them approved my request for extension." That's like a two-cent prayer for a million-dollar result. It wasn't even mustard seed faith; it was a sort of a piggyback prayer relying on prayer that was now seven years old.

The United States Navy Is in Charge

Normally, Sailor would open the mail and distribute to the appropriate department heads to take appropriate action. But the reply Sailor received from the bureau was opened by YNC J. because he handed the reply of Sailor's request to him. The recruiting district would get a good amount of mail daily due largely because of the mission of NRD Harrisburg, enlisting qualified applicants into the navy. There were times when Sailor single-handedly opened and distributed all the mail, and there were times Sailor and YNC J. would open the mail. On the day Sailor received his official reply, both he and the YNC was opening mail, and the orders read,

> The Navy's Enlisted Personnel Action Document that stated Sailor was to be transferred in March 1983 and report to Commander, Amphibious Squadron TWO no later than March 21, 1983.

His world fell apart, and his heart did a palpitation dance. In September 1980, Sailor was officially ordained as a Minister of the

Gospel, sanctioned by the Church of God in Christ. He got married to his fiancée in May of 1980, and they lived in a nice quaint apartment at Twin Lakes Apartments. Life was good, and he was basking on shore duty in Harrisburg, Pennsylvania. He was getting numerous preaching engagements and served as the district Sunday school president and was nominated and selected as the District YPWW president by the district superintendent Belgium B. Life could not have been any better than he was experiencing while stationed at NRD Harrisburg, Pennsylvania.

There were two factors that Sailor overlooked: (1) the United States Navy stepped in and spoke loudly and clearly to show who was in charge in those days in Sailor's life, and (2) Sailor thought he was a minister of the Gospel, but from heaven's throne, he had much more to learn before the true Sermon would be born. Sailor lived a life without prayer in those days and trusted and relied solely on what he had learned in the Bible. He thought very highly of himself. But when he received his decision from the United States Navy that, essentially, "you are going back to sea, Sailor, and this time, it will be the surface navy. Have a nice trip!"

He started praying then and even solicited prayer from others that the navy would reconsider and allow at least a one-year extension. At that point, the commanding officer would offer no additional endorsements, and Sailor could understand from the CO's perspective being in command. If the navy thought it necessary to transfer Sailor back to sea and the CO complied with procedures to request an extension and it was denied, there is no need to continue requesting reconsideration. After all, Sailor was a sailor in the United States Navy, and he, by his own volition, signed the enlistment contract and raised his hand to "defend and obey."

As far as the CO was concerned, his words to Sailor were, "That was that and we appreciate your performance while stationed at NRD Harrisburg, but time to move on, Sailor. Take the same performance and duty responsibility to your next command."

As the saying goes in the navy, "Fair winds and following seas." The commanding officer was a reasonable man, but he was also a military man, and he was by the book and a disciplined leader. Sailor attempted to look at the situation from the commanding officer's eyes, as far as the CO could see, "We gave you a chance and I gave you my best endorsement, and your rating detailer assignment disapproved the request."

The inference was, life goes on Petty Officer Sailor. But it was a *hard denial* Sailor was compelled to accept and deal with. It was a humbling experience as well because Sailor would come to know that he thought way too much of himself in those days and relied way too much on past performance and even past prayers. The next phase of his military career was perceived by Sailor as several years long of spanking from God. He believed that God taught him the fundamental application of faith. During those years, Sailor was bound to travel the road of correction and disciplining of his wayward soul. But looking back, after it was all over, he concluded the core reason for the transfer. What seemed like the center of hell was due to the comfort zone he embraced and enjoyed and a life void of prayer he exhibited. Sailor was about to become indoctrinated into the world of inevitable physical, spiritual, and mental conflict. It was time to enter the extreme path, a path that few people, other than military members, travel. What faced Sailor in the years to come could not have been imagined in the least. In fact, Sailor had no clue of what he was destined to face ahead and foolishly was relying on Mother G.'s prayer of favor. Not realizing that he lost that favor when he failed to continue to trust in and demonstrate his trust in the greatness of God. Sailor had absolutely zero prayer life and an abundance of worldly life. Sailor had to learn that prayer is like a well-oiled machine operating at peak performance. The machine must regularly be lubricated and the oil changed at certain intervals; otherwise, the machine *will* burn out. Sailor took prayer as a onetime "shop till you drop" type of action and all your problems are fixed. Heart-wrenching, spirit-led, soul-searching prayer was needed in the life of Sailor. The type of prayer and power to change individuals and alter the plans of man. Sailor had yet to know that type of prayer, and it was the type of prayer and the lesson God had in store to teach the wayward soul of Sailor, who was filled up with knowledge.

12

TRANSITION AND AWARENESS

Twin Lakes Apartments to Uptown Harrisburg

Sailor's fiancée, now his wife, legally married for the first time, had to move from Twin Lakes Apartments to Uptown Harrisburg with DB, his mother-in-law. He identifies her as DB for deep sentimental reasons and personal privacy concerns. Sailor was preparing to leave his wife, who he loved and was enjoying the early days of his marriage. But the time had come for him to transfer to his next duty station. He was filled with great apprehension, a lot of fear, and anger. His new set of orders transferred him to Beirut, Lebanon, on board an amphibious carrier ship. He was not sure what that all entailed. In his heart and mind, he was still attached to his first command at VS-31 in Cecil Field, Florida. He loved the entire tour of duty with VS-31 and both aircraft carrier experiences. He enjoyed the fun and exciting time at NRD Harrisburg because of the once-in-a-lifetime hometown duty. But now he was about to face the real surface navy on board an amphibious ship. In the mind of Sailor, he was not a shipboard sailor and hadn't learned how to navigate the seas from that perspective. His first duty command in the navy spoiled him immensely, and he forgot that he was in the armed forces. There are no guarantees all duty stations were going to be fun in the sun. He thought he was too good to be assigned to a ship as ship's company, and he felt he did not belong on board ships as primary assignment. After all those years on shore duty preaching what he thought to be faith, there was a lot of fear in his heart. He was clueless what to expect, and he was about to enter an environment that could care less about one's faith or calling as a minister. He was also angry because he believed his prayer was not answered for the one-year extension he requested at NRD Harrisburg. Essentially, he was still relying on a prayer that was seven years old. He failed to understand that prayer was for that time, and that time had passed away. At any rate, he had to transfer, and the following may sound disrespectful, but you will understand as you continue reading.

His mother-in-law, DB, was the mother of mothers in his life at a time he needed one. He hates to recall how he felt between her and his biological mother. But DB was more of a mother many times to Sailor than his biological mother, and Sailor loved DB like she was his mother. She was always there when he needed her, and she was always understanding, compassionate, and loving. When he and his wife had their first child, DB gladly babysat for them *every single day*. When Sailor fell into sin and committed the seemingly unpardonable sin of adultery, DB continued to be a mother and continued to love Sailor as her own son. The love she had for Sailor was incomprehensible to Sailor, considering the love that Sailor had for his biological mother. Sailor could not figure that strange relationship out, but in his heart, she became his second mother who treated him like she was his only mother. At this juncture in Sailor's life, salvation and Christianity became confusing to him, trying to figure out how his biological mother, whom he has known all his life, appeared to him as the saint of saints, yet his mother-in-law, whom he had only known since marrying her daughter, did not appear to be a saint of saints. But DB treated Sailor as a saint and embraced him as her own son. He became flustered over the years, until the death of his biological mother, of how he felt closer to his mother-in-law than his biological mother. When growing up as a child, he loved his mother to no end and thought the world of her. Now as a married adult serving in the United States Navy, it seemed his biological mother was distant from him in many ways. But Sailor yearned so much for the mother he once knew as a boy. It would not be until some years later that it all became clear to Sailor and saddening as well. What began to surprise Sailor at every bend in the road and turn at the corner was the things and perceptions people harbor in their heart even up to the day they die. Living can be liberating, but for many who name the name of Christ, their life is a jumble of hurt, pain, negative feelings, and wrong perceptions. But people seem to love harboring things in their heart instead of unveiling their true feelings to get the monkey off their back. Sailor's life going forward would become a mountain peak of emotions and a deep valley of despair. But he would slowly learn how to get rid of the monkey on his back and the demons in his soul.

Where they lived at Uptown was extremely cramped to Sailor after coming from Twin Lakes Apartments. The apartment was small also, but at least it had more than one room, and it was their place and they had total freedom inside their place. Woodbine street was a small, tiny room up on the third floor, with all their clothes stacked in the room. They did not have the freedom of using the restroom whenever they wanted, nor the freedom to walk to the restroom in their birthday suit if they wanted. They did not have the freedom to go to the kitchen for a snack or the freedom to be intimate all night if they wanted. The room was very cramped and a boatload of disadvantageous. But because they had no other place to go and because DB gladly offered to them to live there while in transit, Sailor was *extremely* appreciative and gladly accepted. The loss of freedom and the disadvantageous imposed upon him and his wife, Sailor managed to overlook day by day, though they stared him in the face minute by minute. The Bible says a tree is known by the fruit it bears, but that tree can have a cloudy perception by the onlooker. Does the fruit define who the real person is, or does the unripe fruit define what the person is going through? It's not always easy to discern the real essence and Bible definition of salvation that resides in one's heart. But if DB's actions during her lifetime are but a taste of the fruit of salvation and what one looks like being saved, then she must be a queen among those who are in eternity now. Sailor truly believes that his biological mother did have salvation, but the fruit of her salvation lacked many biblical qualities. The reason he began to question the validity of the Christian salvation, or perhaps, his biological mother. The transfer from NRD Harrisburg was the quintessential reaping and sowing in his life that his soul needed. It was time for him to learn about his mother and his family, and what he would learn would be the raw facts of who he was and who he was not. The love for his biological mother not once *ever* diminished. He continued to love her immensely while continuing to seek her acceptance and involvement in his life in and out of church. But she respectfully declined by her own actions to become actively involved in Sailor's life and his siblings' lives as well, creating in his heart a devastating reality of negative emotions to overcome. That's just the emotions concerning his mother. There was also all the other stuff he discovered about himself and the stuff yet to experience.

Mother

Sailor noticed the breakdown in the relationship with his mother when he decided to marry his fiancée. He realized that Mom had this uncanny belief and acceptance about another church girl Sailor was involved with. Before he left for the navy, the other church girl got pregnant, supposedly by TJ. Mom, from old school, Southern old school, expected TJ to marry that church girl. Sailor was disturbed by his mother's view and how she accepted Sailor as the father of the baby. There were many people that agreed the child did not look like Sailor, but his mother went back and forth initially in accepting the child. Those times were disturbing. Early on Mom said the child resembled the girl's firstborn—the girl already had a son by another man. And as the child grew, the girl would oftentimes take the child over to Sailor's mother while in church, and his mother, in a weird way, became attached to the child. Maybe, just maybe, that was just a paternal mother's love for children. At least, that thought was comforting to Sailor, but not satisfying to the reality of what he was dealing with. The girl, in a manipulative, skillful manner, convinced Sailor's mother that Sailor was the father. Except for a few of the girls' close friends and other people, there was sort of an unspoken consensus the child did not resemble Sailor. But the child *did* resemble the girl's firstborn son. Consequently, Sailor's mother, being of the old school of Southern thinking, felt Sailor should have married the girl. One of Sailor's sister-in-law, whom he perceived as a "whisperer" about the whole thing, also influenced his mother to believe that Sailor was the father. None of Sailor's siblings believed he was the father, and *none* of them embraced the child as kin. Sailor's seven brothers and five sisters, as far as he knows, never embraced the child as belonging to Sailor. Typically, among that many brothers and sisters, *someone* would have said, "Hey, Sailor, she does look a little like you," but no one ever said so, or ever brought up the prospect of Sailor being the father from the day the child was born. In fact, the older the child became, the more the child resembled the girl's firstborn. But Sailor's mother, she seemed to be convinced otherwise, and that was the beginning of the end of a close relationship Sailor had with his mother from the days of his youth. At times, Sailor's mother mentioned to him about marrying his ex-girlfriend, but when he met his fiancée, his mother was excited to know that Sailor's fiancée would one day become his wife—a smart, working, intelligent lady. That's the way Mom's generation looked at relationship: are you marrying a smart, intelligent, financially sound girl? Or is she someone that's going to work your fingers to the bone and drive you into the poor house? Sailor's mother was torn in her heart because of her upbringing. She appeared to believe that morally and ethically, her son should be marrying the girl with the baby. But she also wanted her son to marry a lady that had some smarts and class. What to do? Unfortunately, Sailor felt like he got screwed. His mother chose to distance herself from him over a conniving, manipulative, skillful woman because of a baby born out of wedlock. It was widely known that the church girl was still seeing her firstborn's father. That information comes from solid eyewitnesses, reputable sources. Sailor felt that his mother should have supported him against all odds and helped him fight this thing to know the truth. Instead, Mom assumed that since Sailor was previously engaged to the mother, it was his baby, and she expected him to make it right. Sailor did not receive any advice at the time, except for a few encouraging words from Fred. But the expectation from Mom and a select few was, "Go ahead and marry the girl whether you have proof or not. You're a Christian. Make it right." The old-time religious environment Sailor grew up in did not allow him to be offered the option of getting a DNA test to ascertain the truth. They just did not think that way, for the most part, and getting a blood test was insulting. Yep! He never got a blood test because he was trying to be an honest Christian man and accept the child. After all, he had been sleeping with the girl before he went in the navy, and he had been engaged to her. Asinine reasons, but a reflection of Sailor's lack of maturity and experience that literally cost him the next eighteen years of his life. Not just the obvious financial cost, but emotionally and spiritually, the situation beset Sailor *every single day*. He wrestled and wrestled on many fronts the entire time the child was growing up into adulthood. But at this point in time in Sailor's life, what does it really matter? Where is the redress? Where is the honesty? Where is the true resolution of the truth? Only the Most High Elohym Yahuah knows the truth—and the devil. The young lady has since gotten married and has children of her own. It's just one of those things among perhaps a multitude of men in the world. Sailor now has a platinum class membership in becoming a statistic among men who got captured by a woman involving maternity and child support. One GREAT undeniable "lessons learned" when it comes to sex, women, and fatherhood. Please don't misconstrue Sailor's desire at this point about the situation. There is only one resolution—the truth, nothing but the truth. If Sailor had conclusive evidence that he was the father, he would have had *no problem* being the father, as he still does today. Sad to say, proof has never been introduced into the mix and throughout the life of the child. Over the years, Sailor spoke with and treated her as a daughter, his daughter. The mother of his alleged daughter has always, *always* been elusive and holier than thou. The situation is a tough one because those who may know are not talking and the naked truth has been hidden for more than forty years.

Sex and Hookers (1) Rated PG-13

Sailor had great doubt about the maternity of a child with good reason because of certain facts. When TJ, left Harrisburg, Pennsylvania, in 1976 for the United States Navy he had given his then-girlfriend a diamond ring and became engaged to her. All the while the older man was still in the other girl's life. Once he gave her the ring, he never saw her and the other man together, but he knew he was involved because he would see the older man's car parked at her place. When TJ questioned her about the older man's car at her place, she would tell him he was either dropping off "their" son or picking him up. She would also tell TJ how he would give her money for "their" son. An extreme novice and youthful foolishness arrested his mind and passion for sex. TJ felt he could not deny that kind of quasi-relationship because, in the mind of young TJ, the man was obligated to financially take care of "his" son, even though TJ was engaged to her. Sailor desperately wished someone would have taken him by the seat of his pants and slapped some sense into his youthful ignorant mind. What enchanted TJ the most with this woman is the liberal and free sex he was having with her. It was liberal because every time they were together, she almost sanctimoniously said she did not want to have sex. But she never allowed him to leave her place without having sex. TJ fought and fought within his young inexperienced mind to respect her as a Christian lady and not appear to be seeing her just for sex. But every time they were together, he *always* gave in to the temptation. She kept him spellbound in his inexperienced mind because she always would cry, sometimes crocodile tears, and TJ would give into her false denial and his useless fighting, and they would have sex repeatedly. As a young seventeen-year-old boy about to turn eighteen prior to leaving for the United States Navy the relationship he had with her was purely a sexual relationship. TJ did not know how, nor did he attempt to deal with the other issues going on. Sex had solidified what he misinterpreted as love and the freedom to have sex with her had given life to the fleshly relationship. The truth of the matter is this sort of thing occurs time after time after time in many a young man's life. Indiscriminate sex paves the road for bad relationships based on personal freedom and private decision to engage in promiscuity. TJ would one day mourn his own son at the time the Sailor would emerge into the full range of the Sermon. Sadly, the new young TJ would walk in the spitting images of his father, precisely at the same age that his father's soul had been taken captive with unrighteous sexual activity. TJ was not a man but was dealing with issues that were of an adult and man responsibility. Had he been a grown man, he should have told her first child's father to take care of business downtown at Domestic Relations. Since the responsibility of a financial nature was the case, at least, that's what she told TJ, "He's picking up his son and he gave me money for him." Since the old man was allegedly giving her money for their son, he should have handled his business through the process of domestic relations. TJ was engaged to the church girl, and the old man did not seem to have any intentions whatsoever to steal her heart away from TJ. It was TJ who was engaged to marry her under false pretense and shallow relationship. He was swimming in adult issues that should have been handled by an adult man. An experienced woman offered her body and gave what she knew would be enticing to a seventeen-year-old teenager still in high school; sex became a driving force in the life of TJ, the Sailor, for decades. Succinctly, this is the solid reason Sailor drawing the conclusion of her being manipulative, cunning and entrapping. Of course, at this point in Sailor's life, there is no cause to be drawn from this and no reparations sought or apology necessary. But perhaps in the growing experience in the life of some young man involved with an older woman or two young people of the same age might spare yourself such agony and pain. In the long run, she was the *only* lady that TJ had unprotected sex with between the age of seventeen and twenty-one. Back then condoms were not strongly suggested, nor were they advertised as much as they are today. HIV was not a known sexually transmitted disease, which means the United States government had not launched their chemical warfare on unsuspecting people. The creation of the HIV virus has been detailed and researched by the valiant efforts of the late Dr. Boyd E. Graves.

The events in the young TJ's life enabled Sailor to connect his own dots involving the church girl of the world. When Sailor traveled overseas with the navy on board the USS *Independence* (CV-62) in 1977 and the USS *Dwight D. Eisenhower* (CVN-69), he experienced an out-of-control young man. The truth of the matter is that back then, everything was exciting to Sailor. He met older men that he respected and enjoyed hanging out with them. But the irony is that many of them respected Sailor because of his faith and his ability to talk his faith and even convince them of certain biblical principles. But the growing temptation of a young seventeen-year-old teenager and the exposure to sex with his church fiancée prior to leaving home opened the door of sinful exploration. He was never 100 percent agreeable to his actions, but he pursued them, nonetheless. As the world of sexual sins introduced itself to Sailor, he thought Naples, Italy, was the only place where condoms were required.

He met many women while overseas but did not feel safe or comfortable engaging in sex with them. He was able to maintain a smidgen of spiritual fortitude not only to walk the other way at times but not even hang out with the older brothers. He knew their agenda included stopping by the bars and clubs looking for women. But in Naples, Italy, it was a little different because the girls at least had a good supply of condoms. Company policy was to wear a condom and properly wear the condom. All those girls could not have been any older than twenty-five years old. A few times he went to the whorehouse, the girl would put the condom on to ensure it was put on correctly and covered all necessary parts. At nineteen years old, overseas, he thought that was safe enough to get what he wanted and to satisfy his fleshly lust. In boot camp, the recruits had to watch videos of the risk of having unprotected sex. Classroom instruction included viewing images of blisters, cankers, and the explanation of sexually transmitted diseases. And of course, pregnancy is always the number one risk factor. The most detailed education TJ received in those days was learned in navy boot camp during classroom training sessions. Even though condoms are not a guarantee, at least they cut in half the chances of getting a girl pregnant and reduced the risk of contracting a communicable disease. Every time Sailor had an experience with one of those petite prostitutes, he *never* had an episode with an infection or burning sensation when urinating the entire time he was overseas!

Hell, he thought to himself, *I never even had crabs because of those prostitutes*. What luck. God having mercy on his ignorance? Or could it be he *never* got infected with any communicable disease during the time of his fornicating life with prostitutes overseas? Granted, those girls undoubtedly were not squeaky clean, and they were not virtuous. Nonetheless, Sailor concluded that the correct use of the condom was successful in completing the job it was designed to do.

When Sailor returned to the United States after a long arduous seven-month deployment to the Mediterranean Sea, naturally he could not wait to go home and see family and friends and his fiancée. When he went home and spent quality time with his family, he made sure that he would spend time with his fiancée—the church girl who had come into his life while he was still in high school and who already had a son. The father of the son was still in her life. Upon seeing her after returning from overseas, he was happy and couldn't wait to be alone with her. She had her own place, and being alone with her was not a problem to arrange. He did not give much thought to it then, but her son was rarely around when they spent time together. It seemed the father of her son would make it possible that Sailor could be alone so she could continue to lead him down a path of seduction. The prevailing thought of Sailor decades later is that her goal was getting every benefit and military privilege had they gotten married. Sailor and even the man of the Sermon know that is a strong accusation. But why was it never a problem with the father of her son keeping their son when Sailor was around? Sailor had a few times when he had words with the father, but nothing serious because Sailor looked at him as an older man, and he was not sure how to take the old man. In his heart and from the eyes of God, Sailor respected the old man because of his upbringing to respect his elders. Even in that unstable relationship with the women who had a son by an older man, twice the age of TJ, he respected the old man. When Sailor returned to the United States, he could not take leave until some weeks later because the more senior military men had first privileges to go on leave. This fact also solidifies in Sailor's mind the deep uncertainty of fathering the child. When his time arrived that he could take leave after being overseas for seven months, he leaped on the opportunity to go on furlough. While on furlough, he would visit his fiancée but did not go home to his parents' house until 12:00 or 1:00 a.m. and a few times 2:30 a.m. It was totally disrespectful to his mother and his father, who was an ordained minister in the Church of God in Christ. Sailor felt because he had entered the navy and he was engaged to her, he could do his own thing. He was not necessarily being rebellious or disrespectful, but he had just returned home from living a life of adulthood. It was not easy for him to change that pattern of staying out into the wee hours of the morning. His pop would say things to him every now and then like, "Son, you staying over that girl's house too late." Or he would say, "Son, what you are doing is not Christian like." And his mom would say, "Son, you need to be careful about kissing on that girl."

He knew very well what they meant, but many times he wished they would have just sat his butt down and barked out orders like, "Hey, we know you are in the military, but if you are going to come home on furlough and stay here, you have got to respect our rules and be in the house before midnight." And they could have straight-up said, "Boy, having sex with her, you need to be very careful because when she gets pregnant, your military life and globetrotting for a long while will be disrupted."

Sailor knows beyond the shadow of a doubt that he would have appreciated any one of those approaches from his parents. Sadly, they did not know how to talk to Sailor about sex, women, and fatherhood. He does not blame them for his actions and walks in forgiveness toward them of their actions toward him by not directly parenting his soul. Sailor's actions were based entirely on the personal decisions he made and the ungodly demonic influence of sexual spirits that haunted him and his brothers for decades. It would not be long thereafter that the influence and compelling desire of lustful spirits in the life of Sailor would become crystal clear. Sailor was home about two weeks, and he spent a lot of time with his girlfriend, and almost like not skipping a beat, sex with her was free, liberal, and the main course of the day. This is not meant to be taken in a derogatory manner or to sound like Sailor is putting her down, because, at the time, he was loving her liberality and did not feel terribly wrong knowing they had plans to get married. One of the most deceptive, ungodly and selfish surmisings any young man and women can make is that because you are engaged to get married, it's all right to have sex. This is probably preaching to the choir, as the saying goes, but would to God that some young teenager who is on the engagement path will get the message and diligently change course.

The brief visit at home after touring the Mediterranean for seven months would teach Sailor one of the greatest lessons he possibly could learn about women. Had he learned the lessons he should have, the future experiences would never have occurred. Because of the demonic track record and assignment unleashed upon the males of his family, Sailor failed to learn his lesson. The future would yield other ungodly relationships to unfold, which precipitated his voluntary fall from grace. Just like the first week, the second week home on furlough involved sex, sex, sex. Any time of the day, any day of the week in all positions they could experiment with and think of. Then the absolute unexpected, carelessness, promiscuity lifestyle was the beginning of rocking Sailor's world. It was the elementary phase of many rocks in his world to come. Exactly three days before he was about to leave home to return to Cecil Field, Florida, where his unit was stationed, *exactly three days before he left home*. Sailor recalls vividly to this day when he went to the bathroom at his parents' house. For the first time, ever in his life he experienced something he only read about in books. He had an uncontrollable need to urinate, and when he went to the bathroom, like a bolt of lightning and an unprotected metal object jammed into an electrical socket, he experienced *the most extreme*, almost *unbearable* burning sensation when urinating. He stood at the toilet in his parents' house, stopping himself from urinating and trying to urinate in spurts because the burning sensation was incredibly agonizing. Sailor felt like climbing up the wall and running his fingernails across the wall and yelling to the top of his voice and grabbing the steel radiator—with his teeth! He could not imagine what was going on, and to top things off, his urine was dark, and I mean dark brown. Granted, he did not drink a lot of water in those days, but his urine should not have been that dark. It was like the color of the water in a toilet when utility workers are working on the sewer lines and your toilet water turns brown. Sailor's urine was equal to that color of brown, and it burned like the deepest part of hell to urinate. The unexpected hot discharge of urine left him confused, afraid, and speechless.

What is going on! he thought.

When he finished urinating, he was literally popping sweat glands like an erupting volcano. Sailor's shirt and face were drenched with an immediate flow of sweat from the fear and anticipation of having to finish urinating. Backing up urine into his bladder would have equally toxic and life-threatening results. Sailor was terrified to finish urinating! He had three days left at home on furlough and resolved to spend most of the time with his siblings. He was in a mummified state, not knowing what to feel or how to enjoy the last three days on furlough. The remainder of those three days became cloudy over the years. He did not go and see the church girl during those three days. He was trying to sort out in his mind what just happened. The last three days were erased in antiquity because Sailor's was delirious and his thoughts were senseless and unintelligible. He had no answers for what he was feeling, and he trembled to think his fiancée infected him with a communicable disease. The two-week furlough, in one instant, went from all the excitement of being home and freedom of having sex to the deepest low of the valley of sin. He had to fly back to Jacksonville, Florida, and the entire time on the plane when he had to use the restroom, the uncontrollable sweating began with just the thought of urinating. He was hoping and praying that it would not burn as bad later, but his hopes and prayers were useless. Every time he went to the restroom on the plane, the burning sensation was a repeat performance. Gripping the door handle of the restroom. Tensing his body and sweating profusely. Untold, unexplainable discomfort. When he arrived back to the barracks at NAS Cecil Field, Florida, the hellfire urinating had not left. It remained just as loud and present as when it began. The agony was unbelievably painful and was archiving in his mind one of the most sensational, painful experiences ever.

There was only one conclusion he could draw. He had to face the possibility and fact that the women he was about to marry had just infected him with a communicable disease. And to top things off, she was still involved with her first child's father. Horrifying thoughts coming to that conclusion, but what was he left with? He was endlessly furious and angry, day in and day out. He was so angry that the veins in his head were popping out. Sailor had never been that angry in his life but would experience that anger even more intensified years later. Yes, he had his lustful escapades with prostitutes while overseas, but if there is any justification in his sinful acts, he used protection. The entire time he was overseas, not once did he have any problem with urinating. He did not see his fiancée until about sixty days after he had sex with the prostitutes. Not once did he have an excruciating burning sensation while urinating when he was overseas. The experience with the venereal disease did not occur until about sixty days after the prostitutes and a few days after he had unprotected sex with his fiancée. You do the math! When he returned to Cecil Field, Florida, he could not wait one more day without checking into sick call. The following day, he told his supervisor that he had to go to the infirmary because he did not feel well. He could not remember what he did on the last three days left while he was on furlough. But he can remember when he went to the infirmary like it was yesterday. The three days have been lost in utter eternal darkness, like being lost in the woods at night. Going to the infirmary was like a pinhead of light pointing in a direction to come out of that darkness. Sailor walked to the infirmary on base, about a one-mile walk, and the whole time he was asking God to forgive him for his licentious lifestyle and ridiculously asking God not to let him have a sexually transmitted disease. Almost like when your parents tell you not to touch the stove because you will get burnt often children ignore the parent's instructions. Sailor's parents were trying to tell him when he was coming in the house early in the morning, but he kept touching the HOT oven. His fiancée was hot and burning from a previous relationship, and Sailor was the newest sucker on the block, gullible and inexperienced and lustful. She simply gave him what he wanted, and it was nothing for her to accommodate TJ's sexual appetite. But it seemed, she gave Sailor more than what he desired and more than what he could ever expect in his lifetime.

Sick Call

Sailor walked over to medical taking his good ol' time because he was not in a hurry to get to medical just to hear them confirm what he suspected. He can still see in his mind's eye walking to the infirmary. When he finally made it into the building, he had to sign in for sick call. It was 8:30 on a Monday morning, and he had just arrived back to the base on the previous Saturday morning. Regretfully, he had to spend the remainder of the weekend in agonizing pain. He stayed in his barracks room the entire weekend curled up like a baby and loathed the thought of having to go to the bathroom. He almost dehydrated himself over that weekend because he drank nothing and ate very little. He was doing everything he possibly could not to fill his bladder with any fluids. Unnecessary urinating was his intense focus the entire weekend. He did not think he could take much of the excruciating pain. What he was feeling was emotional hurt, anger, to the point if he had a firearm, he probably would have committed senseless murder. He felt lied to and cheated on. He felt disgraced and like filthy dirt was flowing through his veins. Each time he urinated he felt dirty, DIRTY, dirty! And the thought of the dirt deep inside his blood system began to unravel in his mind. It was becoming clear the seriousness and uncleanliness mentioned about sin in the Bible. He was beginning to connect with what God was talking about because in his soul he understood what it feels like to be sinfully dirty.

After signing in at sick call, he sat there waiting what seemed like almost an eternity and he felt himself having to go to the bathroom, but he held it until the corpsmen called his name. A petty officer second class hospital corpsman called Sailor's name. Sailor had to embarrassingly write down in the logbook what his symptoms were along with his rank, name, and social security number. Back in those days, you wrote down your whole social security number because identity theft and electronic crimes on personal computers were not an active threat then. Personal computers were not available to the public until some ten years later. Writing down social security numbers was common military practice then. If the record log could be retrieved from 1977 at the medical clinic on base at Naval Air Station Cecil Field, Florida, you would see the following entry within the pages: Seaman (SN) Timothy J. Sailor, xxx-xx-xx75 burning when I urinate. But you would see the whole Social Security Number. You would see the date, the time, and the year. The corpsman called him in the back into a room and gave him a cup and said just like this: "Go piss in here up to the line and bring it back and then have a seat." Just like that.

Sailor felt like a dirty, filthy piece of meat with a number on a page. He reasoned within his heart and thought to himself, *This is the navy. I'm dealing with sailors, and I screwed up by having unprotected sex. No one has to be sympathetic and nice to me because of my stupidity.*

After a few minutes, the corpsman called Sailor back to his office, and back in those days you could smoke inside a building. In the small office space, the corpsman and Sailor were sitting. The corpsman pulled out a cigarette and slowly lit the cigarette. He directed Sailor to have a seat and looked directly at him without any expression of any kind! Sailor looked at the corpsman with a deadening smile on his face, and Sailor had no life whatsoever because he could only imagine what the corpsman was about to say. After Sailor sat down, he looked directly at him. He didn't look away or around the room. He made it plain that he was talking to Sailor. The corpsman wanted it to be clear in Sailor's mind when he said to Sailor, "You have gonorrhea."

The deadening smile Sailor had on his face took a nosedive and died hard. The corpsman took a couple puffs on his cigarette, turned his head slightly to the right, twisted his mouth, and slowly expelled the smoke in the room.

"Damn it! Damn it to hell!" Sailor said out loud. He felt like he was in some interrogation room being investigated by some mobster the way the corpsman was carrying on. Smoking and taking his time to talk and looking very, very serious while talking to Sailor.

In hindsight, Sailor supposes the corpsman was being professional and trying to be calm about the matter because he didn't want to terribly upset Sailor. Afraid and nervous sitting in front of the corpsman, Sailor thought medical had to report his incident to the commanding officer, and he thought he would be discharged out of the navy. But thank God it did not happen that way. However, when the corpsman spoke that soul-wrenching, ugly word, Sailor's eyes immediately filled with water, and he became absolutely speechless and began shaking while sitting in the chair. He could not believe that he was contaminated with a communicable sexually transmitted disease. He had always been healthy and in perfect physical condition. A venereal disease would disrupt his young life in many ways and turn his attention away from every woman for a brief season. "What am I doing with VD?"

That question was not half as important as the next question in his mind, *WHO gave me gonorrhea?*

The process of elimination was not too difficult to figure in Sailor's mind. The normal gestation period for gonorrhea is anywhere from three to thirty days and the prostitutes he had sex with in Naples was at least sixty something days ago, at least sixty. And not only the time factor involved, but the establishment compelled its clients to use condoms. The service provider put on the clients themselves to make sure the condoms were on correctly. There was never a time the condom broke, and it remained on the entire time of illicit sex, which left Sailor with one other possibility. He had sex with his fiancée just a few days ago and several days the week before. So, in essence, he had a three- to seven-day period before he began to experience the excruciating burning sensation while urinating.

The corpsman asked the next embarrassing question, "Do you know who you may have contracted this from?"

Sailor was too embarrassed and hurt to look the corpsman in the eye. With tears flooding his tear ducts and his voice shaky, he said "I'm pretty sure I know."

The corpsman then said, "You need to let them know and tell them to go for treatment."

Sailor, who did not give a shit about the person who infected him, said, "Okay," and then the corpsman said, "We are going to treat you today, and you cannot have sex for at least a week or two."

Sailor had no problem with that because he had just gotten burned for the first time in his life and did not want to jeopardize his health by it happening again. The treatment they were about to administer would reach the peak of hurt and pain and embarrassment, anger, and frustration. Sailor wanted to just lie down like a sheep about to be slaughtered. He sank deep into an emotional abyss that he desired to trash his faith, his life, and screw the attempt to be a Christian. He would come to understand years later that his faith and life of trying to be a Christian was not his problem. His problem was the trash and garbage that was very much alive in his heart.

The corpsman told Sailor to go into the next room and pull his pants all the way down, including his underpants, and lay on the bed. He told Sailor to lay on his stomach, and he would come back in with another hospital corpsman. Sailor complied with his instructions without hesitation but with fear and apprehension and indescribable shame. Within seconds, both corpsmen entered the room where Sailor was laying on a cold, hard hospital bed. Both corpsmen was holding in their hands a syringe with a needle about the size of an unsharpened pencil. Sailor became numb in his mind and stared at the wall in a lifeless state.

One of the corpsmen said, "This is going to hurt, I will not lie to you. Just lay perfectly still."

His words were true to the Gospel. Sailor felt those needles sinking into his lifeless ass with pain almost equal to the burning urination. When they inserted the needles, immediately tears flowed from his eyes as if they had disrupted a nerve that went directly to his eye duct. He could not control the onslaught of tears that flowed. He did not cry with a sound, just the flowing of tears, as if his soul was being washed and cleansed from the filth. The antibiotics they discharged into his system was warm, and he felt it entering his lifeless body and into the cavity walls of his veins. Sailor had been hurt, pained, pissed, angry, frustrated, and confused. Sex with the girl he thought he loved had now humbled him, but he still lacked clear answers for years to come. This by far was the most painful and embarrassing moment of his military career—getting infected with gonorrhea by the woman he thought he loved and was about to marry. Not only did he draw the conclusion that she infected him based on his reasoning, but another rock-solid evidence that the possibility of her infecting him came straight from her acknowledgment. She did not verbalize the possibility of her infecting him, but what she wrote to Sailor in the other letter was evidence, at least in his mind, that merited consideration.

Leaving His Wife

Sailor had just spent thirty-six months of recruiting duty at home virtually in his own backyard while serving on active duty in the United States Navy. An opportunity that he would *never* have again in life. What his senior leaders thought would never happen for him, had happened, and now he was on his way back to the fleet. But he was leaving with substantial baggage on his shoulder, the type of baggage that had the potential of all kinds of emotional traumas. Sailor was tattered in heart and mind because his mother accepted him as the father of the little girl. In many ways, he was angry with his mother because she repeatedly embraced a child whom he and many others did not believe was his daughter. But he had no proof of his suspicions. Sailor had not gotten a DNA test and felt almost condemned requesting one and presumed that he heard from God in prayer to "leave it alone." Sailor's thinking and shallow faith in those days were just as messed up as the multitudes of religions that exist. Torn and tattered in spirit because he did not want to transfer and leave his new wife. He was upset because his request for extension was denied, and he had just received his paper ordination from the bishop of COGIC as a licensed minister. The long history of Christian thinking and the upbringing of his parents persuaded Sailor that he was wrong for not accepting the little girl as his daughter, yet right for making attempts to develop a father-daughter relationship with her. It would be decades later that he began to see that right is what is honest and true, especially with untampered documentation and court-related proof. At the time, Sailor had neither! All he could claim in those days was faith in a muddled type of Christianity and religious practices. A myriad of beliefs among a sea of Christian denominations. In short, Sailor was imprisoned in the confusion of religion that bound him for years, among a people that may have meant well, but was wrongly led.

March 1983, Sailor was beginning a new travel experience into a phase of his life that would seriously distress his Christianity. He would be compelled to put into practice the things he learned during his first tour of duty. It was not until his transfer from NRD Harrisburg that *all* the words and guidance given to him by his friend Guy H. when he was assigned to VS-31, on board the USS *Independence* (CV-62), piece by piece, would become clear. He held on to the experiences learned during his first tour of duty like he held on to the experiences of North 18th Street and the projects. At this point in Sailor's career, North 18th Street and the projects were no more than a chapter about someone's life he read in a book somewhere. The reality of Sailor's life had now become so overwhelming and compelling that all he could see was the discomfort and pain of being torn apart from his wife. Uncle Sam was now in control of his destiny, so he thought. The interest in the Bible and the depths of truth within the pages of the Bible and the relationship one can obtain with the Almighty would begin to come alive during this tour of duty. At the same time, the real self, *deep* down inside the dark chasm of his heart would also become alive. The darkness in his heart would manifest itself for years to come. The transfer back to the fleet was just the beginning of the next phase of lessons for him, defining who and what salvation is. He would become stripped bare of soul, spirit, and mind to uncover the dark of darkness inside his soul. Sailor had become the epitome of Matthew 6:23: "But if thine eye be evil, thy whole body shall be full of darkness." The young lad Sailor was completely clueless of the depth of darkness that had invaded his foolish mind and soul. He anticipated moving forward, but he was so, so depressed and apprehensive about leaving his wife. Worry was on his mind about entering hostile territory in Beirut, Lebanon. In those days the world's attention was focused on the Iran hostage crisis from 1979 to 1981, 444 days, involving 52 Americans. Look at the map and find Beirut to the far left and you will notice that Syria is to the right of Beirut and Iraq is to the right of Syria. The next largest country to the right of Iraq is Iran. Sailor would be a stone's throw away from the place that just spent over a year in the headlines of the United States. The entire world was captivated by the hostage situation. It was the early days of terrorist activity against America and American citizens. Little did he know at the time that he would be among the pioneers, so to speak, of the beginning of terrorism against America. Terrorism at large was a new form of war with unsettling fears. This was the baby stage of active fear that would one day hit the United States of America with dreadful and frightening killing activity. Death in massive form would grip the very foundation of the heartland and strike fear instantaneously in the heart of every American. Sailor did not fully understand at the time the impact those days would have on current times. But he would grow up *fast* and learn *quickly* how it all fit together. The enormous woes thrust upon the country he loved so very much would become crystal clear. America the beautiful, America the brave, America the red, white, and blue would one day become America the chastised in the judgment of God.

The day he left his wife from the cramped little room on Woodbine street is a memory that is seared in his brain. He stood in the doorway of their small room staring directly into her eyes trying to assure her that all is well and everything would be all right. He mentioned something about praying to God. His prayer would be that he would get to come back home. The religious and Christianity mentality continued to saturate his mind. Instead of accepting his responsibility and continuing on to his new tour of duty, he expected God somehow to miraculously turn it all around and cancel the orders. She cried a little but not much in front of him, and he held back his tears but reserved them for later. His pride convinced him to be a strong military sailor for his wife and return home in one piece so he did not cry. He spent weeks away from his wife while at training school for leadership and management at Little Creek, Virginia. This trip would be his very first time traveling to Norfolk and Little Creek Virginia alone, and it would be a place that he would come to love years later. Even to this day, Sailor many times questioned why he returned to Harrisburg, Pennsylvania, to live after all the places he traveled to.

Norfolk and Commuting

The travel to Norfolk took him every bit of six hours plus because he drove very slowly. The speed limit back in those days was 55 miles per hour even through West Virginia. Most of the time he drove fifty miles per hour because he was not in much of a hurry getting too far away from the memories of Woodbine Street knowing his wife was still there. The slower he drove, the more he remembered just leaving home, and he was not in a hurry for those memories to fade like the projects, North 18th Street and VS-31. He wanted to hold on to the images of his wife in his mind for days, months, years so he drove slowly on to Interstate, Baltimore beltway, Washington beltway, Interstate and Interstate to Little Creek Naval Station, Little Creek, Virginia. But the tears he held back while staring in the eyes of his wife found their cue. He purposely drove fifty miles per hour and even slower at times. His thoughts were largely due to him crying and wiping his eyes to clear his vision while driving. For about the first two hours or so on the highway, Sailor could not help but cry. This was not like the time when he first left home at eighteen years old. This was different, making it a different type of tear. Sailor was not sure if he would return home from this tour of duty. This was the real thing, the mission, and purpose of the military. Conflict, armed conflict, and US government instigated military campaigns. He thought it was unfair and not right that he had to leave his wife. He continued to struggle with the thought of his mother abandoning her own son for the likes of a manipulative woman. He was unsure about him being the father of a little girl who was two years old at the time.

He wanted everything to be clear and straightened out before he left, and *nothing* seemed to be going his way. He was nursing his own private pity party and thought of his party as his own personal dilemma that no one would understand. His entire drive to Little Creek was occupied with sifting through, sorting through, and trying to figure out the why. The classic thoughts and whys and why me? The typical pity party with the main ingredient of spiritual immaturity. What life basically boils down to is spiritual awareness and spiritual aptitude involving the things of God. Sailor did not understand the depth of such a view, nor does the average person understand the purpose and reason for the experiences in their lives. Especially at the time they are going through. It is usually in hindsight that we all see and understand. Therein lies the constant complaining and self-pity and nobody understands and this and that and all the other multitude of reasons most rationalize with themselves. Amphibious Squadron TWO duty would expose Sailor to weariness and phenomenal aspect of life that he only heard about. He would come to know by experience that all things and that means "ALL things work together for good to them that love God, to them who are the called according to his purpose" (Rom. 8:28). At seventeen years old, Sailor entered the delayed entry program in preparation for enlisting in the United States Navy. He did not really expect to see any hostile situations or the beginning of hostilities against America or threaten the freedom of other countries. But the new terrorism type of war would escalate almost overnight into world terrorism. In fact, the very word *terrorism* was not a word on the streets of the United States of America at that time. Sailor thought he would travel the world like the recruiter told him and sold him on the navy and visit exotic places and come back home a world traveler. No one even mentioned the threats on his life or the possibility of dying in his sleep while attacked by Muslim extremist. No one told him about the personal battles he would have to face and overcome that devastated his faith and annihilated his religion. No one told him about being on the verge of becoming a rebellious extreme radical black man. No one told him that in his heart he would revive a spirit of hate against white people and some black people. And no one told him how God would charter a course for him that *only* he would know the outcome. God placed him on a path of his own training and military enlistment. Years later, Sailor would conclude that he was among many like the Scripture say "and they shall be all taught of God" (John 6:45). And the Scripture also shows us that those taught of God are enlisted into HIS army as HIS soldiers (2 Tim. 2:4). The army of God will be trained to do battle against the powers of darkness and God's archenemy, Satan, the devil (Rev. 19:14, 19). But this conclusion of Sailor would be the Sermon coming into fruition. But for now, Sailor was still in control of nursing his personal sad feelings and woe-is-me mentality.

Vacation at Virginia Beach

After two weeks of leadership training at Little Creek, Virginia, Naval Station, Sailor spent a few days with his wife at the beach. This would be the last time spent with her before he entered extreme hell. Nothing will and has ever compared to that time since. It would be the imminent tour of duty on board the USS *Guadalcanal* (LPH-7) stationed off the coast of Beirut, Lebanon. In comparison, *nothing* in his life would match the anger, frustration, unhappiness, sadness, and sinful thoughts and intentions like being on board ship in Beirut, Lebanon. If his first tour of duty with VS-31 was like a pleasure excursion of seeing the world, his third tour of duty would be the extreme opposite, literally on a real-time deadly scale. But before entering that hell hole, Sailor spent some time with his wife on their first vacation in Virginia Beach. They stayed at the Royal Clipper Hotel on Atlantic Boulevard in Virginia Beach. It was March 1983 and kind of chilly. The beach was not crowded at all not being peak vacation time. The room rate was a measly $35 per night, but this was over thirty years ago. That same room today is something like $140 a night, a huge difference in inflation and the economy. At the time, there was not much fancy about the Royal Clipper, but being alone with his wife on the beach overlooking the Atlantic Ocean was satisfying to Sailor. It was those few moments he needed with her before entering his soul-searching battle. They walked the beach, she with a winter coat on and Sailor with a small jacket and black cap. Being a sailor, the breeze from the ocean and the cool temperature was just right for him, but his wife, from the inner city, had much adjusting to do. Sailor was all too excited that she was there with him and could have stayed on the beach in Virginia the remainder of his days. In those days, he was very much in love with his wife and did not want to let her out of his sight. Over the years to come, that love nightmarishly would take a turn for the worst. The love he had for her in those days was masked by many things and parental influence. Each page of Sailor's life would only be understood by him years after the page had been turned. He is convinced one of his faults was returning to Harrisburg, Pennsylvania. His native city filled with controversy and issues and things he created himself and problems embedded among people and with people. Not that one can totally escape the challenges, obstacles, and temptations of life, but many internal and external things can be overcome by simply changing your environment and geographical location. If there ever was a time that Sailor failed to hear the voice of God, it was when he *did not* relocate to Virginia. He learned the city. He learned the roads. He learned the travel routes. He even learned the state and government office buildings downtown. It was Sailor's mind and NOT his spirit that directed him back to Harrisburg, Pennsylvania, after his first tour of duty had ended.

Years later, Sailor would begin to understand that moving away from familiar surroundings and growing up was the best thing for him. He acclimated into brand-new surroundings with brand-new people and it opening up a life-changing time for him. The desire to be around family is not always the most profitable and right thing to do. The desire to hang on to his siblings and want to be around them is what Sailor would discover of his life. Much progress can be hampered because of family and familiarity. He began to consider the Holy Scriptures when God directly told Abram to move away from family and familiarity that he would establish him in another location and make him another man. God actually gave Abram a new name meaning "father of many" (Gen.

12 through 17). Relocating from Harrisburg, Pennsylvania, was something Sailor felt he was led to do, but something he failed to do because he had his own agenda. His agenda stunted his growth and caused him to sink into an unimaginable life of sin involving repeated adultery and fornication. Years after getting out of the navy he returned to Harrisburg, Pennsylvania, a continuing saga of bad choices. The headlines of ministers falling and scandals against their person involving sex and money, he had now become part of the same, without the headlines. But inwardly, Sailor knew he was the headline of heaven, and his public demoralization and fall would be forthcoming if he did not change his ways. The circumstances leading up to the fall and demoralization of Sailor will be discovered later. But for now, when his wife came to Virginia with him, it was a peaceful, satisfying, relaxed, and unhurried stay at the Royal Clipper hotel. The walks on the beach were memorable and sentimental. During those days, he would often step back into time to relive those moments spent with her. He could feel the ocean breeze, smell the ocean, and hear the waves. He could see his wife standing on the beach. He could see her walking toward him and feel her embrace and her emotions. He could hear her voice and feel every part of her body, and though she had a winter coat on, her body was pleasingly warm. Her smile was like the luminous rays of the sun. Her touch was like the softness of a newborn baby, and her skin was like the radiant glow of the moon. Sailor was moved with excitement and enjoyment, knowing she was standing there with him, as if the entire world and the ocean before them had to give them special attention. There were other people around walking on the beach and doing different things. But as Sailor noticed the other people, they were more like peripheral images. His wife, being at Virginia Beach with him in a new city he had learned, became the center of all his attention. There was a slight overcast of clouds just about every day they were there, but somehow he was able to overlook the overcast of clouds and enjoy the moment.

Those days were brief, only a few days, but they were long enough to enjoy and remain a lifetime in his mind. Those days masked everything involving Harrisburg, Pennsylvania, including the maternity situation involving the other girl. Those days masked every concern he had about leaving his wife. However, during that time a tragedy struck, that was like pouring salt into an open wound. Sailor asked the question in his mind, *Why don't the devil just leave us alone sometimes?* Sailor would learn the answer to that question one day and would also realize the blame does not always rest squarely on the devil. Furthermore, Satan's actions against mankind are part of the growth process in developing relationship with God. So the devil acts like the devil, lives like the devil, and kills like the devil. One must overcome the devil and all his ways because he is a wily foe. The ability and capability to overcome the powers of darkness are promised by God. Mental and spiritual victory over the devil can be overcome. In his quest to know God, Sailor would come to know him by his true name, Elohym Yahuah. But until the fullness of time when the manifestation of the relationship and walk of a true believer with Elohym Yahuah, one must deal with and endure through the heinous acts of the devil.

Sissy, a young lady in her thirties, first cousin and a good friend of his wife and family, passed away due to a brain aneurysm. A deep chasm of sad moments was immediately unleashed in both of their hearts. Sailor immediately interpreted the clouds as a manifestation of her passing. He struggled within to continue enjoying the remainder of the time with his wife. In a place he loved and the time he was immensely enjoying, his wife fell into grief and bereavement over the loss of one of her good friends. Sailor was pretty much speechless as to an explanation why God would allow such death to occur in a lovely young person. Sailor did not know her at all but trusted his wife's relationship with her that she must have been a wonderful individual. Consequently, for the remainder of the time in Virginia Beach, his wife's sadness became his sadness during a time he wanted to enjoy their time together. He struggled to understand the circumstances, and he sought God for something to say to comfort her. Life becomes filled with unanswered questions at the behemoth of such things. Sailor wondered why it happened and why it happened that way. He was filled with unanswered questions for this and that. He questioned God in search of an answer and was left with little clue and silence on many occasions. As time goes on and one learns a smidgen of the ways and truth of Elohym Yahuah, many unanswered questions become clear. And though the reason behind certain deaths and sudden tragedies is not always easy to accept, it is comforting and saddening, nonetheless, to know why these things happen.

13

TOUR OF DUTY NAVAL STATION LITTLE CREEK, VIRGINIA

A Time of Deep Reflection
Deep in the Mirk and Mire

> Deliver me out of the mire, and let me not sink: let me be delivered from them that hate me, and out of the deep waters.
>
> —Psalm 69:14

M*ire* is defined as "wet spongy earth, often deep mud or slush." You can come upon it in the wetlands of marsh areas throughout the earth. In the United States, it is mostly found in Southern states like Louisiana, Mississippi, Georgia, and Florida. Sailor once found himself in mire at the edge of its parameter, in Cecil Field, Florida, outside the base, off 103rd Street. Sailor and Brother C. were taking pictures and observing the F-14 fly-bys. Sailor had stepped a little too close to the edge of the marsh and his feet and legs began to sink rapidly. Brother C. was right behind Sailor, and only one of Sailor's legs had connected with the mire in the marsh. Both gave a loud yell, and instantaneously, Brother C. leaped forward enough and grabbed Sailor by the shirt and yanked him, seemingly, with all his strength and pulled him out of the mire. Sailor could only imagine the horrid outcome had he been exploring the marsh area of Florida alone. But the thing with the mirk and mire is that it quickly got a hold of his leg when he stepped into it. It was like the mire owned Sailor and was not going to release him no matter what. The mire was very thick and soggy and wet and mushy, and with every move to step backward, it seemed to pull him forward and down. There was nothing to grab on to and impossible to run the other way. Brother C., for all intents and purposes, was his savior that day. God was and is the sovereign over his life, but he certainly places people in our lives to act as human deliverers. Consider Moses, Joshua, Sampson, and all the mighty men of valor in the Bible, God used their humanness and physical strength many times to set his people free.

The mire in the marshlands of Florida would be a premonition of the mire in Sailor's life he would waddle in the years to come. The weakness of the earth around the foundation of his life would come to an uncontrollable shift in his foundation. Women and sex are the curse of the lust of the flesh that inevitably cools down and in some cases, totally extinguishes whatever inspirational fire a man may have. Sailor's fire was, like the prophet said, "shut up in my bones." It was a fire of the Holy Ghost and a fire of discharging in undeniable speech the Word of God. But God's Word would become silent for the most part through the lips of clay without an audience or a following. Sailor's voice became hidden among the deep crevasse of sin for years to come. A defiant perspective on widely accepted worldly issues and virtually a silent voice in the scheme of things concerning heaven and hell. Silence, obscurity, nothingness would become the lot of his life of five-plus years. But this lot was certainly not by divine commission rather by human decision and lustful actions laboriously justified by human reason. He would find Scripture to justify what he was feeling. When would it end? When would he see the true light and accept the voice of God telling him in no uncertain terms, "Leave! Stop! Step far away and rededicate yourself to the real calling and purpose of your life." Without question, at this point, Sailor had entered the ring of sin constructed by the demons of the earth that wage war against the heart of men. Satan, the war instigator, pranced around and around inside the ring refereeing Sailor's thoughts and controlled his soul and abused his flesh. Sailor had become like any other man, week, unbelieving, sluggish, ungodly, undisciplined, and full of sin.

Every single day he read the Bible verse of the day in his Daily Devotional. Each Bible verse gave him solace that his mind had not surrendered totally to the lies of Satan. The experience of his ex-girlfriend that had just infected him with a communicable disease would initiate epic battles in the mind of Sailor. Inside the mirk and mire was filled with pleasure and entertainment and worldly thoughts and actions and human perspectives. His relationship with his church girlfriend was a spinoff of that pleasure under the guise of getting married. It was a hodgepodge of misunderstanding and confusion even with the women stuck with him in the mire. She thought her life was unfolding in a magnanimous way while she rejoiced at the very sight of them being seen together. The time he was with her, he was walking, talking, and living in a mummified state as he took every breath through his lungs. What would unfold in his life minute-by-minute was the unexplainable grace of God upon him. The psalmist talks about making his bed in hell, and never had Sailor imagined that one day he would wake up and realize that he had consigned himself to an emotional hell life. It was not a hell of fire and brimstone, but a hell where worldliness abounds and fleshly desires erupted on end. But he found out that God was also there with him. God was not in the hell of his life in a condemning way but was certainly there by his divine omnipotence. Sailor could sense his presence. He knew his presence and even felt his presence in a very real way.

The Daily Devotional Bible verses he read were like bits of steel from a larger anchor that would one day come together to form a real and lasting anchor of his soul. With every single look at her, he was captivated deeper and deeper into the mire of her flesh. Having sunk to the bottom of the marsh, his soul cried out yelling from deep within the locked captivation of his heart. He could see. He understood clearly the twisted weeds of lust all around his flesh. He knew full well within his mind that he had sunk, and he knew full well how to be raised. But the doing of that thing to raise his soul and spirit was the most tactical calculating battle that Satan had waged against his soul in all his life.

The Daily Devotional Bible verses were like pinheads of light shining through a vast sea of darkness. Every morning that he read a Scripture there was silence, almost a deafening silence. As if no one else was in the dark sea of sin other than he and as if no one else could see the small shining light of the Word of God but him. Every scripture spoke. Every scripture leaped from the page. Every scripture, like a drug addict on crack, called to Sailor each morning. The Word of God was reaching out from the pages of the Bible and had become the Word of God speaking from heaven. God had personified his Word in a way that sounds mystical. Every morning that Sailor rose, he could hear and sense the presence of the Spirit of God. The only hold Satan had on Sailor was in the form of flesh, in a human body. Inside Sailor's spirit, there was a drought of Word, and his spirit began to speak to him in ways he had never experienced before. It seemed that no one else could see his hunger and thirst after righteousness, including his ex-girlfriend and the women he would become involved with in the future. They were all oblivious to what Sailor was experiencing. They, all of them, were only concerned about their seeming happiness and prospect of getting married in a wedded locked cell. Nothing could ever become of the relationships in the eyes of God for a myriad of reasons. Not to mention the relationships were established on ungodly grounds and kept alive by ungodly ways and actions. The time was now, like, now faith is the substance of things hoped for, the evidence of things not seen. Now was the time to disengage, disembark, sever and break the ungodly ties with the plans of Satan. The enemy of the souls of men had launched his most divisive and deceptive assault against Sailor. The battle would rage for several decades, and one day the Sermon would be born from DEEP within the experiences of TJ, the Sailor whose life became the Sermon.

Naval Station Little Creek, Virginia

The tour of duty at Little Creek in this first phase was brief and especially for classroom training. Sailor would spend a measly two weeks at the Navy's Leadership Management Educational Training (LMET) school, training designed to give sailors a brief introduction of leading others as a senior petty officer. The school was exciting and fun, but the TDY, temporary duty, gave Sailor much time to reflect on the overwhelming changes that had occurred in his life. It seemed like yesterday leaving the boat, the USS *Ike* (CVN-69) in Haifa, Israel, and flying over the nuclear stacks on the plane in Middletown, Pennsylvania. The tour of duty at NRD Harrisburg, Pennsylvania, and accepting the call to the ministry was but a brief moment in time, struggling, fighting, and running from himself.

Getting married while on shore duty in Harrisburg, Pennsylvania, and dealing with his ex-girlfriend's dilemma of establishing maternity. Little Creek was essential, a time of deep reflection and a pound of worry about his next permanent duty station in Beirut, Lebanon. Sailor would be stationed onboard the USS *Guadalcanal* (LPH-7) with the embarked Amphibious Squadron Two. Transferring to the Middle East in light of the recent Iran hostage situation had now become the nervous worry of Sailor. Having served his first tour of duty with the Airedale community and debarking the ship when they were in port. The USS *Guadalcanal* (LPH-7) would be his home for the remainder of the two years left on his six-year reenlistment. The idea of being stationed on a ship with an administrative squadron, augmenting ship's company, was the biggest worry in Sailor's life then. How would he adjust to living with ship's company? How would he adjust to being on board ship, not having the liberty of being in a barracks and able to walk on dry land at his leisure? These and other concerns worried Sailor while attending LMET school at the naval station in Little Creek, Virginia.

The two weeks that Sailor was at Naval Station Little Creek, Virginia, he had his three-year-old car with him, just purchased after being at NRD Harrisburg for 1.5 years. The Pontiac Phoenix was nothing of a luxury vehicle, but it was good quality far above the 1972 Ford Pinto. Prior to the Pontiac Phoenix, Sailor had purchased a brand-new Mercury Capri with only sixteen miles on the odometer, two months after being stationed at NRD Harrisburg, Pennsylvania. The Capri was a nice sports car. It was a 5-speed gear shifter in the center console. The car payment was a whopping $179 per month. They were truly the good ol' days, and everything about the Capri was pleasingly satisfying to Sailor—the speed, look, the interior, and the color. He had an in-dash Pioneer cassette deck installed immediately after purchasing the Capri. He had two subwoofers installed in the hatchback section of his car and was planning on installing some nice rims with wide tires on his Capri. He wanted to hold on to the Capri all the way through his time on active duty, even as a second vehicle. Deeply distraught at thoughts of the Capri and the short-lived enjoyment of the car. About one year after being stationed at NRD Harrisburg, on an icy, snowy morning during the workweek, while on his way to work, it would be the very last day he would drive the sporty Capri.

Interstate 81 at North Front Street in Harrisburg, Pennsylvania, would be the accident that would demolish Sailor's Capri. The Capri was the same vehicle he and his fiancée drove off the highway into the grass on interstate 83 while coming back from Norfolk, Virginia. "Bridge freezes before road surface" was a warning Sailor had not yet learned. It wasn't that he was rebellious of the sign, it's just that he did not have training or much experience driving a vehicle in inclement weather. The cool air flowing underneath the overpass had frozen the road surface to clear ice. The speed limit was 55 miles per hour on the highway, and when Sailor arrived at the bridge, he was traveling about 20 miles per hour, way too fast for ice on the road. Immediately when his tires hit the ice, his car began to aggressively fishtail. He made an equal reaction to compensate for the fishtail, seriously overcompensated. He hit the brakes hard. His unskillful action caused the vehicle to spin out of control at 180 degrees. He found himself turning back around with the vehicle in an unstoppable slide toward the direction of the concrete barrier of the bridge. He saw it coming and could do nothing because he lost total control of his Capri. Traditional Christianity had taught him in situations like that when you do not know what to do and you are out of ideas and have no solution, call out the name Jesus. Traveling about 15 or 20 miles per hour right at the point of impact Sailor yelled out the name "*Jesus!*" His nice brand-new Mercury Capri slammed into the concrete barrier at full momentum of its travel speed with Jesus on Sailor's lips. All these thoughts were a deep reflection while at Naval Station Little Creek, and the thoughts forced him to analyze the life of a preacher with sinful actions while stepping up in the pulpit every Sunday morning. He began to question the name of Jesus. He questioned his marriage to his wife. He questioned his duty while at NRD and whatever impact he may have had on others. He came to the startling conclusion that he must be getting rewarded for the life he lived while professing to be a Christian during his first tour of duty and living like a "wild oats" young man. True to line upon line of the verse that says, "Be not deceived; God is not mocked: for whatsoever a man soweth, that shall he also reap. For he that soweth to his flesh shall of the flesh reap corruption, but he that soweth to the Spirit shall of the Spirit reap life everlasting" (Gal. 6:7–8). At NRD Harrisburg, Pennsylvania, little did he know at the time, but Sailor was in the early stages of reaping his sinful actions. Unfortunately, the tape had to play out completely before he would begin to see a smidgen of light full of truth. In the years to come, all his questions would be answered, and yet all his questions would remain questions while searching for answers. The car accident in his Capri resulted in him and his new wife purchasing the Pontiac Phoenix. Sailor would drive the Phoenix back and forth to Norfolk until his departure for the Middle East. The sad story behind the demise of the Phoenix involved both his dearest mother and his youngest sibling. His brother was pretty much along for the ride, so to speak. But the promise of his mother and the failing of her promise continued to irritate the wedge between them. Sailor wanted so desperately to know the Mom of his youth. He wanted so desperately to rekindle the mother-son relationship. But there were factors unbeknownst to him at the time that was eerily affecting his relationship with his mom.

The Hot Chick on the Bus

After the two week LMET training, Sailor would have to leave Little Creek, Virginia, on his way to the USS *Guadalcanal* (LPH-7), anchored off the coast of Beirut, Lebanon. In 1983, the Middle East at the time was the most current hot spot in the world. The Multinational Peacekeeping Force involved in the civil war of Beirut, Lebanon, would reveal itself to Sailor as the ground roots of international terrorism. From those days, terroristic acts against the United States of America and the world would exponentially escalate to untold deadly proportions. The young Sailor was at the grassroots of what most Americans would learn to be terrorism. Of course, terroristic acts against America and against black people in America is nothing new. But the amazing level and attention terrorism gained, the word itself became a household word. Nowadays, everything and everybody is considered terrorism or terroristic threats. But the etymology and use of this word stand as the classic hypocritical actions of the United States of America. The online

Merriam Webster Dictionary succinctly defines *terrorism* as: "a state of being terrified or a state of impressing terror." The dictionary further reveals that terrorism and terrorist was used by the French during a period known as the Reign of Terror (1793–1794). During that time, the French government would punish citizens it thought was against the French Revolution. The state-sponsored gruesome killings of French citizens and whomever else that wicked government thought was against the French Revolution. In a real sense, the denotative meaning of *terrorism* fits the long history of the United States of America since the transatlantic slave trade. State-sponsored gruesome lynching's and inhuman acts were an everyday thing against the black Hebrews for hundreds of years. In a real sense, all the terroristic acts against the United States of America are nothing more than the nation reaping what it sowed.

The American Embassy and the marine headquarters would become targets in a "holy war" of Islamic extremist in Beirut, Lebanon. Sailor was oblivious to international conflict and clueless, like most Americans then, to the acts of terrorism. But this was his time to both grow up and quickly be taught the most eye-opening experience of his lifetime. But before the introduction to all those things, he was still at Naval Station, Little Creek, Virginia, and about to find himself in another sexual temptation that was hard to resist. He had left his Pontiac Phoenix with his younger brother, on the promise of his mother that if anything happened to the car, both she and his brother would make sure they would get it fixed or replaced. Sailor had no problem with that arrangement. After all, he knew very well what it was like not having a car and desiring to have one. His brother was a brand-new driver, and Sailor was confident that he would be a responsible driver and would appreciate having some wheels to get around town. Sailor left his car in the hands of both his mother and his younger brother. In the meantime, while in Little Creek, for just a few more days, it was torture for Sailor to sit around on the ship or stay on the base. He had to get out, if not for nothing but just to go the mall and walk around. The most convenient transportation in those days without a car was the Pentran bus service. Buses would actually drive on the base to pick up passengers and drop passengers off. On the last weekend that Sailor was at Little Creek, he decided to catch a ride on the bus and go to Military Circle Mall just to get off the base and enjoy a little bit of freedom in the United States. He arrived at the mall around 6:00 p.m., and it was not too crowded, and there did not seem to be much going on. He got a bite to eat at McDonald's, walked around a little bit more, and did some window-shopping. All this was his way of fighting against idle thinking and dealing with old memories involving all the stuff in his life. About 9:00 p.m., he decided to catch the bus back to the base so he would not be AWOL. There were a few people standing at the bus stop, and Sailor quietly mingled in with them, not speaking to anyone, and they did not speak either. There was one black girl at the bus stop whom he remembers as, "the chick on the bus." She was talking loud, and it appeared to Sailor that she wanted all the attention. Sailor did not look at her or pay much attention to her because in those days, it seemed to Sailor that it was a cinch for a girl to start talking to him. Considering his sinful condition and now claiming to be a preacher of the Gospel of Jesus Christ, he certainly did not want to pay her any attention. The bus arrived after about twenty minutes or so waiting for it. Sailor, attempting to be low key, allowed everyone at the bus stop to board the bus before him. Lastly, he took his time boarding because he wanted to be as far front in the bus or as far rear in the bus in relation to where the chick on the bus was going to sit. When Sailor boarded the bus, he noticed that she was sitting middle ways of the bus. Great! Sailor thought as he made his way to the rear of the bus where no one was sitting. The bus got underway after all the passengers were seated, and the chick on the bus was still running her mouth. From Sailor's vantage point, he was able to get a glimpse of her. He couldn't see her very well but enough to notice that she appeared to be pretty. She had a nice body, and she was wearing tight-fitting jeans and a nice view of cleavage. At the moment, she was hilarious to him because she was talking so loudly. She also seemed to be talking about nothing very much. She sounded like she was spatting off gibberish.

No sooner had the bus started moving than the chick on the bus snapped up from her seat, almost at military attention. Sailor was looking out the window when he noticed that she was walking toward the rear of the bus closer and closer to Sailor's location. She was still talking, but not as loud as before as she was approaching the seat near Sailor.

He thought to himself, *What is up with this chick? Why did she decide to get up and walk toward me?*

At that point, Sailor became a little concerned, not afraid, but concerned as to what her intentions were. He then fixed his eyes on her, observing her every move as she drew closer and closer to him. She was switching and smiling and began to talk in a softer tone as she looked directly at Sailor. As she got closer to Sailor within perfect view, he noticed that she was actually pretty, with nice clothes on. She had almost like salon hair as she sat down directly across from Sailor. She was looking around out the window and talking smack, which revealed her status. She said that she was cold and bored and had to get back to the base, but she needed a warm body next to hers. For some strange reason, Sailor felt a little uncomfortable knowing now that she was in the navy, but she was acting a fool. She then asked Sailor, "Do you mind if I sit right beside you? I just need a little company, and I can tell you are in the service. What branch?"

Now everything and every suspicion of her took on another facet of the chick on the bus. Sailor discovered that she was in the navy, and it seemed she was looking for someone to hang out with. He said to her, "Sure you can sit here, as long as you promise not to rob me."

They both laughed, and she moved from the seat across the aisle and sat directly beside Sailor as if they were together coming from the mall. At this point, Sailor ignored and did not fight the temptation and invited whatever she was offering that night. He said to her, "You smell very nice. What is that you are wearing?"

She kindly said, with a smile, "It's called Opium. Do you like it?"

Sailor thought he had smelled the fragrance before, and he did—on his wife. Now the entire scene and encounter become eerie and weird to Sailor. Here is a pretty young lady with black negro hair and every strain in order, dressed nice and smells nice, out of nowhere decides she wants to hang out with Sailor. The one problem is the perfume she was wearing reminded him of his wife. What to do? He was tempted very much at a time when he was alone, but not desperate. The one thing that caused great hesitation for him is that every second they were sitting on the bus and talking, her perfume reminded him of his wife. Satan had dangled the proverbial carrot attached to a deep guilty conscience. As every moment dragged along, the chic on the bus became unashamedly forward. She grabbed Sailor's leg and rubbed his knee while saying how cold she was and wanted to get warm tonight. "Are you interested?"

It was the craziest line Sailor had ever heard in his life, and the irony is, a strange woman that he had never met was advancing the seduction. He then looked at her and said, "Are you serious? We don't even know each other and you want to have sex?"

She immediately withdrew her hand and said, "I did not say anything about sex. I just said I want to get warm. That's not sex. I just want a warm body next to mine."

Sailor thought to himself, *What kind of game is the girl playing? Is she undercover? Is she in the navy? What does she really want?*

Sailor fought in his mind and reached deep in his spirit to find reason why he should not take advantage of her offer. But as soon as he began to speak and compromise himself with a strange woman, she hurriedly said, "Oh, this is my stop coming up. Are you getting off with me?"

Sailor did not get off because the stop was about one mile from the base and he could not rely on her getting him a cab or giving him bus fare, and before he could answer, she pulled a sheet of paper out of her purse, jotted down a number, and stuffed the paper in Sailor's hand. "If you change your mind any time before you turn into your bunk, please call me. I'll be up waiting for you, sailor!"

It's not that she knew his name, she knew Sailor was in the navy, and she claimed that she was in the navy also. In a facetious, seductive way, she called him sailor. She hurried down the aisle of the bus to get off and looked back at Sailor with a smile as big as the moon and took a few seconds to stop before debarking the bus and waved at Sailor. "I'll see you later."

Sailor watched her walk down the street as the bus was pulling away, and she waved at the bus, as though she thought Sailor could see her. He pondered and pondered whether he should get off at the next stop and catch up with her. Cell phones did not exist then, so he could not call her from the bus or any location other than a telephone booth. But he watched her switch down the street until he could see her no longer. Then he thought to himself, *What the hell was that all about?*

It wasn't like she was in a brothel and Sailor was about to pay for sexual services, like when he did in Naples, Italy. Hookers don't normally come up to you on the street or on public transportation offering sex in cryptic language. A hooker's first order of business is how much money she is going to get paid, and the chick on the bus said nothing about money or even suggested money. Nonetheless, the entire scene was exciting to Sailor, not to mention totally weird also. Needless to say, Sailor destroyed the telephone number and thought to himself, *That was straight from the pit of hell to get him to regress back into the sex thing with a strange woman.*

After spending thirty-six months on shore duty, preaching what little he understood of the Bible, living with his wife, and striving to walk the straight and narrow, why give in to a piece of loose ass in a one-night stand? Strangely enough, he would never, ever see the chick on the bus in his lifetime and if he were to bump into her, he would not recognize her in a million years. The fact that he resisted the direct temptation from the chick on the bus was a testament to his spiritual growth. Reluctantly, though, at the end of the day, he did not succumb to her advances. The depth and height of trials he would face while onboard the USS *Guadalcanal* (LPH-7) and the USS *Inchon* (LPD-12) while in Beirut, Lebanon, would be the epic spiritual battle he would ever face. The chick on the bus was a small victory for a tough temptation. But the Sermon in Sailor had not been born yet. Sailor was just going through the motions preaching in churches while stationed at NRD Harrisburg, Pennsylvania. During those days, he was yet to know the persecution of hell and death targeted against his soul. Every experience on board the USS *Guadalcanal* (LPH-7) would instantaneously manifest itself as the lion's den of destruction. The manipulative mental games of people and the destructive acts of being in the armed forces would become clear to him. Now would be the time for Sailor to enter the conflict enhanced and birthed by the United States Navy. Nothing in his life would compare to both the spiritual conflict and the mental and physical abuse awaiting him at his new duty station on board the *Guad*, short for *Guadalcanal.*

14

LARNACA AND THE BOAT

Larnaca Cyprus, the Island in the Middle of Nowhere

Modern technology is awesome. Check this out and go online to Google Earth and type in "Black Sea." Once you have been virtually flown around the world to the Black Sea, type in "Turkey." From Turkey, type in "Larnaca, Cyprus," and that's where Sailor's last leg of flying from Philadelphia, Pennsylvania took him on April 6, 1983. All the way across the other side of the planet. An extreme, almost unfathomable distance from the geographical location of the projects and North 18th Street. Sailor had become 100 percent sailor but about to become broken down to the most common nature of man. Once you have found the island of Cyprus to the southeast on the small island itself is a city called Larnax. This city is the ancient town of Kition, now buried under the modern Larnaca. In the Bible, the town is spelled Kittim, of which Javan, a son of Japheth, the son of Noah (Gen. 10:4), settled. This is the same place Sailor erupted into a hellish rebellious attitude from within his soul without one shred of justification. He felt like devils from hell itself was specifically assigned to destroy him. He wanted to cause a lot of hell and made attempts to disrupt the mission at hand. Nonetheless, he did fear what might happen to him, and he worried deeply how God might view him. His fear of God had sunk amidst his jumbled human emotions. His sinful pride gladly filled the gap of his lack of the fear of God. However, it is necessary that you learn about what occurred on the island of Larnaca, Cyprus, in April 1983. The path Sailor chose from the days of a novice youth of North 18th Street, through boot camp and first tour of duty with VS-31. Traveling the European continent and enjoying his new life was about to slam into the proverbial brick wall. Therein lay the beginning of a very unstable and unsettling tour of duty on board the USS *Guadalcanal* (LPH-7).

At latitude 34.917206 north and longitude 33.637843 east lay the small island of Larnaca, a place Sailor never heard of and had no knowledge of its existence up until that point in his life. Learning of new places became quite typical of the port of calls Sailor had while sailing the seas with the US Navy. There are numerous places and locations he never heard of until he read the port of call scheduled for the ship. All the places he visited would be a once in a lifetime experience. Larnaca was one of those places, and once Sailor arrived there, certain events elicited innumerable feelings inside him, and none was stronger than the thought and attempt of insubordination. During that time, he was so overcome with anger and frustration that he totally failed to see how close he had returned to Jerusalem. Had he been alert, focused and astute he would have realized that he was just hours away from Haifa, Israel. Four years earlier, he catapulted from the USS *Dwight D. Eisenhower* (CV-69) on his way to his new duty station. At that time, he had no idea that he would see the port of call of Haifa, Israel, again. Yet he was right there and was not aware of how close he was, again. The Amphibious Task Force did not have liberal leave, but had he been focused instead of basking in his own pity party, getting the opportunity to visit Israel would not have been too difficult. But he blew it again because his frustration and anger ruled his emotions. But this would not be his last time in the vicinity of Israel. He would have one more chance in the near future. Frustration, questions, and anger had reached its peak in the soul of Sailor. There was nowhere else for his jumbled emotions to go or express himself. He quickly resorted to the old adage "from the top of his head," and anything that would come out his mouth was acceptable to him. Beginning with the island of Larnaca, those days where dangerously challenging to him. Test after test and failure after failure he would experience in a barrage of attacks. He had entered the time in his life for the serious development of his soul and awakening of his spirit. The true, naked, almost uncontrollable feelings in his heart were being exposed by his reaction to everything he faced. The cool, calm, happy, satisfied sailor living at home in Harrisburg, Pennsylvania, was about to become crucified and shamed while unsettling the core of his being. Over time, TJ emerged into Sailor, and the merging of the new man was emotionally painful packed with childhood memories. TJ refused to relinquish his youthful life and did not want to give up his past. Likewise, Sailor had to die and die to himself and everything around him. The experience on the island of Larnaca is one experience Sailor remains shameful to reveal who he was. He did not know then that his spirit would remain locked in the prison of his own mind and self if not released by facing the truth. What lay deep inside his heart and what needed to be exposed was the reason for the tour of duty onboard the USS *Guadalcanal* (LPH-7). Larnaca was that place wherein the deepest part of Sailor's heart became exposed to him, like seeing his reflection in a mirror. The lack of fortitude in his spirit became abundantly clear. Larnaca was the beginning of a long hard school of life concerning himself and the man deep inside he was destined to face and overcome. Yes, that real person inside all humankind must be faced in order to grow into the person The Most High envisions one to be. That person, for the most part, is the toughest individual to engage in battle and overcome your own self. Sailor worked day and night attempting to convince himself that he was not as bad as others thought of him. Or as bad as he thought of himself. There exists an uncanny rationalization in all men and women whether good or bad of how they view their own self. The biblical definition of this rationalization is identified in terms that can only be explained by the Most High, He calls it "the nature of sin." Sailor reasoned with himself by thinking, *Hey, I'm no different than anyone else so I might as well go ahead and act crazy.* On the island of Larnaca for about a few hours doing absolutely nothing but hurry up and wait, as the military terms it. Always waiting for something in the service. Stand in line here, stand in line there, stand in a line to get a shot, stand in line to get chow and even stand in line to take a piss, Larnaca was no different. The transition from the plane that brought Sailor from Philadelphia, Pennsylvania, via Rota, Spain, to Larnaca seemed to happen in quick succession. When he arrived at the airport in Rota, Spain, the plane was ready for taxing. In other words, once he arrived at Rota, Spain, there was no layover at all. From one plane to the other. The helicopter he had to board at Larnaca to fly to the boat was waiting—there was very little layover. Sailor had no time to think or reminisce about anything. Like in a movie, all experiences of the past were washed out by the clouds of gloom. On the island of Larnaca, he failed to see the serene tropical ambiance of Larnaca. A strong wave of uncontrollable despair flooded his soul, but he was too angry to cry. About six passengers, the pilot, and copilot had to board a marine helicopter to fly out to the USS *Guadalcanal* (LPH-7). A marine lieutenant colonel gave them a bull shit talk about the size of his testosterone in terms of his gallantry and manhood. Sailor was thinking to himself, *Who gives a shit about this guy and what he is talking about? Let's get this thing over with.*

Those details will come later. In the meantime, Sailor tried his best to transition in his mind from a civilized state of thinking to a military state of mind. It was not an easy transition.

Tropical and Cyrene

April 6, 1983, Sailor landed on the island of Larnaca from Rota, Spain, via Philadelphia, Pennsylvania. Ah, Rota, Spain, Sailor had just left there a little over three years ago on his way to NRD Harrisburg. It seemed like it came around tremendously fast, and he was back on his way, not to the Mediterranean Sea but to the Middle East, the hub of all terrorist activity against the United States of America. Larnaca was a tropical island that he failed to see because his emotions were jumbled and his mind filled with unanswered questions. He could not see the gorgeous beauty the tropical island had to offer, though he was standing on its ground. Sailor's eyes were dim, and his soul was shrouded with darkness of the blackest kind. Darkness akin to a solar or lunar eclipse in the middle of the day. The sun shone for hours, but he could not enjoy its beauty because his emotions and his spirit had been eclipsed with self-pity, immaturity, and sin. His eyes beheld the beauty of the tropical island of Larnaca, and like all the places he traveled, he always sought to see the beauty and enjoy the experience. But at this point in his naval career, he walked in spiritual blindness deep within his being. In his mind, he had been jettisoned from his hometown and his wife and "his" new preaching, he failed to see the beauty of Larnaca, though it stared him directly in his face. His soul and spirit were intense at war against each other like a tornado, hurricane, and tsunami all at once. Each storm inside his soul was a category 5 ready to explode on anybody and anything. Just push the wrong button, or right button, and Sailor would explode and somebody will get hurt, maimed or killed. Yes, it is an utter shame for Sailor to recall these events in his life, but there was a place inside his heart that had been masquerading, unbeknownst to him, all his life. He had to search his heart like a coal miner digging into the crust of the earth. He had to know if the masquerade was intentional or ignorance. And though he was compelled to face the party of the masquerade inside his soul, he vehemently fought what he was feeling and denied what was going on inside as though he was too good to have been transferred to the Middle East. Through it all, the mercy of God was with Sailor and God's grace kept him from his own destruction and possible self-inflicted harm. Sailor would one day learn in its fullness, what grace and mercy are and how all are undeserving of the grace of God. The temperature at Larnaca was soothing, and the sun shone in great strength the beauty of its Creator. Sailor was about to board for the first time, a CH-46 helicopter to fly over the Mediterranean Sea. Directly ahead of them was the Mediterranean Sea with a few white caps amid a relatively calm sea. In fact, where they were standing was almost like a beach. There was sand, a wooden outhouse, and one roll of toilet paper in the outhouse. Mind you, not your typical port-a-potty, this was literally a wooden, almost makeshift toilet shack house. A gentle breeze coming off the sea was blanketing the air, and while Sailor made every attempt to enjoy the beauty of Larnaca, his dimness of sight and darkness of heart prevented him from appreciating the beauty of the tropical land. He was quickly overwhelmed with self-inflicted sorrow, and he wallowed in grief and anger. Much of his frustration stemmed from not being able to enjoy the island. He was angry because he was there against his will. He wanted to reboard the plane and return to Philadelphia, Pennsylvania, an impossible feat. Only God in heaven knows how much he wanted to get back on the plane that had just brought him to Larnaca, Cyprus. Somehow or another he needed to get back on that plane headed for the United States of America. Reboarding the plane, even if he attempted to go absent without leave (AWOL), was a futile thought that would never materialize. Sailor was frustrated because he thought for some reason, he was better than this and should not be in this situation: (1) he just got ordained as a minister of the Gospel, and he thought he should be preaching the Bible to people, (2) he just got married less than three years prior, and he should be home with his new wife. He even found scripture in the Bible to justify his reason.

In Deuteronomy chapter 24 and verse 5, the decree was a man that has taken a new wife shall not go out to war. Eureka! That record in the Bible would become one of his justifications to return back to America and get out of this outfit. But that was misuse and abuse of the Scripture and grossly misinterpretation of the same. Sailor was not feeling the excitement and anticipation the lieutenant colonel and the other sailors were feeling that day on the island of Larnaca. He wanted to leave that island so badly and run toward that plane just before they closed the hatch. It appeared to him the majority of the other sailors and lieutenant colonel was gung ho and ready to move forward into harm's way. They had already put on their life jacket and were ready and positioned at a moment's notice to obey and follow the lieutenant colonel's orders. But as Sailor gazed around at them, they all appeared to have the same blank stare he had. Sailor, on the other hand, the only chocolate drop in the bunch, was still holding his life jacket in his hand. He was listening and keeping his eye on the lieutenant colonel, who, at this point had thoroughly succeeded in adding to his frustration and pushing the right buttons that angered him almost uncontrollably. The beauty and serenity of Larnaca had escaped Sailor's view, and he had sunken deep into a slumber of self-pity. Shame and disrespect would fuel his anger, and his unintelligent mind would make a fool out of him. This would pretty much describe most of his tour of duty on board the USS *Guadalcanal* (LPH-7). Onboard the *Guad*, there was a moment, almost like a small entry in his spirit attempting to shine a smidgen ray of the Son through. But because of the condition of his heart and mind that day on the island of Larnaca, it became increasingly difficult and hard to get through what he was feeling. The condition of Sailor's heart pretty much lasted the entire tour of duty and became intensified day by day on board the USS *Guadalcanal* (LPH-7), anchored off the coast of Beirut, Lebanon.

The Lieutenant Colonel's Talk

The lieutenant colonel was extraordinarily military in every definition of the word. He was over six feet tall and one of the pilots of the CH-46 marine helicopters. His hair was meticulously cut in a box shape with a high fade as he pranced back and forth in front of the six of them. He was enthusiastically explaining the reliabilities, or would you say, the unreliability of the CH-46 helicopter. While pacing back and forth in front of the group, the LTCOL told them how to don the life jacket and "make sure your buddy's jacket is secure properly. Because if one of these babies drop in the 'sink,' you will not have time to make sure your life jacket is on correctly." With the state of mind, Sailor was in that day it was not encouraging for him to hear the pilot of the helicopter that they were five minutes from boarding, telling them they may not make it to their destination. The LTCOL also said they had a high probability of crashing into the sea without warning or getting shot down with a surface to air (SAM) missile from the Hezbollah. The LTCOL then said, "Troops, we will be flying close to the water. Sometimes we will fly a little higher, but most of the time we will be very close to the water." The reason for this is to fly under the radar of the enemy so we will decrease the risk of being shot down by a SAM that will certainly put us in the sea."

Oh hell no! Sailor thought. At this point, he couldn't take any more of the LTCOL's talk and his proud look and what appeared to be his uncompassionate regard for their lives. A slight drizzle of rain had begun at that point, and the sunshine turned into a gray overcast. As Sailor looked up toward the sky, the clouds were gray in color, adding to his morbid self-pity state of mind. May have been, may have not been, but his eyes during those days practically perceived everything to be gray in color. Sailor, like a cork, suddenly removed from a bottle, then blurted out to the colonel, as the colonel was prancing back and forth and said, "Hey, Colonel, why the hell don't we wait until the rain stops instead of defying nature and becoming some sort of heroes."

The colonel didn't skip a beat in his prancing and blurted back, "Because, son, you joined this fine armed forces to protect and defend your nation, and we will do whatever it takes to get the job done. Even in the face of the risk of death or what seems to be insurmountable."

Sailor then blurted out in the most disrespectful manner, "Sounds like we are signing our death warrant."

That did it; Sailor had now found the button of the LTCOL, and he pushed it purposely hard! The colonel stopped dead in his tracks and looked directly at Sailor and said, "Son, you've come a long way and too far in this fine service to become defiant now. You will do what you are told and follow my instructions or I will throw your ass in the sea myself! We do not have time for little boys who want to stay up under their mommy's dress. This is the marines, the navy, the army, and air force joint military operation, and only the strong will survive and return home heroes, and those who do not return home will be remembered. Now, son, you *will* be one or the other. *Do you fucking understand?*"

Sailor's response was a slight head nod and mumbling "hmmm." But the colonel seemed to be satisfied with that lazy unconcerned response. The colonel continued to prance back and forth describing the CH-46 and even said that one of the CH46s malfunctioned just last week and dropped into the sea. That's how he described it—he said it just *dropped* into the sea! This episode in Sailor's military career was becoming increasingly unbearable by the minute, and he was becoming deeply irritated by the second. The colonel did not tell them the fate of the crew and passengers on board, just the fact that a helicopter *just like the one* they were about to board crashed in the sea!

Damn, damn, damn! Sailor thought. He did not want to blurt out again because the colonel had gotten his attention during the earlier verbal exchange. Sailor's thoughts were out of control. Thoughts of wanting to rush the colonel and wrestle him to the ground. Thoughts of wanting to run up to the colonel and punch him directly in his mouth. Thoughts of doing ungodly things to him or anyone else who would attempt to stop him from acting a supreme fool. In retrospect, he shamefully regrets that he felt that way and thought those thoughts against a man of authority. Even if he did not see the mission through his eyes, he was still a man of authority, and Sailor was not raised to outright defy any authority figure. The host of devils that had taken over Sailor's mind and launched a battle against the real man deep inside his soul had begun to manifest themselves, and it didn't look pretty. Immediately after the disrespectful verbal exchange with the lieutenant colonel, Sailor felt horrid as though he had just committed a heinous crime. He was talking back defiantly and was feeling like a problem child to his peers and senior officers. He was facing a man inside his soul he did not know and was furious with him and unhappy with all his surroundings. He took that spirit forward onboard the helicopter and the USS *Guadalcanal* (LPH-7). For the next two years, he wrestled against not only himself but dangerous principalities and powers and rulers of the darkness of this world. Wrestling never was so difficult in all his life. He expected and looked forward to some attack or tragedy to take place while on the tour of duty onboard the USS *Guadalcanal* (LPH-7). All his thoughts were jumbled and stuck inside a maze of wondering and asking question after question to God as to why and why and why was he going through this. The self-pity had overwhelmed him, and he wanted to place blame on someone else of the sole decision he made of entering the armed forces. It wasn't until after the tour of duty that it dawned upon him that he willingly signed the proverbial dotted line back in June of 1976. The tour on board the USS *Guadalcanal* (LPH-7) would reveal itself to be the disturbing shake-up and unraveling of his immature selfish mind and soul. He lived inside his comfortable box that required breaking up in order to be reconstructed in the way of the Most High.

The CH-46 Helicopter Flight

After the colonel had finished his pep talk, the order was given: "Let's go, troops, pick up your stuff, get your shit together, and let's lock and load. We are about to fly into harm's way, say your prayers and have faith in your god, whoever he may be."

Knot after knot was forming in Sailor's stomach, and he thought to himself, *Doesn't this man have anything good or nice to say what about something encouraging?*

But then, why would he? The colonel was over six feet tall and a marine lieutenant colonel whose mind and desire probably wanted to be a soldier in the ancient Roman army or a medieval knight in shining armor. Perhaps he had aspirations of becoming a modern-day war hero. But the bad part about whatever the colonel desired or seen of himself—all his crew and passengers were under his direct authority and were circumstantially compelled to be part of his dream. What a tough spot to be in, someone else's dream, when it appears they are in charge and in some sense has a say over your life. Sailor would learn through the years how to engage in battle over someone else's dream that compelled him to be a part of. He had to learn how to overcome their dream without them controlling his dream. It takes a skilled fighter in the fight of faith to win over those who are over you.

The crew and passengers boarded what seemed to Sailor at this point, the most dreadful, lifeless, big green helicopter of death. Sailor felt like he was boarding a flying coffin, and inside his heart, he surrendered his soul and his spirit into the hands of God. He had reached his end and truly gave up deep inside his spirit. When Sailor boarded the helicopter on the island of Larnaca on April 6, 1983, he boarded what he felt was sure death, and he welcomed it and had settled in his mind that he would be meeting God that day. Boarding through the rear gate of the helo, flashes of his life were almost in digital form as he would embrace growing up for the last time in his memory. Now on board and finding a seat against the bulkhead of the helo, almost like seats were installed as an afterthought. Strapped in with life vest on and protective helmet the engines were started by the pilots. There were three helicopters on the island that day, but only two of them took off. The third helo, Sailor would learn later that it had mechanical problems and was being serviced by the mechanics on the island. The transition from Larnaca to the boat, including the tour of duty on the boat, would become hell in the mind of Sailor. Imagine the sound of a very old car engine hesitating to stay on. The engine would backfire, not idle smoothly, but sounding choppy and like it was going to shut down any minute. That's what both helicopter engines sounded like to Sailor. He was not sure, maybe that's what the performance of those old Vietnam, Korea conflict equipment sounded like. Back in 1983, the armed forces did not have the greatest technology or fighting equipment as it does today. Maybe Sailor was not used to the sound of old stuff, and he nursed and embraced his fear to a level of reality in his own mind. He had accepted death in his heart and ready to meet God if the helicopter were to malfunction while in flight or if a SAM were to strike the helo and destroy the body of the helicopter. At that point, it did not matter to him whatsoever. In his mind, he had accepted whatever fate awaited him while in flight over the Mediterranean Sea in route toward the USS *Guadalcanal* (LPH-7). Was it the words of the lieutenant colonel or a spirit greater than both he and Sailor that had penetrated his weak armor? Sailor's heart and mind had been taken over by a power greater them himself. He had now succumbed to the grips of hell. Whatever it was, Sailor had become pinned down, like a wrestler in the ring on the island of Larnaca, Cyprus. He tragically lost a personal battle while the powers of darkness were salivating in sweet victory over the soul of Sailor.

He was in a morbid state of mind, soaring in the heavens as a thick blanket of dark menacing clouds shrouded the land and sea. The light drizzle that had begun while they were still on the island of Larnaca had now turned into a storm with dark, dark gray clouds. A storm hatched somewhere in the western Mediterranean and had traveled east to wet the Lebanese coast. The horizon of Beirut's gray skyline faded in the clouds as the clouds dumped their rain on the Middle Eastern city. The flight from Larnaca to the flight deck of the USS *Guadalcanal* (LPH-7) took four hours. Sailor is not sure if that was because they were deliberately flying under the enemy radar or if they did sort of a zigzag back and forth to frustrate the enemy radar from getting a good fix on them. Either way, four hours of misery and frustration would drive Sailor's spirit into the pit of despair because it took so long to get to their destination. He became frustrated because they did not get shot down or the craft did not malfunction as the colonel suggested may happen on a mechanically uncertain flying machine. He wished to just end the mental struggle and die. Or at the least, crash and not die, being rescued and then sent to Rota, Spain, for recovery. The seats on board the craft were simply a cushion up against the bulkhead of the helicopter a space large enough for one person to sit. The flight was extremely choppy, no thanks to the storm and the tide of the waves below were threatening. Get the picture, there were very dark gray clouds looming over the crew's heads as if the clouds themselves were creating a menacing situation by appearing to bear down on them. The water beneath them—the pilot was flying about fifty to sixty feet above the sea—was choppy with waves large enough to eliminate all white caps. The sea was boisterous and ready to swallow them whole. The circumstances they were in that day exceeded the proverbial rock and a hard place. By all rights and calculation of odds, they should have never made it to the flight deck of the USS *Guadalcanal* (LPH-7) on April 6, 1983.

The helicopter was hesitating during flight as if the pilot was periodically performing an emergency restart of the engine. There were times they dropped very close to the sea, to the point where the salt and the distinctive smell of the sea was very apparent. Sailor was not sure if the pilot was deliberately trying to induce fear in them or if the old Vietnam helicopters were really having engine trouble. There were eight souls on board that craft, including the pilot and copilot, and as Sailor slowly looked around at the faces of his shipmates, each one had a blank stare. The indoctrination the lieutenant colonel gave to them on the island of Larnaca, Cyprus, virtually wiped clean the minds of Sailor and the other sailors on board. Fear had seized their minds and seized it well. The spirit of fear actually boarded that helicopter with them and was a welcomed passenger on board. Sailor had never known fear like that before in all his life. The spirit of fear must have been up walking around inside that craft staring in the faces of each passenger, zapping them of all intelligent reasoning and survival instincts. They all appeared to have entirely surrendered their mind and soul to *whatever* fate awaited them while flying over the Mediterranean Sea. They were all mentally drained and they all appeared lifeless. Sailor had completely succumbed to the fear onboard the CH-46 and could no longer fight against it for that spirit was way too strong for him in those days. Each passenger's thoughts had been captivated and under the control of the words of one man who seemed to master the skill of speaking fear into the soul and mind of whomever he could. Throughout the flight, the helicopter lost altitude several times until they were within swimming distance of the sea. He observed the other faces turn from white to pale to yellow and some to sickly green, as if a curse had overcome them. Sailor's face, if a mirror were handed to him, would have reflected blankness, emptiness, and eyes that were welled up with tears, but the tears would not run down his face. They just sat there, suspended. Along with the safety helmet and ear protection, Sailor could not hear anyone speaking. Communication was done by hand signals, and one must pay close attention. The experience of that day remains clear, including the loudness and uncomfortable feel of the choppy ride. Up and down, back and forth, sharp yawing and pitching, dropping significantly almost parallel to the sea. Fear transformed into a deafening silence on board the helicopter as the elements themselves appeared to war against the mission. It was similar to the account with Elisha and his servant facing the Syrian army when Elisha's servant became deathly afraid. Elisha prayed that God would open the servant's eyes that he may see and the servant was able to see horses and chariots of fire on the mountain in favor of Elisha (2 Kings 6). While on board the helo, it appeared to Sailor that the presence of fear took on the form or shape of an unseen passenger. The clouds, the rain, and the sea somehow or another was on board the helicopter as fear prevailed. This was the one time in Sailor's life that he believed that a genuine Spirit of mercy was dispatched from heaven to wage battle against the spirit of fear. As they made their approach to the ship, Sailor sensed an uncontrollable need to pray to God about anything. He did not know what to pray for, but the need to pray was somehow or another impregnated into his spirit. He felt a sense of compassion for the other sailors on board when he looked around at their faces. Sailor had accepted and welcomed death upon every soul on board the helicopter that day. But for some reason, when he looked into their eyes, he felt deep sadness for them all. His thoughts began to range from the bliss of what heaven will be like to the torture of what hell would be like. How many of them will go directly to heaven, and how many would go directly to hell, including himself? Sailor did not know the answer to that question, but he did not want any soul onboard to go to hell. Having exhausted his human reason and rebellious emotions and now facing the presence of evil on board the helicopter, the need to pray for all of them was his desperate plea to God as they approached the ship.

The USS Guadalcanal (LPH-7)

Gazing around at the faces of each one of his shipmates on board the helicopter, a faint, almost powerless prayer was born in his soul. Sailor began a mumbled prayer within his soul. A prayer without focus but rather a plea to God for whatever he deemed necessary for each soul on board. Mixed feelings were at war in his soul, asking God to move upon the heart of the pilot in some way to navigate them safely. Even if none of them would ever see the pilot again, Sailor petitioned God to touch the heart of the pilot and sharpen the pilot's flying skill. Anything to allow them to arrive at their destination safely. He felt that if they arrived safely to the ship, their arrival would be a great move of God. Asking God to ease the heart and mind of his shipmates on board, and if they all were destined to die, let them die like warriors, like men, unafraid. There is no other explanation in his mind of what unfolded next. Call it crazy, silly, or even imagination, but he could not express in words enough to let you know what a difference the next event made in his heart. Do you still have a picture of the scene describing the dark gray menacing clouds and the sea raging and winds roaring and high waves beneath them and the presence of fear on board the craft? Remember the heavy downpour of rain beating down on the helicopter and the Lebanese coast? Remember that scene? Basking in grief and sorrow, self-pity, fear, shame, and anger. A small opening in the clouds broke through, and the sun shone through that small opening directly through the window of the helicopter. The ray of sunlight came directly on his back through the window and shone precisely on the face of his shipmate sitting across from him. Instantaneously, the ray of sun shining brought a mild comforting feel of heat on his person and actually lit up the cargo section where he and his shipmates were sitting. Call it what you want to call it, but inside his spirit, he sincerely thought God was using the sun as a tool to comfort him and his shipmates on board the helo. He felt a moment of peace beyond human understanding as the sun was shining through the window of the helicopter. The tears that had welled up in his eyes because he was expecting and had accepted what he thought to be imminent death had now fallen to the deck of the chopper, and his eyes dried up. The faces of his shipmates had somehow or another miraculously went from a pale white face to a good pigmentation of the skin of a Caucasian man. Was the Eternal God in heaven speaking to them without speaking? Was he reassuring them that he knew every detail of hopelessness that had taken up residence in their hearts since arriving on the island of Larnaca? What was he saying, if anything? Is it strange that in the midst of a heavy storm a single ray from the sun shone through the dark clouds precisely at the point of airspace where they were flying? The strength of the sun was reminiscent of when Sailor arrived at his first duty station at Cecile Field, Florida, and the event involving the sun shining through the window. His mind ran the entire stratagem of thoughts trying to figure out what was going on in heaven as they flew in the heavens toward the USS *Guadalcanal* (LPH-7). Or one could simply accept, if not for any other reason, other than wanting to believe, that God in heaven by some unusual way of his own turned the sun in their direction and turned the heat of the sun down to a nice comfortable level. But Sailor thought, *Hey, He is God and the supreme creator of all things, He can turn on, turn off, turn up or turn down anything in the universe he desires to fulfill his ultimate purpose.*

Certain Bible scriptures came to mind prior to the sun shining through like "to be absent from the body is to be present with the Lord (2 Cor. 5:8), and "the dead in Christ shall rise first (I Thess. 4:16). He was ready to die and like a mummy wrapped in a straitjacket wanting the helicopter to plummet down into the sea or get shot down with a SAM to "take him out of his misery." In retrospect, it became apparent to him that he harbored an extreme selfish spirit waddling in a pool of self-pity. It was not so much the circumstances but rather the way he felt about himself and how he felt in relation to other people. He thought he was special in some sense having grasped a good understanding of the Bible and having been sought after by his small circle of local churches to "teach" the Bible. It took him a while to overcome the childish feeling that this must be a mistake for him to be here. Someone *must* have read his orders incorrectly. Perhaps, the detailer typed in his social security number for the orders to the Middle East but should have assigned someone else and not him. Absolute foolish reasoning after foolish reasoning was his way of thinking in those days. Little did he realize then that it was the will of God that put him in the jaws of death, the test of life, and the wilderness experience to be tried. He was way too prideful and arrogant in many ways without trying to be prideful and arrogant. The flight that day onboard the CH-46 was the beginning of a long tedious battle of a humbling experience he was destined to face. There is a verse in the Bible that says, "It is written in the prophets, And they shall be all taught of God. Every man, therefore, that hath heard, and hath learned of the Father cometh unto me" (John 6:45). Sailor can unquestionably say this is what was taking place during those days from the island of Larnaca all the way through the tour of duty stationed off the coast of Beirut Lebanon. It was God who sent Abraham out from his family to learn and receive the promises he had for him. (Gen. 12:1). It was God who strategically and logistically allowed Joseph to be left for dead but raised him up to become second in leadership of ancient Egypt. (Gen. 37–50). It was God who allowed Satan to totally strip Job of everything including his children to ultimately resurrect Job's life and double his possessions. It was God who took a disobedient Jonah and as the Bible puts it "the Lord had prepared a great fish…" especially for Jonah (Jon. 1:17). The list goes on and on to show how God teaches his children and especially how he teaches his men, whom he called to proclaim Divine Truth. At that time, Sailor was clueless of this view, nor did he understand this way of God until years later when it all becomes clear in his heart. Chastisement, life's instruction, and correction is the way of God to mold his children into his Divine Will. According to the Bible, God's way is the same way earthly parents chastise their children, to bring them back in line or to correct them for some wrong they have committed or disobeyed their instructions. God's way of training is no less, however, on a grander scale involving other people, the weather, material things, life, death and the essence of our being. Sailor would discover that he was directly under the mighty hand of God for chastisement. He was under life's instruction and teaching as it related to his faith and belief in what he claimed to have had but was far from what he thought he had.

On Board Another Boat

There is street slang, and there is also navy slang and to call a naval vessel the boat is to use navy slang. Despite the fact, a naval vessel is a large warship berthing anywhere from 200 sailors up to 6,000 sailors (depending on class and type of ship). Most sailors called the ship, the boat and Sailor embraced with his whole heart. He liked it and felt acclimated into the navy world. While the helicopter approached the *Guadalcanal*, which was a few miles off the coast of Beirut, Lebanon, American warships steamed slowly through the water. From the helicopter, it was hard to tell if they were moving at all. The ships left very little visible wake behind them. He looked at the city of Beirut, and then he looked at the ships steaming in the water, and though there was a smidgen of excitement to be a part of this operation, realistically he could not make sense of it all. Having just endured a deep mental battle against the spirit of fear and the prospect of giving up and desiring to die, he reached down into his soul and searched for a sense of excitement. He did not understand the role the United States played in intervening in Beirut, Lebanon's, civil war. His emotions ran from pride to bitterness, to frustration in the short hours it took to transit the Atlantic Ocean. He questioned the decision he made to reenlist and was bitter with himself for having recently married and left his wife miles across the Atlantic Ocean. He was sickened in his mind at the appearance of the enormous tons of steel sitting in the water and abhorred the thought of having to live the next twenty-seven months of his life on board another navy warship. Stationed on board the boat would be a lot different than VS-31 because in the air dale squadron he lived on the shore for about three to four months out of the year, and he knew all his shipmates in the squadron. He was about to board a ship at sea and did not know *anyone* and the ship would spend most of the time at sea. Embarking on Amphibious Squadron was unnerving to him, and he was full of extreme apprehension. As the helo made its final approach and descent on board the flight deck of the USS *Guadalcanal* (LPH-7), the ship appeared to be very small from the air. He glanced at the ship and then the mountains and hills of Beirut, and everything appeared to be in black and white. He could not distinguish between colors mainly because of how he was feeling inside. He supposed what he was seeing through his eyes is how he was feeling within his soul. Morbid, depressed, uncertain, and still harboring the anticipation and possibility of dying during this tour. Considering the circumstances, serving in the armed forces in a hostile environment, death seemed to be inevitable, and his meeting date with death seemed to be drawing closer with every passing minute. The surroundings and the atmosphere on board the boat was swamped with an intense live and active spirit of fear. The feel of death lurked the passageways on the boat and onshore of Beirut, Lebanon.

When the helo touched down on deck on board the USS *Guadalcanal* (LPH-7) and upon exiting the CH-46, all he could see is what appeared to be six, maybe seven feet tall Airedale sailors with all sorts of protective gear on. Hand signals waving in the air, plane captains waving you in their direction. As though it was of the utmost urgency to get off the helicopter and into the ship. Hearing is extremely limited with the protective helmet gear on and the protective safety gear over your ears. They all filed out of the CH-46 with seabag on shoulder in a single file, making their way double-time toward the hatch that would take them inside the ship. Once they arrived inside the boat, the other sailors that were on the helicopter with him vanished in different directions. He does not remember ever seeing them again onboard the *Guadalcanal.* They, in some sense, was like extras in a movie in his struggle with adjusting to being on board ship again. He did not pay attention to which direction they went and does not remember ever seeing them again while onboard. He may have even sat down at the table across from them in the galley during chow time but does not remember what they looked like or who they were. The entire account and tour of duty on board the USS *Guadalcanal* (LPH-7) was all about Sailor and the selfish spirit he harbored deep inside that had to be confronted and slain. In those days, everything was all about Sailor and in retrospect, the answer is clear as to why the emotional roller coaster ride was not fun but rather painful and shamefully demoralizing. He had a difficult time accepting the other side of who he was and why it was so necessary for him to spiritually mature and become the man who he was destined to become. The events on board the USS *Guadalcanal* (LPH-7) turned his stomach and spirit against the United States Navy and everything the armed forces stood for. A roller coaster ride of heralding proportions could not have been imagined in his mind. He knew *nothing* of what to expect and how to deal with what was about to present itself to him for the next twenty-seven months. The first ninety days turned out to be the most intense, unjust, and unfair, with a racism spirit he *never* thought to experience. It all began with a man he perceived at first sight to be a friend, turned out to be a friend but down a path that appeared to him to be a crooked path that ended up as a straight path. Five years ago when he found himself waking up in a bunk bed in a barracks at Cecil Field, Florida, at his first tour of duty, he would find himself again on a bunk bed on board a naval vessel in the midst of extreme hostility in the Middle East. Everything inside of him wanted to turn around and get back on that helicopter to remain a few seconds in the past. While his physical body was walking down the passageway of the USS *Guadalcanal* (LPH-7), his spirit and mind where miles away. His state of mind was very similar to the day he left for the navy. While on the porch saying his good-byes to his family, he was physically there, but his mind was already miles away. A sobering and repeat action for years to come. He purposely rewound *everything* that had just taken place within the last twenty-four hours. The flight from Philadelphia, Pennsylvania, to Rota, Spain; to the island of Larnaca, Sicily; to the episode with the Lieutenant Colonial on the island; to boarding the helicopter on the island and flying to the boat; to landing on the boat. He wanted so, so desperately to rewind and then stop at the point he would be happy with. But even the thoughts of such a thing are the epitome of immature vain thinking. Sailor had to grow up, and he had to grow up regardless if he wanted to or not. The experience that lay ahead on board the USS *Guadalcanal* (LPH-7) would be a memory that would last the remainder of his life. He does not reminisce often about those days; nonetheless, they remain etched in his soul, and he sometimes marvels how he made it through.

15

INTRODUCTION TO PHIBRON

The Adversary and the Crew

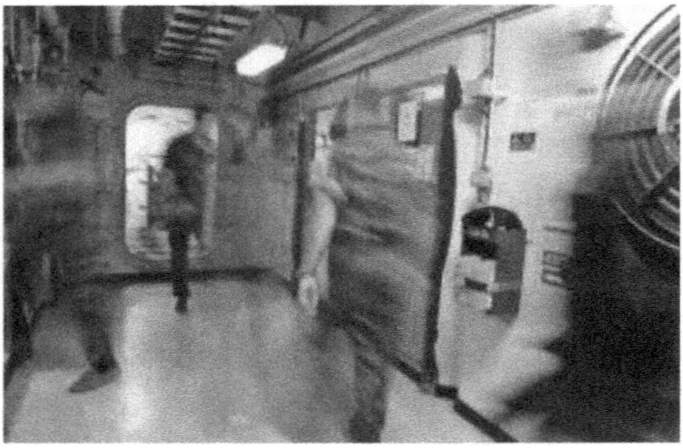

To get from one section to another section on board a navy warship, you must walk down the passageway (civilians call them hallways). To get to the other section, you must cross over what is called a knee knocker. It is simply a raised section at the bottom of the hatch (or doorway for civilians), about ten inches high. This allows for the hatch to securely close in the event of a breach in the hull of the ship, maintaining watertight integrity for that section of the ship. An ingenious safety measure making it not easy to sink a naval vessel as a result of a missile strike, or fire, or any danger that would damage the bulkhead of the ship.

Now on board the *Guadalcanal* (LPH-7), Sailor was making his way into the ship from the flight deck. He looked down the passageway and noticed a dignified-looking gentleman approaching him stepping over knee knocker after knee knocker walking in his direction. He thought to himself, *Thank God, a brother.*

He was the first black man Sailor seen in uniform since leaving the island of Larnaca. The man was about 5'9" with salt-and-pepper hair. Greasy slick hair, thick mustache, and a gold tooth. He looked at Sailor and smiled, revealing his front gold tooth and instead of greeting Sailor with a professional greeting, he extended his hand, with a smirk type of smile, gold tooth and all, and said, "Hello, how you doing? You look like Sweeney."

Sailor gave kind of a faint smile, but deep down inside he was on fire! He hated to be called something he was not or remind someone of another person and especially a person he did not know who they were referring to. Sailor would not have gotten angry had he said, "You look like Denzel Washington, Morgan Freeman, Richard Roundtree, or even Isaac Hayes." Obviously, these are well-known successful black men, and Sailor do not know many people that dislike resembling a successful rich person. But who the hell was Sweeney, he thought. He became immediately uneasy from that point on that he would identify him as some jokester, or prankster. The man wasted no time in passing his mediocre judgment of Sailor and hadn't a clue who Sailor was, nor did Sailor know who he was. At this point in life, Sailor was not even remotely skilled in combating mental games people play and was getting whipped upside his head with every word spoken to him during those days. The man threw a curve at Sailor that he was not expecting, and Sailor did not know what or who he was referring to. Sailor then asked, "Who is Sweeney? A sailor that used to be here?"

He just laughed and didn't answer Sailor, as though his question did not matter. The man turned around facing the direction he had come from and said to Sailor, "C'mon, let's go. They're waiting for you. Wait till they see you. Oh boy, they are going to freak out. This place is a trip!"

Sailor was following close behind, struggling down the passageway with his sea bag on his shoulder and stepping over knee knocker after knee knocker. He was becoming more furious with each step because he felt the first impression of the man was totally unprofessional. Walking the passageway toward the office space that he would be working in with sea bag on his shoulder, Sailor caught a few knee knockers and was furious inside his soul and burnt anger of every impact he encountered with the knee knockers.

Amphibious Squadron 2

The man that met Sailor wore the rank of yeoman first class (YN1), the same rating specialty of Sailor. A first class petty officer is equivalent to a staff sergeant in the army and marines and a technical sergeant in the air force. Sailor was a brand-new second class petty officer and diligently sought to become promoted to first class petty officer. After stepping over ten knee knockers, they arrived at the office space he would be working in for the next ninety days. Unpredictable. If one word could describe living on board a navy warship it would have to be unpredictable. The average young Sailor lives a promiscuous life in many ways and a life that is not acceptable in the eyes of God. At this time in Sailor's life, he did not fear to succumb to such a lifestyle and had only been married three short years greatly desiring to be with his wife. The tour of duty on board the *Guadalcanal* would be nothing like his first experience overseas as a young single nineteen-year-old teenager. On this tour of duty, Sailor was now married and in love with his wife. He did not like the idea of having to spend the next two years with men who seemed to have little regard for one another and who had serious marital problems themselves. Nonetheless, that's the environment he had been dumped in, and like it or not, that's the environment he was compelled to deal with and overcome. The color of a navy warship is gray all over inside and out. The only colors you will see are insignias on the side of aircraft or perhaps at someone's personal bunk. All in all, the ship has no variety of color or of scenery. Sailor's view while on Larnaca and the flight on the helicopter while approaching his final destination of the *Guadalcanal* was on board a large gray vessel. He was mentally overcome with a very depressing mood surrounded by the color gray and thrust into a stressful atmosphere. When they arrived at the workspace, the little three-feet-wide-by-five-and-a-half-feet-high door they had to enter was also the color gray. A normal-size man would have to stoop down to enter, and that description fit all of them, including the senior chief in charge of the office. The following is what transpired to the best of Sailor remembering these events when YN1 opened the door to the administration office and began introducing the crew.

"Here he is, Petty Officer Sailor. This is Senior Chief and this is YN2."

YN2: Hey, welcome aboard. Where you from?
Sailor: Harrisburg, Pennsylvania.
YN2: Where is that at? Close to Philly?
Sailor: About a good two -hour drive west of Philadelphia.
YN2: Oh.

Immediately, Sailor had to remind himself that this is the military and not a group of Christians welcoming him to a new church fellowship. What did he expect, embracing, laughter, excitement or maybe a handshake or two, with the words, "Welcome, welcome!" Why should his new shipmates have any personal liking or acceptance of him? Sailor had to realize that he was no more special than the next guy locked up in a federal institution. He was not only wrestling with his personal feelings but with a host of problems he immediately observed going on, namely the other people that were in the office that day. Van was a young brother sitting at a desk working who YN1 just pointed at unenthusiastically and mumbled something, but really gave little recognition to Van. YN1 said, "There's ah, ah…"

At that point, Van reached up his hand to shake Sailor's and introduced himself. Sailor had enough presence of spirit to pick up that something is ungodly wrong here. The white senior chief sat in his chair and reluctantly shook Sailor's hand while sitting down with gold wire frame glasses looking at Sailor as to think, *Another black man.*

It was apparent the senior chief's thoughts were not professional because the expression on his face told an entire story. The anger and hatred Sailor stepped into that day was unbelievably, unavoidably strong and was the most dreadful emotional time he would ever face. After the introductory of YN2 and the ignoring of the other brothers in the office, Senior Chief quietly and calmly stood up and left the office. Senior Chief said something to YN1 that he had to go to the ship's bridge for something. There was also another brother in the office that turned to shake Sailor's hand and he introduced himself to Sailor. Brother Keith was the other young sailor in the office along with YN2. Both Van and Keith were seaman recruits, pretty much fresh out of boot camp. The office was comprised of four black men, including Sailor, making five set in a very hostile environment onboard a gray naval vessel anchored off the coast of Beirut Lebanon. The mission of the Amphibious Group was to mediate between the radical Islamic factions of Hezbollah and the Palestinian Liberation Organization (PLO). Iran, Syria, Shiites, scud missiles, Islamic fanaticism, jihad, and everything Sailor once feared in a military mission, he was now a part of. Sailor was knee-deep into an atmosphere of hell versus Christianity, masquerading as good that was evil. He was now another military statistic, part of a news article, another sacrifice; somebody no one knew in the headline news on the world's stage of a new type of war. International terrorism would plague the crew and one day change the face of America. Sailor was compelled to either overcome the hellish fear he now faced and return home in victory or die as a coward in some way or another. The United

States Armed Forces was in Lebanon along with the Multinational Peacekeeping Force to help facilitate withdrawal of the PLO fighters from Lebanon. At the time, Sailor new very little about terrorist tactics or the civil war of Beirut, Lebanon, in the Middle East. The acts of terrorism that took place in Beirut, Lebanon, was the groundwork for what would come to the shores of America exactly ten years later. While each American was enjoying the autonomy of a sovereign nation, the pendulum would swing hard in just ten short years and uproot the seemingly untouchable United States of America. Sailor was clueless that he stood at the start and was at the core of the beginning of terrorism against the United States. This undoubtedly served as his crash course of not only the Middle East conflicts but world conflicts. He would come to see and know how the entire military, governmental, and political systems strategically influence certain events to unfold. It became clear to him after meeting his new shipmates and certain factions of the Hezbollah and Islamic radicals, that Beirut, Lebanon, was very explosive both figuratively and literally. Meeting the four brothers would erupt how he felt and it was entirely too much for him to bear. He was very tired of trying to be a Christian or what the Bible says. For Sailor, this was just too much to have to deal with all at once. Like the old saying when it rains it pours. Sailor had just landed in the eye of the storm and could not see a small pinhead of light anywhere around him. Beirut, Lebanon, was the birth of the extremist terrorist attacks on the United States to this day. Sailor was at the grassroots of what many Americans fear today. The very lax approach the Multinational Peacekeeping Force took during those years in Beirut, Lebanon, continued to inspire the hearts of the radical Muslim extremist into what would eventually become September 11, 2001, or 9/11. God had become estranged in the mind of Sailor. He just did not know what to do or what to believe. He had to be very careful of his feelings because there was a part of him that was feeling angry with God and almost wanting God to strike him with a lightning bolt. He wanted to be home, and he wanted to be out of the navy. The cowardice spirit he was harboring had been in him all along throughout his life. He only has God to thank for training him and teaching him how to truly become a warrior and overcome the world.

Kicking the Bunk

It couldn't have been more than two weeks after being on board when he ran into the other side of YN1. Remember now, he had just left home and accustom to sleeping in his nice plush bed in the house on Woodbine Street with his wife. There was no big rush to get out of the bed back home and secondly it was his wife who woke him up. Now almost two weeks later, he is on board a big gray naval warship in a depressing environment, laying on a mattress that is no more than four inches thick. The bunk was big enough for one person to sleep on. Sailor had some serious adjusting to get used to. Back on board the USS *Independence* (CV-62) and the USS *Eisenhower* (CVN-69), he was not married and his home of record was still North 18th Street. Besides, he was younger, and the adjusting back in those days came quite naturally. With the attitude and perspective he was harboring on board the USS *Guadalcanal* (LPH-7), sleeping in that bunk was extremely uncomfortable, and he was now deeply depressed. Sailor could not see life in a positive light, or being in the navy as a good thing during those days. He was one very unhappy individual and sailor. It took exactly twenty-seven months for his perspective to lighten up and began to see the necessity in all his trials and tribulations. But the first ninety days, of which was the time frame the *Guadalcanal* was anchored off the coast of Beirut, Lebanon, was pure, unrefined hell directly from Satan! Many times he truly thought he was going to have either a nervous breakdown or really, really go off on somebody. There were times Sailor did not care what the outcome would be, and he expected to be thrown in the brig. He remembered seeing sailors on board the USS *Independence* (CV-62) who were in the brig, and they were marched back and forth to the chow hall in chains with clean-shaven heads under heavy marine guard.

But this thing with the bunk, he was sleeping sound in that lazy, crazy bunk on the bottom almost parallel to the deck. He was enjoying a nice dream about his wife and living on Woodbine Street in Harrisburg, Pennsylvania. In the dream, he thought the dream was actually real and he really hated to wake up. That's the type of dream he was having. His wife was at the center of the dream, and the dream of her contributed to him sleeping sound. In the dream, he and his wife were actually in the apartment at 1089C Michigan Drive. The place they moved into when we first got married. They were in the kitchen, then walked through the apartment and sat down to watch TV while eating a snack. The sun was shining through the sliding glass door to their small apartment deck. They were talking to one another sitting very close to each other and just relaxing and enjoying one another. In the dream, something became very unstable and the entire dream was rocking back and forth. And the weirdest part about the rocking in the dream is that he and his wife looked at each other when the dream became unstable. They looked at each other as to say, "What is that?" What's happening?"

It's almost like his wife back home knew something was unstable in his life miles and miles across the ocean on board a naval vessel in a hostile situation. He felt himself in the dream becoming hellishly, almost demonically angry. He then heard words in the dream, words he could not distinguish because they seemed out of place for that type of dream. The words got louder and louder and the rocking back and forth of the dream became so unstable the dream fell apart and blew away like small pieces of torn-up paper into the wind. There was blackness at that point, and he opened his eyes to realize that he was dreaming. But he also came face-to-face with a man who was in some way projecting into Sailor's spirit what the man was feeling in his own. The spirit of fear onboard that war vessel in those days was unlike *anything* Sailor had ever known. Fear was bold, imputing, arrogant, and intrusive into everyone's life in some way or another. Sailor was smack dab in the middle of a hellish battle every single day and was compelled to learn how to fight and overcome this thing or be utterly defeated by its strong demonic influence.

YN1 was angry beyond anything Sailor had ever experienced with someone and his anger was directed at Sailor, who had never been so disrespected in such a manner in his whole life. Sailor thought at that moment, *God, what is going on? Why is this happening? What did I do wrong, and where did I do it wrong at? God, don't you know I am a preacher and this should not be happening to me? God, why are you allowing me to go through this? Why?*

You know how it is when you think you are too good to experience certain trials in life. You know how we do when we seek vengeance because of unfair treatment for the crimes and atrocities committed against us. He could not see the necessity of his trials and failed to examine his measly life in comparison to the trials Messiah endured. Not even aware of the scriptural injunction that says, "There hath no temptation taken you but such as is common to man: but God is faithful, who will not suffer you to be tempted above that ye are able; but will with the temptation also make a way to escape, that ye may be able to bear it" (1 Cor. 10:13). The Bible says Messiah was led into the wilderness to be tempted of the devil, Luke 4:1–2. Sailor now heavy into bearing his own cross daily, Luke 9:23. But of course, Sailor did not understand that aspect of life and the fiery darts targeted at him back then. In fact, there wasn't much he understood back then in the way of living and overcoming the tests and trials of life.

Upon waking up, he looked up in the direction the words were coming from because they appeared to be coming from above his head in the dream. He was stunned to see YN1 standing beside his bunk and actually kicking his bunk almost with enough force that a quarterback kicks a football. YN1 was spewing out language that would even shame the devil himself. He was calling Sailor a "lazy son of a bitch, where do you think you are? This is not Hollywood, it's the navy and you are god damn late for watch! You better get your mother-fucking ass out of that bunk and get on watch!" Sailor was YN1's relief for watch, and he was late. Only God in heaven knows that Sailor did not intentionally miss his duty to relieve YN1. He was dreaming about his wife and loving the dream. He actually forgot where he was and thought he was home in his bed sleeping. Back to reality when his supervisor aggressively aroused him from deep sleep. Sailor snapped up out of the bed with just his underwear on ready and poised to get with YN1. But YN1 had walked away yelling something about how he better be up in the office in five minutes or else. Both God and the devil can only know what was going through Sailor's mind at that point. He was beyond furious and ready for whatever would take place next. He thought to himself, *This is my opportunity to get off this boat and out of the navy because I am about to kick me some black ass real good.*

During those days, Sailor was a lean mean—you got it—fighting machine. He was twenty-three years old and in the best shape of his life. He worked out every day, including calisthenics, weights, and martial arts. He still had Bruce Lee books with him in his locker onboard ship. He still practiced the Tao of Bruce Lee Gung Fu with nunchucks and Bo and sometimes with sword. At any rate, YN1 was forty-nine years old, and you could tell he was older and out of shape. YN1 complained about his knees and his back sleeping on navy bunks. He complained about the knee knockers how they put strain and stress on his knees. He would go to sleep sitting in a chair and even doze off to sleep while driving a vehicle. In short, YN1 was absolutely no match for Sailor, and Sailor could not wait to kick YN1's butt for disturbing his sleep in the manner he did and for shattering his dream about his wife. Lastly, for disrespecting him like he was some street punk. What the hell was wrong with that man to think Sailor was going to walk up in the office and bow to YN1's rank and authority. What YN1 did not realize, as the saying goes, he woke a sleeping lion. It was way too much to bear, and YN1 would become the victim of Sailor's deeply entrenched anger. Seems like just yesterday that he left the United States, only to end up on an island Larnaca, Cyprus. From there to the boat anchored off the coast of Beirut, Lebanon, only to enter a depressing environment. The man Sailor was ripe and ready to beat the hell out of someone; anyone. YN1 had just volunteered for that beating, Sailor thought.

The Intent to Be Thrown in the Brig: The Intervening Angel

YN2 was a good brother in Sailor's eyes, although Sailor was very cautious toward him because he hung around YN1. Almost like someone who is up under the skirt of a female leader or brown-nosing with those of senior rank. He learned later that YN2 did not care much for YN1 either, and it was not so much he didn't care for YN1 but he did not like YN1's style of supervision. Sailor quickly learned that YN1 was relentless, coercive, and authoritarian in the most negative way. Sailor came to learn almost twelve months later that YN1 concealed deep personal issues. Nonetheless, Sailor got up out of the bunk and put his pants, T-shirt, shirt, and shoes on in lightning speed. He had to make his way up to the office in record-breaking time while he was still on fire inside his soul. He had to get YN1, and he had to get him now. Open up the brig doors for Sailor, because that's his next stop, after he sees YN1. However, Sailor was about to board one of the most thrilling and heightened emotional roller coaster rides of his life. When Sailor got up to the office, he kicked the door open to the point it slammed into the file cabinet behind it. Thank God no one was standing there, but if so, that didn't matter either. They could have thanked YN1 for his actions. Once the door was open, everyone in the office looks at Sailor almost in dismay, surely wondering, *What's going on?*

YN1 was sitting down at a desk as nothing had happened. YN1 appeared oblivious to what he had just done. Like he could not care less that he angered Sailor. YN1 appeared like he didn't give a damn about Sailor or anybody else, a "just do what I say" kind of impression. This is how it went down:

Sailor: What in the hell is wrong with you, nigga? Don't you know I will kick your black mother-fucking ass! You are certainly screwing with the wrong brother. I'm not going to bow down to your dumb ass, and I'm not going to kiss your black ass. I'm going to kick your black ass, and nobody is going to stop me!

YN1: You betta get outta here, boy. I don't have time for you acting a fool. You betta get outta here.

Sailor: Fool! You ain't seen nothing yet, chump. You goddamn dumb-ass nigga! What gives you the right to kick my bunk like I'm some kind of pussy? I'm about to make you into a pussy when I get done with you.

YN1: I told you, get out of here, boy, and go on your watch. You gonna get hurt, and I mean it.

Sailor: Damn you, mother fucker! All you doing is talking. I'm ready to bust you up! You don't know what I know and how I will kill you, man! I *will* kill you, man, right now! Go ahead and try to kick me now. I will break your dumb mother-fucking ass in half! Get up, punk, get up!

Weeks and months later, Sailor could not believe how he was carrying on. He had lost all respect for rank, authority, and even himself. His mouth had become the epitome of a sailor and he did not care! At the point when he challenged YN1 to get out of his chair, he had actually put his hands on YN1, trying to provoke him to respond. Even though YN1 initiated the confrontation, he was still the stronger man than Sailor because he did not respond even after Sailor put his hands on him. Sailor was spewing out nasty, ugly, ungodly words, prancing around in the small 12 × 15 office with two other brothers in the office. The younger brothers simply got out their chairs and walked out while YN1, YN2, and Sailor was inside the confines of a small hellhole while hell was erupting from within Sailor. Then the unsuspecting intervention from God surprised Sailor to this day. The great mercy of God intervened on Sailor's ignorant fleshly mind and body of the worst kind. God was revealing to Sailor what evils lie in the depths of his soul regardless of his preaching back home at Mount Calvary Church of God in Christ. Sailor had not been tried sufficiently to justify calling himself a preacher. And this was a precursor compared to the ultimate trying that would come from his own brothers some ten years later. Those two brothers he admired and looked up to. The ones he idolized and thought could do no wrong. The ones who pretty much taught him of the world and guided him on his path into the navy. Sailor was a novice in all respects and simply had the Bible as a religious book to massage his spirit. The great Truth of Scripture had not come alive to him, and he was in the worst state of painfully growing. Almost like he was dying on one hand but being reborn on the other, and the act of both death and life was agonizingly painful and shamefully unbearable. He did not know how much more of this he could take and maintain some facade of a sound mind. Unknowingly, he was ready to hand his mind over to Satan on a silver platter. He was ready to become Satan's servant because he desperately wanted revenge against anyone who withstood him. He felt estranged from Messiah, and he felt let down by his mother and lost without his wife. But every day he walked around with his head in the air, appearing to have it all together while all the while deep inside, he was bursting with pain and scars of the past. He had *no one* to share his heart with, nor *anyone* that he felt would understand what he was feeling. So he masqueraded. He played like he was doing well and masked his inner struggles with the knowledge of the use of the English language, by talking a good game.

At that point, YN2, who was standing behind Sailor, reached both his hands forward and almost in a massaging manner gently touched the back of his shoulders and calmly said, "C'mon, T, let's get out of here. C'mon, man, let's go."

Sailor can never forget the intervention of YN2, and though he wanted YN2 to get his hands of him, at the same time, YN2's touch was reassuring Sailor. In an unspoken manner, YN2 was relaying the message to Sailor that aggression against another black man among the company of white men, would be the worst thing Sailor could do. It was the first time that YN2 called Sailor by a nickname, almost like they were best friends for years. Sailor had just met the man just little over a week ago, and everyone else at his new duty station on board the ship. YN2's successful attempt to defuse the tension was to call Sailor "T," and he did not take his hands off Sailor's shoulder. In fact, YN2's touch was almost like a slight rub as though an attempt to relieve the frustration and anger running through the veins of Sailor.

YN2 said again, "T, let's go. You don't want to do this. C'mon, man, let's take a walk."

Sailor was extremely angry and wanting so much for YN1 to stand up or yell back at him or do something, you know, make a false move. YN2 had convinced Sailor that he better leave the office and go up topside and cool down. YN2 continued to nudge Sailor on and gently turned Sailor toward the door to leave. "C'mon, bro, let's go," and they both walked out the office up the passageway toward the bridge. They talked about how unworthy it would be to get busted because of YN1's way of provoking people to anger. The man possessed an uncanny way of getting people angry in an environment that seemed to be unchangeable. The facts were, they were on board a naval warship anchored off the coast of Beirut, Lebanon, under the direct orders of the United States Armed Forces. There was no alternative but adjust, conform, and perform the assigned duties. But YN1 was deeply angry about his life and his past life and anyone who crossed his path was a candidate for ungodly harassment and provoking that would illicit untold anger. YN1 mastered the spirit of provoking one to anger. Sailor has not experienced anyone since YN1 that was so good at provoking one to anger. Sailor had stepped into the trial of his life and was compelled to overcome or doomed to be annihilated.

While walking down the passageway up to the flight deck, YN2 said, "Sailor, YN1 is a very angry man and unhappy with his life. I know that doesn't justify him treating people like shit, but that's the way YN1 is. I've been working with the man for over a year, and there have been times I wanted to punch him in the face myself. But I became aware of the man's shortcomings. Hell, we all have shortcomings, but we don't have to treat other people like shit."

Robbie was rapping to Sailor in a manner like he really cared what would happen to him, and though they both were the same rank (second class petty officers), Sailor was glad that YN2 stepped in and intervened instead of doing nothing. As far as Sailor could see, there was nothing religious about YN2 because he never spoke of his faith. In fact, on the contrary, when he and YN1 got into religious conversations YN2 usually was very negative about preachers and churches. But his actions that day had nothing to do with religion, churches, or Christianity. The Bible says there are times we have interaction with angels (Heb. 13:2), and though Sailor dare not say that YN2 was an angel, the manner in which he intervened had a compassionate and kind implication. YN2 was keeping Sailor's butt out of criminal trouble and dishonorable discharge. Sailor had never been locked up in his life or even almost getting a criminal record, except for the incident in Tijuana, Mexico, back in 1976. But if there ever was a time of Sailor getting locked up, this was the time it almost happened. The intervention of YN2 had to be divinely orchestrated that day in that small 12 × 15 office space on board the USS *Guadalcanal* (LPH-7). The ship was anchored about twenty miles off the coast of Beirut, Lebanon, in an unpredictable hostile area assigned to the Multinational Peacekeeping Force. Had YN2 not intervened the way he did on that day, the outcome of that day would have been the hellish turn around in Sailor's life. His story obviously would have a different outcome and horrible ending. He possibly would not have had the privilege to tell his story. Sailor had every intention of seriously hurting YN1 and consequently destroying his life at least for the next five to six years. The confrontation with YN1 took place in 1983, and Sailor knows he would have gotten a dishonorable discharge and probably incarcerated at the Naval Consolidated Brig in Charleston, South Carolina, for a minute. In fact, he had made up in his mind while he was stretching his legs almost in one step over every knee knocker, on his way up to the workspace to get YN1. He accepted the fact that he was about to go to jail. Sailor was not praying to God to help him—you know how when you get angry you utter a mundane prayer "God, help me that I don't do anything wrong"? Sailor was not praying at all! He was actually running through his mind, like frames in a movie, how he was going to kick YN1's black ass. He was practicing the moves and running the techniques in his mind that he planned to use on YN1 and he was anticipating being swift, maiming, and decisive in his attack. He was angry beyond anything he had ever experienced in his entire life! He wanted deadly revenge, and he wanted it now. In the Bible, the prophet Jeremiah speaks of how the human heart is deceptive and desperately wicked and who can know it (Jer. 17:9). At that time, Sailor had no knowledge of that verse in the Bible; nonetheless, the truth of that Bible verse rang loudly in his life for years thereafter.

The Knot from Within

The quick actions of YN2 opened up a new connection between him and Sailor. He felt like he could talk to YN2 even though YN2's mood swing was unpredictable whenever YN1 was around. When YN1 was not around, YN2 was very civil and intellectual. In many ways, YN1 influenced and controlled YN2's spirit in what Sailor would later understand to be spiritual servitude. YN1 was in control of YN2 while in his presence. The servitude spirit he wielded over YN2 was the beginning of a deep eye-opener for Sailor. It was unbelievable to him at the time the control one person can actually have over another person. Not only was there a strong unearthly presence on board the ship it was as if every word spoken by different ones was masked behind some other intention. Like everyone on board the ship was running some game against the other. On board the USS *Guadalcanal* (LPH-7) anchored off the coast of Beirut, Lebanon, was the most backstabbing, clique environment that Sailor had ever been thrust into. A far cry from his first enlistment. The only tour of duty that would remotely compare to Sailor's first enlistment would not come until some seven years later. But no tour of duty would match VS-31 onboard the USS *Independence* (CV-62) and the USS *Dwight D. Eisenhower* (CVN-69). The travel, the experience, the growing up was an absolute one-of-a-kind opportunity. Filled with excitement and adventure and exploring and learning and gaining knowledge. The likes that he would definitely do over again, yet never experience again in ten lifetimes.

After cooling down to a manageable and reasonable thinking man while talking to YN2, they both arrived at the flag bridge for Sailor to assume the watch for YN1. YN2 then left the flag bridge and went his way back to the office or either to his bunk. Upon arriving on duty on the flag bridge, the officer of the deck, a young lieutenant, played his game like he was cool. He tried to be hip and sort of in the groove. But he was still among the officer rank, and there was an obvious separation between officer and enlisted in that command. At least, between officer and black enlisted in that command. Officers made it clear that they were commissioned by the president of the United States, and they barked out orders similar to a boot camp setting. But in hindsight, the officers were justified because the atmosphere and tension on board that naval vessel hung on the border of insubordination and God forbid mutiny. Who would imagine mutiny onboard a United States naval vessel in the twentieth century? The world having made advancements in sociological and so-called human efforts and civil programs to experience a mutiny on board a United States naval vessel? From the eyes of Sailor, the psychology that prevailed onboard the *Guadalcanal* was not one of pride, duty, and commitment, but rather of survival. Everyone appeared to be watching everyone else and everyone else was watching everyone. As if no one had confidence in anyone's ability and no one dare trust anyone to watch their back. The tour of duty onboard the USS *Guadalcanal* (LPH-7) while anchored off the coast of Beirut, Lebanon, in April of 1983 was the worst tour of duty of Sailor's military career. One might interpret what you have read this far as an intense personality conflict. But as the old saying goes, you would have had to been there. It was more than a single personality conflict. Like a Steven Spielberg suspense and horror, like the very air breathed seemed to be laced with anger and death and pending doom and destruction. The spirit or principality ruling the affairs of men on the shores of Beirut, Lebanon, had engulfed all naval vessels in the theater of operation. When Sailor arrived on the bridge, the lieutenant immediately attacked him with a stern look, like "I'm not listening to what you have to say," and he began to chastise Sailor in the worst way: "You are late! Thirty minutes late! I should write you up. Don't you understand that we are in a hostile environment and *every* crewmember *must* do his part! What do you think this operation would turn out to be if everyone was like you and arrived on watch whenever they felt like it? What then, Petty Officer Sailor?"

"But, but, sir, let me explain."

"I don't want to hear your incompetency! We have enough problems ashore than to have to deal with sailors like you. Now log yourself in as assuming the watch and man the ship to shoreline, you need to be on duty ASAP!"

What calm spirit Sailor had a few minutes ago after talking to YN2 had now escalated like hot lava erupting from an angry volcano. His emotions went from hot to warm to cold to boiling hot in a matter of minutes.

What the hell is happening here at this command? he thought. *Ever since reporting on board from day one when YN1 said I look like Sweeny, nothing, and I mean nothing, is going even reasonably right here. I* hate *this command, and I* hate *these people!*

A jumble of thoughts rushed his mind like a tsunami out of control. His immediate thought was to curse the lieutenant out or either purposely screw things up on watch. But he thought about the episode with the lieutenant colonel on the island of Larnaca. He was not sure what the lieutenant's response would be. Even though the lieutenant looked timid, he talked like he knew his stuff. The lieutenant was not cool like he thought he was. Sailor really had no conflict or issue with him. In fact, this was the first time and only time he ever reprimanded Sailor and had full justification to write him up. Sailor knew he had to really suck this one up and keep his mouth shut because had he opened his mouth to spill out even one word, he was destined to be arrested and thrown in the brig. What Sailor lived in those days was fundamental morals and upbringing. He was not living by the truth of the Scriptures because Scripture had become lost to him. He was quick and thoughtlessly responding to all conflicts in the flesh. His flesh was very much on fire and steaming. Trouble was lurking around the next passageway and beyond the next hatch with his name on it. Each watertight integrity hatch he opened, he shuddered to think what might be on the other side. Big trouble, small trouble, or unrecognized trouble? Life was very difficult for Sailor to categorize trouble in his life then. But on a daily basis during that time in his life trouble had become his bosom buddy. In hindsight, his survival of those days was nothing but the mercy and grace of God. Sailor was an infant in maturity, and patience was unknown to him. He was thrown into the slimy, mushy, ungodliness of the ways of man. He was conforming to the flesh and looking more and more like a man of the world. He had sunk rapidly into the desires and evil ways of Satan. He was overcome with fear of the worst kind, a fear that held his soul and spirit captive of its own free will. At times, he was mindless and thoughtless even with the smallest utterance of some kind of prayer. His prayers had no real focus, and his faith was drained second by second. His hatred for the United States Navy and the crew he was working with had reached the epic of trials and tribulations. The navy became his enemy, an enemy he once loved. Time would reveal, as it often does, the source of the real enemy and the influence and origin of the real trouble. He blamed the navy for his problems, but the navy was only a means of revealing deeper issues residing in the heart of Sailor. He personally struggled with his issues and did not know how to talk about what he was going through. Sailor failed to grasp the enormity of the history of that part of the world. He wasn't sure if the United States Navy really understood its role in historical biblical affairs. The Peacekeeping Force in Beirut, Lebanon, was part of century-long spiritual conflicts. As if all the fallen angels had congregated in the Middle East and all who would attempt to disrupt them would be drawn into the fray. The unseen battled had been waging ever since the dawn of man. Like a scene out of the *Outer Limits* or *One Step Beyond*, the *Guadalcanal* and its battle group were in the hub of a spiritual conflict involving angels and demons. It was impossible not to be affected by the anger and hatred and death that has ruled that region of the world for millennniums. Noah, Moses, Joshua, the ancient Jewish kings, the Judges, and on and on from the Bible has dealt with and succumbed to the depth of the spiritual battles. The United States Navy had now become a part of those everlasting battles. The survival of the Multinational Peacekeeping Force and the individual survival of Sailor depended upon one reality and only one.

The Navy and all its crewmembers would have been wise to seek the Most High. Separation of religion and state is a wrong concept that has brought down the mightiest kingdoms. Therefore, the outcome of the Multinational Peace Keeping Force would be the loss of a number of souls. Sailor would not completely embrace that line of thinking until years into the man of the Sermon.

16

THE AMERICAN EMBASSY

The First Act of Terrorism—Soul-Searching

After the hostile encounter with YN1, Sailor thought to himself, *What could be worse than getting thrown in the brig and getting a dishonorable discharge?* A dishonorable discharge would have been the ultimate disgrace against his family, his church and himself. Had he ended up in jail, he already had his excuse made up with a full explanation. He would simply say, "You just don't understand what I went through from the island of Larnaca to what I was going through onboard the *Guadalcanal*."

He felt that no one would have understood and no one would have had sympathy. But the encounter with YN1 was actually precursor to what lay ahead of the unpredictable times on board the USS *Guadalcanal* amphibious warship, anchored off the coast of Beirut, Lebanon, in 1983. Sailor quickly learned while onboard the ship that frictions were at an all-time high due to the extreme amount of personal stress within the lives of each sailor on board the ship. His first tour of duty with Air Antisubmarine Squadron 31 at nineteen years old was nothing like this tour of duty. It was literally the difference between night and day. In fact, his first tour of duty was more like a controlled, regiment vacation and European excursion. Controlled in the sense that everything was governed by military law and policy. *Regiment* in the sense of a strict code of conduct with serious repercussions. At the end of the day, he was globetrotting at Uncle Sam's expense all over Europe and enjoying every second of it. There were no serious hostile engagements and no wide-scale terrorist threat activity involving the United States of America in those days. The beginning of the worst that occurred at the prepuces of Beirut was the Iran hostages during the transition of the Carter administration into the Reagan administration. As Sailor watched the shame and humiliation of the Iran hostages involving American citizens and military personnel, he knew deep within his soul that somehow or another, he would be part of the events in the Middle East. His first tour of duty unveiled the positive side of the armed forces, and he was enjoying himself immensely seeing this and seeing that and doing this and doing that.

He could not see it then but transferring to Amphibious Squadron Two on board the USS *Guadalcanal* anchored off the coast of Beirut, Lebanon, was the best thing for him at that time in his life. He had to grow up and he had to grow up in the midst of trying times and tumultuous situations. The tour of duty in Beirut, Lebanon, on board the USS *Guadalcanal* (LPH-7) was an unbelievably, huge thorn in the flesh. It was the unraveling of internal exposure of himself along with personality conflict after personality conflict. In other words, in those days Sailor took everything personal which is the recipe for mental breakdown and the gateway into insanity. Sailor had decades ahead of him before he would begin to understand the great victory in not taking things personally. Prior to his tour of duty on board the *Guadalcanal*, Sailor viewed life and interaction with others not as a deadly thing but more from a naive frame of reference. He actually thought everybody liked him, and he made it a point to like everyone he met. The previous temperament of Sailor was friendly, outgoing. He wanted to be accepted and loved by every person. The hostility, prejudice, tension, and explosions of anger took Sailor through a crash course of his true self. He became another actor on the world's stage involving the countless attitudes that reside in all men and women. But Sailor's test was not to understand the attitudes in others as it was to face his own ignorance and masked attitudes that he unknowingly harbored. He was a tremendous culture shock unto himself, both internally and externally. At every turn, he felt he would not survive but would result in doing something idiotic and harmful not only to himself but to anyone who got in his way. He was not ready for what he had to deal with but was compelled to adjust or jeopardize everything he thought he believed and everything he wanted in life. He was at a point many times of surrendering his rank, his faith and his life to defeat. It wasn't the "I want to die" type coward spirit experienced in the past, but a self-sympathy spirit wanting everyone else to feel sorry for him. Going through his trials, it was difficult for him to see the outcome, and all he had was a smidgen of faith. Each day seemed to drag along at a snail's pace. Beirut, Lebanon, at the time was a ninety-day on station Multinational Peacekeeping Force, but it was the longest ninety days of his life. Especially when each day was filled with limited work assignments, and he spent much of the time standing watch on the ship's bridge, monitoring the J24 ship to shoreline connected to the marine headquarters onshore. He would go on watch counting down the hours, "I've got three hours and twenty minutes left on watch." What a miserable thing to do, but you are drawn into that spirit, unbeknownst to yourself and you systematically, unconsciously start counting down how many hours you have left on watch. The days were long, and the watches were arduous. And not only did he count down the hours on watch, he also counted down the days left on the tour of duty. "Eighty days left and we're going back to the States."

But as it often goes in the navy on a Mediterranean or West Pacific military cruise, ninety days could easily turn into 100 days could easily turn into 150 days and on and on. Extensions of tour of duty while on extended deployments was not an uncommon occurrence. So the countdown of eighty days left was simply a psychotherapy attempt to enjoy waking up each morning.

It's Time To Die, Why Didn't It Happen?

The morning of April 18, 1983, began like any other day. An unsuspecting and lax spirit prevailed among the crew. Even while marine sentries stood their posts, acuity and awareness had fallen asleep. Due to the nature of the Multinational Peacekeeping Force, marines walked around with unloaded weapons, .45 calibers strapped to their thighs, unloaded. Military-style rifles and guns on their person, but international rules of engagement forbade them to load their weapons. ROE involving political decisions in an effort to foster peace put all military personnel at risk of uncertain hostile attack resulting in senseless deaths. In an all-out war, weapons are loaded, and the enemy is hunted down with full knowledge of possible casualties. The terrorist form of war falls beyond risky because the "peacemaker" must present himself as the great forgiver of the enemy and show very little signs of aggression. The politicians and military leaders who decided loading weapons in the midst of hostilities was a bad idea should embrace the spirit of grief due to the death of military and civilian personnel. The peacekeeping mission failed on a grand scale. It was marked from its beginning because the international brass and politicians were attempting to broker a peace between millennium of strife between two nations of people. The peacekeeping mission was a military strategy while it should have been a prayerful strategy sought from the highest office in the land, the president of the United States. One would truly think the United States of America should have real lessons learned from centuries of wars in dealing with the enemy. It doesn't matter that it is terrorism, what matters is the nature of armed conflict whether centered on religious beliefs or the acquisition of land. The enemy's objective must be dealt with, *not* the enemy's intent. Hezbollah did not intend to kill the enemies of Islam. Hezbollah's objective is to eradicate all imbeciles who reject the Islamic religion. The deep-rooted beliefs of radical Islamic factions from the hub of its epic center spread throughout the globe has no negotiation or peace objectives. Their main intent is to convert the enemy to the faith of Islam. Those military strategists in the field and the politicians in Washington, DC, who many of them are political scholars, know there is no negotiating with a true, real, avid religious fanatic—be it Christian, Buddhist, or Muslim. To have military rules of engagement of the United States Marine sentries not loading their weapons was a homegrown recipe for the Islamic radicals to totally destroy the marine headquarters. And if the United States had not withdrawn from that explosive arena, the Islamic fanatics would have attempted to sink a naval vessel or two given the once-in-a-lifetime opportunity.

The following images of the USS *Cole* (DDG-67) is proof positive of the objectives of radical Islamic followers. In October 2000, the USS *Cole* (DDG-67) was harbored and refueling in the port of Yemini

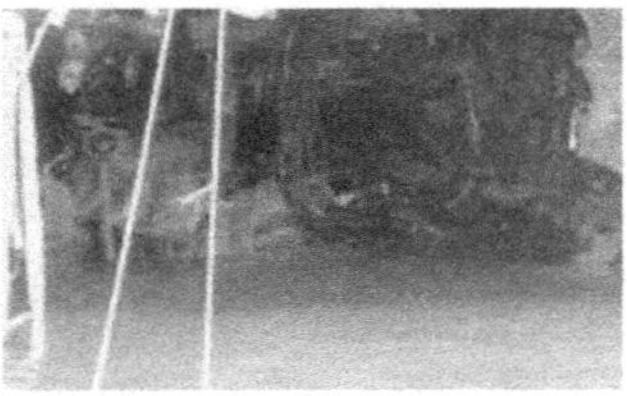
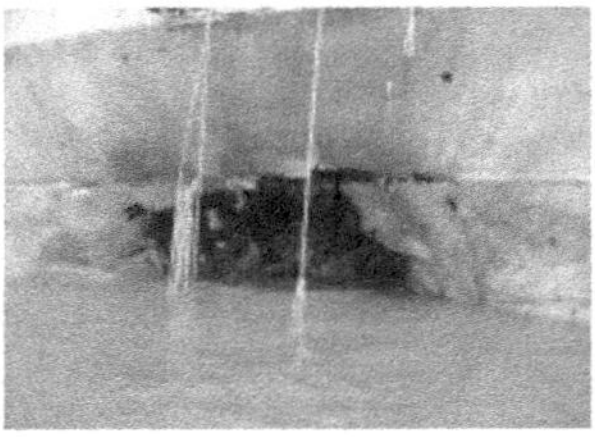

Aden the terrorist group al-Qaeda had proudly claimed the attack upon this US naval vessel. Every Islamic terrorist group in the Middle East and abroad takes glory in attacking and killing, who they term as imbeciles. The fact that seventeen American sailors were killed while not engaged in actual battle and thirty-nine sailors were injured does not matter to the terrorist. Had the United States not pulled out of Beirut, Lebanon, the ship Sailor was on board or any ship in that region undoubtedly would have been attacked as well. The bombing of the American Embassy was the morning terrorist activity began to stretch its heinous death grip across the Atlantic Ocean to reach America. The Beirut explosion began a long string of hostilities against America and her allies that would eventually unnerve and rock the very shores of the United States of America. The Beirut embassy bombing was the grassroots element of terrorism that would one day manifest itself in the very backyard of every American and United States citizen. The powers that be in Washington, DC, the Central Intelligence Agency, the Naval Criminal Investigative Service, the Joint Chiefs of Staff, and all the secret and special agencies that run the country expected and anticipated the day when America would no longer be safe from international terrorist attacks. Sailor did not realize then the potential and momentum of terrorism toward the United States. The act of terrorism was more of a nuisance and disruption into normal daily activity back then and was not dealt with as an act of ongoing war.

But today, in the eyes of a terrorist, terrorism is the standard form of war. The radical Islamic factions and Hezbollah and the Palestinian Liberation Organization have compelled the entire world to be subject to its wrath of religious Jihad. The Holy Koran, being the source of religious faith, fuels the Jihads engaged by Islamic radicals having drawn America into its philosophical and religious war, a war involving both Iran and Syria and eventually all the Middle East. 9/11 and all the terrorist attacks have been brewing over the decades since the days of the bombing of the American Embassy in downtown Beirut, Lebanon. Terrorism will not go away and probably never be dismantled. Even with the withdrawal of American troops from Iraq, the world is still faced with an unstable Middle East instigated, fueled and bullied by the government of the United States of America. All the efforts of the commander in chief George W. Bush and his war on terrorism were quintessential of American politics. It is a war with words and then unjustified military action to cover up their own unjust ways and practices against the Arabian people.

Many political and world commentators claim that 9/11 was simply blowback tracing back to the days of the Soviets invasion of Afghanistan in the late 1970s and 1980s. Notwithstanding, Sailor experienced the early stages of what now is a worldwide campaign against terrorism and the religious debate as to whether the Islamic religion is peaceful or wrathful. Beirut, Lebanon, was the grassroots and earthshaking experience that began to shake up and wake up the inhabitants of the world. Beirut, Lebanon, has become a forgotten Peacekeeping mission with the loss of well over 200 servicemen and women especially of the bombing of the marine headquarters in October 1983. Terroristic act after terroristic act was slowly becoming the frequent modus operandi in dealing with Arab nations abroad and becoming introduced to Westerners in the so-called land of the free.

Since the days of the Korean and Vietnam War, people of the United States of America have been essentially at a time of peace. The land of the free had not known damage and carnage as a result of explosions and destruction on its shores until Beirut, Lebanon, started the momentum. The events of Beirut, Lebanon, reached miles across the ocean to one day invade into the back yards of virtually every America citizen. The Iran hostage crisis from the winter of 1979 through the new year of 1981 was precursor to the Beirut bombings directly aimed at the United States of America. The early days of terrorism against America began with Iranian students holding America hostage for 444 days. Two and a half years later, hostages were no longer a part of the Islamic radical's message to keep the United States at bay. The stakes had become extremely high aiming for the life of any American, especially uniformed armed forces members—1983 American Embassy in Beirut, Lebanon, to 1998 American Embassy in Nairobi, Kenya, to the very shores of the United States of America on September 11, 2001, to even more devastating losses in the future. On October 23, 1983 the United States Marines lost 220 unarmed, unsuspecting, sleeping marines in the barracks at Beirut, Lebanon. Twenty-one other service personnel were included in the loss of life, bringing a grand total of 241 service members who died while fast asleep in their bunks. This by far was the most senseless deaths and cowardly response caused by the powers that be in Washington, DC, against America and the armed forces. Early Sunday morning during the Multinational Peacekeeping Campaign, an act of terrorism aimed at taking lives struck to the very core of the Multinational peacekeepers. Hezbollah and the early stages of many of the Islamic radicals had stepped up their game. The idea, per their deeply seated radical religious beliefs, is to destroy the imbeciles and drive them from their land. Many of the marine corps brothers and sisters feel betrayed by their country that they committed themselves to fight for and defend. Surviving marines and sailors quickly found that the same country, by political jargon and shrewd embodied political interest, failed to defend the senseless deaths of their fallen comrades. President Ronald Regan had approved a retaliatory response to the bombing of the marine headquarters but Defense Secretary Casper Weinberger failed to follow through the retaliation plan by President Ronald Reagan. How can the Defense Secretary or any politician in Washington, DC, especially a member of the president's administration, fail to follow through with an action endorsed by the president? Casper Weinberger's reportedly concerns were it might hurt our relations with other Arab nations. The lives of hundreds of men and women, fathers and mothers, sons and daughters are placed in harm's way daily. When the lightning-fast acts of the venomous snake of terrorism strikes, the politician's main concern is international relationships? Beirut, Lebanon, and the Multinational Peacekeeping force has faded into the annals of American history because the politicians, republican and democrats, want their mess not to be remembered. Vietnam cannot be forgotten because of the sheer scope of America's involvement and great number of loss of soldiers, sailors, airmen, and marines.

The Involvement of Sailor

Sailor had just relieved YN2, who was on watch at the time and walked by him in the passageway when YN2 said to Sailor, "These people are crazy, man. They just bombed the embassy." Sailor remembers the distinct look on YN2's face, one of great despair and frustration. He was no happier then Sailor was to be on board the USS *Guadalcanal* amid an atmosphere that harbored anger and frustration every second on the clock. The inevitable had just happened aimed at the United States government and the beginning of terrorism that would one day change the face of America. When YN2 spoke those words to Sailor, his heart sank into a deep pit of sorrow and frightening fear. Sailor became deeply worried at what might take place following the bombing of the American embassy in Beirut,

Lebanon. Upon assuming the watch on the flag bridge of the USS *Guadalcanal*, he anticipated mayhem that he was not ready for and an evening complete with recording radio transmissions. Detail after detail, that would last well into the night and morning. That day he had just enjoyed a quiet time reflecting on himself and his weak relationship with Messiah, meditating and reading his Bible. He had somewhat gotten himself together following the long transient flight from the United States and the Larnaca experience. He should have been able to interpret the quietness as the calm before the storm. But in those days his interpretation of events was more emotional than spiritual and filled with frustration after frustration. Then a direct attack on the emissaries of the United States of America! Sailor immediately manned the J24 ship to shore phone and was compelled to pick up where YN2 left off.

> "Valuable, valuable—this is Ulcer, over!"
> "Ulcer, this is valuable, over"
> "Valuable, this is Ulcer, are you ready to copy?"
> "Ulcer, this is Valuable—copy, over—begin transmission, over!"

Immediately his ears were glued to the ship to shore phone and his heart pumped faster than any man's heart should bear. The marine's voice on the other end of the J24 sounded like something right out of a World War II movie:

> "Valuable, this is ulcer, there are mass casualties everywhere, do you copy, over!"
> "Ulcer, this is valuable—please say again, slowly and clearly!" "Valuable, this is ulcer, we have mass casualties. Request much assistance, over! The façade of the US Embassy's main section has been totally annihilated, over! There are bodies sprawled in the wreckage—emergency vehicles on the way!"

Explosion rocks U.S. Embassy
in Beirut; 33 are reported dead

The American Embassy in west Beirut, as it appeared before the April 18, 1983 bombing.
Photo courtesy Marine Security Guard School / U.S. Marines in Lebanon 1982-1984
History and Museums Division, Headquarters, U.S.M.C., Washington, D.C.

His personal feelings about everything he experienced in his life up to this point vanished at that moment. His immediate thought after recording the transmission in the log was, *We are about to go to war, and I am in the thick of what is about to happen.* Fear welled up inside him, but it wasn't a cowardice type of fear. It was different, sort of like a reverential fear and respect for human life. He now faced the startling reality of death and how one can lose their life in an instant. He strove with all that was in him to be strong, but he was still not comfortable with the whole environment on board the *Guadalcanal.* He now faced several battles: (1) working with a crew that appeared to be at odds with each other and (2) death and mayhem ashore. While on watch on the flag bridge that day, he looked up to heaven and had one question, only one question: "Why! Why am I here, and why am I recording this?"

Needless to say, he got no answer. He would come to believe one day that God was taking him through the course of life prescribed just for him. All that he thought he knew and all that he understood up to this point in his life was only grade school events in comparison to what was happening then. The Master of Heaven was training

Sailor in his own way to fortify the belief of Sailor's faith and developing in him a soldier spirit. While many souls were lost during the entire Multinational Peacekeeping Force in Beirut, Lebanon, Sailor was spared. Many times, he wanted to know why his life was spared. It was not until the writing of these events in his life that he began to get a glimpse of why his life was spared. Sailor's life since then has been a jigsaw puzzle. A series of ups and downs and uncertainties that he now understands to have been hurdles strategically placed in his way by the enemy of his faith. Other events were intentionally orchestrated by God himself. He was not clear on many occasion which god was doing what in his life and who was to credit for him falling or credit for him standing. Those days in the life of Sailor was an unexplainable labyrinth of confusion and frustration coupled with a good degree of immaturity? What a recipe and combination for sure death. But death was not victorious over Sailor, though present and willing and able to sink its venomous fangs into the heart of Sailor, for some reason death did not prevail over his life then.

Sailor had recorded the transmission accurately and transmitted clearly. The US American Embassy in Beirut, Lebanon, had just been bombed by Islamic radicals and several US American and Lebanese civilians were dead. The thought entered his mind, *This is it! This is what it's all about! This is why I joined the navy over eight years ago.*

An aerial view of the American Embassy as heavy cranes continue to remove rubble from the upper floors on 21 April, 1983, following the terrorist bombing three days earlier.

Photo courtesy of Claude Salhani / U.S. Marines in Lebanon 1982-1984 History and Museums Division, Headquarters, U.S.M.C., Washington, D.C.

His first four years saw nothing but peace, pleasure, and traveling. His remainder years would be void of peace but still some traveling. "This is why I joined the navy, and I have to keep telling myself that." Sailor had to come to grips about what just happened and how he was directly involved in the recording, visual sight and rescuing efforts of severely injured and dead civilians and marines from the cowardice act of terrorism.

Bodies of Death / Both Civilian and Military

One of the strangest feelings occurred after he was relieved from duty on the bridge, he immediately made his way down to the hanger deck where choppers where hurling in the wounded and lifeless within seconds of each flight. He witnessed the severely injured to the ones who had lost their lives all in an effort of keeping the peace in a Lebanese country. He witnessed service members who had been wrapped in field dressings due to dismembered body parts. He heard the moans and the pain of those rocked by the explosion of a senseless terrorist attack. The questions in his mind were absolutely unanswerable that day. He could not figure out his specific role in all this even though he was a member of the armed forces. One of the most pressing thoughts on his mind in those days was missing the opportunity to preach the Bible in a pulpit. Blinded by his own insecurities and selfish emotions he failed to realize that Beirut, Lebanon, was a time when God was preaching to him. Sailor just did not understand the message from God. The life of a true man that loves the Most High is a life tested by the senseless and seemingly unfair acts that happen every day. After a man, or a woman, has endured the deepest and almost life crushing battle against their soul, preaching graduates from the pulpit to the field of reality. Sailor would not realize that his graduation day was years later, even in the midst of the spirit of death among bodies of death.

The USS *Guadalcanal* (LPH-7) would not be the same from that day forward. Everyone on board the ship that day was on pins and needles. A new element of frustration and stress were forcefully added upon the heart and soul of every crewmember. The glitzy type of advertising about the armed forces to woo young people into its service is not always pretty in actuality. Nor is the chain of command always sensible or humanitarian in the protection of their own troops. It was not clear to Sailor until Beirut, Lebanon, when he began to realize the unjust cause and objective of the central powers that run the armed forces. The military of the United States of America perhaps at one time, during the revolutionary and maybe the civil war, served a noble purpose. The military from the days of Vietnam through Beirut and Desert Storm serves a wicked political purpose bolstered by the armed forces ruling powers in Washington, DC. Politicians serve their own political interest to fill their portfolio for reelections. Like Casper Weinberger demonstrated how much he cared by not wanting to retaliate against the terrorist who struck an extremely damaging blow against the United States Marines in Beirut, Lebanon. Sailor believed the United States Military had no right or business interfering with the Lebanese civil war. International intervention during the civil war fought in the United States in the 1800s was debated between the United Kingdom and France, but neither assisted. Other than a few immigrants who fought in the Union Army, essentially, America was on her own, let alone England of which America finds its origin. What philosophical thinking or political interests impresses upon the mind of politicians that take American troops into other countries demanding democracy of those countries? Sailor learned while in boot camp that the one objective of the armed forces was to protect and defend the shores of America in the air, land, and sea. Beirut, Lebanon, and every Arabian country are not the shores of America. World War II involving Germany with Adolf Hitler was justified because Hitler's objective was to exterminate communism in Russia, rule Europe and make his way west to America. As funny as that sounds "rule the world," Adolf Hitler embraced the belief of "ruling" and aggressively demonstrated his belief by invasion after invasion. When war broke out in Europe involving England and then the United States, the entire world was at war. This war was the survival of so-called free countries and democratic societies at the ideals of a world-class terrorist, Adolf Hitler.

Beirut, Lebanon, including Desert Storm, was the quintessential acts of American politics. Neither the Lebanese war involving the Peacekeeping Force or the Middle East war involving the United Nations and England was a justified war according to the mission and objective of the United States Armed Forces. When Sailor was in Beirut defending his country, how so? How was he defending the shores of America in the midst of the Mediterranean Sea, anchored off the coast of a Lebanese shore? Heavily involved in the Lebanese civil war involving Arab people and Israeli people that have been at war since the days of the Bible. How was his involvement and the senseless loss of lives of his comrades fulfilling the philosophy of the American military? Don't get Sailor wrong. He is all for the armed forces and certainly for the residual benefits once served. But Sailor was against the use of the armed forces in conflicts, campaigns, and wars that do not fulfill what they taught him as a recruit—Defend America! Fight for your country, so on and so forth. Sailor concluded that his time served in Beirut, Lebanon, was the Master's way of teaching him the deep-rooted wickedness of the ruling politicians of the world. The brass of the military both for political interest and land interest place well-meaning service men and women in situations destined to fail. It is the politicians and military brass form of battle glory and recognition of fallen soldiers, sailors airmen and marines. Those 241 lives and countless others since the days of Beirut Lebanon did *not* have to happen! Beirut, Lebanon, was not America's war! It was not America's shores. While the bullying and territorial disputes and religious fervor that foster the conflicts in the Middle East are certainly not condoned, the fact remains, they are not America's direct military involvement. At best, the Middle Eastern issues need to be fought by think tanks and political scholars who hold advanced degrees in conflict resolution and hostile takeovers. They fight them anyway from their plush offices in Washington and New York by committing troops to die for them. To commission the United States Armed Forces to go and fight, or show a "strong" military presence only incites the aggressor.

The bodies of death Sailor witnessed on that day in April 1983 was the testimony of the leaders of America from Casper Weinberger to President Ronald Reagan, who could now say these men and women died with honor. But the honor is all theirs and not the men and women who died. If you could ask anyone of the people who died in Beirut or Vietnam, for that matter, how honorable they feel in death, they probably would say "for that cause, it wasn't worth it." Selfish politicians and brainwashed loved ones like to memorialize fallen soldiers, sailors, airmen, and marines. But Sailor is confident that his comrades who died would undoubtedly feel their death was not honorable and their deaths only served the agenda of the White House in Washington, DC.

The bombing of the US Embassy in Beirut that day marked the great unpredictable events that would follow. The remainder of Sailor's tour of duty on station anchored off the coast of Beirut, Lebanon, would involve cleanup of debris and identification of the dead and wounded. Tensions on board ship and land would rise to a life-threatening level. Racism would raise its ugly head through senior officers and cover-up and denial would be the standard operating procedures. Emergency teams and rescue teams worked late into the night only to rise at the crack of dawn to resume operations. The cowardice act of terrorism on the American Embassy in Beirut, Lebanon, would feel the effects of its evil desire for decades to come. The loss of life on the unsuspecting souls from eight stories high was just the beginning of a string of terrorist explosions. But one day in the near future, the same pain and despicable disrespect for human life would come alive on American shores. Little did most Americans know or realize that in those days while deep in the Middle East on board ship, Sailor foresaw a time when these acts would rock the very shores of the coveted red white and blue; the United States of America. All of America on that destined date of the beginning of its fall would stand in unbelievable gasp. Preachers and prophet liars would use Bible to justify the terrorists strike against the United States. America would be likened as ancient Babylon and the predictions in the book of Revelation would be used to attempt to open the eyes of the sleepy.

> And the great city was divided into three parts, and the cities of the nation's fell: and great Babylon came in remembrance before God, to give unto her the cup of the wine of the fierceness of his wrath.
>
> Standing afar off for the fear of her torment, saying, Alas, alas, that great city Babylon, that mighty city! For in one hour is thy judgment come. (Rev. 16:19; 18:10)

It would be decades later when the man of the Sermon would realize the magnitude of what took place. All the Christian religious prophet liars have demonstrated themselves to be clueless and at a loss for an explanation. So in typical fashion, they find Bible verses to explain the terror and show reason for terrorist acts. Fundamentally speaking, they all fail to realize the centuries of unrest in the Middle East, a land marked by the Most High and a national struggle that predates everyone alive today. This would be the conclusion and understanding of Sailor upon the birth of the man of the Sermon.

17

THE AIR TOWER

Amphibious Squadron Two was an operational administrative command typically identified as flagstaff. The title of the commanding officer was commodore. The rank of the commodore was a full bird captain. He was not a rear admiral or two-star. Phibron Two was were generally known as flagstaff. The commodore was in charge of the Mediterranean Amphibious Readiness Group (MARG) on station in Beirut. The flagship at the time was the USS *Guadalcanal* (LPH-7). Flagstaff enjoyed certain privileges that ships company did not have. For instance, when standing in line for chow, flagstaff personnel had head-of-the-line privileges, regardless of rank. That was a privilege Sailor rarely exercised. At this point in his career, he was not about to explain or get into an argument with senior crew members about his privileges to jump them in line. Standing watch on the shores of Beirut, Lebanon, seemed to Sailor to be outside of flag staff's privileged area. It really did not make sense to Sailor why they were tasked with standing watch on shore without any formal training and restricted from bearing arms. The staff stood watch on a rotational basis armed with nothing but a white web duty belt, not even a Billy club. The duty included logging events in the logbook, date, time, and event. Sailor felt like they were a dispensable live commodity to have on record that we kept records while on duty as a part of the Multinational Peacekeeping Force.

Sailor's experience with the air tower was a one-day, one-and-done duty experience. Not because of any shortcomings or inexperience on his part. But largely due to the circumstances and nature of the duty the MARG was assigned to. The memory of his duty in the air tower has blurred over the years and perhaps because it did not impact as greatly as other events during that era. Nonetheless, Sailor can still see in his mind's eye the tower and having gone inside to perform his duty. This particular day was a gorgeous day, a nice sunny warm day. Pretty much that entire week was like a gorgeous summer day. Beirut, Lebanon, is a tropical land. But the serine environment and unpredictable terrorist bombings going on in that city were like dark menacing clouds hovering over the land. The stench of racism revealed its ugly head when Sailor discovered the only people standing watch in the tower were 1, 2, 3, 4, and 5 black squadron men. There was one white guy (E5), who stood watch in the tower, but it seemed all black men assigned to Amphibious Squadron Two had to stand watch in the doomed tower. The squadron was composed of five blacks and about twenty-five white men, and only one white man stood watch in the tower. Coincidence, RHIP (rank has its privileges), or was it pure racism? Sailor was not sure at the time, but it seemed odd to him that the black men appeared to be targeted to go ashore and perform the duty of standing watch in one of the most unstable regions of the world. The one white guy who stood watch didn't mind because he was "fighting for his country." He was pro-military and trying to get promoted. His gung ho was his justification to do whatever his uncle wanted, Uncle Sam. But for Sailor and the other brothers, it was either go ashore and assume the watch or refuse, like some of the white petty officers did. Had any black man refused as their white counterparts did, they would have been written up and definitely served brig time for refusal to perform their duty as a navy sailor. The commodore and the general onshore undoubtedly knew of the plot to destroy the air tower so they placed their most expendable men in harm's way. Terrorist acts would strike again and it seems with a vengeance. Terrorism was a constant nuisance in the mind of Sailor and seemingly had no resolution from the Multinational Peacekeeping Force. Beirut, Lebanon, was not an all-out military conflict, it was a Multinational Peacekeeping Force, the emphasis being on keeping peace. The rhetoric of keeping peace was one of the most careless decisions of Washington politics that cost the lives of 241 marines. Peace was the justification for the marines not loading their weapons. The harm's way they were placed in harbored an alternative, ungodly, wicked motive—to expend the least expendable crewmembers.

Standing Watch, Waiting for Death

At this point in Sailor's military career and tour of duty with Phibron Two embarked on board the USS *Guadalcanal* (LPH-7), he had pretty much lost all sensible reason. He challenged everything and questioned everybody about the goings-on while in Beirut. He consistently and daily encountered conflict after conflict involving personalities, while desperately attempting to respect his senior officers and his supervisor. Giving that respect to the officers and men appointed over him was the most difficult thing in all his life. Nothing has ever compared to the environment or backstabbing since those days. His brief career with the United States Post Office had minor similar experiences. But those experiences with the post office still did not compete with the mayhem and anger and conspiracy that flourished onboard the USS *Guadalcanal* (LPH-7), while off the coast of Beirut, Lebanon. The entire ninety-day anchor in the waters of Beirut was a pure hellish experience in the midst of confusion and unclear mission. That being said, he remembers YN2 saying to him, "Yeah, and we got to stand watch at the tower airport."

Sailor said to him, "Where on land in Beirut?"

"Where else do you think?"

"What are we watching for?"

"Hell, we don't have a weapon or a walkie-talkie. We have this shit beat up piece of phone to contact someone. By the time they respond and answer our call, you'll be dead, man! Do you hear me? You'll be dead!"

From the very first day of reporting to Phibron Two, it seemed nothing was going right for Sailor. Everyone he met in his squadron appeared to be unbelievably negative. It appeared YN2 had nothing to say positive. The brief intervention during the conflict with YN1 was the only time Sailor remember anything positive coming out of YN2's mouth. Sailor was discouraged, depressed, and angry and could not stand being in the midst of an ocean of fear and negativism. Now YN2 is telling him there is a 90 percent chance of him getting blown up and becoming a military sacrificial lamb. The tour of duty with Amphibious Squadron Two may have been easily acceptable in his heart had he not been attacked and overwhelmed by a barrage of fear. In those days he was a distressful person. Everyday was a day of uncertainty if he would live or die. Each event kept him in a state of dismay. He was now being told by the one brother he was attempting to get to know that death may be right around the corner for him. Even with the recent bombing of the American embassy, it still had not registered in Sailor's mind the reality of possibly losing his life in Beirut. Although the overwhelming negative thinking and unrelenting spirit of fear had long before seized his mind and captivated his spirit, it was an unbelievable battle wrestling with the spirit of death. There were times when laying in his bunk, there appeared to be a heavyweight on top of him. It felt like there were times when he could not lift himself out of the bunk, like he was being weighed down by something, which later on he concluded was the manifestation and presence of the spirit of death. Death seemed to prevail on board that ship. Sailor began following the news and listening to the updates every day. He was talking fearful and embracing fear as though he had no other choice. He studied images of Aiyatolo Komeny almost every day. He imagined what it must have been like for the American hostages in Iran for 444 days. He worried deeply that he may become a hostage while standing watch. Too much going on to fast with little time to sort out his thoughts. And now that he had to go ashore and stand watch was the ultimate worry god in his soul. If his skeletal and spirit could have shown through his flesh, one would have noticed his entire bodily form unstable without mercy. Oh, on the outside, he had a stern look on his face and walked with a sense of confidence, but even his walk slowly became slumberous. But on the inside, he worshipped the forceful spirit of fear as his god. Inside the tower reminded him of an old abandoned building that maybe he's seen in an Alfred Hitchcock movie. The equipment was old and the walls were bare, and the windows were stained with mildew and who knows what else. He remembers seeing other men in the tower with him, but he cannot make out their faces. They were from the Multinational Peacekeeping Force, maybe French or from the United Nations. Whoever they were did not matter to Sailor; in fact, they almost did not exist he was so spaced out. One of them was giving Sailor brief instructions on how to operate the emergency phone while the others were making their way down the steps to leave. He was not left alone in the tower, but he does not remember if YN2 was there with him or the French soldier. At any rate, the time spent there was one of the longest four-hour duty ever served in the navy. The watch was uneventful. Nothing happened, *nothing* at all! Idle is no more than an ingredient for Satan to plague your mind with foolish faithless thoughts. He stood a frustrating four-hour watch, with unanswered questions, reminiscing of home, trying to sort out the events over the past few days. His spirit had sunk deathly low into the pit of despair, and he actually was hoping something devastating would happen while he was on watch. He anticipated, sort of expected and desired the tower to be struck with a mortar or bomb explosion. His awareness was not sharp during those four hours, but he would drift in and out of making radio checks to maintain communication with the ship. He even took time to write his wife a letter, of which he held on to long after he returned home, and she showed him the letters he wrote to her. Time crept along slower than a snail's pace, and there were times when it was eerily quiet, so quiet that Sailor expected to hear a loud explosion of something. He hoped they would blow the tower to smithereens with him inside. He truly and actually desired and wanted to die. He was absolutely fed up with all the shit he experienced and at his wit's end with the United States Navy. He panted, worried, thought about his horrible witness as a Christian. That feeling he was having on the boat while lying in his bunk seemed to be the strongest while in the tower, and he was wide awake. All his mind, soul, and spirit had become what he describes as a sheep waiting to be slaughtered. He literally counted down the seconds that his watch would be over. Defenseless, on watch with another man of a French dialect that he could not fluently communicate with. Waiting, worrying, hoping, and welcoming death filled the last few hours of his watch. Toward the end of his watch, void of any activity, locked in the deep quiet of nothingness with a black canvas of death encircling him. Like a hot geyser, he burst into tears. His entire body violently shook as the tears of confusion rushed down his face wearing the most intense look of all his life. No sooner had he begun crying than he heard the sound of a chopper approaching. He looked at his wristwatch out of sheer frustration and pounded on the table and looked at his wristwatch once more. His uneventful four-hour watch had come to an end, and he was about to be relieved. Frustrated, because he had no control over the fact that he was ordered to stand watch. Frustrated, because nothing happened on watch, like an explosion or something—anything to take his mind off everything. But he had to get himself together and stop crying. He took the tail end of his shirt, pulled it out of his pants, and began vigorously wiping the tears away. He could not be seen crying while on watch. He had to maintain his outward "manly man" look while inwardly nursing his personal fears and worries. What seemed like seconds later, his relief was walking up the steps inside the tower, the one white guy in the squadron who was enjoying all the action in Beirut. His relief was gung ho, and

Sailor had no problem turning over the white web belt to his relief so he could leave the tower of death.

His time had come to return to the ship on board the loud, uncertain, flying coffin of death, Marine CH46. He marked time by double-timing to the helo. He was making every attempt to psychologically speed up time so the helo did not have to wait for him. Onboard the helo, strapped in with protective gear and a life vest, the CH-46 took flight, and while the tower was still in sight, an explosion took place on the ground a little distance from the tower. The explosion did not hit the tower or rock the tower, but it rocked every fiber of being inside the soul of Sailor. He turned his head in quick succession, trying to locate where the explosion occurred. He wanted so much for something like that to happen while he was on watch. In his mind, at least it would have speeded up time. *Why the hell didn't something explode when I was down there?* Kind of a stupid question, but it is difficult to translate what he felt during those days. Only brief words can describe what he was going through. The pilot of the helo appeared to be double-timing in flight as Sailor gazed out the window trying to ascertain where the explosion occurred. Pitching and yawing as if the pilot was attempting to avoid hostile radar on the ground, Sailor lost sight of the tower. Time spent in the tower and now flying back to the ship seemed to be brief, like a vapor that comes for a short time, then vanishes away. Everything in his life during those days was brief but entirely too long. Once back on board the ship and his watch was over he returned to his bunk, changed his clothes, laid in his bunk and turned toward the metal wall to somewhat barricade himself from others and resumed his tears of confusion. He cried softly for reasons he did not understand. Why he did not die and why the explosion after his watch was over? He really did not want to die but did not understand why the mercy and grace of God prevailed. Certainly, he lived in a daily situation where he welcomed death and death was present, but it did not happen, and though grateful, he was speechless as to why there was such grace and mercy toward him. In his mind, he deserved to die, but God saw fit, for his reasons alone, to preserve the life of Sailor.

The Devastation of the Tower

The next day when revile was called away, it was time to begin another episode of uncertainty and looming death. Sailor, at this point, had become familiar with the spirit of death, and at times he welcomed his enemy with open arms. He was beyond frustration in a situation and under circumstances he could not change or control. He was being tried beyond anything he thought God would allow. He had forgotten his Christianity and read his Bible every now and then. What he was about to learn next served as wakeup call number two. He had a meeting scheduled with the chaplain at the marine headquarters, which would account for wakeup call number one, but for now, he had to learn that he was not too good to be under the circumstances he was experiencing in the Middle East on board the *Guad*. He failed to realize that God had to teach him things about himself and about his relationship that only God could teach. Time to go to work. He made his way up to the administration office to begin another trying day on board the USS *Guadalcanal* (LPH-7). After getting somewhat of a good night's sleep after standing watch in the tower, rested, but still frustrated, he was ready to go to work. Stepping inside the office, he did not speak to anyone because most of the time they didn't speak back. Sailor had concluded, "What's the point trying to get these guys to accept me and what's the point trying to be positive when these guys are full of overpowering negativism." The irony of Sailor's memory is that he does not remember full days on board the *Guadalcanal*, but he remembers certain events and this one was about to reach down into the core of his spirit and wake him up almost in one call and shake the hell out of him. Yes, hell had entered his soul, and hell was about to be discharged from his thinking and released from his human emotions.

Most of the day had gone by, and YN2 and YN1 were talking. Sailor was not even part of the conversation, but because of the small size of the work space, you could not help but hear everyone's conversation. YN2 said, in the most casual manner, "Yeah, they blew that tower up last night, they shot the hell out of that thing."

Sailor's heart began racing, and he chimed in, "Did you just say they blew up the air tower?"

"Yeah, man, they blew the shit out of that thing. You better be glad you were not in there. You wouldn't be here today asking me questions."

"But I was in there just yesterday standing watch."

"Hell, then you are one lucky son of a bitch because they are scraping dead bodies from that place even now."

Sailor didn't know whether to feel grateful, thankful, afraid or sad. It would seem the explosion that took place as the chopper was getting airborne was meant for the tower. He had *just* been relieved from an uneventful four-hour watch in that very tower. He was in a deep pity party while he was on watch and hoping, kind of expecting they would blow up the tower. Well, they did blow it up, but Sailor was not in it.

YN2 then responded by saying, "Yeah, you don't have to worry about standing watch there. That tower is gone."

Both he and YN1 started laughing like brothers quite often do, bustin' and making fun. YN1 then snickered and said something to the effect, "Yeah, if Sweeney was in there, he probably would have shit his pants right when the mortars hit."

They both laughed like that was the funniest thing that could be said. Sailor, not fully appreciative of the grace of God, asked YN1, "What did you say? You always have something smart mouth to say, mumbling under your breath."

YN1 had to be in his mid to late forties. Sailor did not know and he never asked, but you could tell he was not a twenty- or thirty-year-old man. He may have even been in his fifties. This is what made the entire tour of duty while YN1 was onboard more frustrating because Sailor was not dealing with young boys or even twenty-year-old men. These were full-grown adult men snickering, making fun, and intimidating beyond anything Sailor had ever known in his lifetime.

YN1 replied, "Nothing, man, nothing! Just having fun. You can't take this stuff too seriously. Don't take things so personally."

Sailor blurted out, "Forget you, you dick."

YN1 obviously did not like Sailor's remark and said, "All right now, let's keep it cool."

"Uh-huh, but it's all right for you to make fun and name call, but you want to keep it cool when it's thrown back in your face?"

"All right, Sweeney, all right."

"See what I'm saying? You are a *dick*!"

"Okay, Petty Officer Sailor, that's enough." All the while YN2 was laughing to the point his eyes filled with tears and he was wiping the tears from his eyes. The remainder of that week was perhaps one of the most intensified untrustworthy and disrespectful weeks of the entire tour of duty. Sailor did not remember complete days on board the *Guadalcanal*, but he does remember the destruction of the tower and YN2 and YN1 making a joke out of it. Their lazy, unconcerned attitude helped to deepen Sailor's depressed and frustrating day for the entire week. Both of those brothers were extreme nemesis to Sailor and antagonized him endlessly in a joking way. On one hand, there were times when Sailor and YN2 communicated on a semi-intelligent level. But when YN1 was around, YN2 would inevitably appear to be bosom buddies with the ultimate antagonist to all the brothers in the office. It was not until the destruction of the tower that Sailor began to really look inside his own heart. There were two other brothers in the squadron that Sailor has not said much about up until this point. Both brothers were an encouragement to Sailor in ways they have never known. Their living testimony convicted the wickedness that was manifesting from the heart of Sailor. It was they, the younger brothers, whom Messiah used to minister to Sailor, without them ever saying a word.

The First and Last Sermon—on the Boat

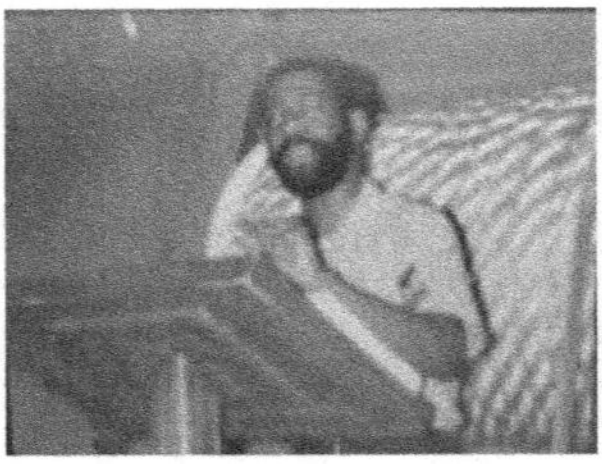

Humility, Sailor did not know what that really meant until he discovered how high minded he really was. Beirut was tailor-made for Sailor by the God of heaven. He did not see, nor did he understand then how the events in Beirut fit his soul to a tee. It would not be until months, even years later, that he would begin to understand why the trying times were especially tailor-made for him. But until that time arrived when he would begin to understand the why and wherefore of his time in Beirut, Lebanon, the emotional roller coaster ride continued. Sailor would be up and down, parallel to the ground and again find himself down and out inside a pity party of his own design. Now these two Christian brothers, young brothers, brother Austin, and brother Van F. had almost an innocent and definitely humble spirit. Sailor attributed their innocence to youthfulness and fairly new in the navy. Nevertheless, they were easy to entreat. They were avid readers of the Bible and would ask questions every now and again of certain verses in the Bible. Sailor sensed they had a genuine and honest desire to know the truth of Scripture and more importantly, a genuineness to live godly lives. Sailor slept in the middle bunk of a three-tier bunk bed. Sailor would become very angry with YN1 and other senior petty officers when he learned of those young brothers being treated wrongly or disrespected in any way. Nonetheless, the Messiah sustained those two godly young men and their lives would become an inspiration to Sailor. Amid all the personal hell Sailor was experiencing, God had a "ram in the bush," of the battle for the soul of men during that time. Sailor did realize that God could keep them young brothers with a sound mind far greater than any way that he tried to help them.

Brother Van F. slept on the bottom bunk at the time, and Sailor remembers waking up one morning hearing a song that sounded heavenly and even to this day the song resonates in his spirit. Brother Van was playing a tape by the Winans, and it was Sailor's very first time hearing of them. The song that he was playing was, "The Question Is." Sailor heard the song in his spirit. He was sleep and heard the song as if God was asking him a question. And when he awoke, the question was still being asked to Sailor. God was asking him a question; he was talking to Sailor's spirit with that song. It was the most melodious, glorious song he could have ever heard while in Beirut, Lebanon. Brother Van F. and Brother Austin were placed in Sailor's life at a time and manner that only God could have orchestrated. The time had come and gone that Sailor needed to really get himself together. He didn't know where to start because he felt his actions were justified in what appeared to be mass confusion. Should he repent for his sinful actions over the years and forget every claiming to be a minister? Should he go to YN1 and ask his forgiveness for disrespecting him and his rank? Should he ask the young brothers to forgive him for not being a living witness of Christianity? He decided that he needed to do all of them. At some point, he spoke with YN1 and asked his forgiveness, and YN1 mumbled something under his breath like, "Yeah, yeah, just remember, you are a second class petty officer and these young boys are watching you."

Sailor wanted to respond by saying something like, "Yeah, and you are the supervisor and senior leading petty officer. They're watching you also."

But Sailor humbled himself and spoke with YN1, not to flare up again and act a fool and idiot, but he spoke with YN1 to make things right with him and with God. YN1 was not easily approachable, and Sailor kind of accepted him as he was, frustrated, apprehensive, and angry. After a few more mild run-ins with him, Sailor learned how to take YN1 in stride, sort of what YN2 said earlier on. But actually, Sailor and YN1 were destined to meet, and their meeting would leave Sailor absolutely speechless and without a thought of any kind. One of the most humbling experiences of Sailor's life was the meeting that could have only been orchestrated by God. The young Christian brothers, both Van F. and Austin, are the two witnesses the Lord used to help steer Sailor back on the right path. He spoke with YN1 and the two young Christian brothers and Sailor made the decision to stop calling himself a minister. Those three actions were the most pressing things on the heart of Sailor in those days. He felt all three actions were the right thing to do. Sailor was thrown into a pit of burning coals, and every move he made and every word that came out of his mouth was hell-bent and hell bound. Having taken the steps he thought was right, now he could begin to relax a little and stop being offended and angry over every battle he had to face. He read his Bible *only* for personal edification. He told everyone that he spoke with to call him either Sailor or Petty Officer Sailor. He had done away with the title pastor or minister or preacher and simply wanted to be known as just another sailor on board. He was beginning to feel a sense of happiness because he no longer carried the burden and impression of Mr. Perfect who knew the Bible. He was free to be just another guy on board the ship going through the same stuff everybody else was going through. It began to dawn upon his thinking that he was not special, and there was no reason he should not be in Beirut, Lebanon, on board the USS *Guadalcanal* (LPH-7). He also told the young brothers they could call him by his first name, both of them continued to demonstrate respect and call him petty officer sailor. Every now and then, they would call Sailor by his first name, and when they called him by his first name, they would chuckle. They knew it wasn't right, and it didn't sound right. But at Sailor's request, they both made small attempts to honor his request by addressing him by his first name.

One day during a Bible study, these brothers were having, as Austin related to Sailor, the conversation came up about having a church service, sort of a revival. Sailor's name was mentioned, and he does not know by whom and why God would even have those brothers think about him. Sailor's testimony as a preacher was not worth the precious time to enter anyone's thoughts. His life at that time was worse than a torn-up sheet of paper into small unrecognizable pieces. Why would those sincere innocent youthful godly men want any part of Sailor? Why? Nonetheless, he can only surmise that from their perspective he had identified himself to them early on upon his arrival that he was a minister of the Gospel. For some stupid, ignorant, novice reason of his, he thought telling people he was a minister meant something. What it exposed Sailor to was the tremendous onslaught from the powers of darkness that he did not expect, nor was he in any way prepared for them. Brother Austin came to Sailor and very humbly and respectfully said, "Brother Sailor, we are planning a revival, and we need a man of God to bring the Word." Most of the young brothers were very junior to Sailor in rank. A few of them were equal to the rank of Sailor, but none higher in rank. So whatever would be the outcome of this so-called revival would fall on the shoulders of Sailor as the principal speaker. Sailor knew he was not ready for that type of backlash and inevitable persecution that would come. He was the ranking leader, and had he accepted the invitation, any persecution afterward would be his! He sort of faintly smiled and looked at brother Austin with disbelief that God would even let those brothers ask him something like that. He was in no position and was not worthy in any way to even read a scripture. But Austin stood there smiling from ear to ear with bated breath, expecting an answer. Austin could tell that Sailor was very hesitant, and he then said, "Pray about it, brother, and let me know by tomorrow!" He chuckled and walked away humming a Gospel tune. Brother Austin was laid back like that every time Sailor seen him, Brother Austin walked around almost without a care in the world. Brother Austin was a good brother to be around. Sailor found himself just wanting to be around him but had to maintain his rank and military bearing around him and the other young brothers. Little did Brother Austin know that Sailor drew off his humble godly spirit. Sailor needed Austin in his life at that time. Austin never tried to verbally teach Sailor anything, but he was always teaching Sailor by his humility and smile and godly spirit. Messiah, in his way, used Austin's spirit to compel Sailor to go to him and ask the question, "Brother Austin, when will the service be? And yes, I will bring the Word."

"Yes, yes, yes, hallelujah!" Austin said.

That brother was so happy, like he had won a million dollars. Sailor had committed himself whether he wanted to be or not, and he really did not want to. But the Scripture of Truth rang in his soul of the prophet Jeremiah when he said, "Then I said, I will not make mention of him, nor speak any more in his name. But his word was in mine heart as a burning fire shut up in my bones, and I was weary with forbearing, and I could not stay." (Jer. 20:9).

If the things Sailor endured so far were not necessarily directed at him, once he would preach the Word of God on a naval vessel, anchored off the coast of Beirut, Lebanon, future trials would have his name personally plastered on it. Days before the Sunday Night Live service, as it was being promoted by Brother Austin and whoever was on the "revival" committee, Sailor prayed and prayed and prayed for forgiveness of his wretched soul. There was even a small hope that something would happen to cancel the service, relieving him of the responsibility to preach the Bible to hungry souls on board a United States naval warship.

Now Is the Day of Salvation

It seemed like almost overnight from the time he checked on board the *Guadalcanal* and meeting YN1, to now, about to crack open the Bible and preach, was a dream, within a dream. The church service was about to go down, God did not stop it and Sailor was now committed to preach. What? he thought. On board the USS *Guadalcanal* (LPH-7) for Sunday Night Live on May 15, 1983 Sailor preached for about one hour. The ship's chaplain was there and the administrative chief petty officer was there and about thirty enlisted men, sailors, and marines. One of the greatest milestones in the life of Sailor was to preach on board a United States naval warship. He was a twenty-five-year-old sailor about to unleash specific devils of persecution that would come his way. The Sunday Night Live service started off nicely, with Brother Todd singing a song invoking the presence of the Almighty. The anticipation of that service and the actual service did not take much invoking of the spirit of God. The brothers on board that ship were thirsty for the spiritual food that comes from heaven. Sailor was not sure that he was the right one to serve the meal. These guys were on fire for and about the truth of God's Word. All Sailor could see was tripping and stumbling over his words to a group of sailors and marines who could not wait to partake of heaven's meal. Brother Todd was the same rank as Sailor and was also a preacher. Sailor did not question why they did not ask Brother Todd to speak instead of him. Brother Todd had been on board the ship as ship's company way longer than Sailor arrived. When Brother Todd was finished singing, the next voice the sailors and marines would hear was that of the speaker. Sailor was nervous and full of apprehension. He felt he failed to fit the bill to be the one speaking the Word of God. For all he knew, anyone of the brothers at that church service could have brought the Word. Sailor could have sat among the "congregation" and received. Nonetheless, he was the speaker, and the time had come for him to step forth hoping God would not smite him or strike him down. Sailor felt most unworthy because he had esteemed himself very high and had allowed his tongue to get away from him. When the time came to speak, he could not see the grace of God had it been personified in front of his face.

Brother Todd sang, "The world is tossing me like a ship upon the sea…in the midst of persecution, stand by me. Thou who rescued Paul and Silas, stand by me. When I'm growing old and feeble, stand by me. When my life becomes a burden, and I'm nearing chilly Jordon, Oh thou lily of the valley, stand by me." You could hear the brothers in the background saying, "Yes, yes, thank you, Jesus, praise the Lord."

Sailor was becoming more apprehensive by the second. All these sailors and marines and the chaplain and a chief petty officer. Sailor perceived the chief petty officer as the religious monitor to see what would be done and what would be said at the church service on board the *Guadalcanal.* The surroundings and fearful thoughts welling up in Sailor's mind was making him begin to sweat. At the time of presenting the Word, his thoughts were, *I can't do this, I can't do this. I need to repent of my own sins.*

He sincerely felt he did not repent enough of his actions and his thoughts and his foul mouth. The closer the time came for Sailor to stand up and begin speaking, the more he felt weighted down in the chair and he could not get up to leave and he was not going to get up to speak. Sailor was locked in the time of his past, unable to get up and leave and afraid to stand up and speak. Before he could make a decision to do one or the other, Brother Hamilton introduced Sailor and said, "Here is Minister Sailor to bring us God's Holy Word."

Why did he have to say "Holy Word"?

Sailor was deeply concerned and positively unworthy in his carnal mind. He had never felt this type of unworthiness in all of his life? He could not forgive himself of the way he had been acting and carrying on like some out of control crazy sailor. Cussing, wanting to fight and hurt someone, anyone. Not asking God to forgive him but becoming more enraged by the second. And now he was standing before thirty-something hungry, sincere, Bible-carrying uncompromising sailors and marines in God's army on board the USS *Guadalcanal* (LPH-7). He thought he was going to freeze up as he had witnessed of different ones back home who were urged to preach by older so-called "missionaries." He has seen person after person, young and old get up on the stage in a church and stand there looking out at the audience while the "missionary" was rubbing their back, saying something like "bless 'em, Lord, bless 'em." Sailor did not want any kind of "bless 'em" from the brothers had he froze up. He would have just categorically said, "I can't do this—I need prayer myself."

Can't really say what or who urged him on, but after he was introduced by Brother Hamilton, he stood up at his place and begin to comment on Brother Todd's song. With full doubt, he proceeded to talk about what he thought was mundane stuff in a low voice failing to annunciate and pronounce his words. He was sort of trying to rush and hurry up and sit down. But it seemed with every word he spoke those brothers were receiving as cool raindrops falling upon every soul. They had no umbrellas up they were fully exposed and got showered upon…with what? Sailor couldn't tell because he did not see himself as a cistern or an encourager. For Sailor, over his lifetime of speaking the Word of God when he felt hopeless and unworthy to speak the hearers where rejoicing beyond what he could understand. Reminiscing in his mind of that day, Sailor cannot recall anything to him worth rejoicing over. But to the sailors and marines onboard in the foscle, they were hearing something Sailor was not. At the beginning of the message, he felt that he was rambling on not really making a point or focusing on any specific truth. In his mind, the preaching was pure unrefined, amateurish speaking, but what he heard they did not hear. And what they heard Sailor did not hear. The entire event was unexplainable to Sailor for day in and day out for years. Is it possible that when speaking under the true unction God somehow intervenes? When a man has fallen to his lowest, untrustworthy state but continues on in blind uncharted faith that God actually causes each person to hear what he wants them to hear? It took Sailor about fifteen minutes into the message that he began to realize how these guys were drinking each word into their spirit like a flowing fountain of clear spring water. They began yelling out things like "Amen! Preach it, brother! Amen, amen!"

Almost like they were drawing out of Sailor something he was clueless that could possibly be inside him. What Word? What message? What speaking? He was almost like a controlled lifeless body being given what to say in his own limited command of the English language. The crescendo of this preaching is when he told them what he would be talking about today, "Now is the day of salvation!" There was an eruption of "amen and amen" and "yes and oh yeah"! Sailor could not get what these brothers were hearing and why such a seemingly elementary thought to any Christian who had been a Christian for some time, would excite these guys the way they were being excited. They continued on by responding with, "Ooooh! Go 'head, Brother! Preach it, preach it."

About thirty minutes into the message, Sailor had become somewhat rested in what was happening, and he gave in to whatever was going on inside of him and whatever those brothers were receiving. He let go of the condemnation he was feeling and buried the negativism and fear and worthlessness he had embraced over the past few weeks of arriving. He stomped to the deck of that boat the pity party he was reveling in and buried the hellish thoughts that plagued him since the island of Larnaca, Italy.

He did not feel completely satisfied or good about what was going on during the time of Sunday Night Live, but he strove to accept what was happening. As he was speaking, the thoughts were racing through his head, *Is the spirit of the Lord really speaking through me? Has God really overlooked my shortcomings and awful witness since arriving on board this naval vessel? Should I really continue on calling myself preaching the Word of God?*

The battle that was raging on inside his soul while speaking to those hungry, acceptant, spiritually needy brothers was a crash course from the God of his grace and mercy upon Sailor's soul. Sailor was done with "himself" and resolved to "himself" to become a regular, normal brother on board ship. He had insisted on being addressed simply as Petty Officer Sailor and not Brother, Minister, or Pastor. He fit the whole description of unworthiness in action, word, and thought. Though his heart's desire was to be true while speaking to those brothers, his soul was grieved at how quickly he became faithless and despairing over the circumstances. His present situation on board the USS *Guadalcanal* (LPH-7) had without mercy immensely overwhelmed him. Throughout the message, he found himself intermittently giving the invitation to come to the Lord. He repeatedly referred to the Word of the Lord in Matthew 11:28 when Jesus said, "Come unto me all ye that labour and are heavy laden, and I will give you rest."

Every time he quoted that Scripture, the brothers became electrified and moved with emotion in the Spirit. They kept saying "Amen, amen, amen! What a time to preach, what a message to give. For truly, if not ever again, the Lord spoke through Sailor at that time in his life when he felt absolutely unworthy to call himself a preacher and absolutely incapable to speak into the lives of men.

Time for Persecution

The Lord had taken over the lips of Sailor, and he was speaking about forty words per minute. He was speaking fast and rapidly that at many times he failed to annunciate, but it did not seem to matter to those men. Their response was a factor in urging him on to preach,

preach, preach, as they were saying. But he continued to wrestle in his own soul as to whether or not he really was preaching. But that Word, as God proclaimed through the prophet in the book of Isaiah 55:11, "So shall my word be that goeth forth out of my mouth: it shall not return unto me void." On that day, at that hour, in that place, onboard a United States Naval Vessel anchored in harm's way, souls gave their heart to the Son of God. He would eventually lose contact with many of those brothers since then, but the ones who cried out to Messiah for Salvation is the record that God keeps of them. The Bible says there is joy in the presence of the angels of God over one sinner that repents (Luke 15:10). So when that one brother among those brothers yelled out, "Messiah, save me!" heaven became joyous. His cry to the Lord sparked others to respond in kind. When Sailor heard that one brother yell out to Messiah for salvation, it became apparent to him the individual personal tests he went through over the past few weeks was from the pit of hell in an effort to silence him and destroy what testimony he may have developed. That Sunday Night Live service on board the USS *Guadalcanal* (LPH-7), anchored off the coast of Beirut, Lebanon, was the first and last time he spoke on board an American warship. It was a milestone in his life and an uncertain one in the beginning. But it turned out to be worth the trials and tribulations he had been experiencing since reporting to the command. But that was just the beginning of what would turn out to illicit direct and certain persecutions from the ranking officers, both enlisted and commissioned. From that day, the young brothers were all excited and full of overflowing zeal. He did not really hang out with them because of being the senior petty officer among them, and in his mind he had to maintain military bearing and leadership. They had a zeal to spread the Word of God on board the ship beyond what he had at the time. In his mind, he was attempting to exercise some wisdom knowing that they all were still members of the armed forces isolated onboard a naval vessel. Their mission was not to convert the ship's crew, although the thought was nice, the young brothers appeared to be trying to do just that. The Scripture came to my mind of the words of Messiah when he said, "Render therefore unto Caesar the things which are Caesar's, and unto God the things that are God's" (Matt. 22:21). He knew there would be some backlash if those young brothers continued on the path they were. But at the same time, he did not want to be the one to tell them to stop. He was new on board and had just experienced hell in his soul, then called upon to bring the Word of God, now what? Tell these brothers to stop spreading the truth of Scripture *just because* they were on a United States naval vessel? He thought to himself, *When does this roller coaster ride end?* Leadership comes with the responsibility of leading, but he did not feel up to the task to lead those young brothers away from spreading the Word of God, which required the wisdom of God to do so.

Nonetheless, one day the chaplain, a man about 6 feet 4'5" inches and appeared to weigh about 200 something pounds. He wasn't fat, just a big man, and could be intimidating looking to someone of Sailor's stature. The chaplain knocked on the administration door of where Sailor was working and called Sailor out into the passageway. "Petty Officer Sailor, you need to get these sailors under control."

"What are they doing, sir?" he asked.

"They are passing out tracks and trying to convert people of other faiths. This is not acceptable, Petty Officer Sailor!"

Initially, Sailor got angry but was able to maintain composure in the chaplain's presence. He thought, *Why is he confronting me about what they are doing? They don't work for me. They are brothers in the Lord that I met on board the ship. Why must I get them under control?*

And somehow or another Sailor mustered up the courage to respectfully ask the chaplain that question. "Sir, I've only been on board this ship for thirty days. I have only met these sailors since reporting on board. They do not work for me or report to me for any duty. What responsibility do I have to get them under control?"

"Because, Petty Officer Sailor, they look to you and look up to you as though you are their leader of sorts."

"But, sir, that's fine and all—"

"All nothing! I am telling you to get with them and explain to them the way things work around here. You are a member of the United States Navy, and they need to understand their priorities...and you also. Now take care of it, Petty Officer Sailor, do you understand?"

Unlike the incident on the Island of Larnaca with the lieutenant colonel, Sailor had regained a sense of respect since the tower destruction. He responded to the chaplain in a calm voice and said, "Sir, I will talk with the men."

"Fine, that's all I want you to do."

Immediately negative thoughts entered his mind like, *Why in the hell didn't he just ask me to look into the allegations and talk to the brothers?*

But he was able to disregard acting on those negative thoughts and respectfully complied with the chaplain's orders. The chaplain then, almost in an arrogant manner, walked away without a thank-you or any other response. Sailor knew then that he had now become the target of persecution involving the religion of Christianity versus the United States Navy. How do you approach and tell young brothers who were full of zeal to use discretion and wisdom in spreading the truth of the Gospel? These guys were already defensive and suspect of senior ranking petty officers and commissioned officers. Sailor is now the new kid on the block, so to speak, and have now been ordered to tell the young brothers, be careful about spreading the Gospel message. These brothers were young and strong, both mentally and physically. This was not going to be an easy task to accomplish by any means. Sailor somehow or another had to suggest to these young brothers that they have a little bit too much zeal under the circumstances. Uncle Sam does not appreciate them on his naval vessel preaching about Jesus Christ. This particular persecution and test was something Sailor neither desired nor wanted to endure. Leaving the ship to escape the task of talking to the brothers was no option. Where was he going to go, and what was he going to do? He was compelled to follow through with the chaplain's orders, *especially* after the chaplain heard Sailor share the Word of God. The test and persecution from the chaplain appeared to have a personal element involved. Sailor perceived the chaplain to be saying, "I want you to stop these guys from trying to do my job. I am the one to preach, convert, and console, not you young uneducated sailors." That was the perception of Sailor concerning the chaplain of whom Sailor never heard the chaplain share the Gospel message. The chaplain appeared to be more politically correct and wore his uniform with pride and military bearing. Nothing especially wrong with that but does personal pride and military bearing circumvent the Gospel message of Messiah? Sailor's thinking was he would have suggested a wiser manner in which the young brothers may have shared their faith instead of ordering him to "get them under control." He sought the wisdom of God to find a time to speak with the brothers in the most humble manner he knew. Having just preached onboard this naval vessel at Brother Austin's request, he did not want to be perceived as one of the petty officers "barking out orders and trying to tell them what to do." With courage and strength of mind, he spoke with Austin to the effect of only sharing your faith when you are not on duty. He was a couple of suggestions short of telling them to cease and desist, as the chaplain had suggested. Sailor's approach to Brother Austin was, "I'm not telling you guys to stop sharing the Gospel, but you must use godly wisdom, because '*they*,' big brother, is watching."

The young brothers continued sharing the Gospel message, despite Sailor's words to them, and they also began to address Sailor as Petty Officer Sailor instead of Sailor or Brother Sailor. Sailor knew there was a perceived change of view of him to the young brothers, but somehow or another they all made it through those times and remained brothers in the Lord, despite the "all up in your face" spirit of division that was attempting to come between them. It was the classic "world" system in the form of the United States Navy against believers in Christ applying pressure to conform and "watch yourself and your religious proselytizing.

They all continued on with brief times of prayer and extemporaneous Bible studies in the form of a single question that led to further discussion. Those were intense times of rightly dividing the word of truth and intense times of spiritual growth in ways Sailor could not see at the time. It would not be until years later, like most of the Beirut experience, that Sailor would see the relevancy of having spent time there. He has made attempt after attempt to contact some of those Brothers since those days and has been successful with staying in contact with two brothers. Never since then has he met a group of brothers in the Lord that were able to take and endure such persecution. Lies and hateful remarks and disrespect attacked them all in shiploads of persecution. Even a spirit of discord showed its ugly head but was quickly silenced. The list goes on and on and on of what they endured and Sailor had never met a group of brothers like the brothers he was stationed with on board the USS *Guadalcanal* (LPH-7), anchored off the coast of Beirut, Lebanon. The most revealing aspect of the entire situation is that they were not brothers attending a church building every Sunday or weekday. They were a group of brothers stationed onboard a naval vessel, but they understood the necessity of fellowship with one another. What obstacle they were faced with at any time was handled respectfully and brotherly. Unlike what Sailor has experienced inside a church building among so-called Christian brothers on land. The circumstances and the confinement onboard a ship at sea compel you to be real or be revealed as fake. The brothers on board the USS *Guadalcanal* (LPH-7), was compelled to be real. Although someone said to Sailor of some of the brothers that their salvation was akin to jailbird Christianity. In that, as long as they were at sea and in need of a spiritual strength they chose Christianity. But as soon as they returned to the United States and were off the ship, they chose their former life. Either way, while they were on board that ship in the midst of unwelcomed, hostile situation, those brothers were impressive in Bible knowledge and were a joy to be around when the spirit of despair struck the vessel. One cannot engage in spiritual battles at levels beyond their faith without another who helps to keep you encouraged. Like the prophet Amos said when he was moved to ask the question, "Can two walk together except they be agreed? (Amos 3:3).

18

THE ENCOUNTER WITH THE CHAPLAIN

The Car Wreck

The lieutenant Sailor worked for called him in his office within a few days of arriving on board to deliver a message to him and these are the lieutenant's exact words: "Petty Officer Sailor, I received a message from the American Red Cross. Apparently, there was a vehicle accident involving your family."

Can you imagine all that he had gone through up to this point only to get an American Red Cross message informing him of a tragedy back home? At this point in his life, he did not feel worthy at all to be called a minister of the Gospel, let alone to be identified as a Christian. He felt like his life and world was under the scrutinizing microscope of Satan. How much more of these trials could he sustain? Sailor asked the lieutenant, "What happened? Is everyone all right? Was my wife involved?" His eyes immediately filled with tears while having difficultly trying to maintain some facade of strength and not appear to act like a baby. Sailor was asking questions to the lieutenant nonstop, and the lieutenant said, "Now calm down. The message read your brother was driving your car and had an accident. Everyone is fine. Your wife sent a message, and she is all right."

Images of the crashed-up 1981 Pontiac Phoenix that Sailor allowed his younger brother to drive while he was away. His brother was fairly new with driver's license, and Sailor thought he was doing a good thing by letting him keep his car. In fact, it was Sailor's mother who persuaded him to "let your brother keep your car." Sailor supposed that wasn't a bad thing to let his brother, young with license and young with driving experience, have a nice car to drive around. Sailor's mother promised to be fully responsible for any damages that may occur while his younger brother was the custodian of his car. When the accident happened, Sailor never got the details as to what actually happened, only a broken conversation with his wife over a ham radio system while in the midst of a torn region of the world. It was one of those things in life he just had to say, "Oh well, thank God no one was hurt or killed!" The vehicle accident was the main reason Sailor had the once-in-a-lifetime privilege of being inside the marine barracks.

He then asked the lieutenant, "Is there some way I can call home and talk to my wife?" Back then, no cell phones or internet existed. Ham radio stations on board the ship was the primary means of verbal communication with loved ones back home. Ham radios were only used for official business and emergencies involving crew members. Sailor's situation was not classified as an emergency, and he understood that. But he thought there had to be some means onshore that would allow him to talk to his wife. The lieutenant said he would check and see if Sailor could make that phone call back to his wife in the United States. A couple days went by before the lieutenant notified Sailor that he could go ashore and make the call. The lieutenant was enthused about making those arrangements for Sailor, but Sailor was new on board the squadron and absolutely inexperienced with military conflict and missions. This was Sailor's first actual military involvement that included other nations of the world and radical Islamic jihadist. Prior to reporting to PHIBRON TWO, as you have learned, Sailor's previous military duty was cushy San Diego, CA, at VS-41, NAS Cecil Field, Florida, at VS-31, while traveling the globe and cushy NRD Harrisburg, Pennsylvania. His initial tour of duty was pleasure stuff and not to be considered actual field duty type military. But all in all, he needed this experience to understand a variety of situations and circumstances life was compelled to issue to him. He was about to get woken up real fast onshore in the marine barracks in Beirut, Lebanon. And the most unlikely person that was the instrument to wake up Sailor's novice soul would be a so-called man of the cloth. Whether viewed as right or wrong, the words of the marine chaplain would enlighten something inside Sailor that would change his perspective and educate him of the other side of the military and the other side of himself.

The Chaplain: A Man of God?

Up until this point in Sailor's military career, he had always respected and sort of looked up to navy and marine corps chaplains. Even though he did not completely understand their mission because they were formally educated commissioned officers that received a paycheck from Uncle Sam. They were commissioned to manage and perform religious services of all faiths. The role of a chaplain conflicted with Sailor's limited understanding in those days of how a minister could justifiably and seemingly without conscience have a word for all faiths. If what he had been taught about God and religion, then there is only one God and one religion, Christianity, in the guise of the Church of God in Christ. In other words, if a person was not in the Church of God in Christ they couldn't possibly be saved and they were on their way to hell. In those days, Sailor nursed an infantile understanding of Christianity, the Church of God in

Christ, religion, heaven, and hell. Without question, he was about to be introduced to the other side of Christianity, masked by titles and manmade authority, shrouded inside military boundaries. Chaplains appeared to be a breed of their own in a religious world of their own creation. Over Sailor's lifetime, he has met chaplains who he respected and thought good of, and he has met chaplains who he thought lacked the spirit of God and were formally and intellectually driven. Sailor did not know how to classify the chaplain that he would meet in the marine barracks. The chaplain was definitely military and marine all the way. In the mind of Sailor, the chaplain, probably, looking at the scrawniness of Sailor, did not seem to have any interest in the need for Sailor to hear a word, if not only a voice from home. Sailor's situation to the chaplain in the marine barracks was obviously, absolutely, insignificant. As life goes on, only significant things in your life that impacted who you are today remain with clarity in your soul. On that day, Sailor had to board the marine CH46 once again, the same type of helicopter that he flew onboard from the island of Larnaca, Italy. The harrowing experience flying over the ocean for hours in threatening inclement weather. But this trip was worth the flight because having the rare opportunity to speak with his wife was worth the trip. The lieutenant had made the arrangements, and the day before the flight, the lieutenant popped in the office and said, "Petty Officer Sailor, you will be going ashore tomorrow at 0900. Be ready, because this is the only chance you will get to make that call. Don't think you will get this opportunity often." Sailor was elated that the lieutenant made those arrangements, but he also felt the lieutenant made the arrangements against his better judgment. But there was some sense of compassion in his heart because he did not have to make the arrangements at all since there were no severe injuries or loss of life involving the vehicle accident. The lieutenant was just being nice, he supposes. When tomorrow arrived, Sailor could not get out of his bunk fast enough and quick shower and threw on his working blues. He was on deck within a millisecond, knowing if he missed the transportation, he would not get another chance. Going ashore under the circumstances, was a privilege, it was not a right to leave the boat just to make a phone call back to the United States. Sailor can never forget visiting the marine barracks and talking to the chaplain that faithful awakening day. The chaplain pissed Sailor off that he forgot the chaplain's name on purpose. Even though he does not remember his name, he is certain he could identify him even today if he were to see him. He had never in his life wanted to punch a minister, or chaplain, never. But he became enraged inside his soul and was actually two seconds from striking the chaplain with all his might on that day. The chaplain was very skilled in intimidating Sailor, and Sailor was having great difficulty controlling his feelings, nor could he control the conversation he was having with the chaplain. It was if the chaplain was getting joy out of belittling Sailor and causing Sailor to feel that his reason for wanting to call home was very insignificant and a waste of his time. Here is what happened on the day Sailor visited the marine barracks in Beirut, Lebanon, to talk to the chaplain, the man of God:

Chaplain: Good morning, uh, Petty Officer Sailor, is it?
Sailor: Yes, sir! (with a grin from ear to ear)
Chaplain: What can I do for you?
Sailor: Chaplain, sir, there has been a vehicle accident back home, and I would like to call my wife.
Chaplain: Was anybody hurt or killed?
Sailor: No sir, I just wanted to talk to my wife about the situation. I just checked onboard a few days ago and I am a minister. (Sailor really, really, thought that would mean something to the chaplain and impress him).
Chaplain: That's nice, but you said no one was hurt or killed.
Sailor: No, sir, no one! Thank God.

Sailor thought he was making some headway with the man of God, the marine chaplain, by identifying himself as a preacher. Sailor was kissing the chaplain's butt by trying to talk the God talk to him. Certainly, the chaplain could relate to Sailor's approach, and certainly, he would grant Sailor's request. But then something changed from the chaplain's smile to almost a Cheshire cat devious smile—you know, like Alice in Wonderland?

Chaplain: If I understood you correctly, Petty Officer Sailor, you did say no one was hurt or killed?

Sailor: Yes, sir! No one was injured. My wife is an emotional wreck because I just left the United States, and I let my brother keep my car and he got involved in a car accident.

Chaplain: Petty Officer Sailor, you must be out of your mind! Why would I let you make a phone call because your brother wrecked your car? I have marines here who have lost mother, father, son, and daughter that I have had to emergency ship back to the States. I have a marine whose wife had a miscarriage in the eighth month of her pregnancy, and you want to make a phone call because of a measly little car accident!

Sailor was bewildered. His thoughts were thrown into emptiness, and he wore a look of despair. He felt worthless and useless. He began to drop his head. He could no longer look the chaplain in the face. The chaplain continued on.

Chaplain: Look up at me when I am talking to you, Petty Officer Sailor! You need to get your priorities straight, son. I can't let you make a phone call on an official piece of equipment because you don't know how to handle a car accident. Do you have insurance? I said look at me when I am talking to you!

Sailor: Yes, sir!

Chaplain: Well then, you have to take the shit along with everyone else and learn how to handle these types of situations whether you like it or not. Now you seem like a fine young man, but I have a duty to serve those in need of real service. A car accident is not a real service, *especially* when no one was injured and no one died. You did say no one died, didn't you? Your brother is still alive, isn't he? He is not dead, is he?

Damn it to hell! What the fuck is wrong with this guy? Sailor thought, but he dared not say what he thought.

Sailor: Yes, sir. My brother is still alive, and no one was injured or hurt.

Sailor's voice went from excited to meet the chaplain and talk with him to emotionally intimidated and whimsical sounding voice. He actually thought they were pretty much done and that the chaplain would tell him to return to the ship and that was that. But he seemed to be getting pleasure out of interrogating Sailor. The full armored sentries would interrupt the meeting Sailor had with the chaplain just to ask him a question or two. The chaplain would take the time to answer them, and Sailor had to sit there and wait until the sentries were done talking to the chaplain.

Chaplain: You do understand my position, don't you? I mean if I let every Tom, Dick, and Harry make phone calls back to the United States I would clog up the communication device that we use for emergencies. I'm sorry your car was destroyed, but I am glad no one was injured or killed. You do understand, don't you?

Sailor hesitated.

Chaplain: Petty Officer Sailor, did you hear me question you? You do understand my position, don't you?

Sailor: Yeah! I understand!

Chaplain: Now don't get disrespectful, Petty Officer Sailor. I am still your superior officer, and you are an enlisted man. We both have a job to perform, and we must perform our duty with dignity and honor. Now do you understand my position?

Sailor: I understand…sir!

Only God knows the fervor in Sailor's heart to either spit in his face, kick his desk over, or punch him directly in the mouth. Sailor was only restrained by the intimidating look of those six-foot-tall marines standing outside the chaplain's office. Had it not been for those marines standing outside his office, Sailor is certain he would have for the second time in his career, ended up in the brig. He slumped down in the chair and disregarded his military position of sitting up straight in the chair. He could not even fake a smile from when he first entered into the chaplain's space. He was void of respect and honor and immediately found himself hating this white man who was blushing while he was interrogating and intimidating Sailor. All Sailor wanted was to make a quick phone call. With Sailor's last response to his demanding, unnecessary questioning he went on explaining to Sailor the pride and dignity in which the marines are serving their country. He told Sailor that he should share that same pride and honor and dignity and serve America while part of the Multinational Peacekeeping mission. He even went as far as to introduce an element of racism and said to Sailor, "Being a black man, you should understand the hard times and unrest in the country of Beirut, Lebanon." As though Sailor needed a history lesson on slavery and blacks in America. "What the *hell* did all that have to do with me wanting to make a phone call? Why didn't this guy just say sure, you can make your call." Or say, "I'm sorry, but I cannot authorize that because it doesn't fall within the parameters of an emergency according to marine policy and Department of Defense regulations."

Believe it or not, Sailor would have taken that type of reply much quicker than what the chaplain, the man of God, was doing to his mind. The chaplain was truly "the devil's advocate" in taking Sailor through intense mental and emotional changes on that day. Those changes would solidify his mental state the remainder of his duty on station in Beirut, Lebanon.

The remainder of the lecture from the chaplain was a brief history lesson on the marines and the navy and military campaigns and the service the marines provide to the great United States of America. Sailor had to wait for the next helo returning to the ship, and that was a couple of hours. So in the meantime, he was compelled to listen to the soft voice in which the chaplain was speaking about stuff Sailor *did not* care about. Yes, soft voice, because he did not raise his voice while speaking with Sailor. He did stress and emphasize certain things that he said, but not once did he raise his voice at Sailor. He was very intellectual and long-winded with his explanations. He purposely twisted Sailor's mind and his thoughts so as to jumble Sailor's thinking. He was good at doing that and Sailor had come under the interrogative ability of the chaplain to control his mind and thoughts. Without a doubt, Sailor really believes that the chaplain knew that Sailor wanted to strike him in the face, and Sailor really believes he was instigating and urging him on to react to him violently. Had Sailor done so, that would have been the end of his military career, notwithstanding, undoubtedly, there would be physical harm to his body because he is certain those marines would have beat the crap out of him. Even though Sailor was into kung fu and he still worked out on board ship, those marines were much larger than he, and they had weapons in their hands with flap jackets on and helmets and so on.

During the Reagan administration, the rules of engagement (ROE) was to have non-lethal weapons (NLW), but the Marines still had weapons in their hands. An interesting article to read about ROE and NLW is by Major D. B. Hall, United States Marine Corps at http://www.globalsecurity.org/military/library/report/1997/Hall.htm. He basically says Rules of Engagement and nonlethal weapons is a deadly combination. The months to follow for the Multinational Peacekeeping in Beirut, Lebanon, would help to prove his theory.

The most frustrating thing of that entire encounter with the chaplain, the man of God, was that after all that interrogated talk, the chaplain made arrangements for Sailor to use the ham radio to call home.

What a jerk, Sailor thought. *Why did he take me through all that mess with the questioning and intimidation to finally allow me to call home?*

The chaplain told Sailor, "You have five minutes to talk, and then you must end your conversation because this Ham radio system must be kept open."

It was the second time during Sailor's military career that he used a ham radio. The first time was on board the USS *Independence* (CV-62) when the commanding officer allowed sailors onboard the ship to call back home to their loved ones. No such thing as cell phones or personal computers. Ham radio is antiquated technology only used by skilled old-school operators today. There may be a few techies who use them today, but with the onslaught of the personal computer industry and cell phone technology, ham radio operator would be really old stuff. Nonetheless, Sailor got the opportunity to speak to his wife, and he had to inform her that after every transmission, or word, you have to say "over." Your voice on ham radio does not sound like your own, and with that, you have to trust and know the person you are speaking with is actually the person you know.

They spoke every bit of five minutes while she was crying the entire time explaining to Sailor what had happened and how his mother was treating her. She told Sailor that his mother told her that she could not help her and that she is sorry for the accident. Sailor recalls both his mother and brother vowing to take full responsibility if something were to happen to their car. Well, the time had come, and something happened to the car. Sailor wondered what happened to the responsibility to be responsible if something happened to his car? Something happened to that responsibility—it vanished away. His mother apologized for the accident, and that was the end of that situation. It took Sailor years afterward to look at his mother the same as he did when he was a boy. It seemed and appeared she was in the early stages of distancing herself from her son. He had always helped his mother in many ways and always loved her dearly. But he could not seem to conquer her distancing herself from him. The car was material, and he really did not focus on that loss. It was the diminishing of the relationship with his mother that was the greater loss. Nonetheless, he enjoyed every second of hearing his wife's voice and the brief sweet touch of home. In his mind's eye, he could see her and touch her as his heart raced and his emotions were raised from a flattened state of dismay after speaking with the chaplain. She did not sound like his wife, but she sounded good because he was talking to her and he heard her voice, even masked with the "over" stuff. His wife asked him a few times, "Sailor, is this you? You don't sound like yourself." He had to explain to her the squelching sound she was hearing and the communication device they were using was not like your everyday home telephone, but it was good to talk.

Back to the Boat

After almost two hours of grueling unnecessary questioning by a "preacher" in a uniform of the United States Marine Corps, Sailor was mentally drained and physically exhausted. Anyone could have walked up to him and said, "Hey, Petty Officer Sailor, jump in the sea, drown yourself," and he probably would have complied. That sounds crazy, but the chaplain had managed to drain all reasonable thinking from Sailor's mind. He had never met anyone who was so skilled in playing the mind game. Not even in boot camp did he ever feel so intimidated. Maybe the environment under the circumstances in Beirut, Lebanon, had a lot to do with the great success of intimidation. Sailor felt his mind was wiped clean from a man he would intrinsically trust. One thing for sure, he knew that he had become hopeless, faithless, and without any sense of pride, dignity, or honor. He returned back to the boat that same day on a helicopter having met the chaplain of the 22nd Marine Amphibious Unit and what a chaplain he was. He was the religious Christianized man of God. In hindsight, he does not really fault the chaplain for the point he was making, he thought the chaplain could have made his point more tactfully. He also felt greatly offended that the chaplain insinuated "as a black man you should understand hard times." What did that have to do with anything? That statement regurgitated almost twenty times the hatred he felt as far back as Marshall Elementary School—the time the white female principal choked tears from the young TJ. The racial hate birthed in his soul in the days of his youth from his teachers, both white male and female, seemed to haunt Sailor.

But he knew that hate was not a characteristic of God. Amid all the confusion he was deeply a part of, he now was struggling with the spirit of hate within his soul all because a "religious" man prodded and poked and provoked him to hate. Upon arrival back to the boat, he reported to his duty station in the administration office. It could not have been a half an hour when his lieutenant came into the office and with a smile on his face said to Sailor, "How'd it go, Petty Officer Sailor?"

Sailor looked at him and said, "Rotten, sir!"

"What do you mean 'rotten,' Petty Officer Sailor?"

"I mean rotten! The chaplain did allow me to make the phone call after an intense round of interrogation, and I don't think that was right."

"Well, Petty Officer Sailor, we are engaged in a military operation that you swore to uphold and defend, and I am sorry about your experience with the chaplain, but I did my part, life goes on." Just like that he said, "life goes on." The truthful thing about the lieutenant's statement is that he did do his part. He did not have to make the arrangements to allow Sailor to make the phone call, but he did. Sailor wanted to go on a rampage and kick everybody's ass! Especially those white officers who did not seem to give a damn about the black sailors. At the time he did not think about the apparent coincidence when he returned to the boat. It was not until months later that he really pondered what occurred that day. Why would the lieutenant hurriedly make his way to the administrative office just to ask him how things went when he was very hesitant about sending Sailor ashore to talk to the chaplain? Why would he come into the office with a smile on his face as though he was happy Sailor went ashore to make his phone call under extreme tension and stress? Sailor's thoughts months later, after they had returned to the United States, is that the lieutenant was heavily involved in Sailor's interrogation. Sailor believes the lieutenant suggested to the chaplain to give Sailor a good reaming out and wake Sailor up to what his primary duties and responsibilities are with the United States Navy. He can only surmise that because the whole negative environment that prevailed on board the USS *Guadalcanal* (LPH-7). There was a crystal-clear separation between black crewmembers and white officers. There was a clear biased duty assignment between black and white sailors. The black sailors that had some sense of authority onboard the *Guadalcanal* (LPH-7) and received good assignments were like black people who try to act white. That concept works both ways—you have whites who try to act black. But in this case, it was the blacks who tried to act white, and maybe that was part of the game Sailor did not know how to play which was partially his reason for taking *everything* personally. After the lieutenant made his despairing comments to Sailor about his visit with the chaplain, the lieutenant said, "Okay, men, let's get back to work," and he slithered out of the office. Sailor did not see him for the rest of that day.

After that brief exchange with the lieutenant, YN2 said to Sailor "T, these people are crazy. Don't you believe a word they say and don't get to close to them. They will screw you up man." All YN1 did was chuckle and told Sailor to get to work. Sailor, still in a deep cultural shock, did whatever anyone told him to do at the moment and would have committed a criminal act if suggested to him. When YN1 told him to get to work, Sailor sat down and mindlessly began doing something until YN1 threw a pile of work on his desk and said, "Do this and get it done before you leave today." YN1 then left the office, and Sailor did not see him for the rest of the day. YN2 looked at Sailor and shrugged his shoulders. YN2 was careful of what he would say about or against YN1 because YN1 was the supervisor of both YN2 and Sailor. Both YN2 and Sailor were the same rank and dealt with each other on pins and needles.

Time drifted away aimlessly as Sailor remained in the administrative office all day unproductively working and pondering gloom. That day was one of the most depressing, sad, sad days of all his life. He had sunk into the deepest depressive state that he did not know was possible. He was terribly missing his wife, and a vehicle accident had occurred a few days earlier without him knowing the details. He was questioned endlessly to use the ham radio, and he thought the questioning was unjustified. He returned to the actual gray ship, while his soul and spirit had become extremely parched. It appeared to him that everyone in his new command was not accepting him, and there was nowhere to go outside of the confines of the ship. When the workday was over, he had several options: Go on deck and walk around in a circle. Go back to his bunk and listen to some music or write his wife a letter. Go to the weight room and lift some weights and work out to relieve some stress and tension or just do nothing. He was directionless, so he went back to his bunk in the aft of the ship. His bunk was close to the deck. He got undressed down to his boxer shorts, climbed in his bunk, pulled the curtains closed, and tied them. He then put his pillow over his face and softly cried and cried and cried until he fell off to sleep.

He *never* could have imagined anything like this while living in the projects or growing up on North 18th Street. His mind and worldly experience had taken quantum leaps above his friends back home. The ride he took to boot camp from the Harrisburg train station while certain choir members were on the boarding dock singing his song "You Know Lord, Whether I'm Right You Know Lord, Whether I'm Wrong," all had become faded memories of an ancient story. He even vainly wished he could have gone back to those days just prior to entering the navy and suspended time and lived the rest of his days over and over again never entering the navy. Sailor had become lost in time, wishing, wanting, remembering times and events that would *never* be a reality again. Such is the case for all humankind, and how many times have you or Sailor vainly desired to relive the past? The words of the preacher in the book of Ecclesiastes were alive in the heart of Sailor in those days: "Vanity of vanities, saith the Preacher, vanity of vanity; all is vanity," Even childhood and youthfulness is vanity (Eccles. 1:2; 11:10). Vanity is something he did not fully understand in those days, but vanity is the life he lived day after day after day. He desired that he would at least be a living testimony to other soldiers, sailors, airmen, and marines who would find themselves in similar circumstances under similar conditions. To overcome the spirit of vanity one must overcome the spirit of the devil. Satan loves to have you bask in what was and what could have been when *every* lesson taught to us is to be graduated from and moved on to higher learning. Sailor's graduation would not come until years later, actually a full decade later. But Sailor would experience a whole world full of vanity upon leaving the navy and would one day come face-to-face with the goodness of God. At this point, he was deep in the thick of training, not from the navy, but training from the Most High that was unraveling, removing and revealing to him the despair in which Sailor was living his life. The remainder of the time on board the USS *Guadalcanal* (LPH-7), anchored off the coast of Beirut, Lebanon, would be a series of separation among the office staff. There were brief moments of controlled relaxation—a steel beach picnic or two. That's when the ship throws a cookout on deck, being a steel ship; hence "steel beach picnic." Those times were few, because the mission in Beirut, Lebanon, had demanded strict political-military posture. But failed on many occasions, both the mission and its troops.

The Barracks of Death

A one-time look and entrance inside the marine barracks ashore at Beirut, Lebanon, would be the memory of memories for Sailor. This is an aerial view of what Sailor calls, "The Barracks of Death." Never in his lifetime did he ever imagine the type of brushes with death he would encounter. The American embassy, the air tower and now, unbeknownst to him, the most devastating would be the marine barracks in Beirut, Lebanon. This is the place where he had just left talking to the marine chaplain, the man of God. This is the place that may have never been a memory had it not been for the inevitable devastation on the horizon. He would have always remembered his encounter with the chaplain, but not necessarily the place of the encounter. Both of them together managed to enhance the encounter with the chaplain. To this day, with every fleeting thought of the encounter with the chaplain, the barracks and the chaplain remain crystal clear in Sailor's mind. It's one of those things he does not particularly wish to remember, but it is one of those things he cannot forget. In April 1983, a few days after Sailor's arrival on board the USS *Guadalcanal* (LPH-7), he had the one-time privilege of entering this barracks. Beirut is a lovely place to visit with its tropical surroundings, but at the time Sailor was there under the circumstances his eyes were extremely dim. He could not see beauty had it been standing directly in front of him, and it was the tropical Beirut, Lebanon. His spirit was sinfully dry, and his faith had been stretched to almost nonexistence. The only thoughts pressing on his mind in those days was how he could somehow or another get back to the United States. He believes his perspective would have been totally different had the United States Armed Forces been engaged in actual war. But this was a politically driven, politically operated and politically doomed mission that reaped mundane responses of the attacks in Beirut, Lebanon. Essentially, the Multinational Peacekeeping Force were sitting ducks because its mission was politically motivated attempts of peace in the region. All that would unfold from the point of the attack on the marine barracks would reveal the true nature of the mission from the terrorist perspective. Negotiations were *all* politically motivated, and the United States Government, overseeing the United States Military had trained its service members how to die while sleeping. It was simple: don't be ready. Secure all weapons and do not load your weapon. Sleep at ease like you are sleeping in your bed at home. That was the implied training that would one Sunday morning bring great bereavement to the people of the United States of America.

Sometime in late August, early September of 1983, the tour of duty on station at Beirut, Lebanon, for MARG 3-83 came to an end. Every day up to the return of the *Guad* at Naval Station Norfolk, VA, continued to present tests and trials and great tribulations. MARG 3-83 was relieved by MARG 3-84/85 by the USS *Inchon* (LPH-12), the next flagship Sailor would serve on upon the return of the *Inchon* to the States. The USS *Inchon* would present a weird change in attitude, circumstances, and leadership. Sailor would be the senior petty officer in the administration office, and things would be unbelievably different. But for now, let's finish out the most devastating part of his first tour in Beirut, Lebanon.

19

THE ULTIMATE DEVASTATION

241 United States Marines Plus Sailors

The main thought pressing on Sailor's mind in those days was how he could somehow or another get back to the United States. At least stationed in perhaps Washington or Virginia. On board ship in Beirut, Lebanon, was not his idea of being in the navy. His initial enlistment in the United States Navy and the tour of duties he enjoyed gave him a one-sided perspective of being in the navy. Sailor reported for duty to Amphibious Squadron TWO, embarked on board the USS *Guadalcanal* (LPH-7), with the birth of a new type of war. The United States of America had deployed to the Middle Eastern nation of Beirut, Lebanon, the fighting force of the US Marines and the US Navy. It would be the death of 220 marines, 18 sailors, and 3 soldiers, bringing the total death in a single act of aggression to 241 armed forces members. The cowardly attack on the building serving as the marine barracks for the battalion landing team (BLT), would go down in forgotten history as the deadliest attack on the United States Armed Forces since Vietnam War. Official reports claim a number of French peacekeepers also died in the blast along with an elderly Lebanese man who was known to operate a concession stand.

A few weeks after his tour of duty had ended in Beirut, Lebanon, and having returned to the United States of America, he was able to get much needed time away from the navy and the big gray naval warship. The time he spent home with his wife while living with her mother on Woodbine St. was refreshing, but very brief. At least that time allowed him to reflect on the events that unfolded while in Beirut, Lebanon. Every second that he arrived on the island of Larnaca to returning to the United States, seemed to have flown by but crept along while actually going through. Having returned back to Norfolk Naval Station in Virginia, it was business as usual. Home will always be a brief touch of his reality, but the fact he was still on active duty meant he would have to leave home again. Every departure from Harrisburg felt to him like he was just passing through and that he may or may not see home again. As a United States Navy sailor, one could find themselves in any part of the world, any day of the week or week of the month or months of the year. But for now, home felt good, and it was time to return to his church at Mount Calvary and give his "look at me" testimony and bask in what he felt was acceptance of the church folk at Mount Calvary. But that time would never arrive. While he was sitting in the pulpit next to an older minister friend, Brother Brown, without provocation, leaned over toward Sailor and whispered in Sailor's ear, "Do you know what happened in Beirut, Lebanon, this morning?"

Sailor actually sat up erect in the chair on the pulpit and looked at Elder Brown with the most startled look on his face and said,

"What? What do you know about Beirut, Lebanon?" Kind of disrespectfully, but not meaning to be disrespectful. Furthermore, Sailor had *just* returned home to the United States, and Sailor was the one in the navy, so how is it that this older gentleman knew something about Beirut, Lebanon, and Sailor did not know? Sailor *just* returned back to the United States from Beirut, Lebanon, Elder Brown was rooted in traditional religion of Christianity, but he was very much aware of the error of Christian practices. But for some reason or another, Elder Brown did not have the drive or overwhelming zeal to speak against the error.

He attempted to on occasion but was mentally beat down by those of more formal education. What a travesty of the educated who think all they have to do is explain something away and their words are to be taken as the Gospel. But Elder Brown stood his ground at least but was not combative and not challenging when it came to discussing the Bible. The memory of that day on the pulpit with Elder Brown remains vivid to Sailor.

On a Sunday morning with the church full, Sailor's parents were there, and everyone was there expecting Sailor to say something of significance. Sailor was surprised that Brother Brown, an older man, frail body, would be interested in military affairs. However, he was by far the *only* minister that Sailor knew in those days that would talk military stuff with him. He seemed to be inspired by United States military missions. Elder Brown was the first who revealed to Sailor that the marine barracks in Beirut, Lebanon, was just bombed. Sailor was struggling to get himself together because of the question Elder Brown had just asked him. He then looked *directly* into Elder Brown's eyes and said, "Where did you hear that from? Who told you that?"

He quickly got a hold of himself and came to grips of where he was sitting and who he was talking to. He then reworded his question to him immediately and said, "Elder Brown, where did you hear that from, sir?"

"This morning on the radio before I came to church, there was an emergency announcement that the United States Marine

Headquarters in Beirut, Lebanon, was just bombed, and they expect about two hundred-something marines are dead."

All the excitement of being home had immediately vanished away from Sailor. He felt deep flutters in his stomach. He became cold, and chills ran up his spine and through his entire body as though someone had just poured an ice-cold bucket of water on his naked body. He felt like he was about to pass out. He began to sweat, and in his mind he *knew* everybody in that church could see that he was not feeling well. Sadly enough, no one seemed to pay attention to Sailor but Elder Brown. He could not believe what Elder Brown just told him. He did not want to believe what Elder Brown just said to him. He was hoping that Elder Brown heard the wrong information on the news report. Like in a movie of sorts, his spirit was immediately transported back to the region of the Middle East in Beirut, Lebanon, and he could *vividly* see, feel, and hear the sights and sounds of being in Beirut, Lebanon. His mind ran through every second of the day he was in the barracks talking to the chaplain. Almost like he blacked out sitting up straight in the pulpit chair but had been transported in mind and spirit to Beirut, Lebanon. The military-owned him for the most part, and no matter where he traveled to, in a millisecond, he could return to the location. Just a few weeks ago, he was in that same barracks pretty much all day on the day he had the appointment with the chaplain. And now he had just been told by the most unlikely source that about two hundred-something fellow service members of the United States Marines had just lost their lives. Sailor knew all along that the MARG presence in that torn region of the world they were the proverbial sitting-duck situation. Two hundred-something marines were sleeping in their bunks when a suicide bomber vehicle was able to penetrate the bivouac and without mercy slayed the marines, sailors, and soldiers of the Multinational Peacekeeping Force while they were in their bunks asleep. Some undoubtedly were awake and up moving around, but others would never ever see the light of day on this side of heaven. Sailor's eyes immediately filled with tears, and his knees became weak and his body felt lifeless. His thoughts began to wander all over the place. Elder Brown looked at him and said, "Are you all right, son?"

Sailor looked at him, eyes filled with tears, and said, "No, sir, I'm not." How could Elder Brown possible know what Sailor was feeling? How could anyone in that church know what he was feeling? When to Sailor, if anyone was truly spiritual, someone should have picked up on the powerful bereaved spirit that was in the house. Nonetheless, he did not blame the church folk for how he was feeling—they did not know. Their world was a world of church confined to the four corners of Harrisburg, Pennsylvania. How could they possibly know the depth and uncertainty of life and the surety of death? But Sailor is eternally grateful that at least Elder Brown, the most unlikely source of information, was there to offer compassion, of which Sailor desperately needed.

The thoughts of his mind took over his entire being, *Why was I not in there when that happened? Why was I spared and why didn't anything happen to me while I was directly in the midst of the terrorist activity in Beirut, Lebanon?*

You might think, why even have those thoughts? Be grateful you are alive and nothing happened to you. But given the ungodly, inconsistent, weak testimony of a Christian Sailor was supposed to be, in his mind, he expected to be, at any time to open his eyes in death. Even down through the years after his Beirut experience, he had fallen to the state of sinful actions again and he expected death at any minute. But it did not come during those days, nor the days he thought it might come. He continuously lived in a cloud of death as God navigated him through the cloud. He wondered and thought and wept and repented and wept again and repented again. Sorrow flooded his soul for the senseless loss of lives over a mission and time when the rules of engagement were not to return fire. The Multinational Peacekeeping Force mission employed extreme laxation and was the root cause of taking the life of America's finest fighting men. The ruling factor of Beirut's mission was the attempt in mediation of the United States of America who placed Sailor's brother, your sons, your children in a useless, military façade, politically driven Multinational Peacekeeping mission that failed miserably. Elder Brown realized that when he told Sailor of the heinous acts committed by the terrorist, instantaneously bereavement flooded Sailor's soul and Sailor was unable to contain the bereavement. Elder Brown reached over and placed his hand on Sailor's shoulder and began praying for Sailor while his head was bowed. Sailor did not bow his head so much out of reverence as he did because of deep, deep sorrow and unanswered questions. The remainder of that day became a blur and the excited testimony Sailor intended to share to the people had just been ripped from his soul. When Elder Brown told Sailor of the news of what just happened that morning on October 23, 1983, bereavement became the shadow of Sailor the remainder of the time he was home. He repeatedly ran over and over in his mind what it must have been like for the deceased Marines and for the surviving marines. For those who lost their lives in a millennium-long torn region of the world had now been numbered with the ancient fallen soldiers. The Middle East is an ongoing war between a nation of people that preexisted Americans by at least two thousand years.

These military men lay in their bunks on Saturday evening, not having a clue they would never see Sunday morning come to light. There may have been many who had just woken up and never made it out of the barracks after the explosion. Many, if not all, who died, probably said a prayer before lying down on Saturday evening, and they all undoubtedly expected to return home someday. But their home would not be what they were familiar with on this earth. They would enter into an eternal home forever in their final resting place.

Of those who survived and were part of the cleanup and identification crew, what trauma, what hurt and pain, what great loss they felt. To see your fallen brothers lying under a mess of concrete and debris is a memory that even the grace of God battles to help you overcome. You trained with these marines, broke bread with them, and even others grew up with one another from childhood. Within seconds, all that was and all that you knew of them is no more than a memory seared in your brain. That's what Sailor remembers from the American embassy explosion in April of the same year. The death toll quickly rose over several days of searching for survivors. In the end, 241 American servicemen—220 marines, 18 navy personnel, and 3 army soldiers. Some reports claim this was the deadliest single-day death toll for the United States Marine Corps since the battle of Iwo Jima (2,500 in one day). And the deadliest single-day death toll for the United States military since 243 killed on January 31, 1968, the first day of the Tet Offensive in the Vietnam War.

Politicians Are Liars That Kill

Given the statistics of death tolls for service members as far back as World War II, you would think lessons learned would have taught the ruling powers of America a lesson. But the embodied politics in the nation's capital continued to play the diplomacy and ridiculous rhetoric game. President Ronald Reagan planned to target the Sheikh Abdullah barracks in Baalbek, Lebanon, which housed Iranian Revolutionary Guards. The Revolutionary Guards were believed to be training Hezbollah fighters. Sailor believed and continues to believe till this day that a surgically targeted strike should have been launched against Hezbollah, the radical Shiite militant groups and the Revolutionary Guards. A decisive military strike in the early days of terrorism would have at least put the terrorist in great disarray. Apart from doing nothing, the inevitable would reveal itself a few short years later when the shores of the United States of America would be rocked with terrorism mayhem. Now all of sudden America wants to remember and never forget 9/11 but how quickly she wants to tell black Hebrews to forget the carnage she inflicted on her slaves from Africa for four hundred years. Such is the hypocrisy of a hypocritical nation. Thank shrewd politics in Washington, DC, for their ability to foresee 9/11 and do nothing. The ruling powers in Washington for the nation at the time knew who the Hezbollah were and their religious ideology. In the 1980s, the Reagan Administration knew and understood the devout mission of terrorist to kill who they call imbeciles. But the politicians in Washington, DC, essentially let them get away with murder at the expense of national security for America.

Sailor wrestled with the fact that the president of the United States of America would decide to take direct retaliatory action against these terrorist group but nothing actually was done. The president actually called the terrorist act a "despicable act." But Sailor learned later by taking no action of the United States that his words were no more than political rhetoric. In all the years of Sailor's life, a constant struggled existed with him believing the words of politicians, whether good intentions or not. The system of the world's government has proven itself to be entrenched in some form of corruption. And with good men attempting to upheaval the corruption, somehow or another their good intentions are buried by some politically correct philosophical thought. How is it that Secretary of Defense Caspar Weinberger was able to abort what the president intended to do against the terrorist? Defense Secretary Weinberger was more concerned about the United States relations with other Arab nations instead of the lives of his sailors, marines, and soldiers. The Defense Secretary should have realized how the Multinational Peacekeeping mission was not being successful and should have employed the "eye for an eye" principle. That's how Sailor felt about the whole thing. Even though an "eye for an eye" is not good Christian thinking, it must be understood that the military does not exist to necessarily abide by Christian principles. The military exists to defend and support the nation of America and collaborate with the friends of the United States. The United States of America's involvement in the Multinational Peacekeeping Force was made in the interest of the Lebanese people and the state of Israel. America's sailors and marines were essentially fulfilling their duty but simultaneously were expendable at the behemoth of American politics. Sneak, surprise, and cowardly attack upon those sleeping marines in their barracks, in their bunks, demanded a surgically retaliatory strike. Not in the coward manner when the terrorist would be asleep like they did against the marines, but in a manner of broad daylight given the extreme firepower and CIA and military intelligence that was in the region. The most heinous crimes of the United States of America's government are their ability and knowledge and power to specifically identify and annihilate the enemy. But the politicians chose to fulfill their own agenda involving their own strategy, which cost the lives of countless soldiers, sailors, airmen, Marines, and civilians.

Typically, Sailor does not like blaming anyone for what happens in life, but in this situation the decision made especially by Defense Secretary Casper Weinberger was a decision that would reap deadly results directly on the shores of America ten short years later. February 1993 would be America's orientation and introduction to acts of terrorism against the US government and its civilians. It would seem that the 1993 bombing of the World Trade Center was somewhat of a dress rehearsal that would fulfill the nightmarish dream of al Qaeda even eight years from 1993; as the FBI described 9/11. Remember the 1951 movie *The Day the Earth Stood Still* and the 2008 remake? There was an article written on FDNewYork.com website titled, "The Day the World Shook." It amazed Sailor that the world is in crisis when the terrorist who began their plot during the Beirut, Lebanon, civil war against America, all of a sudden shakes the world when it hits the shores of the United States. The Middle Eastern people have lived their entire existence being shaken and terrorized and lives disrupted to the point many have become accustomed to extreme civil disruptions. But the leaders in Washington, DC, who make the decisions whether to engage their soldiers in armed conflict or embark them on a military mission are the same ones who turn their backs when military and civilian lives are lost.

As far back as the beginning of World War II when the Japanese bombed Pearl Harbor, this nation was not at war with the Germans or the fascist of Europe. But the president of the United States then, Franklin Delano Roosevelt, desired to enter the war in order to fight fascism in America and Europe. Sailor is not a journalist nor a columnist for that matter, but he discovered over the years of his life that reading and research and studying American and world history develops a certain amount of awareness.

http://www.fbi.gov/news/stories/2008/
february/tradebom_022608

Much of what Sailor has read and discovered since the days of the projects and North 18th Street would be debated by the most expert scholars, but no one can deny the outcome of the decisions made from the political leaders in Washington, DC. Did over three thousand souls die at Pearl Harbor because of the decisions and provoking and power-hungry leaders in the nation's capital? About 81 percent of the American people were against entering a war involving Hitler's Germany in Europe. Even during that era, it was a known fact that FDR yearned to enter the war. But the price that would be paid would be the lives of American servicemen and women. In fact, every president should be guided by a reverential "godly" decision whether to put American troops in harm's way. The presidents themselves do not enter the battlefield and fight for something they started. One may think that thought to be odd and absurd, but it appears United States presidents all seem to have this drive toward a one-world government with themselves at the helm. In ancient times, kings fought on the battlefield with their troops. Though democracy is not a kingdom in the strictest sense, the presidents of this democracy many times lead as though they are king. Concerning Pearl Harbor, even Eleanor Roosevelt wrote in one of her columns that "we all expected this." One of the bloodiest battles of all time was the battle at Okinawa involving the United States Marines resulting in more than 100,000 dead. The Japanese offered a complete surrender before the battle of Okinawa, but the president of the United States did not accept their surrender by saying "they have not suffered enough." If such a statement was made by the president of the United States, what does that say about his true motive and death of America's own soldiers? By conventional military procedures, the president should have accepted Japan's surrender, why keep fighting when your opponent surrenders? That same type of shrewd political spirit continued all the way through the Vietnam War, where upward of 60,000 military deaths occur in that unjustified war? Lyndon Bain Johnson is considered one of the most controversial presidents in particular of his handling of the Vietnam War. President Johnson was publicly and knowingly associated with a certain contractor by the name of Brown and Root then, now known as Kellogg, Brown, and Root, or KBR. The contractor was awarded significant contracts to build bases, airstrips and military structures totaling 380 million dollars. Typically this type of work is done by Navy Seabees or the Army Core of Engineers. But this particular contractor had a good old boy relationship with the Texan Governor now, president of the United States. The name of the contractor during the Vietnam War was the "Vietnam builders." This contractor has been associated with power in the White House all the way through the Iraqi War of the twenty-first century. Among other things, LBJ's presidency involved sweetheart contracts from the White House and war profiteering. Which brings us to the American embassy in Beirut, Lebanon, and the marine headquarters also in Beirut, Lebanon. Sailor's microscopic information and discovery of the real truth that goes on behind what the public may perceive as a justified war, military campaign or military peacekeeping mission, generally have extreme alternative motives by some of the most powerful decision-makers on the planet.

Back to the Boat

The time Sailor spent home after returning from Beirut, Lebanon, and the information about the marine headquarter bombing had become an intense, sad, and emotional time of his life. It seemed nothing could compare to those days, and it seemed they would never end. At that point in his military career, there was sad report after sad report, and though he had enjoyed being a member of the United States Navy, he was becoming disheartened and dissatisfied with being on active duty. Sailor was seeing another side of what he thought to be the greatest navy and military on the planet. He found himself deeply involved in an organization that made him do things and be a part of things he did not agree with. He found himself even attempting the conscientious objector card, which he now sees as a purely coward spirit, especially at a time when the military was an all-volunteer force; the draft was not implemented when Sailor enlisted. It was strictly his decision and his decision alone. But after becoming exposed to the unreal, unbelievable, politically driven stuff that he was seeing and hearing he decided to conscientiously object "for religious reasons." His reasoning and overwhelmed thoughts caused him to think crap. All of sudden, Sailor was filled with the idea to "conscientiously object." Nothing became of the conscientious objection idea it was like a fleeting thought. When he returned to Norfolk, after a brief stay at home and filled with sorrow, he had to face the fact that he was still on active duty. It was time to return to his duties in Norfolk, VA embarked now on board the USS *Inchon* (LPH-12). During this time frame, he seized the opportunity to learn his way around Norfolk and Virginia Beach, Virginia. He would travel back and forth to home every weekend especially to be with his wife. She was his primary and only reason for visiting his home of record. He made attempts periodically to convince her to come along with him and move to the Norfolk area. But he was uncertain of many things in those days and sort of went with the flow, as the saying goes. After exposure to the other side of the navy and becoming aware of the political involvement of the missions, he was uncertain whether he would stay in the navy or actually get out after this tour of duty. On board USS *Inchon* (LPH-12), assigned to commander, Amphibious Squadron Two would be his last active duty time for a while.

Back in Norfolk, while the ship was in port at Pier 7, he had pretty much nothing to do but ride around Norfolk in the evening reminiscing of his wife being there with him. He talked to her on the phone practically every night and throughout the weekends that he had duty on board ship. Sailor remembers those days vividly as if they were actually yesterday. They were long uneventful days, and the uneventful days were strictly his fault. There were plenty of constructive things he could have been doing like preparing himself for getting off active duty. But he chose to be in a slumber of sorts, trying to figure out how he ended up on board the *Inchon* after having the illustrious tour of duty during his first enlistment. He embraced extreme pity party for himself during those days, and to even remember those times is almost sinful just to think about the type of man he was. Nonetheless, every day after duty and sometimes while on duty, he sat on deck of the USS *Inchon* and sometimes walked throughout the naval base listening to music. He recorded song after song from the radio for his own listening pleasure. He was being introduced to new Gospel artists because he spent a good portion of the day listening to music attempting to calm his spirit and answer in his mind why this tour of duty in the Amphibious Navy. He would much rather be at sea because time does move along faster while at sea, even though it did not seem like it at times. Being at sea appeared to move time alone because he was constantly active while the ship was at sea. The choice between being at sea or onshore, ironically, for Sailor it helped to maintain his sanity by keeping his mind engaged. The reprieve of the tour of duty on board the USS *Inchon* (LPH-12) versus the tour of duty on board the USS *Guadalcanal* (LPH-7) was that YN1 transferred sometime shortly after returning back from Beirut and YN2 could not wait to get out of the navy. Before the *Inchon* got underway again headed toward the Mediterranean, both the men that were the greatest antagonist of Sailor of all time were gone. Many of the officers Sailor perceived as bias toward blacks had also transferred and the white senior chief in charge of the office who Sailor strongly felt did not like blacks, at least the black men that he was supervisor of. At any rate, they all transferred or got out of the navy. Even the commodore had transferred, and a new commodore assumed duty, Captain D. L. Strole, USN, the type of commanding officer Sailor was used to. Captain Strole treated his men with a real honest sense of dignity and respect, regardless of the color of his crew's skin. He had the uncanny ability to cause Sailor to feel like belonging to the navy again. Getting advanced to E6, first class petty officer, also attributed to caressing Sailor's attitude and depressed mentality that he had embraced. On the upcoming Mediterranean cruise onboard the USS *Inchon* (LPH-12), Sailor was now the senior man in the office, the LPO, leading petty officer of the young brothers in his shop. Much of what would occur from this point on was now on the shoulders of Sailor because every senior enlisted and officer that Sailor perceived as a problem to him in personality conflicts were *all* gone! What an enormous, tremendous breath of fresh air that was. But still, he had much to learn about himself and his insecurities and his indecisions and fear and anger and "backsliding" due to a deep spirit of sin. The days ahead on board the USS *Inchon* (LPH-12) would prove if he had learned anything that he should have learned from the past. The scriptural injunction is to forget the past and press toward the future. But the past serves as a great learning lesson in the experiences of life. If what one experiences is not learned in one's life, then the past will inevitably repeat itself in some way or another.

YNC Johnson and YN1

October 1984, the USS *Hermitage*, USS *Newport*, USS *Sumter*, USS *Shreveport*, and USS *Inchon* (flagship) got underway for a seven-month deployment to the Mediterranean. This would make Sailor's fourth time on a Med cruise to Europe, and this cruise would be unlike any Sailor had ever set sail with. The circumstances and surroundings were the difference between night and day as opposed to the USS *Guadalcanal.* On his fourth Med. cruise, he would be the leading petty officer, and there would be a brand-new chief petty officer in the admin office. The commanding officer was new, and basically there was an entirely new crew with commander, Amphibious Squadron Two. A far cry from what he was introduced to over a year ago when he checked on board in April 1983. Something about this Med. cruise would be reminiscent of his earlier and younger days with VS-31. He would deeply miss his wife. He had been through enough up to this point that he had learned how to adjust and dispense with the babyish mind-set and ungodly worldly tongue of profanity. The new yeoman chief (YNC) checked on board a few weeks before CPO transferred. The new YNC was a NAVET (navy veteran) who had just come from a two-weeks orientation from the naval training center, Great Lakes, Illinois. YNC Johnson was soft-spoken, mature, intelligent, and formally educated. Sailor thought the remainder of his tour with COMPHIBRON Two would be ugly and unprofessional. But when he met YNC Johnson, they connected immediately because Sailor could see the unmitigated professionalism in YNC Johnson. He also was very discerning to pick up on the friction that prevailed in the office between CPO and those whom he supervised, including Sailor. It was like second nature that Sailor found it his place to bend YNC's ear every day, complaining about the unprofessionalism and lack of good leadership in the office. YNC Johnson would repeatedly say to Sailor, "I hear what you are saying, but you need to calm down because the people you are referring to will be gone very soon, and on this cruise and on this boat, you will be in charge. Wait, your time is coming, and then you can do things the way you rightly see fit."

Sailor liked the new chief! He liked his style, and he liked his rationale. YNC Johnson was never loud and always spoke with a sense of authority and peace of mind and heart. Sailor hadn't worked for a chief like that since the days of VS-31 when he was an E-3 seaman. YNC Johnson was always in the teaching and instructing mode, and Sailor found himself becoming unbelievably relaxed being a part of the Amphibious Squadron TWO. Sailor questioned YNC about everything, professionally and worldly, because he was so easy to communicate with. When anticipating a new member of the crew to be checking onboard and especially if the new member is senior to you in rank, you don't know what to expect. But when Sailor met YNC Johnson, they connected immediately because of his apparent experience and maturity. In the mind and heart of Sailor, he was almost urging the days along so both YN2 and CPO could depart the command. Even though he was biased of them being there, he was ready to be released from their hellish influence. Sailor could not help himself because the time he spent working with those guys was one of the most trying times of his life. They both managed to somehow or another reveal to Sailor the depth of despair, anger and even hatred that resided in his soul. Perhaps it was that dead part of Sailor that he did not understand and not necessarily the men he called antagonist.

Brand-New Chief Petty Officer

As the military career of Sailor was coming to a close, there was one last event that occurred involving the new CPO YNC. In one setting, CPO would leave a lasting impression upon Sailor and reveal a beacon of the compassionate side of Sailor. Prior to CPO transferring from COMPHIBRON TWO, he had asked Sailor if he would go out to breakfast with him on base at Norfolk Naval Station. Sailor mentioned it to YNC Johnson and said he was not interested in spending any time with the newly promoted chief petty officer. Sailor had to come to grips that while he did respect CPO, he could not stand him or his brand of Christianity. Chief Johnson looked at Sailor with cigarette in his mouth; back in those days, you could smoke on board ship and offices. For the first time, YNC Johnson called Sailor by his first name, Sailor, instead of the military formal address as Petty Officer Sailor. In his soft-spoken but authoritative voice, Chief Johnson said, "Sailor, you never know what will come out of this. He may want to share some things with you that will help you understand his ways."

Sailor did not care about his ways or his problems. YN1 at that time, dished out to Sailor extreme grief and persecution. What possibly could he say to Sailor that would make him understand why he was so unhappy and next to impossible to get along with? Argumentative, sarcastic, mean, uncompassionate, so on and so forth. Sailor did not care to listen and did not care to want to know what problems CPO had. As far as Sailor was concerned, his problems were his problems and not mine.

"Why should I, and why do I want to listen to what he has to say, let alone go to breakfast with him?"

The chief said, "Sailor, you are being irrational and immature. I would not have expected that from you. Maybe some of the younger petty officers, but not you."

Sailor wasn't sure if his new chief was playing a mind game on him or if his remarks were genuine. At any rate, Sailor respected his opinion and discernment well enough to accept what he said, "Okay, Chief! I'll go to breakfast with him and listen to what he has to say, but only because you suggested I do so."

"No, no, Sailor, don't go on my behalf. Go because in your heart you never know what good may come out of your meeting with him."

"I still don't see your view, Chief, but I respect your opinion and words of wisdom."

"Heck, I don't know if they are words of wisdom or just experience talking."

"Whatever, Chief, I'll go."

"Good decision, Sailor, and I don't think you will regret it. I really don't."

While the *Inchon* was docked at pier 7 on a gorgeous day in the office, Chief Petty Officer said to Sailor, "I want you to go to breakfast with me tomorrow. You going to do that, man?"

"I guess so, Chief."

"Don't let me twist your arm. Either you're going to go to breakfast or not."

"Look, Chief, I said I would, okay?"

"All right, meet me at the Exchange, at the restaurant section. They make some good grits and bacon." CPO appeared to be very excited about Sailor going to breakfast with him, and Sailor was reprehensibly apprehensive and on defense to sit down with a man he couldn't bear to look in the face because he could not stand being around him. Sailor did not like CPO or his ways or his brand of Christianity. But Sailor would learn that was not his call; rather, it was his personal problems that he harbored in the depths of his own heart. It was not Chief Petty Officer that was his problem, but rather his own self and his own weaknesses and shortcomings. Sailor, a newly ordained so-called preacher, judged a man and condemned the man without knowing who the man really was or his real struggles. Sailor prayed the night before and asked God to please, please help him because he did not know what to say to the chief and he did not want to be around him outside of duty and certainly did not want go to breakfast with him. A knot of great proportions formed in Sailor's stomach, and just the thought of eating breakfast with the Chief made it difficult for Sailor to swallow. In his mind, he was about to sit down and eat with one of the greatest antagonist of his life that he had ever known up to this point. Sailor was naïve that the entire "working" relationship and acquaintance with CPO was preparing him for the greatest test he would have to endure his entire life, decades into the future.

The time had come on a weekend while Sailor had duty and the chief was on his last leg of duty with COMPHIBRON TWO. Chief was preparing to transfer and probably would never see Sailor again. Sailor would have been content just shaking his hand on the deck of the boat, on second thought, rather had just said goodbye and not even watched him walk down the gangplank. At the end of all the selfish, spiritually immature thoughts Sailor was harboring, he did take the advice of his new Chief Johnson, and he met with CPO at the Exchange. The new CPO ordered breakfast for both of them and he insisted that he would pay for the breakfast. Immediately, Sailor was surprised that the chief paid for breakfast for both of them, and he said, "Thank you, Chief."

"No problem, Tim."

Wait! CPO addressed Sailor by his first name, Tim?

What is he doing calling me Tim? Sailor thought. When the chief addressed Sailor as Tim, that huge wall of defense that Sailor had built, began to crumble away, bit by bit. Not in one jolt, because Sailor was still apprehensive about the entire encounter eating breakfast with the chief. Grits, bacon and eggs, toast, and coffee was the order of choice for both of them. The chief then said, "Don't you want some OJ? Breakfast would not be good without a good glass of orange juice."

"Sure, Chief."

They started eating immediately after receiving their order, and the chief was making those grits look real good. His fork kept scraping the plate, stirring the grits. Chief was enjoying his meal, and Sailor, still apprehensive, was trying to enjoy his. Then out of nowhere, absolutely and totally unexpected, the chief started crying, real tears, and he was still eating his food. Sailor was stunned as he watched teardrop after teardrop slowly drop into his grits, but Chief did not skip a beat eating them.

Immediately Sailor thought, *This guy is faking, trying to get me to empathize with him about something.* But then Sailor thought, *Why would a grown man cry like the chief was crying and nothing be wrong?*

Like a completely unexpected rainstorm with dark menacing clouds, the cry of the chief intensified of what appeared to Sailor from the depths of his heart. Real, live unrehearsed tears! Sailor was speechless while the chief had stopped eating and continued crying from his soul. Sailor could not believe what he was witnessing, and he did not know what to say. Sailor just sat there, becoming overwhelmed with emotion, trying to figure out what was going on inside this man's heart and soul. He never considered himself a good comforter of the bereaved or anyone going through a tough time in their life. Sailor was lost, not knowing what to do or what to say. His eyes filled with tears, not on the scale of the chief, but partly because he did not know what to say to a grown man sitting directly across from him crying like a lost soul with no friends in the world.

Humility and Compassion

Both the chief and Sailor needed help. Both were speechless toward each other. The man that had antagonized Sailor in the worst way for the past two years was now crying at the breakfast table, and for what? Sailor had not a clue. Sailor was concerned that other people in the restaurant would notice the chief crying and may come over to the table to offer help. But Sailor would not know what to say to anyone that may have come over to the table. But no one seemed to be paying attention to what was going on at their table. In fact, it was not too crowded that morning perhaps because they had arrived pretty early, and there were not many customers that early in the morning. What seemed like long minutes of him crying and Sailor looking at the chief and searching, searching, digging deep inside for what to say, he could only ask the most obvious question: "Chief, what's wrong? Are you all right?"

"No! My life is miserable. My wife is leaving me, and I don't know what to do. I read the Bible almost every day, and I'm not always sure what it is saying, and I wish I understood the Bible like you."

Sailor wanted to yell out, "Man, I don't know anything!"

At that time in Sailor's life, the Bible might as well be foreign to him also. He said to the chief, "Man, I *don't* always know what the Bible is saying or how to apply its truths. Please don't use me as an example."

"Yeah, but you at least seem to be really sincere about what you believe, and you at least seem to be trying to live what is in the good book."

The time had arrived for the moment for Sailor to stop guessing what to say because he was becoming drained in his spirit in responding to a man he did not know, nor did he know what to say. From the innermost regions of Sailor's soul, he cried out to God and said, "God, please help me because I am lost. I do not know what to do about this situation or what to reasonably say to this man."

The chief continued to say, "I'm lost and on my way to hell. What do I do?"

That day, if none other in the life of Sailor did he truly rely on the Spirit of God to intervene. At the next word Sailor would speak to the chief would not be his own, but a truly divine intervention of the spirit of God. "Chief, what do you want?"

"I don't want to be lost."

"Then you must begin, right here, at this table, to believe that book you have been studying and allow the Lord of that book to become real to you. Chief, the first thing you must do is ask the Lord to forgive you of your sins and believe he is faithful to forgive. You must not reason in your mind of how sinful you have been but accept by faith his great forgiving love for all mankind."

"How do I do that, Sailor?"

"Let's start by confessing Jesus Christ as your Lord and Savior by asking him to come into your heart."

"How?"

"You must believe that God has sent the Lord to die on the cross for your sins, and you must confess with your mouth the Lord Jesus and that God has raised him from the dead, and according to the Bible, you will be saved from your sins."

This was Sailor's limited understanding and Sailor's Christian upbringing. But at any rate, he believes God moved in and responded to both their ignorance. The chief began to repeat those words and confessed aloud at the table of breakfast for the Lord to forgive him of his sins and come into his life. Genuine or not, played on the emotions of Sailor or not, Sailor had to believe that what took place on that morning at the Exchange Restaurant at the Naval Station in Norfolk, Virginia, was that a soul came to the Lord. A soul being a full-grown man that Sailor had only met over a year ago under circumstances and in an environment that was by far the greatest test in his life up to that point. Beirut, Lebanon, at that moment in time, at that location in America, like a battering ram, broke into the heart of Sailor and revealed to him at that moment that it was all worth it. How could he have possibly known that the man he viewed as a nemesis and persecutor of the faith would one day confess the faith in genuine repentance? How could he have known that all that he felt and believed about the chief was not what he felt about him but how disconnected himself was with the Master of Heaven. CPO was struggling with issues in his life that Sailor did not have a clue about. Sailor thought he was the only one going through such a tough time onboard the *Guadalcanal*. Sailor *only* looked at himself and his weaknesses and nursed his ungodliness. Sailor sought deliverance from the boat and wanted to go back home and a bunch of mess that you just read. When, if he were able to see at the time, everything was about God molding him into his image. But all he could see was his own prejudices against the United States Navy, his leading petty officer and the white officers in the command. Sailor was at war with the wrong enemy. He wared against people instead of knowing the enemy who wars against the soul of men from the powers of darkness.

At an instance, Sailor grew exponentially while assessing the past two years of his life serving with CPO. The tour of duty embarked with COMPHIBRON TWO, serving with YN1 at the time, was unexplainable on every level. But the breakfast with the new CPO was answered within minutes of eating. YN2 said YN1 was a confused, unhappy man, and Chief Johnson said YN1 had personal issues that neither Sailor nor he knew about. The witness of Sailor and the impression he gave to YN1 was an incredible revelation. If only YN1 had a clue that Sailor was just as confused, unhappy, and a grand sinner, perhaps greater than YN1, would the outcome have been different? But actually, that question is irrelevant because the outcome, apparently, was the will of God.

There is a verse in the Bible that says, "Thou knowest my downsitting and mine uprising, thou understandest my thought afar off" (Psalm 139:2). Sailor found hope and comfort in that verse concluding that God knew the outcome and the reason and purpose for he and YN1 to cross paths in life. To that end, both men finished their breakfast, stood up, and shook each other's hand with a firm grip. Sailor said to the chief, "Fair winds and following seas…shipmate!"

CPO smiled and said, "Likewise, YN1 Sailor!"

It was the first time and last time the chief addressed Sailor in a professional manner, demonstrating a small degree of respect. The disagreements, arguments, anger, and desire to physically fight YN1 two years ago all ended that day. The absolute misunderstanding of the man and the hatred that Sailor developed in his heart against YN1 all of a sudden fell apart in the mind of Sailor, and he envisioned those tough times dissolving for all eternity. On that day, he watched the chief until he walked out of his sight, and close to forty years would pass and he would never, ever see the chief again. As the chief walked away, Sailor stared at him feeling great empathy, sadness, and a small degree of happiness. He missed the interaction with the chief, and he missed the chief. An astounding reversal of emotions and thoughts overtook Sailor as CPO faded in the distance.

20

TOUR OF DUTY

The USS Inchon (LPH-12)
Fourth and Final Mediterranean Cruise

Everything about this cruise would remind Sailor of his first experiences with the navy on his first Mediterranean cruise. The first cruise he went on in 1977 on board the USS *Independence* (CV-62) was filled with nothing but excitement. Absent of the whorehouses because on this cruise, he was the senior petty officer and role model to younger sailors. Younger brothers looked up to Sailor, and by this time his life had returned back to the right path. On MARG 3-84/85 cruise, he would not even look at a woman in lust but was more concerned about living the Christian life. There would still be encounters with scores of beautiful women, but his heart desired nothing but doing what was right. One of the motivating factors of not desiring other women was the fact that he was married while on his final Med. cruise. He got married one year after being on shore duty he wanted to spend as much time with his new wife that he possibly could. He knew that after shore duty would end, he would be going back to sea. He made every possible attempt not to go back to sea but was unsuccessful in his attempt. To the point of mentally draining and physically taxing talking to different ministers for moral support. Sailor petitioned his senior clergy to write letters on his behalf. He thought if they would let the navy know that he was needed to remain on shore duty because he was nominated and selected for official office in the church. The late B. Baxter had recommended and nominated Sailor as the District Sunday School and YPWW President of the Commonwealth of Pennsylvania Church of God in Christ. But Sailor would not serve one day in that position as his time on shore duty was quickly coming to an end. The United States Navy prevailed over the desires of Sailor, and he was ordered to return back to sea duty. Exceedingly disheartened that his request was not approved and to ease his mind, he reasoned with himself.

After all, I did enter an all-volunteer force, and I did sign the contract to obey the orders of those appointed over me, he thought.

His reasoning was 100 percent true, but not reassuring enough to ease the unrest in his mind. In that situation, the United States Navy was in charge and Sailor had to obey the orders of the navy. The USS *Inchon* duty was one year after the USS *Guadalcanal* (LPH-7) duty involving Beirut, Lebanon. The Amphibious Squadron staff cross decked to the *Inchon* for MARG 3-84/85 Med. cruise. In 1984 in late October, the USS *Inchon* (LPH12) got underway from Norfolk Naval Station on its way to the Mediterranean Sea. This would be Sailor's fourth time transiting the Atlantic Ocean, traveling to familiar places and visiting new places on this cruise. Everything about this cruise was fabulous from the beginning to the end. In many ways, he could not wait to get underway because to Sailor, time moved fast while at sea. Sailor was motivated by another reason for this cruise to get underway—the expectation of his enlistment coming to an end. The old term *EAOS*, then *EOS*, which stood for, "End of Active Obligated Service and End of Obligated Service," would be approaching for Sailor.

A pastime small talk among many sailors was, "When is your EAOS?" It was as if EAOS was a magical number, but it was an exciting thing to talk about. Sailor departed on board the USS *Inchon* (LPH-7) broaching the conversation that his EAOS arrives after this cruise. MARG 3-84/85 with Amphibious Squadron TWO on board the USS *Inchon* (LPH-12) would bring Sailor closer to the end of enlistment, and he would make a decision that one day he would regret. Embarking on Med. cruises was kind of like entering an imaginary portal that would catapult Sailor through time to the end of his travels. He always experienced mixed emotions. Let's go and get it done. Let's not go because it's six long months away from home. He was not aware of the regretful decision he would make, but he would learn, like many decisions he had made over the years. Getting off active duty was totally and absolutely his decision, though he relied upon the input of others. In the words of the late Dr. Ralph Abernathy, "By comparison, my childhood seems like a painted landscape in a museum, but my days as a soldier are carved in granite, a few incidents, some of them irrelevant, still standing in bold relief after the erosion of forty years." Sailor had matured extensively and noticeably from the days of his first enlistment, but he had not yet become settled in making life-changing decisions. It is foolish and absolutely useless to wish he would not have gotten out of the navy, but the good, if any, is the depth of what he learned about himself. MARG 3-84/85 Med cruise was kind of a going-away cruise in his eyes because this cruise reminisced of his earlier days with VS-31. His first military Mediterranean cruise was filled with fun and excitement and a multitude of sinful actions. MARG 3-84/85 would bring with it the anticipation of getting out of the navy or staying in. He had grown up significantly from the days of crying and being sad and wrestling with his own emotions or getting pissed off with people and things. It was his heart's desire to be in control of himself and his emotions. The philosophical words Fred used to dump on Sailor and the sinful worldly life he had picked up from Bay, both were becoming distant memories, barely alive in his mind. Sailor had begun to look deep inside his own heart and search for what he knew to be true and right. He began to hunger and thirst for right living and immutable truth and confidence and assurance in his own words. He thought it necessary and essential to become solely a separate individual created by God to esteem his name. MARG 3-84/85 cruise would be the second time Sailor opened his mind to the beauty and wonder of God's creation and the spirit of closeness with him. Like most of life's experiences, he did not know what to expect during MARG 3-84/85, but he knew it would not be like prior Med. cruises. He became a preacher "of sorts" on board the ship seemingly without restrictions. The spirit of wisdom and maturity allowed Sailor to tactfully share the truth of the Word of God, without appearing to be proselytizing crewmembers. He was far from being a godly man in his eyes, but others perceived him as a man of God. An unexpected type of sermon had formed in the life of Sailor from a year and a half ago where the devil himself would have argued with God about the salvation of Sailor. The devil would have presented to God without question the sinful ways of Sailor and laughed while saying to God, "There is no way in hell he is godly." Since the days of the *Guadalcanal*, the life of Sailor had changed, and Sailor would imagine God would say to the devil "there is no way in heaven that he belongs to you."

YN2 Admin and the Imperials

The cruise began with Sailor's mind on God and ended with his mind on God. There was this guy who worked in the ship's admin office that Sailor never would have guessed they would become good acquaintances. They did not hang out together, and Sailor does not remember ever going on a guided tour with him. It seemed to Sailor they were only friends on board the ship. Sailor does not remember the guy's name or much about him. But for the purposes of identification, he will be called Petty Officer Admin. The thing that connected them together was the music he was playing in his workspace.

One day Sailor had to drop off a document at the administrative office Petty Officer Admin worked in, and Sailor heard the music the guy was playing. As Sailor made his approach to the administrative office, it seemed the music was perfectly clear and the lyrics sang with precision. Petty Officer Admin was playing his music a little louder than normal, but no one was complaining. When Sailor stepped in Petty Officer Admin's, office he turned the music down but still loud enough for Sailor to hear it. Petty Officer Admin smiled at Sailor like he didn't have a care in the world, and Sailor looked at him with an amazed look thinking, *This guy is pretty bold to play that kind of music onboard a Naval warship.*

Petty Officer Admin continued to enjoy his music as nothing else mattered and no one else mattered. He then looked up at Sailor and asked, "Hey, Petty Officer Sailor, may I help you with something?"

"Yes, who is that you are playing on your tape player?"

Quickly, almost immediately, business now became pleasure, and he turned the tunes up a little louder and asked Sailor to sit down. He then reached in one of his cabinets and pulled out what looked like a storage case full of cassette tapes of nothing but Gospel music.

Sailor thought, *This is crazy. What is this guy doing with all these Gospel tapes onboard a naval vessel?*

But to Petty Officer Admin, the *Inchon* was his ship, and he owned his workspace as the leading petty officer. At first glance, Petty Officer Admin seemed to be very content being in the United States Navy. A revelation immediately was birthed in Sailor's spirit. He thought, *It does not matter what circumstances you are in, rather what is in you, be it frustration, anger, discontent or peace.*

From Sailor's eyes, the navy fit Petty Officer Admin well. Deep down inside Sailor's heart, he wanted the navy to fit him also, and he wanted to be fit for the navy. But because of past experiences, Sailor had developed a bitter taste in his mouth toward the navy and was really trying to regain the enthusiasm he once held. Sailor sat down in Petty Officer Admin's office and pretty much forgot why he went to his office. Petty Officer Admin pulled out a blank case and said, "This is who is playing right now. Imperials. Yes, they're good, aren't they?"

"Yes, I like the sound and their style and harmonizing."

Petty Officer Admin then pulled out a blank cassette and rewound the tape that was playing, inserted the blank cassette, and began recording.

Sailor thought to himself, *Why is this guy so generous with his music, and why is he recording this tape for me without me asking?*

They kept talking for a few minutes while the tape was recording, and he began to show Sailor his collection of at least two hundred-plus Gospel artists on board a naval vessel in his office at sea. Sailor maybe had twenty tapes at best at his bunk stored away in his locker. Back in those days, Sailor had developed and learned to be prejudice against white Christian men. In Sailor's mind, they just did not see eye to eye when it came to the Bible and church. He really did not want to get too close to Petty Officer Admin and call himself being his friend because he did not know how, nor did he want to deal with the differences in how they believed. But the music he was playing had captivated the soul of Sailor, and he desperately needed some good sounds while onboard ship again on his way back overseas.

"There's a storm on the horizon…let the wind blow." That is the song Petty Officer Admin was playing that day. The rhythm and sound were very nice and spoke to Sailor's soul having left home again and this time having left his wife. Sailor needed the assurance and comfort that he was not alone, though, in many ways, he was alone. But with the wind blowing in his life and the storm attempting to rage again, his spirit needed to be at peace. The introduction of the Imperials during MARG 3-84/85 Mediterranean cruise did just that. Sailor would find himself back and forth to Petty Officer Admin's workspace looking for new music. Sailor purchased packs of blank cassettes from the ship's store and took over to Petty Officer Admin, and he seemed to be more than happy to record songs for Sailor. He offered to pay Admin for his time and troubles, but Admin never asked for, nor did he want any money from Sailor to record Gospel music for him. It was the most unusual "friendship" Sailor had ever encountered. It was like they were best friends only on the ship. In hindsight, Sailor attributes that limited friendship due to his own apprehensions and prejudice thoughts and bad experiences. During MARG 3-84/85, Sailor and Admin became pretty good friends, but only through and because of his Gospel music. Sailor still concealed within his soul a distance of most white people and continued, for the most part, not allowing others within his selfish boundaries. The song the Imperials were singing was refreshing and yet sort of predictive of one of the greatest trials ever yet to come. The storm would be monumental on a personal, spiritual, and mental level the likes Sailor never, ever would have imagined in his lifetime.

MARG 3-84/85 Mediterranean Cruise

Malaga, Spain, Livorno, Italy, Toulon, France, Palma de Majorca, Catania, Sicily, Istanbul, Turkey, Genoa, Italy, Marseilles, France, Naples, Italy, and Cartegena, Spain was a nice Med. cruise, to say the least. Sailor's indoctrination with terrorism in Beirut, Lebanon, when most Americans were clueless of such diabolical acts, had seen a reprieve for now, and it seemed the Master of Heaven would allow this final typical Mediterranean cruise on active duty. MARG 3-84/85 would be a Mediterranean cruise similar to the first two cruises he had enjoyed during his first enlistment. All the crybaby stuff and cursing and drinking and hating and everything else of the flesh would not have its way during this cruise. MARG 3-84/85 cruise would certainly be reminiscent of days gone by. In Malaga, Spain, he would purchase genuine white pearls for his wife and was very excited about buying them. Toulon, France, he would purchase a robe and slippers for himself that he held on to for a long time until they began to wear out. Palma de Majorca he would purchase another set of white pearls for his wife that she held on to as long as Sailor could remember. Istanbul, Turkey, was an experience of experiences as he beheld a public hanging in the square of Istanbul. Unlike America, an eye for an eye was pretty much still in place in those days. He would also purchase two suits from a vendor on the streets of Turkey that he held on to for years until they began to wear out. In fact, he had those two suits years after he and his wife moved into their newly built home. Naples, Italy is the 6th fleet's home away from home with the Allied Forces Southern Europe (AFSOUTH) home-based there. AFSOUTH has since been deactivated in 2004 and reorganized as Allied Forces Joint Command (JFC). JFC is part of the North Atlantic Treaty Organization (NATO) coalition to face the challenges of the new millennium warfare. There was much to do in Naples, Italy, in and around the area. From Naples, Sailor could travel to Rome, Italy, or Pompeii or pretty much anywhere within the region.

The Two Chaps in the Dark Alley

He greatly anticipated getting underway for MARG 3-84/85 cruise because, in many ways, he was anticipating making the decision whether to stay in or get out of the navy. October 1984, the USS *Inchon* (LPH-12) boatswain mate called away on the 1MC "underway, shift colors." It was a sweet sound to Sailor because he knew everything would be different, and he looked forward to an overseas experience similar to his very first experience. Furthermore, the staff was fairly new with a new commodore. Captain Strolle reminded Sailor of his first commanding officer in VS-31, his first permanent duty station. Captain Strolle was laid back, soft-spoken and seemed to care about his crew. Just like his first commanding officer in VS-31. Petty Officer Sailor could talk to Captain Strolle and hold a reasonably intelligent conversation with him. Unlike the previous commodore, Captain George D.B. Sailor felt great distance and the entire unit was not close with one another, all because the leadership plainly created a separation between officer and men. But with Captain Strolle, things were back to normal as Sailor saw it. MARG 3-84/85 would bring forth an experienced sailor of the seas and also put Sailor at an emotional crossroad whether to stay in or get off active duty. First port of call was Naples, Italy, and Sailor was very, very familiar with the territory and how to get around on his own. Only but for the grace of God that nothing happened to him as he walked around and went to places in Naples on his own. There were a few times that he hung out with shipmates, but for the most part, he was on his own up and down the streets of Naples, Italy. Picking up a few souvenirs, knowing that this may very well be his last time in Italy, he casually strolled by the Galleria Umberto, which is at the base of the road that leads to the whorehouse. Almost as far as one can see up the narrow road is a little whorehouse filled with young girls ready for a $50 payoff to sell their bodies. Sailor was tempted, although he told himself that he would not entertain those thoughts, the familiarity and even the certain smell of Naples, Italy, brought the temptation very intensely. Secondly, walking the streets by himself with an idle mind, so to speak, urged the tempting thoughts on. He paced back and forth inside the Galleria, aimlessly window-shopping, thinking about the young whores. He figured while it was day, he could make his way up the narrow alley and take care of his lustful desire one more time and make it back to the boat before nightfall. But that time would never arrive. He walked out of the Galleria, walked back in the Galleria, walked back out of the Galleria, and did this several times. Playing Russian Roulette with time, he decided to walk up the alley at a very fast pace, hurrying to get to the whorehouse. At this time, the sun was setting, and it was beginning to get dark. He thought to himself, *I should have gone up here when I first thought about it. Now it's starting to get dark, and it will be dark when I leave the whorehouse.*

He started taking slow strides up the cobblestone road toward the place of sin he enjoyed seven years ago. But this time he was all alone, figuring that he knew the territory and was on familiar ground. The thing is, he was so misguided and drawn to old sins that he was careless in his thinking. There was absolutely no one on board the *Inchon* or in his unit, COMPHIBRON TWO, that he could even suggest going with him. Somehow, he was being called to that place. He did not want to go but was unable to resist. Everything inside his soul cried out to him to cease the foolishness and turn around and get out of that place before grace ceases to be grace upon his foolish heart. As he was approaching Momma Rosa's, he could hear the loud music and even smell the distinct nasty musty odor. The smell seemed to be intensified a thousand times compared to his first experience. He almost stopped in his tracks because of the smell alone. He still needed some prodding, and the next event that unfolded continues to baffle Sailor to this day when he thinks about it. About three quarters of the way up the now dark alley, towards the whorehouse a couple of guys walked passed him, seemingly minding their own business. One of the guys looked back at a person in a doorway and yelled out, "We will bring some fool back!"

Stunned and absolutely bewildered, Sailor stopped in his tracks and had the nerve to ask the guy, "What did you say?"

The guy said, "We are bringing food back. What's it to you?"

Sailor replied, "I could have sworn you said *fool*!"

One of them said to Sailor, "Mate, you better lay off the hard stuff and get your ass off the streets before you get killed."

The two chaps walked down the dark alley laughing as loud as they could, as though they were at a comedy show enjoying every minute of the act. Sailor stood there watching them as they walked away and faded into the dark night. It took Sailor all but five seconds to follow in their footsteps at a fast pace that he started jogging, then he decided to run as if competing in a track and field event. Spooked at the whole coincidence, or premonition, or subliminal message of sorts, he ran without looking backward. Less than five minutes, he was back at the Galleria looking around for the two chaps he just encountered. He could not find them anywhere in the Galleria or any store. Actually, he does not remember seeing them coming out of a building or coming from around the corner while they were in the alley. It was like all of a sudden, they were walking past him in the alley when he spotted them, and then, all of a sudden, they were gone. The encounter with the two chaps in the dark alley was very mind-blowing to Sailor and very questionable of the real existence of the two chaps.

He purposely kept his eyes on them as they were walking toward the Galleria, and when he began to run, he was actually about to catch up with them. Once they entered the Galleria among other people, his eyes straight on them, they vanished out of his sight. It wasn't like they were walking fast or even picked up their pace. The two chaps were walking at a very normal pace, one in which anyone could have caught up with them and overtaken them. How is it possible that they vanished out of his sight when they were within a stone's throw away from Sailor? He stood there in the Galleria, unambiguously gazing around, intensely combing the area for those two chaps. He just wanted to talk to them, say something to them, mainly to validate that they were real. He reasoned and reasoned in his mind that the encounter with the two chaps was just his imagination on overload, sort of a chastisement because he was not authorized to be in that area of town. But he could not conclude as to their response to him. He asked them a question, and they gave him a reply. He was so discombobulated, because he wanted to go to the whorehouse, but he was deeply concerned about the "message" coming from two complete strangers. If they were really not there, how does one answer the reply they gave to him? Over time Sailor chose to let the memory and the encounter fade because he knew of no way to validate what happened that dark night in the dark alley in Naples, Italy. The two chaps in the dark alley remain a totally unanswerable encounter to this day for Sailor. The temptation of visiting the whorehouse and the unexplainable encounter with the two chaps began to cause Sailor to evaluate his own actions. Had God brought him this far without any incident with foreign nationals or the government of the United States, of which he was a representative in the military? He had experienced close encounters with the Italian police and the Navy Shore Patrol years before on his first and second Med. cruise. Why continue to risk getting caught or busted by continuing to visit unauthorized locations, just to spend a few unsafe times with a million whores, a million or so, because only God knows how many sailors and marines the whores had spent time with before Sailor ever touched them? What was the meaning of the encounter with the two chaps in the dark alley? Why were they there at the precise time Sailor was taking his trek toward the whorehouse? Why did the word *food* sound like *fool* to Sailor? Many questions not answered, and he was way too embarrassed to ask anyone their thoughts at the risk of revealing to others what he was contemplating doing. There would be other invitations here and there throughout the cruise, and one other encounter that shook him to the core of his soul.

The Witch That Was a Whore

In those days, a typical Mediterranean cruise would be anywhere from six to nine months. As the cruise is winding down to the end of the deployment, the possibility of the cruise getting extended due to international conflict always exists. A month or so had passed since the temptation of going to the whorehouse and the encounter with the two chaps in the dark alley. Sailor kept himself busy in every fashion and manner he could think of. Sailor made sure he companied himself with other crew members on every visit to a new country from that point on. He went on guided tours and bought souvenirs, searching for ways of non-self-serving in which to spend his money. Like his first tour of duty to the Mediterranean, he thought that would be the most productive and safe way to spend his time. He continued to go on tour and continued to take pictures, making every attempt to avoid the thought and possibility of whoring. He would not learn until decades later, it does not matter what you are doing activity-wise, but what actually resides in the depth of one's heart that leads to what you are doing and what activity you engage in. Sailor was trying desperately to run from himself. At the time, he did not realize that self was his major battle and worst enemy.

Sometime in April 1985, just a few short weeks shy of returning to the United States at Naval Station Norfolk. Sailor was feeling proud of himself thinking that he had overcome the lustful spirit of whoring with strange women, as spoken of in the Scriptures. But a brief stop in England would not only give him the weirdest experience of his life but, in some sense, make him feel naked standing in front of a host of evil eyes bearing down into his soul. The ship would make two more stops before transiting the Atlantic Ocean, and Sailor would get the opportunity to travel to London, England. The brief stop to the Netherlands would spark the old temptation of lustful thoughts. If Sailor thought the red-light district in New Orleans was decadent, he hadn't yet been exposed to the shops in the Netherlands, which was not in his favor. He remembers hearing all the talk about the brothels in the Netherlands where prostitution was legal. You could actually walk down certain streets, sort of window-shopping as prostitute after prostitute would stand behind a clear plate glass window, displaying all the bodily flesh they had to offer. Sailor knew full well that if he went window-shopping for women selling their bodies, on display, like a candy store with all sorts of sweets in the window, that would be the resurrection of the demise of his soul. He convinced himself over and over that there was no need to see scantily dressed women standing in a display window. Even if he wanted to view the sights, just to say that he had been there and seen naked women for himself, standing in the prostitute window. The way he would avoid the temptation was to go on a guided tour, purchase some souvenirs, and return to the ship at the end of the day. However, Murphy's law, the devil, or his own thoughts, one of the three, engaged him by association with the wrong crowd or group of dudes from the ship. The tour he took of Amsterdam, Holland, was nice and relaxing, to say the least. The windmills, sunken gardens, water levels almost parallel to the road and just being in another foreign country to add to his global travels, was exciting enough for him. But the sins of the Father played itself out in Sailor in ways he seems not to be able to control. He prayed for strength to resist the temptation, but gave life to the idea of the sin by thinking, thinking and thinking about the experience and what it would be like to see and do the things of worldly pleasure. This was a clear indication to Sailor that deep inside the core of his soul lay a desire and life that was 180 degrees from the life he was raised to believe. But many times, there was an undeniable "living on the edge" that continued to drive Sailor, even with the positive experiences he had at church back home. Once out of the territory of familiar religious, Christian experience, lay the real man that was frightening to look at. His next temptation would occur on a cool breezy evening after taking in the sites of Amsterdam Holland. He was with a good mixture of black and white crewmembers on the guided tour. After the tour, about half of the group decided they wanted to visit the red-light district.

By Massimo Catarinella - Own work, CC BY-SA 3.0, https://commons.wikimedia.org/w/index.php?curid=3829152

It sparked a forbidden excitement in Sailor, but at the same time, a battle raged inside his soul, attempting to deny the desire to see all the talk about prostitutes standing in the window. He also felt the event would be like going to a department store window-shopping to decide which store you wanted to enter and sample the ware. The idea of prostitutes "legally" for sale *blew* the novice mind of Sailor but kept his interest. Some of the guys on the tour, maybe about ten of them, out of a crew of about fifteen, decided to return to the ship and settle in. Sailor, actually physically tired and wanting to return to the ship and lay his tired butt down, opted to tag along with the promiscuous other crewmembers. Sailor and about five other guys excitedly made their way down to the place similar to the image above to see what all the fuss was about. How real is this thing about women tempting the very testosterone right out of the ejaculatory duct of the male anatomy? Sailor wanted to know, and now that he had someone to investigate along with him, reluctantly and with bated breath, he accepted the temptation. There were several problems with this visit that plagued Sailor in the back of his mind, but he justified his actions as a sailor, that it was a once-in-a-lifetime experience. Nonetheless, sin is sin whether it is one time or multiple times. But for Sailor, at the time, his fleshly reasoning and overactive sexual drive outweighed his Christian upbringing. Secondly, how could he not think about his wife back home in the United States? How could he justify the curse of sexual sins that followed him all his youthful life? The young TJ may have been oblivious to sexual activity unless it was brought alive through ideas, thoughts, and suggestions from one of his boyhood idols. Lastly, he was out of money, tired, and hungry but driven by desire of the basest nature. This was the last night in port then the ship would be getting underway early morning. Whatever he was going to experience would be brief, if anything at all. Six guys come strolling around the corner, making their entrance into the red-light district. True to its name, the street, buildings, and even people had a hint of red cast upon them. It was as if the aura of the environment somehow or another painted everything red. Or was Sailor just that enamored by what he was about to see? In the mind of Sailor, all the talk about the red-light district caused a perception of the area and the people to have a hint of red cast upon them? Or maybe the red lustful appeal of the women inside the windows was overpowering every other tint and color. Nonetheless, as these guys started walking down the street, gazing, looking, unhurried, stopping and gawking, Sailor was captivated by the lust of the desire of the flesh of the women in the window. Every woman in the window seemingly wore a beautiful smile as if to say, "I am especially here for you tonight. What is your pleasure?" But Sailor had enough presence of mind to realize they were working women, selling their body to whoever would be willing to pay for their service. Seductive, sexual, sensual service of the sinfully good time. He knew the smile was not especially for him, but he felt they smiled especially at him. After about ten minutes of walking, looking, smiling, and gawking, two of the guys in the group said they were about to engage themselves into the women for sale. In fact, they said it just like that, "Hey, we are about to engage the women. They are *beautiful*."

Was it real beauty or an imitation of a masked, cloaked evil, sinful thing? How can real beauty be purchased for a half an hour or so? The same so-called beauty purchased by a thousand men before? How? One in whom untold John's have "engaged" them for untold dollar amounts and untold sexual acts. But Sailor did not really care about all that reasoning and so-called theological thinking, he was just as much interested as his other shipmates. He just did not have any more money and besides being tired and hungry was pretty confident that his stamina would be next to none.

Torn between desire and compelled by overwhelming lust drawing his spirit into a captivating high and rush of imagined eroticism. He became thoughtless and without focus as to what he should be doing and what decision he should make. One of the guys offered to loan him a few dollars until next payday so they all could enjoy themselves on the last night of liberty. But Sailor respectfully declined the offer from the guy. He really did not want to have sex with an internationally known prostitute in Amsterdam, Holland. The guys were pretty cool about it, and Sailor was able to convince one of the other guys to walk back to the ship with him, both of them, tired and hungry. The other dudes lost themselves under the cover of darkness while inundated with the red-light district, engaging the prostitutes of their choice. Sailor, the entire time walking back to the ship with his other shipmate, could not get the images out of his mind of what he had just seen. He carefully and in detail, recalled the white flesh and black flesh, and even certain positions some of the women were sitting in and the luring spell-bound desire of them. It was like all the lustful demons of hell had launched an attack on his mind, and he could not get his thoughts clear to see his way. His shipmate said to him a couple of times, "Hey, Sailor, you all right? Can't get your mind off that pussy for sale back there, can you?"

They both laughed and continued walking toward the pier to the ship. The shipmate walking with Sailor was a little older and seemed to be a lot more settled in life. He pretty much was just hanging out with the other guys. But he at least helped Sailor to focus on returning back to the ship and for a brief moment, helped to turn Sailor's mind to the right way. But that wouldn't last for long, because the battle was raging inside the soul of Sailor, and the only one able to quiet the storm and defeat the raging serpent of sin was Messiah. Desperately and deeply searching for the truth and how to live that truth has been the lot of Sailor from day one of his natural life.

A few more weeks and Sailor would be back in the United States of America and the relieving thought of going back to America was comforting to him. One more port of call would be the last he would see of the European continent for a few years. Upon arriving back to the ship, it seemed the night passed away in a brief moment of time. Once on board ship, he took a quick shower and made haste to get to his bunk because he was fatigued, both mentally and physically. The next thing he remembers was "now set the sea and anchor detail." They were underway for Portsmouth, England, sailing west but would make one more stop. Sailor would take a trip to London to see the Changing of the Guard. Swing by 10 Downey Street and cross the Thames River and Saint Peter's Basilica. The time he spent in London was thrilling and educational with a few shipmates he hung out with. Traveled to Leeds Castle in Maidstone, Kent, and also took an educational trip to Edinburgh, Scotland, where the famous King James VI ruled and the King James Version of the Bible was born. This trip by far kept him productively occupied and learning historical things worth remembering. The old saying "an idle mind is the devil's workshop" found its place in Sailor during the evenings and days he had duty on board ship. But the curse of the lustful spirit that plagues the soul of men and women, out of nowhere, he thought about the prostitutes in Amsterdam, Holland, and only imagined what it would have been like satisfying his desire with them. One unfortunate evening when he had nothing to do because he had taken several guided tours of England. He went to a club with a couple other guys, and it appeared the shipmates he went with was armed and ready for any action they could possible get into. The first place they visited was a little on the upscale end. Without any prethought of certain consequences of right and wrong, he looked for a woman just to talk to. At this point, he stopped fighting the desire that was resurrected while in Amsterdam and decided to just go out and talk—that's all, talk.

They arrived at a club of which the name Sailor does not remember probably because of the incident that occurred at the club. The place was very active that night as men and women strolled into a nightclub with the music of the Bee Gees playing. The music wasn't too loud but was just right. The song Night Fever was pleasingly playing in the club. The rock group Bee Gees reminded Sailor of his friend JM from his first tour of duty. JM drove around Florida in his streamlined light blue Cadillac, seemed to always have the Bee Gees playing. "Night Fever" was one of those songs that elicited certain feelings and desires in Sailor. Old thoughts, old passions, and old desires uncontrollably resurrected in the soul of Sailor in London, England, when he saw all the beautiful women in the club. The shipmates he was with that evening were aggressively talking to the women. They were on the dance floor bumping and grinding and feeling parts of their body that only spoke one message. When it came to women, Sailor was never the one to be aggressive, loud, and in-your-face type of approach. Rather, he was laid-back, cool, a smooth talker, with suggestive facial expressions. He spotted a woman sitting by herself when her friends got up from the table. He politely made his way over to her table and noticed that she was a buxom and proportionately built woman. She had a complexion that seemed to him at the time to radiate with attention. As he walked toward her table, she noticed him and looked directly at him, batting her eyes, as to welcome the attention. Closer and closer to her table, he quickly increased his stride and straightened his posture as to present a strong young man ready for sexual pleasure. But initially, all he wanted to do was talk and spend time with a female, having been on board ship surrounded by men for months. Back in those days, women were not authorized to be on a sea-going vessel. It was just unheard of and thought to be uncontrollable. Thoughts ranged from a love boat scenario to children out of wedlock. But today, with women on board naval vessels, it doesn't seem as drastic as thought of in the early 1980s. Within seconds, he was at her table, and she slowly and methodically crossed her legs to expose parts of her thigh, increasing her body language all the while as Sailor approached her. "Hey, how are you doing tonight beautiful?"

"I am fine and yourself, handsome? How are you? My name is Kathy, with a *K*."

It's funny of all the stuff Sailor experienced and even people he met, somehow or another Kathy's name stands out to him.

The conversation was satisfying to Sailor, and the fragrance she wore was hypnotically appealing. They talked about the military, nothing classified, basic questions like, "Do you like being in the service, and if you had to, would you do it again."

After about ten minutes of talking, she suggested that they go to her place and that she would drop Sailor off at the pier whenever he would be ready to leave. Immediately, he thought about the experience he had in Naples, Italy, a few years ago with the crossdresser outside of the bar when he was with his homies. He was uncontrollably desirous to be with her and was greatly influenced by the recent temptation in Amsterdam, Holland. But was also paranoid that she would cause harm to him or get him over to her place and men would be there to rob him and cause bodily harm to him. He asked her direct, no-holds-barred questions like, "You are not setting me up, are you? Hell, I could stay here with my friends and leave with them and remain safe."

She laughed and politely reached for Sailor's hand and said, "Sailor, you came over to me, and I willingly accepted your company, because everything about you was interesting to me."

That wasn't enough for Sailor to feel safe, but somehow or another, she was able to convince Sailor to go with her. When they left the club, Sailor made it a point to let his shipmates know what he was doing, and strangely enough, she offered her address to them to let them know where they would be. That gave him a little comfort, but he continued to accommodate her. The remainder of events is a memory that Sailor will never forget. 43 Marylebone Place is where they arrive at, and it was the same address she gave to his shipmates. The comfort level now began to turn into excitement.

She said, "See, I don't have time for trouble or any investigation from the United States Military. It's just you and me at my place to get to know each other better. Isn't that what you wanted?" Sailor smiled and just nodded his head in satisfaction. Once inside 43 Marylebone Place, it was a fresh clean smell, neatly decorated. She lit a few candles softly burning and lit a few sweet-smelling incenses. They sat down on her couch and continued talking. But out of nowhere, she said, "I'm a little psychic at times, but I have to feel it before I can speak."

Sailor, attempting to be polite and chuckled, thinking to himself that was unusual, who cares about psychic right now because he was there for one reason and one reason only. But she convinced him to let her tell him about his background. He laughed and wore a huge smile thinking, *Okay, what harm can she cause by talking foolishly?*

"Go ahead, what do you know about me."

"Well, I don't really know you in reality, but as I said to you, sometimes I am psychic."

"Okay, Ms. Psychic, what is it that you need to psych about me?" Sailor, now responding in a sharp tone and insinuating extreme facetiousness. All that would change in a matter of seconds after she began to delineate her psychic assessment of Sailor. He was chewing gum with a smirk on his face becoming bored with her antics because he did not go over her place to be "psyched" out.

It was almost as if she cast a spell of some sort on him filled with sexual temptation that was intensely uncontrollable. She reared back further on the couch, crossing her legs exposing all there was to see. She never took her eyes off Sailor with a smile. She was never moved by Sailor's smart remarks. But Sailor was greatly distracted looking at her semi-exposed flesh. How could he concentrate on what she was about to say? She took the thoughts, feelings, and desire for any sexual pleasure from Sailor she acted like a master at mind manipulation and soul captivation. "Sailor, you come from a large family, a deeply religious family."

Okay, he thought, *a "lucky" shot in the dark. I mean, what where the odds to correctly identify a black man's life then?* he thought.

But as she continued and all the while exposing more and more of her flesh, the gum he was chewing became dry in his mouth and the smirk on Sailor's face quickly began to fade. Sailor became not only irritated but ready to run away from her back to club to hook up with his shipmates. "Your father was a preacher and the disciplinarian, and your mother was a kind woman that you loved very deeply." At this point, Sailor was becoming afraid of the woman he met in the club in London, England.

He immediately thought, *Is this broad a witch? How can that be? A real witch? This is more than just mere psychic ability.* He became fidgety, couldn't sit still, scratching his head, rubbing his leg.

"Your parents had, what, thirteen, fourteen children, and all of them are still alive. You had two brothers that you really looked up to. And you—"

"STOP! What the *hell* are you doing? How do you know all that? Who the hell are you women!? I *will* fuck you up right here, right now!" The spirit of cursing and wanting to fight attacked Sailor in an instant!

She stopped talking immediately and said, "Oh baby, I'm sorry, I didn't mean to upset you, I told you that there are times when I am psychic. I meant absolutely no harm, Sailor!" At that point, she had nothing but her bra and underpants on, and Sailor did not even realize that she had gotten undressed. Surprisingly, she then said, "Was I correct on what I said?"

"Hey, it does not matter, we are done with that introduction of you."

Sailor was eyeballing her body as she moved closer to him, caressing and apologizing and being gentle with her approach. His soul had become totally submissive to what she wanted to do, and he allowed her to, more or less, satisfy herself. He was hypnotized yet desirous while maintaining a small sense of his own thoughts. He knew that he should leave the witch's place and return to his shipmates, but he was spellbound both by her magic and her naked body. She worked unholy magic on Sailor while simultaneously arousing eroticism within his soul. How is it even possible for such a thing to occur? How and what did she do, without any use of drugs or alcohol? Unless, unless, her place was inundated with a wicked spirit to drench *anyone* who she desired to fulfill her own lustful desires.

The candles, the incense, the dimly lit lights, the soft new age sounding music playing, and the unknown smell of the fragrance inside her house—did that combination work magic on the mind and soul of Sailor as she, the witch, tantalized his mind with her snake tongue? Sailor kind of blacked out into a sexual high and eroticism that he did not even know was possible. All he wanted to do, once he arrived at her place was to have sex and then leave. But she had a mind, body, and soul control over him that had become the most unusual experience of any fornication or adulterous encounter Sailor had *ever* experienced. By the time he left the house of the witch, he was full of unanswered questions that followed him all the way through the trans-Atlantic trip back to the United States of America. Sailor had concluded on his own that Kathy was a witch that worked magic on him from the moment he spotted her in the nightclub. He assessed the encounter with her from the second he spotted her for years into his future. Never, ever coming to a plausible explanation of what he experienced with her. He also decided that the sex with her was really not that great anyway. Was it because she was in control as it seemed to immensely please her? Sailor was under the craziest spell of his life and could not wait to get out of her presence.

He had no explanation for what happened that night at Kathy's place in London, England, but tried his best to figure out what happened. The second he spotted her in the nightclub, there were about four other women sitting at the table with her. Strangely enough, when he spotted Kathy and looked at her, the other women, as if on cue, stood up and mingled around inside the club. As he made his approach to her, no one, *no one* else got her attention and no one came over to the table they were sitting at. Sailor concluded over the years that was strange because, in a nightclub, someone is always encroaching on someone else. Nightclubs are loud, boisterous, tempting, testosterone spilling all on the floor and a place full of ultimate vanity. He does remember one man coming over to the table, looked to be a cook. He wore what looked like a white chef's uniform. Sailor remembers Kathy looked up and spoke to the man, and as she was telling him everything is fine, the man was looking at Sailor. He then looked up at the man, sort of with a grit, and then turned his head. The man then walked away from the table, and that was that. Nothing else seen or heard of him the rest of the time they were in the nightclub. At the end of his unexplainable deep encounter with Kathy—the woman he was apprehensive of identifying as a witch, though had no other explanation for her actions—she remained true to her word and actually accompanied Sailor back to the pier and gave him a brief hug and said, "If you are ever in London, England, again, Sailor, please look me up," handing him her phone number.

Sailor nodded his head, took the paper with her number on it, turned, and walked toward the ship and made no attempt to look back at her. Sailor was pissed, bewildered, and wished he had never met her. But just before he got on board the ship, he could not resist looking back, just to get one last glimpse at her. He noticed that she was walking away, prancing at every stride, head in the air, as to gesture that she was seeking another John to work her magic. Sailor, apparently, was not a lasting memory in her mind. Everything about her body language as she walked away spoke untold volumes that she was an expert in witchcraft against lonely, wayward, seafaring, unfaithful sailors. Sailor folded up the paper that had her phone number, placed the number in his pant pocket, waited until the ship got underway at sea, politely walked to the starboard side of the ship, and tossed the number into the Mediterranean Sea. At the greatest desire to have sex with a prostitute, she is one prostitute he desired *not* to remember or be tempted to contact her, had he visited London, England, again. He sometimes wondered if she was an actual human being or a manifestation of a wicked spirit in the body of a human being. The idea is not totally impossible as some weird accounts are recorded in the Bible of human and spiritual beings interacting. He strove in his thinking to forget, forget, and forget the whole encounter over the years, and this is the first time that part of his escapades and sinful acts have ever been revealed.

London, England, will be remembered not because of the historical and fairy tale lifestyle of the King and Queen, but because Sailor met for the first time, what he perceived to be a witch. Kathy had all the makings and seductive ways of mind and spirit of a person heavily involved in magic of some sort. How, then do you explain what she did? Sailor had *never*, ever seen her prior to that night in the nightclub. And she would haunt his thoughts for years to come until the real, true Messiah would take over the life of Sailor. His life would enter a labyrinth of visitations with different women in almost every town and city he visited or lived. A heavy curse that would plague him for years came alive in his soul. Who, if anyone, would imagine that Sailor was on the run from himself and from the devil of hell? The man of the Sermon would be a man of unending battles until the real Sermon began to come into view. Since those days and that night with Kathy, she and all her antics have faded into eternity past, and though this part of his life was necessary to know, he in no way misses those times. He sincerely wishes the possibility would exist to eradicate *any* of life's experiences that are damning to the soul and shameful to all who know.

21

A DEAD LIFE WITH A NEW BEGINNING

An entirely new life began from the last days on active duty, and yet the Sermon had not even begun to come into fruition. Those days were filled with the most extreme lies and image of life ever to be witnessed by Sailor. After a long fourteen years of marriage to the lady he thought was his mate for the rest of life, his life would significantly change. Two lovely children were born to Sailor and his wife, the women he thought the world of during his days on active duty. All that would change in a few years after building a home and establishing a life, a life complete with Christian rhetoric and church image that would one day undeniably rock the world of Sailor. He would die a thousand deaths and weep from the pit of hell more than the days of his childish homesickness. He would experience the loneliest days of his life for years to follow. It would seem and appear that all those Christian friends, brothers, and sisters he once knew and fellowshipped with turned their entire back on him.

It was like they all did an about-face on Sailor. From the most trusted older Christians to the most critical Christian upon Sailor and his ministry. Sailor was viewed as one of the worst Christians within his sphere of Christian relationships. A few men of the Christian faith appeared to care about Sailor's plight and would lend their ear and humble advice—only a few. It was the beginning of the most distressing days he would experience.

But until his spiritual and impending physical death, he would raise two of the most beautiful children he desired to raise. His son and his daughter were the father-child happiness of his marriage. Sailor's wife was his sweetheart upon entering the United States Navy. But that dear sweetheart relationship would one day explode in the worst evil manner imaginable. The following account in Sailor's life will basically be summarized in order to impact the demise of Sailor. The Sermon would not and could not fully emerge until Sailor was dead. It was not the physical aspect of Sailor dying, but most impactful was his spiritual death. The spiritual death of Sailor would shake, greatly disturb, and anger many of his so-called Christians. His siblings would experience perhaps the most disturbing and emotional reaction to his spiritual death. But the death of Sailor was definitely necessary for the life of the Sermon to come forth.

But those children of his, his son and his daughter, without question he would live that part of his life over if reliving one's life was the least bit possible. He loved his children with all his heart, and he enjoyed raising them and instructing them. He earnestly strove to impute into their mind and spirit a life that would please God. He taught, instructed, directed, and advised them on every level. Sailor's son and daughter were compelled by Sailor to view John Bunyan's *The Pilgrim's Progress*, both in animated form and real people version. *The Pilgrim's Progress* is a Christian allegory of the transition from this world into the world to come. It is an epic story written in the mid-1600s and regarded as significant English literature. *The Pilgrim's Progress* has never been out of print since its first printing. His son and daughter were tasked with learning the character's name and the significance of those characters, like:

> Christian, Evangelist, Obstinate, Mr. Worldly Wiseman, Good-will Keeper of the Wicket Gate, Interpreter, Three Shining Ones, Formalist, Hypocrisy, and a host of other names that reflect perspectives and people of the world.

These real-life attitudes and perspectives personified in the form of characters in a play were hoped to make a lasting impression on his children. At one point, both Sailor's son and daughter were sharp in identifying the name of the characters and their ways. They sincerely began to ask questions about why certain characters were the way they were. They had come to accept and expect the fathering of Sailor, because in many ways he was a strict father. His daughter once posted on Facebook that Sailor treated them both as recruits. But she did acknowledge that he was the best father in the world. Sailor laughed and gave kind of a smile, figuring that all children who had a good relationship with their parents might say the same thing.

Church

On December 25, 1994, Sailor started a nonprofit church approved with a tax-exempt from the IRS. Several people showed up, and the church grew to seventy-five core individuals. From 1994 through 2012, the church fluctuated between eighty and a hundred people, no consistency, just visitors on an irregular basis. All said and done, the church dwindled down to about twenty-five regular attendees by June 2012. During that window of operation, Sailor periodically invited his siblings, almost on a consistent, sporadic basis, if that makes sense. Of all his siblings, including his parents, everyone attended one of his services at least once. The ones who never ever attended were two younger brothers and one younger sister. His older sister who lived a distance away was separated by miles. During those days, his two younger brothers did not seem the least bit interested in the Bible and appeared to careless of Sailor's church and teaching. One brother and Sailor had conversations about the Bible as often as the moon turns blue. Lol! His older sister never had real issues with the Bible; in fact, she is the sister of Atlanta, Georgia, who was always in Sailor's life as a distant consoler and comforter. Jr. attended at least once with Melvin as they are close in age, Jr. being the oldest of Sailor's siblings. When Jr. attended, Sailor felt that he was more "impressed" with the speaking and the knowledge than he was seeking to know the truth to deliver his soul. Nonetheless, Sailor knows that Jr. judges him and his actions based on his understanding of Christianity and church folk. Sailor took blame in the half view he held of him, but Jr. was always viewed by Sailor as a seasoned, knowledgeable, wise man of the world, and he had a good discernment of personal issues people held. Sailor often looked to Jr. for advice, comment and even direction in some areas. But those interactions with Jr. were few and far between.

When it came to church service and attending church, both son and daughter were compelled to submit and follow along with their parents. Church, in many ways, was typical of Christian gatherings. His son was learning how to record the services, and his daughter was there because she had no other options. Respectful and kind they both were, Sailor knew beyond the shadow of a doubt they did not want to be in church every Sunday. All in all, they were good and respectable children who followed the leading of their parents. Sailor was able to persuade his followers the authenticity of his preaching and the simple revelation of his understanding of Scripture, basking in the typicality of Christian gatherings, including announcements, singing, and nowadays, praise singers. Reading of certain Bible verses and whatnot, he was not even in the birth canal for the Sermon to come forth. At the time, Sailor was convinced and felt good about himself that what he was doing, following in the steps of his father, was the right thing to do. But of all the sinful things Sailor engaged in over the past twenty-plus years of his life, the Sermon was still years in the future to manifest. His children, like himself when at their age, had very little sense of urgency for the things of church. Their lack of urgency for church service and church stuff rest squarely on the shoulders of Sailor. Like his father, he allowed the vices of life to hold him captive and also invade his home. Those years of globetrotting overseas and visiting whorehouse after whorehouse and nightclub after nightclub would manifest itself in his family. The scriptural injunction about the sins of the father is revisited in his children. Deuteronomy 24:16, Numbers 14:18, and Ezekiel 18:19–20 all speak to this curse. Perhaps had Sailor understood and applied the Scriptural truth in his youth the sins of his children could have been avoided. The continuing saga of Sailor's exposure to the world and inviting of sinful practices would ruin his home, his life, and his preaching to the slab of death. The death of one, Sailor, and the birth of the other, the man of the Sermon, would be *the* most painful, lonely and revealing experience of all his life. The evidence of the revelation and proof of the facts would completely uproot all previous Christian experiences.

It has been said that one's life preaches way louder than one's words. Sailor became a student of words and linguistics. He fell in love with knowledge, and learning the Bible became the fulcrum of his life. He embraced the literary text and diligently studied the written text. Not that he disregarded the spiritual aspect like prayer, fasting, spiritual discernment, and "hearing from God." But study, study, study became the primary focal point infusing knowledge in his soul. With that, he was able to greatly mask the real man, that man the Bible says should reflect who we are when reading the Bible.

> For if any be a hearer of the word and not a doer, he is like unto a man beholding his natural face in a glass. (James 1:23)

Sailor believed every word in the Bible to the best of his understanding. It was just that one thing, that one area that he battled with all his life. Does it make sense that no one understood? Does it matter that no one really cared? Anyway, one thing he did know is that all have sinned and come short of the glory of God (Rom. 3:23). The idea of personal sins resident in the lives of all humans became Sailor's consolation to continue preaching and teaching. But the battle with self, the battle with demons, the battle with his past was not over yet. There were many battles and hills to climb and valleys to experience before the actualization of the Sermon would be realized.

The Strange Woman

Somewhere around the years 1993 up to 1994, Sailor would begin on a ministry trek all in an effort to expose the horrors of darkness in sinful practices. He served as an associate minister in a local church after getting off active duty. Both he and his senior pastor had begun to develop a reputation as "sons of thunder." They were becoming a household name around town. Family members admired them while other family members rejected them and their preaching. Sailor himself would be short of being viewed as a scholar of scholars. Said to him by his senior pastor at one time, "Sailor, you are on the cutting edge of teaching! A force to be reckoned with. Anointed. Knowledgeable and full of power."

These words, though not required to motivate Sailor, did impact his thinking and his being. Only he knows full well his wicked past and present state of battles. He truly and honestly wished and desired that being married would curb and dismantle the demons he picked up while overseas. Alas, his marriage came with its own set of demons and fleshly woes. But for Sailor at the time, the Word was his comfort and the Word was his mask.

After all those years in the United States Navy, Sailor is now a civilian employed with the United States Postal Service as a customer service supervisor. Going to work under the cover of darkness at 4:00 a.m., 5:00 a.m., and sometimes 3:30 a.m., he would find his soul wandering with shifty eyes. It was around that time that his marriage began to feel the cause and effect of wandering eyes. Inevitably, there would be a scantily dressed woman on the street, somewhere, someplace aimlessly walking. To his vexation of spirit, he had become addicted at stopping and saying hello, or something that would get their attention. And as the Scriptures say, "Seek and you shall find, knock and the door will be opened, seeking and knocking was a sinful plague that had attached itself to Sailor. The plague was not yet dead nor buried within his soul.

It was approximately 3:50 a.m., and he was on his way to work at the United States Post Office in Harrisburg, Pennsylvania. It was a very foggy morning, the kind that makes you think you may see something, like a deer darting out on the road, a possum, or some other kind of animal scurrying across the street, trying to miss the car but using the car's lights to run across the street. He was not really expecting anything more unusual than that. By the time he turned onto 7th Street in the city of Harrisburg, the expectation of something running across the street was out of his mind. But then something very strange and totally unexpected began to unfold. Out of nowhere, he spotted, about a half a block away from where he was driving, a person in the middle of the street. Sailor has always been very alert in the morning for the very reason of the unexpected driving on the early morning dark roads. After the deadly ride coming from Norfolk, Virginia, in 1979 with his fiancée, he made it a point to be awake and alert while driving. He also made it a point to visually scan his surroundings while driving, spot checking his rearview mirror and looking ahead of the immediate spot of his vehicle. Suddenly, he saw something from the middle of the street moving toward his vehicle. There was a person in the street. He *did not* see anyone walking from the sidewalk into the street. He did not see anyone walking in the street or up the street. The fog was not that thick as to hide a figure moving in the street. The streetlights aided somewhat to be able to look a half a block ahead of his vehicle. All conditions were reasonable to enable him to see if someone was on the sidewalk and walk into the street or if someone was walking up the street. But what he saw was someone walking *from* the middle of the street to the other side. It was next to impossible that he would not have seen this person walking from some direction, but *from* the middle of the street was very strange to this day.

He was not afraid whatsoever largely because of the sin engaged in the past. In many ways, in his heart, he expected or suspected a female looking for some promiscuity. But his heart and mind were not pointed in that direction. He was not interested, nor was he feeling lust or desire or looking. Mind you, the Sunday service on the day before, Sailor preached part 2 of the sermon "The Spirit World." The congregation of souls was greatly encouraged by the message. They gave testimony after testimony about the revealing truth and activity of evil and angelic powers.

So the next day, Monday, would be his test and trial from the demonic world. Most Mondays were complete with test after test after test after preaching on Sunday. But that Monday, it seems a direct hit came against Sailor as he was the bull's-eye of Satan and hell. A direct attack from the pit of hell. A test and trial of demonic proportion, more than a mere fiery dart. But rather, a demon either in human form or a human of lustful and demonic influence purposely sent by Satan. Akin to Paul's thorn in the flesh sent by Satan to buffet Sailor all his life. As he approached the figure in the street coming closer and closer to the person, an arm was raised in the air, motioning him to pull over, under the cover of darkness and eerie fog with a temperature of 50 degrees, It was now about 3:58 a.m. A yellowish street light was shining down on the figure in the street. As he got closer, he could see sweat pants, black boots, and what looked like a poncho covering the figures back and head. A light mist of rain was wetting the ground, and the entire scene reminded one of something out of an Alfred Hitchcock movie. It just didn't look right or feel right. But for the remnant of lust in his heart, he couldn't help himself but to stop and see what the person wanted. He stopped in the middle of the street, didn't pull over. There was clearly no other motorist on the road at that time. No need to pull over, just stop. As the person approached his car, he could see clearly that it looked like a woman. She, or it, got in the car with a movement that was un-human, almost imitating robotic dancing that kids perform today. (I will say *passenger* just for reference). The passenger's movement was in a choppy, broken-up manner, as if not a real person. Or, one might imagine, a person wearing a robot suit. That is the only way he knows how to describe her, or its, movement. Everything about the movement and body language of the person did not seem right.

Upon entering Sailor's car, the passenger said, "My, you sure do smell good."

The voice sounded like a man's voice and a women's voice at the same time. Sailor *did not* like the voice *at all*! He drove off with the passenger in his car. She reached over very casually and gently touched his leg and said, "What do you want? Why are you out here?"

Sailor tried all within his being to be cordial. He said to the passenger, "I thought you needed a ride somewhere. I thought you were headed somewhere."

The whole time the passenger was interrupting Sailor and trying to get his attention to what she wanted and desired. The passenger then said, "I need some help" all the while smiling from ear to ear. The passenger then said, "I really suck a mean one."

Sailor immediately said with urgency of spirit, "Oh no, I thought you really needed a ride."

The passenger quickly became irritated and reminded Sailor of her purpose and desire.

Sailor then said, "Where do you want me to drop you off?"

He made a quick turn void of her input onto the next street (Ross Street) and then down to Jefferson and Curtain, and he let her get out of the car. She was very unhappy and lost all composure, and the smile she had then turned into the most gruesome and ugly frown Sailor had ever seen. But she left the car without an argument or confrontation. But when she got out of the car, within a matter of seconds she was nowhere to be seen! Visibility was very clear upon leaving the foggy area with the passenger. He actually did a U-turn and drove around the block and down the narrow Moore Street looking for her, just to confirm she was real, to no avail; he did not find her and could not imagine how she was able to escape his view within seconds.

Sailor will always believe that experience was a direct attack from the pit of hell. He knew then the degree of his battles with the powers of darkness had reached the extreme level of trials. He also knew that Satan saw that he was losing his influence of the lustful spirit in Sailor's life. Hell had discharged an actual lustful demon to attack Sailor head-on in real life. The situation, the appearance, the movements, and the smell. Oh yes, he failed to mention the smell of the passenger. Sort of like sulfur, but not overbearing. Could have been she was smoking a cigarette, but the sulfur smell was way stronger than any cigarette Sailor had ever smelled.

What do you make of that? As esoteric as that may sound, the encounter was real, and Sailor will never forget that passenger, only because the experience was very weird and unexplainable. Other attacks from hell would follow in Sailor's ministry life, but as this one was resisted, the others would also be resisted. The whole scene appeared to be right out of an spooky Alfred Hitchcock or Steven Spielberg movie. Filled with sensuality and wickedness to awaken the lustful spirit that abides within the heart of man. That spirit once lived in full force in Sailor's heart. After the experience with the strange woman, Sailor basked for a brief moment in sweet victory but condemned himself in his lack of ability to resist temptation.

It was one small victory on Sailor's part that would upset the very regions of hell and demons would not rest until they were able to touch his physical life.

In the near future, hell itself would attack Sailor, who at that time was coming into the Sermon phase. He took a quick scan of his life and likened his demise somewhat to Job of the Bible. He had lost everything precious to him and had not a clue how to regain what he lost.

Missionary

For more than twenty years, Sailor was known as a "preacher's preacher." In other words, his preaching could teach other preachers sound Bible interpretation skills. From the year 1980 until the year 2012, he preached and preached and preached. He attained a who's who, at least in central Pennsylvania, of a good expository preacher. He had developed a reputation as a good Bible teacher, a scholar of sorts without formally being a biblical scholar. In the mind of Sailor, he was going places and about to impact the world with his ministry. He expected a church membership of hundreds, if not thousands. But his superfluity expectation would never come to pass. In fact, it would never enter the realm and the possibility of coming to pass. There were way too many forces working against the young Sailor. For all practical intents and purposes, he was ill-equipped to deal with and overcome the barrage of personal battles, church rhetoric, and church politics. He started his own church in the basement of his home on December 25, 1994, with an attendance of about ten people. That membership would fluctuate from ten to about fifty over an eighteen-year period. Until one day, among many confused days, the membership would drastically drop back down to ten people. Some of those he thought were his trusted friends and confidants would turn their back on him in complete disgust. His ex-wife's family would categorically disown him, as though they were the most righteous people on earth. At least, that's how Sailor/the man of the Sermon felt.

Some would refuse him entry into their homes, and some would not even communicate with him after he willingly stepped down from preaching. As these events were unfolding in Sailor's life, he knew full well why it was happening. Others viewed him as the "man of God" while others separated themselves from him as if they had a clue or knew something he did not know they knew. At any rate, he was feeling the pain and observing the dismantling of what he deemed a call from God to start the ministry. Christians and the Christian religion can be horribly unforgiving and judgmental in an unbelievable manner. But this thing was not so much about Christianity as it was clearly the breaking, the death, and the revealing to Sailor his lifelong nemesis that had to die. The Sermon was beginning to come into view, but not the view from Sailor, but the view from the hand of providence to strip Sailor of himself.

As he preached, he learned. As he learned, he preached. At the beginning of his preaching, much of his sermons were regurgitating the preaching of internationally known preachers. In other words, he studied them, like a boxer studies his opponents before entering the ring. He mocked them, almost their every word. He rested strongly on the faith, name it and claim it concept. Oh my, that faith stuff had to go because it had a mountain of holes and void of sound doctrine. It failed the litmus test of the authenticity of interpreting Scripture. But he had to learn, and he had to learn the way of the Most High. A term he would scripturally and passionately embrace years later. But in the meantime, he continued to preach his brand of Christianity, which sounded like and appeared to be superior to the faith message. His ministry would bear the emphasis and central thought of having a pure heart. This scripturally sound truth of a pure heart was introduced to Sailor while station at Naval Air Station Willow Grove in 1990–1993. There he met seemingly a wandering sailor stationed at NAS Willow Grove who was an avid Christian. His Christianity was way different than the brothers he met and befriended at NAS Cecil Field, Florida, during his very first enlistment. Sailor and the wandering sailor became friends, and Sailor saw fit to confide in his new friend. They talked about Sailor's church, his preaching, and his family. His new friend invited Sailor to visit his church in Michigan. That visitation would not occur until Sailor was discharged from the navy. He kept in touch with his new friend almost on a daily basis, excited and overjoyed thinking that he had come into a deeper revelation of what it takes to live a Christian life. When the time came to travel to Michigan, Sailor packed up his entire family with his wife and made one of the most exciting trips of his ministry life. Going to meet Missionary, who already had a reputation of a seasoned woman of God. Sailor's family enjoyed a wonderful week while berthed at the private home of Bishop and Missionary. Of course, the upcoming Sunday, Sailor would be the guest speaker. Sailor's new friend had talked him up so much that both Missionary and her husband could not wait to meet Sailor. When that Sunday arrived, the church was full with all its members, estimated to be about fifty or so people. Sailor had gotten used to that attendance number, although when he was an associate minister prior to starting his own church, it was nothing to preach to two hundred to three hundred people. But for now it was about fifty people he would be breaking the Word of life too. Sailor was introduced by one of the deacons in the church, and Sailor was given a glaring introduction, as if Sailor was a well-known speaker. In the heart of Sailor, he knew he was no more than a perpetrator masked with the Bible in an articulate manner. When he arose to take the podium and crack open the Bible, he read what is commonly known as the beatitudes in the Gospel of Matthew. He read the entire text and then backed tracked to verse 8:

> Blessed are the pure in heart; for they shall see God.

He then engaged himself into a hyped frenzy and began to discharge words from the Bible in machine-gun manner, making reference every now and then to having a pure heart and that without having a pure heart, you will be lost and condemned to the fires of hell. With that, he was unable to finish his message because Missionary stood up in such a manner to capture everyone's attention in that small church.

She yelled at the top of her voice, "*You are an angel! God sent an angel to tell the people! Say it, son! Say it!*"

The congregants all agreed with the words of Missionary, and the church erupted into a blissful high of elation. Sailor did not properly finish his message. The service sort of ended with that, and the altar call was made and hands laid on by both Missionary and her husband. It was a very exciting time for Sailor and the needed confirmation he desired by a seasoned woman of God. Her husband could have made that declaration also, it didn't matter to Sailor. What mattered is both were spiritual parents and well up in age. Did she hurt Sailor, or did she help Sailor by uttering those words, "*You are an angel*"?

In Sailor's mind, he did not feel comfortable thinking that he was an angel or acting in the capacity of an angel. But that's what Missionary said, and that's what everyone believed at the time. With that awesome and impactful declaration from the one women of God that Sailor admired and respected, he moved forward, accepting his sort of angelic calling to teach the people about God, Jesus Christ, and the Christian life. He was now confirmed in his own mind that God specifically called him and tasked him with a mission to expound on Scripture in the most direct manner possible. He would operate in his ministry in that capacity of mind for the next fifteen years or so. Teaching and teaching and expounding and expounding. He, in his own mind, became a biblical expositor to be reckoned with and respected for his no-frills form of preaching.

One of the most heart-wrenching things occurred with the life of Missionary. When Sailor and his family met Missionary, they discovered that she was legally blind. His friend may have told him she was blind, but Sailor does not remember—it was so long ago. She was a pianist and a singer. One could easily imagine that in her younger days, she demonstrated great talent in both piano and song. She was well-liked and well respected in the church and in the community.

From that time forward, Sailor's church would take on a new name and new focus. The Christian Assembly Fellowship would brim with possibility. Every Sunday service would be a day and time of expectation from the congregants. Sailor would proudly and reverentially strut into the church, ready to do battle against the powers of darkness. At least, that's what he thought. There would be glimpses of light dispensed among the people, and there would be hidden treasure chests unlocked. While the battled raged in the soul of Sailor, his preaching would reach an all-time high in the minds of men and women who heard him speak.

The time would come that Missionary would pass through this world, which is the lot of all men and women. When Sailor heard of her passing, he intensely wept. He took time off work so that he and his family could attend her funeral. They took the long journey up north to pay their respects to a woman of God. Her husband had passed away sometime before her, and when Sailor and his family arrived in Michigan, they found the place to the funeral home. Sadly when they arrived at the funeral home, the door was locked, and no one near to answer their knocking. Sailor paced back and forth, not believing that they were not allowed to enter the funeral home. After that long drive out of the deepest respect and heartfelt sympathy, no one would open the door. If he remembers correctly, they stayed in Michigan for a few hours, even went over a church member's house. They were baffled as to why they could not enter the funeral home. Later that evening, the executor of Missionary and her husband, also the head deacon, asked Sailor and his family to meet him at Missionary's home. When they arrived at Missionary's home, he called them in and said a few mundane words like the funeral was private. What was this guy talking about private? Sailor thought. Missionary was Sailor's mentor, his spiritual mother, his advisor, *his* angel! He then handed Sailor a card and said, "Don't open it until you arrive home." It almost sounded like some secret mission in the military. He said, "We don't want you to be worried or bothered. You can return home safely."

Sailor and his family turned and walked out of the house of the one lady that he highly respected and greatly missed. On the road back home, his wife opened the envelope and a crisp $100 bill was inside with a message that Sailor cannot remember. He actually did not care about the money or the message. He cared about the passing of his dear spiritual mother and mentor in the Lord. He drove most of the way back home with teary eyes and asked his wife to take the wheel after a few hours of driving. He struggled to make sense of the whole thing and why they were restricted from the funeral. Missionary was 105 years old when she passed away. But her confirming words to Sailor would motivate him and drive him to the end of his ministry. His ministry would take a nosedive and splatter all over the concrete and it would seem *no one* would even lift his head to assist. Sailor had to die on his own and alone, void of *anyone* attempting to understand his plight.

Months after her passing, Sailor continued to struggle in attempting to make sense of the rejection from the deacon, now the new pastor of the Michigan Christian Assembly Church. Missionary and her husband were the owners of a good amount of land, both their dwelling place and acres of property further up north in Michigan. Sailor hesitantly concluded the new pastor, formerly deacon, falsely perceived that Sailor may have been interested in beneficiary of their property. Sailor resolved in his own mind the new pastor was quickly shutting *any* possibility of Sailor receiving a small parcel of grass. But if that were the case of telling Sailor and his family to return to Pennsylvania, he may never know. Sailor's only intent and purpose was to pay his last respects to his adopted spiritual mother and friend. When it came to the actions of the new pastor, Sailor also concluded such is the case among many Christians, suspect, apprehension and distrust.

Preaching and teaching from that point became intense! A direct bull's-eye aim to all and everyone who visited the church he pastored. No one was exempt from the fiery, almost indignant and judgmental message that Sailor dished out. In his heart, he only intended to wake up the sleeper in the life of his fellow Christians. But the message he taught had not even awoken his own spirit. How could he awaken his fellow man and women? But he laboriously led the cavalry and intently remained on the wall as a pastor with a small amount of knowledge to share with all who would dare to listen. His heart yearned to be true, but his past, very much alive, compelled him to perpetuate and live the exorbitant life of a lie. His wife, his children, and his fellow Christian had elevated him to the level of untouchable. Even though they never expressed that perspective, it was clear Sailor was viewed as a warrior of warriors. A general in the battle. A leader of the souls of men and women. A man of God with a special anointing and calling. But all that superlative perspective would one day come crumbling down, almost in free-fall fashion, to the great dismay of all who observed Sailor's progress. Internally, he was never a bad, calculating, and evil person, but he was still asleep while he thought he was awake. Such is the lot of most Christians, it seemed to Sailor, as he continued to search and study and seek God's intervention in his jumbled-up life.

Those Darn Pesky Massage Parlors

Just to digress a little in order to amplify the great personal trials that were ongoing in Sailor's life. When he met his new friend at Willow Grove Air Station, he continued to wrestle with the seemingly unbreakable addiction to prostitution. Sailor was continually worried about getting arrested if he would proposition a prostitute on the street in the city of brotherly love: Philadelphia, PA. His pure fleshly reasoning to reduce the risk was to frequent massage parlors around the Naval Air Station. The idea of visiting massage parlors was birthed in his mind and came alive in his soul precisely at the time his father was hospitalized. His dad spent almost thirty days in the hospital with no clear diagnosis of his condition. Sailor was still on active duty during the time of his dad's hospitalization and would come home to visit as often as he could. There was much prayer for the healing and recovery of his dad, and Sailor spent many hours visiting him in the hospital. It was also a time of the deepest wedge being formed between his boyhood mentors, Frederick E. and Bay. Those days were filled with great turbulence and unrest. He had never seen or imagined such an awful time among his siblings and parents. In many ways, that episode in Sailor's life may have hastened Sailor's demise in one way or another. Massage parlors had never been a thought in Sailor's mind, and the first visit to one was a new excitement, almost equal to the first whorehouse visit in Italy. But each visit was simultaneously a very cold and hot experience—cold in the sense that the acts and deeds performed were lifeless, routine, and dry yet uncannily attractive and hot in the sense that every visit frightened Sailor that he would meet his new maker soon: the devil. Because, clearly, he was acting like a child of the devil masquerading very well in a full coat of armor of the Bible. The entire time he was at the Naval Air Station, these visits were frequent and costly. There were two totally unexplained events that enveloped Sailor's mind in a frenzy of deep fear and shame. When his dad was in the hospital, he had a condition that would cause him to throw up, without warning, some thick, green mucus that had a foul smell. This is the same dad that rescued his life when he was the young TJ running in the projects from his older brother Fred. But now something horrid and wicked had arrested his dad and captivated Sailor. He does not remember ever getting a clear explanation of what the mucus was and what was causing the frequent throw-ups. If he did, Sailor does not remember because the events of those days were mentally and spiritually overwhelming him with boatloads of fearful concerns and emotions.

At one point, Sailor leaned over to his father and asked him, "Do you have something you want to tell me?" During his entire time in the hospital, his dad could not talk, but he motioned with his eyes that he wanted to tell Sailor something. Sailor put his ear as close as he could to his dad, trying to make out the word he was struggling to utter. Any word! Some word! It didn't matter! What was he trying to tell Sailor? Breathing had become sporadic for his dad, and communication was all but lost, other than his facial expressions and raised eyebrows. Sailor thought he was able to make out two words his dad struggled to say: "don't" and "go."

Don't do what and go where? It did not make sense to Sailor, and he was unable to piece together any sentence his father was attempting to form. His feeble attempt to speak would be the last time Sailor would hear a word from his father. It was the saddest time ever in the mind of Sailor. The circumstances that existed then did not have to be in the mind of Sailor. He did not have to die in the manner he did and at the age he did. Sailor was convinced that his time on earth was drastically cut short.

Nonetheless, prior to his dad's death, as Sailor was traveling back to Willow Grove one evening, on the dark highway about midnight, he instantaneously felt sick with flu-like symptoms. He then had the uncontrollable urge to throw up, and he pulled alongside the dark road, opened the door of his car, and spilled the contents onto the ground. The weirdest thing is that what he threw up looked *exactly* like the stuff his dad was throwing up in the hospital—exactly like it! His immediate thought was, *What in the hell is this? How is this possible?*

That experience happened a few more times up to the time of his father's passing, and then it ceased. This is the very first time this is being revealed to anyone because who, if any, would understand or make sense out of it?

Daryl is a fictitious name of a brother on board the Naval Air Station who appeared to be very sincere in his Christian faith. Daryl also had a very good understanding of the Bible and spoke with a great depth of knowledge and interpretation. He was laid back, soft-spoken, intelligent, and always perfectly groomed. He had a nice car and was all about the business of the Lord. One night Sailor had stepped out from the base to one of those massage parlors and stayed at the parlor way beyond what he should have. Subsequently, he missed the last bus going by the Naval Air Station. Lyft, Uber, and all the modern transportation services did not exist at the time. He didn't have any more money to call a cab and his only option was to walk back to the base. According to Google, the Pennsylvania turnpike is 4 miles from the main gate of the Naval Air Station, and Sailor was another 4 miles from the PA turnpike to the massage parlor. Essentially, he had to trek at least 8.5 or 9 miles back to the base, so he started walking at a very fast pace. He had walked most of the distance and wasn't too far from the base when a nice SUV pulled alongside him. The driver rolled down the passenger window and without hesitation said, "Sailor, get in." Just like that, "Sailor, get in."

Sailor figured God offered a small degree of grace for Daryl to drive by, but Sailor had already trekked about 8 miles before getting picked up. At this time, it was about one in the morning. Daryl was a no-frills guy and did not mince words.

He asked Sailor, "Where are you coming from man this late in the evening?" He was driving at a slow speed while looking at Sailor, attempting to get his complete attention. Of course, Sailor could not directly answer that question because Daryl truly was a deep, sincere brother about the truth and had a good discernment of things. So Sailor simply said, "Oh, just walking."

"C'mon, man! I know better than that! You don't have to give me details, but you really need to hear the voice of God! There are several things wrong with this picture. I'm not your father, or counselor for that matter, but I am concerned about your well-being and your relationship with God."

All Sailor could do was listen and take in what Daryl was saying. There was simply no argument or discussion necessary. Sailor concluded that the mercy and grace of God are way beyond what he ever imagined. Time after time throughout Sailor's naval career, mercy and grace kept him, shielded him, and led him in the midst of his sinful nature.

Upon arrival at the barracks, Daryl dropped Sailor off and said, "I'm praying for you, man. Don't fail this opportunity God is giving you to spiritually grow up."

That was the very last time Sailor ever saw Daryl again. He thinks Daryl transferred, and that's all he wishes to attribute it to—Daryl transferred. The words of Daryl dug deep in the crevices of Sailor's heart, and when Sailor returned to his barracks at Naval Air Station Willow Grove, he got on his knees and wept bitterly about his confused life.

22

THE END IS NOT PRETTY

The Fires of Hell

Hell's fire would burn intently on the day hell entered the house on North 18th Street. Around the year 1990 or so, Sailor would begin down the drudged road of death. At that time, he did not know that he was on a path of death. Spiritual death that would send powerful waves of strong emotion throughout central Pennsylvania. Imagine a lost, confused child of the projects and risky young adult of North 18th Street turned into a sailor of the world would impact the world he lived in. The Church of God in Christ in the Keystone State of Pennsylvania and Independent churches would feel the impact of Sailor's spiritual death and the demise of his ministry. Imagine. There would be talk after talk after talk and rejection after rejection after rejection from Christians. People he knew of long ago growing up in the Christian faith would actually turn their head at the site of Sailor. Ministers, so-called missionaries and evangelists would not even much as say hello to Sailor. The death was instantaneously but slowly brewing with each encounter of a fellow Christian. It was a scary time. It was a frightening time. It was a painful and unexplainable time. Almost like he was smitten with the plague of leprosy where all those Christian brothers and sisters he once admired and loved seen him as the greatest sinner of all time. Was it because the message he preached for years was condemning in their minds? Was it because they felt he deserved what he got? Sort of like a ship without a sail, as it was so frequently termed among COGIC ministers. Whatever their perspective, he felt like his life had fallen beyond rock bottom, and it seemed *no one* was the least bit interested in his view and his story. And as the story goes, he accepted the fact that his spiritual life and leadership role was being nailed in a coffin of religious judgmental Christianity. His solace was to reason in his mind that all who judged him and consigned him to an eternal hell simply did not know the full story. His story began in the projects and caught up with him in his ministry. When the Sermon comes into fruition, he realized that such is the lot of all men and women, and such is the judging of all who don't know or understand the tribulations of life.

He calls his idolized brothers that he grew up with "the Three." They were the most influential men in his life as a boy into a teenager into a man. The days of the projects and North 18th Street would one day erupt into a battle of deep emotional pain for Sailor, the likes of which he never, ever imagined would happen in his lifetime and never from two of the three he admired. A family meeting was the thing in those days sort of airing out some differences. At the time, Sailor thought that to be a good thing. At least it brought everyone together for a brief moment of talking. But this family meeting would be the worst of the worst and best outcome as Sailor seen it and understood the reasons. He would stand face-to-face with his boyhood mentors, the two he immeasurably idolized and worshipped in his own way. The two he thought were the coolest brothers in the world. There was three: Lawrence, Bay, and Frederick E. But only two of the three would be confrontational to the point of a nervous breakdown for Sailor. The breakdown did not occur in actual terms, but inside the heart of Sailor, there was a breakdown of great proportion.

On a day in the summer of 1995, Sailor met with his most admired and trusted brothers that shaped and formed his life into who he had become. Prior to that meeting date, tension and disagreement flourished like an entrenched river between two of the three. On one hand, Sailor was the only known public Christian preacher of the family. He did not know the perspective his other siblings had of him, not one hundred percent. But he knew they all had a rejection type of respect, but respect, nonetheless. Once he overheard one of his sisters say, "Sailor is into his own world." That statement was baffling to him because he thought at least she understood the objective of Sailor's preaching. Anyways, the three had come into a level of understanding and religious practice that conflicted with traditional Christianity. Sailor strove within his heart not only to reason with his trusted and loved brothers but to share and instruct them of the expository aspect of the Bible. They would not hear a word he said, because for real, in their minds, Sailor was still the younger and they the older. Sailor was still the student and they the teacher. That old "I'm older than you," thinking mentality was the greatest division that fueled their separation. They, both Bay and Frederick E., had gotten to a point where they refused everything Sailor preached and taught. They were profoundly convinced that their God of Christianity revealed great truth to them. They were persuaded that Sailor was no more than a baby of Christianity stuck in the tradition of Christian practices. On that note, they were correct that Sailor was stuck in formalized Christianity and the tenants of faith expressed in Christianity. With that, "stuck in traditional Christianity" was actually the fortification of Sailor's life that mercy and grace would sustain him. The Most High, whom Sailor would embrace at the Sermon level, preserved Sailor for such a time as this. Every one of his siblings was there in the house that day except Lawrence and Jr. in the living room of N. 18th Street hell erupted in the most arrogant and disrespectful manner that entrenched itself in Sailor's mind for eternity. How can it be that Frederick E. and Bay would withstand Sailor as a man when in Sailor's youth he revered them in the most worshipful manner? *How is this happening, and why is it happening?* thought Sailor. Bay was the ringleader, standing in the middle of the floor, while Frederick E. was sitting off to the side, observing in silence up to a point. An unexplainable tension filled the room that day, and everyone was emotionally charged with unrestful anticipation. Different ones were silent and waiting with bated breath, nervous as to what was about to be revealed.

Bay kicked off the meeting by saying, "God called me to save the family and that everyone must adhere to what I have to say." There was a lot of other things that came forth from the mouth of Bay that Sailor does not remember. Sailor had prayed all night, literally, all night petitioning God to take charge of his tongue and give him what to say. Sailor loved those two brothers like no other, especially because they were real mentors in his life. He was not about to, nor did he want, to have a verbal fight with them. He desperately needed God's intervention and help because he was in great despair. Why this is happening would not be clear to Sailor until the demise of two of the Three. Bay spoke of many ideas and things that just did not agree with biblical interpretation and the written Word of God. But his delivery and message were so forceful that all who did not know what to believe, believed what he said, to some extent. But when it appeared, he was done with his rant, he said, "But Sailor! Sailor is in error, and Sailor has demons with him that is leading him down the wrong path. Sailor *must* submit to the Will of God or face great demise in his life."

Actually, Bay's assessment was correct based on Sailor's life from the days of leaving home to enlisting in the navy. Sailor did have demons with him, and he was on a path to a great demise. He would fall from grace, and he would divorce his wife. But the manner in which Bay went forth to reveal those things was not in sync with Scripture. The Most High himself said in Jeremiah 31:3, "I have loved you with an everlasting love, therefore I shall draw you with loving commitment."

Even the Most High has compassion and great forgiveness for the sins of man. He is long-suffering and kind and understanding and forgiving. The sins Sailor willingly engaged in was the personal demons he wrestled with and sinful ways he embraced. He never did anything against any one person, nor did he swindle, scam, steal, or lie against people. His lie was against himself as he perpetrated being a man of integrity in the office of a pastor/teacher of the Gospel. Had Bay approached Sailor privately to share with him that he must cease and desist his sinful ways, restoration in the life of Sailor may have been possible then. Was Bay disrupting a process that Sailor himself had to go through? Was Bay overstepping his grounds due to the misguided zeal in his heart, or was there another substance influencing his actions? Sailor does know narcotics and alcohol played a huge part in Bay's life. Don't you remember it was Bay who introduced Sailor, then TJ, to alcohol? The same with Sailor and scores of men and women—alcohol and drugs plague the life of Christians and non-Christians. But the assessment of Bay's life is not the focus of Sailor's story. That was just a tidbit of factual information to consider while continuing to read. Bay's comments came as a tremendous shock to everyone in the room, and Sailor's mother chimed in and said, "No! Not Sailor! He is a man of God, and he preaches the Bible like no other I have heard—"

Her comments were abruptly interrupted by Bay when he said, "You must submit to God and not intervene with what we are saying. Listen and do not rest upon your human understanding." In hindsight, the man of the sermon cringes when he thinks about Bay's unfortunate response to mom. The Scriptures are absolutely clear on honoring one's parents. Sailor had learned some time ago, it's now what you say, rather how you say it. Bay's approach to the women who carried him in her womb for 9 months and raised him with all the motherly love she understood, warranted respect and honor for her. Perhaps his disrespect for her was the first of several check marks against him in the eyes of The Most High.

Sailor likes to think that his siblings on that day were in two categories: (1) onlookers with nothing to say because they just did not know what to say and (2) hearers that desperately wanted to defend the truth, regardless of who is singled out. But the two were very aggressive and forceful, and everyone remained in silence waiting for a response from Sailor. The Most High was about to jump into the mind and heart of Sailor at a time when Sailor did not know the Most High. Sailor sat in a recliner chair, in a reclined position, with his hand on his chin. He was intently listening and observing with great discernment beyond his studies and beyond his capability to know. He watched and he listened, and he loved the two like never before. His heart bled in great pain to see them in such a state of elevated high void of sound biblical teaching and understanding.

One thing Sailor had acquired by the mercy and infusion of the spirit of God was a good understanding and interpretation of the Bible. The knowledge that was bestowed upon him was the anchor of his mind and the truth inscribed in his heart. Had he not had those two life-giving elements of the Bible; he would have been just like any other sibling. Not knowing what to say and not knowing what to believe. When Bay drastically, almost unexpectedly, shifted the focus from what their alleged calling was for the family, too, but Sailor, quiet as a mouse, held everyone captive in the room that day. They all waited, wondered, and watched Sailor for a response. But Sailor had literally prayed all night and really all night. The scriptural injunction of praying in your secret closet is what Sailor had done prior to the family meeting. The promise of the Father that he would reward you openly is what the Father did on that day. On that day, Sailor was calm as the calming sea with a gentle breeze blowing across the ocean. Because what he was about to engage in was an ocean of confusion and years of oppression of the two that he deeply loved and admired.

When Bay said, "But Sailor," he looked directly at Sailor, as to say, "I'm talking about you. Now what you going to do?" Apparently, the expectation of Bay was for Sailor to openly repent in front of the family and submit to his assertive, misguided words that allegedly God called them to. But little did Bay realize that Sailor had spent deep, heartfelt, soul-searching prayer with God. Sailor prayed like praying Hyde, almost making imprints of his knees on the floor. On cue, Sailor calmly and slowly stood up and unassumingly approached Bay and stood within nose length, face-to-face in the most respectful manner to his older brother. Nonetheless, he had fiery indignation for the confusion and deception caused by the devil to destroy the family by Bay's own words. Bay was not being used by God to save the family, but Satan's objective was to divide, conquer, and destroy. The thief comes not but to steal, kill and to destroy (John 10:10).

"Man! What are you talking about? You have lost your mind, and you are very blind! Do you not realize how both you and Frederick E. influenced my entire life? Do you not know how I followed in your steps all my youthful and much of my adult life? Why would I be trying to withstand you? I have loved you with a genuine love that is rarely found between siblings!"

Sailor was on fire! The fire of Ruach HaKodesh (whom he would come to embrace in the future) was all over and inside Sailor unlike he had ever experienced in his past. Sailor did not have one ounce of fear and was ready for the toughest battle he would face. He never took his eyes off Bay. I mean, he was *directly* looking into the soul of a lost brother. The soul of Bay was clear for Sailor to see as he gazed into the eyes of his brother, penetrating deep into his soul. His mentor was lost and confused, and Bay did not even know where he was in his lost state. Bay was crying deep from within his soul for acceptance and love and was able to use mental psychology on the entire family, except for Sailor. In the midst of Sailor's rebuttal and plea for his most trusted and loved brothers of the past to wake up, a voice rang out with the haughtiness of the devil and said, "I'm not impressed!"

Immediately, another younger voice rang out and said, "I don't think he is trying to be impressive." Both voices were like timid fiery darts that had absolutely no impact on Sailor's focus. He was there to slay and dismantle years of oppression in the heart of his beloved brothers and silence the lies of the devil. After those two voices were heard, silence prevailed in the room, and Sailor continued to speak into the soul of his brother with the greatest compassion and love he could find from within. Sailor spoke and spoke without interruption from that point on. As far as Sailor was concerned at that point, everyone else in the room did not exist. This battle was squarely between Sailor, Bay and the spirit of division and confusion. Sailor's talk must have lasted less than thirty minutes, but it seemed hours because the situation and circumstances involved were years of spiritual oppression and confusion. But it only took a few minutes to dismantle the public exhibition of the Two with tender loving care. In the end, silence rained down in the entire room for about two minutes when Sailor was finished arresting the spirit of his older brother under the leading of the Most High. Bay then said to Sailor in the company of his mom and other siblings, "I didn't know that. I'm sorry. Please forgive me."

This would be the very last time Sailor and Bay communicated face to face to settle years of confusion. With that, the man of the Sermon would come to realize and understand that what took place that day was for the good for Bay, Sailor and his siblings; if they could see.

He and Sailor embraced, as Sailor slowly wiped tears from his eyes. Just a few that erupted from within. Nothing dramatic, but more emotionally charged because of the love he had for those two guys. Everyone else began to embrace both Sailor, Bay, and Frederick E. It seemed it took some time for Frederick E. to make his way to Sailor because Frederick E. was not impressed and the prideful state he was in was not ready to humble itself. But they embraced each other, and from that day Sailor would not see or hear from Frederick E. until he learned of the death of his most admired and trusted friend.

The Three

They were the most valuable and important people in the life of TJ, who grew into the Sailor, and the Sailor would be the extent of their influence in his life.

> And we know that all matters work together for good to those who love Elohym, to those who are called according to His purpose. (Romiyim 8:23 / Rom.)

Ronald (a.k.a. Bay)

Every conversation held between Bay and TJ was like one might imagine talking to God. TJ greatly admired and looked up to Bay, and in his eyes, Bay was faultless. This was the deepest and most unassuming ignorance held in the heart of a boy that really knew no better. It would not become apparent to TJ until years into the life of Sailor the reverence he had for his brothers was a reverence he should have never held. Nonetheless, until that understanding, and truth would present itself to him, Bay continued to be persuasive to TJ. In December 2009, Sailor had *just* spoken with Bay over the phone for about three to four hours, not knowing at the time that it would be the very last and most inspiring conversation he had with Bay. It was a time of repentance and forgiveness. Bay had just spent five or more years in prison for an act of sin many believe he took the fall for. Talking to Bay on the phone that day was a time of acknowledgment and understanding. It was a time of bearing all for the sake of restoring all. For about three hours or so, Sailor was beaming with the radiance of the sun as they talked over the phone. It was like old times, but a brand-new conversation with an awesome focus. Sailor wore one of the biggest smiles he ever had at that point in his life. While talking to Bay over the phone *every single* disagreement and misunderstanding of the past was washed away by a mighty ocean of cleanliness. In an instant, Sailor forgot they once disagreed and were seriously at odds with one another. It was like both of them experienced a new birth of sorts into the unfolding of a brand-new friendship. Ah man! That talk will last for eternity in the mind of Sailor. The Sermon will only fortify that talk as the most genuine ever held between both of them. Not to mention the most reverential talk in honor of the Most High void of stroking each other's personal views and opinion. Did Bay know? Was he expecting and did God reveal to him, or did Bay simply give up on life? At any rate, Sailor would never, ever hold a conversation with Bay from that night onward.

On January 6, 2010, Sailor received a call from his oldest brother at the dawning of the day. Sailor answered the call with excitement because his oldest brother was calling him on the phone.

"Sailor, good morning, how are you doing? Are you sitting down? Please sit down."

One cannot imagine how that sounded to Sailor, because Jr. was not one to joke or play around. Jr. was always intense when he spoke to you because he was a man of great worldly experience and you almost wanted to draw the words out of him.

"Bay is dead! He dropped dead on his way to work at the train station."

A deafening silence overcame Sailor, and a blank stare into emptiness invaded his mind. "Please tell me this is not true—please!"

That was rejection and unreasonable thinking that swept across Sailor's brain because he already knew that Jr. did not play like that. Reasoning escaped the mind of Sailor, given the circumstance and the death of one of his greatest mentors. After Jr. further explained Bay's death and they hung up the phone, Sailor slumped down on his couch and covered his face and intensely wept even greater than the passing of his parents. He wept and wept and wept into the night. He paced the floor, wondering why and how it could happen. They had just talked on the phone a couple of weeks ago. Why did God take Bay? Or greater still, why did Bay not take care of himself? For years, Sailor yearned for that old-time brother relationship and looked forward to his return. But when that return arrived, Bay's time on this earth was cut short at a young age of fifty-eight. Bay's passing was at the precipice of Sailor stepping into the Sermon. Bay appeared to be interested and desirous of entering the life of the Sermon with Sailor, but that day would never come.

A significant portion of Bay's life and how Sailor viewed him impacted Sailor in more ways than one. Sailor was deeply saddened at the passing of Bay, and Bay's heart and soul cry for direction, acceptance, and recognition!

Relationship with women has always been a problem for the boys in Sailor's family, some to a greater degree than others but a problem, nonetheless. What Sailor learned that it was not so much the women as it was the relationship. He concluded that his earthly father was by no means a mentor in the area of companionship and relationship. The more Sailor thought, the more his heart sank in deep despair for a man he admired and looked up to while he was growing into adulthood. Sailor was further saddened that many things he proclaimed and spoke to family members and declared of himself, and his brother Fred has come as a witness and testimony against both of them. What a terribly sad, overwhelming thing! In the Bible when Moshe told the Pharaoh about the impending judgment of the Most High, the last declaration Moshe made to Pharaoh was "the next plague shall come out of your own mouth." Sailor held on to his sadness for years, especially when the thought of them came to his mind. If he thinks too long about their lives, it becomes difficult for him not to weep.

Both Bay and Fred's influence in the life of Sailor would fill several pages in a book. The difficulty for Sailor was how to incorporate their passing into a book. How would he account for Fred's disappearance? The eyes of Sailor began to see that Bay was not only unhappy like Sailor was, Bay, like Sailor, was a confused man in his theology. When it looked like he was finally dismantling years of "religious" walls and other personal hindrances in his heart, death struck with absolutely no warning. As far as Sailor knows, there were no warnings, but it's hard to tell because Bay lived alone and maybe that's what he wanted—death. Sailor honestly believes that Bay saw it coming, understood the finality of what was about to happen and possibly embraced the fact that he would die an obscure death. His life of fifty-eight years overwhelmed his spirit and his will to live by taking care of himself. We all carry heredity hypertension and high cholesterol, but both of them can be controlled and overcome by a healthy diet and a stringent lifestyle of exercise. Sure, he rode his bike, but he ate like an undisciplined youth. Unless he drank water at work, Sailor saw no signs of water in his room. Bay lived the last days of his earthly life in a halfway house somewhere in Atlanta, Georgia. Sailor took his final trek to Atlanta in the days of Bay's passing, to reminisce and gather his own personal information of his brother's death. At discovery of the room Bay lived in and entering the room, an immediate spirit of grief overtook Sailor and the deep loneliness Sailor felt was revealing to him. His eyes instantaneously filled with tears and clouded his vision for a minute. He stood in the room looking around and seeing a man who had fallen from a place of honor and respect. He tried to get a picture of how his mentor lived out his last days. There were no empty water bottles. There were no water bottles in his refrigerator, and hydrant water simply would have been unhealthy. The selfish side of Sailor wants to say to Bay that he let him down. But the reality side of Sailor tells him that Bay let himself down! Sailor loves him even to this day and befriends Fred deeply in his heart. But with Bay's passing and Fred's disappearance, they both have taught Sailor an enormous amount of truth and things of humanity more than they will ever, ever know. On the heels of Bay's passing would be the second of the three, Lawrence, who would follow in the path of Bay not just six months later. Those years were full of despair, confusion, and bereavement for Sailor on a daily basis, and who could even possibly know what Sailor was feeling and experiencing? Who could know anything? Sailor was completely masked within the pages of the Bible and hidden within the sins of his heart.

Lawrence

Any time spent with Lawrence was like spending time with a historian of world experiences. Like sailing on the deepest ocean. Like climbing the highest mountain. Lawrence had a life of experience like neither of the two. Being a Vietnam vet and being on the front line and sprayed with Agent Orange from the illustrious United States–backed government, Lawrence was uniquely unique. The conversations Sailor held with Lawrence were few only because of the distance and the Christian thinking of Sailor. While Christianity has been impressively captivating in the world of religion, Sailor's take on the Bible would cause an unintentional separation with him and Lawrence. But they would spend days together and hours discussing the ravages of life and the temptations to overcome. The Veteran's Hospital in Pennsylvania would be the last days spent on this earth for Lawrence. At that time in Sailor's life, he was on the mountain peak of being a Christian Pastor and even harbored a puffed-up spirit. The entire message of faith and the misguided belief of being a Christian all contributed to the great fall of Sailor. He made a few visits to the VA to talk to and be with his brother whom he vigorously stood in the gap on the streets of Harrisburg. Remember that time when TJ was prepared and ready to fight two guys on behalf of Lawrence? This was the same Lawrence he wanted to fight for his life but from a different perspective. He would visit Lawrence and pray for him as death was stalking his beloved brother. Sailor had just lost one of his greatest mentors in the person of Bay, and he could not bear to lose another rock. Those days were filled with bereavement, and at times it seemed it would not end anytime soon.

At the bedside of Lawrence, Sailor presented his brand of Christianity to his admired brother. Sailor asked Lawrence if he'd mind having prayer? Lawrence passionately said no, he would not mind and Sailor, in the typical Christian manner, spoke about Jesus Christ and the forgiveness of sins. There is a verse in the Bible that says the Most High overlooks our ignorance: "Truly, then, having overlooked these times of ignorance, Elohym now commands all men everywhere to repent" (Ma'asei/Acts 17:30).

All Sailor can believe is that in his ignorance, the Most High gave ear to the Christian prayer of Sailor for his brother Lawrence and saved his soul.

Frederick E.

He was by far the greatest influence in the life of TJ who became the Sailor. Frederick E. and the young TJ shared the same room on the third floor once they moved to North 18th Street. It was in this room that Frederick E. carefully and methodically imputed into the young mind of TJ the intricacies of life. Every single morning—and I mean *every* single morning—Frederick E. would talk to TJ about life in the most philosophical manner to impress upon his mind. TJ awoke every single day with the expectation of hearing some deep word from Frederick E. He thrived on the words his older brother told him. He looked forward and expected *anything* Frederick E. would tell him. To TJ, Frederick E. was the coolest and most suave influence upon the naive life of the young lad. Day after day, it would seem their talks would have no end. It would seem Frederick E. would graduate to become a world-known figure of great knowledge and experience. TJ looked forward to and expected nothing but greatness in the future life of Frederick E. No one could match the mind and deepness of what Frederick E. had to share with TJ. He became the life source and very blood of the mind of an impressionable young man. TJ thought the world of Frederick E. and placed him on the highest pedestal known to man. Every word he spoke to the young lad was like setting anchor to a mighty war ship. Frederick E. fundamentally anchored the wayward soul of the young boy TJ. Frederick E.'s words would carry TJ into the life of Sailor all the way up to the point in time of the family meeting on that emotionally charged day. If anyone would have suggested the relationship TJ had with Frederick E. would one day become alienated, Sailor would have physically fought them. TJ, the Sailor, could never, ever have imagined that one day they would be deeply separated in thought and belief. Sailor cried for months and years after the passing of the greatest mentor in his life as a young boy. Frederick E. went into hiding sometime after the family meeting and was not heard of or seen by Sailor until some two years later when it was discovered he had passed away. One of the most unlikely sources in the family researched and found out that Frederick E. had died. One of the saddest things is that when Sailor conducted his own inquiry, he discovered that Frederick E. was a hospice patient in a care home. The most direct source of Frederick E.'s passing was a hospice nurse, who attended to Frederick E. She claims that he did not want his family to know of his condition and not to contact his family. That information seriously disturbed Sailor, and he questioned her and questioned her. She was very compassionate answering the questions and patiently enduring the conversation with Sailor. He will never forget the day it was confirmed that Frederick E. had died. He was at work at the Pennsylvania Department of Transportation, and when he hung up the phone, he stood up in absolute shock. The director of his agency was standing nearby, and she compassionately asked Sailor, "Are you all right? What's wrong, Sailor?"

He instantaneously burst into tears when she compassionately touched his shoulder. He hurriedly told her that he just received word that his brother was dead. His whereabouts had been unknown for two years or more. The director made every humanly attempt to console Sailor, but she just did not understand the impact Frederick E. made in Sailor's life. She would never know. Sailor then turned away from her in full dismay and began walking to get away from the inside of the building. No one in that workplace would ever know what he was feeling that day. Anger, pain, dismay, confusion and complete disappointment at Frederick E. that he allowed himself to digress to the very opposite of what Sailor thought of him. Sailor them walked off the job. He chose to walk down five flights of steps instead of taking the elevator for fear of someone wanting to know if he was all right. Who could console him? Who would understand and know a morsel of what he was feeling? Frederick E. was dead at such a young age of sixty but with a lifetime of investment into the life of Sailor. He made it down to the street level of the building and politely walked away from work. In the wide-open street on a very clear day, he was walking down Sixth street to his car, uncontrollably crying and shaking and crying, not noticing anyone passing by him. All he could see in his mind's eye, his best friend and brother no longer here, but dead. How could Frederick E. die? How? He expected more of the life of Frederick E., certainly not death at sixty years old. There was no one that could console him. That's because no one would understand the love and relationship he had with the coolest and most suave brother of all time—Frederick E.

Sailor's two boyhood idols, Bay never attended Sailor's church. Sailor believed had everything to do with the difference of their age, they were older than him. Stupid yeah, but people are like that, and many siblings are separated by age when it comes to who knows more than the other. But it really isn't about who knows more, rather sharing what you know to help one another. Anyways, Bay never attended, but he and Sailor always talked about spiritual stuff. The one-time Frederick E. did attend, his sole purpose was to debunk everything Sailor said. It was on a Wednesday night Bible study, and Frederick E. became belligerent, loud, prideful, and ungodly assertive. However, Sailor knew at the time he was doing drugs, possibly crack and from that time, their relationship miserably declined. It would be four years later that discovery that Fred was dead and had been dead for two years when Sailor got the news. What a sad, sad epitaph—to privately die in the confines of a room in hospice when in life he came from a large family. Nothing can make Sailor believe that Fred had to die that way; Fred *chose* to isolate himself, for reasons of delirium.

The Three, without a doubt, were the most powerful instructional teachers in the young life of TJ, and their lessons would carry over into the life of Sailor. But when the Sailor died and the Sermon began to come into view, all of TJ's and Sailor's dependency on the Three would slowly become lessons of the eternal past. Rest in peace, Three.

23

THE DEATH OF SAILOR

Skeletons Are Never Pretty

Skeletons many times can look scary. They are used as props especially during Halloween. When you look at a skeleton, you may think of a dead life or something hidden in the proverbial closet. At fifty-nine and a half years old, Sailor stared death in the face, and for the first time in his life, he was deathly afraid. It was the most fearful time of all his life. In the course of his demise, he decided to release all his skeletons. He let them all out of the closet. The skeletons got mad, and they also condemned him for letting them out. Sailor was told by one preacher, "Even though you let the skeletons out, don't stop preaching." *What a noble thought and traditional Christian practice*, Sailor thought. "Keep hiding your skeletons while you preach to the people. By the way, few, if any, actually know about the skeletons. It's best to just keep them hidden."

But those troublesome demonic skeletons plagued the bejesus out of Sailor. Those skeletons were always reminding him of himself and how he loved to keep them in the closet. In fact, they loved the closet, and Sailor was very comfortable with them locked in the deepest part of his soul. The skeletons did not say much. They did not require any attention. They did not require a meal, and they did not care if people knew they existed. Sailor remembers when he released the first batch of skeletons to the people, those people yelled, screamed, cried, and prophesied something...duh! Something. He found that a few months later into a few years later those people were still scared at the sight of his skeletons. I mean, it wasn't Sailor's intent to frighten them. He just got sick and tired of those darn irritating skeletons. It was as if the people would have preferred the skeletons of Sailor to stay locked up. That thought scared Sailor, and he could not understand why the people wanted Sailor to keep the skeletons locked inside. What! Keep your skeletons in the closet and perpetuate something you are not. The idea that people would prefer one to keep hid the active sins in their life upset Sailor about their Christianity. Those Christian folk like to hid things if the thing is still active. Who wants people to know the truth about them, even if the Bible says: "Confess your faults one to another, and pray . . . (James 5:16). Pray! Nope! They would prefer to be angry and reject you for seemingly lying to them and perpetuating a lie. Sailor had become a man full of skeletons in the closet while he was actually sleepwalking in the flesh.

Oh well, it has been the experience of Sailor that his blessings of sixty years to observe that essentially, people do not like the truth. They also do not like exposing lies when it's about them. They would prefer to project a lie and live in a world of "likes" and acceptance rather than stand alone and be rejected. In retrospect, letting those skeletons free and observing the reactions of those who first viewed the skeletons was kind of hilarious. Sailor did not mean that in a derogatory way. What was learned by Sailor is that sometimes we think people are something that they are not. Sailor thought they would handle those skeletons in a mature spiritual manner. But much to his chagrin, the skeletons were embraced more than the man who released them. Sailor released them in search of integrity, honesty, and truth, but he sadly realized the people preferred the skeletons remain silent and the man perpetuate louder and louder. Messiah was despised and rejected of men, and Messiah never put his trust in the arms of flesh. Sailor became thankful that he can experience a smidgen of the type of rejection that Messiah knew. The one aspect of Messiah's cross Sailor cannot bear is that he cannot and will not ever die for the sins of the world. But he certainly could feel the pain of Messiah and become familiar with the rejection Messiah had of men. By the way, those skeletons are out roaming somewhere looking for a home. They love familiarity, so don't keep any of your skeletons too long because the ones Sailor released are still mad, and they love to make their victims miserable. On the lonely path of death that began over ten years prior, Messiah woke Sailor up, and he has become eternally grateful to Elohym Yahuah. But his awakening would be a painful shock of the frailty of life and the unforgiving outlook of death. Sailor now strives to stay woke.

The Announcement of Death

Seventeen years later from that family meeting on N. 18th Street, Sailor would meet his demise, an indirect fulfilling of that word from the mouth of Bay. In the year 2012, Sailor opened the door of his sinful life without specifically naming the sins he committed. His church, his marriage, and his life not only would become exposed to the Christian Church he preached to but the entire world. At least, the Christian world he lived in. In July of 2012, the following is a copy of the actual statement read by Sailor, in an attempt to be real and get his life right with The Most High Elohym Yahuah:

> GOOD MORNING BROTHERS AND SISTERS
>
> I BEGIN MY STATEMENT WITH DEEP, DEEP AND SINCERE REGRET AND SORROW FOR HOW THIS MAY LEAVE SOME OF YOU TODAY. MANY OF YOU HAVE VERY GOOD DISCERNMENT AND I'M SURE WITHOUT A DOUBT HAVE NOTICED OBVIOUS SPIRITUAL BATTLES AMONG THOSE IN THIS FELLOWSHIP. WHILE I AM CAREFUL NOT TO BLAME MYSELF FOR SITUATIONS IN BROTHERS AND SISTERS LIVES—I MUST POINT

THE FINGER AT MYSELF AS A SPIRITUAL LEADER FOR BEING THE CAUSE AND EFFECT IN DEEPENING THE BATTLES. THE BIBLE RECORD IN PROVERBS 27 VERSE 5 SAYS "OPEN REBUKE IS BETTER THAN SECRET LOVE." TODAYS REBUKE IS SQUARELY AGAINST ME. I HAVE STROVE OVER THE YEARS TO WALK AND LIVE AS HONESTLY AS I POSSIBLY COULD. BUT OVER THE LAST 13 YEARS I HAVE FALLEN INTO DEEP CHASMS OF DISHONEST WAYS AND PRACTICES. IT MAY BE DIFFICULT AND EVEN UNBELIEVABLE FOR SOME OF YOU TO HEAR THIS OR BEAR IT—BUT AS I GET OLDER I REALIZE HOW SHORT LIFE IS AND THAT LIVING AN HONEST LIFE IS PARAMOUNT OF ALL ELSE.

THE APOSTLE PAUL ON SEVERAL OCCASSIONS ADDRESSED THE NEED TO BE HONEST IN OUR DAILY LIVES. IN ROMANS 13:13 HE SAYS THAT WE SHOULD WALK A HONEST LIFE. IN II CORINTHIANS 13:7 HE SAYS THAT WE SHOULD DO THAT WHICH IS HONEST "...THOUGH WE BE AS REPROBATES." THE WRITER OF THE BOOK OF HEBREWS ADMONISHES US TO HAVE A GOOD CONSCIENCE IN ALL THINGS WILLING TO LIVE HONESTLY. PLEASE FORGIVE ME AS MUCH AS IS WITHIN YOUR HEART TO ALLOW ME TO ONCE AND FOR ALL BE HONEST IN MY LIFE!. . . I AM REGRETFULLY INFORMING YOU TODAY THAT IN MY HEART AND SOUL I BELIEVE

I HAVE TO STEP DOWN FROM LEADING ALL THE PRECIOUS SOULS UNDER MY STEWARDSHIP. I KNOW THIS COMES AS A PONDING SURPRISE TO MOST OF YOU AND PERHAPS UNBELIEVABLE TO HEAR. NOT ONLY MUST I LIVE A HONEST LIFE I AM DAILY CONCERNED AND PRAYERFUL ABOUT THOSE WHOM I LEAD. EACH INDIVIDUAL PERSON UNDER THE SOUND OF MY VOICE IS WORTH PURE GOLD IN THE SIGHT OF GOD. MY LIFE OVER THE YEARS SHALL NOT CONTINUE TO BE A FACTOR IN STAINING THAT GOLD.

THE PROPHET ISAIAH IN CHAPTER 1 TALKS ABOUT THE WHOLE HEAD BEING SICK. THE HEAD BEING SICK HAS A DEFINITE IMPACT ON THE BODY THAT FOLLOWS. MY (SPIRITUAL) SICKNESS ESPECIALLY OVER THE PAST 13 YEARS; I BELIEVE, HAS BEEN A FACTOR IN THE LOSS OF A FEW PRECIOUS, DEAR, GODLY PEOPLE. I AM DEEPLY SADDEN BECAUSE OF THAT LOSS. BUT THEIR LOSS WAS A CATALYST BEHIND MY DECISION TO TRULY BE HONEST BEFORE THE PEOPLE I HAVE MINISTERED TO FOR YEARS. THE BIBLE IS ABSOLUTELY CLEAR ON THE WALK OF EVERY SINGLE BELIEVER IN CHRIST. BUT WHEN IT COMES TO THE LEADER OF THOSE BELIEVERS THE BIBLE AND GOD SPARE NO WIGGLE ROOM. A LEADER MUST BE BLAMELESS AS DELINEATED THROUGHOUT THE BIBLE. IN GENESIS 44 • "AND YE SHALL BE

BLAMELESS." • JOSHUA 2:17 "WE (WILL BE) BLAMELESS. • LUKE 1:6 "WALKING IN ALL THE ORDINANCES…BLAMELESS."

• PHILIPPIANS 2:15 "THAT YE MAY BE BLAMELESS…" • PHILIPPIANS 3:6 "… BLAMELESS." • I THESSALONIANS 5:23 "… BE PRESERVED BLAMELESS." • II PETER 3:14 "THAT YE MAY BE FOUND IN HIM… BLAMELESS."

I CORINTHIANS 1:8, I TIMOTHY 3:10, TITUS 1:6, 7 AND ESPECIALLY I TIMOTHY 3:2

"A BISHOP THEN MUST BE BLAMELESS, THE HUSBAND OF ONE WIFE, VIGILANT, SOBER, OF GOOD BEHAVIOUR, GIVEN TO HOSPITALITY, APT TO TEACH." MY WIFE WOULD URGE ME TO BE ALL THE WAY HONEST SINCE YOU'RE BEING HONEST. OVER THE YEARS I HAVE NOT BEEN A BLAMELESS HUSBAND TO MY WIFE AND HAVE NOT RECENTLY BEEN A BLAMELESS HUSBAND. WHILE WE ALL HAVE MADE BAD AND EVEN UNGODLY DECISIONS IN OUR LIVES—A LEADER MUST BE LEAD OF THE HOLY SPIRIT OF GOD AND WALK IN THE STEPS OF CHRIST IN ALL AREAS OF HIS LIFE. PLEASE, BROTHERS AND SISTERS, I AM ASKING YOUR FORGIVENESS FROM THE DEPTHS OF MY HEART FOR HOW THIS MAY BE IMPACTING YOU NOW IN HEARING THIS. BUT YOU SHOULD KNOW THIS WAS NOT A HASTY

DECISION, RATHER A THOUGHT OUT AND PRAYERFUL ACTION TO TAKE THIS STEP IN LIEU OF BIBLICAL TRUTH AND PRINCIPLE. THE ONE GOOD THING ABOUT KNOWING THE BIBLE AND BELIEVING THE TRUTH CONTAINED WITHIN ITS PAGES—A TRUE, SINCERE, HEART AND SOUL BELIEVER IN GOD MUST PRACTICE THE TRUTH AS IT FALLS UPON THE WAYS AND ACTIONS IN THEIR OWN LIFE. PLEASE FORGIVE ME FOR BELIEVING THAT I MUST PRACTICE WHAT I PREACH AT THIS TIME IN MY LIFE. I KNOW MANY OF YOU WILL NOT AGREE WITH MY ACTIONS TODAY AND MAY EVEN BE BALKING AT ME TO STAND UP HERE AND READ THIS. BUT I BELIEVE THE LORD GAVE IT TO ME THIS WAY BECAUSE I DID NOT WANT TO LEAVE THE MOST VITAL STONES UNTURNED AS IT RELATES TO ME HAVING BEEN YOUR PASTOR.

I HAVE LIKENED MYSELF OVER MANY YEARS AS A TYPE OF JONAH. GOD TOLD JONAH TO GO TO NINAVAH TO TELL THE PEOPLE TO REPENT. JONAH TRIED TO RUN (AS YOU KNOW), BUT WHILE ON THE BOAT OF ESCAPE A GREAT TEMPEST AROSE AND BEGAN TO TOSS THE BOAT TO AND FRO. THE CREW BEGAN TO THROW CARGO OVER THE SIDE TO LIGHTEN THE LOAD OF THE SEA GOING VESSEL BUT THE STORM BECAME MORE VIOLENT AND THE BIBLE SAYS "THE SHIP WAS LIKE TO BE BROKEN." THE

BIBLE ALSO SAYS THAT THE LORD SENT OUT A GREAT WIND INTO THE SEA AND THERE WAS A MIGHTY TEMPEST IN THE SEA. WHO WE ASSOCIATE WITHIN THE SEA OF LIFE HAS A DEFINITE INFLUENCE AND IMPACT ON OUR OWN LIVES—ESPECIALLY IN THE AREA OF RELIGION AND SPIRITUALITY. WHEN THE CAPTAIN OF THE BOAT AND THE CREW HEARD WHAT JONAH HAD TO SAY ABOUT WHY THE STORM RAGED AGAINST THEM AND JONAH TOLD THEM HE WAS THE CAUSE THEY BECAME AFRAID AND ASKED JONAH WHAT SHALL WE DO. SURPRISINGLY, JONAH'S RESPONSE WAS "CAST ME INTO THE SEA AND THE STORM IN YOUR LIVES WILL CEASE." A MAN OVERBOARD IS A DREADFUL THING AND THE CREW DID NOT WANT TO HEED TO JONAH'S REQUEST. NONETHELESS, AS THEY ROWED HARDER AND HARDER—THE STORM BECAME THE MORE UNBEARABLE. AMAZINGLY, WHEN THEY CAST JONAH INTO THE SEA THE BIBLE SAYS "AND THE SEA CEASED FROM HER RAGING." THIS MAY OR MAY NOT BE COMFORTING FOR YOU TO HEAR BUT I MUST BY MY OWN PRESENCE OF MIND STEP DOWN FROM PILOTING THIS MINISTRY AT THE CONCERN I HAVE OF YOUR OWN SPIRITUAL BATTLES MANY OF YOU, AND MANY WHO HAVE ATTENDED HERE ARE FACING. MY STORM IS YOUR BATTLE IN MANY WAYS. PLEASE FORGIVE ME BROTHER AND SISTER FOR SUCH AN

ANNOUNCEMENT TO MAKE TO YOU TODAY.

I HOPE AND PRAY THAT WHAT I HAVE TAUGHT TO YOU OVER THE MANY YEARS WILL SOMEHOW OR ANOTHER RESONATE DEEP WITHIN YOUR SPIRIT. I HOPE AND PRAY THAT MY GODLY DECISION TO STEP DOWN WILL NOT NEGATIVELY IMPACT YOUR LIFE AS GOD AND JESUS ARE YOUR TRUE LEADERS. I HAVE FOUGHT IN THE SERVICE OF MY LORD AND I HAVE BEEN SPIRITUALLY WOUNDED AND PINNED TO THE MAT BY THE POWERS OF DARKNESS OVER THE YEARS. BUT I TRULY BELIEVE THE MOST HONEST AND TRUTHFUL THING TO DO TODAY IS TO OBEY WHAT I BELIEVE THE LORD HAS GIVEN ME TO SAY AND DO BECAUSE HE NOT ONLY LOVES YOU – BUT HE DOES LOVE ME IN SPITE OF MY WOUNDED SOUL. I URGE YOU NOT TO VIEW ME AS A HIRELING BECAUSE I HAVE FACED THE ONSLAUGHT OF THE DEVIL OVER MANY SPIRITUAL THINGS. I HAVE NOT RUN IN THE FACE OF HARD DISAGREEMENT OR ACCUSATIONS OF BEING A FALSE PROPHET. BUT I HAVE WRESTLED WITH MY OWN FIGHT THAT HAS SPREAD ITSELF INTO YOUR LIVES. IT IS THAT WRESTLING THAT I PRAY YOU WILL NO LONGER HAVE TO CONTEND WITH DUE TO MY OWN UNGODLY ACTIONS. I HOPE THAT OVER THE YEARS I HAVE NOT PORTRAYED MYSELF AS BEING FAULTLESS OR ANY OTHER

THING THAN A MAN. IT ACTUALLY IS MY HUMANESS, BY AND THROUGH THE SPIRIT THAT I MUST FACE AND BE HONEST WITH AND BE LED OF GOD'S SPIRIT. I URGE YOU IN ONE FINAL PLEA TO PLEASE FORGIVE ME FOR MY ACTIONS OVER THE YEARS AND PLEASE VIEW THIS ACTION TODAY AS COMING FROM A HEART OF STRIVING TO BE HONEST AND TRUTHFUL AND HUMAN, BUT SPIRITUAL. YOU ARE ON MY HEART EACH DAY AND MY PRAYER IS THAT GOD WOULD CERTAINLY REVIVE YOUR SPIRIT WITH THE TRUTH OF SCRIPTURE THAT HAS KEPT YOU ALL.

TO GOD BE THE GLORY—EVEN WHEN WE DON'T UNDERSTAND! FOREVER—IN HIS SERVICE—PASTOR TIM —HIS BONDSERVANT.

That announcement on that Sunday morning was the releasing of Sailor's skeletons, and when those skeletons were released, it frightened everyone in the room that day. It was not Sailor's intent to present a real-life horror story to the people; rather, his intent was to reveal to the people his total unworthiness of preaching to them. He also was beckoning deep within his soul for maybe even one warrior to uphold him. Instead, they all rejected him like the plague and from that day forward for decades afterward, turned their back on Sailor, who would one day meet his Sermon. Effectively, on that day Sailor died, he no longer existed. He was no longer relevant as it goes with Christian preachers. His name—Brother, Pastor Sailor—undoubtedly died on the lips and mind of all who once knew him. He specifically remembers one of the deacons of that church gave a glaring, almost superficial, esoteric word. You know how in the Christian religion different ones are known to perpetuate some kind of word from God? This brother had stopped speaking to Sailor for quite some time prior to the announcement. But when Sailor made his regrettable announcement, in brief, the deacon said the following:

> God is not through with you yet! You need to get yourself together and get this ministry together! If you think you are equal to the men in the Bible, like Moses, Elijah or the Apostles of the New Testament, you are wrong! You need to rise above this and move forward in this ministry!

Internally, Sailor was smiling and laughing because how is it that all of a sudden, the deacon wanted to give a word to Sailor, instead of embracing Sailor at a time when Sailor beckoned to him? How is it that his word was almost equally condemning as the sins committed by Sailor? Does condemnation beget condemnation? Does all attempt to come clean and be honest beget judgmental remarks? Does the idea of pursuing integrity in the face of secret sins beget attempting to forgo the shame of embarrassment? It appeared in the mind of Sailor that the deacon had a personal desire of not being embarrassed by being a part of the Christian Church. When it comes down to it, life is never about one's personal desires and likes, rather about one's personal relationship with the Most High Elohym Yahuah. The deacon's words fell on unstable ground, and not once were his words given a moment of consideration, because what he was saying was unquestionably inaccurate. If at any time he knew the heart, mind, and soul of Sailor, he would have discerned the unadulterated need of Sailor to come clean and remain clean. But he, like everyone else in that room, failed to understand anything Sailor was doing that day. Sailor was directly under the leading of Ruach HaKodesh, and it frightened everyone under the sound of his voice.

It was at this moment in time that his relationship with his wife plunged to the ground, straight down like a hydrogen bomb! Her countenance exploded within her soul. Her denial rang loud and clear to all who knew them. Her rejection of Sailor was sealed in the unforgivable, angry, uncompassionate, and unbelievable synapsis of her brain. This would be the breaking point in which Sailor would begin his wilderness experience for the next seven years or so on his own. But concerning his marriage, let's digress for a brief moment to address the murder of satisfaction. Prior to the demise of the ministry, a few years back Sailor's daughter became pregnant at a very young age. Sailor learned of her pregnancy through a phone conversation with his wife at the time. It was then that he realized how his home had fallen and all his sins came crashing down on his head. That pricey little house located on the outskirts of the city would come to a screeching halt. At the time, it seemed like all of sudden these things happened. But in retrospect, the outcome of Sailor's demise had been cooking for the last forty years. It had just arrived at the point in Sailor's life that he was well done, and it was time for the real man to be served. At a time and day, he purposely has forgotten, he and his wife were discussing—no, angrily arguing as to how the daughter became pregnant. Actually, all that talk and arguing was really insignificant because it was what it was, and it was not totally unusual for a young girl to get pregnant. Who really cares whose fault it was and how and when it happened? C'mon, for real, what does that matter? What really mattered is what are we going to do. Even in Sailor's condemned and fallen state, he has always respected life and appreciated the gift of children. The Christian thing to do was to let the process unfold and become an unexpected granddaddy and grandmother. But his wife would reveal one of the most damaging and startling things about her when she uttered the following words: "She has to get an abortion. She can't have this baby! Do you know how this will look? You, the pastor, and your daughter pregnant!"

Hell had brazenly invaded the home of Sailor, and at this point, he was powerless to evict hell from his pricey little home located outside the city. The entrance of hell had made itself welcomed as Sailor welcomed the practice of hell in his own soul over thirty years ago. "Do not be led astray: Elohym is not mocked, for whatever a man sows, that he shall also reap. Because he who sows to his own flesh shall reap corruption from the flesh" (Galatiyim 6:7–8; Gal.) would become the reaping and sowing of Sailor in death for the next seven years. His wife revealed in one instant the depth of her Christianity and the selfishness of her own soul. Every year thereafter, Sailor died deeper and deeper into a lifeless hell. Sailor would learn and perceive that much of Christian practices, and perhaps other religions also, was filled with image after image after image. In other words, she unveiled to Sailor how that her Christianity was all about her image and not about the truth of Elohym Yahuah. Sailor literally ran out the house for fear of reacting to her in a threatening and deadly manner. On that day, hell took over Sailor's home. He no longer had a home and would not secure one for another seven plus years. He didn't know then, but seven years would be the time of the completion of his death and would begin the resurrection of the life gracefully bestowed upon him by the Most High. Seven years reminded him of the time the Babylonian king Nebuchadnezzar was driven into the wilderness and smitten with what is known as boanthropy. Boanthropy is a psychological disorder that causes a person to believe they are an ox, cow, or generally of the bovine species. These individuals believe this to the extent of adopting bovine behaviors, such as walking on all fours and eating grass. Medical research also concluded that boanthropy many times are associated with dreams. In the book of Daniel, the Babylonian king Nebuchadnezzar had a very disturbing dream concerning his kingdom and the events involved at the end of man's reign. Suffice it to say that Sailor had a number of dreams around that time in his life. His ministry, his home, and his marriage were being tried by hell fire. Dreams that would require another story in order to tell the story. At the end of the day, those dreams would manifest in the life of Sailor, and Sailor would die a thousand deaths until he no longer existed.

Effectively on that day in that place when Sailor gave his statement for stepping down from the perpetrated Christian ministry, the Sermon was born. And like the birth of a natural child, Sailor's labor pains and actual birth was not only painful to him, but the onlookers could not stand his pain. When Sailor stepped down from preaching and following the Christian religion, namely because of his faults, he stepped into the entire sermon of his life. Stepping down was the eulogy as the Sermon was now coming into view. The past forty years or so was the text taken for Sailor when he was unaware that our lives speak the message and not our words. He had been physically battered by the enemy of our soul. He lived a confused and unexplainable youthful life as fear was his companion of what lay ahead. He wrestled with demons of hell while enjoying their presence. He lied about who he really was because he was afraid of the truth. He sinned and sinned and sinned like a wayward child let loose in a candy store. To this day, all those Christian people have become faded distant props, sort of like manikins in a department store. Standing aimlessly on the sideline watching without expression or life. Still pictures of people he once knew.

24

ASLEEP BUT AWAKE

The Awakening

When Sailor relocated to Virginia, the outline of the Sermon would become clearer and clearer. Relationship with women has always been the compulsory struggle in the life of TJ, who became the Sailor and would find his fulfillment in the Sermon. Virginia would present an entirely new view and a profound new understanding. Sailor never would have imagined that relocating to another state would wake his sleepy dark soul out of the pit of religion. How could leaving his home of record to a place where he knew no one only to discover how sleep he was. It would be like when Yahuah told Abraham to leave his family into a place he would show him. Sailor was thrust into a new world he was clueless existed. The proverbial light came on inside of him, and the awesome resurrection of his spirit came alive from the Most High Elohym Yahuah. One of the first things he would begin to learn was that all the names and people in the Christian Bible have been fabricated throughout the years of Christianity. Since the dissolving of his marriage, he was in many ways searching for that perfect mate that would complement his journey. For a brief moment, his relationship with the Virginia lady opened an unexpected doorway into the Sermon.

During those years, Sailor was absolutely dead—he died in July 2012 when he released his skeletons. All who did not understand his death, in their mind, had consigned him to the fiery streams of hell. Little did everyone know that in July 2012 Sailor had entered the birth canal of the Sermon, but who could possibly see that then? Who? Not even Sailor was able to comprehend the depth of his stepping down, nor was he able to comprehend how wide his spiritual eyes would open. Sailor discovered the unsettling and revealing truth about the matter like God is really Elohym, and his name is really Yahuah in Hebrew. The title *god* is actually arbitrary and does not identify the Esteemed One of the Hebrew Scriptures. Now the Hebrew language is vitally important because the Scriptures were written in Hebrew. The Septuagint and Greek stuff came on scene sometime later in the process of time. The most unsettling truth of the matter when it comes to religion and Christianity is the name of Messiah. Yahusha HaMashiach is the undisputed truth of the name of Messiah. That fact changes everything, and the discovery of the true Hebrews of the Bible was absolutely earth-shattering to the late Sailor. The foundation of the Sermon was being laid, and the unveiling of the Sermon was the entire life of TJ into the Sailor who died in public because the Most High Elohym Yahuah buried the Sailor in open display of everyone. All that the Sailor was and all that he had learned over the sixty-plus years of his life, was now dead, never to rise again. With that, he posted the following on social media, tagging certain ones in order for them to spread the word:

> I want to vent to certain people. Not everybody, just certain ones because everyone on here did not know the old me. Life is about learning, growing, experience and sharing what you have learned. There was a time in my life when I was a jerk, and some would say a "jack ass." That's what my ex wife called me…a "jack ass." I thought more of myself than I should have. I preached

and taught the Bible like there was no tomorrow. But I was not clear on how to comprehend that understanding of the Bible and understanding people and treating people with kindness. Some have even accused me of thinking "I know everything."

Well, actually, I do not think that. I actually think I am a student in a perpetual class. I love to learn, and I love to understand what I learn. I also love to share what I learn, even now, being way over the hill. LOL!! I am still learning. So, for all the certain people, wherever and whoever you may be, I ask your deepest forgiveness for the old Sailor. I agree he was a jerk! Please understand, I continue to study, research, and conduct a comparative analysis of religion and life. But my treatment of people has become the most aware thing that I must do. I have to treat everyone the same. I love all people and for every case I gave the wrong impression, I ask again for your true, heartfelt, deepest forgiveness. Sometimes I weep, not because I am sad because that's not the case. I weep because now, I have found who I am. You know, we go through that thing trying to "find ourselves." What our worth is and what our mission in life. I humbly ask your forgiveness because as I was searching for me and the love of The Most High; I treated people unkindly many times. I ask again for your true, heartfelt, deepest forgiveness. I want the world to know that I not only regret the man you knew of the past, but he no longer lives in the way I treat others. Don't get me wrong. I am a strong advocate for the way of The Most High and the integrity of The Scriptures. But that does not mean I have to treat

> others unkindly. Recent events in my life have taught me perhaps the greatest lesson I needed to learn. How to treat others! But if this post does not satisfy you acknowledging my human faults of the past, feel free to call me and I will give you a personal plea to forgive me for treating you badly. In His Love Forever His Bond-Servant & Watchman."

This post was responded to and liked with a barrage of people even the most unlikely ones in the mind of Sailor. Remember that family talk with Bay and Frederick E. and that younger voice that rang out, "I don't think he's trying to impress?" She was an unlikely one who gave an encouraging comment. Unlikely, because the Sailor had not spoken to her since the days of that meeting. But you never know who is watching and observing your life and waiting for your eternal demise but amazed at your divine recovery.

Cross Over

In the course of the Sermon developing, Yahuah would bring into the life of the Sermon certain seasoned and articulate Ahchs (brothers). One of which would be Dr. Kenneth Howard, Pastor of New Breed Assembly, Assistant Professor, Ecumenical Theological Seminary, Professor, Oakland Community College, Grace College. Dr. Howard would pour into the Ruach (spirit) of the Sermon a level of knowledge the late Sailor searched for and searched for all his life. Dr. Howard would shine the proverbial light of lights into the life of the Sermon and uncover almost taboo information. The Ahch of the Sermon petitioned Dr. Howard on several occasions, requesting his permission to quote him concerning Christianity. Here are a few of Dr. Howard's message:

> Salvation isn't being preached anymore. Salvation messages are being slowly replaced by church growth strategies, personal development

> strategies, seeker-friendly messages, purpose-driven speeches, prosperity points, and strategies for comfortable living. Yup, Christianity is better known as a dispensary of blessing rather than disciples.

The Sermon viewed this perspective in the infancy of his resurrected life but was not clear on how to present these facts. As these profound facts were coming into view for the Sermon, Dr. Howard continued to pour into the ruach of the Sermon.

> "Interesting! Orthodox traditions are not trying to whitewash the truth. There are thousands of images like this in Europe, Asia Minor, Ethiopia, and Levant. There were no "white images" of Christ until the Medieval and Renaissance eras (Cesare Borgia). So before we make statements like, "why does it matter?" and "why are you making this about color?" please go ask those who initially made it about color by changing the image of the Messiah into their likeness. What were they trying to hide? Let's hold them accountable, not those of us who are called to dispel lies manufactured to deceive people by making Yahusha (so-called Jesus) into an iconography that represents a false narrative to oppress people of color for centuries. If the dominant culture knew that the Jesus whom they say that they worship was a black Negroid man, I wonder if it would change their views on racism?

As if these facts were not enough, Dr. Howard continues to lead the people of Yahuah from the land of our captivity into the land of promise. The following would be the canon explosion into the life of the Sermon that would awaken the message of the Sermon:

> Christianity is undeniably the religion of slavery. Christianity is based on the premises of many Negroes not knowing who we are. To acknowledge that Bantus Negroes are the Hebrews of Scriptures will only disrupt the false narrative and historical lies of Modern Christianity. Christianity is branded on Negroes lack of identity and when one discovers this hidden-in-plain-sight truth and become vocal about it or the role that Bantus/Israelites play in the Scriptures, that person is labeled as divisive, heretical, pro-black and racist.

Virginia was the state of the exciting entrance into TJ's new world of the military. Over forty something years later, Virginia would be the state in which the Sermon would become alive in its full state of being. Exposure to the wisdom and knowledge of Dr. Kenneth Howard and getting up out of the bed of slavery, the eyes of the Sermon became wide open. All that was and all that was misunderstood and all that was life-threatening to TJ, the Sailor, are now clear. It is not always clear in one's life the direction and purpose of living, but when Yahuah is known, all becomes known. That isn't to say or suggest that anyone person knows everything, but everything can be understood in its context. Hebraism and the culture of the people of Yisrael latched itself onto the mind and thinking of the man of the Sermon. The cover of lies, deliberate manipulation of the entire Christian world was all at once exposed. The confused life of the young TJ and the sinful life of Sailor was the sermon in the making. The text was laid when Christianity was introduced into the everyday life of TJ as a boy. Nothing, in his mind then, could compare to what it meant and how he felt to be identified as a Christian. All the years of searching and searching and learning and learning were not entirely wasted but were necessary for the clear revelation forthcoming.

The Sermon under Attack from Hell

As the learning of the Sermon was unfolding and all seemed well, on a day that was gorgeous, to say the least—the sun was shining, and the temperature was a cool 80 degrees Fahrenheit. But for a brief moment, Sailor resurrected in the form of lust. Having spent some time with an old female acquaintance and experiencing a resurgence of mild depression, he acted upon the remnant of his wicked desire. A little over an hour later while driving home on that super gorgeous day, it was as if a streak of lightning shot from one end of his chest to the other in a frightening manner. It was the first time he had ever felt such pain in all his life. He could only imagine what was happening and could only fret of the outcome with what was happening. On that day in the state of Virginia in the state of his awakening, three weeks shy of when the man of the Sermon would turn sixty years old. He was struck in quick succession with symptoms of what he thought maybe a heart attack. Within a millisecond, the symptoms escalated with every single breath he took. He immediately became depressed! Losing all composure! Fading in and out of consciousness while fighting to maintain consciousness!

HaShatan, the Scripture says, "Watch, because your adversary the devil walks about like a roaring lion, seeking someone to devour." On that day, the devil seized the Sermon with the hellish intent to silence the Sermon once and for all. HaShatan would shut the Sermon down before he ever had the opportunity to become a voice of the message. HaShatan was vigorously desirous to remove every opportunity for the man of the Sermon to testify. HaShatan had instantly pierced through the weakened armor and closed a valve in the heart of the infant Sermon. The man of the Sermon trembled to think of what a cardiac arrest would be like. The experience was horrifying to describe in simple words, but the best effort will be put forth in order that you may step into the realm of the Sermon's impending death. It was like all of sudden being electrocuted throughout every neural network of his body as uncontrollable fear overwhelmed his mind. He feared in the worst way that his heart was about to stop pumping blood. Every thought he had intensified with every thought that would come to mind. One of the amazing unexplainable things during this encounter with the angel of death, Sailor instantaneously thought about his entire life.

From the days of the projects when he ran that race with Frederick E. and slammed into the concrete ground. All the way through the days of North 18th Street when he would ride the bus with Mom to go pay bills. When he first laid eyes on the Eliminator 3 to the time, he first took the bike outside. Entering the navy. Leaving for the navy. The train ride to Great Lakes, Illinois, and crying inside his cubicle. Arriving at boot camp and the eight weeks spent at Recruit Training Center Great Lakes. His first duty command to all his Mediterranean cruises on board the ship. His thoughts went on and on.

He was reliving every event in his life and trying to reason at the moment why that was important to remember then. *Why am I thinking about my entire life? Why don't these thoughts cease? I can't control them!*

With each memory of his short life, his body reacted in a profusely drenching manner. As if someone poured a full bucket of water on him from head to toe, he was drenched in his own sweat. His anxiety level had awakened the full limits of stress sweat. His body reacted to his thoughts and compelled him to slump over because he was losing all human strength to sit up straight. His shirt and pants began to stick to his body because he was now, within seconds, in full anxiety stress and life was quickly, but slowly seeping away from his body. Breathing was excruciating, and with every breath, he could taste, smell, and feel the grips of death. There was absolutely no control over what he was feeling. Instantaneously he cried, not from the pain but from the loneliness of dying alone and that no one knew he was dying. He quickly became disoriented, afraid, helpless, and even hopeless, not knowing if his entire bodily functions were about to shut down. He was overcome with the thought and prospect that shortly he would be staring eternity in the face. In this case, his thoughts literally ran wild, and it was difficult and the most challenge event of all his life, just to capture any reasonable thought. That gorgeous day of the sun shining seemed to even shine brighter and brighter while in the small confines of his car while darkness was looming, and an unwanted passenger was sitting directly beside him. He couldn't fight! He couldn't say a word! He knew but did not know who had invaded his vehicle and who was ripping his life right from under his feet, so to speak.

He was not ready! He was not ready to meet the Most High Elohym Yahuah. The man of the Sermon loves the Most High and his Commandments and all that has been revealed to him. But the fact HaShatan got that close and gripped the very existence of his brief life awakened a reality in his soul that death was determined to kill him. Life is but a vapor, the Scripture says, and that vapor life was being withdrawn from his soul without mercy. Fear does not adequately describe what the man of the Sermon was feeling and thinking on that day. To be frightened was a small element of the deeper reality of his existence. The man of the Sermon was about to enter into eternity, and not knowing who he would face once entering the eternal portal remains an unexplainable thought. Time was coming to a standstill as he continued to drive his vehicle. Hearing and sight became shadowy because he was fading in and out of consciousness. He doesn't even know how that is possible, but he does remember being at one point on the road and then at another point, not remember traveling the distance. He could see other vehicles at the traffic light up ahead and wasn't sure if they were moving or sitting still. As he approached the traffic light, it seemed that not one vehicle was moving while the light he was approaching was clearly red. He remembers driving about two, three miles per hour straight toward the red traffic light he was approaching. Still, the opposing traffic was not moving at all. Strange and unexplainable other than the angel of life was actually, in a very real way, watching over and guiding the wayward infant man of the Sermon. The traffic light experience occurred two more times as the man of the Sermon slowly and as carefully as his consciousness would allow him drove right through three red lights. He has no remembrance of any motorist blowing their horn or flashing their lights. He does not even remember any reaction by any other motorist, other than silence. A deafening silence prevailed during the entire event of his date of death.

The only thing he could hear and see was his heart slowing down while the pumping of his blood was incredibly loud in his own ears. He felt like for a brief moment, he stepped into eternity as he was fading in and out of consciousness. He imagined. He beheld. He felt and he knew he was no longer on this earth, but he could feel in real-time that he was stuck inside his body inside a dying vehicle of both body and soul and car. The next phase of his pending death as he began to shake like a loose leaf falling from a dead tree. The leaf itself was already dead as it was rapidly approaching the ground. Nothing made sense, and everything, including one small breath, was precious. A weird type of homesickness seized his mind, and a loud cry of the greatest despair known to man was screaming from his soul. He began to intensely miss all his siblings and his once deeply held marriage with his ex-wife. His children all came to mind. He could see their faces one by one, as if they were just staring at him, looking and wondering what he was going to do with this thing of dying. He could not answer them because he did not have the slightest clue of an answer for himself. But no one could hear him. Absolutely no one on the planet could possibly know the great depth of despair he was in. By that time, he had driven maybe two blocks. His body had unwillingly slumped over the steering wheel, and his physical strength was totally depleted. At that point, he could not confess anything! He could not claim anything! Only one word came to mind, while every other word and reality of life swiftly became an eternal faded memory. The man of the Sermon managed to look up toward heaven, and he simply cried out, "Mercy!" Please have mercy!" All his Christian learning and lessons on faith were actually irrelevant in the face of death. The Ruach inspired in that small parcel of life that was left in his soul to ask for Mercy. The man of the Sermon actually yelled at the top of his voice, "YAHUAH, HAVE MERCY ON MY SOUL! PLEASE, MY ESTEEMED MASTER, NOT LIKE THIS! PLEASE HAVE MERCY!"

That yell took valuable seconds away from his life, and he struggled to breathe. Yelling out like that was way too much for him to bear, and he became drenched with an awful amount of body fluid. As if a second bucket of water was poured on him. Like really, is someone trying to drown him at the same time? The Ruach enabled him to drive one more block, and almost instinctively, he reached for his cell phone, not knowing how much longer his cell would have battery life. The Ruach guided his shaking, almost lifeless fingers because he had no composure left, and his vision was nearly gone. He could see, but it was like dark menacing clouds were around his eyes. Breathing was sporadic. He was forcing out each breath, like an emergency pump about to stop pumping water at any minute.

He intuitively dialed 911! He then accidentally hung up and dropped the phone in his lap because he did not have the strength to hold on to it. He was terribly disoriented. The man of the Sermon was still crawling in his new life but was actively and physically dying at that moment! But 911 called right back! Imagine that? They asked a series of questions: "What is the problem? Where are you located? Are you alone?"

It seemed like they asked him a thousand questions that were endlessly frustrating and shot his blood pressure to stroke level. The Ruach gave him just enough strength to say to them, "I am dying… and I need help immediately!"

It was complete torture to utter those few words. The last thing he remembers is the 911 caller saying, "Hang in there. Help is on the way!" Those were the very last words the man of the Sermon heard. He then dropped the phone again and carelessly drove into the side of the curb nearby. He was traveling about two miles per hour, but it was as if he was assisted the entire drive into the curb. When he closed his eyes, he seriously did not expect to open them again on this side of heaven. With eyes closed, he thought he heard the ambulance in the distance, but his hearing was faint in a lethal way. The sound of the siren didn't seem to be getting close. It was a faint sound that seemed to be hovering in time. His sense of direction was entirely lost. He did not know where he was, and he had completely relinquished all will to live. He welcomed death, reluctantly, but he welcomed it, nonetheless. He did not know where the ambulance was approaching from. It seemed like it was behind him. It seemed like it was approaching from in front of him. It even seemed like it was above him. Reason, rationale, intelligence, knowledge, and every other human quality had washed out from his soul. The man of the Sermon expected to die any minute! He then blacked out, completely slumped over the steering wheel. He knows he had blacked out because after hearing "hang in there, help is on the way," the next thing he remembers was the medic knocking on the driver door saying, "Sir, sir, we are here to help you."

He looked up at the medic with weakened eyelids that did not want to open. His eyes were opening and closing, but more closed than open. He was like an infant opening his eyes for the first time. Actually, it took great strength to pump blood for his eyes to function normally. Anxiety ruled in his heart without mercy. The medics then proceeded to carefully remove him from his vehicle. Those medics were unbelievably tender, passionate, and careful in the performance of their duties. He felt from the simple touch of their hand to the tone of their voice they were not performing their secular job; rather, they were guided by the power of the Ruach HaKodesh. They were way too comforting to simply be men doing their job. At least the thought brought a semblance of peace to the dying man of fifty-nine and a half years old. For the moment of vanity, he felt like they were family members helping him out of his car. The entire ride to the hospital in the ambulance was an experience the man of the Sermon will never forget. His life and soul had come to the point of hell while his physical existence was in the hands of mercy and heaven smiled down on him. From that point, the remainder of the experience occurred in frames. Like one frame after another. For example, he remembers them helping him out of the car, with extreme care. Amazing that was. It was like he was family to them. Nonetheless, the next memory was he was in the ambulance. Then they were driving at a very fast rate of speed, almost like a movie scene. Then one of the medics said, "Sir, you are having a heart attack."

He thought, *Having? When is it going to end?*

He asked them, "Did you get my cell phone? Someone needs to know where I am, please, please..." Those words were redirecting his blood flow in the most lethal manner. He now understands why they say, "Be still, don't talk."

The medic said, "We got your phone, sir, but it will do you no good because it looks like it's dead!"

The man of the Sermon would discover sometime later that his phone had 1 percent battery charge left, possibly 2 percent when he made his call to 911.

Vaguely remembering the arrival at the ER, it was like looking through a foggy window as several nurses and he supposes, internes was staring at him while the head nurse and the doctor relentlessly impressed upon him with question after question. The doctor and the nurse were in his face close up asking him, "what is your name?" "When is your birthday?" "We need to operate NOW, or put you on medicine, but if we do that, your heart attack is sure to return soon!" They continued to persist in asking him what you want us to do-operate or medicine. The man of the Sermon yelled with the last amount of strength he had and said YES! YES! The doctor then said, "does that mean yes operate and insert a stent, or do you want the medicine?" The man of the Sermon, almost in a drunken stupor yelled one last word-OPERATE! Time and events then quickly passed by the infant Sermon and he remembers slowly opening his eyes in the recovery room. Yahuah saw fit to answer his deep sincere prayer and offer the man of the Sermon a renewed lease on life.

The outline of the Sermon continues to be written, and the message of the Sermon is continually alive with hope, promise, and obedience to the Most High Elohym Yahuah and his Ben, Yahusha HaMashiach. The man of the Sermon quickly learned there is a difference between perspective and perception.

One problem that is prevalent among some Christians is the lack of ability to discern between perspective and perception. There is a song by Katy Perry called "Wide Awake": "Everything you see ain't always what it seems. Falling from cloud nine, crashing from the high. God knows that I tried, seeing the bright side, I'm not blind anymore."

Now the perception may be why reference a secular song to illustrate the perspective of the man of the Sermon? In light of that question, consider this: why did Elohym identify the king of the Babylonian kingdom, Nebuchadrezzar, as "HIS servant?" knowing that Babylon has always been a heathen kingdom opposed to the Esteem of the Most High (Yirmeyahu 25:9/Jeremiah). Also, you see that Elohym commanded the prophet Hosea to take a wife of whoredoms to illustrate the relationship his people had created with the heathen of the land and how they had departed from Elohym (the entire book of Hosea). But human perception would not agree with any association of the righteous with the unrighteous. Nonetheless, the perspective of the Most High Elohym Yahuah is always to illustrate a spiritual truth.

Elohym always declares a things end from its beginning (Yeshayahu 46:10/Isa.), and when your walk with him is sealed deep in your heart, your actions have already been judged by him from the beginning of your life unto the end. It is easy to pass human judgment on the actions of others because your perception of what appears to be obvious. But from Elohym 's perspective of the end from the beginning, all one can do is judge the fruit of the tree thereafter. When you perceive someone to be wrong, is it truly from a biblical perspective or from your human perception? Don't accept the misunderstanding of judging by saying, "Don't judge me and I will not judge you." Judging your actions and judging between right and wrong is always in order as from the biblical perspective. "But he who is spiritual discerns indeed all matters, but he himself is discerned by no one." The KJV uses the word "judge" (Qorintiyim Aleph 2:15; 4:41 Cor.). When you perceive judging to be a wrong act, then the wrong of others many times go unaccounted for. The Bible does not forbid judging the actions of men and women between right and wrong. Rather, the Bible forbids condemning men and women because of their actions.

> For all have sinned and fall short of the esteem of Elohym . (Romiyim 3:23/Rom.)

A life full of great trials and tribulations would reveal to the man of the sermon that everything is not what it seems. Perception is best rooted in the Will of the Most High as life is rightly viewed from Yahuah's perspective.

Precious

The man of the Sermon is about to embark on the international stage of learning that the Most High intended for him on the day he was born sixty something years ago. Elohym Yahuah is the only one who knows the end from the beginning. All the life of TJ, the sailor who deathly struggled to become the sermon, was orchestrated by the counsel of heaven.

After nearly twenty years of writing about the Sailor and the Sermon, Precious became the most unlikely candidate and catalyst to massage his mind into the beginning stages of the Sermon. She became a well of encouragement and motivation inspiring the heart and mind of the Sermon to finish the work he started. Years and years of conflict, misunderstanding, religion, and Christianity with Sailor's ex-wife halted everything in his life from moving forward. Sometimes we just do not understand the direction one's life is going until coming out of the woods of life. Precious not only was the encouraging voice but would become the mountain peak out of the valley of despair.

The culture of Hebraism was foreign to her but the willingness to learn was sparked inside her. Much discovery and understanding of the ways of a Hebrew Yisraelite would have to be born in her soul. Early on in this story, it was discovered that relationship has always been the main issue with TJ and the Sailor.

Frederick E.

There was a guy I once knew many, many years ago. Every word he spoke caused me to grow. I thought he was the coolest of them all. I always pictured him ten feet tall. But as life brings its toils and snares, many times our perspective will change, and we all need prayer.

I picked his brain from time to time, always seeking advice with the mountain I had to climb. He always had something very smooth to say. I never once imagined that one day he, or I, might stray. But something came in that detached us for a while, and that something would cause me never again to see him smile.

We all make choices, and some may have a vision. But life, for the most part, comes forth from the heart of our decisions. He chose and I chose to walk the road we did, but I have attempted to copy him from the days of a kid. But one day I awoke and was grateful for his lead. I no longer required, nor had the desire for him to continue to feed. The sleeper had awoken, and thanks to his words, I once and for all became as free as a bird. I hope and pray that he is truly free today because there was a time when we both have gone astray. In memory of a brother lost but found.

Bay

It's been years now since my homie took flight. I wonder sometimes in his passing, did he do me right? But then I realize, it wasn't my fight he had to fight, his relationship was with the Most High, and he fought diligently all his life.

All my life, I strove to walk in his steps. There was none cooler than Bay, and to me, he was the best! He walked with a confidence that only the Most High can give. Sometimes I wonder, why couldn't he continue to live?

But the enemy of our soul always throws his hellish darts. Life has its snares and sometimes a boatload of troubles. No matter how Bay lived his life, at the end of the day, he was still my brother. He left this world not knowing how much I loved him so. He cracked open my mind with worldly wisdom and broad perspectives that caused the child in me to grow.

Bay was the mentor. He was cool, sharp, suave, and he always influenced me to think. It was because of the words of Bay that my initial tour of duty in the military helped me to float and not sink. When dealt with the trials of life in the military, my initial thoughts were, "What would Bay say? What would Bay do? What would be his perspective on this trial that I face?" One thing for sure, it was Bay's words that guided me to rely on God's grace.

Bay had flaws and shortcomings, as we all do, *every single day*! It was Bay and Fred, whom the Most High used to get me started on my way. When I left home for the first time to enter the armed forces of the United States, the steps of Bay were on my mind. From youth, he kept me encouraged. But this is not about me. It's about the brother I will always love. I sincerely hope and pray that he is resting in peace with the Most High above.

Dad

He's the man with the super plan. As he talked, he never squawked. Every word he spoke resonated with grace. But as TJ and the Sailor listened, seldom did he grasp of grace. Decades later, his words became elementary to the man of the Sermon. His knowledge was unique but informal. Never attending even one college. From what I perceived, his life was very rugged, and he was simply attempting to shape the Sermon's mind and soul into a Christian man. When TJ left home, he said to him, "You'll make it." And now I would like to yell from the mountaintop, "The sleeper has awakened!"

Maturity

If you have been blessed to live past forty years of age, you completely understand that time flies. One day you are a teenager and the next day you can't believe how teenagers dress. The world is a grown-up world with grown-up circumstances and responsibilities.

Life's journey is similar to us all, but the path taken on our journey differs in many respects. This particular journey has come to an end and a brand-new journey has begun. The circumstances of the new journey remain the same. For instance, knowing the perfect will of Elohym Yahuah and the truth of Scripture or et' sef'-er א ת Cephher (Divine Book). Proclaiming and publishing the culture and laws and commandments of that Divine Book. And lastly, relationship as defined and outlined in the Scriptures of the Most High Elohym Yahuah. The Sermon and the man of the Sermon remain alive and well, and all previous men have been buried by the hand of Yahuah. Shalam Wa Barawak Ahch Wa Ahcwath. To the esteem of the Most High Elohym Yahuah.

CPSIA information can be obtained
at www.ICGtesting.com
Printed in the USA
LVHW111039280820
664156LV00001B/13

9 781648 950551